Collins

COBUILD

Pocket

English-English-Bangla

Dictionary

ইংরাজী–ইংরাজী–বাংলা

Exclusively marketed by Ratna Sagar Pvt. Ltd.
in the Indian Subcontinent only

HarperCollins Publishers
Westerhill Road
Bishopbriggs
Glasgow
G642QT

First Edition 2011

Reprint 10 9 8 7 6 5 4 3 2 1 0

ISBN 978-0-00-741545-8

www.collinslanguage.com

A catalogue record for this book is available from
the British Library

Typeset by CoralHub Ltd. India
Artwork by Q2A Media

Printed in India by Gopsons Papers Ltd.

Acknowledgements

We would like to thank those authors and
publishers who kindly gave permission for
copyright material to be used in the Collins
Word Web. We would also like to thank Times
Newspapers Ltd for providing valuable data.

Contents

সূচি

Editorial consultant সম্পাদকীয় পরামর্শদাতা

Suchita Singh
Formerly Co-ordinator, Lexical Build Project,
Central Institute of Indian Languages

Translation co-ordination অনুবাদের সমন্বয়ন

Ajit Shirodkar

Translators অনুবাদক

Prachi Banerjee
Gopal Chowdhury

Editors সম্পাদক

Shalini Bansal
Suchitra Choudhury-Talukdar
Gerry Breslin
Lucy Cooper
Kerry Ferguson
Anne Robertson

Editor-in-chief প্রধান সম্পাদক

Dr Elaine Higgleton

Abbreviations সংক্ষেপিত রূপ

abbr	abbreviation
adj	adjective
adv	adverb
conj	conjunction
det	determiner
excl	exclamation
n	noun
npl	plural noun
num	numeral
prep	preposition
pron	pronoun
US	American English
v	verb
vi	intransitive verb
vt	transitive verb

Using this Dictionary

Entry words
Entry words are printed in blue bold type.

abbreviation

Inflected forms
The inflected forms of verbs, nouns, adjectives, abbreviations, and numerals are printed in black bold type in brackets.

abduct (**abducts, abducting, abducted**)

Parts of speech
Parts of speech are abbreviated and printed in italics. When a word can be used as more than one part of speech, the change of part of speech is shown after an empty arrow.

about *adv* **About** means near to something.
প্রায় ▷ *prep* **About** means to do with.

Definitions
Definitions give the meaning of the word. In the definition, the entry word is printed in black bold.

abroad *adv* If you go **abroad**, you go to a foreign country.

Usage and regional labels
Usage and regional labels are printed in italics in brackets after the definition.

consequently *adv* **Consequently** means as a result. (*formal*)

Translations
Translations come after the definition and give the equivalent of the entry word in Bangla.

abolition *n* The **abolition** of something is its formal ending. বিলুপ্তি

Examples
Example sentences are printed in italics and show how the word is used.

consist of *v* Something that **consists of** particular things or people is formed from them. তৈরী হয় *The cabin consisted of two small rooms.*

এই অভিধানের প্রয়োগ

এন্ট্রী শব্দ
এন্ট্রী শব্দগুলোকে নীল রঙে বোল্ড টাইপে ছাপা হয়েছে।

> **abbreviation**

বিভক্তি ও প্রত্যায় রূপ
ক্রিয়াপদ, বিশেষ্য, বিশেষণ এবং সংখ্যাগুলোকে ব্র্যাকিটের ভিতরে কালো রঙে বোল্ড টাইপে ছাপা হয়েছে।

> **abduct (abducts, abducting, abducted)**

বিশেষ্য শব্দ
বিশেষ্য শব্দগুলো কে সংক্ষেপিত রূপে এবং বাঁকা ছাঁদের অক্ষরে ছাপা হয়েছে। যখন একটি শব্দকে একের চেয়ে বেশি ভাবে প্রয়োগ করা যেতে পারে তখন একটি খালি তীর রূপী চিহ্নের পর সেই বিশেষ্য শব্দটিকে দেখানো হয়েছে।

> **about** *adv* **About** means near to something.
> প্রায় ▷ *prep* **About** means to do with.

অর্থ
অর্থ শব্দের মানে বোঝায়। অর্থে, এন্ট্রী শব্দটিকে কালো রঙে বোল্ড টাইপে ছাপা হয়েছে।

> **abroad** *adv* If you go **abroad**, you go to a
> foreign country.

প্রয়োগবিধি এবং আঞ্চলিক লেবল
প্রয়োগবিধি এবং আঞ্চলিক লেবলগুলোকে ব্র্যাকিটের ভিতরে এবং বাঁকা ছাঁদের অক্ষরে অর্থের পর ছাপা হয়েছে।

> **consequently** *adv* **Consequently** means as a
> result. *(formal)*

অনুবাদ
অনুবাদগুলোকে অর্থের পর লেখা হয়েছে। অনুবাদগুলো এন্ট্রী শব্দের সমার্থক বাংলা শব্দ প্রদান করে।

> **abolition** *n* The **abolition** of something is its
> formal ending. বিলুপ্তি

উদাহরণ
উদাহরণ বাক্যগুলোকে বাঁকা ছাঁদের অক্ষরে ছাপা হয়েছে এবং এরা দেখায় যে শব্দটিকে কি ভাবে প্রয়োগ করা হয়।

> **consist of** *v* Something that **consists of**
> particular things or people is formed from them.
> তৈরী হয় *The cabin consisted of two small rooms.*

a

a *det* You use **a** or **an** before a noun when people may not know which person or thing you are talking about. একটি *A waiter came in with a glass of water.*

abandon (abandons, abandoning, abandoned) *vt* If you **abandon** a thing, place, or person, you leave them permanently or for a long time. পরিত্যক্ত

abbreviation (abbreviations) *n* An **abbreviation** is a short form of a word or phrase. সংক্ষিপ্তকরণ,

abdomen (abdomens) *n* Your **abdomen** is the part of your body below your chest where your stomach is. (formal) পেট

abduct (abducts, abducting, abducted) *vt* If someone **is abducted**, he or she is taken away illegally. অপহরণ করা

ability (abilities) *n* Your **ability** is the quality or skill that you have which makes it possible for you to do something. সামর্থ্য

able (abler, ablest) *adj* An **able** person is clever or good at doing something. সক্ষম

abnormal *adj* Someone or something that is **abnormal** is unusual in a way that is worrying. (formal) অস্বাভাবিক

abolish (abolishes, abolishing, abolished) *vt* If someone in authority **abolishes** a practice or organization, they put an end to it. বিলোপ করা

abolition *n* The **abolition** of something is its formal ending. বিলুপ্তি

about *adv* **About** means near to something. প্রায় ▷ *prep* **About** means to do with. সম্বন্ধে *This book is about history.*

above *prep* If something is **above** another thing, it is over it or higher than it. ওপরে *Lift the ball above your head.*

abroad *adv* If you go **abroad**, you go to a foreign country. বিদেশ

abrupt *adj* An **abrupt** action is very sudden and often unpleasant. আকস্মিক

abruptly *adv* If you do something **abruptly**, you do it in an abrupt manner. আকস্মিকভাবে

abscess (abscesses) *n* An **abscess** is a painful swelling containing pus. পুঁজভর্তি ফোড়া

absence (absences) *n* The **absence** of someone or something is the fact that they are not there. অনুপস্থিতি

absent *adj* If someone or something is **absent** from a place or situation, they are not there. অনুপস্থিত

absent-minded *adj* An **absent-minded** person is very forgetful or does not pay attention to what they are doing. অমনোযোগী

absolutely *adv* **Absolutely** means totally and completely. পুরোপুরিভাবে

abstract *adj* An **abstract** idea or way of thinking is based on general ideas rather than on real things and events. মূর্ত

absurd *adj* If you say that something is **absurd**, you think that it is ridiculous or that it does not make sense. উদ্ভট

Abu Dhabi *n* **Abu Dhabi** is an emirate in south-east Arabia, on the southern coast of the Persian Gulf. আবুধাবি

academic *adj* **Academic** means relating to life or work in schools, colleges, and universities. শিক্ষাগত

academic year (academic years) *n* The **academic year** is the period of the year during which students attend school or university. শিক্ষাবর্ষ

academy (academies) *n* A school or college specializing in a particular subject is sometimes called an **academy**. শিক্ষাপ্রতিষ্ঠান

accelerate (**accelerates, accelerating, accelerated**) *v* If the rate of something **accelerates**, or if something **accelerates** it, it gets faster. গতি বাড়ানো

acceleration *n* The **acceleration** of a process is the fact that it is getting faster. গতিবৃদ্ধি

accelerator (**accelerators**) *n* In a vehicle, the **accelerator** is the pedal you press to go faster. গতিবর্ধক যন্ত্রাংশ

accept (**accepts, accepting, accepted**) *v* If you **accept** something that you have been offered, you say yes to it or agree to take it. গ্রহণ করা

acceptable *adj* If a situation or action is **acceptable**, people approve of it. গ্রহণযোগ্য

access (**accesses, accessing, accessed**) *n* If you have **access** to a building or other place, you are able to go into it. অধিগম্যতা ▷ *vt* If you **access** something, especially information held on a computer, you succeed in finding or obtaining it. ব্যবহার করতে পারা

accessible *adj* If a place is **accessible**, you are able to reach it or get into it. গমনের যোগ্য

accessory (**accessories**) *n* **Accessories** are extra parts added to something to make it more useful or decorative. সহায়ক বস্তু

accident (**accidents**) *n* An **accident** is something nasty that happens, and that hurts someone. দুর্ঘটনা ▷ *n* If something happens by **accident**, you do not expect it to happen. দৈবক্রমে

accidental *adj* An **accidental** event happens by chance or as the result of an accident. দুর্ঘটনাজনিত অবস্থা

accidentally *adv* If something happens **accidentally**, it happens by chance or as the result of an accident, and is not deliberately intended. দুর্ঘটনাক্রমে

accident and emergency *n* The **accident and emergency** is the room or department in a hospital where people who have severe injuries or sudden illness are taken for

emergency treatment. দুর্ঘটনাজনিত জরুরী বিভাগ

accident insurance *n* **Accident insurance** is insurance providing compensation for accidental injury or death. দুর্ঘটনাজনিত বিমা

accommodate (**accommodates, accommodating, accommodated**) *vt* If a building or space can **accommodate** someone or something, it has enough room for them. জায়গা দেওয়া

accommodation *n* **Accommodation** is used to refer to rooms or buildings where people live, stay, or work. বাসস্থান

accompany (**accompanies, accompanying, accompanied**) *vt* If you **accompany** someone, you go somewhere with them. (*formal*) সঙ্গ দেওয়া

accomplice (**accomplices**) *n* An **accomplice** is a person who helps to commit a crime. শাগরেদ

accordingly *adv* You use **accordingly** to say that one thing happens as a result of another thing. পরিণামে

according to *prep* You say **according to** somebody to show that you are only repeating what you have read or heard, and that it may not be true. অনুসারে *They drove away in a white van, according to the news.* ▷ *prep* If somebody does something **according to** a set of rules, they follow those rules. অনুসারে *They played the game according to the rules.*

accordion

(**accordions**) *n*
An **accordion** is a
musical instrument
in the shape of a
box which you hold
in your hands. You
play it by pressing

keys and buttons on the side, while moving
the two ends in and out. অ্যাকর্ডিয়ান

account (**accounts**) *n* An **account** is a written or spoken report of something that has happened. বিবরণ ▷ *n* If you have an

account with a bank, you leave money with the bank and take it out when you need it. ব্যাংকের অ্যাকাউন্ট

accountable *adj* If you are **accountable** for something that you do, you are responsible for it. দায়বদ্ধ

accountancy *n* **Accountancy** is the work of keeping financial accounts. হিসাবশাস্ত্র

accountant (**accountants**) *n* An **accountant** is a person whose job is to keep financial accounts. হিসাবরক্ষক

account for *v* If you can **account for** something, you can explain it or give the necessary information about it. উত্তর দেওয়া *How do you account for the missing money?*

account number (**account numbers**) *n* Your **account number** is the unique number of your account with something such as a bank. অ্যাকাউন্ট নম্বর

accuracy *n* The **accuracy** of information or measurements is their quality of being true or correct. যথার্থতা

accurate *adj* Something that is **accurate** is correct to a detailed level. যথার্থ

accurately *adv* **Accurately** means in an accurate manner. যথার্থভাবে

accusation (**accusations**) *n* If you make an **accusation** against someone, you express the belief that they have done something wrong. নালিশ

accuse (**accuses, accusing, accused**) *vt* If you **accuse** someone of something, you say that you believe they did something wrong or dishonest. দোষারোপ করা

accused (**accused**) *n* **The accused** refers to the person or people charged with a crime. অভিযুক্ত

ace (**aces**) *n* An **ace** is a playing card with a single symbol on it. তাসখেলার টেক্কা

ache (**aches, aching, ached**) *n* An **ache** is a steady, fairly strong pain in a part of your body. ব্যথা ▷ *vi* If you **ache** or a part of your body **aches**, you feel a steady, fairly strong pain. ব্যথা করা

achieve (**achieves, achieving, achieved**) *vt* If you **achieve** a particular aim or effect, you succeed in doing it or causing it to happen, usually after a lot of effort. অর্জন করা

achievement (**achievements**) *n* An **achievement** is something which someone has succeeded in doing, especially after a lot of effort. কীর্তি

acid (**acids**) *n* An **acid** is a chemical, usually a liquid, that can burn your skin and cause damage to other substances. অম্ল

acid rain *n* **Acid rain** is rain that damages plants, rivers, and buildings because it contains acid released into the atmosphere from factories and other industrial processes. অম্লবর্ষণ

acknowledgement *n* An **acknowledgement** of something is a statement or action that recognizes that it is true. প্রাপ্তিস্বীকার

acne *n* **Acne** is a skin disease which causes spots on the face and neck. ব্রণ

acorn (**acorns**) *n* An **acorn** is a pale oval nut that is the fruit of an oak tree. ওকগাছের ফল

acoustic *adj* An **acoustic** musical instrument is one which is not electric. অবৈদ্যুতিক বাদ্যযন্ত্র

acre (**acres**) *n* An **acre** is a unit of area equal to 4840 square yards or approximately 4047 square metres. জমির মাপ

acrobat (**acrobats**) *n* An **acrobat** is an entertainer who performs difficult physical acts such as jumping and balancing, especially in a circus. শারীরিক কসরতে দক্ষ

acronym (**acronyms**) *n* An **acronym** is a word made of the initial letters of the words in a phrase, especially when this is the name of an organization such as NATO. বিভিন্ন শব্দের প্রথম অক্ষর সমন্বয়ে গঠিত শব্দ

across *prep* If someone goes **across** a place, they go from one side of it to the other. ওপারে *She walked across the road.*

act (**acts, acting, acted**) *n* An **act** is an action or thing that someone does. কর্ম ▷ *vi*

When you **act**, you do something. কাজ করা ▷ *vi* If you **act** in a play or film, you pretend to be one of the people in it. অভিনয় করা

acting *adj* You use **acting** before the title of a job to indicate that someone is doing that job temporarily. কার্যনির্বাহী ▷ *n* **Acting** is the activity or profession of performing in plays or films. অভিনয়

action *n* **Action** is doing something for a particular purpose. ক্রিয়া

active *adj* An **active** person is energetic and always busy. সক্রিয়

activity *n* **Activity** is a situation in which a lot of things are happening. ক্রিয়াকলাপ

actor (**actors**) *n* An **actor** is someone whose job is acting in plays or films. অভিনেতা

actress (**actresses**) *n* An **actress** is a woman whose job is acting in plays or films. অভিনেত্রী

actual *adj* **Actual** is used to emphasize that you are referring to something real or genuine. প্রকৃত

actually *adv* You use **actually** to indicate that a situation exists or that it is true. প্রকৃতঅর্থে

acupuncture *n* **Acupuncture** is the treatment of a person's illness or pain by sticking small needles into their body. সূচ ফুটিয়ে চিকিৎসা

AD *abbr* You use **AD** in dates to indicate a number of years or centuries since the year in which Jesus Christ is believed to have been born. খ্রীষ্টাব্দ/খ্রীষ্টের জন্মের পর থেকে শুরু যে বছর

ad (**ads**) *abbr* An **ad** is an announcement in a newspaper, on television, or on a poster about something such as a product, event, or job. (*informal*) বিজ্ঞাপন

adapt (**adapts, adapting, adapted**) *vi* If you **adapt** to a new situation, you change your ideas or behaviour in order to deal with it. মানিয়ে নেওয়া

adaptor (**adaptors**) *n* An **adaptor** is a special device for connecting electrical equipment to a power supply, or for connecting different pieces of electrical or electronic equipment together. অ্যাডাপ্টর

add (**adds, adding, added**) *vt* If you **add** one thing to another, you put it with the other thing. মেশানো ▷ *vt* If you **add** numbers together, you find out how many they make together. যোগ করা

addict (**addicts**) *n* An **addict** is someone who cannot stop taking harmful drugs. নেশাসক্ত

addicted *adj* Someone who is **addicted** to a harmful drug cannot stop taking it. নেশার প্রতি আসক্ত

additional *adj* **Additional** things are extra things apart from the ones already present. অতিরিক্ত

additive (**additives**) *n* An **additive** is a substance which is added to food by the manufacturer for a particular purpose, such as colouring it. যা যোগ করা হয়

address (**addresses**) *n* If you give an **address** to a group of people, you give a speech to them. ভাষণ ▷ *n* Your **address** is the number of the house, the name of the street, and the town where you live or work. ঠিকানা

address book (**address books**) *n* An **address book** is a book in which you write people's names and addresses. ঠিকানা লেখবার বই

add up *v* If you **add up** numbers or amounts, or if you **add** them **up**, you calculate their total. যোগ করা *Add up the total of those six games.*

adjacent *adj* If two things are **adjacent**, they are next to each other. সংলগ্ন

adjective (**adjectives**) *n* An **adjective** is a word such as 'big' or 'beautiful' that describes a person or thing. Adjectives usually come before nouns or after verbs like 'be' or 'feel'. বিশেষণ

adjust (**adjusts, adjusting, adjusted**) *v* When you **adjust** to a new situation, you get used to it by changing your behaviour or your ideas. অভিযোজন

adjustable *adj* If something is **adjustable**, it can be changed to different positions or sizes. অভিযোজনযোগ্য

adjustment (**adjustments**) *n* An **adjustment** is a change that is made to something such as a machine or a way of doing something. অভিযোজন

administration *n* **Administration** is the range of activities connected with organizing and supervising the way that an organization functions. প্রশাসন

administrative *adj* **Administrative** work involves organizing and supervising an organization. প্রশাসনিক

admiration *n* **Admiration** is a feeling of great liking and respect. শ্রদ্ধা

admire (**admires, admiring, admired**) *vt* If you **admire** someone or something, you like and respect them. শ্রদ্ধা করা

admission (**admissions**) *n* If you gain **admission** to a place or organization, you are allowed to enter it or join it. ভর্তি

admit (**admits, admitting, admitted**) *vt* If someone **is admitted** to a place or organization, they are allowed to enter it or join it. ভর্তি হওয়া ▷ *v* If you **admit** that something bad or embarrassing is true, you agree, often reluctantly, that it is true. স্বীকার করা

admittance *n* **Admittance** is the act of entering a place or institution or the right to enter it. প্রবেশাধিকার

adolescence *n* **Adolescence** is the period of your life in which you develop from being a child into being an adult. বয়ঃসন্ধিকাল

adolescent (**adolescents**) *n* An **adolescent** is a young person who is no longer a child but who has not yet become an adult. বয়ঃসন্ধিতে উপনীত

adopt (**adopts, adopting, adopted**) *vt* If you **adopt** someone else's child, you take it into your own family and make it legally your own. দত্তক নেওয়া

adopted *adj* An **adopted** child is one which has been adopted. দত্তকরূপে গৃহীত

adoption (**adoptions**) *n* **Adoption** is the act of adopting a child. দত্তকগ্রহণ

adore (**adores, adoring, adored**) *vt* If you **adore** someone, you love and admire them. আরাধনা করা

Adriatic *adj* **Adriatic** means of or relating to the Adriatic Sea, or to the inhabitants of its coast or islands. অ্যাড্রিয়াটিক সাগরের সাথে সম্পর্কযুক্ত

Adriatic Sea *n* The **Adriatic Sea** is an arm of the Mediterranean between Italy and the Balkan Peninsula. অ্যাড্রিয়াটিক সাগর

adult (**adults**) *n* An **adult** is a mature, fully developed person. An adult has reached the age when they are legally responsible for their actions. প্রাপ্ত বয়স্ক

adult education *n* **Adult education** is education for adults in a variety of subjects, most of which are practical, not academic. Classes are often held in the evenings. বয়স্ক শিক্ষা

advance (**advances, advancing, advanced**) *n* An **advance** is money which is lent or paid to someone before they would normally receive it. আগাম ▷ *vi* To **advance** means to move forward, often in order to attack someone. এগিয়ে যাওয়া

advanced *adj* An **advanced** system, method, or design is modern and has been developed from an earlier version of the same thing. উন্নত

advantage (**advantages**) *n* An **advantage** is something that puts you in a better position than other people. সুযোগ

advent *n* The **advent** of something is the fact of it starting or coming into existence. (*formal*) সমাগম

adventure (**adventures**) *n* An **adventure** is a series of events that you become involved in that are unusual, exciting, and perhaps dangerous. অভিযান

adventurous *adj* An **adventurous** person is willing to take risks and eager to have new experiences. দুঃসাহসপূর্ণ

adverb (**adverbs**) *n* In grammar, an **adverb** is a word such as 'slowly' or 'very' which adds information about time, place, or manner. বিশেষণের বিশেষণ

adversary (**adversaries**) *n* Your **adversary** is someone you are competing with or fighting against. প্রতিপক্ষ

advert (**adverts**) *n* An **advert** is an announcement in a newspaper, on television, or on a poster about something such as a product, event, or job. ঘোষণা বা প্রচার

advertise (**advertises, advertising, advertised**) *v* If you **advertise**, or **advertise** something such as a product, event, or job, you tell people about it in newspapers, on television, or on posters. বিজ্ঞাপন দেওয়া

advertisement (**advertisements**) *n* An **advertisement** is an announcement in a newspaper, on television, or on a poster that tells people about a product, event, or job vacancy. (*written*) বিজ্ঞাপন

advertising *n* **Advertising** is the business activity of encouraging people to buy products, go to events, or apply for jobs. বিজ্ঞাপনদেওয়া

advice *n* If you give someone **advice**, you tell them what you think they should do. পরামর্শ

advisable *adj* If you tell someone that it is **advisable** to do something, you are

suggesting that they should do it. (*formal*) সংগত

advise (**advises, advising, advised**) *vt* If you **advise** someone to do something, you tell them what you think they should do. উপদেশ দেওয়া

aerial (**aerials**) *n* An **aerial** is a piece of metal equipment that receives television or radio signals. এরিয়াল

aerobics *npl* **Aerobics** is a form of exercise which increases the amount of oxygen in your blood and strengthens your heart and lungs. অ্যারোবিক ব্যায়াম

aerosol (**aerosols**) *n* An **aerosol** is a small container in which a liquid such as paint is kept under pressure. When you press a button, the liquid is forced out as a fine spray or foam. চাপের মধ্যে তরল রাখার পাত্র

affair (**affairs**) *n* You refer to an event as an **affair** when you are talking about it in a general way. ঘটনা

affect (**affects, affecting, affected**) *vt* When something **affects** someone or something, it influences them or causes them to change. প্রভাবিত করা

affectionate *adj* If you are **affectionate**, you show your fondness for another person in your behaviour. স্নেহ

afford (**affords, affording, afforded**) *vt* If you cannot **afford** something, you do not have enough money to pay for it. খরচ করবার সামর্থ

affordable *adj* If something is **affordable**, people have enough money to buy it. খরচসাধ্য

Afghan (**Afghans**) *adj* **Afghan** means belonging or relating to Afghanistan, or to its people or language. আফগানিস্হান সম্পর্কিত ▷ *n* An **Afghan** is a person from Afghanistan. আফগানিস্হান-বাসী

Afghanistan *n* **Afghanistan** is a republic in central Asia. আফগানিস্হান

afraid *adj* If you are **afraid** of someone or **afraid** to do something, you are frightened because you think that something horrible is going to happen. ভীত

Africa *n* **Africa** is the second largest of the continents. It is located to the south of Europe. আফ্রিকা

African (Africans) *adj* **African** means belonging or relating to the continent of Africa. আফ্রিকা সম্পর্কিত ▷ *n* An **African** is someone who comes from Africa. আফ্রিকার অধিবাসী

Afrikaans *n* **Afrikaans** is one of the official languages of South Africa. আফ্রিকান্স

Afrikaner (Afrikaners) *n* An **Afrikaner** is one of the white people in South Africa whose ancestors were Dutch. আফ্রিকার শ্বেতাঙ্গ অধিবাসী

after *conj* If something happens **after** another thing, it happens later than it. পরে *He arrived after I had left.* ▷ *prep* If something happens **after** another thing, it happens later than it. পরে *I watched television after dinner.* ▷ *prep* If you go **after** a person or thing, you follow them or chase them. পিছনে *They ran after her.*

afternoon (afternoons) *n* The **afternoon** is the part of each day which begins at 12 o'clock lunchtime and ends at about six o'clock. অপরাহ্ন

afters *npl* **Afters** is a dessert or sweet. (*informal*) মিষ্টি

aftershave *n* **Aftershave** is a liquid with a pleasant smell that men sometimes put on their faces after shaving. আফটারশেভ

afterwards *adv* If something is done or happens **afterwards**, it is done or happens later than a particular event or time that has already been described. পরে

again *adv* If something happens **again**, it happens another time. পুনর্বার

against *prep* If something is **against** another thing, it is touching it. হেলান দেওয়া *He leaned against the wall.* ▷ *prep* If you play **against** someone in a game, you try to beat them. বিপক্ষে *The two teams played against one another.*

age (ages) *n* Your **age** is the number of years that you have lived. বয়স

aged *adj* You use **aged** followed by a number to say how old someone is. বয়স্ক

age limit (age limits) *n* An **age limit** is the oldest or youngest age at which you are allowed under particular regulations to do something. বয়সের সীমা

agency (agencies) *n* An **agency** is a business which provides services for a person or another business. এজেন্সী

agenda (agendas) *n* An **agenda** is a list of items to be discussed at a meeting. সভার বিষয়তালিকা

agent (agents) *n* An **agent** is someone who arranges work or business for someone else. এজেন্ট

aggressive *adj* An **aggressive** person behaves angrily or violently towards other people. আক্রমণাত্মক

AGM (AGMs) *abbr* The **AGM** of a company or organization is a meeting which it holds once a year in order to discuss the previous year's activities and accounts. **AGM** is an abbreviation for 'Annual General Meeting'. বার্ষিক সাধারণ সভা

ago *adv* You use **ago** to talk about a time in the past. আগে

agree (agrees, agreeing, agreed) *v* If you **agree** with someone, you have the same opinion about something. একমত হওয়া

agreed *adj* If people are **agreed** on something, they have reached a joint decision on it or have the same opinion about it. সহমত পোষণ করা

agreement (agreements) *n* An **agreement** is a decision that two or more people, groups, or countries have made together. মিলিত চুক্তি

agricultural *adj* **Agricultural** means involving or relating to agriculture. কৃষিভিত্তিক

agriculture *n* **Agriculture** is farming and the methods used to look after crops and animals. কৃষি

ahead *adv* Someone who is **ahead** of another person is in front of them. সামনে

aid *n* **Aid** is money, equipment, or services that are provided for people, countries, or organizations who need them but cannot provide them for themselves. অনুদান

AIDS *n* **AIDS** is an illness which destroys the natural system of protection that the body has against disease. **AIDS** is an abbreviation for 'acquired immune deficiency syndrome'. এডস্ রোগ

aim (**aims, aiming, aimed**) *n* The **aim** of something that you do is the purpose for which you do it. লক্ষ্য ▷ *v* If you **aim** for something or **aim** to do it, you plan or hope to achieve it. লক্ষ্য স্থির করা

air *n* **Air** is the mixture of gases which forms the earth's atmosphere and which we breathe. বায়ু

airbag (**airbags**) *n* An **airbag** is a safety device in a car which automatically fills with air if the car crashes, and is designed to protect the people in the car when they are thrown forward in the crash. হাওয়াভর্তি ব্যাগ

air-conditioned *adj* If a room is **air-conditioned**, the air in it is kept cool and dry by means of a special machine. শীততাপ নিয়ন্ত্রিত

air conditioning *n* **Air conditioning** is a method of providing buildings and vehicles with cool air. শীততাপ নিয়ন্ত্রণ

aircraft (**aircraft**) *n* An **aircraft** is a vehicle which can fly, for example an aeroplane or a helicopter. বিমান

air force (**air forces**) *n* An **air force** is the part of a country's military organization that is concerned with fighting in the air. বিমানবাহিনী

air hostess (**air hostesses**) *n* An **air hostess** is a woman whose job is to look after passengers in an aircraft. (*old-fashioned*) বিমানসেবিকা

airline (**airlines**) *n* An **airline** is a company which provides regular services carrying people or goods in aeroplanes. বিমান পরিষেবা

airmail *n* **Airmail** is the system of sending letters, parcels, and goods by air. বিমান বাহিত মেল

airport (**airports**) *n* An **airport** is a place where aircraft land and take off, usually with a lot of buildings and facilities. বিমানবন্দর

airsick *adj* If you are **airsick**, you are sick or nauseated from travelling in an aircraft. বিমান-সফর জনিত অসুস্থতা

airspace *n* A country's **airspace** is the part of the sky that is over that country and is considered to belong to that country. এয়ারস্পেস

airtight *adj* If a container is **airtight**, its lid fits so tightly that no air can get in or out. বায়ুনিরোধী

air traffic controller (**air traffic controllers**) *n* An **air traffic controller** is someone whose job is to organize the routes that aircraft should follow, and to tell pilots by radio which routes they should take. বিমান চলাচল নিয়ন্ত্রক

aisle (**aisles**) *n* An **aisle** is a long narrow gap that people can walk along between rows of seats in a public building such as a church, or between rows of shelves in a supermarket. আইল/দুটি আসনের মধ্যবর্তী রাস্তা

alarm *n* **Alarm** is a feeling of fear or anxiety that something unpleasant or dangerous might happen. সতর্কবার্তা

alarm clock (**alarm clocks**) *n* An **alarm clock** is a clock that you can set to make a noise so that it wakes you up at a particular time. অ্যালার্ম ঘড়ি

alarming *adj* Something that is **alarming** makes you feel afraid or anxious that something unpleasant or dangerous might happen. আশঙ্কাসূচক

Albania *n* **Albania** is a republic in south-east Europe, on the Balkan Peninsula. আলবেনিয়া

Albanian (**Albanians**) *adj* **Albanian** means belonging or relating to Albania, its people, language, or culture. আলবেনিয়া সম্পর্কিত ▷ *n* An **Albanian** is a person who comes from Albania. আলবেনীয় ▷ An **Albanian** is the language spoken by people who live in Albania. আলবেনীয় ভাষা

album (**albums**) *n* An **album** is a CD, record, or cassette with music on it. গানের অ্যালবাম

alcohol *n* Drinks that can make people drunk, such as beer, wine, and whisky, can be referred to as **alcohol**. সুরা

alcohol-free *adj* Beer or wine which is **alcohol-free** contains only a trace of alcohol. সুরা-বর্জিত

alcoholic (**alcoholics**) *adj* **Alcoholic** drinks contain alcohol. সুরাসক্ত ▷ An **alcoholic** is someone who is addicted to alcohol. সুরাপানে আসক্ত

alert (**alerts, alerting, alerted**) *adj* If you are **alert**, you are paying full attention to things around you and are ready to deal with anything that might happen. সতর্ক ▷ *vt* If you **alert** someone to a situation, especially a dangerous or unpleasant situation, you tell them about it. সতর্ক করা

Algeria *n* **Algeria** is a republic in north-west Africa, on the Mediterranean. আলজেরিয়া

Algerian (**Algerians**) *adj* **Algerian** means belonging or relating to Algeria, or its people or culture. আলজেরিয়া সম্পর্কিত ▷ *n* An **Algerian** is an Algerian citizen or a person of Algerian origin. আলজেরীয়

alias *prep* You use **alias** when you are mentioning another name that someone, especially a criminal or an actor, is known by. ছদ্মনাম ...*the defendant Pericles Pericleous, alias Peter Smith.*

alibi (**alibis**) *n* If you have an **alibi**, you can prove that you were somewhere else when a crime was committed. ওজর

alien (**aliens**) *n* An **alien** is someone who is not a legal citizen of the country in which they live. (*formal*) বর্হিদেশীয়

alive *adj* If people or animals are **alive**, they are living. জীবিত

all *det* You use **all** to talk about everything, everyone, or the whole of something. সমস্ত *Did you eat all of it?* ▷ *pron* You use **all** to talk about everything, everyone, or the whole of something. সকল *We make our own hair-care products, all based on herbal recipes.*

Allah *n* **Allah** is the name of God in Islam. আল্লা

allegation (**allegations**) *n* An **allegation** is a statement saying that someone has done something wrong. দোষারোপ

alleged *adj* An **alleged** fact has been stated but has not been proved to be true. (*formal*) কথিত

allergic *adj* If you are **allergic** to something, or have an **allergic** reaction to it, you become ill or get a rash when you eat it, smell it, or touch it. বিমুখ

allergy (**allergies**) *n* If you have a particular **allergy**, you become ill or get a rash when you eat, smell, or touch something that does not normally make people ill. অ্যালার্জি

alley (**alleys**) *n* An **alley** or **alleyway** is a narrow passage or street with buildings or walls on both sides. সংকীর্ণ রাস্তা

alliance (**alliances**) *n* An **alliance** is a group of countries or political parties that are formally united and working together because they have similar aims. জোট

alligator (**alligators**) *n* An **alligator** is a large reptile with short legs, a long tail and very powerful jaws. কুমির প্রজাতির

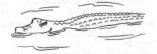

allow (**allows, allowing, allowed**) *vt* If someone **is allowed** to do something, it is all right for them to do it. অনুমতি দেওয়া/ অনুমতি প্রদান করা

all right *adv* If something goes **all right**, it happens in a satisfactory manner. (*informal*)

একদম ঠিক ▷ *adj* If you say that something is **all right**, you mean that it is good enough. (*informal*) ঠিক আছে

ally (**allies**) *n* An **ally** is a country, organization, or person that helps and supports another. সন্ধিস্থাপন

almond (**almonds**) *n* An **almond** is a kind of pale oval nut. কাঠবাদাম

almost *adv* **Almost** means very nearly. প্রায়

alone *adj* When you are **alone**, you are not with any other people. একা

along *prep* If you walk **along** a road or other place, you move towards one end of it. বরাবর *We walked along the street.* ▷ *adv* If you bring something **along** when you go somewhere, you bring it with you. সঙ্গে

aloud *adv* When you speak or read **aloud**, you speak so that other people can hear you. উচ্চস্বরে

alphabet (**alphabets**) *n* The **alphabet** is the set of letters in a fixed order which is used for writing the words of a language. বর্ণমালা

Alps *npl* The **Alps** are a mountain range in south central Europe. আল্পস্ পর্বতমালা

already *adv* You use **already** to show that something has happened before the present time. এরই মধ্যে

also *adv* You use **also** to give more information about something. এছাড়াও

altar (**altars**) *n* An **altar** is a holy table in a church or temple. বেদি

alter (**alters, altering, altered**) *v* If something **alters**, or if you **alter** it, it changes. অদলবদল করা

alternate *adj* **Alternate** actions, events, or processes regularly occur after each other. পালাক্রম

alternative (**alternatives**) *adj* An **alternative** plan or offer is different from the one that you already have, and can be done or used instead. পালাক্রমিক ▷ *n* If one thing is an **alternative** to another, the first can be found, used, or done instead of the second. বিকল্প

alternatively *adv* You use **alternatively** to introduce a suggestion or to mention something different from what has just been stated. পরিবর্তে

although *conj* You use **although** to add information that changes what you have already said. যদিও *They all play basketball, although on different teams.* ▷ *conj* You use **although** to start talking about an idea that is not what you would expect. যদিও *I can remember seeing it on TV, although I was only six.*

altitude (**altitudes**) *n* If something is at a particular **altitude**, it is at that height above sea level. উচ্চতা

altogether *adv* If you say that different numbers of people or things add up to something **altogether**, you mean that you have counted all of them. সবশুদ্ধ

aluminium *n* **Aluminium** is a lightweight metal used for making things such as cooking equipment and aircraft parts. অ্যালুমিনিয়াম

always *adv* If you **always** do something, you do it every time or all the time. সর্বদা

Alzheimer's disease *n* **Alzheimer's disease** is a condition in which a person's brain gradually stops working properly. আলজাইমার অসুখ

a.m. *abbr* **a.m.** after a number indicates that the number refers to a particular time between midnight and noon. এ. এম./মধ্যরাত্রি এবং মধ্যাহ্নের মধ্যবর্তী সময় এর দ্বারা চিহ্নিত হয়

amateur (**amateurs**) *n* An **amateur** is someone who does a particular activity as a hobby, not as a job. অপেশাদার

amaze (**amazes, amazing, amazed**) *vt* If something **amazes** you, it surprises you very much. বিস্ময়

amazed *adj* If you are **amazed**, you are very surprised. বিস্মিত

amazing *adj* If something is **amazing**, it is very surprising and makes you feel pleasure or admiration. বিস্ময়কর

ambassador (**ambassadors**) *n* An **ambassador** is an important official living in a foreign country who represents the government of his or her own country. দূত

amber *n* **Amber** is a hard yellowish-brown substance used for making jewellery. হলুদ রং এর মণি

ambition (ambitions) *n* If you have an **ambition** to achieve something, you want very much to achieve it. উচ্চাভিলাষ

ambitious *adj* Someone who is **ambitious** wants to be successful, rich, or powerful. উচ্চাভিলাষী

ambulance (ambulances) *n* An **ambulance** is a vehicle for taking people to and from hospital. অ্যাম্বুলেনস্

amenities *npl* **Amenities** are things such as shopping centres or sports facilities that are for people's convenience or enjoyment. সুযোগসুবিধা

America *n* **America** is the American continent, including North, South, and Central America. আমেরিকা মহাদেশ

American (Americans) *adj* **American** means belonging or relating to the United States of America, or to its people or culture. আমেরিকা সম্পর্কিত ▷ *n* An **American** is a person who comes from the United States of America. আমেরিকা বাসী

American football *n* **American football** is a game similar to rugby that is played by two teams of eleven players using an oval-shaped ball. আমেরিকার ফুটবল খেলা

among *prep* Someone or something that is **among** a group of things or people has them around them. মধ্যে *There were children sitting among adults.* ▷ *prep* If something

happens **among** a group of people, it happens in that group. মধ্যে *Discuss it among yourselves.*

amount (amounts) *n* An **amount** of something is how much of it you have, need, or get. পরিমাণ/টাকার অংকের পরিমাণ

amp (amps) *n* An **amp** is a unit which is used for measuring electric current. অ্যাম্প

amplifier (amplifiers) *n* An **amplifier** is an electronic device in a radio or stereo system, which causes sounds or signals to become louder. আওয়াজ পরিবর্ধক

amuse (amuses, amusing, amused) *vt* If something **amuses** you, it makes you want to laugh or smile. হাসানো

amusement arcade (amusement arcades) *n* An **amusement arcade** is a place where you can play games on machines which work when you put money in them. চিত্তবিনোদনের জায়গা

an *det* **An** means the same as **a**, but you use **an** before words that begin with the sound of **a, e, i, o,** or **u.** একটি *He started eating an apple.*

anaemic *adj* Someone who is **anaemic** suffers from a medical condition in which there are too few red cells in their blood, making them feel tired and look pale. রক্তাল্পতার রোগী

anaesthetic (anaesthetics) *n* **Anaesthetic** is a substance used to stop you feeling pain during an operation. অজ্ঞান করবার ওষুধ

analyse (analyses, analysing, analysed) *vt* If you **analyse** something, you consider it or examine it in order to understand it or to find out what it consists of. বিশ্লেষণ করা

analysis (analyses) *n* **Analysis** is the process of considering something or examining it in order to understand it or to find out what it consists of. বিশ্লেষণ

ancestor (ancestors) *n* Your **ancestors** are the people from whom you are descended. পূর্বপুরুষ

anchor (anchors) *n* An **anchor** is a heavy hooked object at the end of a chain that is dropped from a boat into the water to make the boat stay in one place. নোঙর

anchovy (**anchovies**) *n* **Anchovies** are small fish that live in the sea. They are often eaten salted. ছোট সামুদ্রিক মাছ

ancient *adj* **Ancient** means very old, or having existed for a long time. প্রাচীনকালের

and *conj* You use **and** to join two or more words or ideas. এবং *She and her husband have already gone.*

Andes *npl* The **Andes** are a major mountain system of South America. আন্ডিজ পর্বতমালা

Andorra *n* **Andorra** is a small, mountainous country in south-west Europe, between France and Spain. অ্যান্ডোরা

angel (**angels**) *n* **Angels** are spiritual beings that some people believe are God's messengers and servants in heaven. দেবদূত

anger *n* **Anger** is the strong emotion that you feel when you think someone has behaved in an unfair, cruel, or unacceptable way. ক্রোধ

angina *n* **Angina** is severe pain in the chest and left arm, caused by heart disease. আঞ্জাইনা

angle (**angles**) *n* An **angle** is the difference in direction between two lines or surfaces. Angles are measured in degrees. কোণ

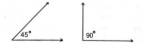

angler (**anglers**) *n* An **angler** is someone who fishes with a fishing rod as a hobby. মৎসশিকারী

angling *n* **Angling** is the activity of fishing with a fishing rod. ছিপের সাহায্যে মাছ ধরা

Angola *n* **Angola** is a republic in south-west Africa, on the Atlantic. অ্যাঙ্গোলা

Angolan (**Angolans**) *adj* **Angolan** means belonging or relating to Angola or its

people. অ্যাঙ্গোলা সম্পর্কিত ▷ *n* An **Angolan** is someone who comes from Angola. অ্যাঙ্গোলা-বাসী

angry (**angrier, angriest**) *adj* When you are **angry**, you feel strong emotion about something that you consider unfair, cruel, or insulting. রাগী

animal (**animals**) *n* Any living creature other than a human being can be referred to as an **animal**. জন্তু

aniseed *n* **Aniseed** is a substance made from the seeds of the anise plant. It is used as a flavouring in sweets, drinks, and medicine. মৌরী

ankle (**ankles**) *n* Your **ankle** is the joint where your foot joins your leg. গোড়ালি

anniversary (**anniversaries**) *n* An **anniversary** is a date which is remembered or celebrated because a special event happened on that date in a previous year. বার্ষিকী

announce (**announces, announcing, announced**) *vt* If you **announce** something, you tell people about it publicly or officially. ঘোষণা করা

announcement (**announcements**) *n* An **announcement** is a public statement which gives information about something that has happened or that will happen. ঘোষণা

annoy (**annoys, annoying, annoyed**) *vt* If someone **annoys** you, they make you quite angry and impatient. বিরক্ত

annoying *adj* An **annoying** person or action makes you feel quite angry and impatient. বিরক্তিকর

annual *adj* **Annual** means happening or done once every year. বার্ষিক

annually *adv* If something happens **annually**, it happens once every year. বার্ষিকভাবে

anonymous *adj* If you remain **anonymous** when you do something, you do not let people know that you were the person who did it. অনামী

anorak (anoraks) n An **anorak** is a warm waterproof jacket, usually with a hood. ফারের জ্যাকেট

anorexia n **Anorexia** or **anorexia nervosa** is an illness in which a person refuses to eat enough because they have a fear of becoming fat. অ্যানোরেক্সিয়া একটি রোগ

anorexic adj If someone is **anorexic**, they are suffering from anorexia and so are very thin. অ্যানোরেক্সিয়া রোগী

another det You use **another** to mean one more. অন্য একটি She ate another cake.

answer (answers, answering, answered) n An **answer** is something that you say or write when you answer someone. উত্তর ▷ v When you **answer** someone who has asked you something, you say something back to them. উত্তর দেওয়া

answering machine (answering machines) n An **answering machine** is a device which records telephone messages while you are out. উত্তর দেওয়ার যন্ত্র

answerphone (answerphones) n An **answerphone** is a device which you connect to your telephone and which records telephone calls while you are out. উত্তর দেওয়ার যন্ত্র (ফোনের সাথে সংযুক্ত)

ant (ants) n **Ants** are small crawling insects that live in large groups. পিঁপড়ে

antagonize (antagonizes, antagonizing, antagonized) vt If you **antagonize** someone, you make them feel hostile towards you. শত্রুভাবাপন্ন করে তোলা

Antarctic n The **Antarctic** is the area around the South Pole. দক্ষিণ মেরু

Antarctica n **Antarctica** is a continent around the South Pole. It is extremely cold and there is very little light in winter and very little darkness in summer. অ্যান্টার্কটিকা মহাদেশ

antelope (antelopes, antelope) n An **antelope** is an animal like a deer, with long legs and horns, that lives in Africa or Asia. Antelopes are graceful and can run fast. কৃষ্ণসার হরিণ

antenatal adj **Antenatal** means relating to the medical care of women when they are expecting a baby. গর্ভবতী নারীর পরিচর্যা

anthem (anthems) n An **anthem** is a song or hymn written for a special occasion. স্তুতিমূলক গান

anthropology n **Anthropology** is the study of people, society, and culture. নৃতত্ত্ববিদ্যা

antibiotic (antibiotics) n **Antibiotics** are drugs that are used in medicine to kill bacteria and to cure infections. সংক্রমণরোধী ওষুধ

antibody (antibodies) n **Antibodies** are substances which your body produces in order to fight diseases. অ্যান্টিবডি

anticlockwise adv If something is moving **anticlockwise**, it is moving in the opposite direction to the direction in which the hands of a clock move. ঘড়ির কাঁটার বিপরীতমুখে

antidepressant (antidepressants) n An **antidepressant** is a drug which is used to treat people who are suffering from depression. অবসাদ-প্রতিরোধক

antidote (antidotes) n An **antidote** is a chemical substance that controls the effect of a poison. বিষনাশক পদার্থ

antifreeze n **Antifreeze** is a liquid which is added to water to stop it freezing. It is used in car radiators in cold weather. জমাট-প্রতিরোধক

antihistamine (antihistamines) n An **antihistamine** is a drug that is used to treat allergies. অ্যালার্জির ওষুধ

antiperspirant (antiperspirants) n An **antiperspirant** is a substance that you put on your skin to stop you from sweating. ঘামনাশক পদার্থ

antique (antiques) n An **antique** is an old object which is valuable because of its beauty or rarity. প্রাচীনকালের দুর্মূল্য বস্তু

antique shop (antique shops) n An **antique shop** is a shop where antiques are sold. দুর্মূল্য বস্তুর দোকান

antiseptic (**antiseptics**) *n* **Antiseptic** kills harmful bacteria. অ্যান্টিসেপটিক

anxiety (**anxieties**) *n* **Anxiety** is a feeling of nervousness or worry. উদ্বেগ

any *det* You use **any** to mean some of a thing. কোন *Is there any juice left?* ▷ *pron* **Any** is used in negative sentences to show that no person or thing is involved. যে কেউ *The children needed new clothes and we couldn't afford any.* ▷ *det* You use **any** to show that it does not matter which one. যে কোন *Take any book you want.*

anybody *pron* You use **anybody** to talk about a person, when it does not matter which one. যে কেউ *Is there anybody there?*

anyhow *adv* You use **anyhow** to give the idea that something is true even though other things have been said. যাইহোক

anymore *adv* If something used to happen or is not true **anymore**, it has stopped happening or is no longer true. আর নয়

anyone *pron* You use **anyone** to talk about a person, when it does not matter who. কাউকে *Don't tell anyone.*

anything *pron* You use **anything** to talk about a thing, when it does not matter which one. কোন জিনিস *I can't see anything.*

anytime *adv* You use **anytime** to mean a point in time that is not fixed. যে কোন সময়

anyway *adv* You use **anyway** or **anyhow** to give the idea that something is true even though other things have been said. যাইহোক

anywhere *adv* You use **anywhere** to talk about a place, when it does not matter which one. যে কোন জায়গায়

apart *adv* When things are **apart**, there is a space or a distance between them. ব্যবধানে ▷ *adv* If you take something **apart**, you take it to pieces. খুলে ফেলা

apart from *prep* You use **apart from** when you are giving an exception to a general statement. এ ছাড়া *The room was empty apart from one man sitting beside the fire.*

apartment (**apartments**) *n* An **apartment** is a set of rooms for living in, usually on one floor of a large building. অ্যাপার্টমেন্ট

aperitif (**aperitifs**) *n* An **aperitif** is an alcoholic drink that you have before a meal. মদ্যবিশেষ

aperture (**apertures**) *n* An **aperture** is a narrow hole or gap. (*formal*) সরু গর্ত

apologize (**apologizes, apologizing, apologized**) *vi* When you **apologize** to someone, you say that you are sorry that you have hurt them or caused trouble for them. ক্ষমা চাওয়া

apology (**apologies**) *n* An **apology** is something that you say or write in order to tell someone that you are sorry that you have hurt them or caused trouble for them. ক্ষমা

apostrophe (**apostrophes**) *n* An **apostrophe** is the mark ' that shows that one or more letters have been removed from a word, as in 'isn't'. It is also added to nouns to show possession, as in 'the girl's doll'. অ্যাপস্ট্রফি, একটি চিহ্ন

appalling *adj* Something that is **appalling** is so bad that it shocks you. মর্মঘাতী

apparatus (**apparatuses**) *n* The **apparatus** of an organization or system is its structure and method of operation. যন্ত্রপাতি

apparent *adj* An **apparent** situation seems to be the case, although you cannot be certain that it is. প্রত্যক্ষ

apparently *adv* You use **apparently** to refer to something that seems to be the case although it may not be. আপাতরূপে

appeal (**appeals, appealing, appealed**) *n* An **appeal** is a serious and urgent request. গুরুত্বপূর্ণ আবেদন ▷ *vi* If you **appeal** to someone to do something, you make a serious and urgent request to them. জরুরী আবেদন করা

appear (**appears, appearing, appeared**) *vt* If something **appears** to be the way you describe it, it seems that way. প্রকাশ পাওয়া

appearance (appearances) *n* When someone makes an **appearance** at a public event or in a broadcast, they take part in it. অংশ নেওয়া

appendicitis *n* **Appendicitis** is an illness in which a person's appendix is infected and painful. অ্যাপিন্ডিসাইটিস

appetite (appetites) *n* Your **appetite** is your desire to eat. ক্ষুধার ইচ্ছা

applaud (applauds, applauding, applauded) *v* When a group of people **applaud** or **applaud** someone, they clap their hands to show that they have enjoyed a performance. হাততালির মাধ্যমে প্রশংসা করা

applause *n* **Applause** is the noise made by a group of people clapping their hands to show approval. হাততালি দিয়ে প্রশংসা

apple (apples) *n* An **apple** is a round fruit with a smooth skin and firm white flesh. আপেল

apple pie (apple pies) *n* An **apple pie** is a kind of pie made with apples. আপেলের পিঠা

appliance (appliances) *n* An **appliance** is a device such as a vacuum cleaner that does a particular job in your home. (*formal*) সরঞ্জাম

applicant (applicants) *n* An **applicant** for a job or position is someone who applies for it. আবেদনকারী

application (applications) *n* An **application** for something such as a job or a place at a college is a formal written request to be given it. আবেদন

application form (application forms) *n* An **application form** is a formal written request for something such as a job or membership of an organization. আবেদনপত্র

apply (applies, applying, applied) *v* If you **apply** for something or to something, you ask to be allowed to have it or do it. আবেদন করা

appoint (appoints, appointing, appointed) *vt* If you **appoint** someone to a job or post, you formally choose them for it. নিয়োগ করা

appointment (appointments) *n* The **appointment** of a person to a particular job is the choice of that person to do it. নিয়োগ

appreciate (appreciates, appreciating, appreciated) *vt* If you **appreciate** something, you like it because you recognize its good qualities. প্রশংসা করা

apprehensive *adj* Someone who is **apprehensive** is afraid that something bad may happen. শঙ্কিত

apprentice (apprentices) *n* An **apprentice** is a person who works with someone in order to learn their skill. শিক্ষার্থী

approach (approaches, approaching, approached) *v* When you **approach** something, you get closer to it. প্রস্তাব রাখা

appropriate *adj* Something that is **appropriate** is suitable or acceptable for a particular situation. যথাযথ

approval *n* If a plan or request gets someone's **approval**, they agree to it. অনুমোদন

approve (approves, approving, approved) *vi* If you **approve** of something or someone, you like them or think they are good. অনুমোদন করা

approximate *adj* **Approximate** figures are close to the correct figure, but are not exact. আনুমানিক

approximately *adv* **Approximately** means close to, around, or roughly. আনুমানিকভাবে

apricot (apricots) *n* An **apricot** is a small, soft, round fruit with yellow-orange flesh and a stone inside. খোবানি

April (Aprils) *n* **April** is the fourth month of the year in the Western calendar. এপ্রিল

April Fools' Day *n* In the West, **April Fools' Day** is the 1st of April, the day on which people traditionally play tricks on each other. "এপ্রিল ফুল" দিবস

apron (aprons) *n* An **apron** is a piece of clothing that you put on over the front of your clothes to prevent them from getting dirty. ঢলঢলে বহির্বাস

aquarium (**aquariums, aquaria**) *n* An **aquarium** is a building, often in a zoo, where fish and underwater animals are kept. অ্যাকোয়ারিয়াম

Aquarius *n* **Aquarius** is one of the twelve signs of the zodiac. Its symbol is a person pouring water. People who are born between 20th January and 18th February come under this sign. কুম্ভ রাশি

Arab (**Arabs**) *adj* **Arab** means belonging or relating to Arabs or to their countries or customs. আরব দেশের ▷ *n* **Arabs** are people who speak Arabic and who come from the Middle East and parts of North Africa. আরবীয়

Arabic *n* **Arabic** is a language that is spoken in the Middle East and in parts of North Africa. আরবি ভাষা ▷ *adj* Something that is **Arabic** belongs or relates to the language, writing, or culture of the Arabs. আরবদেশীয়

arbitration *n* **Arbitration** is the judging of a dispute between people or groups by someone who is not involved. সালিশি

arch (**arches**) *n* An **arch** is a structure which is made when two columns join at the top in a curve. খিলান

archaeologist (**archaeologists**) *n* An **archaeologist** is a person who studies the

past by examining the remains of things such as buildings and tools. পুরাতাত্ত্বিক

archaeology *n* **Archaeology** is the study of the past by examining the remains of things such as buildings and tools. পুরাতত্ত্ব

architect (**architects**) *n* An **architect** is a person who designs buildings. স্থপতি

architecture *n* **Architecture** is the art of designing and constructing buildings. স্থাপত্যবিদ্যা

archive (**archives**) *n* **Archives** are collections of documents that contain information about the history of an organization or group of people. সংরক্ষণাগার

Arctic *n* **The Arctic** is the area of the world around the North Pole. It is extremely cold and there is very little light in winter and very little darkness in summer. সুমেরু অঞ্চল

Arctic Circle *n* **The Arctic Circle** is an imaginary line drawn around the northern part of the world at approximately 66° North. সুমেরু বলয়

Arctic Ocean *n* The **Arctic Ocean** is the ocean surrounding the North Pole, north of the Arctic Circle. সুমেরু মহাসাগর

area (**areas**) *n* An **area** is a particular part of a city, a country, or the world. অঞ্চল

Argentina *n* **Argentina** is a republic in southern South America. আর্জেন্টিনা

Argentinian (**Argentinians**) *adj* **Argentinian** means belonging or relating to Argentina or its people. আর্জেন্টিনা সম্পর্কিত ▷ *n* An **Argentinian** is someone who comes from Argentina. আর্জেন্টিনা-বাসী

argue (**argues, arguing, argued**) *vi* If you **argue** with someone, you disagree with them about something, often angrily. তর্কবিতর্ক করা

argument (**arguments**) *n* If people have an **argument**, they disagree with each other, often angrily. তর্কবিতর্ক

Aries *n* **Aries** is one of the twelve signs of the zodiac. Its symbol is a ram. People who are born between 21st March and 19th April come under this sign. মেষ রাশি

arm (**arms**) *n* Your **arms** are the two parts of your body between your shoulders and your hands. বাহু

armchair (**armchairs**) *n* An **armchair** is a comfortable chair with a support on each side for your arms. আর্মচেয়ার

armed *adj* Someone who is **armed** is carrying a weapon. সশস্ত্র

Armenia *n* **Armenia** is a republic in north-west Asia. আর্মেনিয়া

Armenian (**Armenians**) *adj* **Armenian** means of or relating to Armenia, its inhabitants, their language, or the Armenian Church. আর্মেনিয়া সম্পর্কিত ▷ *n* An **Armenian** is a native or inhabitant of Armenia or an Armenian-speaking person elsewhere. আর্মেনিয়া-বাসী ▷ *n* **Armenian** is the language spoken by people who live in Armenia. আর্মেনিয়ান ভাষা

armour *n* In former times, **armour** was special metal clothing that soldiers wore for protection in battle. বর্ম

armpit (**armpits**) *n* Your **armpits** are the areas of your body under your arms where your arms join your shoulders. বগল

army (**armies**) *n* An **army** is a large organized group of people who are armed and trained to fight. সেনাবাহিনী

aroma (**aromas**) *n* An **aroma** is a strong pleasant smell. সুগন্ধ

aromatherapy *n* **Aromatherapy** is a type of treatment which involves massaging the body with special fragrant oils. সুগন্ধ-চিকিৎসা

around *adv* **Around** means surrounding, or on all sides of. আশপাশে ▷ *prep* Things or people that are **around** a place or object surround it or are on all sides of it. চারিধারে *There were lots of people around her.* ▷ *prep* You use **around** to say that something is in every part of a place. চারিধারে *His toys lay around the room.* ▷ *prep* **Around** means near to something. প্রায় *We left around noon.*

arrange (**arranges**, **arranging**, **arranged**) *v* If you **arrange** something, you make plans for it to happen. আয়োজন করা ▷ *vt* If you **arrange** things somewhere, you put them in a way that looks tidy or pretty. সাজিয়ে রাখা

arrangement (**arrangements**) *n* **Arrangements** are plans and preparations which you make so that something can happen. ব্যবস্থাপনা

arrears *npl* **Arrears** are amounts of money that someone owes. If someone is **in arrears** with regular payments, they have not paid them. বকেয়া

arrest (**arrests**, **arresting**, **arrested**) *n* An **arrest** is the act of taking a person into custody, especially under lawful authority. গ্রেপ্তার ▷ *vt* If the police **arrest** you, they take charge of you and take you to a police station, because they believe you may have committed a crime. গ্রেপ্তার করা

arrival (**arrivals**) *n* Your **arrival** at a place is the act of arriving there. আগমন

arrive (**arrives**, **arriving**, **arrived**) *vi* When you **arrive** at a place, you reach it at the end of a journey. পৌঁছে যাওয়া ✦

arrogant *adj* If you say that someone is **arrogant**, you disapprove of them because they behave as if they are better than other people. উদ্ধত

arrow (**arrows**) *n* An **arrow** is a long, thin stick with a sharp point at one end. তীর ▷ *n* An **arrow** is a sign that shows you which way to go. তীরচিহ্ন

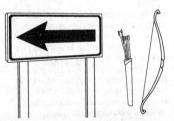

arson n **Arson** is the crime of deliberately setting fire to a building or vehicle. আগুন ধরিয়ে দেওয়ার মত ইচ্ছাকৃত অপরাধ

art n **Art** is paintings, drawings, and sculpture which are beautiful or which express an artist's ideas. চারুকলা

artery (**arteries**) n Your **arteries** are the tubes that carry blood from your heart to the rest of your body. ধমনী

art gallery (**art galleries**) n An **art gallery** is a building where paintings and other works of art are shown to the public. শিল্প প্যালারি

arthritis n **Arthritis** is a condition in which the joints in someone's body are swollen and painful. গেঁটেবাত

artichoke (**artichokes**) n An **artichoke** or a **globe artichoke** is a round vegetable with thick green leaves arranged like the petals of a flower. এক ধরনের সবুজ সবজি

article (**articles**) n An **article** is a piece of writing in a newspaper or magazine. প্রবন্ধ

artificial adj **Artificial** objects, materials, or situations do not occur naturally and are created by people. কৃত্রিম

artist (**artists**) n An **artist** is someone who draws, paints, or produces other works of art. শিল্পী

artistic adj Someone who is **artistic** is good at drawing or painting, or arranging things in a beautiful way. শিল্পসম্পন্ন

art school (**art schools**) n An **art school** is a college that specializes in art. চারুকলা বিদ্যালয়

as conj If one thing happens **as** a different thing happens, it happens at the same time. যখনই We shut the door behind us as we entered. ▷ prep You use **as** when you are talking about somebody's job. হিসাবে He works as a doctor.

asap abbr **Asap** is an abbreviation for 'as soon as possible'. যত তাড়াতাড়ি সম্ভব

as ... as adv You use the structure **as ... as** when you are comparing things, or emphasizing how large or small something is. মত

ashamed adj If someone is **ashamed** of something or someone, they feel embarrassed about it or guilty because of it. লজ্জিত

ashtray (**ashtrays**) n An **ashtray** is a small dish in which people put the ash from their cigarettes and cigars. ছাইদানি

Ash Wednesday n **Ash Wednesday** is the first day of Lent. খ্রীষ্টানদের চল্লিশ দিনব্যাপী উৎসবের প্রথম দিন এটি

Asia n **Asia** is the largest of the continents, bordering on the Arctic Ocean, the Pacific Ocean, the Indian Ocean, and the Mediterranean and Red Seas in the west. এশিয়া বৃহত্তম মহাদেশ

Asian (**Asians**) adj **Asian** means belonging or relating to Asia. এশিয়া সম্পর্কিত ▷ n An **Asian** is a person who comes from a country or region in Asia. এশিয়ার অধিবাসী

aside adv If you move something **aside**, you move it to one side of you. একপাশে

ask (**asks, asking, asked**) vt If you **ask** someone a question, you say that you want to know something. জিজ্ঞাসা করা

ask for v If you **ask for** something, you say that you want it. চাওয়া She asked for some sweets.

asleep adj Someone who is **asleep** is sleeping. ঘুমন্ত

asparagus n **Asparagus** is a vegetable with green shoots that you cook and eat. অ্যাসপ্যারাগাস/একপ্রকারের জলজ উত্তিদ

aspect (**aspects**) *n* An **aspect** of something is one of the parts of its character or nature. দিক

aspirin (**aspirins, aspirin**) *n* **Aspirin** is a mild drug which reduces pain and fever. ব্যথানাশক ওষুধ

assembly (**assemblies**) *n* An **assembly** is a group of people gathered together for a particular purpose. সমাবেশ

asset (**assets**) *n* If something that you have is an **asset**, it is useful to you. সম্পদ

assignment (**assignments**) *n* An **assignment** is a piece of work that you are given to do, as part of your job or studies. কাজ

assistance *n* If you give someone **assistance**, you help them. সহায়তা

assistant (**assistants**) *n* Someone's **assistant** is a person who helps them in their work. সহায়ক

associate (**associates**) *adj* **Associate** is used before a rank or title to indicate a slightly different or lower rank or title. সহযোগী ▷ *n* Your **associates** are your business colleagues. সঙ্গী

association (**associations**) *n* An **association** is an official group of people who have the same occupation, aim, or interest. সমিতি

assortment (**assortments**) *n* An **assortment** is a group of similar things that have different sizes, colours, or qualities. সংগ্রহ

assume (**assumes, assuming, assumed**) *vt* If you **assume** that something is true, you suppose that it is true, sometimes wrongly. অনুমান করা

assure (**assures, assuring, assured**) *vt* If you **assure** someone that something is true or will happen, you tell them that it is the case, to make them less worried. নিশ্চিত করা

asthma *n* **Asthma** is an illness which affects the chest and makes breathing difficult. হাঁপানি

astonish (**astonishes, astonishing, astonished**) *vt* If someone or something

astonishes you, they surprise you very much. বিস্ময়

astonished *adj* If you are **astonished** by something, you are very surprised about it. বিস্মিত

astonishing *adj* Something that is **astonishing** is very surprising. বিস্ময়কর

astrology *n* **Astrology** is the study of the movements of the planets, sun, moon, and stars in the belief that they can influence people's lives. জ্যোতিষশাস্ত্র

astronaut (**astronauts**) *n* An **astronaut** is a person who travels in a spacecraft. মহাকাশচারী

astronomy *n* **Astronomy** is the scientific study of the stars, planets, and other natural objects in space. জ্যোতির্বিদ্যা

asylum (**asylums**) *n* If a government gives a person from another country **asylum**, they allow them to stay, usually because they are unable to return home safely for political reasons. আশ্রয় দান

asylum seeker (**asylum seekers**) *n* An **asylum seeker** is a person who is trying to get asylum in a foreign country. আশ্রয় খোঁজে যারা

at *prep* You use **at** to say where or when something happens or where it is. কোন স্থানে *I'll meet you at the information desk at seven o'clock.*

atheist (**atheists**) *n* An **atheist** is a person who believes that there is no God. নাস্তিক

athlete (**athletes**) *n* An **athlete** is a person who takes part in athletics competitions. ক্রীড়াবিদ

athletic *adj* **Athletic** means relating to athletes and athletics. ক্রীড়াবিষয়ক

athletics *npl* **Athletics** consists of sports such as running, the high jump, and the javelin. ক্রীড়া

Atlantic Ocean *n* The **Atlantic Ocean** is the second largest ocean in the world. আটলান্টিক মহাসমুদ্র

atlas (**atlases**) *n* An **atlas** is a book of maps. মানচিত্রের বই

at least *adv* **At least** means not less than. কমপক্ষে

atmosphere (**atmospheres**) *n* A planet's **atmosphere** is the layer of air or other gas around it. বায়ুমণ্ডল

atom (**atoms**) *n* An **atom** is the smallest possible amount of a chemical element. পরমাণু

atom bomb (**atom bombs**) *n* An **atom bomb** is a bomb that causes an explosion by a sudden release of energy that results from splitting atoms. পারমাণবিক বোমা

atomic *adj* **Atomic** means relating to atoms or to the power produced by splitting atoms. পরমাণুসংক্রান্ত

attach (**attaches, attaching, attached**) *vt* If you **attach** something to an object, you join it or fasten it to the object. যুক্ত করা

attached *adj* If you are **attached** to someone or something, you care deeply about them. যুক্ত

attachment (**attachments**) *n* An **attachment** to someone or something is a love or liking for them. সংযুক্তি

attack (**attacks, attacking, attacked**) *n* An **attack** is the act or an instance of attacking. আক্রমণ ▷ *v* To **attack** a person or place means to try to hurt or damage them using physical violence. আক্রমণ করা

attempt (**attempts, attempting, attempted**) *n* If you make an **attempt** to do something, you try to do it, often without success. চেষ্টা ▷ *vt* If you **attempt** to do something, especially something difficult, you try to do it. চেষ্টা করা

attend (**attends, attending, attended**) *v* If you **attend** a meeting or other event, you are at it. উপস্থিত হওয়া

attendance *n* Someone's **attendance** at an event or an institution is the fact that they are present at the event or go regularly to the institution. উপস্থিতি

attention *n* If something has your **attention** or if you are paying **attention** to it, you have noticed it and are interested in it. মনোযোগ

attic (**attics**) *n* An **attic** is a room at the top of a house, just below the roof. চিলেকোঠার ঘর

attitude (**attitudes**) *n* Your **attitude** to something is the way you think and feel about it. হাবভাব

attract (**attracts, attracting, attracted**) *vt* If something **attracts** people or animals, it has features that cause them to come to it. আকর্ষণ করা

attraction (**attractions**) *n* **Attraction** is a feeling of liking someone. আকর্ষণ

attractive *adj* An **attractive** person or thing is pleasant to look at. আকর্ষণীয়

aubergine (**aubergines**) *n* An **aubergine** is a vegetable with a smooth purple skin. বেগুন

auburn *adj* **Auburn** hair is reddish brown. লালচে বাদামী

auction (**auctions**) *n* An **auction** is a sale where goods are sold to the person who offers the highest price. নিলাম

audience (**audiences**) *n* The **audience** is all the people who are watching or listening to a play, concert, film, or programme. দর্শক

audit (**audits, auditing, audited**) *n* An **audit** is an inspection, correction, and verification of business accounts, conducted by an independent qualified accountant. হিসাব নিরীক্ষণ ▷ *vt* When an accountant **audits** an organization's accounts, he or she examines the accounts officially in order to make sure that they have been done correctly. হিসাব নিরীক্ষণ করা

audition (**auditions**) *n* An **audition** is a short performance given by an actor, dancer, or musician so that someone can decide if they are good enough to be in a play, film, or orchestra. স্বর-শ্রুতি পরীক্ষা

auditor (**auditors**) *n* An **auditor** is an accountant who officially examines the accounts of organizations. হিসাব নিরীক্ষক

August (**Augusts**) *n* **August** is the eighth month of the year in the Western calendar. আগস্ট মাস

aunt (**aunts**) *n* Your **aunt** is the sister of your mother or father, or the wife of your uncle. পিসি, মাসি, কাকিমা, জেঠিমা

auntie (**aunties**) *n* Someone's **auntie** is the sister of their mother or father, or the wife of their uncle. (*informal*) পিসি, মাসি, কাকিমা, জেঠিমা

au pair (**au pairs**) *n* An **au pair** is a young person who lives with a family in a foreign country in order to learn their language and help around the house. একজন অল্পবয়স্ক ব্যক্তি যে বিদেশে কোন পরিবারে থেকে তাদের ভাষা, ঐতিহ্য শেখে

austerity *n* **Austerity** is a situation in which people's living standards are reduced because of economic difficulties. মিতব্যয়িতা

Australasia *n* **Australasia** is Australia, New Zealand, and neighbouring islands in the South Pacific Ocean. অস্ট্রেলেশিয়া অস্ট্রেলিয়া, নিউজিল্যান্ড এবং সন্নিহিত দ্বীপপুঞ্জ

Australia *n* **Australia** is a country located between the Indian Ocean and the Pacific. অস্ট্রেলিয়া

Australian (**Australians**) *adj* **Australian** means belonging or relating to Australia, or to its people or culture. অস্ট্রেলিয়া সম্পর্কিত ▷ *n* An **Australian** is someone who comes from Australia. অস্ট্রেলিয়া-বাসী

Austria *n* **Austria** is a republic in central Europe. অস্ট্রিয়া

Austrian (**Austrians**) *adj* **Austrian** means belonging or relating to Austria, or to its people or culture. অস্ট্রিয়া সম্পর্কিত ▷ *n* An **Austrian** is a person who comes from Austria. অস্ট্রিয়া-বাসী

authentic *adj* If something is **authentic**, it is genuine or accurate. নির্ভরযোগ্য

author (**authors**) *n* The **author** of a piece of writing is the person who wrote it. লেখক

authorize (**authorizes, authorizing, authorized**) *vt* If someone **authorizes** something, they give their official permission for it to happen. অনুমোদন

autobiography (**autobiographies**) *n* Your **autobiography** is an account of your life, which you write yourself. আত্মজীবনী

autograph (**autographs**) *n* An **autograph** is the signature of someone famous which is specially written for a fan to keep. অটোগ্রাফ

automatic *adj* An **automatic** machine or device is one which has controls that enable it to perform a task without needing to be constantly operated by a person. স্বয়ংক্রিয়

automatically *adv* If you do something **automatically**, you do it without thinking about it. স্বয়ংক্রিয়ভাবে

autonomous *adj* An **autonomous** country, organization, or group governs or controls itself rather than being controlled by anyone else. স্বশাসিত

autonomy *n* If a country, person, or group has **autonomy**, they control themselves rather than being controlled by others. স্বায়ত্তশাসন

autumn (**autumns**) *n* **Autumn** is the season between summer and winter. শরৎকাল

availability *n* The **availability** of something is the ease with which you can find it or obtain it. লভ্যতা

available *adj* If something is **available**, you can use it or obtain it. লভ্য

avalanche (**avalanches**) *n* An **avalanche** is a large mass of snow or rock that falls down the side of a mountain. বরফের ধস

avenue (**avenues**) *n* An **avenue** is a wide road, with shops or houses on each side. চওড়া রাস্তা

average (**averages**) *adj* If you describe a figure as **average**, you mean that it represents a numerical average. গড়পড়তা মান ▷ *n* An **average** is the result that you get when you add two or more numbers together and divide the total by the number of numbers you added together. গড়

avocado (**avocados**) *n* An **avocado** is a fruit in the shape of a pear with a dark green skin and a large stone inside it. আভোকাডো

avoid (**avoids, avoiding, avoided**) *vt* If you **avoid** something unpleasant that might happen, you take action in order to prevent it from happening. এড়িয়ে যাওয়া

awake (**awakes, awaking, awoke, awoken**) *adj* If you are **awake**, you are not sleeping. জাগ্রত ▷ *v* When you **awake**, or when something **awakes** you, you wake up. (*literary*) জেগে থাকা

award (**awards**) *n* An **award** is a prize or certificate you get for doing something well. পুরস্কার

aware *adj* If you are **aware** of a fact or situation, you know about it. সচেতন

away *adv* If someone moves **away** from a place, they move so that they are not there any more. চলে যাওয়া ▷ *adv* If you put something **away**, you put it where it should be. সরিয়ে রাখা

away match (**away matches**) *n* When a sports team plays an **away match**, it plays on its opponents' ground. প্রতিপক্ষের মাঠে যে খেলা হয়

awful *adj* If you say that someone or something is **awful**, you dislike that person or thing or you think that they are not very good. জঘন্য

awfully *adv* You use **awfully** to emphasize how much of a quality someone or something has. প্রচণ্ডভাবে

awkward *adj* An **awkward** situation is embarrassing and difficult to deal with. উদ্ভট

axe (**axes**) *n* An **axe** is a tool used for chopping wood. It consists of a blade attached to the end of a long handle. কুঠার

axle (**axles**) *n* An **axle** is a rod connecting a pair of wheels on a car or other vehicle. গাড়ীর চাকার রড

Azerbaijan *n* **Azerbaijan** is a republic in north-west Asia. আজারবাইজান

Azerbaijani (**Azerbaijanis**) *adj* **Azerbaijani** means belonging or relating to Azerbaijan. আজারবাইজান সম্পর্কিত ▷ *n* An **Azerbaijani** is a native or inhabitant of Azerbaijan. আজারবাইজান-বাসী

b

BA (BAs) abbr A **BA** is a first degree in an arts or social science subject. **BA** is an abbreviation for 'Bachelor of Arts'. সাহিত্যে স্নাতক

baby (babies) n A **baby** is a very young child that cannot yet walk or talk. শিশু

baby milk n **Baby milk** is a powder which you mix with water to make artificial milk for babies. শিশুদের দুধ

baby's bottle (babies' bottles) n A **baby's bottle** is a drinking container used by babies. It has a special rubber part at the top through which they can suck their drink. শিশুদের দুধ খাওয়ার বোতল

babysit (babysits, babysitting, babysat) v If you **babysit** for someone or **babysit** their children, you look after their children while they are out. শিশু পরিচর্যা করা

babysitter (babysitters) n A **babysitter** is a person who looks after someone's children while they are out. শিশু পরিচর্যাকারী

babysitting n **Babysitting** is the action of looking after someone's children while they are out. শিশু পরিচর্যা

baby wipe (baby wipes) n A **baby wipe** is a disposable moistened medicated paper towel, usually supplied in a plastic drum or packet, used for cleaning babies. শিশুদের পরিষ্কার করার তোয়ালে

bachelor (bachelors) n A **bachelor** is a man who has never married. অবিবাহিত

back (backs, backing, backed) adj **Back** is used to refer to the part of something that is farthest from the front. পেছনে ▷ adv If you move **back**, you move away from the way you are facing. বিপরীত দিকে ▷ n Your **back** is the part of your body from your neck to your bottom. পিঠ ▷ vi If a building **backs** onto something, the back of it faces that thing. পেছনের দিকে ▷ n The **back** of something is the side or part of it that is farthest from the front. পিছনে

backache (backaches) n **Backache** is a dull pain in your back. পিঠে ব্যথা

backbone (backbones) n Your **backbone** is the column of small linked bones along the middle of your back. মেরুদণ্ড

backfire (backfires, backfiring, backfired) vi If a plan **backfires**, it has the opposite result to the one that was intended. অসফল হওয়া

background (backgrounds) n Your **background** is the kind of family you come from and the kind of education you have had. পরিচয়

backing (backings) n **Backing** is money, resources, or support given to a person or organization. সাহায্য

back out v If you **back out**, you decide not to do something that you previously agreed to do. সরে আসা They backed out of the project.

backpack (backpacks) n A **backpack** is a bag with straps that go over your shoulders, so that you can carry things on your back when you are walking or climbing. পেছনে ঝোলানোর ব্যাগ

backpacker (backpackers) n A **backpacker** is a person who goes travelling with a backpack. পেছনে ঝোলা বয়ে নিয়ে যাওয়া ভ্রমণকারী

backpacking n If you go **backpacking**, you go travelling with a backpack. ভ্রমণ

back pain n **Back pain** is pain that you feel in your back. পিঠের ব্যথা/কোমরের ব্যথা

backside (**backsides**) *n* Your **backside** is the part of your body that you sit on. (*informal*) শরীরের পেছনের অংশ

backslash (**backslashes**) *n* A **backslash** is the mark \. বাঁ দিকে হেলানো একটি চিহ্ন

backstroke *n* **Backstroke** is a swimming stroke that you do on your back. ব্যাকস্ট্রোক(সাঁতারের একটি ভঙ্গী)

back up (**backups**) *v* If someone or something **backs up** a statement, they show that it is true. সমর্থন করা *He didn't have any proof to back up his story.* ▷ *n* **Backup** consists of extra equipment or people that you can get help or support from if necessary. সহায়ক

backwards *adv* If you move **backwards**, you move in the direction behind you. পিছনের দিকে ▷ *adv* If you do something **backwards**, you do it the opposite of the usual way. উল্টোদিকে

bacon *n* **Bacon** is salted or smoked meat taken from the back or sides of a pig. লবণে জারিত শুয়োরের মাংস

bacteria *npl* **Bacteria** are very small organisms which can cause disease. জীবাণু

bad (**worse**, **worst**) *adj* Something that is **bad** is not nice or good. খারাপ ▷ *adj* Someone who is **bad** does things they should not do. মন্দ

badge (**badges**) *n* A **badge** is a small piece of metal or cloth showing a design or words, which you attach to your clothes. ব্যাজ

badger (**badgers**) *n* A **badger** is a wild animal with a white head with two wide black stripes on it. একজাতীয় ক্ষুদ্র নিশাচর প্রাণী

badly *adv* If you do something **badly**, you do it with very little success or effect. বাজে ভাবে

badminton *n* **Badminton** is a game played on a rectangular court by two or four players. They hit a feathered object called a shuttlecock across a high net. ব্যাডমিন্টন

bad-tempered *adj* If you are **bad-tempered**, you are not cheerful and get angry easily. বদরাগী

baffled *adj* If you are **baffled** by something, you cannot understand or explain it. বিভ্রান্ত

bag (**bags**) *n* A **bag** is a container made of paper, plastic, or leather which you use to carry things. ব্যাগ/থলে

baggage *n* Your **baggage** consists of the suitcases and bags that you take with you when you travel. মালপত্র

baggy (**baggier**, **baggiest**) *adj* **Baggy** clothes hang loosely on your body. ঢিলে-ঢালা পোষাক

bagpipes *npl* **Bagpipes** are a musical instrument that are played by blowing air through a pipe into a bag, and then squeezing the bag to force the air out through other pipes. হাওয়াবাদিত বাদ্যযন্ত্র

Bahamas *npl* The **Bahamas** are a group of over 700 coral islands in the Caribbean. বাহামাস দ্বীপপুঞ্জ

Bahrain *n* **Bahrain** is a country on the Persian Gulf that consists of several islands. বাহরিন

bail *n* **Bail** is a sum of money that an arrested person or someone else puts forward as a guarantee that the arrested person will attend their trial in a law court. If the arrested person does not attend it, the money is lost. জামিন

bake (bakes, baking, baked) *vi* If you **bake**, you spend some time preparing and mixing together ingredients to make bread, cakes, pies, or other food which is cooked in the oven. সেঁকা

baked *adj* **Baked** food is cooked in the oven. সেঁকা খাবার

baked potato (baked potatoes) *n* A **baked potato** is a large potato that has been baked with its skin on. সেঁকা আলু

baker (bakers) *n* A **baker** is a person whose job is to bake and sell bread and cakes. রুটিওয়ালা

bakery (bakeries) *n* A **bakery** is a building where bread and cakes are baked, or the shop where they are sold. বেকারী

baking *n* **Baking** is the activity of cooking bread or cakes in an oven. রুটি তৈরী করার পদ্ধতি

baking powder (baking powders) *n* **Baking powder** is an ingredient used in cake making. It causes cakes to rise when they are in the oven. বেকিং পাউডার

balance *n* **Balance** is the steadiness that someone or something has when they are balanced on something. ভারসাম্য

balanced *adj* A **balanced** account or report is fair and reasonable. সামঞ্জস্যপূর্ণ

balance sheet (balance sheets) *n* A **balance sheet** is a written statement of the amount of money and property that a company or person has, including amounts of money that are owed or are owing. ব্যালেন্স শিট

balcony (balconies) *n* A **balcony** is a platform on the outside of a building with a wall or railing around it. ঝুলবারান্দা

bald (balder, baldest) *adj* Someone who is **bald** has little or no hair on the top of their head. টেকো

Balkan *adj* **Balkan** means of or relating to the Balkan Peninsula or the Balkan Mountains, or to the Balkan States or their inhabitants. বলকান উপদ্বীপ সম্বন্ধীয়

ball (balls) *n* A **ball** is a round object used in games such as football. বল ▷ n A **ball** is a large formal dance. বলনৃত্য

ballerina (ballerinas) *n* A **ballerina** is a woman ballet dancer. ব্যালে নর্তকী

ballet *n* **Ballet** is a type of artistic dancing with carefully planned movements. ব্যালে নৃত্য

ballet dancer (ballet dancers) *n* A **ballet dancer** is a dancer who does ballet, especially as a profession. ব্যালে নর্তক/নর্তকী

ballet shoes *npl* **Ballet shoes** are special soft, light shoes that ballet dancers wear. ব্যালে নৃত্যের জুতো

balloon (balloons) *n* A **balloon** is a small, thin, rubber bag that becomes larger when you blow air into it. বেলুন

ballpoint (ballpoints) *n* A **ballpoint** or a **ballpoint pen** is a pen with a very small metal ball at the end which transfers the ink from the pen onto a surface. বল পেন

ballroom dancing *n* **Ballroom dancing** is a type of dancing in which a man and a woman dance together using fixed sequences of steps and movements. বলরুম নৃত্য

bamboo (bamboos) *n* **Bamboo** is a tall tropical plant with hard hollow stems. বাঁশ

ban (bans, banning, banned) *n* A **ban** is an official ruling that something must not be done, shown, or used. নিষিদ্ধ ▷ vt To **ban** something means to state officially that it must not be done, shown, or used. নিষিদ্ধ করা

banana (bananas) *n* A **banana** is a long curved fruit with a yellow skin. কলা

band (bands) *n* A **band** is a group of people who play music together. ব্যান্ড ▷ n

A **band** is a narrow strip of material that you put around something. ফেট্টি

bandage (**bandages, bandaging, bandaged**) *n* A **bandage** is a long strip of cloth that is tied around a wounded part of someone's body in order to protect or support it. ব্যান্ডেজ ▷ *vt* If you **bandage** a wound or part of someone's body, you tie a bandage round it. ব্যান্ডেজ করা

bang (**bangs, banging, banged**) *n* A **bang** is a sudden loud noise such as an explosion. প্রচন্ড জোরে আওয়াজ ▷ *v* If you **bang** something such as a door, or if it **bangs**, it closes suddenly with a loud noise. সজোরে ধাক্কা মারা

Bangladesh *n* **Bangladesh** is a republic in South Asia, formerly the Eastern Province of Pakistan. বাংলাদেশ

Bangladeshi (**Bangladeshis**) *adj* **Bangladeshi** means belonging to or relating to Bangladesh, or to its people or culture. বাংলাদেশীয় ▷ *n* The **Bangladeshis** are the people who come from Bangladesh. বাংলাদেশি

banister (**banisters**) *n* A **banister** is a rail supported by posts and fixed along the side of a staircase. সিঁড়ির রেলিং

banjo (**banjos**) *n* A **banjo** is a musical instrument that looks like a guitar with a circular body, a long neck, and four or more strings. একপ্রকার বাদ্যযন্ত্র

bank (**banks**) *n* A **bank** is the ground beside a river. নদীর পাড় ▷ *n* A **bank** is a place where people can keep their money. ব্যাংক

bank account (**bank accounts**) *n* A **bank account** is an arrangement with a bank which allows you to keep your money in the bank and to take some out when you need it. ব্যাংক অ্যাকাউন্ট

bank balance (**bank balances**) *n* Your **bank balance** is the amount of money that you have in your bank account at a particular time. ব্যাংক ব্যালেন্স

bank charges *npl* **Bank charges** are an amount of money that you have to pay to

your bank, for example, if you have spent more money than you have in your account. ব্যাংক চার্জেস

banker (**bankers**) *n* A **banker** is someone involved in banking at a senior level. ব্যাংকের উচ্চপদছ কর্মচারী

bank holiday (**bank holidays**) *n* A **bank holiday** is a public holiday. ব্যাংকের ছুটির দিন

banknote (**banknotes**) *n* A **banknote** is a piece of paper money. ব্যাংকের নোট বা মুদ্রা

bankrupt *adj* People or organizations that go **bankrupt** do not have enough money to pay their debts. দেউলিয়া

bank statement (**bank statements**) *n* A **bank statement** is a printed document showing all the money paid into and taken out of a bank account. ব্যাংক স্টেটমেন্ট

banned *adj* If something is **banned**, it has been stated officially that it must not be done, shown, or used. নিষিদ্ধ

bar (**bars**) *n* A **bar** is a long, thin piece of wood or metal. গরাদ ▷ *n* A **bar** is a place where people buy and drink alcoholic drinks. উঁড়িখানা

Barbados *n* **Barbados** is an island in the Caribbean, in the east Lesser Antilles. বার্বাডোজ দ্বীপ

barbaric *adj* **Barbaric** behaviour is extremely cruel. বর্বর আচরণ

barbecue (**barbecues**) *n* A **barbecue** is a grill used to cook food outdoors. মাংস ঝলসানোর উনুন

barbed wire *n* **Barbed wire** is strong wire with sharp points sticking out of it, which is used to make fences. কাঁটা তার

barber (**barbers**) *n* A **barber** is a man whose job is cutting men's hair. নাপিত

bare (**barer, barest, bares, baring, bared**) *adj* If a part of your body is **bare**, it is not covered by any clothes. খালি ▷ *adj* If something is **bare**, it has nothing on top of it or inside it. ফাঁকা ▷ *vt* If you **bare** something, you show it. উন্মোচন করা

barefoot *adj* If you are **barefoot** or **barefooted**, you are wearing nothing on your feet. খালি-পা ▷ *adv* If you do something **barefoot**, you do it while wearing nothing on your feet. খালি পায়ে

barely *adv* You use **barely** to say that something is only just true or possible. খুব কম

bargain (**bargains**) *n* Something that is a **bargain** is good value, usually because it has been sold at a lower price than normal. দরাদরি

barge (**barges**) *n* A **barge** is a narrow boat with a flat bottom, used for carrying heavy loads. মালবাহী নৌকা

bark (**barks, barking, barked**) *vi* When a dog **barks**, it makes a short, loud noise. চিৎকার করা

barley *n* **Barley** is a crop which has seeds that are used in the production of food, beer, and whisky. বার্লি

barn (**barns**) *n* A **barn** is a building on a farm in which crops or animal food are kept. গোলাবাড়ি

barrel (**barrels**) *n* A **barrel** is a large round container for liquids or food. Barrels are usually wider in the middle than at the top or bottom. পিপে

barrier (**barriers**) *n* A **barrier** is something such as a law or policy that makes it difficult or impossible for something to happen. প্রতিবন্ধক

base (**bases**) *n* The **base** of something is its lowest edge or part, or the part at which it is attached to something else. ভিত

baseball *n* **Baseball** is a game that is played with a bat and a ball on a large field by two teams of nine players. Players must hit the ball and run around four bases to score. বেসবল

baseball cap (**baseball caps**) *n* A **baseball cap** is a close-fitting thin cap with a deep peak. বেসবল টুপি

based *adj* If one thing is **based** on another, the first thing is developed from the second one. ভিত্তি করে

basement (**basements**) *n* The **basement** of a building is an area partly or completely below ground level, with a room or rooms in it. বাড়ির মাটির তলার অংশ

bash (**bashes, bashing, bashed**) *n* A **bash** is a party or celebration. (*informal*) কোলাহলপূর্ণ অনুষ্ঠান ▷ *vt* If you **bash** someone or something, you hit them hard in a rough way. (*informal*) সজোরে ধাক্কা মারা

basic *adj* You use **basic** to describe things, activities, and principles that are very important or necessary, and on which others depend. মৌলিক

basically *adv* You use **basically** for emphasis when you are stating an opinion, or when you are making an important statement about something. মূলতঃ

basics *npl* The **basics** of something are its simplest, most important elements, ideas, or principles, in contrast to more complicated or detailed ones. প্রাথমিক

basil *n* **Basil** is a strong-smelling and strong-tasting herb that is used in cooking, especially with tomatoes. তুলসী

basin (**basins**) *n* A **basin** is a deep bowl that you use for holding liquids, or for mixing food in. খাদ্য বা পানীয় রাখার পাত্র

basis (**bases**) *n* If something happens or is done on a particular **basis**, it happens or is done in that way. ভিত্তি

basket (**baskets**) *n* A **basket** is a container made of thin strips of cane, metal or plastic woven together. ঝুড়ি

basketball *n* **Basketball** is a game in which two teams of five players each try to throw a large ball through a round net hanging from a high metal ring. বাস্কেটবল

Basque (**Basques**) *adj* **Basque** means relating to, denoting, or characteristic of the Basques or their language. বাস্ক সম্বন্ধীয় ▷ *n* The **Basques** are a people of unknown origin living around the western Pyrenees in France and Spain. পিরেনিজ পর্বতাঞ্চলের অধিবাসী ▷ *n* **Basque** is the language spoken by the Basque people. বাস্ক ভাষা

bass (basses) n A **bass** is a man with a deep singing voice. গম্ভীর গলার লোক

bass drum (bass drums) n A **bass drum** is a large shallow drum of low and indefinite pitch. ব্যাস ড্রাম বাদ্যযন্ত্র

bassoon (bassoons) n A **bassoon** is a large musical instrument of the woodwind family that is shaped like a tube and played by blowing into a curved metal pipe. ব্যাসুন

bat (bats) n A **bat** is a special stick that you use to hit a ball in some games. ব্যাট ▷ n A **bat** is a small animal that looks like a mouse with wings. **Bats** come out to fly at night. বাদুড়

bath (baths) n A **bath** is a container which you fill with water and sit in while you wash your body. স্নানের পাত্র

bathe (bathes, bathing, bathed) vi When you **bathe** in a sea, river, or lake, you swim or play there. (formal) স্নান করা

bathing suit (bathing suits) n A **bathing suit** is a piece of clothing which people wear when they go swimming. সাঁতার কাটার পরিধান

bathrobe (bathrobes) n A **bathrobe** is a loose piece of clothing made of the same material as towels. You wear it before or after you have a bath or a swim. স্নানের পরে পরার জন্য পরিধান

bathroom (bathrooms) n A **bathroom** is a room in a house that contains a bath or shower, a washbasin, and sometimes a toilet. স্নানঘর

baths npl A **baths** is a public building containing a swimming pool, and sometimes other facilities that people can use to have a wash or a bath. স্নানাগার

bath towel (bath towels) n A **bath towel** is a very large towel used for drying your body after you have had a bath or shower. স্নান করার তোয়ালে

bathtub (bathtubs) n A **bathtub** is a container which you fill with water and sit in while you wash your body. স্নানের বড় গামলা

batter n **Batter** is a mixture of flour, eggs, and milk used to make pancakes. ফেটানো ময়দা, ডিম ইত্যাদি

battery (batteries) n **Batteries** are the devices that you put in electrical items to provide the power that makes them work. ব্যাটারী

battle (battles) n In a war, a **battle** is a fight between armies or between groups of ships or planes. যুদ্ধ

battleship (battleships) n A **battleship** is a very large, heavily armoured warship. যুদ্ধজাহাজ

bay (bays) n A **bay** is a part of a coastline where the land curves inwards. উপসাগর

bay leaf (bay leaves) n A **bay leaf** is a leaf of an evergreen tree that can be dried and used as a herb in cooking. তেজপাতা

BC abbr You use **BC** in dates to indicate a number of years or centuries before the year in which Jesus Christ is believed to have been born. খ্রীষ্টপূর্ব

be (am, are, is, being, was, were, been) v You use **be** to say what a person or thing is like. হওয়া She is very young. ▷ v You use **be** to say that something is there. থাকা There is a tree in the garden.

beach (beaches) n A **beach** is an area of sand or pebbles by the sea. সমুদ্রতট

bead (beads) n **Beads** are small pieces of coloured glass, wood, or plastic with a hole through the middle which are used for jewellery or decoration. পুঁতি

beak (beaks) n A bird's **beak** is the hard curved or pointed part of its mouth. ঠোঁট

beam (beams) n A **beam** of light is a line of light that shines from an object such as a torch or the sun. আলোকরশ্মি

bean (beans) n **Beans** are the pods of a climbing plant, or the seeds that the pods contain, which are eaten as a vegetable. বীন-ঔটিযুক্ত ফলধারী লতা

beansprouts npl **Beansprouts** are small, long, thin shoots grown from beans. মটর গাছের অঙ্কুর

bear (bears) *n* A **bear** is a big, strong animal with thick fur and sharp claws. ভালুক

bear (bears, bearing, bore, borne) *vt* If you **bear** something somewhere, you carry it there. (*literary*) বহন করা

beard (beards) *n* A man's **beard** is the hair that grows on his chin and cheeks. দাড়ি

bearded *adj* A **bearded** man has a beard. শ্মশ্রুময়

bear up *v* If you **bear up** when experiencing problems, you remain cheerful and show courage in spite of them. ধৈর্য ধরা *How's she bearing up?*

beat (beats, beating, beaten) *n* A **beat** is a regular sound or rhythm. তাল ▷ *vt* If you **beat** something, you keep hitting it. মারা ▷ *vt* If you **beat** someone in a game or a competition, you do better than they do. হারিয়ে দেওয়া

beautiful *adj* **Beautiful** means attractive to look at. সুন্দর

beautifully *adv* If you do something **beautifully**, you do it in a beautiful manner. সুন্দরভাবে

beauty *n* **Beauty** is the state or quality of being beautiful. সৌন্দর্য

beauty salon (beauty salons) *n* A **beauty salon** is a place where women can go to have beauty treatments, for example to have their hair, nails or make-up done. রূপচর্চার স্থান

beauty spot (beauty spots) *n* A **beauty spot** is a place in the country that is popular because of its beautiful scenery. সুন্দর স্থান

beaver (beavers) *n* A **beaver** is a furry animal like a large rat with a big flat tail. বড় ইঁদুরের মত ধারালো দাঁতওয়ালা প্রাণী

because *conj* You use **because** to say why something happens. কারণ *I went to bed because I was tired.*

become (becomes, becoming, became) *v* If one thing **becomes** another thing, it starts to be that thing. রূপান্তরিত হওয়া

bed (beds) *n* A **bed** is a piece of furniture that you lie on when you sleep. বিছানা

bed and breakfast *n* **Bed and breakfast** is a system of accommodation in a hotel or guest house in which you pay for a room for the night and for breakfast the following morning. The abbreviation 'B&B' is also used. শোয়া এবং জলখাবার

bedclothes *npl* **Bedclothes** are the sheets and covers which you put on a bed. বিছানার চাদর

bedding *n* **Bedding** consists of sheets, blankets, and other covers used on beds. বিছানা

bed linen *n* **Bed linen** is sheets and pillowcases. বিছানার চাদর এবং বালিশ

bedroom (bedrooms) *n* A **bedroom** is a room which is used for sleeping in. শোয়ার ঘর

bedside lamp (bedside lamps) *n* A **bedside lamp** is a lamp that you have next to your bed. খাটসংলগ্ন ল্যাম্প

bedside table (bedside tables) *n* A **bedside table** is a small table usually with shelves or drawers, that you have next to your bed. খাটসংলগ্ন টেবিল

bedsit (bedsits) *n* A **bedsit** is a room you rent which you use for both living in and sleeping in. ছোট ঘর

bedspread (bedspreads) *n* A **bedspread** is a decorative cover which is put over a bed, on top of the sheets and blankets. বিছানার চাদর

bedtime *n* Your **bedtime** is the time when you usually go to bed. ঘুমানোর সময়

bee (bees) *n* A **bee** is an insect with a yellow-and-black striped body that makes a buzzing noise as it flies. Bees make honey. মৌমাছি

beech (beeches) *n* A **beech** or a **beech tree** is a tree with a smooth grey trunk. একধরণের গাছ

beef *n* **Beef** is the meat of a cow, bull, or ox. গরুর মাংস

beefburger (beefburgers) *n* A **beefburger** is minced meat which has been shaped into a flat circle. রান্না করা গরুর মাংস

beeper (**beepers**) *n* A **beeper** is a portable device that makes a beeping noise, usually to tell you to phone someone or to remind you to do something. (*informal*) ফোনের শব্দ সৃষ্টি করার যন্ত্র

beer (**beers**) *n* **Beer** is a bitter alcoholic drink made from grain. বীয়ার

beetle (**beetles**) *n* A **beetle** is an insect with a hard covering to its body. গুবরেপোকা

beetroot (**beetroots**) *n* **Beetroot** is a dark red root vegetable which can be cooked or pickled. বীট

before *adv* You use **before** when you are talking about a previous time. আগে ▷ *conj* If you do something **before** someone else, you do it when they have not yet done it. সামনে *Before I got to the ball, someone else kicked it away.* ▷ *prep* If one thing happens **before** another thing, it happens earlier than it. আগে *My birthday is just before his.*

beforehand *adv* If you do something **beforehand**, you do it earlier than a particular event. পূর্ব থেকে

beg (**begs, begging, begged**) *v* If you **beg** someone to do something, you ask them anxiously or eagerly to do it. ভিক্ষা করা

beggar (**beggars**) *n* A **beggar** is someone who lives by asking people for money or food. ভিক্ষুক

begin (**begins, beginning, began, begun**) *vt* If you **begin** to do something, you start to do it. শুরু করা

beginner (**beginners**) *n* A **beginner** is someone who has just started learning to do something and cannot do it well yet. শিক্ষানবিশ

beginning (**beginnings**) *n* The **beginning** of something is the first part of it. শুরু

behave (**behaves, behaving, behaved**) *vi* The way you **behave** is the way that you do and say things. আচরণ করা ▷ *vt* If you **behave** yourself, you are good. ভালো আচরণ করা

behaviour *n* A person's **behaviour** is the way they behave. আচরণ

behind (**behinds**) *adv* **Behind** means in or to a position further back. পেছনে ▷ *n* Your **behind** is the part of your body that you sit on. পেছনের দিকে ▷ *prep* If something is **behind** another thing, it is at the back of it. পিছনে *He stood behind his desk.*

beige *adj* Something that is **beige** is pale brown in colour. হালকা হলদে-বাদামী রঙ

Beijing *n* **Beijing** is the capital of the People's Republic of China. বেজিং

Belarus *n* **Belarus** is a republic in eastern Europe. বেলারুস

Belarussian (**Belarussians**) *adj* **Belarussian** means of, relating to, or characteristic of Belarus, its people, or their language. বেলারুস সম্বন্ধীয় ▷ *n* A **Belarussian** is a native or inhabitant of Belarus. বেলারুসবাসী ▷ *n* **Belarussian** is the official language of Belarus. বেলারুসীয়

Belgian (**Belgians**) *adj* **Belgian** means belonging or relating to Belgium or to its people. বেলজিয়াম সম্বন্ধীয় ▷ *n* A **Belgian** is a native or inhabitant of Belgium. বেলজিয়ামবাসী

Belgium *n* **Belgium** is a country in north-west Europe. বেলজিয়াম

belief (**beliefs**) *n* **Belief** is a feeling of certainty that something exists, is true, or is good. বিশ্বাস

believe (**believed, believing, believes**) *vt* If you **believe** that something is true, you think that it is true. (*formal*) বিশ্বাস করা ▷ *vi* If you **believe** in things such as God, fairies, or miracles, you are sure that they exist or happen. বিশ্বাস রাখা

bell (**bells**) *n* A **bell** is a device that makes a ringing sound which attracts people's attention. ঘন্টা

belly (**bellies**) *n* A person's or animal's **belly** is their stomach or abdomen. পেট

belly button (**belly buttons**) *n* Your **belly button** is the small round thing in the centre of your stomach. (*informal*) নাভি

belong (**belongs, belonging, belonged**) *vi* If something **belongs** somewhere, that is where it should be. যথাস্থানে থাকা ▷ vi If you **belong** to a group of people, you are one of them. কোন কিছুর অন্তর্ভুক্ত

belongings npl Your **belongings** are the things that you own. জিনিষপত্র

belong to v If something **belongs to** you, you own it. কারোর নিজের হওয়া The house had belonged to her family for three or four generations.

below adv **Below** means at or to a lower position or place. নীচে ▷ prep If something is **below** another thing, it is lower down than it. নীচে His shoes were below his bed.

belt (belts) n A **belt** is a strip of leather or cloth that you fasten round your waist. বেল্ট

bench (benches) n A **bench** is a long seat of wood or metal. বেঞ্চ

bend (bends, bending, bent) n A **bend** in a road, river, or pipe is a curved part in it. বাঁক ▷ vi When you **bend**, you move the top part of your body downwards and forwards. নুয়ে পড়া

bend down v When you **bend down**, you move the top part of your body downwards and forwards. নীচে ঝোঁকা He bent down to tie his laces.

bend over v When you **bend over**, you move the top part of your body downwards and forwards. কোন কিছুর ওপরে ঝোঁকা I bent over and kissed her cheek.

beneath prep If something is **beneath** another thing, it is below it. তলায় The dog was beneath the table.

benefit (benefits, benefiting, benefited) n The **benefit** of something is the help that you get from it or the advantage that results from it. সুবিধা ▷ v If you **benefit** from something or if it **benefits** you, it helps you or improves your life. সুবিধা ভোগ করা

bent adj Something that is **bent** is not straight. ঝোঁকানো ▷ adj If you say that someone in a position of responsibility is **bent**, you mean that they are dishonest or do illegal things. অসাধু

beret (berets) n A **beret** is a circular, flat hat that is made of soft material and has no brim. নরম কাপড়ের তৈরী টুপি

berry (berries) n **Berries** are small round fruit that grow on a bush or a tree. জাম

berth (berths) n A **berth** is a bed on a boat or train, or in a caravan. ট্রেনে, জাহাজে ঘুমানোর স্থান

beside prep If something is **beside** another thing, it is next to it. পাশে He sat down beside me.

besides adv You use **besides** when you want to give another reason for something. এছাড়াও ▷ prep **Besides** means as well as. ছাড়া Besides being tall, they're strong and clever.

best adj If you say that something is **best**, you mean that it is better than all the others. সর্বশ্রেষ্ঠ ▷ adv You use **best** to say that something is better than all the others. শ্রেষ্ঠ

best-before date (best-before dates) n The **best-before date** on a food container is the date by which the food should be used before it starts to decay. তারিখের পূর্বে ব্যবহার সর্বাধিক উত্তম

best man n The **best man** at a wedding is the man who assists the bridegroom. নিতবর

bestseller (bestsellers) n A **bestseller** is a book of which a very large number of copies have been sold. সর্বাধিক বিক্রয়

bet (bets, betting) n A **bet** is an agreement between two parties that a sum of money will be paid by the loser to the party who correctly predicts the outcome of an event. বাজি ▷ v If you **bet** on the result of a horse race, football game, or other event, you give someone a sum of money which they give you back with extra money if the result is what you predicted, or which they keep if it is not. বাজি রাখা

betray (betrays, betraying, betrayed) vt If you **betray** someone who trusts you, you do something which hurts and disappoints them. বিশ্বাসঘাতকতা করা

better *adj* You use **better** to mean that a thing is very good compared to another thing. উৎকৃষ্টতর ▷ *adv* You use **better** to mean that someone or something does something very well compared to another person or thing. অধিকতর ভালো ▷ *adj* If you feel **better**, you do not feel ill any more. সুস্থ বোধ করা

between *prep* If you are **between** two things, one of them is on one side of you and the other is on the other side. মধ্যে *She stood between her two brothers.*

bewildered *adj* If you are **bewildered**, you are very confused and cannot understand something or decide what you should do. দিধাগ্রস্ত

beyond *prep* Something that is **beyond** a place is on the other side of it, or farther away than it. ছাড়িয়ে *On his right was a garden, and beyond it there was a large house.*

biased *adj* Someone or something that is **biased** towards one thing is more concerned with it than with other things. পক্ষপাতদুষ্ট

bib (**bibs**) *n* A **bib** is a piece of cloth or plastic which is worn by very young children to protect their clothes while they are eating. নালপোষ

Bible *n* The **Bible** is the sacred book of the Christian religion. বাইবেল

bicarbonate of soda *n* **Bicarbonate of soda** is a white powder which is used in baking to make cakes rise, and also as a medicine for your stomach. সোডা বাইকার্বোনেট

bicycle (**bicycles**) *n* A **bicycle** is a vehicle with two wheels which you ride by sitting on it and pushing two pedals with your feet. বাইসাইকেল

bicycle pump (**bicycle pumps**) *n* A **bicycle pump** is a hand pump for pumping air into the tyres of a bicycle. বাইসাইকেল পাম্প

bid (**bids**, **bade**, **bidden**) *n* If you make a **bid** for something that is being sold, you

say that you will pay a certain amount of money for it. নীলাম ▷ *v* If you **bid** for something that somebody is selling, you offer to pay a price that you think is fair. নীলাম করা

bifocals *npl* **Bifocals** are glasses with lenses made in two halves. The top part is for looking at things some distance away, and the bottom part is for reading and looking at things that are close. দুই ফোকাস যুক্ত চশমা

big (**bigger**, **biggest**) *adj* A person or thing that is **big** is large in size. বিরাট

bigheaded *adj* If you describe someone as **bigheaded**, you disapprove of them because they think they are very clever and know everything. বড় মাথাবিশিষ্ট

bike (**bikes**) *n* A **bike** is a vehicle with two wheels which you ride by sitting on it and pushing two pedals with your feet. (*informal*) বাইক

bikini (**bikinis**) *n* A **bikini** is a two-piece swimming costume worn by women. বিকিনি

bilingual *adj* **Bilingual** means involving or using two languages. দ্বৈভাষিক

bill (**bills**) *n* A **bill** is a written statement of money that you owe for goods or services. বিল ▷ *n* In parliament, a **bill** is a formal statement of a proposed new law that is discussed and then voted on. আইনের খসড়া

billiards *npl* **Billiards** is a game played on a large table, in which you use a long stick called a cue to hit small heavy balls against each other or into pockets around the sides of the table. বিলিয়ার্ড

billion (**billions**) *num* A **billion** is the number 1,000,000,000. একশো কোটি

bin (**bins**) *n* A **bin** is a container that you put rubbish in. আবর্জনা ফেলার পাত্র

bingo *n* **Bingo** is a game in which players aim to match the numbers that someone calls out with the numbers on a card that they have been given. তাসের জুয়া

binoculars *npl* **Binoculars** consist of two small telescopes joined together side by side, which you look through in order to see things that are a long way away. দূরবীন

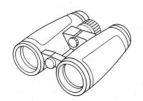

biochemistry n **Biochemistry** is the study of the chemical processes that happen in living things. জৈব রসায়ন

biodegradable adj Something that is **biodegradable** breaks down or decays naturally without any special scientific treatment, and can therefore be thrown away without causing pollution. জীবাণুবিয়োজ্য

biography (**biographies**) n A **biography** of a person is an account of their life, written by someone else. জীবনচরিত

biological adj **Biological** is used to describe processes and states that occur in the bodies and cells of living things. জীববিদ্যাসংক্রান্ত

biology n **Biology** is the science concerned with the study of living things. জীববিদ্যা

biometric adj **Biometric** tests and devices use biological information about a person to create a detailed record of their personal characteristics. বায়োমেট্রিক

birch (**birches**) n A **birch** is a tall tree with thin branches. ভুজগাছ

bird (**birds**) n A **bird** is a creature with feathers and wings. পাখি

bird flu n **Bird flu** is a virus which can be transmitted from chickens, ducks, and other birds to people. বার্ড ফ্লু

bird of prey (**birds of prey**) n A **bird of prey** is a bird such as an eagle or a hawk that kills and eats other birds and animals. ঈগল জাতীয় পাখি

birdwatching n **Birdwatching** is the activity of watching and studying wild birds in their natural surroundings. বন্য পাখিদের নিরীক্ষণ

Biro® (**Biros**) n A **Biro** is a pen with a small metal ball at its tip. বিরো®

birth (**births**) n When a baby is born, you refer to this event as its **birth**. জন্ম

birth certificate (**birth certificates**) n Your **birth certificate** is an official document which gives details of your birth, such as the date and place of your birth, and the names of your parents. জন্ম পরিচয়পত্র

birthday (**birthdays**) n Your **birthday** is the anniversary of the date on which you were born. জন্মদিন

birthplace (**birthplaces**) n Your **birthplace** is the place where you were born. (written) জন্মস্থান

biscuit (**biscuits**) n A **biscuit** is a small flat cake that is crisp and usually sweet. বিস্কুট

bit (**bits**) n A **bit** of something is a small amount of it, or a small part of it. অল্প

bitch (**bitches**) n A **bitch** is a female dog. মাদি কুকুর

bite (**bites, biting, bit, bitten**) n A **bite** of something, especially food, is the action of biting it. কামড় ▷ v If you **bite** something, you use your teeth to cut into it, for example in order to eat it or break it. If an animal or person **bites** you, they use their teeth to hurt or injure you. কামড়ানো

bitter (**bitterest**) adj In a **bitter** argument, people argue very angrily. তিক্ত

black (**blacker, blackest**) adj Something that is **black** is of the darkest colour that there is, the colour of the sky at night when there is no light at all. কালো

blackberry (**blackberries**) n A **blackberry** is a small dark purple fruit. কালোজাম

BlackBerry® (**Blackberries**) n A **BlackBerry** is a mobile computing device that allows you to send and receive email. ব্ল্যাকবেরি

blackbird (**blackbirds**) n A **blackbird** is a common European bird. The male has black feathers and a yellow beak, and the female has brown feathers. ব্ল্যাকবার্ড

blackboard (**blackboards**) n A **blackboard** is a dark-coloured board which teachers write on with chalk. ব্ল্যাকবোর্ড

black coffee (**black coffees**) n **Black coffee** has no milk or cream added to it. কালো কফি

blackcurrant (**blackcurrants**) n **Blackcurrants** are very small, dark purple fruits that grow in bunches. কালো কিসমিস

black ice n **Black ice** is a thin, transparent layer of ice on a road or path that is very difficult to see. রাস্তায় পড়ে থাকে বরফের টুকরো

blackmail (**blackmails, blackmailing, blackmailed**) n **Blackmail** is the action of threatening to reveal a secret about someone, unless they do something you tell them to do, such as giving you money. গোপন তথ্য ফাঁস না করার বদলে টাকা নেওয়া ▷ vt If one person **blackmails** another person, they use blackmail against them. গোপন তথ্য ফাঁস না করার বদলে দাবি করা

blackout (**blackouts**) n A **blackout** is a period of time during a war in which the buildings in an area are made dark for safety reasons. যুদ্ধকালীন নিষ্প্রদীপ অবস্থা

bladder (**bladders**) n Your **bladder** is the part of your body where urine is held until it leaves your body. মূত্রাশয়

blade (**blades**) n The **blade** of a knife, axe, or saw is the sharp edge of it that is used for cutting. ব্লেড

blame (**blames, blaming, blamed**) vt If you **blame** a person or thing for something bad, you believe or say that they are responsible for it or that they caused it. দোষারোপ করা ▷ n The **blame** for something bad that has happened is the responsibility for causing it or letting it happen. দোষ

blank (**blanks**) adj Something that is **blank** has nothing on it. খালি ▷ n A **blank** is a space which is left in a piece of writing or on a printed form for you to fill in particular information. শূন্যস্থান

blank cheque (**blank cheques**) n If someone is given a **blank cheque**, they are given the authority to spend as much money as they need or want. ফাঁকা চেক

blanket (**blankets**) n A **blanket** is a large piece of thick cloth, especially one which you put on a bed to keep you warm. কম্বল

blast (**blasts**) n A **blast** is a big explosion. বিস্ফোরণ

blatant adj If you describe something you think is bad as **blatant**, you mean that it is very obvious. অশোভন

blaze (**blazes**) n A **blaze** is a large fire in which things are damaged. অগ্নিকান্ড

blazer (**blazers**) n A **blazer** is a kind of jacket. ব্লেজার

bleach n **Bleach** is a chemical that is used to make cloth white, or to clean things thoroughly. কাপড় সাদা বা জিনিস পরিষ্কার করার রাসায়নিক

bleached adj Something that is **bleached** has been made lighter in colour. রং ফিকে হওয়া কাপড়

bleak (**bleaker, bleakest**) adj If a situation is **bleak**, it is bad, and seems unlikely to improve. আনন্দহীন

bleed (**bleeds, bleeding, bled**) vi When you **bleed**, you lose blood from your body as a result of injury or illness. রক্তপাত

blender (**blenders**) n A **blender** is an electrical kitchen appliance used for mixing liquids and soft foods together or turning fruit or vegetables into liquid. মিশ্রক

bless (**blesses, blessing, blessed**) vt When a priest **blesses** people or things, he or she asks for God's favour and protection for them. আশীর্বাদ করা

blind (**blinds**) adj Someone who is **blind** is unable to see because their eyes are damaged. অন্ধ

blindfold (blindfolds, blindfolding, blindfolded) *n* A **blindfold** is a strip of cloth that is tied over someone's eyes so that they cannot see. চোখের কালো পটি ▷ *vt* If you **blindfold** someone, you tie a strip of cloth over their eyes. চোখে কালো পটি পরানো

blink (blinks, blinking, blinked) *v* When you **blink** or when you **blink** your eyes, you shut your eyes and very quickly open them again. চোখ পিটপিট করা

bliss *n* **Bliss** is a state of complete happiness. আনন্দ

blister (blisters) *n* A **blister** is a painful swelling containing clear liquid on the surface of your skin. জলফোস্কা

blizzard (blizzards) *n* A **blizzard** is a storm in which snow falls heavily and there are strong winds. তুষারঝড়

block (blocks, blocking, blocked) *n* A **block** of a substance is a large rectangular piece of it. কোন বস্তুর আয়তাকার টুকরো ▷ *n* In a town, a **block** is a group of buildings with streets on all four sides. বিভাগ ▷ *n* A **block** is an obstruction or hindrance. বাধা ▷ *vt* To **block** a road or channel means to put something across or in it so that nothing can go through it or along it. রাস্তা অবরোধ করা

blockage (blockages) *n* A **blockage** in a pipe or tunnel is something that is blocking it. আটক

blocked *adj* If something is **blocked**, it is completely closed so that nothing can get through it. বন্ধ

blog (blogs, blogging, blogged) *v* When you **blog**, you update a website containing a diary or journal. ব্লগ লেখা

bloke (blokes) *n* A **bloke** is a man. (*informal*) পুরুষ

blonde (blonder, blondest) *adj* Someone who has **blonde** hair has pale-coloured hair. ফর্সা

blood *n* **Blood** is the red liquid that flows inside your body. রক্ত

blood group (blood groups) *n* Someone's **blood group** is the type of blood that they have in their body. There are four main types: A, B, AB, and O. রক্তের গ্রুপ

blood poisoning *n* **Blood poisoning** is a serious illness resulting from an infection in your blood. রক্ত দূষণ

blood pressure *n* Your **blood pressure** is a measure of the force with which blood is pumped around your body. রক্তচাপ

blood test (blood tests) *n* A **blood test** is a medical examination of a sample of your blood. রক্ত পরীক্ষা

blossom (blossoms, blossoming, blossomed) *n* **Blossom** is the flowers that appear on a tree before the fruit. কুঁড়ি ▷ *vi* If someone or something **blossoms**, they develop good, attractive, or successful qualities. সফল হওয়া

blouse (blouses) *n* A **blouse** is a kind of shirt worn by girls or women. ব্লাউজ

blow (blowing, blew, blows) *n* Someone receives a **blow** when someone or something hits them. আক্রমণ ▷ *vi* When the wind **blows**, it moves the air. প্রবাহিত হওয়া ▷ *vt* When you **blow**, you push air out of your mouth. ফুঁ দেওয়া

blow-dry *n* A **blow-dry** is a method of styling the hair while drying it with a hand-held hairdryer. চুল শোকানোর পদ্ধতি

blow up *v* If someone **blows** something **up**, or if it **blows up**, it is destroyed by an explosion. বিস্ফোরণ করা *Their boat blew up.*

blue (bluer, bluest) *adj* Something that is **blue** is the colour of the sky on a sunny day. নীল

blueberry (blueberries) *n* A **blueberry** is a small dark blue fruit that is found in North America. ব্লু বেরী

blues *npl* **The blues** is a type of music which was developed by African-American musicians in the southern United States. It is characterized by a slow tempo and a strong rhythm. ব্লুজ

bluff (**bluffs, bluffing, bluffed**) n A **bluff** is an attempt to make someone believe that you will do something when you do not really intend to do it. ধাপ্পা ▷ v If you **bluff**, you try to make someone believe that you will do something although you do not really intend to do it, or that you know something you do not really know it. ধাপ্পা দেওয়া

blunder (**blunders**) n A **blunder** is a stupid or careless mistake. বিরাট বড় ভুল

blunt (**blunter, bluntest**) adj If you are **blunt**, you say exactly what you think without trying to be polite. বোকা

blush (**blushes, blushing, blushed**) vi When you **blush**, your face becomes redder than usual because you are ashamed or embarrassed. লজ্জা পাওয়া

blusher (**blushers**) n **Blusher** is a coloured substance that women put on their cheeks. ব্লাশার

board (**boards**) n The **board** of a company or organization is the group of people who control it. বোর্ড/পর্ষদ ▷ n A **board** is a flat piece of wood, plastic, or cardboard which is used for a particular purpose. পাটাতন

boarder (**boarders**) n A **boarder** is a pupil who lives at school during the term. আবাসিক

board game (**board games**) n A **board game** is a game such as chess or backgammon, which people play by moving small objects around on a board. বোর্ড-গেম

boarding school (**boarding schools**) n A **boarding school** is a school where the pupils live during the term. বোর্ডিং স্কুল

boast (**boasts, boasting, boasted**) vi If someone **boasts** about something that they have done or that they own, they talk about it very proudly, in a way that other people may find irritating or offensive. গর্ব করা

boat (**boats**) n A **boat** is something in which people can travel across water. নৌকা

body (**bodies**) n Your **body** is all your physical parts, including your head, arms, and legs. দেহ

bodybuilding n **Bodybuilding** is the activity of doing special exercises regularly in order to make your muscles grow bigger. শরীরচর্চা

bodyguard (**bodyguards**) n Someone's **bodyguard** is the person or group of people employed to protect them. দেহরক্ষী

bog (**bogs**) n A **bog** is a wet muddy area of land. নরম মাটি

boil (**boils, boiling, boiled**) vt When you **boil** food, you cook it in water that is boiling. ফোটানো ▷ vi When water **boils**, it becomes very hot, and you can see bubbles in it and steam coming from it. ফোটা

boiled adj Food that is **boiled** is cooked in boiling water. সিদ্ধ

boiled egg (**boiled eggs**) n A **boiled egg** is an egg that has been cooked in its shell in boiling water. সিদ্ধ ডিম

boiler (**boilers**) n A **boiler** is a device which burns fuel to provide hot water. বয়লার

boiling adj Something that is **boiling** is very hot. ফোটানো

boil over v When a liquid that is being heated **boils over**, it rises and flows over the edge of the container. ফুটে ছিটকানো *Heat the liquid in a large, wide container so it doesn't boil over.*

Bolivia n **Bolivia** is an inland republic in central South America. বলিভিয়া

Bolivian (**Bolivians**) adj **Bolivian** means belonging or relating to Bolivia or its people. বলিভিয়া সংক্রান্ত ▷ n A **Bolivian** is a person who comes from Bolivia. বলিভিয়ার বাসিন্দা

bolt (**bolts**) n A **bolt** is a long metal object which screws into a nut and is used to fasten things together. বল্টু

bomb (**bombs, bombing, bombed**) n A **bomb** is a device which explodes, damaging a large area or killing people.

বোমা ▷ vt When a place **is bombed**, it is attacked with bombs. বোমাবাজি করা

bombing (**bombings**) n **Bombing** is the action of attacking a place with bombs. বোমাবর্ষন

bond (**bonds**) n A **bond** between people is a close link between them, for example feelings of love, or a special agreement. বন্ধন

bone (**bones**) n Your **bones** are the hard parts inside your body which together form your skeleton. হাড়

bone dry adj If you say that something is **bone dry**, you are emphasizing that it is very dry indeed. খুব শুকনো

bonfire (**bonfires**) n A **bonfire** is a fire built outdoors, usually to burn rubbish. কুটোর আগুন

bonnet (**bonnets**) n The **bonnet** of a car is the metal cover over the engine at the front. বনেট

bonus (**bonuses**) n A **bonus** is an amount of money that is added to someone's pay, usually because they have worked very hard. বোনাস

book (**books, booking, booked**) n A **book** consists of pieces of paper, usually with words printed on them, which are fastened together and fixed inside a cover of strong paper or cardboard. বই ▷ vt When you **book** something such as a hotel room or a ticket, you arrange to have it or use it at a particular time. সংরক্ষণ করা

bookcase (**bookcases**) n A **bookcase** is a piece of furniture with shelves for books. বইয়ের তাক

booking (**bookings**) n A **booking** is the arrangement that you make when you book something such as a hotel room, a table at a restaurant, a theatre seat, or a place on public transport. সংরক্ষণ

booklet (**booklets**) n A **booklet** is a small paperback book, containing information on a particular subject. পুস্তিকা

bookmark (**bookmarks**) n A **bookmark** is a narrow piece of card or cloth that you put

between the pages of a book so that you can find a particular page easily. বুকমার্ক

bookshelf (**bookshelves**) n A **bookshelf** is a shelf on which you keep books. বই রাখার তাক

bookshop (**bookshops**) n A **bookshop** is a shop where books are sold. বইয়ের দোকান

boost (**boosts, boosting, boosted**) vt If one thing **boosts** another, it causes it to increase, improve, or be more successful. তুলে ধরা

boot (**boots**) n **Boots** are strong heavy shoes that cover your whole foot and the lower part of your leg. জুতো

booze n **Booze** is alcoholic drink. (informal) মদ

border (**borders**) n The **border** between two countries is the dividing line between them. সীমানা

bore (**bores, boring, bored**) vt If someone or something **bores** you, you find them dull and uninteresting. একঘেয়েমি করে তোলা

bored adj If you are **bored**, you feel tired and impatient because you are not interested in something or because you have nothing to do. একঘেয়েমি

boredom n **Boredom** is the state of being bored. ক্লান্তিময় অবস্থা

boring adj If you say that someone or something is **boring**, you think that they are very dull and uninteresting. বিরক্তিকর

born adj You use **born** to describe someone who has a natural ability to do a particular activity or job. For example, a **born** cook has a natural ability to cook well. জন্মগত যোগ্যতা

borrow (**borrows, borrowing, borrowed**) vt If you **borrow** something that belongs to someone else, you take it, usually with their permission, intending to return it. ধার করা

Bosnia n **Bosnia** is a region of central Bosnia-Herzegovina. বসনিয়া

Bosnia-Herzegovina n **Bosnia-Herzegovina** is a country in south-west

Europe, which was part of Yugoslavia until 1991. বসনিয়া-হার্জেগোভিনা

Bosnian (**Bosnians**) *adj* **Bosnian** means of or relating to Bosnia or its inhabitants. বসনিয়া সংক্রান্ত ▷ *n* A **Bosnian** is a native or inhabitant of Bosnia. বসনিয়ার বাসিন্দা

boss (**bosses**) *n* Your **boss** is the person in charge of the organization or department where you work. কর্মকর্তা

boss around *v* If you say that someone **bosses** you **around**, you mean that they keep telling you what to do in a way that is irritating. আদেশ দেওয়া

bossy *adj* If someone is **bossy**, they enjoy telling people what to do. প্রভুত্বপরায়ণ

both *det* You use **both** to mean two people or two things together. উভয় *He put both books in the drawer.* ▷ *pron* You use **both** when you are saying that something is true about two people or things. উভয় *The woman and her friend, both aged 50, were arrested.*

bother (**bothers, bothering, bothered**) *v* If you do not **bother** to do something or if you do not **bother** with it, you do not do it, consider it, or use it because you think it is unnecessary or because you are too lazy. চিন্তা না করা

Botswana *n* **Botswana** is a republic in southern Africa. বটসোয়ানা

bottle (**bottles**) *n* A **bottle** is a glass or plastic container in which drinks and other liquids are kept. বোতল

bottle bank (**bottle banks**) *n* A **bottle bank** is a large container into which people can put empty bottles so that the glass can be used again. খালি বোতল রাখার স্থান

bottle-opener (**bottle-openers**) *n* A **bottle-opener** is a metal device for removing caps or tops from bottles. বোতল খোলার জিনিস

bottom (**bottoms**) *adj* The **bottom** thing is the lowest one. তলার দিকে ▷ *n* The **bottom** of something is its lowest part. তলদেশ ▷ *n*

Your **bottom** is the part of your body that you sit on. নিতম্ব

bounce (**bounces, bouncing, bounced**) *v* When an object such as a ball **bounces** or when you **bounce** it, it moves upwards from a surface or away from it immediately after hitting it. লাফানো

boundary (**boundaries**) *n* The **boundary** of an area of land is an imaginary line that separates it from other areas. সীমারেখা

bouquet (**bouquets**) *n* A **bouquet** is a bunch of flowers arranged in an attractive way. ফুলের তোড়া

bow (**bows**) *n* A **bow** is a long, curved piece of wood with a string stretched between the two ends, that is used to send arrows through the air. ধনুক ▷ *n* A **bow** is a knot that you use to tie laces and ribbons. গিঁট

bow (**bows, bowing, bowed**) *vi* When you **bow**, you bend your body towards someone as a polite way of saying hello or thanking them. মাথা ঝোঁকানো

bowels *npl* Your **bowels** are the tubes in your body through which digested food passes from your stomach to your anus. অন্ত্র

bowl (**bowls**) *n* A **bowl** is a circular container with a wide uncovered top that is used for mixing and serving food. পাত্র

bowling *n* **Bowling** is a game in which you roll a heavy ball down a narrow track towards a group of wooden objects and try to knock down as many of them as possible. বোলিং

bowling alley (**bowling alleys**) *n* A **bowling alley** is a building which contains several tracks for bowling. বোলিং অ্যালি

bow tie (**bow ties**) *n* A **bow tie** is a tie in the form of a bow. Bow ties are worn by men, especially for formal occasions. বো-টাই

box (**boxes**) *n* A **box** is a square or rectangular container with stiff sides and sometimes a lid. বাক্স

boxer (**boxers**) *n* A **boxer** is someone who takes part in the sport of boxing. বক্সার

boxer shorts *npl* **Boxer shorts** are loose-fitting men's underpants that are shaped like the shorts worn by boxers. ঢিলে হাফ প্যান্ট

boxing *n* **Boxing** is a sport in which two people wearing padded gloves fight, using only their hands. মুষ্টিযুদ্ধ

box office (**box offices**) *n* The **box office** in a theatre or cinema is the place where the tickets are sold. টিকিট অফিস

boy (**boys**) *n* A **boy** is a male child. বালক

boyfriend (**boyfriends**) *n* Someone's **boyfriend** is the man or boy with whom they are having a romantic relationship. ছেলে বন্ধু

bra (**bras**) *n* A **bra** is a piece of underwear that a woman wears to support her breasts. বক্ষবন্ধনী

brace (**braces**) *n* A **brace** is a device attached to a person's leg to strengthen or support it. বন্ধনী

bracelet (**bracelets**) *n* A **bracelet** is a piece of jewellery that you wear round your wrist. কব্জি-বন্ধনী

braces *npl* **Braces** are a pair of straps that you wear over your shoulders to prevent your trousers from falling down. জোড়া ফিতে

brackets *npl* **Brackets** are a pair of written marks that you place round a word, expression, or sentence in order to indicate that you are giving extra information. বন্ধনী

brain (**brains**) *n* Your **brain** is the organ inside your head that controls your body's activities and enables you to think and to feel things. মস্তিষ্ক

brainy (**brainier, brainiest**) *adj* Someone who is **brainy** is clever and good at learning. (*informal*) বুদ্ধিমান

brake (**brakes, braking, braked**) *n* A vehicle's **brakes** are devices that make it go slower or stop. ব্রেক ▷ *v* When a vehicle or its driver **brakes**, or when a driver **brakes** a vehicle, the driver makes it slow down or stop by using the brakes. ব্রেক কষা

brake light (**brake lights**) *n* A **brake light** is a red light attached to the rear of a motor vehicle that lights up when the brakes are applied, serving as a warning to following drivers. ব্রেক লাইট

bran *n* **Bran** consists of small brown flakes that are left when wheat grains have been used to make white flour. তুষ

branch (**branches**) *n* The **branches** of a tree are the parts that grow out from its trunk. শাখা

brand (**brands**) *n* A **brand** of a product is the version made by one particular manufacturer. ব্র্যান্ড

brand name (**brand names**) *n* A product's **brand name** is the name the manufacturer gives it and under which it is sold. ব্র্যান্ডের নাম

brand-new *adj* Something that is **brand-new** is completely new. আনকোরা নতুন

brandy (**brandies**) *n* **Brandy** is a strong alcoholic drink. ব্র্যান্ডি

brass *n* **Brass** is a yellow metal made from copper and zinc. পিতল

brass band (**brass bands**) *n* A **brass band** is a band that is made up of brass and percussion instruments. পিতলের বাদ্যযন্ত্রের বাদক সম্প্রদায়

brat (**brats**) *n* If you call a child a **brat**, you disapprove of their bad or annoying behaviour. (*informal*) ছোকরা

brave (**braver, bravest**) *adj* Someone who is **brave** is willing to do dangerous things, and does not show fear in difficult or dangerous situations. সাহসী

bravery n **Bravery** is brave behaviour or the quality of being brave. সাহসিকতা

Brazil n **Brazil** is a country in South America. ব্রাজিল

Brazilian (**Brazilians**) adj **Brazilian** means belonging or relating to Brazil, or to its people or culture. ব্রাজিল সংক্রান্ত ▷ n A **Brazilian** is a person who comes from Brazil. ব্রাজিলের বাসিন্দা

bread n **Bread** is a food made from flour, water, and often yeast. পাউরুটি

bread bin (**bread bins**) n A **bread bin** is a wooden, metal, or plastic container for storing bread. পাউরুটি রাখার জায়গা

breadcrumbs npl **Breadcrumbs** are tiny pieces of dry bread. They are used in cooking. শুকনো পাউরুটি গুঁড়ো

bread roll (**bread rolls**) n A **bread roll** is a small piece of bread that is round or long and is made to be eaten by one person. ব্রেডরোল

break (**breaks**, **breaking**, **broke**, **broken**) n A **break** is the result of breaking. ভাঙ্গা ▷ v When something **breaks**, or when you **break** it, it goes into pieces. ভেঙে যাওয়া ▷ v If a machine **breaks**, or if you **break** it, it stops working. অকেজো হয়ে যাওয়া

break down (**breakdowns**) v If a machine or a vehicle **breaks down**, it stops working. বিকল হয়ে যাওয়া Their car broke down. ▷ n The **breakdown** of a system, plan, or discussion is its failure or ending. অচল হয়ে যাওয়া

breakdown truck (**breakdown trucks**) n A **breakdown truck** is a truck which is used to pull broken or damaged cars and other vehicles. অচল গাড়ি বয়ে নিয়ে যাওয়ার ট্রাক

breakdown van (**breakdown vans**) n A **breakdown van** is a motor vehicle which is used to pull broken or damaged vehicles. অচল গাড়ি বয়ে নিয়ে যাওয়ার ভ্যান

breakfast (**breakfasts**) n **Breakfast** is the first meal of the day, which is usually eaten early in the morning. প্রাতরাশ

break in (**break-ins**) v If someone **breaks in**, they get into a building by force. তালা ভেঙে ঘরে ঢোকা The robbers broke in and stole a valuable painting. ▷ n When there is a **break-in**, someone gets into a building by force. তালা ভেঙে ঘরে ঢুকেছে

break up v When something **breaks up** or when you **break** it **up**, it separates or is divided into several smaller parts. টুকরো হয়ে যাওয়া Break up the chocolate and melt it.

breast (**breasts**) n A woman's **breasts** are the two soft round pieces of flesh on her chest that can produce milk to feed a baby. স্তন

breast-feed (**breast-feeds**, **breast-feeding**, **breast-fed**) v When a woman **breast-feeds**, or **breast-feeds** her baby, she feeds her baby with milk from her breasts, rather than from a bottle. স্তন্য পান করানো

breaststroke n **Breaststroke** is a swimming stroke which you do lying on your front, and making circular movements with your arms and legs. ব্রেস্ট স্ট্রোক

breath (**breaths**) n Your **breath** is the air which you take into and let out of your lungs when you breathe. নিঃশ্বাস

Breathalyser® (**Breathalysers**) n A **Breathalyser** is a bag or electronic device that the police use to test whether a driver has drunk too much alcohol. ব্রেথালাইসার

breathe (**breathes**, **breathing**, **breathed**) v When people or animals **breathe**, they take air into their lungs and let it out again. নিঃশ্বাস নেওয়া

breathe in v When you **breathe in**, you take some air into your lungs. নিঃশ্বাস গ্রহণ করা She breathed in deeply.

breathe out v When you **breathe out**, you send air out of your lungs through your nose or mouth. নিঃশ্বাস বার করা Breathe out and bring your knees in toward your chest.

breathing n **Breathing** is the passage of air into and out of the lungs to supply the body with oxygen. শ্বাস-প্রশ্বাস

breed (breeds, breeding, bred) n A **breed** of animal is a particular type of it. এক প্রজাতির প্রাণী ▷ vt If you **breed** animals or plants, you keep them for the purpose of producing more animals or plants. বংশবৃদ্ধি করা

breeze (breezes) n A **breeze** is a gentle wind. মৃদু বাতাস

brewery (breweries) n A **brewery** is a place where beer is made. ভাটিখানা

bribe (bribes, bribing, bribed) vt If one person **bribes** another, they give them a bribe. ঘুষ দেওয়া

bribery n **Bribery** is the action of giving someone a bribe. ঘুষ দেওয়া

brick (bricks) n **Bricks** are rectangular blocks of baked clay used for building walls. ইঁট

bricklayer (bricklayers) n A **bricklayer** is a person whose job is to build walls using bricks. রাজমিস্ত্রী

bride (brides) n A **bride** is a woman who is getting married or who has just got married. কনে

bridegroom (bridegrooms) n A **bridegroom** is a man who is getting married. বর

bridesmaid (bridesmaids) n A **bridesmaid** is a woman or a girl who helps a bride on her wedding day. কনের সহচরী

bridge (bridges) n A **bridge** is a structure built over a river, road, or railway so that people or vehicles can cross from one side to the other. সেতু

brief (briefer, briefest) adj Something that is **brief** lasts for only a short time. স্বল্পস্থায়ী

briefcase (briefcases) n A **briefcase** is a case for carrying documents. ব্রিফকেস

briefing (briefings) n A **briefing** is a meeting at which information or instructions are given to people. নির্দেশাবলী

briefly adv Something that happens **briefly** happens for a very short period of time. সংক্ষিপ্তাকারে

briefs npl Men's or women's underpants can be referred to as **briefs**. ছেলে বা মেয়েদের জাঙিয়া

bright (brighter, brightest) adj A **bright** colour is very easy to see. উজ্জ্বল ▷ adj Something that is **bright** shines with a lot of light. ঝলমলে

brilliant adj If you describe people or ideas as **brilliant**, you mean that they are extremely clever. মেধাবী

bring (brings, bringing, brought) vt If you **bring** something, you take it with you when you go somewhere. বহন করা

bring back v If something **brings back** a memory, it makes you start thinking about it. ফিরিয়ে আনা Your article brought back sad memories for me.

bring forward v If you **bring forward** an event, you arrange for it to take place at an earlier time than had been planned. আগে নিয়ে যাওয়া He had to bring forward an 11 o'clock meeting.

bring up v If you **bring up** a child, you look after it until it is grown up. বড় করে তোলা She brought up four children.

Britain n **Britain** is the island consisting of England, Scotland, and Wales, which together with Northern Ireland makes up the United Kingdom. ব্রিটেন

British adj **British** means belonging or relating to Great Britain. ব্রিটেন সংক্রান্ত ▷ npl The **British** are the people who come from Great Britain. ব্রিটেনের বাসিন্দা

broad (broader, broadest) adj Something that is **broad** is wide. চওড়া

broadband n **Broadband** is a method of sending many electronic messages at the same time by using a wide range of frequencies. ব্রডব্যান্ড

broad bean (**broad beans**) n **Broad beans** are flat round beans that are light green in colour and are eaten as a vegetable. বরবটি

broadcast (**broadcasts, broadcasting**) n A **broadcast** is something that you hear on the radio or see on television. সম্প্রচার ▷ v To **broadcast** a programme means to send it out by radio waves, so that it can be heard on the radio or seen on television. সম্প্রচার করা

broad-minded adj Someone who is **broad-minded** does not disapprove of actions or attitudes that many other people disapprove of. খোলা মনের

broccoli n **Broccoli** is a vegetable with green stalks and green or purple flower buds. ব্রকোলি

brochure (**brochures**) n A **brochure** is a booklet with pictures that gives you information about a product or service. ইস্তাহার

broke adj If you are **broke**, you have no money. (informal) সর্বস্বান্ত

broken adj A **broken** line is not continuous but has gaps in it. খন্ডিত

broken down adj A **broken down** vehicle or machine no longer works because it has something wrong with it. ভাঙা

broker (**brokers**) n A **broker** is a person whose job is to buy and sell shares, foreign money, or goods for other people. দালাল

bronchitis n **Bronchitis** is an illness like a very bad cough, in which your bronchial tubes become sore and infected. ব্রঙ্কাইটিস

bronze n **Bronze** is a yellowish-brown metal made from copper and tin. কাঁসা

brooch (**brooches**) n A **brooch** is a small piece of jewellery which can be pinned on a dress, blouse, or coat. ব্রোচ

broom (**brooms**) n A **broom** is a long-handled brush which is used to sweep the floor. ঝাড়ু

broth (**broths**) n **Broth** is a kind of soup. It usually has vegetables or rice in it. মাংসের ঝোল

brother (**brothers**) n Your **brother** is a boy or a man who has the same parents as you. ভাই

brother-in-law (**brothers-in-law**) n Someone's **brother-in-law** is the brother of their husband or wife, or the man who is married to their sister. দেওর

brown (**browner, brownest**) adj Something that is **brown** is the colour of earth or of wood. বাদামী

brown bread n **Brown bread** is made from grains that have not had their outer layers removed. লাল পাউরুটি

brown rice n **Brown rice** is unpolished rice, in which the grains retain the outer yellowish-brown layer (bran). লাল চাল

browse (**browses, browsing, browsed**) vi If you **browse** in a shop, you look at things in a fairly casual way, in the hope that you might find something you like. ঘেঁটে দেখা

browser (**browsers**) n A **browser** is a piece of computer software that you use to search for information on the Internet. ব্রাউজার

bruise (**bruises**) n A **bruise** is an injury which appears as a purple or dark mark on your body. কালসিটে

brush (**brushes, brushing, brushed**) n A **brush** is an object with a large number of bristles fixed to it. You use brushes for painting, for cleaning things, and for tidying your hair. ব্রাশ ▷ vt If you **brush** something or **brush** something such as dirt off it, you clean it or tidy it using a brush. ব্রাশ করা

Brussels sprouts *npl* **Brussels sprouts** are vegetables that look like tiny cabbages. বাঁধাকপির মত দেখতে সবজি

brutal *adj* A **brutal** act or person is cruel and violent. পাশবিক

bubble (**bubbles**) *n* **Bubbles** are small balls of air or gas in a liquid. বুদবুদ

bubble bath *n* **Bubble bath** is a liquid that smells nice and makes a lot of bubbles when you add it to your bath water. সাবান জলে স্নান

bubble gum *n* **Bubble gum** is a sweet substance similar to chewing gum. You can blow it out of your mouth so it makes the shape of a bubble. বাবল গাম

bucket (**buckets**) *n* A **bucket** is a deep round metal or plastic container with a handle. বালতি

buckle (**buckles**) *n* A **buckle** is a piece of metal or plastic attached to one end of a belt or strap, which is used to fasten it. আংটা

Buddha *n* **Buddha** is the title given to Gautama Siddhartha, the religious teacher and founder of Buddhism. বুদ্ধ

Buddhism *n* **Buddhism** is a religion which teaches that the way to end suffering is by overcoming your desires. বৌদ্ধ ধর্ম

Buddhist (**Buddhists**) *adj* **Buddhist** means relating or referring to Buddhism. বৌদ্ধ ধর্ম সংক্রান্ত ▷ *n* A **Buddhist** is a person whose religion is Buddhism. বৌদ্ধ

budgerigar (**budgerigars**) *n* **Budgerigars** are small, brightly-coloured birds from Australia. বাজরিগার

budget (**budgets**) *n* Your **budget** is the amount of money that you have available to spend. The **budget** for something is the amount of money that a person, organization, or country has available to spend on it. বাজেট

budgie (**budgies**) *n* **Budgies** are small, brightly-coloured birds from Australia. (*informal*) বাজী

buffalo (**buffaloes, buffalo**) *n* A **buffalo** is a wild animal like a large cow with long curved horns. মোষ

buffet (**buffets**) *n* A **buffet** is a meal of cold food at a special occasion. Guests usually help themselves to the food. স্বয়ং পরিবেশন ভোজ

buffet car (**buffet cars**) *n* On a train, the **buffet car** is the carriage where food is sold. বুফে গাড়ি

bug (**bugs**) *n* A **bug** is a tiny insect, especially one that causes damage. (*informal*) ছারপোকা

bugged *adj* If a place or a telephone is **bugged**, tiny microphones have been hidden in it which transmit what people are saying. আড়ি পেতে শোনা

buggy (**buggies**) *n* A **buggy** is a small folding seat with wheels, which a young child can sit in and which can be pushed around. চাকা লাগানো মোড়া চেয়ার

build (**builds, building, built**) *vt* If you **build** a structure, you make it by joining things together. নির্মাণ করা

builder (**builders**) *n* A **builder** is a person whose job is to build or repair buildings. নির্মাণকর্তা

building (**buildings**) *n* A **building** is a structure with a roof and walls, such as a house. ভবন

building site (building sites) *n* A **building site** is an area of land on which a building or a group of buildings is in the process of being built or altered. নির্মাণস্থল

bulb (bulbs) *n* A **bulb** is an onion-shaped root that grows into a plant. কন্দ ▷ A **bulb** is the glass part of an electric lamp which gives out light when electricity passes through it. বাল্ব

Bulgaria *n* **Bulgaria** is a republic in south-east Europe, on the Balkan Peninsula on the Black Sea. বুলগেরিয়া

Bulgarian (Bulgarians) *adj* **Bulgarian** means belonging or relating to Bulgaria, or to its people, language, or culture. বুলগেরিয়া সংক্রান্ত ▷ *n* A **Bulgarian** is a person who comes from Bulgaria. বুলগেরিয়ার বাসিন্দা ▷ *n* **Bulgarian** is the main language spoken by people who live in Bulgaria. বুলগেরিয়ান ভাষা

bulimia *n* **Bulimia** or **bulimia nervosa** is a mental illness in which a person eats very large amounts and then makes themselves vomit. বুলিমিয়া

bull (bulls) *n* A **bull** is a male animal of the cow family. ষাঁড়

bulldozer (bulldozers) *n* A **bulldozer** is a large tractor with a broad metal blade at the front, used for moving earth or knocking down buildings. বুলডোজার

bullet (bullets) *n* A **bullet** is a small piece of metal which is fired from a gun. বুলেট

bulletin board (bulletin boards) *n* A **bulletin board** is a board which is usually attached to a wall in order to display notices giving information about something. সংবাদ বিবৃতি বোর্ড

bully (bullies, bullying, bullied) *n* A **bully** is someone who uses their strength or power to hurt or frighten other people. মস্তান ▷ *vt* If someone **bullies** you, they use their strength or power to hurt or frighten you. মস্তানি করা

bum (bums) *n* Your **bum** is the part of your body which you sit on. (*informal*) পাছা

bum bag (bum bags) *n* A **bum bag** consists of a small bag attached to a belt which you wear round your waist. You use it to carry things such as money and keys. বেল্টে লাগানো ছোট ব্যাগ

bumblebee (bumblebees) *n* A **bumblebee** is a large hairy bee. গুঁড়যুক্ত বড় মৌমাছি

bump (bumps) *n* A **bump** is an accidental knock or collision. ধাক্কা

bumper (bumpers) *n* **Bumpers** are bars at the front and back of a vehicle which protect it if it bumps into something. বাম্পার

bump into *v* If you **bump into** someone you know, you meet them by chance. (*informal*) হঠাৎ দেখা হওয়া I *bumped into a friend of yours today.*

bumpy (bumpier, bumpiest) *adj* A **bumpy** road or path has a lot of bumps on it. উঁচুনীচু

bun (buns) *n* A **bun** is a small round cake. ছোট গোলাকৃতি কেক

bunch (bunches) *n* A **bunch** of things is a group of them. (*informal*) দল

bungalow (bungalows) *n* A **bungalow** is a house with only one storey. বাংলো

bungee jumping *n* If someone goes **bungee jumping**, they jump from a high place such as a bridge or cliff with a long piece of strong elastic cord tied around their ankle connecting them to the bridge or cliff. উঁচু স্থান থেকে লাফানো

bunion (bunions) *n* A **bunion** is a large painful lump on the first joint of a person's big toe. কুল আঁটি

bunk (bunks) *n* A **bunk** is a bed fixed to a wall, especially in a ship or caravan. বাংক

bunk beds *npl* **Bunk beds** are two beds fixed one above the other in a frame. দুতলা বিছানা

buoy (buoys) *n* A **buoy** is a floating object that shows ships and boats where they can go and warns them of danger. নোঙর করা ভাসমান বস্তু

burden (burdens) *n* Something that is a **burden** causes you a lot of worry or hard work. বোঝা

bureaucracy (bureaucracies) n A
bureaucracy is an administrative system
operated by a large number of officials.
আমলাতন্ত্র

bureau de change (bureaux de change)
n A **bureau de change** is a place where
foreign currencies can be exchanged. বুরো
ডে চেঞ্জ

burger (burgers) n A **burger** is a flat round
mass of meat or vegetables, which is grilled
or fried. বার্গার

burglar (burglars) n A **burglar** is a thief
who breaks into houses and steals things.
সিঁধকাটা চোর

burglar alarm (burglar alarms) n A
burglar alarm is an electric device that
makes a bell ring loudly if someone tries to
enter a building by force. চোরঘন্টি

burglary (burglaries) n If someone
commits a **burglary**, they enter a building
by force and steal things. সিঁধকেটে চুরি

burgle (burgles, burgling, burgled) vt If
a house **is burgled**, someone breaks in and
steals things. সিঁধকেটে ঢোকা

Burmese n A **Burmese** is a person who
comes from Myanmar. বার্মার বাসিন্দা ▷ n
Burmese is the main language spoken by
the people who live in Myanmar. বার্মীজ ভাষা

burn (burns, burning, burned, burnt)
n A **burn** is an injury caused by fire or
something very hot. পোড়ার ক্ষত ▷ vi If
something is **burning**, it is on fire. জ্বলা ▷ vt
If you **burn** something, you destroy it or
damage it with fire. জ্বালিয়ে দেওয়া ▷ vt If you
burn yourself, you touch something that is
hot and get hurt. পুড়ে যাওয়া

burn down v If a building **burns down** or
if someone **burns it down**, it is completely
destroyed by fire. জ্বলে যাওয়া Anarchists
burnt down a restaurant.

burp (burps, burping, burped) n A **burp**
is a noise someone makes because air from
their stomach has been forced up through
their throat. ঢেঁকুর ▷ vi When someone
burps, they make a noise because air from

their stomach has been forced up through
their throat. ঢেঁকুর তোলা

burst (bursts, bursting) v When
something **bursts** or when you **burst** it, it
suddenly splits open, and air or some other
substance comes out. বিস্ফোরিত হওয়া

bury (buries, burying, buried) vt If you
bury something, you put it into a hole in
the ground and cover it up, often in order to
hide it. কবর দেওয়া

bus (buses) n A **bus** is a large motor vehicle
which carries passengers. বাস

bus conductor (bus conductors) n A
bus conductor is the person whose job
is to sell tickets to the passengers. বাস
কন্ডাক্টর

bush (bushes) n A **bush** is a dense cluster
of shrubs. ঝোপ-ঝাড় ▷ n A **bush** is a plant
which is like a very small tree. গুল্ম

business n **Business** is work relating to the
production, buying, and selling of goods or
services. ব্যবসায়

businessman (businessmen) n A
businessman is a man who works in
business. ব্যবসায়ী

businesswoman (businesswomen) n A
businesswoman is a woman who works in
business. মহিলা ব্যবসায়ী

busker (buskers) n A **busker** is a person
who sings or plays music for money in
streets and other public places. রাস্তার
গায়ক

bus station (bus stations) n A **bus station**
or **coach station** is a place where buses or
coaches start a journey. বাস স্টেশন

bus stop (bus stops) n A **bus stop** is a
place on a road where buses stop to let
passengers on and off. বাস স্টপ

bust (busts) n A **bust** is a statue of
someone's head and shoulders. মাথা এবং
বুকের মূর্তি

bus ticket (bus tickets) n A **bus ticket** is a
small, official piece of paper or card which
shows that you have paid for a journey on a
bus. বাস টিকিট

busy (busier, busiest) *adj* If you are **busy**, you have a lot of things to do. ব্যস্ত ▷ *adj* A **busy** place is full of people. জনবহুল

busy signal (busy signals) *n* A **busy signal** is a repeated single note heard on a telephone when the number called is already in use. ব্যস্ত সিগনাল

but *conj* You use **but** to say something that is different than what you have just said. কিন্তু *Heat the milk until it is very hot but not boiling.*

butcher (butchers) *n* A **butcher** is a shopkeeper who sells meat. কসাই ▷ *n* A **butcher** or a **butcher's** is a shop where meat is sold. কসাইয়ের দোকান

butter *n* **Butter** is a yellowish substance made from cream which you spread on bread or use in cooking. মাখন

buttercup (buttercups) *n* A **buttercup** is a small plant with bright yellow flowers. ঝুমকো লতা

butterfly (butterflies) *n* A **butterfly** is an insect with large colourful wings and a thin body. প্রজাপতি

buttocks *npl* Your **buttocks** are the two rounded fleshy parts of your body that you sit on. নিতম্ব

button (buttons) *n* **Buttons** are small hard objects sewn on to pieces of clothing, which you use to fasten the clothing. বোতাম

buy (buys, buying, bought) *vt* If you **buy** something, you obtain it by paying money for it. কেনা

buyer (buyers) *n* A **buyer** is a person who is buying something or who intends to buy it. ক্রেতা

buyout (buyouts) *n* A **buyout** is the buying of a company, especially by its managers or employees. বিক্রিত কোম্পানী

by *prep* If something is done **by** a person or thing, that person or thing does it. দ্বারা *Dinner was cooked by the children.*

bye! *excl* **Bye!** is another way of saying goodbye. (*informal*) বিদায়

bye-bye! *excl* **Bye-bye!** is another way of saying goodbye. (*informal*) বিদায় সম্ভাষণ

bypass (bypasses) *n* A **bypass** is a surgical operation performed on or near the heart, in which the flow of blood is redirected so that it does not flow through a part of the heart that is diseased or blocked. বাইপাস

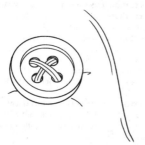

C

cab (**cabs**) *n* A **cab** is a taxi. ট্যাক্সি

cabbage (**cabbages**) *n* A **cabbage** is a round vegetable with green leaves. বাঁধাকপি

cabin (**cabins**) *n* A **cabin** is a small room in a ship or boat, or one of the areas inside a plane. কেবিন

cabin crew (**cabin crews**) *n* The **cabin crew** on an aircraft are the people whose job is to look after the passengers. বিমানসেবক

cabinet (**cabinets**) *n* A **cabinet** is a cupboard used for storing things or for displaying objects in. আলমারি

cable (**cables**) *n* A **cable** is a thick wire which is used to carry electricity or electronic signals. কেবল/প্লাস্টিক মোড়া ইলেকট্রিকের তার

cable car (**cable cars**) *n* A **cable car** is a vehicle for taking people up mountains or steep hills. It is pulled by a moving cable. কেবলচালিত গাড়ি

cable television *n* **Cable television** is a television system in which signals are sent along wires rather than by radio waves. কেবল টিভি

cactus (**cactuses, cacti**) *n* A **cactus** is a desert plant with a thick stem, often with spikes. ক্যাকটাস/কাঁটাওয়ালা গাছ

cadet (**cadets**) *n* A **cadet** is a young person who is being trained in the armed forces or police. সশস্ত্রবাহিনী/পুলিস-প্রশিক্ষণপ্রাপ্ত ছেলে/ পুলিস-প্রশিক্ষণপ্রাপ্ত মেয়ে

cafeteria (**cafeterias**) *n* A **cafeteria** is a self-service restaurant in a large shop or workplace. স্বয়ংপরিবেশন রেস্তোরাঁ

caffeine *n* **Caffeine** is a chemical substance found in coffee, tea, and cocoa, which makes you more active. ক্যাফিন

café (**cafés**) *n* A **café** is a place where simple meals, snacks, and drinks are sold. রেস্তোরাঁ

cage (**cages**) *n* A **cage** is a structure of wire or metal bars in which birds or animals are kept. খাঁচা

cagoule (**cagoules**) *n* A **cagoule** is a lightweight usually knee-length type of anorak. হালকা ওজনের হাঁটু পর্যন্ত ঢাকা বর্ষাতি

cake (**cakes**) *n* A **cake** is a sweet food made by baking a mixture of flour, eggs, sugar, and fat. কেক

calcium *n* **Calcium** is a soft white element found in bones and teeth, and also in limestone, chalk, and marble. ক্যালসিয়াম

calculate (**calculates, calculating, calculated**) *vt* If you **calculate** a number or amount, you work it out by doing some arithmetic. গণনা করা

calculation (**calculations**) *n* A **calculation** is something that you think about and work out mathematically. গণনা

calculator (**calculators**) *n* A **calculator** is a small electronic device used for doing mathematical calculations. যন্ত্রগণক

calendar (**calendars**) *n* A **calendar** is a chart or device which displays the date and the day of the week, and often the whole of a particular year. ক্যালেন্ডর/তারিখ, দিন সম্বলিত তালিকা

calf (**calves**) *n* A **calf** is a young cow. বাছুর ▷ Your **calves** are the thick parts at the backs of your legs, between your ankles and your knees. পায়ের ডিম

call (calls, calling, called) *n* When you make a telephone **call**, you telephone someone. ফোন করা ▷ *vt* If you **call** someone something, you give them a name. ডাকা ▷ *vt* If you **call** something, you say it in a loud voice. চিৎকার করে ডাকা ▷ *v* If you **call** someone, you talk to them on the telephone. টেলিফোন করা

call back *v* If you **call** someone **back**, you telephone them again or in return for a telephone call that they have made to you earlier. টেলিফোনের প্রত্যুত্তর *OK, I'll call you back around three o'clock.*

call box (call boxes) *n* A **call box** is a small shelter in the street in which there is a public telephone. জনগণের জন্য টেলিফোন

call centre (call centres) *n* A **call centre** is an office where people work answering or making telephone calls for a company. কলসেন্টার

call for *v* If you **call for** someone or something, you go to collect them. দাবি করা *I shall be calling for you at seven o'clock.*

call off *v* If you **call off** an event, you cancel it. বাতিল করা *The wedding was called off.*

calm (calmer, calmest) *adj* A **calm** person does not show or feel any worry, anger, or excitement. শান্ত

calm down *v* If you **calm down** or if someone **calms** you **down**, you become less upset or excited. শান্ত করা/শান্ত হওয়া *I'll try a herbal remedy to calm him down.*

calorie (calories) *n* A **calorie** is a unit of measurement for the energy value of food. ক্যালোরি

Cambodia *n* **Cambodia** is a country in south-east Asia. কাম্বোডিয়া

Cambodian (Cambodians) *adj* **Cambodian** means of or relating to Cambodia or its inhabitants. কাম্বোডিয়ার সাথে সম্পর্কযুক্ত ▷ *n* A **Cambodian** is a native or inhabitant of Cambodia. কাম্বোডিয়া-বাসী

camcorder (camcorders) *n* A **camcorder** is a portable video camera. ক্যাম-কর্ডার/ বহনযোগ্য ভিডিও ক্যামেরা

camel (camels) *n* A **camel** is a desert animal with one or two humps on its back. উট

camera (cameras) *n* A **camera** is a piece of equipment for taking photographs or for making a film. ক্যামেরা

cameraman (cameramen) *n* A **cameraman** is a person who operates a television or film camera. চিত্রগ্রাহক/ক্যামেরা-ম্যান

camera phone (camera phones) *n* A **camera phone** is a mobile phone that can also take photographs. মোবাইল ক্যামেরা-ফোন

Cameroon *n* **Cameroon** is a republic in West Africa, on the Gulf of Guinea. ক্যামেরুন

camp (camps, camping, camped) *n* A **camp** is a place where people live or stay in tents or caravans. শিবির/ছাউনি ▷ *vi* If you **camp** somewhere, you stay there in a tent or caravan. ছাউনি ফেলা

campaign (campaigns) *n* A **campaign** is a planned set of activities that people carry out over a period of time in order to achieve something such as social or political change. অভিযান

camp bed (camp beds) *n* A **camp bed** is a small bed that you can fold up. বহনযোগ্য খাট

camper (campers) *n* A **camper** is a person who goes camping. ক্যাম্পার

camping *n* **Camping** is the action of staying in a tent or caravan. ছাউনিতে থাকা

campsite (**campsites**) *n* A **campsite** or a **camping site** is a place where people who are on holiday can stay in tents. ছাউনিস্থল

campus (**campuses**) *n* A **campus** is the area of land containing the main buildings of a college or university. ক্যাম্পস/বিশ্ববিদ্যালয় বা কলেজ চত্বর

can *v* If you **can** do something, you are able to do it. করতে পারা *I can swim.*

can (**cans**) *n* A **can** is a metal container for food or drink. কৌটো

Canada *n* **Canada** is a country in North America. কানাডা

Canadian (**Canadians**) *adj* **Canadian** means belonging or relating to Canada, or to its people or culture. কানাডার সঙ্গে সম্পর্কিত ▷ *n* A **Canadian** is a Canadian citizen, or a person of Canadian origin. কানাডা-বাসী

canal (**canals**) *n* A **canal** is a long, narrow, man-made stretch of water. খাল

Canaries *npl* The **Canaries** are a group of islands in the Atlantic, off the northwest coast of Africa. ক্যানারিস দ্বীপপুঞ্জ

canary (**canaries**) *n* **Canaries** are small yellow birds which sing beautifully. ক্যানারি

cancel (**cancels, cancelling, cancelled**) *v* If you **cancel** an order or an arrangement, you stop it from happening. বাতিল করা

cancellation (**cancellations**) *n* **Cancellation** is the fact or an instance of cancelling. বাতিল

Cancer *n* **Cancer** is one of the twelve signs of the zodiac. Its symbol is a crab. People who are born between the 21st of June and the 22nd of July come under this sign. কর্কট রাশি

cancer (**cancers**) *n* **Cancer** is a serious illness in which abnormal body cells increase, producing growths. ক্যান্সার

candidate (**candidates**) *n* A **candidate** is someone who is being considered for a position. প্রার্থী

candle (**candles**) *n* A **candle** is a stick of hard wax with a piece of string called a wick through the middle. You light the wick so the candle produces light. মোমবাতি

candlestick (**candlesticks**) *n* A **candlestick** is a narrow object with a hole at the top which holds a candle. মোমবাতিদানি

candyfloss *n* **Candyfloss** is a large pink or white mass of sugar threads that is eaten from a stick. It is sold at fairs or other outdoor events. হাওয়া-মিঠাই

canister (**canisters**) *n* A **canister** is a metal container. ক্যানেস্তারা

canned *adj* **Canned** music, laughter, or applause on a television or radio programme has been recorded beforehand and is added to the programme to make it sound as if there is a live audience. সংরক্ষিত

canoe (**canoes**) *n* A **canoe** is a small narrow boat that you row using a paddle. ডিঙি নৌকা

canoeing *n* **Canoeing** is the sport of using and racing a canoe. ডিঙি নৌকার প্রতিযোগিতা

can opener (**can openers**) *n* A **can opener** is a tool that is used for opening cans of food. খাবারের টিন খোলার যন্ত্র

canteen (**canteens**) *n* A **canteen** is a place in a factory, office, or shop where the workers can have meals. ক্যান্টিন/ভোজনালয়

canter (**canters, cantering, cantered**) *vi* When a horse **canters**, it moves at a speed that is slower than a gallop but faster than a trot. ঘোড়ার স্বচ্ছন্দ দৌড়

canvas (**canvases**) *n* **Canvas** is strong heavy cloth used for making tents, sails, and bags. একধরনের মোটা কাপড়

canvass (**canvasses, canvassing, canvassed**) *vi* If you **canvass** for a person or political party, you try to persuade people to vote for them. প্রচার

cap (**caps**) *n* A **cap** is a soft flat hat usually worn by men or boys. টুপি

capable *adj* If you are **capable** of doing something, you are able to do it. সমর্থ

capacity (**capacities**) *n* Your **capacity** for something is your ability to do it, or the amount of it that you are able to do. সামর্থ্য

capital (**capitals**) *n* **Capital** is money that you use to start a business. মূলধন ▷ The **capital** of a country is the main city, where the country's leaders work. রাজধানী ▷ n A **capital** is a big letter of the alphabet, for example A or R. বড়হাতের অক্ষর

capitalism *n* **Capitalism** is an economic and political system in which property, business, and industry are owned by private individuals and not by the state. পুঁজিবাদ

capital punishment *n* **Capital punishment** is the legal killing of a person who has committed a serious crime. মৃত্যুদণ্ড

Capricorn *n* **Capricorn** is one of the twelve signs of the zodiac. Its symbol is a goat. People who are born between the 22nd of December and the 19th of January come under this sign. মকর রাশি

capsize (**capsizes, capsizing, capsized**) *v* If you **capsize** a boat or if it **capsizes**, it turns upside down in the water. নৌকা উল্টে যাওয়া

capsule (**capsules**) *n* A **capsule** is a small container with powdered or liquid medicine inside, which you swallow whole. ক্যাপসুল

captain (**captains**) *n* In the army, navy, and some other armed forces, a **captain** is an officer of middle rank. ক্যাপ্টেন

caption (**captions**) *n* The **caption** of a picture consists of the words printed underneath. শিরোনাম

capture (**captures, capturing, captured**) *vt* If you **capture** someone or something, you catch them and keep them somewhere so that they cannot leave. আটক করা

car (**cars**) *n* A **car** is a motor vehicle with room for a small number of passengers. মোটরগাড়ী

carafe (**carafes**) *n* A **carafe** is a glass container in which you serve water or wine. জল দেওয়ার পাত্র/মদ দেওয়ার পাত্র

caramel (**caramels**) *n* A **caramel** is a chewy sweet food made from sugar, butter, and milk. ক্যারামেল

carat (**carats**) *n* A **carat** is a unit equal to 0.2 grams used for measuring the weight of diamonds and other precious stones. ক্যারাট/সোনা-হীরে ওজনের মাপ

caravan (**caravans**) *n* A **caravan** is a vehicle without an engine that can be pulled by a car or van. It contains beds and cooking equipment so that people can live or spend their holidays in it. ক্যারাভ্যান

carbohydrate (**carbohydrates**) *n* **Carbohydrates** are energy-giving substances found in foods such as sugar and bread. শর্করা

carbon *n* **Carbon** is a chemical element that diamonds and coal are made of. অঙ্গার

carbon footprint (**carbon footprints**) *n* Your **carbon footprint** is a measure of the amount of carbon dioxide released into the atmosphere by your activities over a particular period. পরিবেশে কার্বন-ডাই-অক্সাইডের পরিমাপক

carburettor (**carburettors**) *n* A **carburettor** is the part of an engine, usually in a car, in which air and petrol are mixed together to form a vapour which can be burned. কার্বুরেটর

card (**cards**) *n* A **card** is a folded piece of stiff paper that has a picture on the front and a message inside. You send **cards** to people at special times, like birthdays. কার্ড ▷ n **Card** is stiff paper. কার্ড ▷ n **Cards** are pieces of stiff paper with numbers or pictures on them that you use for playing games. তাস

cardboard *n* **Cardboard** is thick stiff paper used to make boxes and other containers. শক্ত কাগজের বোর্ড

cardigan (cardigans) n A **cardigan** is a knitted woollen garment that fastens at the front. বোতামওয়ালা উলের পোশাক

cardphone (card phones) n A **cardphone** is a public telephone operated by the insertion of a phonecard instead of coins. কার্ড-ফোন

care (cares, caring, cared) n **Care** is very careful attention. যত্ন ▷ vi If you **care** about something, you think that it is important. যত্ন নেওয়া ▷ vi If you **care** for a person or an animal, you look after them. দেখভাল করা

career (careers) n Your **career** is your job or profession. পেশা

careful adj If you are **careful**, you pay attention to what you are doing in order to avoid damage or mistakes. সতর্ক

carefully adv If you do something **carefully**, you pay attention to what you are doing, in order to avoid damage or mistakes. সতর্কভাবে

careless adj If you are **careless**, you do not pay enough attention to what you are doing, and so you make mistakes. অসতর্ক

caretaker (caretakers) n A **caretaker** is someone who looks after a building and the area around it. দেখভাল করেন যিনি

car ferry n A **car ferry** is a boat that transports vehicles and passengers, usually across rivers or short stretches of sea. গাড়ী পারাপারের নৌকা

cargo (cargoes) n The **cargo** of a ship or plane is the goods that it is carrying. মালপত্র

car hire n **Car hire** is the activity or process of hiring a car. ভাড়া গাড়ী

Caribbean adj **Caribbean** means belonging or relating to the Caribbean Sea and its islands, or to its people. ক্যারিবিয়ান দ্বীপপুঞ্জের সঙ্গে সম্পর্কিত ▷ n The **Caribbean** is the sea which is between the West Indies, Central America and the north coast of South America. ক্যারিবিয়ান সাগর

caring adj A **caring** person is affectionate, helpful, and sympathetic. দরদী

car insurance n **Car insurance** is an arrangement in which you pay money to a company, and they pay money to you if you have an accident in your car or if your car is stolen. গাড়ীর বিমা

car keys npl **Car keys** are a set of keys that you use to lock and unlock a car and to start and stop its engine. গাড়ীর চাবি

carnation (carnations) n A **carnation** is a plant with white, pink, or red flowers. একপ্রকারের ফুল গাছ

carnival (carnivals) n A **carnival** is a public festival with music, processions, and dancing. খ্রীষ্টানদের উৎসব

carol (carols) n **Carols** are Christian religious songs that are sung at Christmas. খ্রীষ্টধর্মের গান

car park (car parks) n A **car park** is an area or building where people can leave their cars. গাড়ী রাখবার জায়গা

carpenter (carpenters) n A **carpenter** is a person whose job is making and repairing wooden things. ছুতোর

carpentry n **Carpentry** is the activity of making and repairing wooden things. কাঠের কাজ

carpet (carpets) n A **carpet** is a thick covering for a floor or staircase, made of wool or a similar material. কার্পেট

car rental n **Car rental** is the activity or process of renting a car. গাড়ী-ভাড়া

carriage (carriages) n A **carriage** is one of the separate sections of a train that carries passengers. রেলগাড়ী

carrier bag (carrier bags) n A **carrier bag** is a paper or plastic bag with handles. প্লাস্টিকের ব্যাগ

carrot (carrots) n **Carrots** are long, thin, orange-coloured vegetables that grow under the ground. গাজর

carry (carries, carrying, carried) vt If you **carry** something, you take it with you, holding it so that it does not touch the ground. বহন করা

carrycot (**carrycots**) *n* A **carrycot** is a small bed for babies which has handles so it can be carried. হাতলওয়ালা শিশুদের খাট

carry on *v* If you **carry on** doing something, you continue to do it. চালিয়ে যাওয়া *The assistant carried on talking.*

carry out *v* If you **carry out** a threat, task, or instruction, you do it or act according to it. নির্দেশমত কাজ করা *The police carried out the arrests.*

cart (**carts**) *n* A **cart** is an old-fashioned wooden vehicle, usually pulled by an animal. গরুর গাড়ী

carton (**cartons**) *n* A **carton** is a plastic or cardboard container in which food or drink is sold. কার্ডবোর্ড/কাগজের বক্স

cartoon (**cartoons**) *n* A **cartoon** is a funny drawing. কার্টুন ▷ *n* A **cartoon** is a film that uses drawings, not real people or things. কার্টুন ফিল্ম

cartridge (**cartridges**) *n* In a gun, a **cartridge** is a tube containing a bullet and an explosive substance. কার্তুজ

carve (**carves, carving, carved**) *v* If you **carve** an object, you cut it out of stone or wood. You **carve** wood or stone in order to make the object. খোদাই করা

car wash (**car washes**) *n* A **car wash** is a place with special equipment, where you can pay to have your car washed. গাড়ী ধোওয়ার জায়গা

case (**cases**) *n* A **case** is a particular situation, especially one that you are using as an example. ক্ষেত্র ▷ *n* A **case** is a container that is used to hold or carry something. বাক্স

cash *n* **Cash** is money, especially money in the form of notes and coins. নগদ

cash dispenser (**cash dispensers**) *n* A **cash dispenser** is a machine built into the wall of a bank or other building, which allows people to take out money from their bank account using a special card. নগদ-পরিবেশক

cashew (**cashews**) *n* A **cashew** or a **cashew nut** is a curved nut that you can eat. কাজু

cashier (**cashiers**) *n* A **cashier** is the person that customers pay money to or get money from in a shop or bank. কোষাধ্যক্ষ

cashmere *n* **Cashmere** is a kind of very fine soft wool. সূক্ষ্ম নরম উল

cash register (**cash registers**) *n* A **cash register** is a machine in a shop, pub, or restaurant that is used to add up and record how much money people pay, and in which the money is kept. নগদ নিবন্ধকরণের যন্ত্র

casino (**casinos**) *n* A **casino** is a place where people play gambling games. ক্যাসিনো

casserole (**casseroles**) *n* A **casserole** is a meal made by cooking food in liquid in an oven. তরল রাখবার পাত্র

cassette (**cassettes**) *n* A **cassette** is a small, flat, rectangular, plastic container with magnetic tape inside, which is used for recording and playing back sounds. ক্যাসেট

cast (**casts**) *n* The **cast** of a play or film is all the people who act in it. নাটকের চরিত্র

castle (**castles**) *n* A **castle** is a large building with thick, high walls that was built in the past to protect people during wars and battles. দুর্গ

casual *adj* If you are **casual**, you are relaxed and not very concerned about what is happening. ঘরোয়া

casually *adv* If you do something **casually**, you do it in a relaxed and unconcerned way. ঘরোয়াভাবে

casualty (**casualties**) *n* A **casualty** is a person who is injured or killed in a war or accident. দুর্ঘটনায় আহত/দুর্ঘটনায় নিহত

cat (**cats**) *n* A **cat** is a small furry animal with a tail, whiskers, and sharp claws. বিড়াল

catalogue (catalogues) n A **catalogue** is a list of things, such as the goods you can buy from a company. ক্যাটালগ/জিনিসের তালিকা

catalytic converter (catalytic converters) n A **catalytic converter** is a device which is fitted to a car's exhaust to reduce the pollution coming from it. গাড়ীর থেকে নির্গত দূষণ কম করবার সরঞ্জামবিশেষ

cataract (cataracts) n A **cataract** is a large waterfall or rapids. জলপ্রপাত ▷ n A **cataract** is a layer that has grown over a person's eye that prevents them from seeing properly. চোখের ছানি

catarrh n **Catarrh** is a medical condition in which a lot of mucus is produced in your nose and throat. You may get catarrh when you have a cold. সর্দি, নাসিকা ও গলার প্রদাহ

catastrophe (catastrophes) n A **catastrophe** is an unexpected event that causes great suffering or damage. আচমকা বিপর্যয়

catch (catches, catching, caught) vt If you **catch** a person or animal, you capture them. ধরা ▷ vt If you **catch** something that is moving, you take hold of it while it is in the air. লুফে নেওয়া ▷ vt If you **catch** a bus or a train, you get on it. ধরা ▷ vt If you **catch** an illness, you become ill with it. অসুখে পড়া

catching adj If an illness or a disease is **catching**, it is easily passed on or given to someone else. ছোঁয়াচে

catch up v If you **catch up** with someone, you reach them by moving faster than them. ছুঁয়ে ফেলা I ran faster to catch up with him.

category (categories) n If people or things are divided into **categories**, they are divided into groups according to their qualities and characteristics. শ্রেণীবিভাগ

catering n **Catering** is the activity or business of providing food for people. খাদ্য সরবরাহের ব্যবসা

caterpillar (caterpillars) n A **caterpillar** is a small worm-like animal that eventually develops into a butterfly or moth. শুঁয়োপোকা

cathedral (cathedrals) n A **cathedral** is a large important Christian church which has a bishop in charge of it. বড় গির্জা

cattle npl **Cattle** are cows and bulls. গবাদি পশু

Caucasus n The **Caucasus** is a mountain range in south-west Russia. ককেশাস পর্বতমালা

cauliflower (cauliflowers) n A **cauliflower** is a large, round, white vegetable surrounded by green leaves. ফুলকপি

cause (causes, causing, caused) n The **cause** of an event is the thing that makes it happen. কারণ ▷ n A **cause** is an aim which a group of people supports or is fighting for. উদ্দেশ্য ▷ vt To **cause** something, usually something bad, means to make it happen. খারাপ কিছু ঘটা

caution n **Caution** is great care taken in order to avoid danger. সাবধানতা

cautious adj A **cautious** person acts very carefully in order to avoid danger. সাবধান

cautiously adv If you do something **cautiously**, you do it very carefully in order to avoid possible danger. সাবধানে

cave (caves) n A **cave** is a large hole in the side of a cliff or hill, or under the ground. গুহা

CCTV abbr **CCTV** is an abbreviation for 'closed-circuit television'. সিসিটিভি/"ক্লোজড সার্কিট টেলিভিশন"

CD (CDs) n A **CD** is a small shiny disc on which music or information is stored. **CD** is an abbreviation for 'compact disc'. সিডি

CD burner (CD burners) n A **CD burner** is a piece of computer equipment that you use for copying data from a computer onto a CD. সিডি-কপি করার যন্ত্র

CD player (CD players) n A **CD player** is a machine on which you can play CDs. সিডি বাজানোর যন্ত্র

CD-ROM (CD-ROMs) n A **CD-ROM** is a disc which can be read by a computer, and on which a large amount of data is stored. সিডি-রোম

ceasefire (**ceasefires**) *n* A **ceasefire** is an arrangement in which countries at war agree to stop fighting for a time. সাময়িক যুদ্ধবিরতির ব্যবস্থা

ceiling (**ceilings**) *n* A **ceiling** is the top inside surface of a room. ছাদ

celebrate (**celebrates, celebrating, celebrated**) *v* If you **celebrate**, or **celebrate** something, you do something enjoyable because of a special occasion. উৎসব পালন করা

celebration (**celebrations**) *n* A **celebration** is a special enjoyable event that people organize because something pleasant has happened or because it is someone's birthday or anniversary. উৎসব পালন

celebrity (**celebrities**) *n* A **celebrity** is someone who is famous. বিখ্যাত ব্যক্তি

celery *n* **Celery** is a vegetable with long pale green stalks. শাকবিশেষ

cell (**cells**) *n* A **cell** is the smallest part of an animal or plant. Animals and plants are made up of millions of cells. কোষ

cellar (**cellars**) *n* A **cellar** is a room underneath a building. সেলার/মাটির নিচে ঘর

cello (**cellos**) *n* A **cello** is a musical instrument that looks like a large violin. You hold it upright and play it sitting down. সেলো/একপ্রকার বাদ্যবিশেষ

cement *n* **Cement** is a grey powder which is mixed with sand and water in order to make concrete. সিমেন্ট

cemetery (**cemeteries**) *n* A **cemetery** is a place where dead people are buried. কবরখানা

census (**censuses**) *n* A **census** is an official survey of the population of a country. জনগণনা

cent (**cents**) *n* A **cent** is a small unit of money in many countries. সেন্ট

centenary (**centenaries**) *n* A **centenary** is the one hundredth anniversary of an event. শতবার্ষিকী

centimetre (**centimetres**) *n* A **centimetre** is a unit of length equal to ten millimetres or one-hundredth of a metre. সেন্টিমিটার

central *adj* Something that is **central** is in the middle of a place or area. কেন্দ্রীয়

Central African Republic *n* The **Central African Republic** is a country of central Africa. মধ্য-আফ্রিকান প্রজাতন্ত্র

Central America *n* **Central America** is an area joining the continents of North and South America, extending from the south border of Mexico to the north-west border of Colombia. মধ্য-আমেরিকা

central heating *n* **Central heating** is a heating system in which water or air is heated and passed round a building through pipes and radiators. কেন্দ্রীয় তাপ পরিবহন ব্যবস্থা

centre (**centres**) *n* The **centre** of something is the middle of it. কেন্দ্র

century (**centuries**) *n* A **century** is one hundred years. শতবর্ষ

CEO (**CEOs**) *abbr* **CEO** is an abbreviation for 'chief executive officer'. সি.ই.ও./"চিফ এক্সিকিউটিভ অফিসার"

ceramic *adj* **Ceramic** means of, relating to, or made of clay that has been heated to a very high temperature so that it becomes hard. চিনামাটির তৈরী

cereal (**cereals**) *n* A **cereal** is a food made from grains that you eat with milk for breakfast. শস্যদানা থেকে তৈরি খাবার ▷ *n* A **cereal** is a kind of plant, for example wheat or rice. The seeds of **cereals** are used for food. শস্যদানা

ceremony (**ceremonies**) *n* A **ceremony** is a formal event such as a wedding or a coronation. সামাজিক অনুষ্ঠান

certain *adj* If you are **certain** about something, you know it is true. নিশ্চিত

certainly *adv* You can use **certainly** to emphasize what you are saying. নিশ্চিতভাবে

certainty (**certainties**) *n* **Certainty** is the state of having no doubts at all. নিশ্চয়তা

certificate (**certificates**) *n* A **certificate** is an official document which states that particular facts are true, or which you receive when you have successfully completed a course of study or training. সংসাপত্র

Chad *n* **Chad** is a republic in north central Africa. চ্যাড/উত্তর-মধ্য আফ্রিকার একটি প্রজাতন্ত্র

chain (**chains**) *n* A **chain** consists of metal rings connected together in a line. শৃঙ্খল

chair (**chairs**) *n* A **chair** is a piece of furniture for one person to sit on, with a back and four legs. চেয়ার

chairlift (**chairlifts**) *n* A **chairlift** is a line of chairs that hang from a moving cable and carry people up and down a mountain or ski slope. চেয়ার-লিফট/পাহাড়ী জায়গায় এর সাহায্যে মানুষ ওঠানামা করে

chairman (**chairmen**) *n* The **chairman** of a meeting or organization is the person in charge of it. সভাপতি

chalk *n* **Chalk** is soft white rock. খড়ি

challenge (**challenges, challenging, challenged**) *n* A **challenge** is something new and difficult which requires great effort and determination. চ্যালেঞ্জ/সাহস ও ঝুঁকি ▷ *vt* If you **challenge** ideas or people, you question their truth, value, or authority. প্রশ্ন করা/চ্যালেঞ্জ গ্রহণ করা

challenging *adj* A **challenging** job or activity requires great effort and determination. সাহসিকতাপূর্ণ/ঝুঁকিপূর্ণ

chambermaid (**chambermaids**) *n* A **chambermaid** is a woman who cleans and tidies the bedrooms in a hotel. হোটেলের পরিচারিকা

champagne (**champagnes**) *n* **Champagne** is an expensive French sparkling white wine. ফরাসী ওয়াইন

champion (**champions**) *n* A **champion** is someone who has won the first prize in a competition. শ্রেষ্ঠ প্রতিযোগি/প্রথমশ্রেণীর বিজয়ী

championship (**championships**) *n* A **championship** is a competition to find the best player or team in a particular sport. প্রতিযোগিতা

chance (**chances**) *n* If there is a **chance** of something happening, it is possible that it will happen. সুযোগ

change (**changes, changing, changed**) *n* If there is a **change** in something, it becomes different. পরিবর্তন ▷ *vi* When you **change**, you put on different clothes. পোষাক পরিবর্তন করা ▷ *v* When you **change** something, or when it **changes**, it becomes different. বদলানো ▷ *n* **Change** is the money that you get back when you pay too much for something. মূল্যফেরত

changeable *adj* Someone or something that is **changeable** is likely to change many times. পরিবর্তনযোগ্য

changing room (**changing rooms**) *n* A **changing room** is a room where you can change your clothes and usually have a shower, for example at a sports centre. পোশাক পরিবর্তনের ঘর

channel (**channels**) *n* A **channel** is a wavelength on which television programmes are broadcast. চ্যানেল/টিভির চ্যানেল

chaos *n* **Chaos** is a state of complete disorder and confusion. চূড়ান্ত বিশৃঙ্খলা

chaotic *adj* If a situation is **chaotic**, it is in a state of disorder and confusion. চূড়ান্ত বিশৃঙ্খলাযুক্ত

chap (**chaps**) *n* A **chap** is a man or boy. (*informal*) ছোট ছেলে বা লোক

chapel (**chapels**) *n* A **chapel** is a part of a Christian church which has its own altar and which is used for private prayer. চ্যাপেল/খ্রীষ্টানদের ব্যক্তিগত প্রার্থনাঘর

chapter (**chapters**) *n* A **chapter** is one of the parts that a book is divided into. অধ্যায়

character (**characters**) *n* Your **character** is the kind of person you are. চরিত্র ▷ *n* A **character** is a person in a story or a film. গল্পের অথবা ফিল্মের চরিত্র

characteristic (**characteristics**) *n* A **characteristic** is a quality or feature that is typical of someone or something. বৈশিষ্ট্য

charcoal *n* **Charcoal** is a black substance used as a fuel and for drawing, obtained by burning wood without much air. কাঠকয়লা

charge (**charges**, **charging**, **charged**) *n* A **charge** is an amount of money that you have to pay for a service. মূল্য ▷ *n* A **charge** is a formal accusation that someone has committed a crime. অভিযোগে ▷ *n* An electrical **charge** is an amount of electricity that is held in or carried by something. বিদ্যুৎশক্তির পরিমাণ বোঝাতে ▷ *v* If you **charge** someone an amount of money, you ask them to pay that amount for something. মূল্য ধার্য করা ▷ *vt* When the police **charge** someone, they formally accuse them of having done something illegal. অভিযোগে দায়ী করা ▷ *vt* To **charge** a battery means to pass an electrical current through it to make it more powerful or to make it last longer. বিদ্যুৎশক্তি পরিবাহিত হওয়া

charger (**chargers**) *n* A **charger** is a device used for charging or recharging batteries. যা দিয়ে চার্জ করা হয়

charity (**charities**) *n* A **charity** is an organization which raises money to help people who are ill, disabled, or poor. দাতব্য প্রতিষ্ঠান

charity shop (**charity shops**) *n* A **charity shop** is a shop that sells used goods cheaply and gives its profits to a charity. সস্তার বিপণি

charm (**charms**) *n* **Charm** is the quality of being attractive and pleasant. মাধুর্য

charming *adj* If someone or something is **charming**, they are very pleasant and attractive. মধুর

chart (**charts**) *n* A **chart** is a diagram or graph which displays information. তথ্যতালিকা

chase (**chases**, **chasing**, **chased**) *n* A **chase** is the act of chasing someone. পশ্চাদ্ধাবন ▷ *vt* If you **chase** someone, you run after them or follow them in order to catch them or force them to leave a place. পশ্চাদ্ধাবন করা

chat (**chats**, **chatting**, **chatted**) *n* A **chat** is informal conversation or talk conducted in an easy familiar manner. চ্যাট/হালকা কথাবার্তা ▷ *vi* When people **chat**, they talk to each other in an informal and friendly way. চ্যাট/হালকা কথাবার্তা বলা

chatroom (**chatrooms**) *n* A **chatroom** is a site on the Internet, or another computer network, where users have group discussions by electronic mail, typically about one subject. ইন্টারনেটের চ্যাটরুম

chat show (**chat shows**) *n* A **chat show** is a television or radio show in which an interviewer and his or her guests talk in a friendly, informal way about different topics. চ্যাট শো/হালকা কথাবার্তা বলার শো

chauffeur (**chauffeurs**) *n* A **chauffeur** is a person whose job is to drive and look after another person's car. ব্যক্তিগত ড্রাইভার

chauvinist (**chauvinists**) *n* A **chauvinist** is a man who believes that men are naturally better and more important than women. পুরুষদের শ্রেষ্ঠতায় বিশ্বাসী

cheap (**cheaper, cheapest**) *adj* **Cheap** goods or services cost less money than usual or than you expected. সস্তা

cheat (**cheats, cheating, cheated**) *n* Someone who is a **cheat** does not obey a set of rules which they should be obeying. ঠগ ▷ *vi* When someone **cheats**, they do not obey a set of rules which they should be obeying, for example in a game or exam. ঠকানো

Chechnya *n* **Chechnya** is a republic that is part of south Russia. চেচনিয়া

check (**checks, checking, checked**) *n* A **check** is a control, especially a rapid or informal one, designed to ensure accuracy, progress, etc. নিয়ন্ত্রণ ▷ *v* If you **check** something such as a piece of information or a document, you make sure that it is correct or satisfactory. পরীক্ষা করা

checked *adj* Something that is **checked** has a pattern of small squares, usually of two colours. দুই রঙ এর চৌকো ডিজাইন

check in (**check-ins**) *v* When you **check in** or **check into** a hotel or clinic, you arrive and go through the necessary procedures before staying there. চেক-ইন/নাম-ঠিকানা নিবন্ধকরণ *He checked in at the hotel and asked to see the manager.*

check out (**checkouts**) *v* When you **check out** of a hotel, you pay the bill and leave. হোটেলের বিল মেটানো *They packed and checked out of the hotel.* ▷ *n* In a supermarket, a **checkout** is a counter where you pay for your goods. বিলপ্রদান

check-up (**check-ups**) *n* A **check-up** is a routine examination by a doctor or dentist. শারীরিক পরীক্ষা

cheek (**cheeks**) *n* Your **cheeks** are the sides of your face below your eyes. গাল

cheekbone (**cheekbones**) *n* Your **cheekbones** are the two bones in your face just below your eyes. গালের হাড়

cheeky (**cheekier, cheekiest**) *adj* Someone who is **cheeky** is rude to someone they ought to respect, but often in a charming or amusing way. বিনয়ী

cheer (**cheers, cheering, cheered**) *n* A **cheer** is a shout or cry of approval, encouragement, etc. আনন্দের চিৎকার ▷ *v* When people **cheer**, they shout loudly to show their approval or to encourage someone who is doing something such as taking part in a game. আনন্দে চিৎকার করা

cheerful *adj* A **cheerful** person is happy. উৎফুল্ল

cheerio! *excl* People sometimes say '**Cheerio!**' as a way of saying goodbye. (*informal*) বিদায়ধ্বনি

cheers! *excl* **Cheers!** is a word that people say to each other as they lift up their glasses to drink. চিয়ার্স/মদ্যপায়ীরা এই শব্দটি বলে মদ্যপান শুরু করে।

cheese (**cheeses**) *n* **Cheese** is a solid food made from milk. দুগ্ধজাত জিনিস

chef (**chefs**) *n* A **chef** is a cook in a restaurant or hotel. হোটেলের পাচক

chemical (**chemicals**) *n* **Chemicals** are substances that are used in or made by a chemical process. রাসায়নিক বস্তু

chemist (**chemists**) *n* A **chemist** is a specially qualified person who prepares and sells medicines. রসায়নবিদ ▷ *n* A **chemist** or a **chemist's** is a place where medicines are sold or given out. ওষুধের দোকান

chemistry *n* **Chemistry** is the scientific study of the characteristics and composition of substances. রসায়ন

cheque (**cheques**) *n* A **cheque** is a printed form on which you write an amount of money and say who it is to be paid to. Your bank then pays the money to that person from your account. ব্যাঙ্কের চেক

chequebook (**chequebooks**) n A **chequebook** is a book containing detachable blank cheques and issued by a bank or building society to holders of cheque accounts. ব্যাংকের চেকবই

cherry (**cherries**) n **Cherries** are small, round fruit with red or black skins. চেরীফল

chess n **Chess** is a game for two people played on a board with 64 black and white squares. Each player has 16 pieces including a King. The aim is to trap your opponent's King. দাবা

chest (**chests**) n Your **chest** is the top part of the front of your body. বক্ষস্থল ▷ n A **chest** is a large heavy box, used for storing things. সিন্দুক

chestnut (**chestnuts**) n A **chestnut** or **chestnut tree** is a tall tree with broad leaves. বাদাম

chest of drawers (**chests of drawers**) n A **chest of drawers** is a low, flat piece of furniture with drawers in which you keep clothes and other things. ড্রয়ারওয়ালা আলমারি

chew (**chews, chewing, chewed**) v When you **chew** food, you break it up with your teeth and make it easier to swallow. চিবানো

chewing gum n **Chewing gum** is a kind of sweet that you can chew for a long time. You do not swallow it. চিউইং গাম/চিবানোর মিষ্টি গাম

chick (**chicks**) n A **chick** is a baby bird. মুরগীর বাচ্ছা

chicken (**chickens**) n A **chicken** is a bird that is kept on a farm for its eggs and meat. মুরগী ▷ n **Chicken** is the meat that comes from chickens. মুরগীর মাংস

chickenpox n **Chickenpox** is a disease which gives you a high temperature and red spots that itch. বসন্ত রোগ

chickpea (**chickpeas**) n **Chickpeas** are hard round seeds that look like pale-brown peas. They can be cooked and eaten. ছোলার ডাল

chief (**chiefs**) adj **Chief** is used in the job titles of the most senior worker or workers of a particular kind in an organization. মুখ্য ▷ n The **chief** of an organization or department is its leader or the person in charge of it. প্রধান

child (**children**) n A **child** is a human being who is not yet an adult. শিশু

childcare n **Childcare** refers to looking after children. শিশুর যত্ন

childhood (**childhoods**) n A person's **childhood** is the time when they are a child. শৈশব

childish adj **Childish** means relating to or typical of a child. শিশুসুলভ

childminder (**childminders**) n A **childminder** is someone whose job it is to look after children when the children's parents are away or are at work. Childminders usually work in their own homes. শিশু-পালক/শিশু-পালয়িত্রী

Chile n **Chile** is a republic in South America, on the Pacific. চিলি

Chilean (**Chileans**) adj **Chilean** means of or relating to Chile or its inhabitants. চিলির সাথে সম্পর্কিত ▷ n A **Chilean** is a native or inhabitant of Chile. চিলির অধিবাসী

chill (**chills, chilling, chilled**) v To **chill** something means to make it cold. ঠান্ডা করা

chilli (**chillies, chillis**) n **Chillies** are small red or green seed pods with a hot, spicy taste. লঙ্কা

chilly (**chillier, chilliest**) adj **Chilly** means uncomfortably cold. অসহ্য ঠান্ডা

chimney (**chimneys**) n A **chimney** is a pipe above a fireplace or furnace through which smoke can go up into the air. চিমনি

chimpanzee (**chimpanzees**) n A **chimpanzee** is a kind of small African ape. শিম্পাঞ্জি

chin (**chins**) n Your **chin** is the part of your face below your mouth and above your neck. থুতনি

China n **China** is a republic in East Asia. চীন প্রজাতন্ত্র

china n **China** or **china clay** is a very thin clay used to make cups, plates, and ornaments. চীনামাটি

Chinese (**Chinese**) *adj* **Chinese** means relating to or belonging to China, or its people, languages, or culture. চীনের সাথে সম্পর্কিত ▷ *n* The **Chinese** are the people who come from China. চীন-বাসী ▷ The languages that are spoken in China, especially Mandarin, are often referred to as **Chinese**. চীনা ভাষা

chip (**chips, chipping, chipped**) *n* A **chip** is a small piece which has been broken off something. ছোট টুকরো ▷ *n* A **chip** is a very small part that controls a piece of electronic equipment. সিলিকনের ছোট টুকরো ▷ *vt* If you **chip** something, you break a small piece off it by accident. টুকরো করা

chips *npl* **Chips** or potato **chips** are thin pieces of potato fried in hot oil. আলুভাজা

chiropodist (**chiropodists**) *n* A **chiropodist** is a person whose job is to treat and care for people's feet. পায়ের চিকিৎসক

chisel (**chisels**) *n* A **chisel** is a tool that has a long metal blade with a sharp edge at the end. It is used for cutting and shaping wood and stone. ছেনি

chives *npl* **Chives** are long, thin, hollow green leaves which are cut into small pieces and added to food to give it a flavour similar to onions. পেঁয়াজের মত গন্ধবিশিষ্ট গুল্ম

chlorine *n* **Chlorine** is a gas that is used to disinfect water and to make cleaning products. একপ্রকার গ্যাস

chocolate (**chocolates**) *n* **Chocolate** is a sweet food made from cocoa beans. কোকো বীজের তৈরী মিষ্টান্ন

choice (**choices**) *n* If there is a **choice** of things, there are several of them and you can choose the one you want. পছন্দ

choir (**choirs**) *n* A **choir** is a group of people who sing together. সমবেত গায়কবৃন্দ

choke (**chokes, choking, choked**) *v* When you **choke** or when something **chokes** you, you cannot breathe properly or get enough air into your lungs. শ্বাসরোধ হওয়া

cholesterol *n* **Cholesterol** is a substance that exists in the fat, tissues, and blood of all animals. Too much cholesterol in a person's blood can cause heart disease. কোলেস্টেরল

choose (**chooses, choosing, chose, chosen**) *v* If you **choose** someone or something from all the people or things that are available, you decide to have that person or thing. বাছাই করা

chop (**chops, chopping, chopped**) *n* A **chop** is a small piece of meat cut from the ribs of a sheep or pig. মাংসের ছোট টুকরো ▷ *vt* If you **chop** something, you cut it into pieces with a knife or axe. ছোট টুকরো করা

chopsticks *npl* **Chopsticks** are a pair of thin sticks which people in Asia use to eat their food. চীনার খাবার কাঠি

chosen *adj* Something that is **chosen** has been selected or picked out. বাছাই করা হয়েছে

Christ *n* **Christ** is one of the names of Jesus, whom Christians believe to be the son of God and whose teachings are the basis of Christianity. যীশু খ্রীষ্ট

Christian (**Christians**) *adj* **Christian** means relating to Christianity or Christians. খ্রীষ্টধর্মের সাথে সম্পর্কিত ▷ *n* A **Christian** is someone who follows the teachings of Jesus Christ. যীশুর অনুগামী

Christianity *n* **Christianity** is a religion based on the teachings of Jesus Christ. খ্রীষ্টধর্ম

Christmas (**Christmases**) *n* **Christmas** is the period around the 25th of December when Christians celebrate the birth of Jesus Christ. বড়দিনের উৎসব

Christmas card (**Christmas cards**) *n* **Christmas cards** are cards with greetings, which people send to their friends and family at Christmas. বড়দিনের শুভেচ্ছা কার্ড

Christmas Eve *n* **Christmas Eve** is the 24th of December. প্রাক্-বড়দিন

Christmas tree (**Christmas trees**) *n* A **Christmas tree** is a real or artificial fir tree, which people put in their houses at

Christmas and decorate with lights and balls. খ্রীষ্টমাসে সাজানোর গাছ

chrome n **Chrome** is a hard silver-coloured metal, used to coat other metals. ক্রোমিয়াম

chronic adj A **chronic** illness lasts for a very long time. দুররোগ্য

chrysanthemum (**chrysanthemums**) n A **chrysanthemum** is a large garden flower with many long, thin petals. চন্দ্রমল্লিকা ফুল

chubby (**chubbier, chubbiest**) adj A **chubby** person is rather fat. মোটাসোটা

chunk (**chunks**) n A **chunk** of something is a thick solid piece of it. খণ্ড

church (**churches**) n A **church** is a building in which Christians worship. গীর্জা

cider (**ciders**) n **Cider** is an alcoholic drink made from apples. সিডার/আপেল থেকে প্রস্তুত সুরা

cigar (**cigars**) n **Cigars** are rolls of dried tobacco leaves which people smoke. চুরুট

cigarette (**cigarettes**) n **Cigarettes** are small tubes of paper containing tobacco which people smoke. সিগারেট

cigarette lighter (**cigarette lighters**) n A **cigarette lighter** is a device which produces a small flame when you press a switch and which you use to light a cigarette or cigar. সিগারেট ধরাবার সরঞ্জাম

cinema (**cinemas**) n A **cinema** is a place where people go to watch films. সিনেমা

cinnamon n **Cinnamon** is a spice used for flavouring sweet food. দারুচিনি

circle (**circles**) n A **circle** is a round shape. Every part of its edge is the same distance from the centre. চক্র

circuit (**circuits**) n An electrical **circuit** is a complete route which an electric current can flow around. বর্তনী

circular adj Something that is **circular** is shaped like a circle. চক্রাকার

circulation n The **circulation** of something is the passing of it around, or the spreading of it among a group of people. সঞ্চালন

circumstances npl Your **circumstances** are the conditions of your life, especially the amount of money that you have. পরিস্থিতি

circus (**circuses**) n A **circus** is a travelling show performed in a large tent, with performers such as clowns and trained animals. সার্কাস

citizen (**citizens**) n If someone is a **citizen** of a country, they are legally accepted as belonging to that country. নাগরিক

citizenship n If you have **citizenship** of a country, you are legally accepted as belonging to it. নাগরিকত্ব

city (**cities**) n A **city** is a large town. শহর

city centre (**city centres**) n The **city centre** is the busiest part of a city, where most of the shops and businesses are. শহরের ব্যস্ততম স্থান

civilian (**civilians**) adj In a military situation, **civilian** is used to describe people or things that are not military. অসামরিক ব্যক্তি ▷ n A **civilian** is anyone who is not a member of the armed forces. সাধারণ নাগরিক যে সশস্ত্র বাহিনীর সদস্য নয়

civilization (**civilizations**) n A **civilization** is a human society with its own social organization and culture. সভ্যতা

civil rights npl **Civil rights** are the rights that people have to equal treatment and equal opportunities, whatever their race, sex, or religion. নাগরিক অধিকার

civil servant (**civil servants**) n A **civil servant** is a person who works in the Civil Service. অসামরিক চাকুরে

civil war (**civil wars**) n A **civil war** is a war which is fought between different groups of people living in the same country. গৃহযুদ্ধ

claim (**claims, claiming, claimed**) n A **claim** is something which someone says which they cannot prove and which may be false. দাবি ▷ vt If you say that someone **claims** that something is true, you mean they say that it is true but you are not sure whether or not they are telling the truth. দাবি করা

claim form (claim forms) n A **claim form** is a formal written request to the government, an insurance company, or another organization for money that you think you are entitled to according to their rules. দাবিপত্র

clap (claps, clapping, clapped) v When you **clap**, you hit your hands together to show appreciation or attract attention. হাততালি দেওয়া

clarify (clarifies, clarifying, clarified) vt To **clarify** something means to make it easier to understand. (formal) স্পষ্ট করা

clarinet (clarinets) n A **clarinet** is a wind instrument with a single reed in its mouthpiece. ক্লারিওনেট বাদ্যযন্ত্র

clash (clashes, clashing, clashed) vi When people **clash**, they fight, argue, or disagree with each other. দ্বন্দ্ব হওয়া

clasp (clasps) n A **clasp** is a small metal fastening. আংটা

class (classes) n A **class** is a group of pupils or students who are taught together. শ্রেণী

classic (classics) adj A **classic** example of something that has all the features which you expect that kind of thing to have. সর্বোত্তম ▷ n A **classic** is a piece of writing, film, or piece of music of high quality that has become a standard against which similar things are judged. উচ্চমার্গের

classical adj You use **classical** to describe something that is traditional in form, style, or content. পরম্পরাগত

classmate (classmates) n Your **classmates** are students in the same class as you at school or college. সহপাঠী

classroom (classrooms) n A **classroom** is a room in a school where lessons take place. শ্রেণীকক্ষ

classroom assistant (classroom assistants) n A **classroom assistant** is a person whose job is to help a schoolteacher in the classroom. শ্রেণীকক্ষ-সহায়ক

clause (clauses) n A **clause** is a section of a legal document. দফা

claustrophobic adj You describe a place or situation as **claustrophobic** when it makes you feel uncomfortable and unhappy because you are enclosed or restricted. আটকে থাকার অনুভূতি হয় যার

claw (claws) n The **claws** of a bird or animal are the thin curved nails on its feet. থাবা

clay n **Clay** is a type of earth that is soft when it is wet and hard when it is baked dry. মাটি

clean (cleaner, cleanest, cleans, cleaning, cleaned) adj Something that is **clean** does not have any dirt or marks on it. পরিষ্কার ▷ vt When you **clean** something, you take all the dirt off it. পরিষ্কার করা

cleaner (cleaners) n A **cleaner** is someone who is employed to clean the rooms and furniture inside a building or someone whose job is to clean a particular type of thing. সাফাই কর্মী

cleaning n **Cleaning** is the action of making something clean. সাফাই

cleaning lady (cleaning ladies) n A **cleaning lady** is a woman who is employed to clean the rooms and furniture in a building. মহিলা সাফাইকর্মী

cleanser (cleansers) n A **cleanser** is a liquid or cream that you use for cleaning something, especially your skin. ত্বক-পরিষ্কারক

cleansing lotion (cleansing lotions) n **Cleansing lotion** is a liquid or cream that you use for cleaning your skin. ত্বক পরিষ্কার করবার লোশন

clear (clearer, clearest, clears, clearing, cleared) adj If something is **clear**, it is easy to understand, to see, or to hear. স্পষ্ট ▷ adj If something like glass or plastic is **clear**, you can see through it. স্বচ্ছ ▷ adj If a place is **clear**, it does not have anything there that you do not want. ফাঁকা ▷ vt When you **clear** a place, you take away all the things you do not want there. সাফ করা

clearly adv **Clearly** means in a manner that is easy to understand, see, or hear. স্পষ্টরূপে

clear off *v* If you tell someone to **clear off**, you are telling them in a rude way to go away. (*informal*) বেরিয়ে যেতে বলা *The boys told me to clear off.*

clear up *v* When you **clear up**, or when you **clear** a place **up**, you tidy a place and put things away. পরিষ্কার করা *I cleared up my room.*

clementine (**clementines**) *n* A **clementine** is a fruit that looks like a small orange. একধরণের কমলালেবু

clever (**cleverer, cleverest**) *adj* A **clever** person is intelligent and able to understand things easily or to plan things well. চালাক

click (**clicks, clicking, clicked**) *n* A **click** is a short, light often metallic sound. ধাতুর আওয়াজ ▷ *v* If something **clicks** or if you **click** it, it makes a short, sharp sound. আওয়াজ করা

client (**clients**) *n* A **client** is someone for whom a professional person or organization is providing a service or doing some work. গ্রাহক

cliff (**cliffs**) *n* A **cliff** is a high area of land with a very steep side, especially one next to the sea. পাহাড়ের ঢাল

climate (**climates**) *n* The **climate** of a place is the general weather conditions that are typical of it. জলবায়ু

climate change *n* **Climate change** is change that is taking place in the Earth's climate that is believed to be the result of human activity. জলবায়ুর পরিবর্তন

climb (**climbs, climbing, climbed**) *v* If you **climb** something such as a tree, mountain, or ladder, or **climb** up it, you move towards the top of it. If you **climb** down it, you move towards the bottom of it. আরোহণ

climber (**climbers**) *n* A **climber** is someone who climbs rocks or mountains as a sport. আরোহী

climbing *n* **Climbing** is the activity of climbing rocks or mountains. পর্বতারোহন

clinic (**clinics**) *n* A **clinic** is a building where people receive medical advice or treatment. চিকিৎসালয়

clip (**clips**) *n* A **clip** is a small metal or plastic device that is used for holding things together. ক্লিপ

clippers *npl* **Clippers** are a tool used for cutting small amounts from something, especially from someone's hair or nails. কাটার যন্ত্র

cloakroom (**cloakrooms**) *n* A **cloakroom** is a small room in a public building where people can leave their coats. ক্লোকরুম

clock (**clocks**) *n* A **clock** is an instrument, for example in a room or on the outside of a building, that shows you what the time is. ঘড়ি

clockwise *adv* When something is moving **clockwise**, it is moving in a circle in the same direction as the hands on a clock. ঘড়ির কাঁটার অভিমুখে

clog (**clogs**) *n* **Clogs** are heavy leather or wooden shoes with thick wooden soles. কাঠের জুতো

clone (**clones, cloning, cloned**) *n* If someone or something is a **clone** of another person or thing, they are so similar to this person or thing that they seem to be exactly the same as them. নকল ▷ *vt* If you **clone** an animal or plant, you produce it artificially from a cell of another animal or plant, so that it is exactly the same as the original. নকল সৃষ্টি করা

close (**closer, closest, closes, closing, closed**) *adj* If something is **close** to another thing, it is near it. নিকটে ▷ *adv* **Close** means near to something else. কাছাকাছি ▷ *vt* When you **close** something, you shut it. বন্ধ করা

close by *adj* Something that is **close by** is near to you. নিকটে

closed *adj* A **closed** group of people does not welcome new people or ideas from outside. অনুদার

closely *adv* **Closely** means near to something else. নিকটভাবে

closing time (**closing times**) *n* **Closing time** is the time when something such as a shop, library, or pub closes and people have to leave. বন্ধের সময়

closure (**closures**) *n* The **closure** of a business or factory is the permanent shutting of it. বন্ধের অবস্থা

cloth (**cloths**) *n* **Cloth** is material that is used to make things like clothes and curtains. কাপড় ▷ *n* A **cloth** is a piece of material that you use to clean something. মোছার কাপড়

clothes *npl* **Clothes** are the things that people wear, such as shirts, coats, trousers, and dresses. জামাকাপড়

clothes line (**clothes lines**) *n* A **clothes line** is a thin rope on which you hang washing so that it can dry. জামাকাপড় শুকাবার দড়ি

clothes peg (**clothes pegs**) *n* A **clothes peg** is a small device which you use to fasten clothes to a washing line. দড়িতে জামাকাপড় আটকাবার ক্লিপ

clothing *n* **Clothing** is the clothes people wear. জামাকাপড়

cloud (**clouds**) *n* A **cloud** is a mass of water vapour that is seen as a white or grey mass in the sky. মেঘ

cloudy (**cloudier, cloudiest**) *adj* If it is **cloudy**, there are a lot of clouds in the sky. মেঘাচ্ছন্ন

clove (**cloves**) *n* **Cloves** are small dried flower buds used as a spice. লবঙ্গ

clown (**clowns**) *n* A **clown** is a performer who wears funny clothes and bright make-up, and does silly things to make people laugh. জোকার

club (**clubs**) *n* A **club** is an organization of people who are all interested in a particular activity. ক্লাব ▷ *n* A **club** is a thick, heavy stick that can be used as a weapon. গদা

club together *v* If people **club together** to do something, they all give money towards

the cost of it. সংঘবদ্ধ হওয়া *For my thirtieth birthday, my friends clubbed together and bought me a watch.*

clue (**clues**) *n* A **clue** to a problem, mystery, or puzzle is something that helps you find the answer. সূত্র

clumsy (**clumsier, clumsiest**) *adj* A **clumsy** person moves or handles things in an awkward way. উদ্ভট

clutch (**clutches**) *n* If you are in another person's **clutches**, that person has control over you. কবলে

clutter *n* **Clutter** is a lot of unnecessary or useless things in an untidy state. অগোছাল অবস্থা

coach (**coaches**) *n* A **coach** is someone who trains a person or team of people in a particular sport. প্রশিক্ষক ▷ *n* A **coach** is a large comfortable bus that carries passengers on long journeys. বড় বাস

coal *n* **Coal** is a hard black substance taken from underground and burned as fuel. কয়লা

coarse (**coarser, coarsest**) *adj* **Coarse** things have a rough texture. মোটা

coast (**coasts**) *n* The **coast** is an area of land next to the sea. উপকূল

coastguard (**coastguards**) *n* A **coastguard** is an official who watches the sea near a coast, in order to get help when it is needed and to prevent smuggling. উপকূলরক্ষী

coat (**coats**) *n* A **coat** is a piece of clothing with long sleeves worn over your other clothes when you go outside. কোট

coathanger (**coat hangers**) *n* A **coathanger** is a curved piece of wood, metal, or plastic that you hang a piece of clothing on. কোট ঝোলাবার হ্যাঙ্গার

cobweb (**cobwebs**) *n* A **cobweb** is the fine net that a spider makes in order to catch insects. মাকড়সার জাল

cock (**cocks**) *n* A **cock** is an adult male chicken. বড় মোরগ

cockerel (**cockerels**) *n* A **cockerel** is a young male chicken. ছোট মোরগ

cockpit (**cockpits**) n The **cockpit** in a small plane or racing car is the part where the pilot or driver sits. ককপিট/বিমানচালনা হান

cockroach (**cockroaches**) n A **cockroach** is a large brown insect that is often found in dirty or damp places. আরশোলা

cocktail (**cocktails**) n A **cocktail** is an alcoholic drink containing several ingredients. ককটেল/মদের সংমিশ্রণ

cocoa n **Cocoa** is a brown powder used in making chocolate. কোকো

coconut (**coconuts**) n A **coconut** is a very large nut with a hairy shell, white flesh, and milky juice inside. নারকেল

cod (**cods, cod**) n A **cod** is a large sea fish with white flesh. একপ্রকার সামুদ্রিক মাছ

code (**codes**) n A **code** is a set of rules about how people should behave. নিয়ম

coeliac adj **Coeliac** means of or relating to the abdomen. পেটসংক্রান্ত

coffee (**coffees**) n **Coffee** is the roasted beans of the coffee plant. কফি

coffee bean (**coffee beans**) n **Coffee beans** are small dark-brown beans that are roasted and ground to make coffee. They are the seeds of the coffee plant. কফির বীজ

coffeepot (**coffeepots**) n A **coffeepot** is a tall narrow pot with a spout and a lid, in which coffee is made or served. কফির পাত্র

coffee table (**coffee tables**) n A **coffee table** is a small low table in a living room. কফির টেবিল

coffin (**coffins**) n A **coffin** is a box in which a dead body is buried or cremated. কফিন/শবাধার

coin (**coins**) n A **coin** is a small piece of metal used as money. মুদ্রা

coincide (**coincides, coinciding, coincided**) vi If one event **coincides** with another, they happen at the same time. সহঘটিত

coincidence (**coincidences**) n A **coincidence** happens when two or more things occur at the same time by chance. সহঘটন

Coke® (**Cokes**) n **Coke** is a sweet, brown, non-alcoholic fizzy drink. কোক

colander (**colanders**) n A **colander** is a container in the shape of a bowl with holes in it which you wash or drain food in. ছিদ্রযুক্ত পাত্র

cold (**colder, coldest, colds**) adj If something is **cold**, it is not hot. ঠান্ডা ▷ n When you have a **cold**, you sneeze and cough a lot, and you have a sore throat. সর্দি ▷ adj If you are **cold**, you do not feel comfortable because you are not warm enough. শীত লাগা

cold sore (**cold sores**) n **Cold sores** are small sore spots that sometimes appear on or near someone's lips and nose when they have a cold. জ্বর ফোস্কা

coleslaw n **Coleslaw** is a salad of chopped raw cabbage, carrots, onions, and sometimes other vegetables, usually with mayonnaise. একপ্রকার স্যালাড

collaborate (**collaborates, collaborating, collaborated**) vi When people **collaborate**, they work together on a particular project. সহযোগিতা করা

collapse (**collapses, collapsing, collapsed**) vi If a building or other structure **collapses**, it falls down very suddenly. ধসে পড়া

collar (**collars**) n The **collar** of a shirt or jacket is the part that goes around your neck. কলার ▷ n A **collar** is a band that goes around the neck of a dog or cat. গলাবন্ধনী

collarbone (**collarbones**) n Your **collarbones** are the two long bones which run from your throat to your shoulders. গলার হাড়

colleague (**colleagues**) n Your **colleagues** are the people you work with, especially in a professional job. সহকর্মী

C

collect (collects, collecting, collected) vt If you **collect** things, you bring them together. সংগ্রহ করা ▷ vt If you **collect** someone from a place, you go there and take them away. নিয়ে নেওয়া

collection (collections) n A **collection** of things is a group of similar things that you have deliberately acquired, usually over a period of time. সংগ্রহ

collective (collectives) adj **Collective** means shared by or involving every member of a group of people. সমষ্টিগত ▷ n A **collective** is a business or farm whose employees share the decision-making and the profits. সমিতি

collector (collectors) n A **collector** is a person who collects things of a particular type as a hobby. সংগ্রাহক

college (colleges) n A **college** is an institution where students study after they have left school. কলেজ

collide (collides, colliding, collided) vi If people or vehicles **collide**, they bump into each other. মুখোমুখি সংঘর্ষ হওয়া

collie (collies) n A **collie** or a **collie dog** is a dog with long hair and a long, narrow nose. একধরণের কুকুর

colliery (collieries) n A **colliery** is a coal mine. কয়লাখনি

collision (collisions) n A **collision** occurs when a moving object hits something. মুখোমুখি সংঘর্ষ

Colombia n **Colombia** is a republic in north-west South America. কলম্বিয়া

Colombian (Colombians) adj **Colombian** means belonging or relating to Colombia or its people or culture. কলম্বিয়ার সাথে সম্পর্কিত ▷ n A **Colombian** is a Colombian citizen, or a person of Colombian origin. কলম্বিয়া-বাসী

colon (colons) n A **colon** is the punctuation mark :. যতিচিহ্ন

colonel (colonels) n A **colonel** is a senior officer in an army, air force, or the marines. কর্নেল

colour (colours) n The **colour** of something is the appearance that it has as a result of reflecting light. Red, blue, and green are colours. রং

colour-blind adj Someone who is **colour-blind** cannot see the difference between colours, especially between red and green. বর্ণান্ধ

colourful adj Something that is **colourful** has bright colours. বর্ণময়

colouring n Someone's **colouring** is the colour of their hair, skin, and eyes. কিছুর রং

column (columns) n A **column** is a tall solid cylinder, especially one supporting part of a building. স্তম্ভ

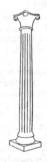

coma (comas) n If someone is in a **coma**, they are deeply unconscious. কোমা

comb (combs, combing, combed) n A **comb** is a flat piece of plastic or metal with narrow pointed teeth along one side, which you use to tidy your hair. চিরুনি ▷ vt When you **comb** your hair, you tidy it using a comb. চুল আঁচড়ানো

combination (combinations) n A **combination** is a mixture of things. সংমিশ্রণ

combine (combines, combining, combined) v If you **combine** two or more things, or if they **combine**, they exist or join together. সংমিশ্রিত করা

come (comes, coming, came) *vi* When you **come** to a place, you move towards it or arrive there. আসা

come back *v* If someone **comes back** to a place, they return to it. ফিরে আসা *I came back to my hometown and decided to be a photographer.*

comedian (comedians) *n* A **comedian** is an entertainer whose job is to make people laugh by telling jokes. কৌতুকশিল্পী

come down *v* If the cost, level, or amount of something **comes down**, it becomes less than it was before. কমে যাওয়া *The price of petrol is coming down.*

comedy *n* **Comedy** consists of types of entertainment that are intended to make people laugh. হাস্যরস

come from *v* If someone or something **comes from** a particular place or thing, that place or thing is their origin or source. উৎস থেকে আসা *Half the students come from abroad.*

come in *v* If information or a report **comes in**, you receive it. পাওয়া *Reports are now coming in of trouble at the event.*

come out *v* When a new product **comes out**, it becomes available to the public. প্রকাশিত হওয়া *The actor has a new movie coming out.*

come round *v* When someone who is unconscious **comes round** or **comes around**, they recover consciousness. চেতনা ফিরে পাওয়া *When I came round I was on the kitchen floor.*

comet (comets) *n* A **comet** is an object that travels around the sun leaving a bright trail behind it. ধূমকেতু

come up *v* If someone **comes up** to you, they walk over to you. কাছে আসা *Her cat came up and rubbed itself against their legs.*

comfortable *adj* You describe things such as furniture as **comfortable** when they make you feel physically relaxed. আরামদায়ক

comic (comics) *n* A **comic** is an entertainer who tells jokes in order to make people laugh. হাস্যরসশিল্পী

comic book (comic books) *n* A **comic book** is a magazine that contains stories told in pictures. হাস্যরসাত্মক বই

comic strip (comic strips) *n* A **comic strip** is a series of drawings that tell a story, especially in a newspaper or magazine. ছবিসম্বলিত গল্প

coming *adj* A **coming** event or time will happen soon. আসন্ন

comma (commas) *n* A **comma** is the punctuation mark ,. ছেদচিহ্ন

command (commands) *n* If you give someone a **command** to do something, you order them to do it. (*written*) আদেশ

comment (comments, commenting, commented) *n* A **comment** is something that you say which expresses your opinion of something or which gives an explanation of it. মন্তব্য ▷ *v* If you **comment** on something, you give your opinion about it or you give an explanation for it. মন্তব্য করা

commentary (commentaries) *n* A **commentary** is a spoken description of an event that is broadcast on radio or television while it is taking place. ভাষ্যপাঠ

commentator (commentators) *n* A **commentator** is a broadcaster who gives a commentary on an event. ভাষ্যকার

commercial (commercials) *n* A **commercial** is an advertisement broadcast on television or radio. বিজ্ঞাপন

commercial break (commercial breaks) *n* A **commercial break** is the interval during a commercial television programme, or between programmes, during which advertisements are shown. বিজ্ঞাপন বিরতি

commission (commissions) *n* A **commission** is a piece of work that someone is asked to do and is paid for. করণীয় কাজ

commit (commits, committing, committed) *vt* If someone **commits** a crime or a sin, they do something illegal or bad. করা

committee (**committees**) *n* A **committee** is a group of people who represent a larger group or organization and make decisions for them. কমিটি

common (**commoner, commonest**) *adj* If something is **common**, it is found in large numbers or it happens often. সাধারণ

common sense *n* **Common sense** is the natural ability to make good judgements and behave sensibly. সাধারণ বুদ্ধি

communicate (**communicates, communicating, communicated**) *vi* If you **communicate** with someone, you give them information, for example by speaking, writing, or sending radio signals. যোগাযোগ স্থাপন করা

communication *n* **Communication** is the act of sharing or exchanging information with someone, for example by speaking, writing, or sending radio signals. যোগাযোগ স্থাপন

communion *n* **Communion** with nature or with a person is the feeling that you are sharing thoughts or feelings with them. চিন্তাভাবনা ভাগ করে নেওয়ার অনুভূতি

communism *n* **Communism** is the political belief that all people are equal and that workers should control the means of producing things. সাম্যবাদ

communist (**communists**) *adj* **Communist** means relating to communism. সাম্যবাদ-সম্পর্কিত ▷ *n* A **communist** is someone who believes in communism. সাম্যবাদী

community (**communities**) *n* The **community** is all the people who live in a particular area or place. সম্প্রদায়

commute (**commutes, commuting, commuted**) *vi* If you **commute**, you travel a long distance to work every day. যাতায়াত করা

commuter (**commuters**) *n* A **commuter** is a person who travels a long distance to work every day. যাতায়াতকারী

compact *adj* Something that is **compact** is small or takes up very little space. ঘন সন্নিবদ্ধ

compact disc (**compact discs**) *n* **Compact discs** are small discs on which sound, especially music, is recorded. The abbreviation 'CD' is also used. কম্প্যাক্ট ডিস্ক/সিডি

companion (**companions**) *n* A **companion** is someone who you spend time with or travel with. সঙ্গী

company (**companies**) *n* A **company** is a business organization that makes money by selling goods or services. কোম্পানী

company car (**company cars**) *n* A **company car** is a car which an employer gives to an employee to use as their own. কোম্পানীর গাড়ি

comparable *adj* Something that is **comparable** to something is roughly similar, for example in amount or importance. তুলনীয়

comparatively *adv* **Comparatively** means compared to something else. তুলনামূলকভাবে

compare (**compares, comparing, compared**) *vt* If you **compare** things, you consider them and discover the differences or similarities between them. তুলনা করা

comparison (**comparisons**) *n* When you make a **comparison** between two or more things, you discover the differences or similarities between them. তুলনা

compartment (**compartments**) *n* A **compartment** is one of the separate sections of a railway carriage. রেলের কামরা

compass (**compasses**) *n* A **compass** is an instrument that you use for finding directions. It has a dial and a magnetic needle that always points to the north. কম্পাস

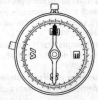

compatible adj If things, systems, or ideas are **compatible**, they work well together or can exist together successfully. সামঞ্জস্যপূর্ণ

compensate (**compensates, compensating, compensated**) vt If someone **is compensated** for something unpleasant which has happened to them, they receive compensation for it. ক্ষতিপূরণ দেওয়া

compensation (**compensations**) n **Compensation** is money that someone who has undergone loss or suffering claims from the person or organization responsible. ক্ষতিপূরণ

compere (**comperes**) n A **compere** is the person who introduces the people taking part in a radio or television show or a live show. অনুষ্ঠান-পরিচালক

compete (**competes, competing, competed**) vi If one person or organization **competes** with another for something, they try to get that thing for themselves and stop the other getting it. প্রতিযোগিতায় নামা

competent adj Someone who is **competent** is efficient and effective. যোগ্যতাসম্পন্ন

competition (**competitions**) n **Competition** is a situation in which two or more people or groups are trying to get something which not everyone can have. প্রতিযোগিতা

competitive adj **Competitive** situations or activities are ones in which people compete with each other. প্রতিযোগিতামূলক

competitor (**competitors**) n A company's **competitors** are other companies that sell similar kinds of goods or services. প্রতিযোগী

complain (**complains, complaining, complained**) v If you **complain** about something, you say you are not satisfied with it. অভিযোগ করা

complaint (**complaints**) n A **complaint** is a statement of dissatisfaction about a situation. অভিযোগ

complementary adj If two different things are **complementary**, they form a complete

unit when they are brought together, or they combine well with each other. (formal) সম্পূরক

complete adj You use **complete** to emphasize that something is as great in extent, degree, or amount as it possibly can be. সম্পূর্ণ

completely adv **Completely** means as much in extent, degree, or amount as possible. সম্পূর্ণভাবে

complex (**complexes**) adj **Complex** things have many different parts and are hard to understand. জটিল ▷ n A **complex** is a group of buildings used for a particular purpose. চত্বর

complexion (**complexions**) n Your **complexion** is the natural colour or condition of the skin on your face. গায়ের রং

complicated adj Something that is **complicated** has many parts and is therefore difficult to understand. জটিল

complication (**complications**) n A **complication** is a problem or difficulty. জটিলতা

compliment (**compliments, complimenting, complimented**) n A **compliment** is a polite remark that you say to someone to show that you like their appearance, appreciate their qualities, or approve of what they have done. প্রশংসা ▷ vt If you **compliment** someone, you say something nice about them. প্রশংসা করা

complimentary adj If you are **complimentary** about something, you express admiration for it. সম্মানসূচক

component (**components**) n The **components** of something are its parts. উপাদান

composer (**composers**) n A **composer** is a person who writes music. সুরস্রষ্টা

composition (**compositions**) n The **composition** of something is the things that it consists of and the way that they are arranged. গঠন

comprehension n **Comprehension** is the ability to understand something or the process of understanding something. (formal) বোধশক্তি

comprehensive adj Something that is **comprehensive** includes everything necessary or relevant. বিস্তৃত

compromise (**compromises, compromising, compromised**) n A **compromise** is a situation in which people accept something slightly different from what they really want. আপোস ▷ vi If you **compromise** with someone, you reach an agreement with them in which you both give up something that you originally wanted. You can also say that two people or groups **compromise**. আপোস করা

compulsory adj If something is **compulsory**, you must do it because a law or someone in authority says you must. আবশ্যক

computer (**computers**) n A **computer** is an electronic machine which makes quick calculations and deals with large amounts of information. কম্পিউটার

computer game (**computer games**) n A **computer game** is a game that you play on a computer or on a small portable piece of electronic equipment. কম্পিউটার গেম

computer science n **Computer science** is the study of computers and their application. কম্পিউটার বিজ্ঞান

computing n **Computing** is the activity of using a computer and writing programs for it. কম্পিউটার ব্যবহার

concentrate (**concentrates, concentrating, concentrated**) vi If you **concentrate** on something, you give it all your attention. মনঃসংযোগ করা

concentration n **Concentration** on something involves giving all your attention to it. মনঃসংযোগ

concern (**concerns**) n **Concern** is worry about a situation. চিন্তা

concerned adj If you are **concerned** about something, you are worried about it. চিন্তিত

concerning prep You use **concerning** to show what a piece of information is about. (formal) বিষয়ে Contact the teacher for more information concerning the class.

concert (**concerts**) n A **concert** is a performance of music. ঐকতান

concerto (**concerti, concertos**) n A **concerto** is a piece of music for a solo instrument and an orchestra. একক বাজনা

concession (**concessions**) n If you make a **concession** to someone, you agree to let them do or have something, especially in order to end an argument or conflict. ছাড়

concise adj Something that is **concise** gives all the necessary information in a very brief form. সংক্ষিপ্ত

conclude (**concludes, concluding, concluded**) vt If you **conclude** that something is true, you decide that it is true using the facts you know. নিষ্পত্তি ঘটানো

conclusion (**conclusions**) n When you come to a **conclusion**, you decide that something is true after you have thought about it carefully. সিদ্ধান্ত

concrete n **Concrete** is a substance used for building. It is made from cement, sand, small stones, and water. কংক্রিট

concussion n If you suffer **concussion** after you hit your head, you lose consciousness or feel sick or confused. ঝাঁকুনি

condemn (**condemns, condemning, condemned**) vt If you **condemn** something, you say that it is bad and unacceptable. দোষারোপ করা

condensation n **Condensation** consists of small drops of water which form when warm water vapour or steam touches a cold surface such as a window. ঘনীভবন

condition (**conditions**) n The **condition** of someone or something is the state they are in. অবস্থা

conditional adj If a situation or agreement is **conditional** on something, it will only happen if this thing happens. শর্তাধীন

conditioner (**conditioners**) n A **conditioner** is a substance which you can put on your hair after you have washed it to make it softer. কন্ডিশনার

condom (**condoms**) n A **condom** is a rubber covering which a man wears on his penis as a contraceptive. কন্ডোম

conduct (**conducts, conducting, conducted**) vt When you **conduct** an activity or task, you organize it and carry it out. পরিচালনা

conductor (**conductors**) n A **conductor** is a person who stands in front of an orchestra or choir and directs its performance. পরিচালক

cone (**cones**) n A **cone** is a shape with a circular base and smooth curved sides ending in a point at the top. শঙ্কু

conference (**conferences**) n A **conference** is a meeting, often lasting a few days, which is organized on a particular subject. সম্মেলন

confess (**confesses, confessing, confessed**) v If you **confess** to doing something wrong or something that you are ashamed of, you admit that you did it. স্বীকার করা

confession (**confessions**) n A **confession** is a signed statement by someone in which they admit that they have committed a particular crime. স্বীকারোক্তি

confetti npl **Confetti** is small pieces of coloured paper that people throw over the bride and bridegroom at a wedding. একধরণের কাগজের টুকরো যা বরবধূর মাথায় ফেলা হয়

confidence n If you have **confidence** in someone, you feel you can trust them. আস্থা ▷ n If you have **confidence**, you feel sure about your abilities, qualities, or ideas. প্রত্যয় ▷ n If you tell someone something in **confidence**, you tell them a secret. গোপনে

confident adj If you are **confident** about something, you are certain that it will happen in the way you want it to. প্রত্যয়ী

confidential adj Information that is **confidential** is meant to be kept secret. গোপনীয়

confirm (**confirms, confirming, confirmed**) vt If something **confirms** what you believe, it shows that it is definitely true. সুনিশ্চিত করা

confirmation n **Confirmation** is the act of showing that something you believe is definitely true, or something that shows this. সুনিশ্চিতকরণ

confiscate (**confiscates, confiscating, confiscated**) vt If you **confiscate** something from someone, you take it away from them, often as a punishment. বাজেয়াপ্ত করা

conflict n **Conflict** is serious disagreement and argument. If two people or groups are in **conflict**, they have had a serious disagreement and have not yet reached agreement. দ্বন্দ্ব

confuse (**confuses, confusing, confused**) vt If you **confuse** two things, you get them mixed up, so that you think one is the other. গুলিয়ে ফেলা

confused adj If you are **confused**, you do not know what to do or you do not understand what is happening. হতভম্ব

confusing adj Something that is **confusing** makes it difficult for people to know what to do or what is happening. হতবুদ্ধিকর

confusion n If there is **confusion** about something, the facts are not clear. বিভ্রান্তি

congestion n If there is **congestion** in a place, the place is extremely crowded and blocked with traffic or people. জনবাহুল্য

Congo n The **Congo** is a republic in south central Africa. কংগো

congratulate (**congratulates, congratulating, congratulated**) vt If you **congratulate** someone, you express pleasure for something good that has happened to them, or you praise them for something they have achieved. অভিনন্দিত করা

congratulations npl You say '**congratulations**' to someone in order to congratulate them. অজস্র অভিনন্দন

conifer (**conifers**) n **Conifers** are a group of trees and shrubs, for example pine trees and fir trees, that grow in cooler areas of the world. They have fruit called cones, and very thin leaves called needles which they do not normally lose in winter. পাইন গাছ

conjugation (**conjugations**) n A **conjugation** is one of the different forms of a verb. The form can change according to the number of people it refers to, or according to whether it refers to the past, present, or future. ধাতুরূপ

conjunction (**conjunctions**) n A **conjunction** of two or more things is the occurrence of them at the same time or place. (formal) যোজনা

conjurer (**conjurers**) n A **conjurer** is a person who entertains people by doing magic tricks. জাদুকর

connection (**connections**) n A **connection** is a relationship between two people, groups, or things. সংযোগ

conquer (**conquers, conquering, conquered**) vt If one country or group of people **conquers** another, they take complete control of their land. দখল করা

conscience (**consciences**) n Your **conscience** is the part of your mind that tells you if what you are doing is wrong. If you have a **guilty conscience**, or if you

have something **on** your **conscience**, you feel guilty because you know you have done something wrong. বিবেক

conscientious adj Someone who is **conscientious** is very careful to do their work properly. কর্তব্যনিষ্ঠ

conscious adj If you are **conscious** of something, you notice it or are aware of it. সচেতন

consciousness n Your **consciousness** consists of your mind, thoughts, beliefs, and attitudes. সচেতনতা

consecutive adj **Consecutive** periods of time or events happen one after the other without interruption. ক্রমিক

consensus n A **consensus** is general agreement amongst a group of people. সর্বসম্মতি

consequence (**consequences**) n The **consequences** of something are the results or effects of it. পরিণাম

consequently adv **Consequently** means as a result. (formal) পরিণামে

conservation n **Conservation** is the preservation and protection of the environment. সংরক্ষণ

conservative adj Someone who is **conservative** has right-wing views. রক্ষণশীল

conservatory (**conservatories**) n A **conservatory** is a glass room built onto a house. কাঁচঘর

consider (**considers, considering, considered**) vt If you **consider** a person or thing to be something, this is your opinion of them. বিবেচনা করা

considerate adj A **considerate** person pays attention to the needs, wishes, or feelings of other people. বিবেচক

considering prep You use **considering** to show that you haven't forgotten an important fact. বিবেচনা করে Considering the time, I think we'll have to wait until tomorrow.

consistent adj A **consistent** person always behaves or responds in the same way. অবিচলিত

consist of v Something that **consists of** particular things or people is formed from them. তৈরী হয় *The cabin consisted of two small rooms.*

consonant (**consonants**) n A **consonant** is a sound such as 'p' or 'f' which you pronounce by stopping the air flowing freely through your mouth. ব্যঞ্জনবর্ণ

conspiracy (**conspiracies**) n **Conspiracy** is the secret planning by a group of people to do something wrong or illegal. ষড়যন্ত্র

constant adj Something that is **constant** happens all the time or is always there. একটানা

constantly adv If something happens **constantly**, it happens all the time. অবিরতভাবে

constipated adj Someone who is **constipated** has difficulty in getting rid of solid waste from their body. কোষ্ঠকাঠিন্যযুক্ত

constituency (**constituencies**) n A **constituency** is an area, and the people who live in it. In an election, the people in the constituency choose one person for the government. নির্বাচনকেন্দ্র

constitution (**constitutions**) n The **constitution** is the laws of a country or organization. সংবিধান

construct (**constructs, constructing, constructed**) vt If you **construct** something, you build, make, or create it. গঠন করা

construction (**constructions**) n **Construction** is the building or creating of something. নির্মাণ

constructive adj A **constructive** discussion, comment, or approach is useful and helpful. গঠনমূলক

consul (**consuls**) n A **consul** is a government official who lives in a foreign city and looks after all the people there who are from his or her own country. রাষ্ট্রদূত

consulate (**consulates**) n A **consulate** is the place in a city where a foreign government official works and looks after all the people there who are from his or her own country. রাষ্ট্রদূতের অফিস

consult (**consults, consulting, consulted**) v If you **consult** someone or something, you refer to them for advice or information. You can also **consult** with someone. পরামর্শ

consultant (**consultants**) n A **consultant** is an experienced doctor specializing in one area of medicine. পরামর্শদাতা

consumer (**consumers**) n A **consumer** is a person who buys things or uses services. গ্রাহক

contact (**contacts, contacting, contacted**) n Contact involves meeting or communicating with someone. যোগাযোগ ▷ vt If you **contact** someone, you telephone them or write to them. যোগাযোগ করা

contact lenses npl **Contact lenses** are small lenses that you put on your eyes to help you to see better. কনট্যাক্ট লেন্স

contagious adj A **contagious** disease can be caught by touching people or things that are infected with it. ছোঁয়াচে

contain (**contains, containing, contained**) vt If something such as a box or a room **contains** things, those things are in it. ধারণ করে

container (**containers**) n A **container** is something such as a box or bottle that is used to hold things. পাত্র

contemporary adj **Contemporary** means existing now or at the time you are talking about. সমসাময়িক

contempt n If you have **contempt** for someone or something, you have no respect for them. অবমাননা

content (**contents**) n The **content** of a piece of writing, speech, or television programme is its subject and the ideas expressed in it. বিষয়

content adj If you are **content**, you are happy. খুশী

contents npl The **contents** of a container such as a bottle, box, or room are the things inside it. জিনিষপত্র

contest (**contests**) n A **contest** is a competition or game. প্রতিযোগিতা

contestant (**contestants**) n A **contestant** in a competition or quiz is a person who takes part in it. প্রতিযোগী

context (**contexts**) n The **context** of an idea or event is the general situation in which it occurs. প্রসঙ্গ

continent (**continents**) n A **continent** is a very large area of land, such as Africa or Asia, that consists of several countries. মহাদেশ

continual adj **Continual** means happening without stopping, or happening again and again. নিরবচ্ছিন্ন

continually adv If something happens **continually**, it happens without stopping, or happens again and again. নিরবচ্ছিন্নভাবে

continue (**continues, continuing, continued**) vt If you **continue** to do something, you do not stop doing it. চালিয়ে যাওয়া ▷ vi If something **continues**, it does not stop. চলতে থাকা

continuous adj A **continuous** process or event continues for a period of time without stopping. ধারাবাহিক

contraception n Methods of preventing pregnancy are called **contraception**. জন্মনিয়ন্ত্রণ

contraceptive (**contraceptives**) n A **contraceptive** is a device or pill used to prevent pregnancy. জন্মনিয়ন্ত্রক

contract (**contracts**) n A **contract** is a legal agreement, usually between two companies or between an employer and employee, which involves doing work for a stated sum of money. ঠিকা

contractor (**contractors**) n A **contractor** is a person or company that works for other people or companies. ঠিকাদার

contradict (**contradicts, contradicting, contradicted**) vt If you **contradict** someone, you say or suggest that what they have just said is wrong. বিপরীত কথা বলা

contradiction (**contradictions**) n A **contradiction** is an aspect of a situation which appears to conflict with other aspects, so that they cannot all exist or be successful. বৈপরীত্য

contrary n You use **on the contrary** when you are contradicting what has just been said. বিপরীতে

contrast (**contrasts**) n A **contrast** is a great difference between two or more things. বৈসাদৃশ্য

contribute (**contributes, contributing, contributed**) vi If you **contribute** to something, you say or do something to help make it successful. অবদান রাখা

contribution (**contributions**) n If you make a **contribution** to something, you do something to help make it successful or to produce it. অবদান

control (**controls, controlling, controlled**) n **Control** of an organization, place, or system is the power to make all the important decisions about the way that it is run. নিয়ন্ত্রণ ▷ vt The people who **control** an organization or place have the power to take all the important decisions about the way that it is run. নিয়ন্ত্রণ করা

controversial adj Someone or something that is **controversial** causes intense public argument, disagreement, or disapproval. বিতর্কমূলক

convenient adj Something that is **convenient** is easy, useful, or suitable for a particular purpose. সুবিধাজনক

conventional adj **Conventional** people behave in a way that is accepted as normal in their society. প্রথাসিদ্ধ

conversation (**conversations**) n If you have a **conversation** with someone, you talk to each other, usually in an informal situation. কথোপকথন

convert (**converts, converting, converted**) v To **convert** one thing into another means to change it into a different shape or form. রূপান্তর

convertible (**convertibles**) *adj*
Convertible money can be easily
exchanged for other forms of money.
বিনিময়যোগ্য ▷ *n* A **convertible** is a car
with a soft roof that can be folded down or
removed. হুডখোলা গাড়ী

conveyor belt (**conveyor belts**) *n* A
conveyor belt or a **conveyor** is a
continuously moving strip which is used in
factories to move objects along. কনভেয়ার
বেল্ট

convict (**convicts, convicting, convicted**)
vt If someone **is convicted** of a crime, they
are found guilty of it in a law court. অপরাধী

convince (**convinces, convincing,
convinced**) *vt* If someone or something
convinces you of something, they make
you believe that it is true or that it exists.
প্রত্যয় জাগানো

convincing *adj* If someone or something
is **convincing**, you believe them. প্রত্যয়
জাগায় এমন

convoy (**convoys**) *n* A **convoy** is a group of
vehicles or ships travelling together. কনভয়/
সৌজোয়া গাড়ি

cook (**cooks, cooking, cooked**) *n* A **cook** is
a person whose job is to prepare and cook
food. পাচক ▷ *v* When you **cook**, or **cook** a
meal, you prepare and heat food so it can
be eaten. রান্না করা

cookbook (**cookbooks**) *n* A **cookbook** is
a book that contains recipes for preparing
food. রান্নার বই

cooker (**cookers**) *n* A **cooker** is a large
metal device used for cooking food using
gas or electricity. কুকার

cookery *n* **Cookery** is the activity of
preparing and cooking food. রান্না করবার
পদ্ধতি

cookery book (**cookery books**) *n* A
cookery book is a book that contains
recipes for preparing food. রন্ধনপ্রণালীর বই

cooking *n* **Cooking** is the act of preparing
and heating food so it can be eaten.
রন্ধনকার্য

cool (**cooler, coolest**) *adj* Something that is
cool has a low temperature but is not cold.
শীতল ▷ *adj* If you say that someone is **cool**,
you mean that they are fashionable and
attractive. (*informal*) দারুণ

cooperation *n* **Cooperation** is the action
of working together with or helping
someone. সহযোগিতা

cop (**cops**) *n* A **cop** is a policeman or
policewoman. (*informal*) পুলিশকর্মী

cope (**copes, coping, coped**) *vi* If you **cope**
with a problem, task, or difficult situation,
you deal with it successfully. নির্বাহ করা

copper (**coppers**) *n* **Copper** is a soft
reddish-brown metal. তামা

copy (**copies, copying, copied**) *n* If you
make a **copy** of something, you produce
something that looks like the original thing.
অনুলিপি ▷ *n* A **copy** of a book, newspaper,
or record is one of many identical ones that
have been printed or produced. প্রতিলিপি
▷ *vt* If you **copy** something, you produce
something that looks like the original thing.
নকল করা

copyright (**copyrights**) *n* If someone
has the **copyright** on a piece of writing or
music, it is illegal to reproduce or perform it
without their permission. কপিরাইট

coral (**corals**) *n* **Coral** is a hard substance
formed from the skeletons of very small sea
animals. প্রবাল

cordless *adj* A **cordless** telephone or
piece of electric equipment is operated
by a battery fitted inside it and is not
connected to the electricity mains.
তারবিহীন

corduroy *n* **Corduroy** is thick cotton cloth
with parallel raised lines on the outside.
কর্ডুরয়

core (**cores**) *n* The **core** of a fruit is the
central part containing seeds or pips. ফলের
শাঁস

coriander *n* **Coriander** is a plant with
seeds that are used as a spice and leaves
that are used as a herb. ধনে

cork n **Cork** is a soft light substance which forms the bark of a Mediterranean tree. কর্কগাছ

corkscrew (**corkscrews**) n A **corkscrew** is a device for pulling corks out of bottles. বোতলের ছিপি খোলার সরঞ্জাম

corn n **Corn** refers to crops such as wheat and barley, or their seeds. ভুট্টা

corner (**corners**) n A **corner** is a place where two sides or edges of something meet, or where a road meets another road. কোণ

cornet (**cornets**) n A **cornet** is a musical instrument of the brass family that looks like a small trumpet. বাদ্যযন্ত্র

cornflakes npl **Cornflakes** are small flat pieces of maize that are eaten with milk as a breakfast cereal. কর্ণফ্লেক্স

cornflour n **Cornflour** is a fine white powder made from maize and is used to make sauces thicker. ভুট্টার গুঁড়ো

corporal (**corporals**) n A **corporal** is a non-commissioned officer in the army or United States Marines. কর্পোরাল

corporal punishment n **Corporal punishment** is the punishment of people by hitting them. দৈহিক শাস্তি

corpse (**corpses**) n A **corpse** is a dead body. লাশ

correct (**corrects, correcting, corrected**) adj Something that is **correct** is accurate and has no mistakes. (formal) সঠিক ▷ vt If you **correct** a mistake, problem, or fault, you put it right. ভুল শুধরানো

correction (**corrections**) n A **correction** is something which puts right something that is wrong. সংশোধন

correctly adv If you do something **correctly**, you do it in the correct way. সঠিকভাবে

correspondence n **Correspondence** is the act of writing letters to someone. পত্রলিখন

correspondent (**correspondents**) n A **correspondent** is a television or newspaper reporter. সাংবাদিক

corridor (**corridors**) n A **corridor** is a long passage in a building or train, with rooms on one or both sides. দালান

corrupt adj A **corrupt** person behaves in a way that is morally wrong, especially by doing illegal things for money. দুর্নীতিগ্রস্ত

corruption n **Corruption** is dishonesty and illegal behaviour by people in positions of power. দুর্নীতি

cosmetics npl **Cosmetics** are substances such as lipstick and face powder. বিভিন্ন প্রসাধনী দ্রব্য

cosmetic surgery n **Cosmetic surgery** is surgery done to make a person look more attractive. সৌন্দর্যবর্ধক-শল্যচিকিৎসা

cost (**costs, costing**) n The **cost** of something is the amount of money needed to buy, do, or make it. মূল্য ▷ vt If something **costs** a particular amount of money, you can buy, do, or make it for that amount. মূল্যে

Costa Rica n **Costa Rica** is a republic in Central America. কোস্টা রিকা

cost of living n The **cost of living** is the average amount of money that people need to spend on food, housing, and clothing. সংসার-খরচ

costume (**costumes**) n An actor's or performer's **costume** is the set of clothes they wear while they are performing. পোশাক

cosy (**cosier, cosiest**) adj A **cosy** house or room is comfortable and warm. আরামদায়ক

cot (**cots**) n A **cot** is a bed for a baby, with bars or panels round it so that the baby cannot fall out. বাচ্চার খাট

cottage (**cottages**) *n* A **cottage** is a small house, usually in the country. ছোট বাড়ী

cottage cheese *n* **Cottage cheese** is a soft, white, lumpy cheese made from sour milk. পনির

cotton (**cottons**) *n* **Cotton** is a kind of cloth that is made from the **cotton** plant. সুতির কাপড় ▷ *n* **Cotton** is thread that you use to sew with. সুতো

cotton bud (**cotton buds**) *n* A **cotton bud** is a small stick with a ball of cotton wool at each end, which people use, for example, for applying make-up. তুলোয় জড়ানো কাঠি

cotton wool *n* **Cotton wool** is soft fluffy cotton, often used for applying creams to your skin. তুলোর বল

couch (**couches**) *n* A **couch** is a long soft piece of furniture for sitting or lying on. কোচ

couchette (**couchettes**) *n* A **couchette** is a bed on a train or a boat which is either folded against the wall or used as an ordinary seat during the day. ট্রেনে শোয়ার বিছানা

cough (**coughs, coughing, coughed**) *n* A **cough** is an act, instance, or sound of coughing. কাশি ▷ *vi* When you **cough**, you force air out of your throat with a sudden, harsh noise. You often cough when you are ill, or when you are nervous or want to attract someone's attention. কাশি হওয়া

cough mixture (**cough mixtures**) *n* **Cough mixture** is a liquid medicine that you take when you have a cough. কাশির ওষুধ

could *v* If you say you **could** do something, you mean that you were able to do it. পারা *I could see through the window.*

council (**councils**) *n* A **council** is a group of people elected to govern a town or other area. পরিষদ

council house (**council houses**) *n* A **council house** is a house that is owned by a local council and that people can rent at a low cost. পরিষদীয় ভবন

councillor (**councillors**) *n* A **councillor** is a member of a local council. পরিষদ-সদস্য

count (**counts, counting, counted**) *vi* When you **count**, you say numbers in order, one after the other. পরপর গোনা ▷ *vt* When you **count** all the things in a group, you add them up to see how many there are. গুনে নেওয়া

counter (**counters**) *n* In a shop, a **counter** is a long flat surface at which customers are served. দোকানের কাউন্টার

count on *v* If you **count on** someone or something, you rely on them to support you. ভরসা করা *I can always count on you to cheer me up.*

country (**countries**) *n* A **country** is a part of the world with its own people and laws. দেশ ▷ *n* The **country** is land that is away from towns and cities. There are farms and woods in the **country**. গ্রামাঞ্চল

countryside *n* The **countryside** is land away from towns and cities. শহর থেকে দূরে

couple (**couples**) *n* A **couple** is two people who are married or who are having a romantic relationship. দম্পতি ▷ *det* A **couple** of people or things means two or around two of them. দুই বা তার আশেপাশে *Things should get better in a couple of days.*

courage *n* **Courage** is the quality shown by someone who does something difficult or dangerous, even though they may be afraid. সাহস

courageous *adj* Someone who is **courageous** does something difficult or dangerous, even though they may be afraid. সাহসী

courgette (**courgettes**) *n* **Courgettes** are long thin green vegetables. ঝিঙে

courier (**couriers**) *n* A **courier** is a person who is paid to take letters and parcels direct from one place to another. ক্যারিয়ার

course (**courses**) *n* The **course** of a vehicle is the route along which it is travelling. যাত্রাপথ

court (**courts**) *n* A **court** is a place where a judge and a group of people (= a jury) decide if someone has done something wrong. আদালত ▷ *n* A **court** is a place for playing a game such as tennis. খেলার জায়গা

courtyard (**courtyards**) *n* A **courtyard** is a flat open area of ground surrounded by buildings or walls. অঙ্গন

cousin (**cousins**) *n* Your **cousin** is the child of your uncle or aunt. সম্পর্কিত ভাই-বোন

cover (**covers, covering, covered**) *n* A **cover** is something that you put over another thing. ঢাকা ▷ *vt* If you **cover** something, you put another thing over it. ঢাকা দেওয়া

cover charge (**cover charges**) *n* A **cover charge** is a sum of money that you must pay in some restaurants and nightclubs in addition to the money that you pay there for your food and drink. অতিরিক্ত চার্জ

cow (**cows**) *n* A **cow** is a large female animal kept on farms for its milk. গরু

coward (**cowards**) *n* A **coward** is someone who is easily frightened and avoids dangerous or difficult situations. কাপুরুষ

cowardly *adj* Someone who is **cowardly** is easily frightened and so avoids doing dangerous or difficult things. কাপুরুষোচিত

cowboy (**cowboys**) *n* A **cowboy** is a male character in a western. কাউবয়

crab (**crabs**) *n* A **crab** is a sea creature with a flat round body covered by a shell, and five pairs of legs with claws on the front pair. কাঁকড়া

crack (**cracks, cracking, cracked**) *n* A **crack** is a very narrow gap between two things. ফাঁক ▷ *n* A **crack** is a line on the surface of something when it is slightly damaged. ফাটল ▷ *v* If something **cracks** or if you **crack** it, it becomes damaged, and lines appear on the surface where it has broken. ফাটল ধরা

crack down on *v* If people in authority **crack down on** a group of people, they become stricter in making the group obey rules or laws. দমনাত্মক হওয়া *The police are cracking down on motorists who drive too fast.*

cracked *adj* An object that is **cracked** has lines on its surface because it is damaged. ফাটলযুক্ত

cracker (**crackers**) *n* A **cracker** is a thin crisp savoury biscuit. কুড়মুড়ে বিস্কুট

cradle (**cradles**) *n* A **cradle** is a baby's bed with high sides. দোলনা

craft (**craft**) *n* You can refer to a boat, a spacecraft, or an aircraft as a **craft**. যান

craftsman (**craftsmen**) *n* A **craftsman** is a man who makes things skilfully with his hands. হস্তশিল্পী

cram (**crams, cramming, crammed**) *v* If you **cram** things or people into a place, or if they **cram** it, there are so many of them in it at one time that it is completely full. ঠেসে ভর্তি করা

crammed *adj* If a place is **crammed** with things or people, it is very full of them. ঠাসা

cranberry (**cranberries**) *n* **Cranberries** are red berries with a sour taste. They are often used to make a sauce or jelly that you eat with meat. ক্রেনবেরি

crane (**cranes**) *n* A **crane** is a large bird with a long neck and long legs. **Cranes** live near water. সারস ▷ *n* A **crane** is a tall machine that can lift very heavy things. ক্রেন (যন্ত্র)

crash (**crashes, crashing, crashed**) *n* A **crash** is an accident when a vehicle hits something. গাড়ী দুর্ঘটনা ▷ *vt* If you **crash** a moving vehicle, it hits something. মুখোমুখি ধাক্কা লাগানো ▷ *vi* If a moving vehicle **crashes**, it hits something. মুখোমুখি ধাক্কা লাগা ▷ *n* A **crash** is a sudden, loud noise. আচমকা তীব্র আওয়াজ

crawl (**crawls, crawling, crawled**) *vi* When you **crawl**, you move forward on your hands and knees. হামাগুড়ি দেওয়া

crayfish (**crayfish**) *n* A **crayfish** is a small shellfish with five pairs of legs which lives in rivers and streams. You can eat some types of crayfish. বিশাল গলদাচিংড়ি

crayon (**crayons**) n A **crayon** is a rod of coloured wax used for drawing. মোম-রং

crazy (**crazier, craziest**) adj If you describe someone or something as **crazy**, you think they are very foolish or strange. (informal) উন্মাত্ত

cream adj Something that is **cream** in colour is yellowish-white. ক্রিম ▷ n **Cream** is a thick liquid that is produced from milk. You can use it in cooking or put it on fruit or puddings. ননি

crease (**creases**) n **Creases** are lines that are made in cloth or paper when it is crushed or folded. ভাঁজ

creased adj If something such as cloth or paper is **creased**, there are lines in it because it has been crushed or folded. ভাঁজযুক্ত

create (**creates, creating, created**) vt To **create** something means to cause it to happen or exist. সৃষ্টি করা

creation (**creations**) n The **creation** of something is the act of bringing it into existence. সৃষ্টি

creative adj A **creative** person has the ability to invent and develop original ideas, especially in art. সৃষ্টিশীল

creature (**creatures**) n You can refer to any living thing that is not a plant as a **creature**. জীব

crèche (**crèches**) n A **crèche** is an establishment where preschool children are looked after in the daytime, enabling their parents to work full time. ক্রেশ

credentials npl Your **credentials** are your previous achievements, training, and general background, which indicate that you are qualified to do something. আস্থাপত্র

credible adj **Credible** means able to be trusted or believed. বিশ্বাসযোগ্য

credit n **Credit** is a system where you pay for goods or services several weeks or months after you have received them. ধার

credit card (**credit cards**) n A **credit card** is a plastic card that you use to buy goods on credit. ক্রেডিট কার্ড

creep (**creeps, creeping, crept**) vi If you **creep** somewhere, you move in a very slow and quiet way. হামাগুড়ি দেওয়া ▷ vi If an animal **creeps**, it moves along close to the ground. বুকে হেঁটে চলা

crematorium (**crematoria, crematoriums**) n A **crematorium** is a building in which the bodies of dead people are burned. শ্মশান

cress n **Cress** is a plant with small green leaves that are used in salads or to decorate food. হিংচে শাক

crew (**crews**) n The **crew** of a ship, an aircraft, or a spacecraft consists of the people who work on it and operate it. **Crew** can take the singular or plural form of the verb. বিমান-কর্মীবৃন্দ/জাহাজ-কর্মীবৃন্দ

crew cut (**crew cuts**) n A **crew cut** is a man's hairstyle in which his hair is cut very short. ক্রু-কাট চুল

cricket (**crickets**) n **Cricket** is a game where two teams take turns to hit a ball with a bat and run up and down. ক্রিকেট খেলা ▷ n A **cricket** is a small jumping insect that rubs its wings together to make a high sound. ঝিঁঝিঁ পোকা

crime (**crimes**) n A **crime** is an illegal action or activity for which a person can be punished by law. অপরাধ

criminal (**criminals**) adj **Criminal** means connected with crime. অপরাধ-সম্পর্কিত ▷ n A **criminal** is a person who has committed a crime. অপরাধী

crisis (**crises**) n A **crisis** is a situation in which something or someone is affected by one or more very serious problems. সংকটমুহূর্ত

crisp (**crisper, crispest**) adj **Crisp** food is pleasantly hard and crunchy. মুচমুচে ভাবযুক্ত

crisps npl **Crisps** are very thin slices of fried potato that are eaten cold as a snack. পাতলা আলুভাজা

crispy (crispier, crispiest) adj Food that is **crispy** is pleasantly hard, or has a pleasantly hard surface. মুচমুচে

criterion (criteria) n A **criterion** is a factor on which you judge or decide something. বিচারের মাপকাঠি

critic (critics) n A **critic** is a person who writes reviews and expresses opinions about books, films, music, and art. সমালোচক

critical adj A **critical** time or situation is extremely important. সংকটজনক

criticism (criticisms) n **Criticism** is the action of expressing disapproval of something or someone. সমালোচনা

criticize (criticizes, criticizing, criticized) vt If you **criticize** someone or something, you express your disapproval of them by saying what you think is wrong with them. সমালোচনা করা

Croatia n **Croatia** is a republic in south-east Europe. ক্রোয়েশিয়া

Croatian (Croations) adj **Croatian** means of, relating to, or characteristic of Croatia, its people, or their language. ক্রোয়েশিয়ার সাথে সম্পর্কিত ▷ n A **Croatian** is a native or inhabitant of Croatia. ক্রোয়েশিয়া-বাসী ▷ n **Croatian** is the language that is spoken in Croatia. ক্রোয়েশিয়ান ভাষা

crochet (crochets, crocheting, crocheted) v If you **crochet**, you make cloth by using a needle with a small hook at the end. কুরুশে বোনা

crocodile (crocodiles) n A **crocodile** is a large reptile with a long body. Crocodiles live in rivers. কুমির

crocus (crocuses) n **Crocuses** are small white, yellow, or purple flowers that grow in the early spring. বসন্তকালের ফুল

crook (crooks) n A **crook** is a criminal or a dishonest person. (informal) অপরাধপ্রবণ ব্যক্তি

crop (crops) n **Crops** are plants such as wheat and potatoes that are grown in large quantities for food. ফসল

cross (crosser, crossest, crosses, crossing, crossed) adj If you are **cross**, you feel angry about something. রেগে যাওয়া ▷ n A **cross** is a mark that you write. It looks like **X** or +. ক্রুশ ▷ vt If you **cross** something, you go from one side of it to the other. পার হওয়া

cross-country n **Cross-country** is the sport of running, riding, or skiing across open countryside. ক্রস-কান্ট্রি ক্রীড়া

crossing (crossings) n A **crossing** is a boat journey to the other side of a sea. জাহাজে সাগর পার হওয়া

cross out v If you **cross out** words, you draw a line through them. কেটে দেওয়া He crossed out her name and added his own.

crossroads (crossroads) n A **crossroads** is a place where two roads meet and cross. দুটি রাস্তার সংযোগস্থল

crossword (crosswords) n A **crossword** or a **crossword puzzle** is a word game in which you work out answers to clues, and write the answers in the white squares of a pattern of black and white squares. ক্রস-ওয়ার্ড

crouch down v If you **are crouching down**, your legs are bent under you so that you are close to the ground and leaning forward slightly. উপুড় হয়ে বসা He crouched down and reached under the mattress.

crow (crows) n A **crow** is a large black bird which makes a loud harsh noise. কাক

crowd (crowds) n A **crowd** is a large group of people who have gathered together. লোকের ভিড়

crowded adj A **crowded** place is full of people or things. জনবহুল

crown (crowns) n A **crown** is a circular ornament, usually made of gold and jewels, which a king or queen wears on their head at official ceremonies. মুকুট

crucial adj Something that is **crucial** is extremely important. গুরুত্বপূর্ণ

crucifix (crucifixes) n A **crucifix** is a cross with a figure of Christ on it. ক্রুশে ঝোলানো যীশুর মূর্তি

crude (cruder, crudest) adj Something that is **crude** is simple and not sophisticated. অশোধিত

cruel (crueller, cruellest) adj Someone who is **cruel** deliberately causes pain or distress. নিষ্ঠুর

cruelty (cruelties) n **Cruelty** is behaviour that deliberately causes pain or distress to people or animals. নিষ্ঠুরতা

cruise (cruises) n A **cruise** is a holiday spent on a ship or boat which visits a number of places. জাহাজে প্রমোদভ্রমণ

crumb (crumbs) n **Crumbs** are tiny pieces that fall from bread, biscuits, or cake when you cut or eat them. বিস্কুটের গুঁড়ো

crush (crushes, crushing, crushed) vt To **crush** something means to press it very hard so that its shape is destroyed or so that it breaks into pieces. চূর্ণ করা

crutch (crutches) n A **crutch** is a stick which someone with an injured foot or leg uses to support them when walking. ক্রাচ

cry (cries, crying, cried) n A **cry** is a loud sound that you make with your voice. চেঁচানো ▷ vi When you **cry**, tears come from your eyes. People **cry** when they are sad or hurt. কাঁদা

crystal (crystals) n A **crystal** is a piece of a mineral that has formed naturally into a regular symmetrical shape. স্ফটিক

cub (cubs) n A **cub** is a young wild animal such as a lion, wolf, or bear. সিংহশাবক

Cuba n **Cuba** is a republic and the largest island in the Caribbean, at the entrance to the Gulf of Mexico. কিউবা প্রজাতন্ত্র

Cuban (Cubans) adj **Cuban** means belonging or relating to Cuba, or to its people or culture. কিউবার সঙ্গে সম্পর্কিত ▷ n A **Cuban** is a Cuban citizen, or a person of Cuban origin. কিউবা-বাসী

cube (cubes) n A **cube** is a solid shape with six square surfaces which are all the same size. ঘনক

cubic adj **Cubic** is used to express units of volume. আয়তনের একক

cuckoo (cuckoos) n A **cuckoo** is a grey bird which makes an easily recognizable sound consisting of two quick notes. কোকিল

cucumber (cucumbers) n A **cucumber** is a long dark green vegetable. শশা

cuddle (cuddles, cuddling, cuddled) n A **cuddle** is a close embrace, especially when prolonged. আলিঙ্গন ▷ vt If you **cuddle** someone, you put your arms round them and hold them close as a way of showing your affection. জড়িয়ে ধরা

cue (cues) n A **cue** is something said or done by a performer that is a signal for another performer to begin speaking or to begin doing something. খেই ধরানোর ইঙ্গিত

cufflinks npl **Cufflinks** are small decorative objects used for holding together shirt cuffs around the wrist. কারুকার্যময় হাতের বোতাম

culprit (culprits) n The person who committed a crime or did something wrong can be referred to as the **culprit**. দোষী

cultural adj **Cultural** means relating to the arts generally, or to the arts and customs of a particular society. সাংস্কৃতিক

culture (cultures) n **Culture** consists of activities such as the art, music, literature, and theatre. সংস্কৃতি

cumin n **Cumin** is a sweet-smelling spice, and is popular in cooking. জিরে

cunning adj A **cunning** person is clever and deceitful. ধূর্ত

cup (cups) n A **cup** is a small round container with a handle, which you drink from. কাপ

cupboard (**cupboards**) *n* A **cupboard** is a piece of furniture with doors at the front and usually shelves inside. দেরাজ

curb (**curbs**) *n* A **curb** is something that restrains or holds something else back. প্রতিবন্ধক

cure (**cures, curing, cured**) *n* A **cure** for an illness is a medicine or other treatment that cures the illness. আরোগ্যলাভ ▷ *vt* If a doctor or a medical treatment **cures** someone, or **cures** their illness, they make the person well again. আরোগ্যলাভ করানো

curfew (**curfews**) *n* A **curfew** is a law stating that people must stay inside their houses after a particular time at night. কার্ফু

curious *adj* If you are **curious** about something, you are interested in it and want to learn more about it. কৌতূহলী

curl (**curls**) *n* **Curls** are lengths of hair shaped in curves and circles. কুঞ্চন

curler (**curlers**) *n* **Curlers** are small plastic or metal tubes that women roll their hair round in order to make it curly. চুল কোঁচকানোর সরঞ্জাম

curly (**curlier, curliest**) *adj* **Curly** hair is full of curls. কোঁচকানো

currant (**currants**) *n* **Currants** are small dried black grapes, used especially in cakes. শুকনো কালো আঙুর

currency (**currencies**) *n* The money used in a country is referred to as its **currency**. মুদ্রা

current (**currents**) *adj* Something that is **current** is happening, being done, or being used at the present time. বর্তমান ▷ *n* A **current** is a steady, continuous, flowing movement of water or air. প্রবাহ ▷ *n* An electric **current** is electricity flowing through a wire or circuit. তড়িৎশক্তি

current account (**current accounts**) *n* A **current account** is a bank account which you can take money out of at any time. চালু খাতা

current affairs *npl* **Current affairs** are political events and problems which are discussed in the media. সাম্প্রতিক বিষয়াবলী

currently *adv* **Currently** means at the present time. বর্তমানে

curriculum (**curriculums, curricula**) *n* A **curriculum** is all the different courses of study that are taught in a school, college, or university. পাঠক্রম

curriculum vitae *n* A **curriculum vitae** is a brief written account of your personal details, your education, and jobs you have had, which you send when you are applying for a job. The abbreviation 'CV' is also used. সি.ডি./ব্যক্তিগত বিবরণ

curry (**curries**) *n* **Curry** is an Asian dish made with hot spices. কারি

curry powder (**curry powders**) *n* **Curry powder** is a powder made from a mixture of spices. It is used in cooking, especially when making curry. কারি পাউডার

curse (**curses**) *n* A **curse** is rude or offensive language which someone uses, usually because they are angry. (*written*) অভিশাপ

cursor (**cursors**) *n* On a computer screen, the **cursor** is a small, movable shape which indicates where anything typed by the user will appear. কম্পিউটারের কার্সর

curtain (**curtains**) *n* **Curtains** are hanging pieces of material which you can pull across a window to keep light out or prevent people from looking in. পর্দা

cushion (**cushions**) *n* A **cushion** is a fabric case filled with soft material, which you put on a seat to make it more comfortable. গদিআঁটা

custard *n* **Custard** is a sweet yellow sauce made from milk and eggs or from milk and a powder. It is eaten with puddings. কাস্টার্ড

custody *n* **Custody** is the legal right to look after a child, especially the right given to a child's father or mother when they get divorced. অভিভাবকত্ব

custom (**customs**) *n* A **custom** is an activity, a way of behaving, or an event which is usual or traditional in a particular society or in particular circumstances. রীতিনীতি

customer (**customers**) n A **customer** is someone who buys goods or services, especially from a shop. ক্রেতা

customized adj Something that is **customized** has had its appearance or features changed to suit someone's tastes or needs. চাহিদামাফিক

customs npl **Customs** is the official organization responsible for collecting taxes on goods coming into a country and preventing illegal goods from being brought in. শুল্ক বিভাগ

customs officer (**customs officers**) n A **customs officer** is a person who works for the official organization responsible for collecting taxes on goods coming into a country and preventing illegal goods from being brought in. শুল্ক অধিকারিক

cut (**cuts, cutting**) n A **cut** is a place on your skin where something sharp has gone through it. কাটা চিহ্ন ▷ v If you **cut** something, you use a knife or scissors to divide it into pieces. কাটা ▷ vt If you **cut** yourself, something sharp goes through your skin and blood comes out. কেটে ফেলা

cutback (**cutbacks**) n A **cutback** is a reduction in something. হ্রাসকরণ

cut down v If you **cut down** on something, you use or do less of it. কমানো He cut down on coffee.

cute (**cuter, cutest**) adj **Cute** means pretty or attractive. (informal) মাধুর্যময়

cutlery n The knives, forks, and spoons that you eat with are referred to as **cutlery**. কাঁটা-চামচ

cutlet (**cutlets**) n A **cutlet** is a small piece of meat which is usually fried or grilled. কাটলেট

cut off v If you **cut** something **off**, you cut it with a knife or a similar tool. ছাড়ানো She cut off a large piece of meat.

cutting (**cuttings**) n A **cutting** is a piece of writing cut from a newspaper or magazine. কাগজের কাটা অংশ

cut up v If you **cut** something **up**, you cut it into several pieces. টুকরো করে কাটা Halve the tomatoes, then cut them up.

CV (**CVs**) abbr Your **CV** is a brief written account of your personal details, your education, and jobs you have had, which you send when you are applying for a job. **CV** is an abbreviation for 'curriculum vitae'. সি.ভি./ব্যক্তিগত বিবরণ

cybercafé (**cybercafés**) n A **cybercafé** is a café where people can pay to use the Internet. সাইবার কাফে

cybercrime n **Cybercrime** is the illegal use of computers and the Internet. সাইবার ক্রাইম

cycle (**cycles, cycling, cycled**) n A **cycle** is a bicycle. সাইকেল ▷ n A **cycle** is a series of events or processes that is continually repeated, always in the same order. চক্র ▷ vi If you **cycle**, you ride a bicycle. সাইকেল চড়া

cycle lane (**cycle lanes**) n A **cycle lane** is a part of a road or path that only bicycles are allowed to use. সাইকেল গলি

cycle path (**cycle paths**) n A **cycle path** is a special path on which people can travel by bicycle separately from motor vehicles. শুধুমাত্র সাইকেলের জন্য রাস্তা

cycling n **Cycling** is the action of riding a cycle. সাইকেল চালনা

cyclist (**cyclists**) n A **cyclist** is someone who rides a bicycle. সাইকেল-চালক

cyclone (**cyclones**) n A **cyclone** is a violent tropical storm. ঝড়বিশেষ

cylinder (**cylinders**) n A **cylinder** is a shape or container with flat circular ends and long straight sides. সিলিন্ডার/চোঙ

d

cymbals (**cymbals**) *npl* **Cymbals** are flat circular brass objects that are used as musical instruments. You hit two cymbals together to make a loud noise. মন্দিরা

Cypriot (**Cypriots**) *adj* **Cypriot** means belonging or relating to Cyprus, or to its people or culture. সাইপ্রাসের সঙ্গে সম্পর্কযুক্ত ▷ *n* A **Cypriot** is a Cypriot citizen, or a person of Cypriot origin. সাইপ্রাসের নাগরিক

Cyprus *n* **Cyprus** is an island in the East Mediterranean. সাইপ্রাস একটি দ্বীপ

cyst (**cysts**) *n* A **cyst** is a growth containing liquid that appears inside your body or under your skin. জলভরা কোষ

cystitis *n* **Cystitis** is a bladder infection. প্রস্রাবনলির সংক্রমণ

Czech (**Czechs**) *adj* **Czech** means belonging or relating to the Czech Republic, or to its people, language, or culture. চেক প্রজাতন্ত্রের সঙ্গে সম্পর্কিত ▷ *n* A **Czech** is a person who comes from the Czech Republic. চেক এর অধিবাসী ▷ *n* **Czech** is the language spoken in the Czech Republic. চেক ভাষা

Czech Republic *n* The **Czech Republic** is a country in central Europe. চেক প্রজাতন্ত্র

dad (**dads**) *n* Your **dad** is your father. You can call your dad 'Dad'. (*informal*) বাবা

daddy (**daddies**) *n* Children often call their father **daddy**. (*informal*) বাপি

daffodil (**daffodils**) *n* A **daffodil** is a yellow flower that blooms in the spring. ড্যাফোডিল ফুল/হলুদ রঙের ফুল

daft (**dafter, daftest**) *adj* **Daft** means stupid and not sensible. নির্বোধ

daily *adj* **Daily** means of or occurring every day or every weekday. রোজ ▷ *adv* If something happens **daily**, it happens every day. দৈনিক

dairy (**dairies**) *n* A **dairy** is a shop or company that sells milk, butter, and cheese. ডেয়ারী

dairy produce *n* **Dairy produce** is foods such as butter and cheese that are made from milk. ডেয়ারী প্রস্তুত খাদ্য

dairy products *npl* **Dairy products** are foods such as butter and cheese that are made from milk. ডেয়ারী প্রস্তুত খাদ্যদ্রব্য

daisy (**daisies**) *n* A **daisy** is a small wild flower with a yellow centre and white petals. সাদা পাপড়িযুক্ত বুনো ফুল

dam (**dams**) *n* A **dam** is a wall built across a river to stop the flow of the water and make a lake. বাঁধ

damage (**damages, damaging, damaged**) *n* **Damage** is injury or harm that is caused to something. ক্ষয়ক্ষতি ▷ *vt* If you **damage** something, you injure or harm it. ক্ষতি করা

damp (**damper, dampest**) *adj* Damp
means slightly wet. আর্দ্র

dance (**dances, dancing, danced**) *n* A
dance is a series of steps and rhythmic
movements which you do to music. It is also
a piece of music which people can dance
to. নৃত্য ▷ *vi* When you **dance**, you move
around in time to music. নাচ করা

dancer (**dancers**) *n* A **dancer** is a person
who is dancing, or who earns money by
dancing. নর্তক/নর্তকী

dancing *n* When people dance for
enjoyment or to entertain others, you can
refer to this activity as **dancing**. নৃত্যকলা

dandelion (**dandelions**) *n* A **dandelion**
is a wild plant which has yellow flowers
first, then a fluffy ball of seeds. হলুদ ফুলযুক্ত
গাছ

dandruff *n* Dandruff is small white pieces
of dead skin in someone's hair, or fallen
from someone's hair. খুসকি

Dane (**Danes**) *n* A **Dane** is a person who
comes from Denmark. ডেনমার্ক-বাসী

danger *n* Danger is the possibility that
someone may be harmed or killed. বিপদ

dangerous *adj* If something is **dangerous**,
it may hurt or harm you. বিপজ্জনক

Danish *adj* Danish means relating to or
belonging to Denmark, or to its people,
language, or culture. ডেনমার্ক সম্বন্ধীয় ▷ *n*
Danish is the language spoken in Denmark.
ড্যানিশ ভাষা

dare (**dares, daring, dared**) *vt* If you **dare**
to do something, you are brave enough to
do it. সাহস করা *Most people don't dare to
argue with him.*

daring *adj* A **daring** person does things
which might be dangerous or shocking.
সাহসী

dark (**darker, darkest**) *adj* When it is **dark**,
there is no light or not much light. অন্ধকার
▷ *n* The **dark** is the lack of light in a place.
অন্ধকার ▷ *adj* A **dark** colour is not pale. গাঢ়

darkness *n* Darkness is the lack of light in
a place. আঁধার

darling (**darlings**) *n* You call someone
darling if you love them or like them very
much. প্রিয়তম

dart (**darts**) *n* A **dart** is a small, narrow
object with a sharp point which you can
throw or shoot. ধারালো বস্তু

darts *npl* Darts is a game in which you
throw darts at a round board with numbers
on it. ডার্টস

dash (**dashes, dashing, dashed**) *vi* If you
dash somewhere, you run or go there
quickly and suddenly. ছুটে যাওয়া

dashboard (**dashboards**) *n* The
dashboard in a car is the panel facing the
driver's seat where most of the instruments
and switches are. ড্যাসবোর্ড

data *npl* You can talk about information
as **data**, especially when it is in the form of
facts or numbers. ডেটা

database (**databases**) *n* A **database** is a
collection of data stored in a computer in a
way that makes it easy to obtain. ডেটাবেস

date (**dates**) *n* A **date** is a particular day or
year, for example 7th June 2010, or 1066.
তারিখ

daughter (**daughters**) *n* Your **daughter** is
your female child. কন্যা

daughter-in-law (**daughters-in-law**) *n*
Your **daughter-in-law** is the wife of your
son. পুত্রবধূ

dawn (**dawns**) *n* Dawn is the time of day
when light first appears in the sky, before
the sun rises. প্রভাত

day (**days**) *n* A **day** is the length of time
between one midnight and the next. There
are twenty-four hours in a **day**, and seven
days in a week. দিন ▷ *n* **Day** is the time
when there is light outside. দিনের বেলা

day return (**day returns**) *n* A **day return**
is a train or bus ticket which allows you to
go somewhere and come back on the same
day for a lower price than an ordinary return
ticket. একই দিনে ফেরার টিকিট

daytime *n* Daytime is the part of a day
when it is light. দিনের বেলা

dead *adj* A person, animal, or plant that is **dead** is no longer living. মৃত ▷ *adv* **Dead** means 'precisely' or 'exactly'. সম্পূর্ণভাবে

dead end (**dead ends**) *n* If a street is a **dead end**, there is no way out at one end of it. শেষ প্রান্ত

deadline (**deadlines**) *n* A **deadline** is a time or date before which a particular task must be finished or a particular thing must be done. নির্দিষ্ট সময়সীমা

deaf (**deafer, deafest**) *adj* Someone who is **deaf** is unable to hear anything or is unable to hear very well. কালা

deafening *adj* A **deafening** noise is a very loud noise. কানে তালা লাগার মত আওয়াজ

deal (**deals, dealing, dealt**) *n* If you make a **deal**, you agree to do something with somebody. রফা ▷ *v* If you **deal** playing cards, you give them out to the players in a game of cards. তাস দেওয়া

dealer (**dealers**) *n* A **dealer** is a person whose business involves buying and selling things. ব্যাপারী

deal with *v* When you **deal with** a situation or problem, you do what is necessary to achieve the result you want. সামলানো *How do you deal with an uninvited guest?*

dear (**dearer, dearest**) *adj* You use **dear** to describe someone or something that you feel affection for. প্রিয় ▷ *adj* Something that is **dear** costs a lot of money. (*informal*) দুর্মূল্য

death (**deaths**) *n* **Death** is the end of the life of a person or animal. মৃত্যু

debate (**debates, debating, debated**) *n* A **debate** is a discussion about a subject on which people have different views. বিতর্ক ▷ *vt* When people **debate** a topic, they discuss it fairly formally, putting forward different views. You can also say that one person **debates** a topic with another person. তর্ক করা

debit (**debits, debiting, debited**) *n* A **debit** is a record of the money taken from your bank account. ডেবিট ▷ *vt* When your

bank **debits** your account, money is taken from it and paid to someone else. টাকা কেটে নেওয়া

debit card (**debit cards**) *n* A **debit card** is a bank card that you can use to pay for things. When you use it, the money is taken out of your bank account immediately. ডেবিট কার্ড

debt (**debts**) *n* A **debt** is a sum of money that you owe someone. ঋণ

decade (**decades**) *n* A **decade** is a period of ten years, especially one that begins with a year ending in 0, for example 2000 to 2009. দশক

decaffeinated coffee (**decaffeinated coffees**) *n* **Decaffeinated coffee** has had most of the caffeine removed from it. ডেকাফিনের কফি

decay (**decays, decaying, decayed**) *vi* When something such as a dead body, a dead plant, or a tooth **decays**, it is gradually destroyed by a natural process. ক্ষয়

deceive (**deceives, deceiving, deceived**) *vt* If you **deceive** someone, you make them believe something that is not true. বিশ্বাসঘাতকতা করা

December (**Decembers**) *n* **December** is the twelfth and last month of the year in the Western calendar. ডিসেম্বর

decent *adj* **Decent** means acceptable in standard or quality. উপযুক্ত

decide (**decides, deciding, decided**) *vt* If you **decide** to do something, you choose to do it. স্থির করা

decimal *adj* A **decimal** system involves counting in units of ten. দশমিক

decision (**decisions**) *n* When you make a **decision**, you choose what should be done or which is the best of various alternatives. সিদ্ধান্ত

decisive *adj* If a fact, action, or event is **decisive**, it makes it certain that there will be a particular result. নির্ণায়ক

deck (**decks**) *n* A **deck** on a bus or ship is a downstairs or upstairs area. ডেক

deckchair (**deckchairs**) n A **deckchair** is a simple chair with a folding frame, and a piece of canvas as the seat and back. Deckchairs are usually used on the beach, on a ship, or in the garden. ডেক চেয়ার

declare (**declares, declaring, declared**) vt If you **declare** that something is the case, you say that it is true in a firm, deliberate way. (written) ঘোষনা করা

decorate (**decorates, decorating, decorated**) vt If you **decorate** something, you make it more attractive by adding things to it. সাজানো

decorator (**decorators**) n A **decorator** is a person whose job is to paint houses or put wallpaper up. যে ঘরবাড়ি সাজায়

decrease (**decreases, decreasing, decreased**) n A **decrease** is a reduction in the quantity or size of something. হ্রাস ▷ v When something **decreases**, or when you **decrease** it, it becomes less in quantity, size, or intensity. হ্রাস পাওয়া

dedicated adj If you describe a person as **dedicated**, you mean that they are devoted to a particular purpose or cause. উৎসর্গিত

dedication n **Dedication** is the state of being devoted to a particular purpose or cause. উৎসর্গ

deduct (**deducts, deducting, deducted**) vt When you **deduct** an amount from a total, you subtract it from the total. কেটে নেওয়া

deep (**deeper, deepest**) adj If something is **deep**, it extends a long way down from the ground or from the top surface of something. গভীর

deep-fry (**deep-fries, deep-frying, deep-fried**) vt If you **deep-fry** food, you fry it in a large amount of fat or oil. ছাঁকা তেলে ভাজা

deeply adv **Deeply** means seriously, strongly, or to a great degree. গভীরভাবে

deer (**deer**) n A **deer** is a large wild animal. Male deer usually have large, branching horns. হরিণ

defeat (**defeats, defeating, defeated**) n **Defeat** is the state of being beaten in a battle, game, or contest, or of failing to achieve what you wanted to. পরাজয় ▷ vt If you **defeat** someone, you win a victory over them in a battle or contest. পরাজিত করা

defect (**defects**) n A **defect** is a fault or imperfection in a person or thing. ত্রুটি

defence n **Defence** is action taken to protect someone or something from attack. প্রতিরক্ষা

defend (**defends, defending, defended**) vt If you **defend** someone or something, you take action to protect them. রক্ষা করা

defendant (**defendants**) n The **defendant** in a trial is the person accused of a crime. প্রতিবাদী

defender (**defenders**) n If you are a **defender** of a particular thing or person that has been criticized or attacked, you support that thing or person in public. রক্ষক

deficit (**deficits**) n A **deficit** is the amount by which something is less than the amount that is needed. ঘাটতি

define (**defines, defining, defined**) vt If you **define** something, you say exactly what it is or exactly what it means. অর্থ নির্ধারণ করা

definite adj If something is **definite**, it is firm and clear, and unlikely to be changed. যথার্থ

definitely adv You use **definitely** to emphasize that something is the case and will not change. নিশ্চিতভাবে

definition (**definitions**) n A **definition** of a word or term is a statement giving its meaning, especially in a dictionary. সংজ্ঞা

degree (**degrees**) n You use **degree** to indicate the extent to which something happens or is the case. মাত্রা

degree Celsius (**degrees Celsius**) n A **degree Celsius** is a unit of measurement on the Celsius scale that is used to measure temperatures. ডিগ্রী সেলসিয়াস

degree centigrade (**degrees centigrade**) n A **degree centigrade** is a unit of measurement on the centigrade scale that is used to measure temperatures. ডিগ্রী সেন্টিগ্রেড

degree Fahrenheit (**degrees Fahrenheit**) *n* A **degree Fahrenheit** is a unit of measurement on the Fahrenheit scale that is used to measure temperatures. ডিগ্রী ফারেনহিট

dehydrated *adj* When something such as food is **dehydrated**, all the water is removed from it, often in order to preserve it. নিরুদিত

delay (**delays, delaying, delayed**) *n* If there is a **delay**, something does not happen until later than planned or expected. দেরী ▷ *vt* If you **delay** doing something, you do not do it until a later time. দেরী করা

delayed *adj* If a person or thing is **delayed**, they are made late. বিলম্বিত

delegate (**delegates, delegating, delegated**) *n* A **delegate** is a person chosen to vote or make decisions on behalf of a group of people, especially at a conference or meeting. প্রতিনিধি ▷ *vt* If you **delegate** duties, responsibilities, or power to someone, you give them those duties or responsibilities or that power, so that they can act on your behalf. প্রতিনিধি নিয়োগ করা

delete (**deletes, deleting, deleted**) *vt* If you **delete** something that has been written down or stored in a computer, you cross it out or remove it. বাতিল করা

deliberate *adj* If something that you do is **deliberate**, you intended to do it. স্বেচ্ছায়

deliberately *adv* If you do something **deliberately**, you intended to do it. জেনেশুনে

delicate *adj* Something that is **delicate** is small and beautifully shaped. সূক্ষ্ম

delicatessen (**delicatessens**) *n* A **delicatessen** is a shop that sells unusual or foreign foods. মুখরোচক খাবারের দোকান

delicious *adj* **Delicious** food or drink has an extremely pleasant taste. সুস্বাদু

delight *n* **Delight** is a feeling of very great pleasure. আনন্দ

delighted *adj* If you are **delighted**, you are extremely pleased and excited about something. আনন্দিত

delightful *adj* Someone or something that is **delightful** is very pleasant. তৃপ্তিকর

deliver (**delivers, delivering, delivered**) *vt* If you **deliver** something somewhere, you take it there. প্রদান করা

delivery (**deliveries**) *n* **Delivery** is the act of bringing of letters, parcels, or goods to someone's house or office. প্রদান

demand (**demands, demanding, demanded**) *n* A **demand** is a firm request for something. দাবি ▷ *vt* If you **demand** something such as information or action, you ask for it in a very forceful way. দাবি করা

demanding *adj* A **demanding** job requires a lot of time, energy, or attention. চাহিদাপূর্ণ

demo (**demos**) *n* A **demo** is a march or gathering by a group of people to show their opposition to something or their support for something. (*informal*) প্রদর্শন

democracy *n* **Democracy** is a political system in which people choose their government by voting for them in elections. গণতন্ত্র

democratic *adj* A **democratic** country, organization, or system is governed by representatives who are elected by the people. গণতান্ত্রিক

demolish (**demolishes, demolishing, demolished**) *vt* When a building is **demolished**, it is knocked down, often because it is old or dangerous. ভূমিসাৎ করা

demonstrate (**demonstrates, demonstrating, demonstrated**) *vt* To **demonstrate** a fact or theory means to make it clear to people. প্রদর্শন করা

demonstration (**demonstrations**) *n* A **demonstration** of something is the act of making it clear to people. প্রদর্শন

demonstrator (**demonstrators**) *n* **Demonstrators** are people who are

d

marching or gathering somewhere to show their opposition to something or their support for something. প্রদর্শনকারী

denim n **Denim** is a thick cotton cloth used to make clothes. Jeans are made from denim. সুতির কাপড়

denims npl **Denims** are casual trousers made of denim. সুতির কাপড়ের প্যান্ট

Denmark n **Denmark** is a kingdom in north Europe, between the Baltic and the North Sea. ডেনমার্ক

dense (**denser, densest**) adj Something that is **dense** contains a lot of things or people in relation to its size. ঘন

density (**densities**) n The **density** of something is the extent to which it fills a place. ঘনত্ব

dent (**dents, denting, dented**) n A **dent** is a hollow in the surface of something which has been caused by hitting or pressing it. টোল খাওয়ানো ▷ vt If you **dent** something, you damage it by hitting or pressing it, causing a hollow dip to form in it. টোল খাওয়া

dental adj **Dental** is used to describe things relating to teeth. দন্ত বিষয়ক

dental floss n **Dental floss** is a type of thread that is used to clean the gaps between your teeth. দাঁতের সুতো

dentist (**dentists**) n A **dentist** is a person qualified to treat people's teeth. দন্ত-চিকিৎসক

dentures npl **Dentures** are artificial teeth. কৃত্রিম দাঁত

deny (**denies, denying, denied**) vt If you **deny** something, you say that it is not true. অস্বীকার করা

deodorant (**deodorants**) n **Deodorant** is a substance that you put on your body to reduce or hide the smell of perspiration. দুর্গন্ধনাশক

depart (**departs, departing, departed**) vi To **depart** from a place means to leave it and start a journey to another place. প্রস্থান করা

department (**departments**) n A **department** is one of the sections of a large shop or organization such as a university. বিভাগ

department store (**department stores**) n A **department store** is a large shop which sells many different kinds of goods. বিভাজিত বিপণী

departure (**departures**) n **Departure** is the act of leaving a place or a job. প্রস্থান

departure lounge (**departure lounges**) n In an airport, the **departure lounge** is the place where passengers wait before they get onto their plane. প্রস্থানের জায়গা

depend (**depends, depending, depended**) vi If you say that one thing **depends** on another, you mean that the first thing will be affected or decided by the second. নির্ভর করা

deport (**deports, deporting, deported**) vt If a government **deports** someone, it sends them out of the country. দেশান্তরে পাঠানো

deposit (**deposits**) n A **deposit** is a sum of money given as part payment for something, or as security when you rent something. জমা

depressed adj If you are **depressed**, you are sad and feel you cannot enjoy anything, because your situation is difficult and unpleasant. মনখারাপ

depressing adj Something that is **depressing** makes you feel sad and disappointed. মানসিক বিষন্নতা

depression (**depressions**) *n* Depression is a mental state in which someone feels unhappy and has no energy or enthusiasm. মানসিক বিষণ্ণ

depth (**depths**) *n* The depth of something such as a hole is the distance between its top and bottom surfaces. গভীরতা

deputy head (**deputy heads**) *n* The deputy head of a school is the second most important person after the head teacher. সহকারী প্রধান

descend (**descends, descending, descended**) *v* If you descend, or if you descend something, you move downwards. (*formal*) অবরোহণ করা

describe (**describes, describing, described**) *vt* If you describe someone or something, you say what they are like. বর্ণনা করা

description (**descriptions**) *n* A description of someone or something is a statement which explains what they are or what they look like. বিবরণ

desert (**deserts**) *n* A desert is a large area of land, usually in a hot region, which has almost no water, rain, trees, or plants. মরুভূমি

desert island (**desert islands**) *n* A desert island is a small tropical island, where nobody lives. জনমানবহীন দ্বীপ

deserve (**deserves, deserving, deserved**) *vt* If you say that someone deserves something, you mean that they should have it or do it because of their qualities or actions. যোগ্য হওয়া

design (**designs, designing, designed**) *n* Design is the process and art of planning and making detailed drawings of something. পরিকল্পনা ▷ *vt* When someone designs a garment, building, machine, or other object, they plan it and make a detailed drawing of it from which it can be built or made. পরিকল্পনা করা

designer (**designers**) *n* A designer is a person whose job involves planning the form of a new object. পরিকল্পক

desire (**desires, desiring, desired**) *n* A desire is a strong wish to do or have something. আকাঙ্ক্ষা ▷ *vt* If you desire something, you want it. আকাঙ্ক্ষিত হওয়া

desk (**desks**) *n* A desk is a table which you sit at in order to write or work. ডেস্ক

despair *n* Despair is the feeling that everything is wrong and that nothing will improve. হতাশা

desperate *adj* If you are desperate, you are in such a bad situation that you will try anything to change it. মরিয়া

desperately *adv* If you do something desperately, you are in such a bad situation that you are willing to try anything to achieve it. মরিয়া ভাবে

despise (**despises, despising, despised**) *vt* If you despise someone or something, you hate them very much. হেলাফেলা করা

despite *prep* If you say that one thing is true despite another thing, it's a surprise to you that the first thing is true. সত্ত্বেও *The party was fun, despite the rain.*

dessert (**desserts**) *n* Dessert is something sweet, such as fruit or a pudding, that you eat at the end of a meal. আইসক্রিম

dessert spoon (**dessert spoons**) *n* A dessert spoon is a spoon which is midway between the size of a teaspoon and a tablespoon. You use it to eat desserts. আইসক্রিম খাওয়ার চামচ

destination (**destinations**) *n* Your destination is the place you are going to. গন্তব্যস্থান

destiny (**destinies**) *n* A person's destiny is everything that happens to them during their life, including what will happen in the future. নিয়তি

destroy (**destroys, destroying, destroyed**) *vt* To destroy something means to cause so much damage to it that it is completely ruined or does not exist any more. ধ্বংস করে দেওয়া

destruction n **Destruction** is the act of destroying something, or the state of being destroyed. ধ্বংস

detached house (**detached houses**) n A **detached house** is one that is not joined to any other house. বিছিন্ন বাড়ী

detail (**details**) n The **details** of something are its small, individual features or elements. If you examine or discuss something **in detail**, you examine all these features. বিশদ

detailed adj A **detailed** report or plan contains a lot of details. বিস্তারিত

detective (**detectives**) n A **detective** is someone whose job is to discover the facts about a crime or other situation. গোয়েন্দা

detention (**detentions**) n **Detention** is the arrest or imprisonment of someone, especially for political reasons. আটক

detergent (**detergents**) n **Detergent** is a chemical substance used for washing things such as clothes or dishes. কাপড় কাচার পাউডার

deteriorate (**deteriorates, deteriorating, deteriorated**) vi If something **deteriorates**, it becomes worse. ক্রমশ অবনতি হওয়া

determined adj If you are **determined** to do something, you have made a firm decision to do it and will not let anything stop you. দৃঢ়প্রতিজ্ঞ

detour (**detours**) n If you make a **detour** on a journey, you go by a route which is not the shortest way. আঁকাবাঁকা পথ

devaluation (**devaluations**) n **Devaluation** is an official reduction in the value of a currency. মুদ্রাহ্রাস

devastated adj If you are **devastated** by something, you are very shocked and upset by it. নাশকতা

devastating adj You describe something as **devastating** when it is very damaging or upsetting. নাশকতামূলক

develop (**develops, developing, developed**) vt When someone **develops** something, the thing grows or changes over a period of time and usually becomes more advanced or complete. বানানো ▷ vi When someone or something **develops**, the person or thing grows or changes over a period of time and usually becomes more advanced or complete. প্রকাশিত করা

developing country (**developing countries**) n A **developing country** is a poor country that does not have many industries. উন্নয়নশীল দেশ

development n **Development** is the gradual growth or formation of something. উন্নতি

device (**devices**) n A **device** is an object that has been made for a particular purpose. যন্ত্র

Devil n In Christianity, Judaism, and Islam, **the Devil** is the most powerful evil spirit. শয়তান

devise (**devises, devising, devised**) vt If you **devise** something, you have the idea for it and design it. উদ্ভাবন করা

devoted adj If you are **devoted** to someone or something, you care about them or love them very much. উৎসর্গীকৃত

diabetes n **Diabetes** is a condition in which someone's body is unable to control the level of sugar in their blood. ডায়াবেটিস

diabetic (**diabetics**) adj **Diabetic** means of, relating to, or having diabetes. বহুমূত্র সংক্রান্ত ▷ n A **diabetic** is a person who suffers from diabetes. বহুমূত্র রোগী

diagnosis (**diagnoses**) n **Diagnosis** is identifying what is wrong with someone who is ill or with something that is not working properly. রোগ নির্ণয়

diagonal adj A **diagonal** line or movement goes in a slanting direction. কোনাকুনি

diagram (**diagrams**) n A **diagram** is a drawing which is used to explain something. রেখাচিত্র

dial (**dials, dialling, dialled**) v If you **dial**, or if you **dial** a number, you turn the dial or press the buttons on a telephone. ডায়াল করা

dialect (**dialects**) *n* A **dialect** is a form of a language spoken in a particular area. উপভাষা

dialling code (**dialling codes**) *n* A **dialling code** for a particular city or region is the series of numbers that you have to dial before a particular telephone number if you are making a call to that place from a different area. ডায়াল করার কোড

dialling tone (**dialling tones**) *n* The **dialling tone** is the noise which you hear when you pick up a telephone receiver and which means that you can dial the number you want. ডায়ালিং টোন

dialogue (**dialogues**) *n* Dialogue is communication or discussion between people or groups. সংলাপ

diameter (**diameters**) *n* The **diameter** of a circle or sphere is the length of a straight line through the middle of it. ব্যাস

diamond (**diamonds**) *n* A **diamond** is a kind of jewel that is hard, clear, and shiny. হিরে ▷ *n* A **diamond** is a shape with four straight sides. সমচতুর্ভুজ

diarrhoea *n* When someone has **diarrhoea**, a lot of liquid waste material comes out of their bowels because they are ill. পেট খারাপ

diary (**diaries**) *n* A **diary** is a notebook with a separate space for each day of the year. ডায়েরী

dice (**dice, die**) *npl* Dice are small cubes with one to six spots on each face, used in games. ছক্কা

dictation *n* Dictation is the speaking or reading aloud of words for someone else to write down. শ্রুতলিপি

dictator (**dictators**) *n* A **dictator** is a ruler who has complete power in a country; used showing disapproval. একনায়ক

dictionary (**dictionaries**) *n* A **dictionary** is a book in which the words and phrases of a language are listed, usually in alphabetical order, together with their meanings or their translations in another language. অভিধান

die (**dies, dying, died**) *vi* When people, animals, or plants **die**, they stop living. মারা যাওয়া

diet (**diets, dieting, dieted**) *n* Your **diet** is the type and range of food that you regularly eat. খাবার ▷ *vi* If you **are dieting**, you eat special kinds of food or you eat less food than usual because you are trying to lose weight. খাদ্যসংযম করা

difference (**differences**) *n* The **difference** between things is the way in which they are different from each other. পার্থক্য

different *adj* If two things are **different**, they are not like each other. আলাদা

difficult *adj* If something is **difficult**, it is not easy to do or to understand. কঠিন

difficulty (**difficulties**) *n* A **difficulty** is a problem. অসুবিধা

dig (**digs, digging, dug**) *v* When people or animals **dig**, they make a hole in the ground or in a pile of stones or debris. খোঁড়া

digest (**digests, digesting, digested**) v
When food **digests** or when you **digest** it, it
passes through your body to your stomach.
Your stomach removes the substances that
your body needs and gets rid of the rest.
হজম করা

digestion n **Digestion** is the process of
digesting food. হজম

digger (**diggers**) n A **digger** is a machine
that is used for digging. খনক যন্ত্র

digital adj **Digital** systems record or
transmit information in the form of
thousands of very small signals. ডিজিটাল

digital camera (**digital cameras**) n A
digital camera is a camera that produces
digital images that can be stored on a
computer. ডিজিটাল ক্যামেরা

digital radio n **Digital radio** is radio in
which the signals are transmitted in digital
form and decoded by the radio receiver.
ডিজিটাল রেডিও

digital television n **Digital television**
is television in which the signals are
transmitted in digital form and decoded by
the television receiver. ডিজিটাল টেলিভিশন

digital watch (**digital watches**) n A
digital watch gives information by
displaying numbers rather than by having a
pointer which moves round a dial. ডিজিটাল
ঘড়ি

dignity n If someone behaves with
dignity, they are serious, calm, and
controlled. মর্যাদা

dilemma (**dilemmas**) n A **dilemma** is
a difficult situation in which you have to
choose between two or more alternatives.
উভয় সংকট

dilute (**dilutes, diluting, diluted**) v If a
liquid **is diluted**, it is mixed with water or
another liquid, and becomes weaker. পাতলা
করা ▷ adj A **dilute** liquid is very thin and
weak, usually because it has had water
added to it. পাতলা

dim (**dimmer, dimmest**) adj **Dim** light is
not bright. You can also say that something

is **dim** when the light is not bright enough
to see very well. অস্পষ্ট

dimension (**dimensions**) n A particular
dimension of something is a particular
aspect of it. দিক

diminish (**diminishes, diminishing,
diminished**) v When something
diminishes, its importance, size, or intensity
is reduced. কমে যাওয়া

din n A **din** is a very loud and unpleasant
noise that lasts for some time. হট্টগোল

diner (**diners**) n A **diner** is a small cheap
restaurant that is open all day. (US) ডাইনার

dinghy (**dinghies**) n A **dinghy** is a small
boat that you sail or row. ডিঙিনৌকো

dining car (**dining cars**) n A **dining car** is
a carriage on a train where passengers can
have a meal. খাবার বওয়ার গাড়ী

dining room (**dining rooms**) n The **dining
room** is the room in a house or hotel where
people have their meals. খাবার ঘর

dinner (**dinners**) n **Dinner** is the main
meal of the day, eaten in the evening.
নৈশভোজ

dinner jacket (**dinner jackets**) n A **dinner
jacket** is a jacket, usually black, worn by
men for formal social events. ডিনার জ্যাকেট

dinner party (**dinner parties**) n A **dinner
party** is a social event where a small group
of people are invited to have dinner and
spend the evening at someone's house.
ডিনার পার্টি

dinner time n **Dinner time** is the period of
the day when most people have their main
meal of the day, usually in the evening.
ডিনারের সময়

dinosaur (**dinosaurs**) n **Dinosaurs** were
large reptiles which lived in prehistoric
times. ডায়নোসর

dip (**dips, dipping, dipped**) n A **dip** is
a thick creamy sauce. You dip pieces of
raw vegetable or biscuits into the sauce
and then eat them. সস ▷ vt If you **dip**
something into a liquid, you put it in and
then quickly take it out again. ডোবানো

diploma (diplomas) n A **diploma** is a qualification which may be awarded to a student by a university, college, or high school. ডিপ্লোমা

diplomat (diplomats) n A **diplomat** is a senior official, usually based at an embassy, who negotiates with another country on behalf of his or her own country. কূটনীতিক

diplomatic adj **Diplomatic** means relating to diplomacy and diplomats. কূটনৈতিক

dipstick (dipsticks) n A **dipstick** is a metal rod with marks along one end. It is used to measure the amount of liquid in a container, especially the amount of oil in a car engine. ডিপস্টিক

direct (directs, directing, directed) adj **Direct** means moving towards a place or object, without changing direction and without stopping, for example in a journey. সরাসরি ▷ vt If you **direct** something at a particular thing, you aim or point it at that thing. নির্দেশ দেওয়া

direct debit (direct debits) n If you pay a bill by **direct debit**, you give permission for the company who is owed money to transfer the correct amount from your bank account into theirs, usually every month. ডাইরেক্ট ডেবিট

direction (directions) n A **direction** is the way that you go to get to a place. দিক

directions npl **Directions** are words or pictures that show you how to do something, or how to get somewhere. নির্দেশ

directly adv If you go somewhere **directly**, you go there without changing direction and without stopping. সরাসরিভাবে

director (directors) n The **director** of a play, film, or television programme is the person who decides how it will appear on stage or screen, and who tells the actors and technical staff what to do. পরিচালক

directory (directories) n A **directory** is a book which gives lists of information

such as people's names, addresses, and telephone numbers. তথ্যপঞ্জিকা

directory enquiries npl **Directory enquiries** is a service which you can telephone to find out someone's telephone number. তথ্য অনুসন্ধান

dirt n If there is **dirt** on something, there is dust, mud, or a stain on it. ধুলো

dirty (dirtier, dirtiest) adj If something is **dirty**, it is marked or covered with stains, spots, or mud, and needs to be cleaned. ময়লা

disability (disabilities) n A **disability** is a physical or mental condition that restricts the way someone can live their life. অক্ষমতা

disabled adj Someone who is **disabled** has an illness, injury, or condition that tends to restrict the way that they can live their life, especially by making it difficult for them to move about. অক্ষম

disadvantage (disadvantages) n A **disadvantage** is a part of a situation which causes problems. অসুবিধা

disagree (disagrees, disagreeing, disagreed) vi If you **disagree** with someone, you have a different opinion to them about something. অসম্মত হওয়া

disagreement (disagreements) n **Disagreement** means objecting to something. অসম্মতি

disappear (disappears, disappearing, disappeared) vi If someone or something **disappears**, they go where they cannot be seen or found. অন্তর্হিত হওয়া

disappearance (disappearances) n If you refer to someone's **disappearance**, you are referring to the fact that nobody knows where they have gone. অন্তর্ধান

disappoint (disappoints, disappointing, disappointed) vt If things or people **disappoint** you, they are not as good as you had hoped, or do not do what you hoped they would do. নিরাশ করা

disappointed adj If you are **disappointed**, you are sad because something has not happened or because something is not as good as you hoped it would be. নিরাশ

disappointing *adj* Something that is **disappointing** is not as good or as large as you hoped it would be. নিরাশাজনক

disappointment *n* **Disappointment** is the state of feeling sad because something has not happened or because something is not as good as you hoped it would be. অসফল

disaster (**disasters**) *n* A **disaster** is a very bad accident such as an earthquake or a plane crash. প্রাকৃতিক দুর্যোগ

disastrous *adj* Something that is **disastrous** has extremely bad consequences and effects or is very unsuccessful. সর্বনাশা

disc (**discs**) *n* A **disc** is a flat, circular shape or object. ডিস্ক

discipline *n* **Discipline** is the practice of making people obey rules or standards of behaviour, and punishing them when they do not. অনুশাসন

disc jockey (**disc jockeys**) *n* A **disc jockey** is someone who plays and introduces pop records on the radio or at a club. ডিস্ক জকি

disclose (**discloses, disclosing, disclosed**) *vt* If you **disclose** new or secret information, you tell it to someone. প্রকাশ করা

disco (**discos**) *n* A **disco** is a place or event where people dance to pop music. ডিস্কো

disconnect (**disconnects, disconnecting, disconnected**) *vt* To **disconnect** a piece of equipment means to detach it from its source of power. বিচ্ছিন্ন করা

discount (**discounts**) *n* A **discount** is a reduction in the price of something. ছাড়

discourage (**discourages, discouraging, discouraged**) *vt* If someone or something **discourages** you, they cause you to lose your enthusiasm about doing something. নিরুত্ত করা

discover (**discovers, discovering, discovered**) *vt* If you **discover** something

that you did not know about before, you become aware of it or learn it. আবিষ্কার করা

discretion *n* **Discretion** is the quality of behaving in a quiet and controlled way without attracting attention or giving away private information. (*formal*) বিচক্ষণতা

discrimination *n* **Discrimination** is the practice of treating one person or group of people less fairly or less well than other people or groups. বৈষম্য

discuss (**discusses, discussing, discussed**) *vt* If people **discuss** something, they talk about it, often in order to reach a decision. আলোচনা করা

discussion (**discussions**) *n* If there is **discussion** about something, people talk about it, often in order to reach a decision. আলোচনা

disease (**diseases**) *n* A **disease** is an illness which affects people, animals, or plants. রোগ

disgraceful *adj* If you say that something is **disgraceful**, you disapprove of it strongly জঘন্য

disguise (**disguises, disguising, disguised**) *vt* If you **disguise** yourself, you put on clothes which make you look like someone else or alter your appearance in other ways, so that people will not recognize you. ছদ্মবেশ ধারণ করা

disgusted *adj* If you are **disgusted**, you have a strong feeling of dislike or disapproval. বিরক্ত

disgusting *adj* If you say that something is **disgusting**, you think it is extremely unpleasant or unacceptable. বিরক্তিকর

dish (**dishes**) *n* A **dish** is a shallow container used for cooking or serving food. ডিশ

dishcloth (**dishcloths**) *n* A **dishcloth** is a cloth used to dry dishes after they have been washed. ডিশ মোছার কাপড়

dishonest *adj* If you say someone is **dishonest**, you mean that they are not honest and you cannot trust them. অসৎ

dish towel (**dish towels**) n A **dish towel** is a cloth used to dry dishes after they have been washed. ডিশ তোয়ালে

dishwasher (**dishwashers**) n A **dishwasher** is an electrically operated machine that washes and dries plates, saucepans, and cutlery. ডিসওয়াশার

disinfectant (**disinfectants**) n **Disinfectant** is a substance that kills germs. জীবাণুনাশক

disk (**disks**) n In a computer, the **disk** is the part where information is stored. ডিক্স

disk drive (**disk drives**) n The **disk drive** on a computer is the part that contains the hard disk or into which a disk can be inserted. ডিক্স ড্রাইভ

diskette (**diskettes**) n A **diskette** is a small magnetic disk that used to be used for storing computer data and programs. ডিক্সেট

dislike (**dislikes, disliking, disliked**) vt If you **dislike** someone or something, you consider them to be unpleasant and do not like them. অপছন্দ করা

dismal adj Something that is **dismal** is depressingly bad. হতাশাজনক

dismiss (**dismisses, dismissing, dismissed**) vt If you **dismiss** something, you decide that it is not important enough for you to think about. খারিজ করা

disobedient adj If you are **disobedient**, you deliberately do not do what someone in authority tells you to do, or what a rule or law says that you should do. অবাধ্য

disobey (**disobeys, disobeying, disobeyed**) v When someone **disobeys** a person or an order, they deliberately do not do what they have been told to do. অমান্য করা

dispenser (**dispensers**) n A **dispenser** is a machine or container from which you can get things. পরিবেশক

display (**displays, displaying, displayed**) n **Display** is the act of exhibiting or showing something. প্রদর্শনী ▷ vt If you

display something that you want people to see, you put it in a particular place, so that people can see it easily. প্রদর্শন করা

disposable adj **Disposable** things are designed to be thrown away after use. নিষ্পত্তিযোগ্য

disqualify (**disqualifies, disqualifying, disqualified**) vt When someone **is disqualified** from an event or an activity, they are officially stopped from taking part in it. অনুপযুক্ত ঘোষণা করা

disrupt (**disrupts, disrupting, disrupted**) vt If someone or something **disrupts** an event or process, they cause problems that prevent it from continuing normally. ব্যাহত করা

dissatisfied adj If you are **dissatisfied** with something, you are not content or pleased with it. অসন্তুষ্ট

dissolve (**dissolves, dissolving, dissolved**) v If a substance **dissolves** in liquid, or if you **dissolve** a substance, it mixes with the liquid, becoming weaker until it finally disappears. দ্রবীভূত হওয়া

distance (**distances**) n The **distance** between two places is the amount of space between them. দূরত্ব

distant adj **Distant** means far away. দূরে

distillery (**distilleries**) n A **distillery** is a place where whisky or a similar strong alcoholic drink is made by a process of distilling. ভাটিখানা

distinction (distinctions) n A **distinction** is a difference between similar things. পার্থক্য

distinctive adj Something that is **distinctive** has special qualities that make it easily recognizable. আলাদা

distinguish (distinguishes, distinguishing, distinguished) v If you can **distinguish** one thing from another, you can see or understand the difference between them. পার্থক্য নির্দেশ করা

distract (distracts, distracting, distracted) vt If something **distracts** you, or if it **distracts** your attention, it stops you concentrating. অমনোযোগী করা

distribute (distributes, distributing, distributed) vt If you **distribute** things, you hand them or deliver them to a number of people. বিলি করা

distributor (distributors) n A **distributor** is a company that supplies goods to shops or other businesses. বিতরণকারী

district (districts) n A **district** is an area of a town or country. জেলা

disturb (disturbs, disturbing, disturbed) vt If you **disturb** someone, you interrupt what they are doing and cause them inconvenience. বিরক্ত করা

ditch (ditches, ditching, ditched) n A **ditch** is a long narrow channel cut into the ground at the side of a road or field. খাদ ▷ vt If you **ditch** something, you get rid of it. ফেলে দেওয়া

dive (dives, diving, dived) n A **dive** is a headlong plunge into water, especially one of several formalized movements made as a sport. ডুব ▷ vi If you **dive** into some water, you jump in head-first with your arms held straight above your head. ডুব দেওয়া

diver (divers) n A **diver** is a person who swims under water using special breathing equipment. ডুবুরি

diversion (diversions) n A **diversion** is a special route arranged for traffic when the normal route cannot be used. পরিবর্তিত গতিপথ

divide (divides, dividing, divided) vt If you **divide** something, you make it into smaller pieces. টুকরো করা ▷ vt When you **divide** numbers, you see how many times one number goes into another number. ভাগ করা

diving n **Diving** is the activity of working or looking around underwater, using special breathing equipment. ডুব

diving board (diving boards) n A **diving board** is a board high above a swimming pool from which people can dive into the water. ডাইভিং বোর্ড

division n The **division** of something is the act of separating it into two or more different parts. ভাগ

divorce (divorces) n A **divorce** is the formal ending of a marriage by law. বিবাহবিচ্ছেদ

divorced adj Someone who is **divorced** from their former husband or wife has separated from them and is no longer legally married to them. বিবাহ-বিচ্ছিন্ন

DIY abbr **DIY** is the activity of making or repairing things in your home. **DIY** is an abbreviation for 'do-it-yourself'. বাড়িতে নিজে নিজে করা

dizzy (dizzier, dizziest) adj If you feel **dizzy**, you feel that you are losing your balance and are about to fall. মাথা ঘোরা

DJ (DJs) abbr A **DJ** is someone who plays and introduces pop records on the radio or at a club. ডিজে

DNA n **DNA** is a chemical that is found in all living cells. It contains genetic information. **DNA** is an abbreviation for 'deoxyribonucleic acid'. ডি এন এ

do (does, doing, did, done) vt If you **do** something, you spend some time on it or finish it. করা I tried to do some work.

dock (docks) *n* A **dock** is an enclosed area of water where ships are loaded, unloaded, or repaired. পোতাশ্রয়

doctor (doctors) *n* A **doctor** is someone who is qualified in medicine and treats people who are ill. ডাক্তার

document (documents) *n* A **document** is an official piece of paper with writing on it. নথিপত্র

documentary (documentaries) *n* A **documentary** is a radio or television programme or a film which provides factual information about a particular subject. তথ্যচিত্র

documentation *n* **Documentation** consists of documents which provide a record of something. তথ্যাবলী

documents *npl* **Documents** are official pieces of paper with writing on them. দলিল

dodge (dodges, dodging, dodged) *vi* If you **dodge** somewhere, you move there suddenly to avoid being hit, caught, or seen. লুকিয়ে পড়া

dog (dogs) *n* A **dog** is an animal that is often kept as a pet or used to guard or hunt things. কুকুর

dole *n* The **dole** is money that is given regularly by the government to people who are unemployed. ভাতা

doll (dolls) *n* A **doll** is a child's toy which looks like a small person or baby. পুতুল

dollar (dollars) *n* The **dollar** is a unit of money in the USA, Canada, and some other countries. It is represented by the symbol $. ডলার

dolphin (dolphins) *n* A **dolphin** is a mammal with fins and a pointed nose which lives in the sea. ডলফিন

domestic *adj* **Domestic** political activities and decisions happen or exist within one particular country. দেশী

Dominican Republic *n* The **Dominican Republic** is a republic in the Caribbean, on the eastern side of the island of Hispaniola. ডমিনিক প্রজাতন্ত্র

domino (dominoes) *n* A **domino** is a small rectangular block marked with two groups of spots on one side. **Dominoes** are used for playing various games. ডমিনো

dominoes *npl* **Dominoes** is a game played using small rectangular blocks, called **dominoes**, which are marked with two groups of spots on one side. ডমিনোজ

donate (donates, donating, donated) *vt* If you **donate** something to a charity or other organization, you give it to them. দান করা

done *adj* A task that is **done** has been completed. কৃত

donkey (donkeys) *n* A **donkey** is an animal like a small horse with long ears. গাধা

donor (donors) *n* A **donor** is someone who gives a part of their body or some of their blood to be used by doctors to help a person who is ill. দাতা

door (doors) *n* A **door** is a swinging or sliding piece of wood, glass, or metal, which is used to open and close the entrance to a building, room, cupboard, or vehicle. দরজা

doorbell (**doorbells**) n A **doorbell** is a bell on the outside of a house which you can ring so that the people inside know that you want to see them. দরজার বেল

door handle (**door handles**) n A **door handle** is a small round object or a lever that is attached to a door and is used for opening and closing it. দরজার হাতল

doorman (**doormen**) n A **doorman** is a man who stands at the door of a club, prevents unwanted people from coming in, and makes people leave if they cause trouble. দরজারক্ষী

doorstep (**doorsteps**) n A **doorstep** is a step on the outside of a building, in front of a door. চৌকাঠ

dormitory (**dormitories**) n A **dormitory** is a large bedroom where several people sleep. যৌথ শয়নালয়

dose (**doses**) n A **dose** of a medicine or drug is a measured amount of it. মাত্রা

dot (**dots**) n A **dot** is a very small round mark. বিন্দু

double (**doubles, doubling, doubled**) adj You use **double** to describe a pair of similar things. দুটি ▷ v When something **doubles** or when you **double** it, it becomes twice as great in number, amount, or size. দ্বিগুণ

double bass (**double basses**) n A **double bass** is the largest instrument in the violin family. You play it standing up. ডবল বাস

double glazing n If someone has **double glazing** in their house, their windows are fitted with two layers of glass. People put in double glazing in order to keep buildings warmer or to keep out noise. দু-পাল্লার কাঁচের জানালা

doubt (**doubts, doubting, doubted**) n If you feel **doubt** or **doubts** about something, you feel uncertain about it. সন্দেহ ▷ vt If you **doubt** something, or if you **doubt** whether something is true or possible, you believe that it is probably not true, genuine, or possible. সন্দেহ করা

doubtful adj Something that is **doubtful** seems unlikely or uncertain. সন্দেহজনক

dough n **Dough** is a mixture of flour and water, and sometimes also sugar and fat, which can be cooked to make bread, pastry, and biscuits. ময়দার তাল

doughnut (**doughnuts**) n A **doughnut** is a lump or ring of sweet dough cooked in hot fat. ময়দার মিষ্টি

do up v If you **do** something **up**, you fasten it. গিঁট দেওয়া She did up the buttons.

dove (**doves**) n A **dove** is a white bird that looks like a pigeon. সাদা ঘুঘু

do without v If you **do without** something, you manage or survive in spite of not having it. ছাড়া We can't do without the help of your organisation.

down adv When something moves **down**, it goes from a higher place to a lower place. নিচে

download (**downloads**) vt To **download** data means to transfer it to or from a computer along a line such as a telephone line, a radio link, or a computer network. ডাউনলোড করা

downpour (**downpours**) n A **downpour** is a heavy fall of rain. প্রবল-বর্ষণ

Down's syndrome n **Down's syndrome** is a condition that some people are born with. People who have Down's syndrome have a flat forehead and sloping eyes and lower than average intelligence. ডাউনস্ সিন্ড্রোম

downstairs adj **Downstairs** means situated on the ground floor of a building or on a lower floor than you are. নিচের তলার ▷ adv If you go **downstairs** in a building, you go down a staircase towards the ground floor. সিঁড়ি বেয়ে নিচে

doze (**dozes, dozing, dozed**) vi When you **doze**, you sleep lightly or for a short period, especially during the daytime. ঝিমানো

dozen (**dozens**) num A **dozen** means twelve. বারো

doze off *v* If you **doze off**, you fall into a light sleep. ঘুমিয়ে পড়া *She dozed off for a few moments.*

drab (**drabber, drabbest**) *adj* Something that is **drab** is dull and not attractive or exciting. ম্যাটমেটে

draft (**drafts**) *n* A **draft** is an early version of a letter, book, or speech. খসড়া

drag (**drags, dragging, dragged**) *vt* If you **drag** something or someone somewhere, you pull them there with difficulty. টেনে আনা

dragon (**dragons**) *n* In stories and legends, a **dragon** is an animal like a big lizard. It has wings and claws, and breathes out fire. ড্রাগন

dragonfly (**dragonflies**) *n* A **dragonfly** is a brightly coloured insect with a long thin body and two sets of wings. জলফড়িং

drain (**drains, draining, drained**) *n* A **drain** is a pipe that carries water or sewage away from a place, or an opening in a surface that leads to the pipe. নালী ▷ *v* If you **drain** a liquid from a place or object, you remove the liquid by causing it to flow somewhere else. If a liquid **drains** somewhere, it flows there. নিষ্কাশন করা

draining board (**draining boards**) *n* The **draining board** is the place on a sink unit where things such as cups, plates, and cutlery are put to drain after they have been washed. জল শোকানোর স্থান

drainpipe (**drainpipes**) *n* A **drainpipe** is a pipe attached to the side of a building, through which rainwater flows from the roof into a drain. বাড়ীর ছাদের পাইপ

drama (**dramas**) *n* A **drama** is a serious play for the theatre, television, or radio. নাটক

dramatic *adj* A **dramatic** change is sudden and noticeable. নাটকীয়

drastic *adj* A **drastic** course of action is extreme and is usually taken urgently. চূড়ান্ত

draught (**draughts**) *n* A **draught** is an unwelcome current of air coming into a room or vehicle. হাওয়ার দমক

draughts *npl* **Draughts** is a game for two people, played with 24 round pieces on a board. ড্রটস খেলা

draw (**draws, drawing, drew, drawn**) *v* When you **draw**, or when you **draw** something, you use pens, pencils, or crayons to make a picture. আঁকা ▷ *vi* In a game, if one person or team **draws** with another one, or if two people or teams **draw**, they finish with the same number of points. অমীমাংসিত থাকা ▷ *v* You can use **draw** to indicate that someone or something moves somewhere or is moved there. টেনে আনা

drawback (**drawbacks**) *n* A **drawback** is an aspect of something that makes it less acceptable. অসুবিধা

drawer (**drawers**) *n* A **drawer** is a part of a desk or other piece of furniture that is shaped like a rectangular box. You pull it towards you to open it. ড্রয়ার

drawing (**drawings**) *n* A **drawing** is a picture or plan made by means of lines on a surface, especially one made with a pencil or pen without the use of colour. চিত্র

drawing pin (**drawing pins**) *n* A **drawing pin** is a short pin with a broad, flat top which is used for fastening papers or pictures to a board, wall, or other surface. ড্রয়িং পিন

dreadful *adj* If you say that something is **dreadful**, you mean that it is very unpleasant or very poor in quality. ভয়ঙ্কর

dream (**dreams, dreaming, dreamed, dreamt**) *n* A **dream** is an imaginary series of events that you experience in your mind while you are asleep. স্বপ্ন ▷ *v* When you **dream**, you experience imaginary events in your mind while you are asleep. স্বপ্ন দেখা

drench (**drenches, drenching, drenched**) *vt* To **drench** something or someone means to make them completely wet. ভিজে জবজবে হওয়া

dress (**dresses, dressing, dressed**) n A **dress** is something that a girl or a woman can wear. It covers the body and part of the legs. পোশাক ▷ vi When you **dress**, you put on clothes. সাজগোজ করা

dressed adj If you are **dressed**, you are wearing clothes rather than being naked. তৈরী

dresser (**dressers**) n A **dresser** is a chest of drawers, sometimes with a mirror on the top. সাজার জায়গা

dressing gown (**dressing gowns**) n A **dressing gown** is a loose-fitting coat worn over pyjamas or other night clothes. ড্রেসিং গাউন

dressing table (**dressing tables**) n A **dressing table** is a small table in a bedroom with drawers and a mirror. ড্রেসিং টেবিল

dress up v If you **dress up**, you put on different clothes, in order to look smarter or to disguise yourself. নতুন জামা পরা You do not need to dress up for dinner.

dried adj **Dried** food or milk has had all the water removed from it so that it will last for a long time. শুকনো

drift (**drifts, drifting, drifted**) n A **drift** is a movement away from somewhere or something, or a movement towards somewhere or something different. সঞ্চারণ ▷ vi When something **drifts** somewhere, it is carried there by the wind or by water. স্রোতের টান

drill (**drills, drilling, drilled**) n A **drill** is a tool for making holes. ড্রিল ▷ v When you **drill** into something or **drill** a hole in it, you make a hole using a drill. গর্ত করা

drink (**drinks, drinking, drank, drunk**) n A **drink** is an amount of a liquid which you drink. পানীয় ▷ v When you **drink**, or **drink** a liquid, you take it into your mouth and swallow it. পান করা

drink-driving n **Drink-driving** is the offence of driving a car after drinking more

than the amount of alcohol that is legally allowed. মদ্যপান করে গাড়ী চালানো

drinking water n **Drinking water** is water which it is safe to drink. পানীয় জল

drip (**drips, dripping, dripped**) n A **drip** is a small individual drop of a liquid. ফোঁটা ▷ vi When liquid **drips** somewhere, it falls in small drops. ফোঁটা ফোঁটা করে পড়া

drive (**drives, driving, drove, driven**) n A **drive** is a journey in a vehicle such as a car. গাড়িতে ভ্রমণ ▷ v When someone **drives** a vehicle, they make it go where they want. চালানো

driver (**drivers**) n The **driver** of a vehicle is the person who is driving it. গাড়িচালক

driveway (**driveways**) n A **driveway** is a private road that leads from a public road to a house or garage. ব্যক্তিগত রাস্তা

driving instructor (**driving instructors**) n A **driving instructor** is someone who teaches a people to drive a vehicle. গাড়িচালনার শিক্ষক

driving lesson (**driving lessons**) n A **driving lesson** is a one of a course of lessons during which a person is taught how to do drive a vehicle. গাড়িচালনার পাঠক্রম

driving licence (**driving licences**) n A **driving licence** is a card showing that you are qualified to drive. গাড়িচালনার লাইসেন্স

driving test (**driving tests**) n A **driving test** is a test that must be passed before you are qualified to drive a vehicle. ড্রাইভিং টেস্ট

drizzle n **Drizzle** is light rain falling in fine drops. ঝিরঝিরে হালকা বৃষ্টি

drop (**drops, dropping, dropped**) n If there is a **drop** in something, it quickly becomes less. বিন্দু ▷ v If a level or amount **drops** or if someone or something **drops** it, it quickly becomes less. কমে যাওয়া

drought (**droughts**) n A **drought** is a long period of time during which no rain falls. খরা

drown (**drowns, drowning, drowned**) v When someone **drowns**, or when they **are**

drowned, they die because they have gone under water and cannot breathe. তলিয়ে যাওয়া

drowsy (**drowsier, drowsiest**) *adj* If you are **drowsy**, you feel sleepy and cannot think clearly. নিদ্রাচ্ছন্ন

drug (**drugs**) *n* A **drug** is a chemical substance given to people to treat or prevent an illness or disease. ওষুধ

drum (**drums**) *n* A **drum** is a musical instrument consisting of a skin stretched tightly over a round frame. ড্রাম

drummer (**drummers**) *n* A **drummer** is a person who plays a drum or drums in a band or group. ড্রামবাদক

drunk (**drunks**) *adj* If someone is **drunk**, they have consumed too much alcohol. নেশাগ্রস্ত ▷ *n* A **drunk** is someone who is drunk or who often gets drunk. মাতাল

dry (**drier, dryer, driest, dries, drying, dried**) *adj* If something is **dry**, it has no water or other liquid on it or in it. শুকনো ▷ *v* When you **dry** something, or when it **dries**, it becomes dry. শুকানো

dry cleaner (**dry cleaners**) *n* A **dry cleaner** or a **dry cleaner's** is a shop where things can be dry-cleaned. ড্রাই ক্লিনার

dry-cleaning *n* **Dry-cleaning** is the action or work of dry-cleaning things such as clothes. ড্রাই-ক্লিন করা

dryer (**dryers**) *n* A **dryer** is a machine for drying things, for example clothes or people's hair. ড্রায়ার

dual carriageway (**dual carriageways**) *n* A **dual carriageway** is a road which has two lanes of traffic travelling in each direction with a strip of grass or concrete down the middle to separate the two lots of traffic. উভগামী রাস্তা

dubbed *adj* If a film or soundtrack in a foreign language is **dubbed**, a new soundtrack is added with actors giving a translation. মূল সঙ্গীতে শব্দযোগ

dubious *adj* You describe something as **dubious** when you think it is not

completely honest, safe, or reliable. সন্দেহজনক

duck (**ducks**) *n* A **duck** is a common water bird with short legs and a large flat beak. পাতিহাঁস

due *adj* If something is **due** at a particular time, it is expected to happen or to arrive at that time. পূর্বনির্দিষ্ট তারিখ

due to *prep* If something is **due to** another thing, it is a result of that thing. কারণে *He couldn't do the job, due to pain in his hands.*

dull (**duller, dullest**) *adj* Something that is **dull** is not interesting. নীরস ▷ *adj* A **dull** colour is not bright. অনুজ্জ্বল

dumb *adj* Someone who is **dumb** is completely unable to speak. বোবা

dummy (**dummies**) *n* A **dummy** is a model of a person, often used to display clothes. নকল

dump (**dumps, dumping, dumped**) *n* A **dump** is a site provided for people to leave their rubbish. আস্তাকুঁড় ▷ *vt* If something **is dumped** somewhere, it is put there because it is no longer wanted or needed. (*informal*) আস্তাকুঁড়ে ফেলে দেওয়া

dumpling (**dumplings**) *n* **Dumplings** are small lumps of dough that are cooked and eaten, either with meat and vegetables or as part of a sweet pudding. মাংস বা সজ্বির ফুলুরি

dungarees *npl* **Dungarees** are a one-piece garment consisting of trousers, a piece of cloth which covers your chest, and straps which go over your shoulders. সুতির কাপড়

dungeon (**dungeons**) *n* A **dungeon** is a dark underground prison in a castle. অন্ধকূপ

duration *n* The **duration** of an event or state is the time that it lasts. সময়সীমা

during *prep* If something happens **during** a period of time, it happens between the beginning and the end of that period. চলাকালীন *Storms are common during the winter.*

dusk *n* **Dusk** is the time just before night when it is not yet completely dark. সন্ধ্যা

dust (**dusts, dusting, dusted**) *n* **Dust** consists of very small dry particles of earth, sand, or dirt. ধুলো ▷ *v* When you **dust** or **dust** furniture or other objects, you remove dust from them using a dry cloth. ধুলো ঝাড়া

dustbin (**dustbins**) *n* A **dustbin** is a large container for rubbish. আবর্জনা ফেলার পাত্র

dustman (**dustmen**) *n* A **dustman** is a person whose job is to empty the rubbish from people's dustbins and take it away to be disposed of. ঝাড়ুদার

dustpan (**dustpans**) *n* A **dustpan** is a small flat container made of metal or plastic. You hold it flat on the floor and put dirt and dust into it using a brush. ময়লা তোলার পাত্র

dusty (**dustier, dustiest**) *adj* Something that is **dusty** is covered with dust. ধুলোমাখা

Dutch *adj* **Dutch** means relating to or belonging to the Netherlands, or to its people, language, or culture. নেদারল্যান্ড দেশীয় ▷ *n* **Dutch** is the language spoken in the Netherlands. ডাচ ভাষা

Dutchman (**Dutchmen**) *n* A **Dutchman** is a man who is a native of the Netherlands. নেদারল্যান্ডের পুরুষ

Dutchwoman (**Dutchwomen**) *n* A **Dutchwoman** is a woman who is a native of the Netherlands. নেদারল্যান্ডের নারী

duty (**duties**) *n* **Duty** is the work that you have to do as your job. কাজ

duty-free *adj* **Duty-free** goods are sold at airports or on planes or ships at a cheaper price than usual because they are not taxed. করমুক্ত ▷ *n* **Duty-free** is goods sold at airports or on planes or ships at a cheaper

price than usual because they are not taxed. করমুক্ত জিনিষ

duvet (**duvets**) *n* A **duvet** is a large cover filled with feathers or similar material, which you use to cover yourself in bed. পালকের তৈরী লেপ

DVD (**DVDs**) *n* A **DVD** is a disc similar to a compact disc on which a film or music is recorded. **DVD** is an abbreviation for 'digital video disc' or 'digital versatile disc'. ডিভিডি

DVD burner (**DVD burners**) *n* A **DVD burner** is a piece of computer equipment that you use for copying data from a computer onto a DVD. ডিভিডি বার্ণার

DVD player (**DVD players**) *n* A **DVD player** is a machine for playing DVDs. ডিভিডি প্রেয়ার

dwarf (**dwarves**) *n* In children's stories, a **dwarf** is an imaginary creature that is like a small man. Dwarves often have magical powers. বামন

dye (**dyes, dyeing, dyed**) *n* **Dye** is a substance which is used to dye something. রং ▷ *vt* If you **dye** something, you change its colour by soaking it in a special liquid. রং করা

dynamic *adj* A **dynamic** person is full of energy; used showing approval. দৃঢ়চেতা

dyslexia *n* If someone suffers from **dyslexia**, they have difficulty with reading because of a slight disorder of their brain. ডিসলেক্সিয়া

dyslexic (**dyslexics**) *adj* If someone is **dyslexic**, they have difficulty with reading because of a slight disorder of their brain. পড়তে অসুবিধা

e

each *det* **Each** thing or person in a group means every member as an individual. প্রত্যেকটি *Each book is beautifully illustrated.* ▷ *pron* **Each** means every one. প্রত্যেক *He gave each of us a book.*

eagle (eagles) *n* An **eagle** is a large bird that hunts and kills small animals for food. ঈগল পাখি

ear (ears) *n* Your **ears** are the two parts of your body with which you hear sounds. কান

earache (earaches) *n* **Earache** is a pain in the inside part of your ear. কানে ব্যথা

eardrum (eardrums) *n* Your **eardrums** are the thin pieces of tightly stretched skin inside each ear, which vibrate when sound waves reach them. কানের পর্দা

earlier *adv* **Earlier** is used to refer to a point or period in time before the present or before the one you are talking about. পূর্বে

early (earlier, earliest) *adj* If you are **early**, you arrive before the time that you were expected to come. তাড়াতাড়ি ▷ *adv* **Early** means before the usual time that a particular event or activity happens. আগে ▷ *adj* **Early** means near the first part of something. প্রারম্ভিক

earn (earns, earning, earned) *vt* If you **earn** money, you receive it in return for work that you do. রোজগার করা

earnings *npl* Your **earnings** are the money that you earn by working. রোজগার

earphones *npl* **Earphones** are a small piece of equipment which you wear over or inside your ears so that you can listen to a radio or MP3 player without anyone else hearing. কানের গ্রাহকযন্ত্র

earplugs *npl* **Earplugs** are small pieces of a soft material which you put into your ears to keep out noise, water, or cold air. কানের প্লাগ

earring (earrings) *n* **Earrings** are pieces of jewellery which you attach to your ears. কানের দুল

earth *n* The **earth** is the planet that we live on. পৃথিবী ▷ *n* **Earth** is the soil that plants grow in. মৃত্তিকা

earthquake (earthquakes) *n* An **earthquake** is a shaking of the ground caused by movement of the earth's crust. ভূমিকম্প

easily *adv* You use **easily** to emphasize that something is very likely to happen, or is certainly true. সহজেই

east *adj* The **east** edge, corner, or part of a place or country is the part which is towards the east. পূর্ব-দিক ▷ *adv* If you go **east**, you travel towards the east. পূর্বে ▷ *n* The **east** is the direction in which you look to see the sun rise. পূর্ব-দিকে

eastbound *adj* **Eastbound** roads or vehicles lead to or are travelling towards the east. (*formal*) পূর্ব-দিকে

Easter (Easters) *n* **Easter** is a Christian festival and holiday, when the resurrection of Jesus Christ is celebrated. ইস্টার

Easter egg (Easter eggs) *n* An **Easter egg** is an egg made of chocolate that is given as a present at Easter. In some countries, Easter eggs are hidden and children then look for them. ইস্টার উৎসবের জন্য ডিম

eastern *adj* **Eastern** means in or from the east of a region or country. পূর্ব

easy (easier, easiest) *adj* If a job or action is **easy**, you can do it without difficulty. সহজ

easy chair (easy chairs) *n* An **easy chair** is a large, comfortable padded chair. আরাম কেদারা

easy-going *adj* If you describe someone as **easy-going**, you approve of the fact that that they are not easily worried or upset. অলস

eat (eats, eating, ate, eaten) *v* When you **eat**, you chew and swallow food. খাওয়া

e-book (e-books) *n* An **e-book** is a book which is produced for reading on a computer screen. **E-book** is an abbreviation for 'electronic book'. ইলেকট্রনিক-বই

eccentric *adj* If you say that someone is **eccentric**, you mean that they behave in a strange way, and have habits or opinions that are different from those of most people. অদ্ভুত

echo (echoes) *n* An **echo** is a sound caused by a noise being reflected off a surface such as a wall. প্রতিধ্বনি

ecofriendly *adj* **Ecofriendly** products or services are less harmful to the environment than other similar products or services. বাস্তুতন্ত্র যোগ্য

ecological *adj* **Ecological** means involved with or concerning ecology. বাস্তুবিদ্যা-বিষয়ক

ecology *n* **Ecology** is the study of the relationship between living things and their environment. বাস্তুতন্ত্র

e-commerce *n* **E-commerce** is the buying, selling, and ordering of goods and services using the Internet. ই-কমার্স

economic *adj* **Economic** means concerned with the organization of the money, industry, and trade of a country, region, or society. অর্থনৈতিক

economical *adj* Something that is **economical** does not require a lot of money to operate. কমদামী

economics *npl* **Economics** is the study of the way in which money, industry, and trade are organized in a society. অর্থশাস্ত্র

economist (economists) *n* An **economist** is a person who studies, teaches, or writes about economics. অর্থনীতিবিদ

economize (economizes, economizing, economized) *vi* If you **economize**, you save money by spending it very carefully. পরিমিত ব্যয় করা

economy (economies) *n* The **economy** of a country or region is the system by which money, industry, and trade are organized. অর্থব্যবস্থা

economy class *n* **Economy class** is a class of travel in aircraft, providing less luxurious accommodation than first class at a lower fare. সাধারণ শ্রেণী

ecstasy (ecstasies) *n* **Ecstasy** is a feeling of great happiness. উচ্ছ্বাস

Ecuador *n* **Ecuador** is a republic in South America, on the Pacific. ইকুয়েডর

eczema *n* **Eczema** is a skin condition which makes your skin itch and become sore and broken. চর্মরোগ

edge (edges) *n* The **edge** of something is the place or line where it stops, or the part of it that is furthest from the middle. প্রান্ত

edgy (edgier, edgiest) *adj* If you feel **edgy**, you are nervous and anxious. (*informal*) ভয়াতুর

edible *adj* If something is **edible**, it is safe to eat. ভোজ্য

edition (editions) *n* An **edition** is a particular version of a book, magazine, or newspaper that is printed at one time. সংস্করণ

editor (**editors**) n An **editor** is a person in charge of a newspaper or magazine, or a section of a newspaper or magazine, who makes decisions concerning the contents. সম্পাদক

educated adj **Educated** people have reached a high standard of learning. শিক্ষিত

education (**educations**) n **Education** means learning and teaching. শিক্ষা

educational adj **Educational** matters or institutions are concerned with or relate to education. শিক্ষাগত

eel (**eels**) n An **eel** is a fish with a long, thin body. ইল

effect (**effects**) n An **effect** is a change, reaction, or impression that is caused by something or is the result of something. প্রভাব

effective adj Something that is **effective** produces the intended results. ফলোৎপাদক

effectively adv If you do something **effectively**, you do it well and produce the results that were intended. দক্ষতার সাথে

efficient adj Something or someone that is **efficient** does a job successfully, without wasting time or energy. কার্যকরী

efficiently adv If you do something **efficiently**, you do it successfully, without wasting time or energy. দক্ষতার সাথে

effort (**efforts**) n If you make an **effort** to do something, you try hard to do it. চেষ্টা

e.g. abbr **e.g.** is an abbreviation that means 'for example'. It is used before a noun, or to introduce another sentence. অর্থাৎ

egg (**eggs**) n An **egg** is the rounded object produced by a female bird from which a baby bird later emerges. Reptiles, fish, and insects also produce eggs. ডিম

eggcup (**eggcups**) n An **eggcup** is a small container in which you put a boiled egg while you eat it. ডিম রাখার বাটি

egg white (**egg whites**) n An **egg white** is the clear liquid part of an egg, which becomes white when you cook it. ডিমের সাদা অংশ

egg yolk (**egg yolks**) n An **egg yolk** is the yellow part in the middle of the egg. ডিমের কুসুম

Egypt n **Egypt** is a republic in north-east Africa, on the Mediterranean and Red Sea. মিশর

Egyptian (**Egyptians**) adj **Egyptian** means belonging or relating to Egypt or to its people, language, or culture. মিশর দেশীয় ▷ n The **Egyptians** are the people who come from Egypt. মিশরবাসী

eight num **Eight** is the number 8. আট

eighteen (**eighteens**) num **Eighteen** is the number 18. আঠারো

eighteenth adj The **eighteenth** item in a series is the one that you count as number eighteen. অষ্টাদশীয়

eighth (**eighths**) adj The **eighth** item in a series is the one that you count as number eight. অষ্টম ▷ n An **eighth** is one of eight equal parts of something. এক-অষ্টমাংশ

eighty num **Eighty** is the number 80. আশি

Eire n **Eire** is the Gaelic name for Ireland. আয়ার

either adv You use **either** in negative sentences to mean also. এমনকি ▷ det **Either** means each. প্রতিটি The teams waited at either end of the gym. ▷ pron You can use **either** when there are two things to choose from. অনেকগুলি She wants a husband and children. I don't want either. ▷ det **Either** means one of two things or people. দুটির মধ্যে একটি You can choose either date.

either ... or conj You use **either** in front of the first of two or more alternatives, when you are stating the only possibilities or choices that there are. The other alternatives are introduced by **or**. নতুবা Sightseeing is best done either by tour bus or by bicycles.

elastic n **Elastic** is a rubber material that stretches when you pull it and returns to its original size when you let it go. স্থিতিস্থাপক

elastic band (**elastic bands**) n An **elastic band** is a thin circle of very stretchy rubber that you can put around things in order to hold them together. স্থিতিস্থাপক

Elastoplast® (**Elastoplasts**) *n* **Elastoplast** is a type of sticky tape that you use to cover small cuts on your body. এলাস্টোপ্লাস

elbow (**elbows**) *n* Your **elbow** is the joint where your arm bends in the middle. কনুই

elder *adj* The **elder** of two people is the one who was born first. বড়

elderly *adj* You use **elderly** as a polite way of saying that someone is old. বয়োজ্যেষ্ঠ

eldest *adj* The **eldest** person in a group is the one who was born before all the others. জ্যেষ্ঠ

elect (**elects, electing, elected**) *vt* When people **elect** someone, they choose that person to represent them, by voting. নির্বাচন করা

election (**elections**) *n* An **election** is a process in which people vote to choose a person or group of people to hold an official position. নির্বাচন

electorate (**electorates**) *n* The **electorate** of a country is the people there who have the right to vote in an election. নির্বাচকমণ্ডলী

electric *adj* An **electric** device works by means of electricity. বৈদ্যুতিক

electrical *adj* **Electrical** devices work by means of electricity. বৈদ্যুতিক

electric blanket (**electric blankets**) *n* An **electric blanket** is a blanket with wires inside it which carry an electric current that keeps the blanket warm. বৈদ্যুতিক কম্বল

electrician (**electricians**) *n* An **electrician** is a person whose job is to install and repair electrical equipment. তড়িৎ-বিজ্ঞানবিদ

electricity *n* **Electricity** is a form of energy used for heating and lighting, and to provide power for machines. বিদ্যুৎ শক্তি

electric shock (**electric shocks**) *n* If you get an **electric shock**, you get a sudden painful feeling when you touch something which is connected to a supply of electricity. বৈদ্যুতিক ঝটকা

electronic *adj* An **electronic** device has transistors, silicon chips, or valves which control and change the electric current passing through it. বৈদ্যুতিন

electronics *npl* You can refer to electronic devices, or the part of a piece of equipment that consists of electronic devices, as the **electronics**. ইলেকট্রনিক্স

elegant *adj* If you describe a person or thing as **elegant**, you think they are pleasing and graceful in appearance or style. জাঁকজমকপূর্ণ

element (**elements**) *n* An **element** of something is one of the parts which make up the whole thing. উপাদান

elephant (**elephants**) *n* An **elephant** is a very large animal with a long trunk. হাতি

eleven *num* **Eleven** is the number 11. এগারো

eleventh *adj* The **eleventh** item in a series is the one that you count as number eleven. একাদশ

eliminate (**eliminates, eliminating, eliminated**) *vt* To **eliminate** something means to remove it completely. (*formal*) বিলোপ করা

elm (**elms**) *n* An **elm** is a tree with broad leaves which it loses in autumn. পাতাঝরা গাছ

else *adv* You use **else** after words such as 'someone', and 'everyone', and after question words like 'what', to talk about another person, place, or thing. আর কি

elsewhere *adv* **Elsewhere** means in other places or to another place. অন্যত্র

email (**emails, emailed, emailing**) *n* **Email** is a system of sending written messages electronically from one computer to another. **Email** is an abbreviation of 'electronic mail'. ই-মেল ▷ *v* If you **email** a person, you contact them by electronic mail. ই-মেল করা

email address (**email addresses**) *n* Your **email address** is the combination of letters, numbers, and symbols that people use for sending email to you. ই-মেল ঠিকানা

embankment (embankments) n An **embankment** is a thick wall built of earth, often supporting a railway line or road. টিবি

embarrassed adj A person who is **embarrassed** feels shy, ashamed, or guilty about something. লজ্জিত হওয়া

embarrassing adj Something that is **embarrassing** makes you feel shy or ashamed. অস্বস্তিকর

embassy (embassies) n An **embassy** is a group of officials, headed by an ambassador, who represent their government in a foreign country. দূতাবাস

embroider (embroiders, embroidering, embroidered) vt If cloth is **embroidered** with a design, the design is stitched into it. সূচীশিল্পের দ্বারা সাজানো

embroidery (embroideries) n **Embroidery** consists of designs sewn onto cloth. সূচীশিল্প

emergency (emergencies) n An **emergency** is an unexpected and serious situation such as an accident, which must be dealt with quickly. জরুরী অবস্থা

emergency exit (emergency exits) n The **emergency exit** in a building or on a vehicle is a special doorway that is to be used only in an emergency. আপৎকালীন বহির্গমন

emergency landing (emergency landings) n An **emergency landing** is an occasion when a plane is forced to land, for example, because of a technical problem or bad weather. আপৎকালীন অবতরণ

emigrate (emigrates, emigrating, emigrated) vi If you **emigrate**, you leave your own country to live in another. দেশান্তরে যাওয়া

emotion (emotions) n An **emotion** is a feeling such as happiness, love, fear, anger, or hatred, which can be caused by the situation that you are in or the people you are with. আবেগ

emotional adj **Emotional** means relating to emotions and feelings. আবেগময়

emperor (emperors) n An **emperor** is a man who rules an empire. সম্রাট

emphasize (emphasizes, emphasizing, emphasized) vt To **emphasize** something means to indicate that it is particularly important or true, or to draw special attention to it. জোর দিয়ে উল্লেখ করা

empire (empires) n An **empire** is a group of countries controlled by one powerful country. সাম্রাজ্য

employ (employs, employing, employed) vt If a person or company **employs** you, they pay you to work for them. নিযুক্ত করা

employee (employees) n An **employee** is a person who is paid to work for a company or organization. কর্মচারী

employer (employers) n Your **employer** is the organization or person that you work for. কর্তৃপক্ষ

employment n If you are in **employment**, you have a paid job. চাকুরী

empty (emptier, emptiest, empties, emptying, emptied) adj An **empty** place, vehicle, or container has no people or things in it. খালি ▷ vt If you **empty** a container, or if you **empty** something out of it, you remove its contents. খালি করা

enamel n **Enamel** is a substance which can be heated and put onto metal in order to decorate or protect it. এনামেল

encourage (encourages, encouraging, encouraged) vt If you **encourage** someone, you give them confidence, for example by letting them know that what they are doing is good. উৎসাহ প্রদান করা

encouragement (encouragements) n **Encouragement** is the activity of encouraging someone. উৎসাহ

encouraging adj Something that is **encouraging** gives you hope or confidence. উৎসাহজনক

encyclopaedia (encyclopaedias) n An **encyclopaedia** is a book, set of books, or CD-ROM in which many facts are arranged for reference. বিশ্বকোষ

end (ends, ending, ended) n The **end** of
something is the last part of it. সমাপ্তি ▷ v
When a situation or activity **ends**, or when
something or someone **ends** it, it stops.
শেষ হওয়া

**endanger (endangers, endangering,
endangered)** vt To **endanger** something
or someone means to put them in a
situation where they might be harmed or
destroyed. বিপদ ডেকে আনা

ending n An **ending** is an act of bringing
to or reaching an end. সমাপ্তি

endless adj If you describe something as
endless, you mean that it lasts so long that
it seems as if it will never end. অবিরাম

enemy (enemies) n Your **enemy** is
someone who intends to harm you. শত্রু

energetic adj An **energetic** person has a
lot of energy. চঞ্চল

energy n If you have **energy**, you have
the strength to move around a lot and do
things. কর্মশক্তি ▷ n **Energy** is the power
that makes machines work. শক্তি

engaged adj Someone who is **engaged
in** or **on** a particular activity is doing it or
involved with it. (formal) কর্মরত

engaged tone (engaged tones) n An
engaged tone is a repeated single note
heard on a telephone when the number
called is already in use. ব্যস্ত থাকার টোন

engagement (engagements) n An
engagement is an arrangement that you
have made to do something at a particular
time. অঙ্গীকার

engagement ring (engagement rings) n
An **engagement ring** is a ring worn by a
woman when she is engaged to be married.
আশীর্বাদের আংটি

engine (engines) n An **engine** is a
machine that makes things like cars and
planes move. ইঞ্জিন ▷ n An **engine** is the
front part of a train that pulls it along.
রেলগাড়ির ইঞ্জিন

engineer (engineers) n An **engineer** is
a person who designs, builds, and repairs

machines, or structures such as roads,
railways, and bridges. প্রযুক্তিবিদ / ইঞ্জিনিয়ার

engineering n **Engineering** is the work
of designing and constructing machines
or structures such as roads and bridges.
প্রযুক্তিবিদ্যা / ইঞ্জিনিয়ারিং

England n **England** is the largest division
of Great Britain, bordering on Scotland and
Wales. ইংলন্ড

English adj **English** means belonging
or relating to England. ইংলন্ড দেশীয় ▷ n
English is the language spoken in Great
Britain and Ireland, the United States,
Canada, Australia, and many other
countries. ইংরাজী ভাষা

Englishman (Englishmen) n An
Englishman is a man who comes from
England. ইংরেজ

Englishwoman (Englishwomen) n An
Englishwoman is a woman who comes
from England. ইংরেজ নারী

engrave (engraves, engraving, engraved)
vt If you **engrave** something with a design
or words, you cut the design or words into
its surface. মিনা করা

enjoy (enjoys, enjoying, enjoyed) vt If you
enjoy something, it gives you pleasure and
satisfaction. আনন্দ উপভোগ করা

enjoyable adj Something that is
enjoyable gives you pleasure. উপভোগ্য

enlargement n The **enlargement** of
something is the process or result of
making it bigger. পরিবর্ধন

enormous adj **Enormous** means
extremely large in size, amount, or degree.
বিশাল

enough det If you have **enough** of
something, you have as much as you need.
যথেষ্ট I don't have enough money to buy both
books. ▷ pron **Enough** means as much as is
needed or required. যথেষ্ট Although they are
trying hard, they are not doing enough.

enquire (enquired, enquiring, enquires) v
If you **enquire** about something, you ask for
information about it. (formal) জিজ্ঞাসা করা

enquiry (enquiries) n An **enquiry** is a question which you ask in order to get information. অনুসন্ধান

ensure (ensures, ensuring, ensured) vt To **ensure** that something happens means to make certain that it happens. (formal) সুনিশ্চিত করা

enter (enters, entering, entered) v When you **enter** a place, you come or go into it. (formal) প্রবেশ করা

entertain (entertains, entertaining, entertained) v If you **entertain**, or **entertain** people, you do something that amuses or interests them. আনন্দ প্রদান করা

entertainer (entertainers) n An **entertainer** is a person whose job is to entertain audiences, for example by telling jokes, singing, or dancing. আনন্দ প্রদানকারী

entertaining adj Something that is **entertaining** is amusing or interesting. আমোদজনক

enthusiasm n **Enthusiasm** is great eagerness to do something or to be involved in something. আগ্রহ

enthusiastic adj If you are **enthusiastic** about something, you show how much you like or enjoy it by the way that you behave and talk. অত্যন্ত আগ্রহান্বিত

entire adj You use **entire** when you want to emphasize that you are referring to the whole of something. সমগ্র

entirely adv **Entirely** means completely. সম্পূর্ণভাবে

entrance (entrances) n The **entrance** of a place is the way you get into it. প্রবেশদ্বার

entrance fee (entrance fees) n An **entrance fee** is a sum of money which you pay before you go into somewhere such as a cinema or museum, or which you have to pay in order to join an organization or institution. প্রবেশ-মূল্য

entry (entries) n An **entry** is something that you complete in order to take part in a competition, for example the answers to a set of questions. প্রবেশ

entry phone (entry phones) n An **entry phone** is a type of telephone on the wall next to the entrance to a building enabling a person inside the building to speak to a person outside before opening the door. প্রবেশদ্বারে ফোন

envelope (envelopes) n An **envelope** is the rectangular paper cover in which you send a letter through the post. খাম

envious adj If you are **envious** of someone else, you envy them. ঈর্ষান্বিত

environment (environments) n Someone's **environment** is their surroundings, especially the conditions in which they grow up, live, or work. পরিবেশ

environmental adj **Environmental** means concerned with the protection of the natural world of land, sea, air, plants, and animals. পরিবেশ সুরক্ষা সংক্রান্ত

environmentally friendly adj **Environmentally friendly** products do not harm the environment. পরিবেশ অনুকূল

envy (envies, envying, envied) n **Envy** is the feeling you have when you wish you could have the same thing or quality that someone else has. ঈর্ষা ▷ vt If you **envy** someone, you wish that you had the same things or qualities that they have. ঈর্ষা করা

epidemic (epidemics) n If there is an **epidemic** of a particular disease somewhere, it spreads quickly to a very large number of people there. মহামারী

episode (episodes) n You can refer to an event or a short period of time as an

episode if you want to suggest that it is important or unusual, or has some particular quality. পর্ব

equal (equals, equalling, equalled) *adj* If two things are **equal**, or if one thing is **equal** to another, they are the same in size, number, or value. সমান ▷ *vt* To **equal** something or someone means to be as good or as great as them. সমান করা

equality *n* **Equality** is a situation or state where all the members of a society or group have the same status, rights, and opportunities. সাম্য

equalize (equalizes, equalizing, equalized) *vt* To **equalize** a situation means to give everyone the same rights or opportunities. সমান করা

equation (equations) *n* An **equation** is a mathematical statement saying that two amounts or values are the same, for example 6x4=12x2. সমীকরণ

equator *n* **The equator** is an imaginary line round the middle of the earth, halfway between the North and South poles. নিরক্ষরেখা

Equatorial Guinea *n* **Equatorial Guinea** is a republic of West Africa. নিরক্ষীয় গিনি

equipment *n* **Equipment** consists of the things such as tools or machines which are used for a particular purpose. সরঞ্জাম

equipped *adj* If someone or something is **equipped**, they are provided with the tools or equipment that are needed. সশস্ত্র

equivalent *n* If one amount or value is the **equivalent** of another, they are the same. সমমূল্য

erase (erases, erasing, erased) *vt* If you **erase** a thought or feeling, you destroy it completely so that you can no longer remember it or feel it. মুছে ফেলা

Eritrea *n* **Eritrea** is a small country in north-east Africa, on the Red Sea. এরিট্রিয়া

error (errors) *n* An **error** is a mistake. ক্রুটি

escalator (escalators) *n* An **escalator** is a moving staircase. চলমান সিঁড়ি

escape (escapes, escaping, escaped) *n* Someone's **escape** is the act of getting away from a particular place or situation. পলায়ন ▷ *vi* If you **escape** from a place, you succeed in getting away from it. পলায়ন করা

escort (escorts, escorting, escorted) *vt* If you **escort** someone somewhere, you accompany them there, usually in order to make sure that they leave a place or get to their destination. সঙ্গে নিয়ে যাওয়া

especially *adv* You use **especially** to emphasize that what you are saying applies more to one person or thing than to any others. বিশেষভাবে

espionage *n* **Espionage** is the activity of finding out the political, military, or industrial secrets of your enemies or rivals by using spies. (*formal*) গোয়েন্দাগিরি

essay (**essays**) *n* An **essay** is a piece of writing on a particular subject. প্রবন্ধ

essential *adj* Something that is **essential** is absolutely necessary. প্রয়োজনীয়

estate (**estates**) *n* An **estate** is a large area of land in the country owned by one person or organization. সম্পত্তি

estate agent (**estate agents**) *n* An **estate agent** is someone who works for a company selling houses and land. জমি বাড়ির দালাল

estate car (**estate cars**) *n* An **estate car** is a car with a long body, a door at the rear, and space behind the back seats. সংছা-গাড়ী

estimate (**estimates, estimating, estimated**) *n* An **estimate** is an approximate calculation of a quantity or value. গণনা ▷ *vt* If you **estimate** a quantity or value, you make an approximate judgment or calculation of it. গণনা করা

Estonia *n* **Estonia** is a republic in north-east Europe, on the Gulf of Finland and the Baltic. এস্টোনিয়া

Estonian (**Estonians**) *adj* **Estonian** means of, relating to, or characteristic of Estonia, its people, or their language. এস্টোনিয়া দেশীয় ▷ *n* An **Estonian** is a native or inhabitant of Estonia. এস্টোনিয়ার জনগণ ▷ *n* **Estonian** is the official language of Estonia. এস্টোনিয়ান ভাষা

etc *abbr* **etc** is used at the end of a list to show that you have not given a full list. **etc** is a written abbreviation for 'etcetera'. ইত্যাদি

eternal *adj* Something that is **eternal** lasts for ever. চিরকাল

eternity *n* **Eternity** is time without an end, or a state of existence outside time, especially the state which some people believe they will pass into after they have died. অনন্তকাল

ethical *adj* **Ethical** means relating to beliefs about right and wrong. নৈতিক

Ethiopia *n* **Ethiopia** is a state in north-east Africa, on the Red Sea. ইথিওপিয়া

Ethiopian (**Ethiopians**) *adj* **Ethiopian** means belonging or relating to Ethiopia, or to its people, language, or culture. ইথিওপিয়া দেশীয় ▷ *n* An **Ethiopian** is an Ethiopian citizen, or a person of Ethiopian origin. ইথিওপিয়ার জনগণ

ethnic *adj* **Ethnic** means relating to different racial or cultural groups of people. জনগোষ্ঠীগত

EU *abbr* **The EU** is an organization of European countries which have joint policies on matters such as trade, agriculture, and finance. **EU** is an abbreviation of 'European Union'. ই ইউ

euro (**euros**) *n* The **euro** is a unit of currency that is used by the member countries of the European Union which have joined the European Monetary union. ইউরো

Europe *n* **Europe** is the second smallest continent in the world, situated between western Asia and the Atlantic Ocean. ইউরোপ

European (**Europeans**) *adj* **European** means coming from or relating to Europe. ইউরোপীয় ▷ *n* A **European** is a person who comes from Europe. ইউরোপের জনগণ

European Union *n* **The European Union** is an organization of European countries which have joint policies on matters such as trade, agriculture, and finance. ইউরোপীয়ান ইউনিয়ন

evacuate (**evacuates, evacuating, evacuated**) *v* If people **are evacuated** from a place, they move out of it because it has become dangerous. খালি করা

eve (**eves**) *n* The **eve** of an event is the day before it, or the period of time just before it. আগের দিন

even *adj* Something that is **even** is flat and smooth. মসৃণ ▷ *adv* You use **even** to suggest that what comes just after or just before it in the sentence is surprising.

এমনকি ▷ *adj* An **even** number is a number that you can divide by two, with nothing left over. জোড়

evening (**evenings**) *n* The **evening** is the part of each day between the end of the afternoon and the time when you go to bed. সন্ধ্যাবেলা

evening class (**evening classes**) *n* An **evening class** is a course for adults that is taught in the evening rather than during the day. সান্ধ্য ক্লাস

evening dress *n* **Evening dress** consists of the formal clothes that people wear to formal occasions in the evening. সান্ধ্য পোষাক

event (**events**) *n* An **event** is something that happens. ঘটনা

eventful *adj* If you describe an event or a period of time as **eventful**, you mean that a lot of interesting, exciting, or important things have happened during it. ঘটনাবহুল

eventually *adv* **Eventually** means in the end, especially after a lot of delays, problems, or arguments. ফলত

ever *adv* **Ever** means at any time. কোনদিনও

every *adj* You use **every** to mean all the people or things in a group. প্রতিটি

everybody *pron* **Everybody** means all the people in a group, or all the people in the world. সকলেই *Everybody likes him.*

everyone *pron* **Everyone** means all the people in a group, or all the people in the world. প্রত্যেকে *Everyone knows who she is.*

everything *pron* **Everything** means all of something. সবকিছু *He told me everything that happened.*

everywhere *adv* **Everywhere** means in every place. প্রত্যেক স্থানের

evidence *n* **Evidence** is anything that makes you believe that something is true or exists. প্রামাণ্য তথ্য

evil *adj* If an act or a person is **evil**, they are morally very bad. দুষ্ট

evolution *n* **Evolution** is a process in which animals and plants slowly change over many years. বিবর্তন

ewe (**ewes**) *n* A **ewe** is an adult female sheep. ভেড়ি

exact *adj* Something that is **exact** is correct, accurate, and complete in every way. সঠিক

exactly *adv* **Exactly** means in an exact manner, accurately or precisely. যথাযতভাবে

exaggerate (**exaggerates, exaggerating, exaggerated**) *v* If you **exaggerate**, or **exaggerate** something, you make the thing that you are talking about seem bigger or more important than it actually is. বাড়ানো

exaggeration *n* **Exaggeration**, or an **exaggeration**, is the act of saying that something is bigger, worse, or more important than it really is. অতিরঞ্জন

exam (**exams**) *n* An **exam** is a formal test taken to show your knowledge of a subject. পরীক্ষা

examination (**examinations**) *n* An **examination** is a formal test taken to show your knowledge of a subject. (*formal*) পরীক্ষা

examine (**examines, examining, examined**) *vt* If you **examine** something, you look at it or consider it carefully. পরীক্ষা করা

examiner (**examiners**) *n* An **examiner** is a person who sets or marks an exam. পরীক্ষক

example (**examples**) *n* An **example** is something which represents or is typical of a particular group of things. উদাহরণ

excellent *adj* Something that is **excellent** is very good indeed. অসাধারণ

except *prep* You use **except** or **except for** to show that you are not counting something or somebody. ছাড়া *The shops are open every day except Sunday.*

exception (**exceptions**) *n* An **exception** is a situation, thing, or person that is not included in a general statement. ব্যতিক্রম

exceptional adj You use **exceptional** to describe someone or something that has a particular quality to an unusually high degree. অসাধারণ

excess baggage n On an aeroplane journey, **excess baggage** is luggage that is larger or weighs more than your ticket allows, so that you have to pay extra to take it on board. অতিরিক্ত মালপত্র

excessive adj If something is **excessive**, it is too great in amount or degree. অত্যধিক

exchange (**exchanges, exchanging, exchanged**) vt If two or more people **exchange** things of a particular kind, they give them to each other at the same time. বিনিময় করা

exchange rate (**exchange rates**) n The **exchange rate** of a country's unit of currency is the amount of another country's currency that you get in exchange for it. বিনিময় হার

excited adj If you are **excited**, you are looking forward to something eagerly. উত্তেজিত

exciting adj Something that is **exciting** makes you feel very happy or enthusiastic. উত্তেজনাপ্রবণ

exclamation mark (**exclamation marks**) n An **exclamation mark** is the punctuation mark !. বিস্ময়সূচক চিহ্ন

exclude (**excludes, excluding, excluded**) vt If you **exclude** someone from a place or activity, you prevent them from entering it or taking part in it. বহিষ্কৃত করা

excluding prep You use **excluding** before mentioning a person or thing to show that you are not including them in your statement. ছাড়া This applies to most vertebrates (excluding mammals).

exclusively adv **Exclusively** is used to refer to situations or activities that involve only the thing or things mentioned, and nothing else. একান্তভাবে

excuse (**excuses, excusing, excused**) n An **excuse** is a reason which you give in order to explain why something has been done or has not been done, or to avoid doing something. মার্জনা ▷ vt To **excuse** someone or to **excuse** their behaviour means to provide reasons for their actions, especially when other people disapprove of these actions. মার্জনা করা

execute (**executes, executing, executed**) vt To **execute** someone means to kill them as a punishment. মৃত্যুদণ্ড দেওয়া

execution (**executions**) n **Execution** is the act or process of killing someone as a punishment. মৃত্যুদণ্ড

executive (**executives**) n An **executive** is someone employed by a company at a senior level. নির্বাহক

exercise (**exercises**) n When you do **exercise**, you move your body so that you can keep healthy and strong. (formal) ব্যায়াম ▷ n An **exercise** is something you do to practise what you have learnt. অনুশীলন

exhaust (**exhausts**) n The **exhaust** or the **exhaust pipe** is the pipe which carries the gas out of the engine of a vehicle. নির্গমন পাইপ

exhausted adj If you are **exhausted**, you are very tired. ক্লান্ত

exhaust fumes npl **Exhaust fumes** are the gas or steam that is produced when the engine of a vehicle is running. নির্গত গ্যাস

exhibition (**exhibitions**) n An **exhibition** is a public display of art, products, skills, activities, etc. শিল্প-প্রদর্শনী

ex-husband (**ex-husbands**) n A woman's **ex-husband** was once her husband but is no longer her husband. প্রাক্তন স্বামী

exile n If someone is living in **exile**, they are living in a foreign country because they cannot live in their own country, usually for political reasons. নির্বাসন

exist (exists, existing, existed) *vi* If something **exists**, it is present in the world as a real thing. অস্তিত্ব

exit (exits) *n* An **exit** is a doorway through which you can leave a public building. বাইরে যাওয়ার রাস্তা

exotic *adj* Something that is **exotic** is unusual and interesting, usually because it comes from another country. বিদেশী

expect (expects, expecting, expected) *vt* If you **expect** something to happen, you believe that it will happen. অনুমান করা

expedition (expeditions) *n* An **expedition** is a journey made for a particular purpose such as exploration. অভিযান

expel (expels, expelling, expelled) *vt* If someone **is expelled** from a school or organization, they are officially told to leave because they have behaved badly. বিতাড়িত করা

expenditure (expenditures) *n* **Expenditure** is the spending of money on something, or the money that is spent on something. *(formal)* ব্যয়

expenses *npl* Your **expenses** are the money you spend while doing something in the course of your work, which will be paid back to you afterwards. খরচ

expensive *adj* If something is **expensive**, it costs a lot of money. দামী

experience (experiences) *n* **Experience** is knowledge or skill in a particular job or activity, which you have gained from doing that job or activity. অভিজ্ঞতা

experienced *adj* If you describe someone as **experienced**, you mean that they have been doing a particular job or activity for a long time, and therefore know a lot about it or are very skilful at it. অভিজ্ঞ

experiment (experiments) *n* An **experiment** is a scientific test which is done to discover what happens to something in particular conditions. পরীক্ষা

expert (experts) *n* An **expert** is a person who is very skilled at doing something or who knows a lot about a particular subject. দক্ষ

expire (expires, expiring, expired) *vi* When something such as a contract or a visa **expires**, it comes to an end or is no longer valid. শেষ হয়ে যাওয়া

expiry date (expiry dates) *n* The **expiry date** of an official document or agreement is the date after which it is no longer valid. অন্তিম তারিখ

explain (explains, explaining, explained) *vt* If you **explain** something, you give details about it or describe it so that it can be understood. ব্যাখ্যা করা

explanation (explanations) *n* If you give an **explanation**, you give reasons why something happened, or describe something in detail. ব্যাখ্যা

explode (explodes, exploding, exploded) *vi* If something such as a bomb **explodes**, it bursts with great force. বিস্ফোরণ ঘটা

exploit (exploits, exploiting, exploited) *vt* If someone **exploits** you, they unfairly use your work or ideas and give you little in return. ব্যবহার করা

exploitation *n* **Exploitation** is the act of treating someone unfairly by using their work or ideas and giving them little in return. শোষণ

explore (**explores, exploring, explored**) v If you **explore**, or **explore** a place, you travel around it to find out what it is like. আবিষ্কার করা

explorer (**explorers**) n An **explorer** is someone who travels to places about which very little is known, in order to discover what is there. অনুসন্ধানকারী

explosion (**explosions**) n An **explosion** is a sudden violent burst of energy, for example one caused by a bomb. বিস্ফোরণ

explosive (**explosives**) n An **explosive** is a substance or device that can cause an explosion. বিস্ফোরক

export (**exports, exporting, exported**) n **Export** is the selling of products or raw materials to another country. রপ্তানী ▷ v To **export** products or raw materials means to sell them to another country. রপ্তানী করা

express (**expresses, expressing, expressed**) vt When you **express** an idea or feeling, you show what you think or feel. প্রকাশ করা

expression (**expressions**) n The **expression** of ideas or feelings is the showing of them through words, actions, or art. মুখের ভাব

extension (**extensions**) n An **extension** is a new room or building which is added to an existing building. সম্প্রসারণ

extension cable (**extension cables**) n An **extension cable** is an electrical cable that is connected to the cable on a piece of equipment in order to make it reach further. এক্সটেনশন কেবল

extensive adj Something that is **extensive** covers a large area. বিশাল

extensively adv If you travel **extensively**, you cover a large physical area. বহুদূর ব্যাপী

extent n The **extent** of a situation is how great, important, or serious it is. মাত্রা

exterior adj You use **exterior** to refer to the outside parts of something, or to things that are outside something. বহিঃস্থ

external adj **External** means happening, coming from, or existing outside a place, person, or area of activity. বহিরাগত

extinct adj If a species of animals is **extinct**, it no longer has any living members. লুপ্ত

extinguisher (**extinguishers**) n An **extinguisher** is a metal cylinder which contains water or chemicals at high pressure which can put out fires. নির্বাপকযন্ত্র

extortionate adj If you describe something such as a price as **extortionate**, you are emphasizing that it is much greater than it should be. অতিরিক্ত

extra adj You use **extra** to describe an amount, person, or thing that is added to others of the same kind, or that can be added to others of the same kind. অতিরিক্ত ▷ adv You can use **extra** in front of adjectives and adverbs to emphasize the quality that they are describing. আরো বেশি

extraordinary adj An **extraordinary** person or thing has some extremely good or special quality. অসাধারণ

extravagant adj Someone who is **extravagant** spends more money than they can afford or uses more of something than is reasonable. অসংযত

extreme adj **Extreme** means very great in degree or intensity. চরম

extremely adv You use **extremely** in front of adjectives and adverbs to emphasize that the specified quality is present to a very great degree. খুব

extremism n **Extremism** is the behaviour or beliefs of people who try to bring about political change by using violent or extreme methods. চরমপন্থা

extremist (**extremists**) n If you describe someone as an **extremist**, you disapprove of them because they try to bring about political change by using violent or extreme methods. চরমপন্থী

ex-wife (**ex-wives**) *n* A man's **ex-wife** was once his wife but is no longer his wife. প্রাক্তন-স্ত্রী

eye (**eyes**) *n* Your **eyes** are the parts of your body with which you see. চোখ

eyebrow (**eyebrows**) *n* Your **eyebrows** are the lines of hair which grow above your eyes. ভ্রূ

eye drops *npl* **Eye drops** are a kind of medicine that you put in your eyes one drop at a time. চোখের ড্রপ

eyelash (**eyelashes**) *n* Your **eyelashes** are the hairs which grow on the edges of your eyelids. চোখের লোম

eyelid (**eyelids**) *n* Your **eyelids** are the two flaps of skin which cover your eyes when they are closed. চোখের পাতা

eyeliner (**eyeliners**) *n* **Eyeliner** is a special kind of pencil which some women use on the edges of their eyelids next to their eyelashes in order to look more attractive. আইলাইনার

eye shadow (**eye shadows**) *n* **Eye shadow** is a substance which you can paint on your eyelids in order to make them a different colour. আইশ্যাডো

eyesight *n* Your **eyesight** is your ability to see. চোখের দৃষ্টি

fabric (**fabrics**) *n* **Fabric** is cloth. কাপড়

fabulous *adj* You use **fabulous** to emphasize how wonderful or impressive you think something is. (*informal*) দারুণ

face (**faces, facing, faced**) *n* Your **face** is the front part of your head. মুখ ▷ *vt* To **face** a particular direction means to look directly in that direction. মুখী

face cloth (**face cloths**) *n* A **face cloth** is a small cloth made of towelling which you use for washing yourself. মুখের তোয়ালে

facial (**facials**) *adj* **Facial** is used to describe things that relate to your face. মুখমণ্ডল-সম্পর্কিত ▷ *n* A **facial** is a sort of beauty treatment in which someone's face is massaged, and creams and other substances are rubbed into it. ফেসিয়াল

facilities *npl* **Facilities** are buildings, equipment, or services that are provided for a particular purpose. সুযোগ-সুবিধা

fact (**facts**) *n* **Facts** are pieces of information which can be proved to be true. আসল কথা

factory (**factories**) *n* A **factory** is a large building where machines are used to make goods in large quantities. কারখানা

fade (**fades, fading, faded**) *v* When something **fades**, or when something **fades** it, it slowly becomes less intense in brightness, colour, or sound. বিবর্ণ হয়ে যাওয়া

fail (**fails, failing, failed**) *v* If you **fail** or **fail** to do something that you were trying to do, you do not succeed in doing it. অকৃতকার্য হওয়া

failure (failures) *n* **Failure** is a lack of success in doing or achieving something. অকৃতকার্য

faint (fainter, faintest, faints, fainting, fainted) *adj* Something that is **faint** is not strong or intense. আবছা ▷ *vi* If you **faint**, you lose consciousness for a short time, especially because you are hungry, or because of pain, heat, or shock. অজ্ঞান হওয়া

fair (fairer, fairest, fairs) *adj* If something is **fair**, it seems right because it is the same for everyone. ন্যায্য ▷ *adj* **Fair** hair is pale yellow in colour. ফ্যাকাশে ▷ *n* A **fair** is a place where you can play games to win prizes, and you can ride on special, big machines for fun. মেলা

fairground (fairgrounds) *n* A **fairground** is a part of a park or field where people pay to ride on various machines for amusement or try to win prizes in games. মেলাপ্রাঙ্গন

fairly *adv* **Fairly** means to quite a large degree. ভালমত

fairness *n* **Fairness** is the quality of being reasonable, right, and just. ন্যায়পরতা

fairy (fairies) *n* A **fairy** is an imaginary creature with magical powers. পরী

fairy tale (fairy tales) *n* A **fairy tale** is a story for children involving magical events and imaginary creatures. রূপকথা

faith *n* If you have **faith** in someone or something, you feel confident about their ability or goodness. বিশ্বাস

faithful *adj* If you are **faithful** to a person, organization, or idea, you remain firm in your support for them. বিশ্বাসী

faithfully *adv* If you do something **faithfully**, you remain firm in your support for a person, organization, or idea. বিশ্বস্তভাবে

fake (fakes) *adj* A **fake** fur or a **fake** painting, for example, is a fur or painting that has been made to look valuable or genuine, usually in order to deceive people. লোকঠকানো ▷ *n* A **fake** is an object, person, or act that is not genuine. নকল

fall (falls, falling, fell, fallen) *n* A **fall** is an act of falling. পতন ▷ *vi* If a person or thing **falls**, they move towards the ground suddenly by accident. মাটিতে পড়ে যাওয়া

fall down *v* If a person or thing **falls down**, they move from an upright position, so that they are lying on the ground. নীচে পড়া *He fell down the stairs.*

fall for *v* If you **fall for** someone, you are attracted to them and start loving them. প্রেমে পড়া *I fell for him right away.*

fall out *v* If a person's hair or a tooth **falls out**, it becomes loose and separates from their body. ঝরে পড়া

false *adj* If something is **false**, it is incorrect, untrue, or mistaken. অসত্য

false alarm (false alarms) *n* When you think something dangerous is about to happen, but then discover that you were mistaken, you can say that it was a **false alarm**. ফলস্ অ্যালার্ম

fame *n* If you achieve **fame**, you become very well known. খ্যাতি

familiar *adj* If someone or something is **familiar** to you, you recognize them or know them well. পরিচিত

family (families) *n* A **family** is a group of people who are related to each other, especially parents and their children. পরিবার

famine (famines) *n* A **famine** is a serious shortage of food in a country, which may cause many deaths. দুর্ভিক্ষ

famous *adj* Someone or something that is **famous** is very well known. বিখ্যাত

fan (fans) *n* If you are a **fan** of someone or something, you admire them and are very interested in them. অনুরাগী

fanatic (fanatics) *n* If you describe someone as a **fanatic**, you disapprove of them because you consider their behaviour or opinions to be very extreme. অন্ধ ভক্ত

fan belt (**fan belts**) *n* In a car engine, the **fan belt** is the belt that drives the fan which keeps the engine cool. ফ্যান বেল্ট

fancy (**fancies, fancying, fancied, fancier, fanciest**) *vt* If you **fancy** something, you want to have it or do it. (*informal*) কল্পনা করা ▷ *adj* Something that is **fancy** is special and not ordinary. শৌখীন

fancy dress *n* **Fancy dress** is clothing that you wear to a party at which everyone tries to look like a famous person or a person from a story, from history, or from a particular profession. ফ্যান্সি ড্রেস

fantastic *adj* If you say that something is **fantastic**, you are emphasizing that you think it is very good. (*informal*) খুব সুন্দর

FAQ (**FAQs**) *abbr* **FAQ** is used especially on websites to refer to questions about a particular topic. **FAQ** is an abbreviation for 'frequently asked questions'. প্রায়শই জিজ্ঞাসিত প্রশ্ন

far (**farther, farthest**) *adj* You use **far** to refer to the part that is the greatest distance from the centre. দূর ▷ *adv* If something is **far** away, it is a long way away. দূর

fare (**fares**) *n* The **fare** is the money that you pay for a journey by bus, taxi, train, boat, or aeroplane. ভাড়া

Far East *n* In the West, the expression 'The **Far East**' is used to refer to all the countries of Eastern Asia, including China and Japan. সুদূর প্রাচ্য

farewell! *excl* **Farewell!** means the same as goodbye! বিদায়

farm (**farms**) *n* A **farm** is an area of land consisting of fields and buildings, where crops are grown or animals are raised. খামার

farmer (**farmers**) *n* A **farmer** is a person who owns or manages a farm. কৃষক

farmhouse (**farmhouses**) *n* A **farmhouse** is the main house on a farm, usually where the farmer lives. খামার-বাড়ী

farming *n* **Farming** is the activity of growing crops or keeping animals on a farm. চাষ

Faroe Islands *npl* The **Faroe Islands** are a group of 21 islands in the North Atlantic, between Iceland and the Shetland Islands. ফারো দ্বীপপুঞ্জ

fascinating *adj* If you find something **fascinating**, you find it extremely interesting. মনোমুগ্ধকর

fashion *n* **Fashion** is the area of activity that involves styles of clothing and appearance. কেতা

fashionable *adj* Something that is **fashionable** is popular or approved of at a particular time. কেতাদুরস্ত

fast (**faster, fastest**) *adj* **Fast** means happening, moving, or doing something at great speed. You also use **fast** in questions or statements about speed. দ্রুত ▷ *adv* You use **fast** to say that something happens without any delay. দ্রুতভাবে

fat (**fatter, fattest, fats**) *adj* A **fat** person has a lot of flesh on their body and weighs too much. মোটা ▷ *n* **Fat** is a substance in many foods without your body uses to produce energy. স্নেহপদার্থ

fatal *adj* A **fatal** action has undesirable results. মারাত্মক

fate *n* **Fate** is a power that some people believe controls everything that happens. ভাগ্য

father (**fathers**) *n* Your **father** is your male parent. বাবা

father-in-law (**fathers-in-law**) *n* Your **father-in-law** is the father of your husband or wife. শ্বশুর

fault *n* If a bad or undesirable situation is your **fault**, you caused it or are responsible for it. ক্রটি

faulty *adj* A **faulty** machine or piece of equipment is not working properly. ক্রটিযুক্ত

fauna *npl* Animals, especially those in a particular area, can be referred to as **fauna**. প্রাণীকুল

favour *n* If you regard something or someone with **favour**, you like or support them. আনুকূল্য

favourite (favourites) *adj* Your **favourite** thing or person of a particular type is the one you like most. অত্যন্ত প্রিয় ▷ *n* A **favourite** is a person or thing regarded with especial preference or liking. প্রিয়পাত্র

fax (faxes, faxing, faxed) *n* A **fax** or a **fax machine** is a piece of equipment used to send and receive documents electronically along a telephone line. ফ্যাক্স ▷ *vt* If you **fax** a document, you send a document from one fax machine to another. ফ্যাক্স পাঠানো

fear (fears, fearing, feared) *n* **Fear** is the unpleasant feeling of worry that you get when you think that you are in danger or that something horrible is going to happen. ভয় ▷ *vt* If you **fear** something unpleasant, you are worried that it might happen, or might have happened. ভয় পাওয়া

feasible *adj* If something is **feasible**, it can be done, made, or achieved. সম্ভবপর

feather (feathers) *n* A bird's **feathers** are the light soft things covering its body. পালক

feature (features) *n* A particular **feature** of something is an interesting or important part or characteristic of it. বৈশিষ্ট্য

February (Februaries) *n* **February** is the second month of the year in the Western calendar. ফেব্রুয়ারী

fed up *adj* Someone who is **fed up** is bored or annoyed. (*informal*) তিতিবিরক্ত হওয়া

fee (fees) *n* A **fee** is a sum of money that you pay to be allowed to do something. পারিশ্রমিক

feed (feeds, feeding, fed) *vt* If you **feed** a person or animal, you give them food. খাওয়ানো

feedback *n* When you get **feedback** on your work or progress, someone tells you how well or badly you are doing. প্রতিক্রিয়া

feel (feels, feeling, felt) *v* The way you **feel**, for example happy or sad, or cold or tired, is how you are at the time. বোধ করা ▷ *vt* If you **feel** something, you touch it with your hand to see what it is like. অনুভব করা

feeling (feelings) *n* A **feeling** is an emotion. অনুভূতি

feet *npl* Your **feet** are the parts of your body that are at the ends of your legs, and that you stand on. পদযুগল

felt *n* **Felt** is a type of thick cloth made from wool or other fibres packed tightly together. একধরণের কাপড়

felt-tip (felt-tips) *n* A **felt-tip** or a felt-tip pen is a pen which has a piece of fibre at the end that the ink comes through. ফেল্ট-টিপ পেন

female (females) *adj* Someone who is **female** is a woman or a girl. নারী ▷ *n* Women and girls are sometimes referred to as **females** when they are being considered as a type. মহিলা

feminine *adj* **Feminine** means relating to women or considered typical of or suitable for them. নারী-সংক্রান্ত

feminist (feminists) *n* A **feminist** is a person who believes that women should have the same rights and opportunities as men. নারীবাদী

fence (fences) *n* A **fence** is a barrier made of wood or wire supported by posts. বেড়া

fennel *n* **Fennel** is a plant with a crisp rounded base and feathery leaves. It can be eaten as a vegetable or the leaves can be used as a herb. মৌরীজাতীয় শাক

fern (**ferns**) *n* A **fern** is a plant with long stems, thin leaves, and no flowers. ফার্ন

ferret (**ferrets**) *n* A **ferret** is a small, fierce animal which hunts rabbits and rats. নেউল

ferry (**ferries**) *n* A **ferry** is a boat that carries passengers or vehicles across a river or a narrow stretch of sea. খেয়াতরী

fertile *adj* Land or soil that is **fertile** is able to support a large number of strong healthy plants. উর্বর

fertilizer (**fertilizers**) *n* **Fertilizer** is a substance that you spread on the ground to make plants grow more successfully. সার

festival (**festivals**) *n* A **festival** is an organized series of events and performances. উৎসব

fetch (**fetches, fetching, fetched**) *vt* If you **fetch** something or someone, you go and get them from where they are. তুলে আনা

fever (**fevers**) *n* If you have a **fever**, your temperature is higher than usual because you are ill. জ্বর

few *det* A **few** means some, but not many. অল্প কয়েকটি She gave me a few sweets. ▷ *pron* You use a **few** to refer to a small number of things or people. কয়েকটি The doctors are all busy and a few work more than 100 hours a week.

fewer (**fewest**) *adj* You use **fewer** to indicate that you are talking about a number of people or things that is smaller than another number. অপেক্ষাকৃত কম

fiancé (**fiancés**) *n* A woman's **fiancé** is the man she is engaged to and will marry. হবু-বর

fiancée (**fiancées**) *n* A man's **fiancée** is the woman he is engaged to and will marry. হবু-বউ

fibre (**fibres**) *n* A **fibre** is a thin thread of a natural or artificial substance, especially one used to make cloth or rope. তন্তু

fibreglass *n* **Fibreglass** is plastic strengthened with short, thin threads of glass. ফাইবার গ্লাস

fiction *n* **Fiction** is stories about imaginary people and events. কাল্পনিক কাহিনী

field (**fields**) *n* A **field** is an enclosed area of land where crops are grown or animals are kept. মাঠ

fierce (**fiercer, fiercest**) *adj* A **fierce** animal or person is very aggressive or angry. হিংস্র

fifteen *num* **Fifteen** is the number 15. পনের

fifteenth *adj* The **fifteenth** item in a series is the one that you count as number fifteen. পনের নম্বর

fifth *adj* The **fifth** item in a series is the one that you count as number five. পাঁচ নম্বর

fifty *num* **Fifty** is the number 50. পঞ্চাশ

fifty-fifty *adj* If a division or sharing of something such as money or property between two people is **fifty-fifty**, each person gets half of it. (*informal*) আধা-আধা ▷ *adv* If something such as money or property is divided or shared **fifty-fifty** between two people, each person gets half of it. (*informal*) অর্ধেকভাবে

fig (**figs**) *n* A **fig** is a soft sweet fruit full of tiny seeds. Figs grow on trees in hot countries. ডুমুর

fight (**fights, fighting, fought**) *n* A **fight** against something is an attempt to stop it. লড়াই ▷ *v* If you **fight** something unpleasant, you try in a determined way to prevent it or stop it happening. লড়াই করা

fighting *n* **Fighting** is a battle, struggle, or physical combat. সংগ্রাম

figure (**figures**) *n* A **figure** is a particular amount expressed as a number, especially a statistic. আকৃতি

figure out *v* If you **figure out** a solution to a problem or the reason for something, you succeed in solving it or understanding it. (*informal*) সমাধান খোঁজা His parents could not figure out how to start their new computer.

Fiji *n* **Fiji** is an independent republic, consisting of 844 islands in the south-west Pacific. ফিজি

file (files, filing, filed) n A **file** is a box or folder in which documents are kept. ফাইল ▷ n A **file** is a tool with rough surfaces, used for smoothing and shaping hard materials. উকো ▷ vt If you **file** a document, you put it in the correct file. ফাইলবদ্ধ করা ▷ vt If you **file** an object, you smooth or shape it with a file. মসৃণ করা

Filipino (Filipinos) adj **Filipino** means belonging or relating to the Philippines, or to its people or culture. ফিলিপিন্স দেশীয় ▷ n A **Filipino** is a person who comes from the Philippines. ফিলিপিনের অধিবাসী

fill (fills, filling, filled) v If you **fill** a container or area, or if it **fills**, an amount of something enters it that is enough to make it full. ভর্তি করা

fillet (fillets, filleting, filleted) n A **fillet** of fish or meat is a piece that has no bones in it. ফিলে ▷ vt When you **fillet** fish or meat, you prepare it by taking the bones out. ফিলে তৈরী করা

fill in v When you **fill in** a form, you write information in the spaces on it. পূরণ করা *Fill in the coupon and send it to the address shown.*

fill up v If you **fill** a container **up**, you keep putting or pouring something into it until it is full. পূর্ণ করা *Filling up your car's petrol tank these days is very expensive.*

film (films) n A **film** consists of moving pictures that have been recorded so that they can be shown in a cinema or on television. চলচ্চিত্র

film star (film stars) n A **film star** is a famous actor or actress who appears in films. চলচ্চিত্র-তারকা

filter (filters, filtering, filtered) n A **filter** is a device through which a substance is passed when it is being filtered. ছাঁকনি ▷ vt To **filter** a substance, or to **filter** particles out of a substance, means to pass it through a device which removes the particles from it. ছাঁকা

filthy (filthier, filthiest) adj Something that is **filthy** is very dirty indeed. নোংরা

final (finals) adj In a series of events, things, or people, the **final** one is the last one, or the one that happens at the end. অন্তিম ▷ n A **final** is the last game or contest in a series, which decides the overall winner. চূড়ান্ত

finalize (finalizes, finalizing, finalized) vt If you **finalize** something that you are arranging, you complete the arrangements for it. আয়োজন সম্পূর্ণ করা

finally adv If something **finally** happens, it happens after a long delay. অবশেষে

finance (finances, financing, financed) n **Finance** is funds provided to pay for a project or a purchase, or the provision of these funds. অর্থসংস্থান ▷ vt When someone **finances** something such as a project or a purchase, they provide the money that is needed to pay for them. অর্থবিনিয়োগ

financial adj **Financial** means relating to or involving money. আর্থিক

financial year (financial years) n A **financial year** is a period of twelve months, used by government, business, and other organizations in order to calculate their budgets, profits, and losses. আর্থিক বছর

find (finds, finding, found) vt If you **find** someone or something, you see them or learn where they are. খোঁজা

find out v If you **find** something **out**, you learn it, often by making an effort to do so. খুঁজে বার করা *They wanted to find out the truth.*

fine (finer, finest, fines) adj When the weather is **fine**, it is dry and sunny. মনোরম ▷ adj If you say that you are **fine**, you mean that you are well or happy. ভালো ▷ adj Something that is **fine** is very thin. মিহি ▷ n A **fine** is money that a person is ordered to pay because they have done something wrong. জরিমানা

finger (fingers) n Your **fingers** are the four long moveable parts at the end of your hands. আঙুল

fingernail (fingernails) n Your **fingernails** are the hard areas on the ends of your fingers. আঙুলের নখ

fingerprint (fingerprints) n **Fingerprints** are marks made by a person's fingers which show the lines on the skin. Everyone's fingerprints are different, so they can be used to identify criminals. আঙুলের ছাপ

finish (finishes, finishing, finished) n The **finish** of something is the end of it or the last part of it. সমাপ্তি ▷ vt When you **finish** doing or dealing with something, you do or deal with the last part of it, so that there is no more for you to do or deal with. শেষ করা

finished adj If you are **finished with** something, you are no longer doing it or interested in it. সমাপ্ত

Finland n **Finland** is a republic in north Europe, on the Baltic Sea. ফিনল্যান্ড

Finn (Finns) n The **Finns** are the people of Finland. ফিনল্যান্ডের জনগণ

Finnish adj **Finnish** means belonging or relating to Finland or to its people, language, or culture. ফিনল্যান্ড দেশীয় ▷ n **Finnish** is the language spoken in Finland. ফিনিশীয় ভাষা

fire n **Fire** is the hot, bright flames that come from something that is burning. আগুন

fire alarm (fire alarms) n A **fire alarm** is a device that makes a noise, for example with a bell, to warn people when there is a fire. অগ্নিসংকেত

fire brigade (fire brigades) n The **fire brigade** is an organization which has the job of putting out fires. দমকলবাহিনী

fire escape (fire escapes) n A **fire escape** is a metal staircase on the outside of a building, which can be used to escape from the building if there is a fire. ফায়ার এসকেপ

fire extinguisher (fire extinguishers) n A **fire extinguisher** is a metal cylinder which contains water or chemicals at high pressure which can put out fires. অগ্নি-নির্বাপক যন্ত্র

fireman (firemen) n A **fireman** is a person whose job is to put out fires. দমকলকর্মী

fireplace (fireplaces) n In a room, the **fireplace** is the place where a fire can be lit. ফায়ারপ্লেস

firewall (firewalls) n A **firewall** is a computer system or program that automatically prevents an unauthorized person from gaining access to a computer when it is connected to a network such as the Internet. ফায়ারওয়াল

fireworks npl **Fireworks** are small objects that are lit to entertain people on special occasions. They burn in a bright, attractive, and often noisy way. আতসবাজি

firm (firmer, firmest, firms) adj Something that is **firm** is fairly hard and does not change much in shape when it is pressed. দৃঢ় ▷ n A **firm** is a business selling or producing something. ব্যবসা-প্রতিষ্ঠান

first adj If a person or thing is **first**, they come before all the others. প্রথম ▷ adv If you do something **first**, you do it before anyone else does, or before you do anything else. প্রথমে ▷ n An event that is described as a **first** has never happened before. শুরুর

first aid n **First aid** is medical treatment given as soon as possible to a sick or injured person. প্রাথমিক চিকিৎসা

first-aid kit (first-aid kits) n A **first-aid kit** is a bag or case containing basic medical supplies that are designed to be used on someone who is injured or who suddenly becomes ill. প্রাথমিক চিকিৎসার বাক্স

first-class *adj* Something or someone that is **first-class** is of the highest quality or standard. প্রথম শ্রেণী

firstly *adv* You use **firstly** when you are about to mention the first in a series of items. প্রথমতঃ

first name (first names) *n* Your **first name** is the first of the names that you were given when you were born, as opposed to your family name. প্রথম নাম

fir tree (fir trees) *n* A **fir** or a **fir tree** is a tall pointed tree. ফার গাছ

fiscal *adj* **Fiscal** means related to government money or public money, especially taxes. সরকারী রাজস্বসংক্রান্ত

fiscal year (fiscal years) *n* The **fiscal year** is a twelve-month period beginning and ending in April, which governments and businesses use to plan their finances. সরকারী রাজস্ববর্ষ

fish (fish, fishes, fishing, fished) *n* A **fish** is a creature with a tail and fins that lives in water. মাছ ▷ *vi* If you **fish**, you try to catch fish. মাছধরা

fisherman (fishermen) *n* A **fisherman** is a person who catches fish as a job or for sport. জেলে

fishing *n* **Fishing** is the sport or business of catching fish. মাছধরা

fishing boat (fishing boats) *n* A **fishing boat** is a boat that is used in the business of catching fish. জেলে-নৌকা

fishing rod (fishing rods) *n* A **fishing rod** is a long, thin pole which has a line and hook attached to it and which is used for catching fish. ছিপ

fishing tackle *n* **Fishing tackle** consists of all the equipment that is used in the sport of fishing, such as fishing rods, lines, hooks, and bait. মাছ ধরার দড়ি

fishmonger (fishmongers) *n* A **fishmonger** is a shopkeeper who sells fish. মাছবিক্রেতা

fist (fists) *n* You refer to someone's hand as their **fist** when they have bent their fingers towards their palm. হাতের মুঠো

fit (fitter, fittest, fits, fitting, fitted) *adj* If something is **fit** for a particular purpose, it is suitable for that purpose. উপযুক্ত ▷ *n* If something is a good **fit**, it fits well. মানানসই ▷ *v* If something **fits** you, it is the right size and shape for you. মাপে হওয়া

fit in *v* If you manage to **fit** a person or task **in**, you manage to find time to deal with them. সময় বের করা *I find that I just can't fit in the housework.*

fitted carpet (fitted carpets) *n* A **fitted carpet** is cut to the same shape as a room so that it covers the floor completely. কাটছাঁট করা কার্পেট

fitted kitchen (fitted kitchens) *n* A **fitted kitchen** is a kitchen with units that are attached to the wall. দেওয়াল আলমারিসহ রান্নাঘর

fitted sheet (fitted sheets) *n* A **fitted sheet** is a bedsheet with the corners sewn so that they fit over the corners of the mattress and do not have to be folded. কোনামোড়া মাদুর

fitting room (fitting rooms) *n* A **fitting room** is a room or cubicle in a shop where you can put on clothes to see how they look. ফিটিং রুম

five *num* **Five** is the number 5. পাঁচ

fix (fixes, fixing, fixed) *vt* If you **fix** something to another thing, you join them together. জোড়া লাগানো ▷ *vt* If you **fix** something that is broken, you mend it. মেরামত করা

fixed *adj* You use **fixed** to describe something which stays the same and does not vary. স্থায়ী

fizzy (fizzier, fizziest) adj **Fizzy** drinks are full of little bubbles of gas. বুদ্বুদভরা পানীয়

flabby (flabbier, flabbiest) adj **Flabby** people are rather fat, with loose flesh over their bodies. মেদবহুল

flag (flags) n A **flag** is a piece of coloured cloth used as a sign for something or as a signal. পতাকা

flame (flames) n A **flame** is a hot bright stream of burning gas that comes from something that is burning. অগ্নিশিখা

flamingo (flamingos, flamingoes) n A **flamingo** is a bird with pink feathers, long thin legs, a long neck, and a curved beak. Flamingos live near water in warm countries. ফ্লেমিংগো পাখি

flammable adj **Flammable** chemicals, gases, cloth, or other things catch fire and burn easily. সহজদাহ্য

flan (flans) n A **flan** is a food that has a base and sides of pastry or sponge cake. The base is filled with fruit or savoury food. জ্যামভরা কেক

flannel (flannels) n A **flannel** is a small cloth that you use for washing yourself. ফ্লানেল

flap (flaps, flapping, flapped) v If something that is attached at one end **flaps**, or if you **flap** it, it moves quickly up and down or from side to side. ঝটকানো

flash (flashes, flashing, flashed) n A **flash** of light is a sudden, short burst of it. ঝলকানি ▷ v If a light **flashes**, or if you **flash** a light, it shines brightly and suddenly. ঝলক দেওয়া

flask (flasks) n A **flask** is a bottle used for carrying alcoholic or hot drinks around with you. ফ্লাস্ক

flat (flatter, flattest, flats) adj Something that is **flat** is level and smooth. চ্যাটালো ▷ n A **flat** is a set of rooms for living in, that is part of a larger building. ফ্ল্যাট

flat-screen adj A **flat-screen** television set or computer monitor has a slim flat screen. ফ্ল্যাট-স্ক্রীণ

flatter (flatters, flattering, flattered) vt If someone **flatters** you, they praise you in an exaggerated way that is not sincere. তোষামোদ

flattered adj If you are **flattered** by something that has happened, you are pleased about it because it makes you feel important. প্রশংসায় তুষ্ট

flavour (flavours) n The **flavour** of a food or drink is its taste. সুগন্ধ

flavouring (flavourings) n **Flavourings** are substances that are added to food or drink to give it a particular taste. সুগন্ধকারী বস্তু

flaw (flaws) n A **flaw** in something such as a theory is a mistake in it. খুঁত

flea (fleas) n A **flea** is a small jumping insect that sucks human or animal blood. রক্তচোষা পতঙ্গ

flea market (flea markets) n A **flea market** is an outdoor market which sells cheap used goods and sometimes also very old furniture. পুরানো জিনিসের বাজার

flee (flees, fleeing, fled) v If you **flee**, you escape from something or someone by running away. (written) পলায়ন করা

fleece (fleeces) n A sheep's **fleece** is its coat of wool. লোমশ চামড়া

fleet (fleets) n A **fleet** is an organized group of ships. নৌ-বহর

flex (flexes) n A **flex** is an electric cable containing wires that is connected to an electrical appliance. বিদ্যুৎবাহী তার

flexible adj A **flexible** object or material can be bent easily without breaking. নমনীয়

flexitime n **Flexitime** is a system that allows employees to vary the time that they start or finish work, provided that an agreed total number of hours are spent at work. নমনীয় সময়

flight (flights) n A **flight** is a journey made by flying, usually in an aeroplane. এরোপ্লেন যাত্রা

flight attendant (flight attendants) n On an aeroplane, the **flight attendants** are the people whose job is to look after the passengers and serve their meals. যাত্রার সহযোগী

fling (**flings, flinging, flung**) *vt* If you **fling** something or someone somewhere, you throw them there suddenly, using a lot of force. সজোরে ছুঁড়ে দেওয়া

flip-flops *npl* **Flip-flops** are open shoes which are held on your feet by a strap that goes between your toes. ফ্লিপ-ফ্লপ

flippers *npl* **Flippers** are flat pieces of rubber that you can wear on your feet to help you swim more quickly, especially underwater. ফ্লিপার

flirt (**flirts, flirting, flirted**) *n* A **flirt** is someone who flirts a lot. প্রেমের অভিনয়ে দক্ষ ▷ *vi* If you **flirt** with someone, you behave as if you are sexually attracted to them, in a playful or not very serious way. প্রেমের অভিনয় করা

float (**floats, floating, floated**) *n* A **float** is a light object that is used to help someone or something float in water. হালকা ভাসমান বস্তু ▷ *vi* If something **floats** in a liquid, it stays on top of it. ভাসা ▷ *vi* If something **floats** in the air, it moves slowly through it. ওড়া

flock (**flocks**) *n* A **flock** of birds, sheep, or goats is a group of them. **Flock** can take the singular or plural form of the verb. পাল

flood (**floods, flooding, flooded**) *n* If there is a **flood**, a large amount of water covers an area which is usually dry. বন্যা ▷ *vt* If something such as a river or a burst pipe **floods** an area that is usually dry, it becomes covered with water. জলময় হওয়া ▷ *vi* If an area that is usually dry **floods**, it becomes covered with water. জলে পরিপূর্ণ হওয়া

flooding *n* If **flooding** occurs, an area of land that is usually dry is covered with water after heavy rain or after a river or lake flows over its banks. প্লাবন

floodlight (**floodlights**) *n* **Floodlights** are powerful lamps which are used to light sports grounds and the outsides of public buildings. ফ্লাডলাইট

floor (**floors**) *n* A **floor** is the part of a room that you walk on. মেঝে ▷ A **floor** of a building is all the rooms in it that are at the same height. তলা

flop (**flops**) *n* If something is a **flop**, it is completely unsuccessful. অসফল

floppy disk (**floppy disks**) *n* A **floppy disk** is a small magnetic disk that used to be used for storing computer data and programs. ফ্লপি ডিস্ক

flora *npl* You can refer to plants as **flora**, especially the plants growing in a particular area. (*formal*) বিশেষ কোন অঞ্চলের উদ্ভিদ

florist (**florists**) *n* A **florist** is a shopkeeper who sells flowers and indoor plants. ফুলবিক্রেতা

flour (**flours**) *n* **Flour** is a white or brown powder that is made by grinding grain. It is used to make bread, cakes, and pastry. ময়দা

flow (**flows, flowing, flowed**) *vi* If a liquid, gas, or electrical current **flows** somewhere, it moves there steadily and continuously. প্রবাহ

flower (**flowers, flowering, flowered**) *n* A **flower** is the brightly coloured part of a plant which grows at the end of a stem. ফুল ▷ *vi* When a plant or tree **flowers**, its flowers appear and open. ফুল দেওয়া

flu *n* **Flu** is an illness caused by a virus. The symptoms are like those of a bad cold, but more serious. ভাইরাসবাহিত রোগ

fluent *adj* Someone who is **fluent** in a particular language can speak it easily and correctly. ঝরঝরে

fluorescent *adj* A **fluorescent** surface or colour has a very bright appearance when light is directed onto it. ফ্লুরোসেন্ট

flush (flushes, flushing, flushed) *n* A **flush** is a rosy colour, especially in the cheeks. রক্তিম আভা ▷ *vi* If you **flush**, your face goes red because you are hot or ill, or because you are feeling a strong emotion such as embarrassment or anger. লাল হয়ে যাওয়া

flute (flutes) *n* A **flute** is a musical wind instrument consisting of a long tube with holes in it. You play it by blowing over a hole at one end while holding it sideways. বাঁশি

fly (flies, flying, flew, flown) *n* A **fly** is a small insect with two thin, clear wings. মাছি ▷ *vi* When a bird or aeroplane **flies**, it moves through the air. ওড়া

fly away *v* When something such as a bird, insect, or aircraft **flies away**, it leaves a place by moving through the air. উড়ে চলে যাওয়া *With a flap and a screech, the falcon flew away.*

foal (foals) *n* A **foal** is a very young horse. বাচ্চা ঘোড়া

focus (foci, focuses, focusing, focused) *n* The **focus** of something is the main topic or main thing that it is concerned with. লক্ষ্য ▷ *v* If you **focus** on a particular topic, or if your attention **is focused** on it, you concentrate on it and deal with it. লক্ষ্য নিবদ্ধ করা

foetus (foetuses) *n* A **foetus** is an unborn animal or human being in its later stages of development. ভ্রূণ

fog (fogs) *n* When there is **fog**, there are tiny drops of water in the air which form a thick cloud and make it difficult to see things. কুয়াশা

foggy (foggier, foggiest) *adj* When it is **foggy**, there is fog. কুয়াশাপূর্ণ

fog light (fog lights) *n* A **fog light** is a very bright light on the front or back of a car to help the driver to see or be seen in fog. ফগলাইট

foil *n* **Foil** is metal that is as thin as paper. It is used to wrap food in. মোড়ক

fold (folds, folding, folded) *n* A **fold** in a piece of paper or cloth is a bend that you make in it when you put one part of it over another part and press the edge. ভাঁজ ▷ *vt* If you **fold** something such as a piece of paper or cloth, you bend it so that one part covers another part, often pressing the edge so that it stays in place. ভাঁজ করা

folder (folders) *n* A **folder** is a thin piece of cardboard in which you can keep loose papers. ফোল্ডার

folding *adj* A **folding** piece of furniture, bicycle, etc. can be folded, so that it can be carried or stored in a small space. ভাঁজ করার সুবিধা সমন্বিত

folklore *n* **Folklore** consists of the traditional stories, customs, and habits of a particular community or nation. লোককথা

folk music *n* **Folk music** is music which is traditional or typical of a particular community or nation. লোকসঙ্গীত

follow (follows, following, followed) *v* If you **follow** someone who is going somewhere, you move along behind them. অনুসরণ করা

following *adj* The **following** day, week, or year is the day, week, or year after the one you have just talked about. পরবর্তী

food (foods) *n* **Food** is what people and animals eat. খাদ্য

food poisoning *n* If you get **food poisoning**, you become ill because you have eaten food that has gone bad. খাদ্যে বিষক্রিয়া

food processor (food processors) *n* A **food processor** is a piece of electrical equipment that is used to mix, chop, or beat food, or to make it into a liquid. ফুড প্রসেসর

fool (fools, fooling, fooled) *n* If you call someone a **fool**, you are indicating that you think they are not sensible and show a lack of good judgement. বোকা ▷ *vt* If someone **fools** you, they deceive or trick you. বোকা বানানো

foot (**feet**) *n* Your **feet** are the parts of your body that are at the ends of your legs, and that you stand on. পা

football (**footballs**) *n* **Football** is a game played by two teams of eleven people who kick a ball and try to score goals by getting the ball into a net. ফুটবল খেলা ▷ *n* A **football** is the ball that you use to play football. ফুটবল

footballer (**footballers**) *n* A **footballer** is a person who plays football. ফুটবলার

football match (**football matches**) *n* A **football match** is an organized game that is played between two football teams. ফুটবল ম্যাচ

football player (**football players**) *n* A **football player** is a person who plays football, especially as a profession. ফুটবল খেলোয়াড়

footpath (**footpaths**) *n* A **footpath** is a path for people to walk on. ফুটপাথ

footprint (**footprints**) *n* A **footprint** is the mark of a person's foot or shoe left on a surface. পায়ের ছাপ

footstep (**footsteps**) *n* A **footstep** is the sound made by someone's feet touching the ground when they are walking or running. পদচারণা

for *prep* If something is **for** someone, they will have it or use it. জন্য *These flowers are for you.* ▷ *prep* You use **for** when you are talking about the way in which you use

something. জন্য *This knife is for cutting bread.* ▷ *prep* If someone does something **for** you, they do it so that you do not have to do it. জন্য *I held the door open for the next person.*

forbid (**forbids, forbidding, forbade, forbidden**) *vt* If you **forbid** someone to do something, or if you **forbid** an activity, you order that it must not be done. নিষেধ করা

forbidden *adj* If something is **forbidden**, you are not allowed to do it or have it. নিষিদ্ধ

force (**forces, forcing, forced**) *n* **Force** is power or strength. শক্তি ▷ *vt* If something or someone **forces** you to do something, they make you do it, even though you do not want to. জোর করা

forecast (**forecasts**) *n* A **forecast** is a statement of what is expected to happen in the future, especially in relation to a particular event or situation. পূর্বাভাষ

foreground *n* The **foreground** of a picture is the part that seems nearest to you. ছবির নিকটবর্তী স্থান

forehead (**foreheads**) *n* Your **forehead** is the flat area at the front of your head above your eyebrows and below where your hair grows. কপাল

foreign *adj* Something that is **foreign** comes from or relates to a country that is not your own. বিদেশ

foreigner (**foreigners**) *n* A **foreigner** is someone who belongs to a country that is not your own. বিদেশী

foresee (**foresees, foreseeing, foresaw, foreseen**) *vt* If you **foresee** something, you expect and believe that it will happen. ভবিষ্যদ্বাণী করা

forest (**forests**) *n* A **forest** is a large area where trees grow close together. অরণ্য

forever *adv* Something that will happen or continue **forever** will always happen or continue. চিরদিন

forge (**forges, forging, forged**) *vt* If someone **forges** banknotes, documents, or paintings, they make false copies of them in order to deceive people. জাল করা

forgery n **Forgery** is the crime of making fake banknotes, documents, or paintings. জালিয়াতি

forget (forgets, forgetting, forgot, forgotten) vt If you **forget** something, or if you **forget** how to do something, you cannot think of it or think of how to do it, although you knew in the past. ভুলে যাওয়া

forgive (forgives, forgiving, forgave, forgiven) vt If you **forgive** someone who has done something wrong, you stop being angry with them. ক্ষমা করা

forgotten adj Something that is **forgotten** is no longer remembered or thought about by people. বিস্মৃত

fork (forks) n A **fork** is an implement that you use when you are eating food. It consists of three or four long thin points on the end of a handle. কাঁটাচামচ

form (forms) n A **form** of something is a type or kind of it. রূপ

formal adj **Formal** speech or behaviour is very correct and serious rather than relaxed and friendly, and is used especially in official situations. নিয়মানুগ

formality n **Formality** is speech or behaviour which is correct and serious, rather than relaxed and friendly, and is used especially in official situations. নিয়মানুগত্য

format (formats, formatting, formatted) n The **format** of something is the way it is arranged and presented. ▷ vt To **format** a computer disk means to run a program so that the disk can be written on. তথ্য বিন্যাস করা

former adj You use **former** when you are talking about someone or something in the past. প্রাক্তন

formerly adv If something happened or was **formerly** true, it happened or was true in the past. পূর্বকালে

formula (formulae, formulas) n A **formula** is a plan that is made as a way of dealing with a problem. সূত্র

fort (forts) n A **fort** is a strong building that is used as a military base. দুর্গ

fortnight (fortnights) n A **fortnight** is a period of two weeks. একপক্ষকাল

fortunate adj If someone or something is **fortunate**, they are lucky. সৌভাগ্যবান

fortunately adv **Fortunately** is used to introduce or indicate a statement about an event or situation that is good. সৌভাগ্যবশতঃ

fortune (fortunes) n You can refer to a large sum of money as a **fortune** or a small **fortune** to emphasize how large it is. সৌভাগ্য

forty num **Forty** is the number 40. চল্লিশ

forward (forwards, forwarding, forwarded) adv If you move or look **forward**, you move or look in a direction that is in front of you. সামনের দিকে ▷ vt If a letter or message **is forwarded** to someone, it is sent to the place where they are, after having been sent to a different place earlier. পাঠিয়ে দেওয়া

forward slash (forward slashes) n A **forward slash** is the sloping line (/) that separates letters, words, or numbers. তির্যক চিহ্ন

foster (fosters, fostering, fostered) vt If you **foster** a child, you take him or her into your family as a foster child. পালন করা

foster child (foster children) n A **foster child** is a child looked after temporarily or brought up by people other than its parents. পালিত সন্তান

foul (fouler, foulest, fouls) adj If you describe something as **foul**, you mean it is dirty and smells or tastes unpleasant. দুর্গন্ধযুক্ত ▷ n In sports such as football, a **foul** is an action that is against the rules. ফাউল

foundations npl The **foundations** of a building or other structure are the layer of bricks or concrete below the ground that it is built on. ভিত

fountain (**fountains**) *n* A **fountain** is an ornamental feature in a pool which consists of a jet of water that is forced up into the air by a pump. ঝরণা

fountain pen (**fountain pens**) *n* A **fountain pen** is a pen which uses ink that you have drawn up inside it from a bottle. কলম

four *num* **Four** is the number 4. চার

fourteen *num* **Fourteen** is the number 14. চতুর্দশ

fourteenth *adj* The **fourteenth** item in a series is the one that you count as number fourteen. চতুর্দশতম

fourth *adj* The **fourth** item in a series is the one that you count as number four. চতুর্থ

four-wheel drive (**four-wheel drives**) *n* A **four-wheel drive** is a vehicle in which all four wheels receive power from the engine. যে গাড়ির চার চাকায় শক্তি আসে

fox (**foxes**) *n* A **fox** is a wild animal which looks like a dog and has reddish-brown fur and a thick tail. শিয়াল

fracture (**fractures**) *n* A **fracture** is a crack or break in something. অস্থিভঙ্গ

fragile *adj* If you describe a situation as **fragile**, you mean that it is weak or uncertain and unlikely to be able to resist strong pressure or attack. ভঙ্গুর

frail (**frailer, frailest**) *adj* Someone who is **frail** is not very strong or healthy. দুর্বল

frame (**frames**) *n* The **frame** of a picture or mirror is the part around its edges. কাঠামো

France *n* **France** is a republic in western Europe, between the English Channel, the Mediterranean, and the Atlantic. ফ্রান্স

frankly *adv* You use **frankly** when you are expressing an opinion or feeling to emphasize that you mean what you are saying. খোলাখুলিভাবে

frantic *adj* If someone is **frantic**, they are behaving in a desperate, wild, and

disorganized way, because they are frightened, worried, or in a hurry. প্রমত্ত

fraud (**frauds**) *n* **Fraud** is the crime of gaining money by a trick or lying. জালিয়াতি

freckles *npl* If someone has **freckles**, they have small light brown spots on their skin. মেচেতা

free (**freer, freest, frees, freeing, freed**) *adj* If you are **free**, you can do what you like or go where you like. স্বাধীন ▷ *adj* If something is **free**, you can have it without paying any money for it. বিনামূল্যে ▷ *vt* If you **free** someone of something unpleasant, you remove it from them. মুক্তি দেওয়া

freedom (**freedoms**) *n* **Freedom** is the state of being allowed to do what you want. স্বাধীনতা

free kick (**free kicks**) *n* In a game of football, when there is a **free kick**, the ball is given to a member of one side to kick because a member of the other side has broken a rule. ফ্রী কিক

freelance *adj* Someone who does **freelance** work or who is, for example, a **freelance** journalist or photographer is not employed by one organization, but is paid for each piece of work they do by the organization they do it for. স্বনির্ভর ▷ *adv* If someone works **freelance**, they are not employed by one organization, but are paid for each piece of work they do by the organization they do it for. স্বনির্ভরভাবে

freeze (**freezes, freezing, froze, frozen**) *vi* When water **freezes**, it is so cold that it becomes ice. জমে যাওয়া ▷ *vt* If you **freeze** food, you make it very cold so that it will not go bad. ঠান্ডা করা

freezer (**freezers**) *n* A **freezer** is a fridge in which the temperature is kept below freezing point so that you can store food inside it for long periods. ফ্রিজার

freezing *adj* Something that is **freezing** is very cold. হিমশীতল

freight n **Freight** is the movement of goods by lorries, trains, ships, or aeroplanes. পরিবাহিত মালপত্র

French adj **French** means belonging or relating to France, or to its people, language, or culture. ফ্রান্সদেশীয় ▷ n **French** is the language spoken by people who live in France and in parts of some other countries, including Belgium, Canada, and Switzerland. ফরাসী ভাষা

French beans npl **French beans** are narrow green beans that are eaten as a vegetable. They grow on a tall climbing plant and are the cases that contain the seeds of the plant. ফ্রেঞ্চবীন

French horn (French horns) n A **French horn** is a musical instrument shaped like a long round metal tube with one wide end, which is played by blowing into it. একপ্রকার বাদ্যযন্ত্র

Frenchman (Frenchmen) n A **Frenchman** is a man who comes from France. ফরাসী ভদ্রলোক

Frenchwoman (Frenchwomen) n A **Frenchwoman** is a woman who comes from France. ফরাসী ভদ্রমহিলা

frequency n The **frequency** of an event is the number of times it happens. বারংবারতা

frequent adj If something is **frequent**, it happens often. বারংবার

fresh (fresher, freshest) adj A **fresh** thing or amount replaces or is added to an existing thing or amount. তাজা ▷ adj If food is **fresh**, it has been picked or made a short time ago. টাটকা ▷ adj **Fresh** water has no salt in it. The water in rivers is **fresh**. তাজা ▷ adj **Fresh** air is clean and cool. তাজা

freshen up v If you **freshen** something **up**, you make it clean and pleasant in appearance or smell. তরতাজা করে তোলা A thorough brushing helps to freshen up your mouth.

freshwater fish (freshwater fish, freshwater fishes) n A **freshwater fish** lives in water that is not salty. মিষ্টিজলের মাছ

fret (frets, fretting, fretted) vi If you **fret** about something, you worry about it. উদ্বিগ্ন হওয়া

Friday (Fridays) n **Friday** is the day after Thursday and before Saturday. শুক্রবার

fridge (fridges) n A **fridge** is a large metal container for storing food at low temperatures to keep it fresh. ফ্রিজ

fried adj If food is **fried**, it is cooked in a pan containing hot fat. ভাজা

friend (friends) n A **friend** is someone who you know well and like, but who is not related to you. বন্ধু

friendly (friendlier, friendliest) adj A **friendly** person is kind and pleasant. বন্ধুভাবাপন্ন

friendship (friendships) n A **friendship** is a relationship or state of friendliness between two people who like each other. বন্ধুত্ব

fright n **Fright** is a sudden feeling of fear. প্রচন্ড ভয়

frighten (frightens, frightening, frightened) vt If something or someone **frightens** you, they cause you to suddenly feel afraid or anxious. প্রচন্ড ভয় পাওয়া

frightened adj If you are **frightened**, you feel anxious or afraid. প্রচন্ড ভীত

frightening adj If something is **frightening**, it makes you feel afraid or anxious. প্রচন্ড ভীতিজনক

fringe (fringes) n A **fringe** is hair which is cut so that it hangs over your forehead. ঝুলে থাকা চুলের গোছা

frog (frogs) n A **frog** is a small creature with smooth skin, big eyes, and long back legs which it uses for jumping. ব্যাঙ

from prep If something comes **from** a person, they give it to you or send it to you. কাছ থেকে I received a letter from him yesterday. ▷ prep If someone or something moves **from** a place, they leave it. থেকে Everyone watched as she ran from the room. ▷ prep You use **from** to say what somebody used to make something. থেকে *This bread is made from white flour.*

front (fronts) *adj* **Front** is used to refer to the side or part of something that is towards the front or nearest to the front. সামনে ▷ *n* The **front** of something is the part of it that faces you, or that faces forward, or that you normally see or use. সম্মুখ

frontier (frontiers) *n* A **frontier** is a border between two countries. সীমান্ত অঞ্চল

frost (frosts) *n* When there is **frost** or a **frost**, the temperature outside falls below freezing point and the ground becomes covered in ice crystals. তুষারপাত

frosty (frostier, frostiest) *adj* If the weather is **frosty**, the temperature is below freezing. হিমেল

frown (frowns, frowning, frowned) *vi* When someone **frowns**, their eyebrows become drawn together, because they are annoyed, worried, or puzzled, or because they are concentrating. ভ্রু কোঁচকানো

frozen *adj* If the ground is **frozen**, it has become very hard because the weather is very cold. বরফজমা

fruit (fruit, fruits) *n* **Fruit** is something which grows on a tree or bush and which contains seeds or a stone covered by edible flesh. Apples, oranges, and bananas are all fruit. ফল

fruit juice *n* **Fruit juice** is the liquid that can be obtained from a fruit and drunk. ফলের রস

fruit salad (fruit salads) *n* **Fruit salad** is a mixture of pieces of different kinds of fruit. It is usually eaten as a dessert. ফ্রুট স্যালাড

frustrated *adj* If you are **frustrated**, you are upset or angry because you are unable to do anything about a situation. হতাশাগ্রস্ত

fry (fries, frying, fried) *vt* When you **fry** food, you cook it in a pan containing hot fat. ভাজা

frying pan (frying pans) *n* A **frying pan** is a flat metal pan with a long handle, in which you fry food. ভাজার পাত্র

fuel (fuels) *n* **Fuel** is a substance such as coal, oil, or petrol that is burned to provide heat or power. জ্বালানী

fulfil (fulfils, fulfills, fulfilling, fulfilled) *vt* If you **fulfil** a promise, dream, or ambition, you do what you said or hoped you would do. পূর্ণ করা

full (fuller, fullest) *adj* Something that is **full** contains as much of a substance or as many objects as it can. পরিপূর্ণ

full moon *n* You use **full moon** to describe one of the four phases of the moon, occurring when the earth lies between the sun and the moon so that the moon is visible as a fully illuminated disc. পূর্ণিমা

full stop (full stops) *n* A **full stop** is the punctuation mark . which you use at the end of a sentence when it is not a question or exclamation. দাঁড়ি

full-time *adj* **Full-time** work or study involves working or studying for the whole of each normal working week rather than for part of it. সম্পূর্ণ সময়ের ▷ *adv* If you do something **full-time**, you do it for the whole of each normal working week. সম্পূর্ণ সময়

fully *adv* **Fully** means to the greatest degree or extent possible. সম্পূর্ণভাবে

fumes *npl* **Fumes** are unpleasantly strong or harmful gases or smells. ধোঁয়া

fun *adj* If someone is **fun**, you enjoy their company. If something is **fun**, you enjoy doing it. মজার ▷ *n* You refer to an activity or situation as **fun** if you think it is pleasant and enjoyable. মজা

funds *npl* **Funds** are amounts of money that are available to be spent. তহবিল

funeral (**funerals**) *n* A **funeral** is a ceremony for the burial or cremation of someone who has died. অন্ত্যেষ্টি

funeral parlour (**funeral parlours**) *n* A **funeral parlour** is a place where dead people are prepared for burial or cremation. অন্ত্যেষ্টিক্রিয়া সম্পূর্ণ করবার স্থান

funfair (**funfairs**) *n* A **funfair** is an event held in a park or field at which people pay to ride on various machines for amusement or try to win prizes in games. আনন্দমেলা

funnel (**funnels**) *n* A **funnel** is an object with a wide top and a tube at the bottom, which is used to pour substances into a container. ফানেল

funny (**funnier, funniest**) *adj* If something is **funny**, it makes you laugh. মজার ▷ *adj* **Funny** means strange. আশ্চর্যজনক

fur *n* **Fur** is the thick hair that grows on the bodies of many animals, such as rabbits and bears, and is sometimes used to make clothes or rugs. ফার

fur coat (**fur coats**) *n* A **fur coat** is a coat made from real or artificial fur. ফারের কোট

furious *adj* If someone is **furious**, they are extremely angry. ক্রোধোন্মত্ত

furnished *adj* A **furnished** room or house is available to be rented together with the furniture in it. আসবাবপত্র-সঞ্জিত

furniture *n* **Furniture** consists of large movable objects such as tables, chairs, or beds that are used in a room for sitting or lying on, or for putting things on or in. আসবাবপত্র

further (**furthest**) *adj* A **further** thing or amount is an additional one. অতিরিক্ত ▷ *adv* **Further** means to a greater degree or extent. আরো দূরে

further education *n* **Further education** is the education of people who have left school but who are not at a university or a college of education. স্কুল-পরবর্তী শিক্ষা

fuse (**fuses**) *n* In an electrical appliance, a **fuse** is a wire safety device which melts and stops the electric current if there is a fault. ফিউজ

fuse box (**fuse boxes**) *n* The **fuse box** is the box that contains the fuses for all the electric circuits in a building. It is usually fixed to a wall. ফিউজ বক্স

fuss *n* **Fuss** is anxious or excited behaviour which serves no useful purpose. অকারণে উত্তেজনা

fussy (**fussier, fussiest**) *adj* Someone who is **fussy** is very concerned with unimportant details and is difficult to please. অকারণ উত্তেজিত

future *adj* **Future** things will happen or exist after the present time. আগামী ▷ *n* The **future** is the period of time after the present. ভবিষ্যত

g

Gabon *n* **Gabon** is a republic in west central Africa, on the Atlantic. গ্যাবন

gain (**gains, gaining, gained**) *n* A **gain** is an improvement or increase. লাভ ▷ *vt* If you **gain** something, you acquire it. লাভ করা

gale (**gales**) *n* A **gale** is a very strong wind. প্রবল ঝড়

gall bladder (**gall bladders**) *n* Your **gall bladder** is the organ in your body which contains bile and is next to your liver. পিত্তাশয়

gallery (**galleries**) *n* A **gallery** is a place that has permanent exhibitions of works of art in it. গ্যালারি

gallop (**gallops, galloping, galloped**) *n* A **gallop** is a ride on a horse that is galloping. ঘোড়ার পিঠে লাফিয়ে চলা ▷ *vi* When a horse **gallops**, it runs very fast. লাফানো

gallstone (**gallstones**) *n* A **gallstone** is a small, painful lump which can develop in your gall bladder. পিত্তাশয়ে পাথর

Gambia *n* **Gambia** is a republic in West Africa. গাম্বিয়া

gamble (**gambles, gambling, gambled**) *v* If you **gamble** on something, you take a risk because you hope that something good will happen. জুয়াখেলা

gambler (**gamblers**) *n* A **gambler** is someone who gambles regularly, for example in card games or horse racing. জুয়াড়ি

gambling *n* **Gambling** is the act or activity of betting money, for example in card games or on horse racing. জুয়া

game (**games**) *n* A **game** is something you play that has rules, for example football. খেলা ▷ *n* Children play a **game** when they pretend to be other people. খেলা

games console (**games consoles**) *n* A **games console** is an electronic device used for playing computer games on a television screen. গেমস্ কনসোল

gang (**gangs**) *n* A **gang** is a group of people who join together for some purpose, often criminal. অপরাধীদের দল

gangster (**gangsters**) *n* A **gangster** is a member of a group of violent criminals. অপরাধীদের সদস্য

gap (**gaps**) *n* A **gap** is a space between two things or a hole in something solid. ফাঁক

garage (**garages**) *n* A **garage** is a building where you keep a car. গ্যারেজ ▷ *n* A **garage** is a place where you can get your car repaired. গাড়ি সারাবার জায়গা

garden (**gardens**) *n* A **garden** is an area of land next to a house, with plants, trees, and grass. বাগান

garden centre (**garden centres**) *n* A **garden centre** is a large shop, usually with an outdoor area, where you can buy things for your garden such as plants and gardening tools. গাছের দোকান

gardener (**gardeners**) *n* A **gardener** is a person who is paid to work in someone else's garden. মালী

gardening *n* **Gardening** is the activity of planning and cultivating a garden. বাগান-পরিচর্যা

garlic n **Garlic** is a plant like a small onion, with a strong flavour, which you use in cooking. রসুন

garment (**garments**) n A **garment** is a piece of clothing. পোষাক

gas (**gases**) n A **gas** is any substance that is neither liquid nor solid. গ্যাস

gas cooker (**gas cookers**) n A **gas cooker** is a large metal device for cooking food using gas. গ্যাসকুকার

gasket (**gaskets**) n A **gasket** is a flat piece of soft material that you put between two joined surfaces in a pipe or engine in order to make sure that gas and oil cannot escape. গ্যাসকেট

gate (**gates**) n A **gate** is a structure like a door that you use to enter a field, a garden, or the area around a building. দরজা

gateau (**gateaux**) n A **gateau** is a very rich, elaborate cake, especially one with cream in it. ক্রীম-কেক

gather (**gathers, gathering, gathered**) v When people **gather** somewhere, or if someone **gathers** them together, they come together in a group. জড়ো হওয়া

gauge (**gauges, gauging, gauged**) n A **gauge** is a device that measures the amount or quantity of something and shows the amount measured. ফিতে ▷ vt If you **gauge** something, you measure it or judge it. ফিতে দিয়ে মাপা

gaze (**gazes, gazing, gazed**) vi If you **gaze** at someone or something, you look steadily at them for a long time. একদৃষ্টে তাকানো

gear (**gears**) n A **gear** is a piece of machinery, for example in a car or on a bicycle, which helps to control its movement. গাড়ির গিয়ার ▷ n The **gear** for a particular activity is the equipment and special clothes that you use. সরঞ্জাম

gearbox (**gearboxes**) n A **gearbox** is the system of gears in an engine or vehicle. গিয়ার-বক্স

gear lever (**gear levers**) n A **gear lever** or a **gear stick** is the lever that you use

to change gear in a car or other vehicle. গিয়ার-লিভার

gel (**gels**) n **Gel** is a smooth, soft, jelly-like substance, especially one used to keep your hair in a particular style. জেল ক্রীম

gem (**gems**) n A **gem** is a jewel. রত্ন

Gemini n **Gemini** is one of the twelve signs of the zodiac. Its symbol is a pair of twins. People who are born approximately between 21st May and 20th June come under this sign. মিথুন রাশি

gender (**genders**) n A person's **gender** is the fact that they are male or female. লিঙ্গ

gene (**genes**) n A **gene** is the part of a cell in a living thing which controls its physical characteristics, growth, and development. জিন

general (**generals**) adj If you talk about the **general** situation somewhere or talk about something in **general** terms, you are describing the situation as a whole rather than part of it. সাধারণ ▷ n A **general** is a senior officer in the armed forces, usually in the army. জেনারেল

general anaesthetic (**general anaesthetics**) n A **general anaesthetic** is a substance that doctors use to stop you feeling pain during an operation. It causes you to lose consciousness. সাধারণ অ্যানােস্থেসিয়া

general election (**general elections**) n A **general election** is a time when people choose a new government. সাধারণ নির্বাচন

generalize (**generalizes, generalizing, generalized**) v If you **generalize**, you say something that is usually, but not always, true. সাধারণ রূপ দেওয়া

general knowledge n **General knowledge** is knowledge about many different things, as opposed to detailed knowledge about one particular subject. সাধারণ জ্ঞান

generally adv You use **generally** to summarize a situation, activity, or idea without referring to the particular details of it. সাধারণতঃ

generation (generations) n A **generation** is all the people in a group or country who are of a similar age, especially when they are considered as having the same experiences or attitudes. প্রজন্ম

generator (generators) n A **generator** is a machine which produces electricity. জেনারেটর

generosity n If you refer to someone's **generosity**, you mean that they are generous, especially in doing or giving more than is usual or expected. উদারতা

generous adj A **generous** person gives more of something, especially money, than is usual or expected. উদার

genetic adj You use **genetic** to describe something that is related to genetics or genes. জিনগত

genetically-modified adj **Genetically-modified** plants and animals have had one or more genes changed. The abbreviation **GM** is often used. জিনগতভাবে পরিবর্তিত

genetics n **Genetics** is the study of how characteristics are passed from one generation to another by means of genes. জিনতত্ত্ব

genius n **Genius** is very great ability or skill in something. প্রতিভা

gentle (gentler, gentlest) adj A **gentle** person is kind, mild, and calm. ভদ্র

gentleman (gentlemen) n A **gentleman** is a man from a family of high social standing. ভদ্রলোক

gently adv If you do something **gently** you do it in a kind, mild, and calm manner. ভদ্রভাবে

gents n The **gents** is a public toilet for men. পুরুষদের শৌচালয়

genuine adj Something that is **genuine** is real and exactly what it appears to be. প্রকৃত

geography n **Geography** is the study of the countries of the world and things such as the land, oceans, weather, towns, and population. ভূগোল

geology n **Geology** is the study of the earth's structure, surface, and origins. ভূ-তত্ত্ব

Georgia n **Georgia** is a state of the southeastern United States, on the Atlantic. জর্জিয়া ▷ n **Georgia** is a republic in north-west Asia, on the Black Sea. জর্জিয়া রাষ্ট্র

Georgian (Georgians) adj **Georgian** means belonging to or connected with the republic of Georgia, in north-west Asia, or to its people, language, or culture. জর্জিয়া দেশীয় ▷ n A **Georgian** is a person who comes from the republic of Georgia, in north-west Asia. জর্জিয়ার জনগণ

geranium (geraniums) n A **geranium** is a plant with red, pink, or white flowers. একজাতীয় ফুলেরগাছ

gerbil (gerbils) n A **gerbil** is a small, furry animal. ছোট তীক্ষ্ণদন্তী প্রাণী

geriatric adj **Geriatric** is used to describe things relating to the illnesses and medical care of old people. বয়স্কদের স্বাস্থ্য ও পরিচর্যা সংক্রান্ত বিভাগ

germ (germs) n A **germ** is a very small organism that causes disease. জীবাণু

German (Germans) adj **German** means belonging or relating to Germany, or to its people, language, or culture. জার্মানি দেশীয় ▷ n A **German** is a person who comes from Germany. জার্মানির অধিবাসী ▷ n **German** is the language spoken in Germany, Austria, and parts of Switzerland. জার্মান ভাষা

German measles n **German measles** is a disease which causes you to have a cough, a sore throat, and red spots on your skin. জার্মান মিজলস্ (হাম)

Germany n **Germany** is a country in central Europe. জার্মানি

gesture (gestures) n A **gesture** is a movement that you make with a part of your body, especially your hands, to express emotion or information. অঙ্গভঙ্গি

get (gets, getting, got) v You can use **get** to mean the same as 'become'. পরিণত হওয়া

We should go before it gets dark. ▷ *vi* If you **get** somewhere, you arrive there. পৌঁছানো ▷ *vt* If you **get** something, someone gives it to you. পাওয়া ▷ *vt* If you **get** something, you go to where it is and bring it back. পাওয়া

get away *v* If you **get away**, you succeed in leaving a place or situation that you do not want to be in. অব্যাহতি পাওয়া *The thieves got away through an upstairs window.*

get back *v* If you **get** something **back** after you have lost it or after it has been taken from you, you have it again. ফিরে পাওয়া *You can cancel the contract and get your money back.*

get in *v* When a train, bus, or plane **gets in**, it arrives. পৌঁছানো *Her train gets in at about ten to two.*

get into *v* If you **get into** an activity, you start doing it or being involved in it. যোগদান করা *He was eager to get into politics.*

get off *v* If someone who has broken a law or rule **gets off**, they are not punished, or only slightly punished. মুক্তি পাওয়া *He is likely to get off with a small fine.*

get on *v* If you **get on** with someone, you have a friendly relationship with them. সুসম্পর্ক বজায় রাখা *I get on very well with his wife.*

get out *v* If you **get out**, you leave a place because you want to escape from it, or because you are made to leave it. বেরিয়ে যাওয়া *I told him to leave and get out.*

get over *v* If you **get over** an unpleasant experience or an illness, you recover from it. অতিক্রম করা *It took me a long time to get over the illness.*

get together *v* When people **get together**, they meet in order to discuss something or to spend time together. একত্রিত হওয়া *This is a time for families to get together and enjoy themselves.*

get up *v* If you are sitting or lying and then **get up**, you rise to a standing position. উঠে পড়া *I got up and walked over to where he was.*

Ghana *n* **Ghana** is a republic in West Africa, on the Gulf of Guinea. ঘানা

Ghanaian (**Ghanaians**) *adj* **Ghanaian** means belonging or relating to Ghana, or to its people, language or culture. ঘানা দেশীয় ▷ *n* **Ghanaians** are people who are Ghanaian. ঘানার জনগণ

ghost (**ghosts**) *n* A **ghost** is the spirit of a dead person that someone believes they can see or feel. ভূত

giant (**giants**) *adj* You use **giant** to describe something that is much larger or more important than most other things of its kind. বিশালাকার ▷ *n* A large successful organization or country can be referred to as a **giant**. বিশাল

gift (**gifts**) *n* A **gift** is something that you give someone as a present. উপহার

gifted *adj* A **gifted** person has a natural ability for doing most things or for doing a particular activity. ঈশ্বর-প্রদত্ত

gift voucher (**gift vouchers**) *n* A **gift voucher** is a card or piece of paper that you buy at a shop and give to someone, which entitles the person to exchange it for goods worth the same amount. গিফট ভাউচার

gigantic *adj* If you describe something as **gigantic**, you are emphasizing that it is extremely large in size, amount, or degree. খুব বড় আকারের

giggle (**giggles, giggling, giggled**) *vi* If someone **giggles**, they laugh in a childlike way, because they are amused, nervous, or embarrassed. খিলখিলিয়ে হাসা

gin (**gins**) *n* **Gin** is a colourless alcoholic drink. জিন

ginger *adj* **Ginger** is used to describe things that are orangey-brown in colour. কমলা খয়েরি রংবিশিষ্ট ▷ *n* **Ginger** is the root of a plant that is used to flavour food. It has a sweet spicy flavour. আদা

giraffe (**giraffes**) *n* A **giraffe** is a large African animal with a very long neck, long legs, and dark patches on its body. জিরাফ

girl (**girls**) *n* A **girl** is a female child. মেয়ে

girlfriend (**girlfriends**) *n* Someone's **girlfriend** is a girl or woman with whom they are having a romantic relationship. প্রেমিকা

give (**gives, giving, gave, given**) *vt* If you **give** someone something, you let them have it to keep. দেওয়া

give back *v* If you **give** something **back**, you return it to the person who gave it to you. ফেরত দেওয়া *I gave the textbook back to him.*

give in *v* If you **give in**, you admit that you are defeated or that you cannot do something. হার মানা *All right. I give in. What did you do with it?*

give out *v* If you **give out** a number of things, you distribute them among a group of people. বিতরণ করা *They were giving out leaflets.*

give up *v* If you **give up** something, you stop doing it or having it. ছেড়ে দেওয়া *We almost gave up hope.*

glacier (**glaciers**) *n* A **glacier** is a huge mass of ice which moves very slowly, often down a mountain. হিমবাহ

glad *adj* If you are **glad** about something, you are happy and pleased about it. আনন্দিত

glamorous *adj* If you describe someone or something as **glamorous**, you mean that they are more attractive, exciting, or interesting than ordinary people or things. জৌলুসময়

glance (**glances, glancing, glanced**) *n* A **glance** is a quick look at someone or something. চকিতের দেখা ▷ *vi* If you **glance** at something or someone, you look at them very quickly and then look away again immediately. একনজরে দেখা

gland (**glands**) *n* **Glands** are organs in your body that produce chemical substances which your body needs in order to function. গ্রন্থি

glare (**glares, glaring, glared**) *vi* If you **glare** at someone, you look at them with an angry expression on your face. ঝলসানো চাহনি

glaring *adj* If you describe something bad as **glaring**, you mean that it is very obvious. ক্রোধাম্বিত

glass (**glasses**) *n* **Glass** is a hard, clear material that is used to make things like windows and bottles. It is quite easy to break **glass**. কাঁচ ▷ *n* A **glass** is a container made from **glass** that you can drink out of. গ্লাস

glasses *npl* **Glasses** are two lenses in a frame that some people wear in front of their eyes in order to see better. চশমা

glider (**gliders**) *n* A **glider** is an aircraft without an engine which flies by floating on the air. গ্লাইডার

gliding *n* **Gliding** is the sport or activity of flying in a glider. গ্লাইডারে ওড়া

global *adj* **Global** means concerning or including the whole world. বিশ্বব্যাপী

globalization *n* **Globalization** is the idea that the world is developing a single economy as a result of improved technology and communications. বিশ্বায়ন

global warming *n* The problem of the gradual rise in the earth's temperature is referred to as **global warming**. বিশ্ব উষ্ণায়ন

globe (**globes**) *n* You can refer to the Earth as the **globe**. ভূমণ্ডল

gloomy (**gloomier, gloomiest**) *adj* If a place is **gloomy**, it is almost dark so that you cannot see very well. অন্ধকারাচ্ছন্ন

glorious adj If you describe something as **glorious**, you are emphasizing that it is very beautiful or wonderful. গৌরবপূর্ণ

glory n Glory is fame and admiration that you get for an achievement. মহিমা

glove (gloves) n Gloves are pieces of clothing which cover your hand and wrist and have individual sections for each finger. দস্তানা

glove compartment (glove compartments) n The **glove compartment** in a car is a small cupboard or shelf below the front windscreen. প্রকোষ্ঠ

glucose n Glucose is a type of sugar. গ্লুকোজ

glue (glues, glueing, gluing, glued) n Glue is a sticky substance used for joining things together. আঠা ▷ vt If you **glue** one object to another, you stick them together, using glue. আটকানো

gluten n Gluten is a substance found in cereal grains such as wheat. মাড়

GM abbr GM crops have had one or more genes changed, for example in order to make them resist pests better. **GM** is an abbreviation for 'genetically modified'. জিনগতভাবে পরিবর্তিত

go (goes, going, went, gone) vi If you **go** somewhere, you move there from another place. যাওয়া ▷ v If you say that something is **going** to happen, you mean that it will happen. হতে চলেছে

go after v If you **go after** something, you try to get it, catch it, or hit it. তাড়া করা The company is going after the Asia Pacific market.

go ahead v If someone **goes ahead** with something, they begin to do it or make it. এগিয়ে যাওয়া The board will vote on whether to go ahead with the plan.

goal (goals) n In games such as football or hockey, the **goal** is the space into which the players try to get the ball in order to score. লক্ষ্য

goalkeeper (goalkeepers) n A **goalkeeper** is the player in a sports team whose job is to guard the goal. গোলরক্ষক

goat (goats) n A **goat** is an animal which is a bit bigger than a sheep and has horns. ছাগল

go away v If you **go away**, you leave a place or a person's company. চলে যাওয়া I think we need to go away and think about this.

go back v If something **goes back** to a particular time in the past, it was made or started at that time. অতীতে ফেরা The feud goes back to the 11th century.

go by v If you say that time **goes by**, you mean that it passes. পেরিয়ে যাওয়া I gradually forgot about him as the years went by.

God n The name **God** is given to the spirit or being who is worshipped as the creator and ruler of the world, especially by Christians, Jews, and Muslims. ঈশ্বর

godfather n A powerful man who is at the head of a criminal organization is sometimes referred to as a **godfather**. গডফাদার

go down v If a price, level, or amount **goes down**, it becomes lower than it was. কমে যাওয়া Crime has gone down 70%.

goggles npl Goggles are large glasses that fit closely to your face around your eyes to protect them, for example in a laboratory. রোদচশমা

go in v If the sun **goes in**, it becomes covered by a cloud. ভেতরে ঢুকে যাওয়া The sun went in, and it felt cold.

gold (golds) n Gold is a valuable yellow-coloured metal used for making jewellery, and as an international currency. সোনা

golden adj Something that is **golden** is bright yellow. সোনালী

goldfish (goldfish, goldfishes) n A **goldfish** is a small orange-coloured fish. গোল্ডফিশ

gold-plated adj Something that is **gold-plated** is covered with a very thin layer of gold. সোনার জল দিয়ে নির্মিত

golf n Golf is a game in which you use long sticks called clubs to hit a ball into holes that are spread out over a large area of grassy land. গলফ খেলা

golf club (**golf clubs**) *n* A **golf club** is a long, thin, metal stick with a piece of wood or metal at one end that you use to hit the ball in golf. গলফ খেলার ক্লাব ▷ *n* A **golf club** is a social organization which provides a golf course and a clubhouse for its members. গলফ শেখার ক্লাব

golf course (**golf courses**) *n* A **golf course** is an area of land where people play golf. গলফ খেলার মাঠ

gone *adj* Someone or something that is **gone** is no longer present or no longer exists. বিগত

good (**better, best**) *adj* If you say that something is **good**, you like it. ভাল ▷ *adj* If you are **good**, you behave well. ভাল ▷ *adj* If you are **good** at something, you do it well. পারদর্শী

goodbye! *excl* You say '**goodbye!**' to someone when you or they are leaving, or at the end of a telephone conversation. বিদায়-সম্ভাষণ

good-looking (**better-looking, best-looking**) *adj* A **good-looking** person has an attractive face. সুশ্রী

good-natured *adj* A **good-natured** person or animal is naturally friendly and does not get angry easily. সুন্দর স্বভাব-বিশিষ্ট

goods *npl* **Goods** are things that are made to be sold. জিনিসপত্র

go off *v* If an explosive device or a gun **goes off**, it explodes or fires. বিস্ফোরণ ঘটা *A few minutes later the bomb went off, destroying the vehicle.*

google (**googles, googling, googled**) *v* If you **google** someone or something, you search the Internet for information about them, especially using the website Google®. গুগল্ করা

go on *v* If you **go on** doing something, or **go on with** an activity, you continue to do it. চালিয়ে যাওয়া *She just went on laughing.*

goose (**geese**) *n* A **goose** is a large bird similar to a duck, with a long neck. লম্বা গলাওয়ালা হাঁস

gooseberry (**gooseberries**) *n* A **gooseberry** is a small green fruit that has a sharp taste and is covered with tiny hairs. বৈচিজাতীয় ছোট ফল

goose pimples *npl* If you get **goose pimples**, the hairs on your skin stand up so that it is covered with tiny bumps. ভয়ে বা শীতে গায়ে কাঁটা দেওয়া

go out *v* When you **go out**, you do something enjoyable away from your home, for example you go to a restaurant or the cinema. বাইরে যাওয়া *I'm going out to dinner tonight.*

go past *v* If you **go past** someone or something, you go near them and keep moving, so that they are then behind you. অতিক্রম করা *He went past me and into the hall.*

gorgeous *adj* Someone or something that is **gorgeous** is extremely pleasant or attractive. (*informal*) জমকালো

gorilla (**gorillas**) *n* A **gorilla** is a very large ape. গরিলা

go round *v* If you **go round** to someone's house, you visit them at their house. পৌঁছানো *I went round to his house last night.*

gossip (**gossips, gossiping, gossiped**) *n* **Gossip** is informal conversation, often about other people's private affairs. পরচর্চা ▷ *vi* If you **gossip** with someone, you talk informally with them, especially about other people or local events. পরচর্চা করা

go through *v* If you **go through** a difficult experience or period of time, you experience it. কাটানো *He was going through a very difficult time.*

go up *v* If a price, amount, or level **goes up**, it becomes higher or greater than it was. দাম বাড়া *Interest rates went up.*

government (**governments**) *n* The **government** of a country is the group of people who are responsible for running it. সরকার

GP (**GPs**) *abbr* A **GP** is a doctor who treats all types of illness, instead of specializing in one area of medicine. **GP** is an abbreviation for 'general practitioner'. সাধারণ চিকিৎসক

GPS (**GPSs**) *abbr* **GPS** is a system that uses signals from satellites to find out the position of an object. **GPS** is an abbreviation for 'global positioning system'. জিপিএস

grab (**grabs, grabbing, grabbed**) *vt* If you **grab** something, you take it or pick it up roughly. ছোঁ মেরে নেওয়া

graceful *adj* Someone or something that is **graceful** moves in a smooth and elegant way that is attractive to watch. মাধুর্যমণ্ডিত

grade (**grades**) *n* The **grade** of a product is its quality. মান

gradual *adj* A **gradual** change or process happens in small stages over a long period of time, rather than suddenly. ক্রমিক

gradually *adv* If something changes or is done **gradually**, it changes or is done in small stages over a long period of time, rather than suddenly. পর্যায়ক্রমে

graduate (**graduates**) *n* A **graduate** is a student who has completed a course at a college or university. স্নাতক

graduation *n* **Graduation** is the successful completion of a course of study at a university, college, or school, for which you receive a degree or diploma. স্নাতকত্ব লাভ

graffiti *npl* **Graffiti** is words or pictures that are written or drawn in public places, for example on walls or trains. অশিষ্ট দেওয়াললিখন

grain (**grains**) *n* A **grain** is the seed of a cereal plant, for example rice or wheat. দানাশস্য ▷ *n* A **grain** of something, for example sand or salt, is a tiny piece of it. কণা

gram (**grams**) *n* A **gram** or **gramme** is a unit of weight equal to one thousandth of a kilogram. গ্রাম (ওজনের একক)

grammar *n* **Grammar** is the ways that words can be put together in order to make sentences. ব্যাকরণ

grammatical *adj* **Grammatical** is used to describe something relating to grammar. ব্যাকরণগত

grand (**grander, grandest**) *adj* If you describe a building or landscape as **grand**, you mean that it is splendid or impressive. বিরাট

grandchild (**grandchildren**) *n* Someone's **grandchild** is the child of their son or daughter. নাতি অথবা নাতনি

granddad (**granddads**) *n* Your **granddad** is your grandfather. You can call your granddad 'Granddad'. (*informal*) ঠাকুর্দা

granddaughter (**granddaughters**) *n* Someone's **granddaughter** is the daughter of their son or daughter. নাতনি

grandfather (**grandfathers**) *n* Your **grandfather** is the father of your father or mother. You can call your grandfather 'Grandfather'. ঠাকুর্দা

grandma (**grandmas**) *n* Your **grandma** is your grandmother. You can call your grandma 'Grandma'. (*informal*) ঠাকুমা

grandmother (**grandmothers**) *n* Your **grandmother** is the mother of your father or mother. You can call your grandmother 'Grandmother'. ঠাকুমা

grandpa (**grandpas**) *n* Your **grandpa** is your grandfather. You can call your grandpa 'Grandpa'. (*informal*) ঠাকুর্দা

grandparents *npl* Your **grandparents** are the parents of your father or mother. ঠাকুমা-ঠাকুর্দা

grandson (**grandsons**) *n* Someone's **grandson** is the son of their son or daughter. নাতি

granite *n* **Granite** is a very hard rock used in building. গ্রানাইট

granny (**grannies**) *n* Some people refer to or address their grandmother as **granny**. (*informal*) ঠাকুমা

grant (**grants**) *n* A **grant** is an amount of money that the government or other institution gives to a person or an organization for a particular purpose. অনুদান

grape (**grapes**) *n* **Grapes** are small green or purple fruit that grow in bunches. আঙুর

grapefruit (**grapefruit**, **grapefruits**) *n* A **grapefruit** is a large, round, yellow fruit that has a sharp taste. বাতাপি লেবু

graph (**graphs**) *n* A **graph** is a mathematical diagram which shows the relationship between two or more sets of numbers or measurements. গ্রাফ

graphics *npl* **Graphics** are drawings and pictures that are composed using simple lines and sometimes strong colours. গ্রাফিক্স

grasp (**grasps**, **grasping**, **grasped**) *vt* If you **grasp** something, you take it in your hand and hold it very firmly. আঁকড়ে ধরা

grass (**grasses**) *n* **Grass** is a very common green plant with narrow leaves that forms a layer covering an area of ground. ঘাস ▷ *n* A **grass** is someone who tells the police or other authorities about criminal activities that they know about. (*informal*) পুলিশের চর

grasshopper (**grasshoppers**) *n* A **grasshopper** is an insect with long back legs that jumps high into the air and makes a high, vibrating sound. ফড়িং

grate (**grates**, **grating**, **grated**) *vt* When you **grate** food, you shred it into very small pieces using a tool called a grater. কোরানো

grateful *adj* If you are **grateful** for something that someone has given you or done for you, you are pleased and wish to thank them. কৃতজ্ঞ

grave (**graves**) *n* A **grave** is a place where a dead person is buried. কবর

gravel *n* **Gravel** consists of very small stones. নুড়ি

gravestone (**gravestones**) *n* A **gravestone** is a large stone with words carved into it, which is placed on a grave. কবরের পাথর

graveyard (**graveyards**) *n* A **graveyard** is an area of land where dead people are buried. কবরখানা

gravy *n* **Gravy** is a sauce made from the juices that come from meat when it cooks. মাংসের রসা

grease *n* **Grease** is a thick substance used to oil the moving parts of machines. গ্রীজ

greasy (**greasier**, **greasiest**) *adj* Something that is **greasy** is covered with grease or contains a lot of grease. গ্রীজযুক্ত

great (**greater**, **greatest**) *adj* **Great** means very large. বিশাল ▷ *adj* **Great** means very important. মহৎ ▷ *adj* If you say that something is **great**, you mean that it is very good. সুন্দর

Great Britain *n* **Great Britain** is the island consisting of England, Scotland, and Wales, which together with Northern Ireland makes up the United Kingdom. গ্রেট ব্রিটেন

great-grandfather (**great-grandfathers**) *n* Your **great-grandfather** is the father of your grandmother or grandfather. প্রপিতামহ

great-grandmother (**great-grandmothers**) *n* Your **great-grandmother** is the mother of your grandmother or grandfather. প্রপিতামহী

Greece *n* **Greece** is a republic in south-east Europe. গ্রীস

greedy (**greedier**, **greediest**) *adj* Someone who is **greedy** wants more of something than is necessary or fair. লোভী

Greek (**Greeks**) *adj* **Greek** means belonging or relating to Greece, or to its people, language, or culture. গ্রীসদেশীয় ▷ *n* A **Greek** is a person who comes from Greece. গ্রীসের অধিবাসী ▷ *n* **Greek** is the language spoken in Greece. গ্রীক ভাষা

green (**greener**, **greenest**, **greens**) *adj* Something that is **green** is the colour of grass or leaves. সবুজ ▷ *adj* If you say that someone is **green**, you mean that they have had very little experience of life or a particular job. অনভিজ্ঞ ▷ n **Greens** are members of political movements concerned with the protection of the environment. গ্রীনপার্টি

greengrocer n A **greengrocer** or a **greengrocer's** is a shop that sells fruit and vegetables. ফল ও সজ্জিবিক্রেতা

greenhouse (**greenhouses**) n A **greenhouse** is a glass building in which you grow plants that need to be protected from bad weather. গ্রীনহাউজ

Greenland n **Greenland** is a large island, lying mostly within the Arctic Circle. গ্রীনল্যান্ড

green salad (**green salads**) n A **green salad** is a salad made mainly with lettuce and other green vegetables. গ্রীণ স্যালাড

greet (**greets, greeting, greeted**) vt When you **greet** someone, you say something friendly such as 'hello' when you meet them. সম্ভাষণ করা

greeting (**greetings**) n A **greeting** is something friendly that you say or do when you meet someone. সম্ভাষণ

greetings card (**greetings cards**) n A **greetings card** is a folded card with a picture on the front and greetings inside that you give or send to someone, for example on their birthday. গ্রীটিংস কার্ড

grey (**greyer, greyest**) adj Something that is **grey** is the colour of ashes or of clouds on a rainy day. ধূসর

grey-haired adj A **grey-haired** person has grey hair. পাকা চুলওয়ালা লোক

grid (**grids**) n A **grid** is a pattern of straight lines that cross over each other to form squares. গ্রিড

grief n **Grief** is extreme sadness. তীব্র মনোবেদনা

grill (**grills, grilling, grilled**) n A **grill** is a part of a cooker where food is grilled. উনুনের শিক ▷ vt If you **grill** food, you cook it using strong heat directly above or below it. ঝলসে যাওয়া

grilled adj If food is **grilled**, it is cooked using strong heat directly above or below it. ঝলসানো

grim (**grimmer, grimmest**) adj A situation or news that is **grim** is unpleasant. সাংঘাতিক

grin (**grins, grinning, grinned**) n A **grin** is a broad smile. সদন্ত-হাসি ▷ vi When you **grin**, you smile broadly. দাঁত বার করে হাসা

grind (**grinds, grinding, ground**) vt When something such as corn or coffee **is ground**, it is crushed until it becomes a fine powder. পেষা

grip (**grips, gripping, gripped**) vt If you **grip** something, you take hold of it with your hand and continue to hold it firmly. হাতের মুঠির মধ্যে আসা

gripping adj If something is **gripping**, it holds your interest or attention. উত্তেজক

grit n **Grit** consists of tiny pieces of stone, often put on roads in winter to make them less slippery. কাঁকর

groan (**groans, groaning, groaned**) vi If you **groan**, you make a long, low sound because you are in pain, or because you are upset or unhappy about something. ব্যথায় ককিয়ে ওঠা

grocer (**grocers**) n A **grocer** is a shopkeeper who sells foods such as flour, sugar, and tinned foods. মুদি ▷ n A **grocer** or a **grocer's** is a small shop that sells foods such as flour, sugar, and canned goods. মুদিখানা

groceries npl **Groceries** are foods you buy at a grocer's or at a supermarket. মুদিখানায় লভ্য সামগ্রী

groom (**grooms**) n A **groom** is a man who is getting married. বর

grope (**gropes, groping, groped**) vi If you **grope** for something that you cannot see, you search for it with your hands. হাতড়ানো

gross (**grosser, grossest**) adj You use **gross** to emphasize the degree to which something is unacceptable or unpleasant. পুরোপুরি

grossly adv **Grossly** means in a manner that is unacceptable or unpleasant to a very great degree. স্থূলভাবে

ground (**grounds, grounding, grounded**) n **The ground** is the surface of the earth or the floor of a room. মেঝে/ভূতল ▷ vt If an argument, belief, or opinion **is grounded** in something, that thing is used to justify it. ভিত্তি

ground floor (**ground floors**) n The **ground floor** of a building is the floor that is level or almost level with the ground outside. একতলা

group (**groups**) n A **group** of people or things is a number of them together in one place at one time. দল

grouse (**grouses, grouse**) n A **grouse** is a complaint. অভিযোগ ▷ n **Grouse** are small fat birds which are often shot for sport and can be eaten. বুনো হাঁস

grow (**grows, growing, grew, grown**) vt When you **grow** something, you cause it to develop or increase in size or length. বাড়ানো ▷ vi When something or someone **grows**, they develop and increase in size or intensity. বাড়া

growl (**growls, growling, growled**) vi When a dog or other animal **growls**, it makes a low noise in its throat, usually because it is angry. গরগর করা

grown-up (**grown-ups**) n Children, or people talking to children, often refer to adults as **grown-ups**. পরিণত

growth n The **growth** of something such as an industry, organization, or idea is its development in size, wealth, or importance. বৃদ্ধি

grow up v When someone **grows up**, they gradually change from being a child into being an adult. বেড়ে ওঠা She grew up in this city.

grub (**grubs**) n A **grub** is an insect which has just hatched from its egg. শুঁয়োপোকা

grudge (**grudges**) n If you have a **grudge** against someone, you have unfriendly feelings towards them because they have harmed you in the past. বিদ্বেষ

gruesome adj Something that is **gruesome** is horrible and shocking. ভয়ানক

grumpy (**grumpier, grumpiest**) adj If you say that someone is **grumpy**, you think they are bad-tempered and miserable. বদমেজাজি

guarantee (**guarantees, guaranteeing, guaranteed**) n Something that is a **guarantee** of something else makes it certain that it will happen or that it is true. গ্যারান্টি ▷ vt If one thing **guarantees** another, the first is certain to cause the second thing to happen. গ্যারান্টি দেওয়া

guard (**guards, guarding, guarded**) n A **guard** is someone such as a soldier, police officer, or prison officer who is guarding a particular place or person. রক্ষী ▷ vt If you **guard** a place, person, or object, you watch them carefully, either to protect them or to stop them from escaping. পাহারা দেওয়া

Guatemala n **Guatemala** is a republic in Central America. গুয়েতেমালা

guess (**guesses, guessing, guessed**) n A **guess** is an attempt to give an answer or provide an opinion when you do not know if it is true. আন্দাজ ▷ v If you **guess** something, you give an answer or provide an opinion when you do not know if it is true. আন্দাজ করা

guest (**guests**) n A **guest** is someone who has been invited to stay in your home, attend an event, or appear on a radio or television show. অতিথি

guesthouse (**guesthouses**) n A **guesthouse** is a small hotel. অতিথিশালা

guide (**guides**) n A **guide** is a book that gives you information or instructions to help you do or understand something. পথপ্রদর্শক

guidebook (**guidebooks**) n A **guidebook** is a book that gives tourists information about a town, area, or country. গাইডবুক

guide dog (**guide dogs**) n A **guide dog** is a dog that has been trained to lead a blind person. পথ দেখানো কুকুর

guided tour (**guided tours**) n If someone takes you on a **guided tour** of a place, they show you the place and tell you about it. পথপ্রদর্শিত ভ্রমণ

guilt n **Guilt** is an unhappy feeling that you have because you have done something bad. অপরাধবোধ

guilty (**guiltier, guiltiest**) adj If you feel **guilty**, you feel unhappy because you have done something bad or have failed to do something which you should have done. দোষী

Guinea n **Guinea** is a republic in West Africa, on the Atlantic. গিনি

guinea pig (**guinea pigs**) n If someone is used as a **guinea pig** in an experiment, a drug or other treatment is tested for the first time on them. গিনিপিগ হিসাবে ব্যবহৃত ▷ n A **guinea pig** is a small furry animal without a tail. গিনিপিগ

guitar (**guitars**) n A **guitar** is a wooden musical instrument with six strings which are plucked or strummed. গিটার

Gulf States npl The **Gulf States** are the oil-producing states around the Persian Gulf: Iran, Iraq, Kuwait, Saudi Arabia, Bahrain, Qatar, the United Arab Emirates, and Oman. উপসাগরীয় রাজ্য

gum n **Gum** is a substance, often mint-flavoured, which you chew for a long time but do not swallow. গাম

gun (**guns**) n A **gun** is a weapon from which bullets or pellets are fired. বন্দুক

gust (**gusts**) n A **gust** is a short, strong, sudden rush of wind. আচমকা ঝড়

gut (**guts**) n A person's or animal's **guts** are all their internal organs. নাড়িভুঁড়ি

guy (**guys**) n A **guy** is a man. (informal) লোক

Guyana n **Guyana** is a republic in north-east South America, on the Atlantic. গায়ানা

gym (**gyms**) n A **gym** is a club or room, usually containing special equipment, where people can exercise. জিম

gymnast (**gymnasts**) n A **gymnast** is someone who is trained in gymnastics. জিমন্যাস্টিকে পারদর্শী

gymnastics npl **Gymnastics** consists of physical exercises that develop your strength, co-ordination, and agility. জিমন্যাস্টিকস্

gynaecologist (**gynaecologists**) n A **gynaecologist** is a doctor who specialises in women's diseases and medical conditions. স্ত্রীরোগ-বিশেষজ্ঞ

gypsy (**gypsies**) n A **gypsy** is a member of a race of people who travel from place to place in caravans, rather than living in one place. যাযাবর সম্প্রদায়

habit (**habits**) *n* A **habit** is something that you do often or regularly. অভ্যাস

hack (**hacks, hacking, hacked**) *v* If you **hack** something or **hack** at it, you cut it with strong, rough strokes using a sharp tool such as an axe or knife. ফালা ফালা করে কাটা

hacker (**hackers**) *n* A computer **hacker** is someone who tries to break into computer systems, especially in order to get secret information. হ্যাকার

haddock (**haddock**) *n* A **haddock** is a type of sea fish. কড জাতীয় মাছ

haemorrhoids *npl* **Haemorrhoids** are painful swellings that can appear in the veins inside the anus. হেমারয়েড

haggle (**haggles, haggling, haggled**) *vi* If you **haggle**, you argue about something before reaching an agreement, especially about the cost of something. দর-কষাকষি করা

hail *n* **Hail** consists of tiny balls of ice that fall like rain from the sky. শিলা

hail (**hails, hailing, hailed**) *vt* If a person or event **is hailed** as important or successful, they are praised publicly. সম্ভাষণ জানানো

hair (**hairs**) *n* Your **hair** is the mass of fine thread-like strands that grow on your head. চুল

hairband (**hairbands**) *n* A **hairband** is a strip of fabric or curved plastic worn by women in their hair, that fits closely over the top of the head and behind the ears. হেয়ারব্যান্ড

hairbrush (**hairbrushes**) *n* A **hairbrush** is a brush that you use to brush your hair. চুলের ব্রাশ

haircut (**haircuts**) *n* If you have a **haircut**, someone cuts your hair for you. চুলকাটা

hairdo (**hairdos**) *n* A **hairdo** is the style in which your hair has been cut and arranged. (*informal*) কেশবিন্যাস

hairdresser (**hairdressers**) *n* A **hairdresser** is a person who cuts, washes, and styles people's hair. কেশবিন্যাসকারী ▷ *n* A **hairdresser** or a **hairdresser's** is a place where you can get your hair cut, washed, and shaped. কেশবিন্যাসকারীর দোকান

hairdryer (**hairdryers**) *n* A **hairdryer** is a machine that you use to dry your hair. হেয়ারড্রায়ার

hair gel (**hair gels**) *n* **Hair gel** is a thick substance like jelly that you use to keep your hair in a particular style. চুলে লাগানোর জেলি

hairgrip (**hairgrips**) *n* A **hairgrip** is a small piece of metal or plastic bent back on itself, which you use to hold your hair in position. চুল আটকানোর ক্লিপ

hair spray (**hairsprays**) *n* **Hair spray** is a sticky substance that you spray out of a can onto your hair in order to hold it in place. চুলে লাগানোর স্প্রে

hairstyle (**hairstyles**) *n* Your **hairstyle** is the style in which your hair has been cut or arranged. কেশবিন্যাস

hairy (**hairier, hairiest**) *adj* Someone or something that is **hairy** is covered with a lot of hair. লোমওয়ালা

Haiti *n* **Haiti** is a republic in the Caribbean, on the western side of the island of Hispaniola. হাইতি

half (**halves**) *adj* **Half** means being a half or approximately a half. আধা ▷ *adv* You use **half** to say that something is only partly the case. অর্ধেক ▷ *n* A **half** is one of two equal parts that make up a whole thing. অর্ধেক

half board *n* If you stay at a hotel and have **half board**, your breakfast and evening meal are included in the price of your stay at the hotel, but not your lunch. হোটেল ভাড়াতে লাঞ্চ দেওয়া হয় না

half-hour (**half-hours**) *n* A **half-hour** is a period of 30 minutes. আধ-ঘন্টা

half-price *adj* If something is **half-price**, it costs only half what it usually costs. অর্ধেক দাম ▷ *adv* If you do something **half-price** or if you buy or sell something **half-price**, it costs only half what it usually costs. অর্ধেক দামে

half-term (**half-terms**) *n* **Half-term** is a short holiday in the middle of a school term. ষান্মাসিক

half-time *n* In sport, **half-time** is the short rest period between the two parts of a game. বিরতি

halfway *adv* **Halfway** means in the middle of a place or in between two points, at an equal distance from each of them. মধ্যিখানে

hall (**halls**) *n* In a house or flat, the **hall** is the area just inside the front door. হলঘর

hallway (**hallways**) *n* A **hallway** is the entrance hall of a house or other building. দালান

halt (**halts**) *n* A **halt** is an interruption or end to activity, movement or progress. থেমে যাওয়া

hamburger (**hamburgers**) *n* A **hamburger** is a flat round mass of minced beef, fried and eaten in a bread roll. হ্যামবার্গার

hammer (**hammers**) *n* A **hammer** is a tool used for hitting things. It consists of a heavy piece of metal at the end of a handle. হাতুড়ি

hammock (**hammocks**) *n* A **hammock** is a piece of strong cloth or netting which is hung between two supports and used as a bed. দোলনা বিছানা

hamster (**hamsters**) *n* A **hamster** is a small furry animal which is similar to a mouse. ধেড়ে ইঁদুরের মত প্রাণী

hand (**hands, handing, handed**) *n* Your **hands** are the parts of your body that are at the ends of your arms, and that you use to hold things. A **hand** has four fingers and a thumb. হাত ▷ *vt* If you **hand** something to someone, you pass it to them. দেওয়া

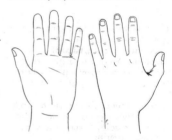

handbag (**handbags**) *n* A **handbag** is a small bag used by women to carry things such as money and keys. হাতব্যাগ

handball *n* **Handball** is a team sport in which the players try to score goals by throwing or hitting a large ball with their hand. হ্যান্ডবল

handbook (**handbooks**) *n* A **handbook** is a book giving advice or instructions on how to do a practical task. নির্দেশিকা

handbrake (**handbrakes**) *n* In a vehicle, the **handbrake** is a brake which the driver operates with his or her hand, for example when parking. হ্যান্ডব্রেক

handcuffs *npl* **Handcuffs** are two metal rings linked by a short chain which are locked round a prisoner's wrists. হাতকড়া

handkerchief (**handkerchiefs**) *n* A **handkerchief** is a small square of fabric which you use for blowing your nose. রুমাল

handle (**handles, handling, handled**)
n A **handle** is the part of something, for
example a tool or a bag, that you use to
hold it. হাতল ▷ *vt* If you **handle** a situation,
you deal with it. পরিচালনা করা ▷ *n* A **handle**
is something that is joined to a door, a
window, or a drawer, that you use to open
and close it. হাতল

handlebars *npl* The **handlebars** of a
bicycle consist of a curved metal bar with
handles at each end which are used for
steering. হাতল

hand luggage *n* When you travel by air,
your **hand luggage** is the luggage you
have with you in the plane, rather than the
luggage that is carried in the hold. হাতে
বওয়ার তল্পিতল্পা

handmade *adj* If something is **handmade**,
it is made without using machines. হাতে
বানানো

hands-free *adj* A **hands-free** phone or
other device can be used without being
held in your hand. হ্যান্ডস্-ফ্রী

hands-free kit (**hands-free kits**) *n* A
hands-free kit is equipment that enables
you to use your mobile phone, for example
while driving, without holding it in your
hand. হ্যান্ডস্-ফ্রী কিট

handsome *adj* A **handsome** man has an
attractive face. সুদর্শন

handwriting *n* Your **handwriting** is your
style of writing with a pen or pencil. হাতের
লেখা

handy (**handier, handiest**) *adj* Something
that is **handy** is useful. সুবিধাজনক

hang (**hangs, hanging, hung**) *vt* If you
hang something somewhere, you fix
the top of it to something so that it does
not touch the ground. ঝোলানো ▷ *vi* If
something **hangs** somewhere, it is attached
at the top so it does not touch the ground.
টাঙানো

hanger (**hangers**) *n* A **hanger** is a curved
piece of metal, plastic or wood used for
hanging clothes on. হ্যাঙ্গার

hang-gliding *n* **Hang-gliding** is the
activity of flying from high places in a type
of glider made from a large piece
of cloth fixed to a frame. The pilot
hangs underneath the glider. হ্যাং-গ্লাইডারে
ওড়া

hang on *v* If you ask someone to **hang
on**, you mean you want them to wait for a
moment. (*informal*) অপেক্ষা করা *Hang on a
second. I'll come with you.*

hangover (**hangovers**) *n* A **hangover** is
a headache and feeling of sickness that
you have after drinking too much alcohol.
খোয়ারি

hang up *v* If you **hang up** or you **hang up**
the phone, you end a phone call. ফোন রেখে
দেওয়া *Don't hang up!*

hankie (**hankies**) *n* A **hankie** is a small
square of fabric which you use for blowing
your nose. (*informal*) রুমাল

happen (**happens, happening, happened**)
vi When something **happens**, it occurs or is
done without being planned. ঘটা

happily *adv* You can add **happily** to a
statement to show that you are glad that
something happened or is true. আনন্দের
ব্যাপার

happiness *n* **Happiness** is feelings of joy
or contentment. সুখ

happy (**happier, happiest**) *adj* Someone
who is **happy** has feelings of joy or
contentment. সুখী

harassment *n* **Harassment** is behaviour
which is intended to trouble or annoy
someone, for example repeated attacks on
them or attempts to cause them problems.
হয়রানি

harbour (**harbours**) *n* A **harbour** is an area
of deep water which is protected from the
sea by land or walls, so that boats can be
left there safely. পোতাশ্রয়

hard (**harder, hardest**) *adj* If something
is **hard**, you have to try a lot to do it or to
understand it. কঠিন ▷ *adj* Something that
is **hard** is solid, and it is not easy to bend it

h

or break it. শক্ত ▷ *adv* If you work **hard**, you work with a lot of effort. কঠোর

hardboard *n* **Hardboard** is a material which is made by pressing very small pieces of wood very closely together to form a thin, slightly flexible sheet. হার্ডবোর্ড

hard disk (**hard disks**) *n* A **hard disk** is a hard plastic disk inside a computer on which data and programs are stored. হার্ড-ডিস্ক

hardly *adv* You use **hardly** to say that something is almost, or only just, true. নামমাত্র ▷ *adv* When you say things like **hardly ever** and **hardly any**, you mean almost never or almost none. খুবই কম বা না

hard shoulder (**hard shoulders**) *n* The **hard shoulder** is the area at the side of a motorway or other road where you are allowed to stop if your car breaks down. রাস্তায় গাড়ি খারাপ হলে থামানোর জায়গা

hard up (**harder up, hardest up**) *adj* If you are **hard up**, you have very little money. (*informal*) অসচ্ছল

hardware *n* Computer **hardware** is computer equipment as opposed to the programs that are written for it. Printers and monitors are computer hardware. হার্ডওয়ার

hare (**hares**) *n* A **hare** is an animal like a large rabbit, but with longer ears and legs. খরগোশ

harm (**harms, harming, harmed**) *vt* To **harm** a person or animal means to cause them physical injury, usually on purpose. ক্ষতি করা

harmful *adj* Something that is **harmful** has a bad effect on someone or something else. ক্ষতিকর

harmless *adj* Something that is **harmless** does not have any bad effects. নিরাপদ

harp (**harps**) *n* A **harp** is a large musical instrument consisting of a triangular frame with vertical strings which you pluck with your fingers. বীণা

harsh (**harsher, harshest**) *adj* **Harsh** climates or living conditions are very

difficult for people, animals, and plants to exist in. রূঢ়

harvest (**harvests, harvesting, harvested**) *n* **The harvest** is the gathering of a crop. ফসল ▷ *vt* When you **harvest** a crop, you gather it in. ফসল কাটা

hastily *adv* If you do something **hastily**, you do it in a hurry, without planning or preparation. তাড়াতাড়ি

hat (**hats**) *n* A **hat** is a covering that you wear on your head. টুপি

hatchback (**hatchbacks**) *n* A **hatchback** is a car with an extra door at the back which opens upwards. পিছন দিকের দরজা ওপরের দিকে খোলা যায় এমন গাড়ি

hate (**hates, hating, hated**) *vt* If you **hate** someone or something, you have an extremely strong feeling of dislike for them. ঘৃণা করা

hatred *n* **Hatred** is an extremely strong feeling of dislike for someone or something. ঘৃণা

haunted *adj* A **haunted** building or other place is one where a ghost regularly appears. ভুতুড়ে

have (**has, having, had**) *v* You use **have** and **has** with another verb to form the present perfect. আছে *Alex hasn't left yet.* ▷ *v* When you **have** something, you feel it, or it happens to you. রয়েছে *I have a bad cold.*

have to *v* You use **have to** when you are saying that something is necessary, obligatory, or must happen. If you do not **have to** do something, it is not necessary or obligatory for you to do it. হবেই *He had to go to Germany.*

hawthorn (**hawthorns**) *n* A **hawthorn** is a small tree which has sharp thorns and produces white or pink flowers. কাঁটাগাছ

hay *n* **Hay** is grass which has been cut and dried so that it can be used to feed animals. খড়

hay fever *n* If someone suffers from **hay fever**, they have an allergy to pollen which makes their nose, throat, and eyes become red and swollen. একধরণের জ্বর

haystack (**haystacks**) *n* A **haystack** is a large, solid pile of hay, often covered with a straw roof to protect it, which is left in the field until it is needed. খড়ের গাদা

hazard warning lights *npl* The **hazard warning lights** on a motor vehicle are small lights set to flash all at the same time to indicate that the vehicle is stopped and blocking the traffic. হ্যাজার্ড লাইট

hazelnut (**hazelnuts**) *n* **Hazelnuts** are nuts from a hazel tree, which can be eaten. হেজল গাছের বাদাম

he *pron* You use **he** to talk about a man, a boy, or a male animal. তিনি (পুরুষ) He could never remember all our names.

head (**heads**, **heading**, **headed**) *n* The **head** of something is the person who is its leader. প্রধান ▷ *n* Your **head** is the part of your body at the top that has your eyes, ears, nose, mouth, and brain in it. মাথা ▷ *vt* If someone or something **heads** a line, they are at the front of it. নেতৃত্ব দেওয়া

headache (**headaches**) *n* If you have a **headache**, you have a pain in your head. মাথাব্যথা

headlight (**headlights**) *n* A vehicle's **headlights** are the large bright lights at the front. হেডলাইট

headline (**headlines**) *n* A **headline** is the title of a newspaper story, printed in large letters at the top of it. শিরোনাম

head office (**head offices**) *n* The **head office** of a company is its main office. মুখ্য কার্যালয়

headphones *npl* **Headphones** are small speakers which you wear over your ears in order to listen to music or other sounds without other people hearing. হেডফান

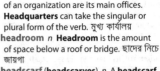

headquarters *npl* The **headquarters**

of an organization are its main offices. **Headquarters** can take the singular or plural form of the verb. মুখ্য কার্যালয়

headroom *n* **Headroom** is the amount of space below a roof or bridge. ছাদের নিচে জায়গা

headscarf (**headscarves**) *n* A **headscarf** is a piece of cloth which some women wear around their heads, for example to keep their hair neat, or as part of their religious beliefs. চুল ঢাকার স্কার্ফ

headteacher (**headteachers**) *n* A **headteacher** is a teacher who is in charge of a school. প্রধান শিক্ষক / শিক্ষিকা

heal (**heals**, **healing**, **healed**) *vi* When an injury such as a broken bone **heals**, it becomes healthy and normal again. সেরে যাওয়া

health *n* Your **health** is the condition of your body. স্বাস্থ্য

healthy (**healthier**, **healthiest**) *adj* Someone who is **healthy** is well and strong and is not often ill. সুস্বাস্থ্যবল ▷ *adj* Something that is **healthy** is good for you. স্বাস্থ্যকর

heap (**heaps**) *n* A **heap** of things is a messy pile of them. স্তূপ

hear (**hears**, **hearing**, **heard**) *v* When you **hear** sounds, you are aware of them because they reach your ears. শোনা

hearing (**hearings**) *n* **Hearing** is the sense which makes it possible for you to be aware of sounds. শ্রবণশক্তি

hearing aid (**hearing aids**) *n* A **hearing aid** is a device which people with hearing difficulties wear in their ear to enable them to hear better. কানে শোনার যন্ত্র

heart (**hearts**) *n* Your **heart** is the organ in your chest that pumps the blood around your body. হৃৎপিণ্ড

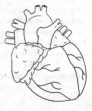

heart attack (**heart attacks**) *n* If someone has a **heart attack**, their heart begins to beat irregularly or stops completely. হৃদরোগে আক্রান্ত হওয়া

heartbroken *adj* Someone who is **heartbroken** is extremely sad and upset. মানসিকভাবে ভেঙে পড়া

heartburn *n* **Heartburn** is a painful burning sensation in your chest, caused by indigestion. বুকজ্বালা করা

heat (**heats, heating, heated**) *n* **Heat** is warmth or the quality of being hot. তাপ ▷ *vt* When you **heat** something, you raise its temperature, for example by using a flame or a special piece of equipment. গরম করা

heater (**heaters**) *n* A **heater** is a piece of equipment which is used to warm a place or to heat water. হিটার

heather *n* **Heather** is a low spreading plant with small purple, pink, or white flowers that grows wild on hills or moorland. জংলি ফুলের গাছ

heating *n* **Heating** is the process or equipment involved in keeping a building warm. হিটিং

heat up *v* When you **heat** something **up**, especially food which has already been cooked and allowed to go cold, you make it hot. পুনরায় গরম করা *She heated up some soup for me.*

heaven *n* In some religions, **heaven** is said to be the place where God lives and where good people go when they die. স্বর্গ

heavily *adv* You can use **heavily** to indicate that something is great in amount, degree, or intensity. গুরুত্বরভাবে

heavy (**heavier, heaviest**) *adj* Something that is **heavy** weighs a lot. ভারি

hedge (**hedges**) *n* A **hedge** is a row of bushes along the edge of a garden, field, or road. ঝোপঝাড়ের সারি

hedgehog (**hedgehogs**) *n* A **hedgehog** is a small brown animal with sharp spikes covering its back. সজারুজাতীয় ছোট প্রাণী

heel (**heels**) *n* Your **heel** is the back part of your foot, just below your ankle. গোড়ালি

height (**heights**) *n* The **height** of a person or thing is their measurement from bottom to top. উচ্চতা

heir (**heirs**) *n* Someone's **heir** is the person who will inherit their money, property, or title when they die. উত্তরাধিকারী

heiress (**heiresses**) *n* An **heiress** is a woman who will inherit property, money, or a title. উত্তরাধিকারিণী

helicopter (**helicopters**) *n* A **helicopter** is an aircraft with no wings. It hovers or moves vertically and horizontally by means of large overhead blades which rotate. হেলিকপ্টার

hell *n* According to some religions, **hell** is the place where the Devil lives, and where wicked people are sent to be punished when they die. নরক

hello! *excl* You say 'hello!' to someone when you meet them. শুনছেন!

helmet (**helmets**) *n* A **helmet** is a hard hat which you wear to protect your head. শিরস্ত্রাণ

help (**helps, helping, helped**) *excl* You shout 'help!' when you are in danger in order to attract someone's attention so that they can come and rescue you. বাঁচাও! ▷ *n* **Help** is the act of helping. সাহায্য ▷ *v* If you **help** someone, you make something easier for them to do, for example by doing part of their work or by giving them advice or money. সাহায্য করা

helpful *adj* If someone is **helpful**, they help you by doing work for you or by giving you advice or information. উপকারী

helpline (**helplines**) *n* A **helpline** is a special telephone service that people can call to get advice about a particular subject. হেল্পলাইন

hen (**hens**) *n* A **hen** is a female chicken. মুরগী

hen night (**hen nights**) *n* A **hen night** is a party for a woman who is getting married very soon, to which only women are invited. আইবুড়োভাত

hepatitis n **Hepatitis** is a serious disease which affects the liver. হেপাটাইটিস

her det You use **her** to say that something belongs to a woman or a girl. তার (নারী) I borrowed her pen. ▷ pron You use **her** to talk about a woman or a girl. তাকে (নারী) I had something to say to her.

herbal tea (**herbal teas**) n **Herbal tea** is tea made from or using herbs. ভেষজ চা

herbs npl **Herbs** are plants whose leaves are used in cookery to add flavour to food, or as a medicine. ঔষধি

here adv **Here** means the place where you are. এখানে

hereditary adj A **hereditary** characteristic or illness is passed on to a child from its parents before it is born. বংশগত

heritage (**heritages**) n A country's **heritage** consists of all the qualities and traditions that have continued over many years, especially when they are considered to be of historical importance. ঐতিহ্য

hernia (**hernias**) n A **hernia** is a medical condition in which one of your internal organs sticks through a weak point in the surrounding tissue. হার্নিয়া

hero (**heroes**) n The **hero** of a book, play, or film is the main male character, who usually has good qualities. নায়ক

heroine (**heroines**) n The **heroine** of a book, play, or film is its main female character, who usually has good qualities. নায়িকা

heron (**herons**) n A **heron** is a large bird which has long legs and a long beak, and which eats fish. সারস

herring (**herring, herrings**) n A **herring** is a long silver-coloured fish. হেরিংমাছ

hers pron You use **hers** to say that something belongs to a woman or a girl. তার (নারী) She said that the bag was hers.

herself pron You use **herself** when you want to say that something a woman or a

girl does has an effect on her. নিজে (নারী) She pulled herself out of the water.

hesitate (**hesitates, hesitating, hesitated**) vi If you **hesitate**, you pause slightly while you are doing something or just before you do it, usually because you are uncertain, embarrassed, or worried. ইতস্ততঃ করা

HGV abbr An **HGV** is a large vehicle such as a lorry. **HGV** is an abbreviation for 'heavy goods vehicle'. বড় মাল গাড়ী

hi! excl In informal situations, you say '**hi!**' to greet someone. একটি সম্ভাষণ

hiccups npl When you have **hiccups**, you make repeated sharp sounds in your throat, often because you have been eating or drinking too quickly. হেঁচকি

hidden adj Something that is **hidden** is not easily noticed. গোপন

hide (**hides, hiding, hid, hidden**) vt If you **hide** something, you put it where no one can see it or find it. লুকিয়ে রাখা ▷ vi If you **hide**, you go somewhere where people cannot easily find you. লুকিয়ে থাকা ▷ vt If you **hide** what you feel, you do not let people know about it. গোপন করা

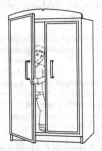

hide-and-seek n **Hide-and-seek** is a children's game in which one player covers his or her eyes until the other players have hidden themselves, and then he or she tries to find them. লুকোচুরি খেলা

hideous *adj* If you say that someone or something is **hideous**, you mean that they are extremely unpleasant or ugly. জঘন্য

hifi (**hifis**) *n* A **hifi** is a set of equipment on which you play CDs and tapes, and which produces stereo sound of very good quality. হাইফাই

high (**higher**, **highest**) *adj* Something that is **high** is tall or is a long way above the ground. উঁচু ▷ *adv* If items are piled **high**, they are arranged in a tall pile. উঁচু ▷ *adj* **High** means great in amount or strength. উঁচু ▷ *adj* A **high** sound or voice goes up a long way. উঁচু

highchair (**highchairs**) *n* A **highchair** is a chair with long legs for a small child to sit in while they are eating. উঁচু চেয়ার

higher education *n* **Higher education** is education at universities and colleges. উচ্চ-শিক্ষা

high-heeled *adj* **High-heeled** shoes are women's shoes that have high heels. উঁচু হিলের জুতো

high heels *npl* You can refer to women's shoes that have high heels as **high heels**. উঁচু-হিল জুতো

high jump *n* The **high jump** is an athletics event which involves jumping over a raised bar. হাই জাম্প

highlight (**highlights**, **highlighting**, **highlighted**) *n* The **highlights** of an event, activity, or period of time are the most interesting or exciting parts of it. উল্লেখযোগ্য ▷ *vt* If you **highlight** a point or problem, you draw attention to it. প্রাধান্য দেওয়া

highlighter (**highlighters**) *n* A **highlighter** is a pen with brightly coloured ink that is used to mark parts of a document. হাইলাইটার কলম

high-rise (**high-rises**) *n* A **high-rise** is a modern building which is very tall and has many levels or floors. বহুতল ভবন

high season *n* The **high season** is the time of year when a place has most tourists or visitors. সেরা মরসুম

Highway Code *n* **The Highway Code** is an official book which contains the rules which tell people how to use public roads safely. হাইওয়ে কোড

hijack (**hijacks**, **hijacking**, **hijacked**) *vt* If someone **hijacks** a plane or other vehicle, they illegally take control of it by force while it is travelling from one place to another. অপহরণ করা

hijacker (**hijackers**) *n* A **hijacker** is a person who hijacks a plane or other vehicle. অপহরণকারী

hike (**hikes**) *n* A **hike** is a long walk in the country, especially one that you go on for pleasure. পায়ে চলা

hiking *n* **Hiking** is the activity of going on long walks in the country, especially for pleasure. পদযাত্রা

hilarious *adj* If something is **hilarious**, it is extremely funny. অত্যন্ত মজার

hill (**hills**) *n* A **hill** is an area of land that is higher than the land that surrounds it, but not as high as a mountain. পাহাড়

hill-walking *n* **Hill-walking** is the activity of walking through hilly country for pleasure. পাহাড়ে হেঁটে বেড়ানো

him *pron* You use **him** to talk about a man or a boy. তাকে (পুরুষ) *We met him at the station.*

himself *pron* You use **himself** when you want to say that something a man or a boy does has an effect on him. নিজে (পুরুষ) *He fell and hurt himself.*

Hindu (**Hindus**) *adj* **Hindu** is used to describe things that belong or relate to Hinduism. হিন্দুধর্ম সংক্রান্ত ▷ *n* A **Hindu** is a person who believes in Hinduism. হিন্দু

Hinduism *n* **Hinduism** is an Indian religion, which has many gods and teaches that people have another life on earth after they die. হিন্দুধর্ম

hinge (**hinges**) *n* A **hinge** is a moveable joint made of metal, wood, or plastic that joins two things so that one of them can swing freely. কবজা

hint (**hints, hinting, hinted**) n A **hint** is a suggestion about something that is made in an indirect way. আভাস ▷ vi If you **hint** at something, you suggest it in an indirect way. সংকেত দেওয়া

hip (**hips**) n Your **hips** are the two areas or bones at the sides of your body between the tops of your legs and your waist. নিতম্ব

hippie (**hippies**) n In the 1960s and 1970s, **hippies** were people who rejected conventional society and tried to live a life based on peace and love. হিপ্পি

hippo (**hippos**) n A **hippo** is a hippopotamus. (informal) জলহস্তী

hippopotamus (**hippopotami, hippopotamuses**) n A **hippopotamus** is a very large African animal with short legs and thick, hairless skin. Hippopotamuses live in and near rivers. জলহস্তী

hire (**hires, hiring, hired**) n You use **hire** to refer to the activity or business of hiring something. ভাড়া ▷ vt If you **hire** someone, you employ them or pay them to do a particular job for you. নিয়োগ করা

his det You use **his** to say that something belongs to a man or a boy. তার(পুরুষ) He showed me his new football. ▷ pron You use **his** to say that something belongs to a man or a boy. তার (পুরুষ) He listened to the advice, but the decision was his.

historian (**historians**) n A **historian** is a person who specializes in the study of history and who writes about it. ইতিহাসকার

historical adj **Historical** people, situations, or things existed in the past and are considered to be a part of history. ঐতিহাসিক

history (**histories**) n You can refer to the events of the past as **history**. You can also refer to the past events which concern a particular topic or place as its **history**. ইতিহাস

hit (**hits, hitting**) n A **hit** is the act of a moving object touching another object very quickly or hard. আঘাত ▷ vt If you

hit something, you touch it with a lot of strength. আঘাত করা

hitch (**hitches**) n A **hitch** is a slight problem. অপ্রত্যাশিত বাধা

hitchhike (**hitchhikes, hitchhiking, hitchhiked**) vi If you **hitchhike**, you travel by getting free lifts from passing vehicles. গাড়িতে লিফট নেওয়া

hitchhiker (**hitchhikers**) n A **hitchhiker** is someone who travels somewhere by getting free lifts from passing vehicles. গাড়িতে লিফট নেওয়া ব্যক্তি

hitchhiking n **Hitchhiking** is the activity or process of travelling by getting lifts from passing vehicles without paying. গাড়িতে লিফট নেওয়া

HIV-negative adj If someone is **HIV-negative**, they are not infected with the HIV virus, which reduces the ability of people's bodies to fight illness and which can cause AIDS. এইচ আই ভি নেগিটিভ

HIV-positive adj If someone is **HIV-positive**, they are infected with the HIV virus, which reduces the ability of people's bodies to fight illness, and they may develop AIDS. এইচ আই ভি পজিটিভ

hobby (**hobbies**) n A **hobby** is something that you enjoy doing in your spare time, for example reading or playing tennis. শখ

hockey n **Hockey** is a sport played between two teams of 11 players who use long curved sticks to hit a small ball and try to score goals. হকি

hold (**holds, holding, held**) vt When you **hold** something, you have it in your hands or your arms. ধরা ▷ vt If something **holds** an amount of something, then that is how much it has room for inside. ধারণ ক্ষমতা

holdall (**holdalls**) n A **holdall** is a strong bag which you use to carry your clothes and other things, for example when you are travelling. বড় ব্যাগ

hold on v If you **hold on** or **hold onto** something, you keep your hand firmly round something. ধরে রাখা *He held on to a coffee cup.*

hold up (**hold-ups**) *v* If someone or something **holds** you **up**, they delay you. অপেক্ষা করিয়ে রাখা *Why were you holding everyone up?* ▷ *n* A **hold-up** is a situation in which someone is threatened with a weapon in order to make them hand over money or valuables. ভয় দেখিয়ে টাকা আদায়

hole (**holes**) *n* A **hole** is an opening or hollow space in something. গর্ত

holiday (**holidays**) *n* A **holiday** is a period of time during which you relax and enjoy yourself away from home. ছুটি

Holland *n* **Holland** is another name for the Netherlands. হল্যান্ড

hollow *adj* Something that is **hollow** has a hole or space inside it. ফাঁপা

holly (**hollies**) *n* **Hollies** are a group of evergreen trees and shrubs which have hard, shiny, prickly leaves, and also have bright red berries in winter. একজাতীয় চিরহরিৎ গুল্ম

holy (**holier, holiest**) *adj* Something that is **holy** is considered to be special because it relates to God or to a particular religion. পবিত্র

home (**homes**) *adv* **Home** means to or at the place where you live. বাড়ি ▷ *n* Your **home** is the place where you live. বাসা

home address (**home addresses**) *n* Your **home address** is the address of your house or flat. বাড়ির ঠিকানা

homeland (**homelands**) *n* Your **homeland** is your native country. (*written*) জন্মভূমি

homeless *adj* **Homeless** people have nowhere to live. গৃহহীন

home-made *adj* **Home-made** things are made in someone's home, rather than in a shop or factory. বাড়িতে তৈরী

home match (**home matches**) *n* When a sports team plays a **home match**, they play a game on their own ground, rather than on the opposing team's ground. নিজের জায়গায় ম্যাচ

homeopathic *adj* **Homeopathic** means relating to or used in homeopathy. হোমিওপ্যাথি সংক্রান্ত

homeopathy *n* **Homeopathy** is a way of treating illness in which the patient is given very small amounts of a drug which would produce symptoms of the illness if taken in large quantities. হোমিওপ্যাথি

home page (**home pages**) *n* On the Internet, a person's or organization's **home page** is the main page of information about them. হোম-পেজ

homesick *adj* If you are **homesick**, you feel unhappy because you are away from home and are missing your family and friends. গৃহাকুল

homework *n* **Homework** is school work given to pupils to do at home. স্কুলের কাজ

Honduras *n* **Honduras** is a republic in Central America. হনডুরাস

honest *adj* If you describe someone as **honest**, you mean that they always tell the truth, and do not try to deceive people or break the law. সৎ

honestly *adv* If you do something **honestly**, you are truthful, and do not try to deceive people or break the law. সৎভাবে

honesty *n* **Honesty** is the quality of being honest. সততা

honey (**honeys**) *n* **Honey** is a sweet, sticky, edible substance made by bees. মধু

honeymoon (**honeymoons**) *n* A **honeymoon** is a holiday taken by a couple who have just married. মধুচন্দ্রিমা

honeysuckle (**honeysuckles**) *n* **Honeysuckle** is a climbing plant with sweet-smelling yellow, pink, or white flowers. সুগন্ধি পুস্পলতা

honour (**honours**) *n* **Honour** means doing what you believe to be right and being confident that you have done what is right. সম্মান

hood (**hoods**) *n* A **hood** is a part of some pieces of clothing which covers your head. গুঠন

hook (hooks) n A hook is a bent piece of metal or plastic that is used for catching or holding things, or for hanging things up. আঁকড়া

hooray! *excl* People sometimes shout 'hooray!' when they are very happy and excited about something. আনন্দধ্বনি!

Hoover® (hoovers) n A Hoover is an electric machine which sucks up dust and dirt from carpets. ধুলোবালি শুষে নেবার বৈদ্যুতিক যন্ত্র

hoover (hoovers, hoovering, hoovered) v If you hoover a carpet, you clean it using a vacuum cleaner. ভ্যাকুয়াম ক্লিনার দিয়ে পরিষ্কার করা

hop (hops, hopping, hopped) vi If you hop, you jump on one foot. একপায়ে লাফানো ▷ vi When animals or birds hop, they jump with two feet together. দুপায়ে লাফানো

hope (hopes, hoping, hoped) n Hope is a feeling of desire and expectation that things will go well in the future. আশা ▷ v If you hope that something is true, or if you hope for something, you want it to be true or to happen, and you usually believe that it is possible or likely. আশা করা

hopeful adj If you are hopeful, you are fairly confident that something that you want to happen will happen. আশাপ্রদ

hopefully adv Hopefully is often used when mentioning something that you hope and are fairly confident will happen. আশাপ্রদভাবে

hopeless adj If you feel hopeless, you feel desperate because there seems to be no possibility of success. আশাহীন

horizon n The horizon is the distant where the sky seems to touch the land or the sea. দিগন্ত

horizontal adj Something that is horizontal is flat and parallel with the ground. অনুভূমিক

hormone (hormones) n A hormone is a chemical, usually occurring naturally in your body, that stimulates certain organs of your body. হরমোন

horn (horns) n On a vehicle such as a car, the horn is the device that makes a loud noise. হর্ন ▷ n A horn is one of the hard bones with sharp points that grow out of some animals' heads. Goats and bulls have horns. শিঙ ▷ n A horn is an instrument that you blow into to make music. হর্ন

horoscope (horoscopes) n Your horoscope is a forecast of events which some people believe will happen to you in the future, based on the position of the stars when you were born. কোষ্ঠী

horrendous adj Something that is horrendous is very bad or unpleasant. ভয়ংকর

horrible adj If you say that someone or something is horrible, you mean that they are very unpleasant. (*informal*) ভয়ানক

horrifying adj If you describe something as horrifying, you mean that it is shocking or disgusting. ভয়ংকর

horror n Horror is a strong feeling of alarm caused by something extremely unpleasant. বিভীষিকা

horror film (horror films) n A horror film is a film that is intended to be very frightening. ভয়াবহ সিনেমা

horse (horses) n A horse is a large animal which people can ride. ঘোড়া

horse racing n Horse racing is a sport in which horses ridden by people called jockeys run in races, sometimes jumping over fences. ঘোড়দৌড়

horseradish *n* **Horseradish** is a small white vegetable that is the root of a crop. It has a very strong sharp taste and is often made into a sauce. মুলো

horse riding *n* **Horse riding** is the activity of riding a horse, especially for enjoyment or as a form of exercise. ঘোড়ায় চড়া

horseshoe (**horseshoes**) *n* A **horseshoe** is a piece of metal shaped like a U which is fixed to a horse's hoof. ঘোড়ার নাল

hose (**hoses**) *n* A **hose** is a long, flexible pipe through which water is carried in order to do things such as put out fires or water gardens. এক ধরণের জলের পাইপ

hosepipe (**hosepipes**) *n* A **hosepipe** is a hose that people use to water their gardens or wash their cars. হোসপাইপ

hospital (**hospitals**) *n* A **hospital** is a place where people who are ill are looked after by doctors and nurses. হাসপাতাল

hospitality *n* **Hospitality** is friendly, welcoming behaviour towards guests or strangers. আতিথেয়তা

host (**hosts**) *n* The **host** at a party is the person who has invited everybody. গৃহকর্তা ▷ *n* A **host** of things is a lot of them. বহু

hostage (**hostages**) *n* A **hostage** is someone who has been captured by a person or organization and who may be killed or injured if people do not do what that person or organization demands. বন্দি

hostel (**hostels**) *n* A **hostel** is a large house where people can stay cheaply for a short time. হোস্টেল

hostile *adj* If someone is **hostile** to another person or to an idea or suggestion, they show their dislike for them in an aggressive way. প্রতিকূল

hot (**hotter, hottest**) *adj* If something is **hot**, it has a high temperature. গরম

hot dog (**hot dogs**) *n* A **hot dog** is a long bread roll with a sausage in it. হট-ডগ

hotel (**hotels**) *n* A **hotel** is a building where people stay, paying for their rooms and meals. হোটেল

hot-water bottle (**hot-water bottles**) *n* A **hot-water bottle** is a rubber container that you fill with hot water and put in a bed to make it warm. গরম জলের বোতল

hour (**hours**) *n* An **hour** is a period of sixty minutes. ঘন্টা

hourly *adj* An **hourly** event happens once every hour. ঘন্টায় ▷ *adv* If something happens **hourly**, it happens once every hour. প্রতি ঘন্টায়

house (**houses**) *n* A **house** is a building in which people live. বাড়ি

household (**households**) *n* A **household** is all the people in a family or group who live together in a house. পরিবার

housewife (**housewives**) *n* A **housewife** is a married woman who does not have a paid job, but instead looks after her home and children. গৃহবধূ

house wine (**house wines**) *n* A restaurant's **house wine** is the cheapest wine it sells, which is not listed by name on the wine list. দেশি মদ

housework *n* **Housework** is the work such as cleaning and cooking that you do in your home. বাড়ির কাজ

hovercraft (**hovercraft**) *n* A **hovercraft** is a vehicle that can travel across land and water. It floats above the land or water on a cushion of air. হোভারক্র্যাফ্ট

how *adv* You use the word **how** when you ask about the way that something happens or the way that you do something. কেমন করে ▷ *adv* You use **how** when you ask about an amount. কত

however *adv* You use **however** when you are saying something that somebody might not expect because of what you have just said. তথাপি

howl (**howls, howling, howled**) *vi* If an animal such as a wolf or a dog **howls**, it makes a long, loud, crying sound. গর্জন করা

HQ (HQs) *abbr* The **HQ** of an organization is the centre or building from which its operations are directed. **HQ** is an abbreviation for 'headquarters'. সদর দপ্তর

hubcap (hubcaps) *n* A **hubcap** is a metal or plastic disc that covers and protects the centre of a wheel on a car, truck, or other vehicle. চাকার মাঝখানের ঢাকনা

hug (hugs, hugging, hugged) *n* If you give someone a **hug**, you put your arms around them and hold them tightly, for example because you like them or are pleased to see them. আলিঙ্গন ▷ *vt* When you **hug** someone, you put your arms around them and hold them tightly, for example because you like them or are pleased to see them. You can also say that two people **hug** each other or that they **hug**. আলিঙ্গন করা

huge (huger, hugest) *adj* Something that is **huge** is extremely large in size, amount, or degree. বিশাল

hull (hulls) *n* The **hull** of a boat is the main part of its body. জাহাজের খোল

hum (hums, humming, hummed) *vi* If something **hums**, it makes a low continuous noise. গুণগুণ করা

human *adj* **Human** means relating to or concerning people. মানব

human being (human beings) *n* A **human being** is a man, woman, or child. মানুষ

humanitarian *adj* If a person or society has **humanitarian** ideas or behaviour, they try to avoid making people suffer or they help people who are suffering. মানবতাবাদী

human rights *npl* **Human rights** are basic rights which many societies believe that all people should have. মানবাধিকার

humble (humbler, humblest) *adj* A **humble** person is not proud and does not believe that they are better than other people. নিরহঙ্কার

humid *adj* You use **humid** to describe an atmosphere or climate that is very damp, and usually very hot. স্যাঁতস্যাঁতে

humidity *n* **Humidity** is dampness in the air. আর্দ্রতা

humorous *adj* If someone or something is **humorous**, they are amusing, especially in a clever or witty way. রসিক

humour *n* You can refer to the amusing things that people say as their **humour**. ব্যঙ্গ

hundred *num* A **hundred** is the number 100. একশো

Hungarian (Hungarians) *adj* **Hungarian** means belonging or relating to Hungary, or to its people, language, or culture. হাঙ্গেরী দেশীয় ▷ *n* A **Hungarian** is a person who comes from Hungary. হাঙ্গেরীর মানুষ

Hungary *n* **Hungary** is a republic in central Europe. হাঙ্গেরী

hunger *n* **Hunger** is the feeling of weakness or discomfort that you get when you need something to eat. ক্ষুধা

hungry (hungrier, hungriest) *adj* When you are **hungry**, you want food. ক্ষুধার্ত

hunt (hunts, hunting, hunted) *vi* If you **hunt** for something, you try to find it. তন্নতন্ন করে খোঁজা ▷ *v* When animals **hunt**, they chase another animal to kill it for food. শিকার করা

hunter (hunters) *n* A **hunter** is a person who hunts wild animals for food or as a sport. শিকারী

hunting *n* **Hunting** is the chasing and killing of wild animals by people or other animals, for food or as a sport. শিকার করা

hurdle (hurdles) *n* A **hurdle** is a difficulty that you must overcome in order to achieve something. বাধা

hurricane (hurricanes) *n* A **hurricane** is a very violent storm with strong winds. ঘূর্ণিঝড়

hurry (hurries, hurrying, hurried) *n* If you are in a **hurry** to do something, you need or want to do something quickly. If you do something in a **hurry**, you do it quickly or suddenly. তাড়াহুড়ো ▷ *vi* If you **hurry** somewhere, you go there quickly. তাড়াহুড়ো করা

h

hurry up *v* If you tell someone to **hurry up**, you are telling them to do something more quickly. তাড়াতাড়ি করা *Hurry up with that coffee, will you.*

hurt (**hurts, hurting, hurt**) *adj* If you are **hurt**, you have been injured. আঘাত ▷ *vt* If you **hurt** yourself or **hurt** a part of your body, you feel pain because you have injured yourself. আঘাত করা

husband (**husbands**) *n* A woman's **husband** is the man she is married to. স্বামী

hut (**huts**) *n* A **hut** is a small, simple building, often made of wood, mud, or grass. কুঁড়েঘর

hyacinth (**hyacinths**) *n* A **hyacinth** is a plant with a lot of small, sweet-smelling flowers growing closely around a single stem. It grows from a bulb and the flowers are usually blue, pink, or white. কচুরিপানা

hydrogen *n* **Hydrogen** is a colourless gas that is the lightest and most common element in the universe. হাইড্রোজেন

hygiene *n* **Hygiene** is the practice of keeping yourself and your surroundings clean, especially in order to prevent the spread of disease. স্বাস্থ্যবিধি

hypermarket (**hypermarkets**) *n* A **hypermarket** is a very large supermarket. হাইপারমার্কেট

hyphen (**hyphens**) *n* A **hyphen** is the punctuation sign (-) used to join words together to make a compound. হাইফেন

I *pron* You use **I** to talk about yourself. আমি *I like cats.*

ice *n* **Ice** is frozen water. বরফ

iceberg (**icebergs**) *n* An **iceberg** is a large, tall piece of ice floating in the sea. হিমশৈল

icebox (**iceboxes**) *n* An **icebox** is a container which is kept cool so that the food and drink inside stays fresh. (*old-fashioned*) ঠাণ্ডা রাখার বাক্স

ice cream (**ice creams**) *n* **Ice cream** is a very cold sweet food made from frozen milk, fats, and sugar. আইসক্রিম

ice cube (**ice cubes**) *n* An **ice cube** is a small square block of ice that you put into a drink in order to make it cold. বরফের টুকরো

ice hockey *n* **Ice hockey** is a game like hockey played on ice. বরফে খেলবার উপযুক্ত হকি

Iceland *n* **Iceland** is an island republic in the North Atlantic, regarded as part of Europe. আইসল্যান্ড

Icelandic *adj* **Icelandic** means belonging or relating to Iceland, or to its people, language, or culture. আইসল্যান্ড দেশীয় ▷ *n* **Icelandic** is the official language of Iceland. আইসল্যান্ডের ভাষা

ice lolly (**ice lollies**) *n* An **ice lolly** is a piece of flavoured ice or ice cream on a stick. বরফের ললি

ice rink (**ice rinks**) *n* An **ice rink** is a level area of ice, usually inside a building, that has been made artificially and kept frozen so that people can skate on it. স্কেটিং করবার জন্য তৈরি করা

ice-skating n **Ice-skating** is a sport or leisure activity which involves people moving about on ice wearing ice-skates. বরফের উপর স্কেটিং

icing n **Icing** is a sweet substance made from powdered sugar that is used to cover and decorate cakes. কেকের ওপরে মিষ্টি দেওয়া

icing sugar n **Icing sugar** is very fine white sugar that is used for making icing and sweets. আইসিং সুগার

icon (**icons**) n If you describe something or someone as an **icon**, you mean that they are important as a symbol of something. আদর্শ স্থানীয়

icy (**icier, iciest**) adj **Icy** air or water is extremely cold. হিমশীতল

ID card abbr An **ID card** is a card with a person's name, photograph, date of birth, and other information on it. পরিচয়-পত্র

idea (**ideas**) n An **idea** is a plan or suggestion. ধারণা

ideal adj The **ideal** person or thing for a particular purpose is the best one for it. আদর্শ

ideally adv If you say that **ideally** a particular thing should happen or be done, you mean that this is what you would like to happen or be done, but you know that this may not be possible or practical. আদর্শগতভাবে

identical adj Things that are **identical** are exactly the same. একরূপ

identification n When someone asks you for **identification**, they are asking to see something such as a passport which proves who you are. সনাক্তকরণ

identify (**identifies, identifying, identified**) vt If you can **identify** someone or something, you can recognize them and say who or what they are. চিহ্নিত করা

identity (**identities**) n Your **identity** is who you are. পরিচয়

identity card (**identity cards**) n An **identity card** is a card with a person's name, photograph, date of birth, and other information about them on it. পরিচয়-পত্র

identity theft n **Identity theft** is the crime of getting personal information about another person without their knowledge, for example in order to gain access to their bank account. অন্যের পরিচয়-তথ্য চুরি করা

ideology (**ideologies**) n An **ideology** is a set of beliefs, especially the political beliefs on which people, parties, or countries base their actions. মতাদর্শ

idiot (**idiots**) n If you call someone an **idiot**, you mean that they are very stupid. মূর্খ

idiotic adj If you call someone or something **idiotic**, you mean that they are very stupid or silly. মূর্খামি

idle adj If you describe someone as **idle** you disapprove of them not doing anything when they should be doing something. অকেজো

i.e. abbr **i.e.** is used to introduce a word or sentence which makes what you have just said clearer or gives details. যেটা হল

if conj You use **if** to talk about things that might happen, or that might have happened. যদি *You can go if you want.* ▢ *If he was there, I didn't see him.*

ignition (**ignitions**) n In a car, the **ignition** is the mechanism which ignites the fuel and starts the engine, usually operated by turning a key. প্রজ্বলন

ignorance n **Ignorance** of something is lack of knowledge about it. অজ্ঞতা

ignorant adj If you refer to someone as **ignorant**, you mean that they do not know much because they are not well educated. If someone is **ignorant** of a fact, they do not know it. অজ্ঞ

ignore (**ignores, ignoring, ignored**) vt If you **ignore** someone or something, you deliberately take no notice of them. অবহেলা করা

ill *adj* Someone who is **ill** is suffering from a disease or a health problem. অসুস্থ

illegal *adj* If something is **illegal**, the law says that it is not allowed. অবৈধ

illegible *adj* Writing that is **illegible** is so unclear that you cannot read it. পড়ার অযোগ্য

illiterate *adj* Someone who is **illiterate** cannot read or write. অশিক্ষিত

illness (**illnesses**) *n* **Illness** is the fact or experience of being ill. অসুস্থতা

ill-treat (**ill-treats, ill-treating, ill-treated**) *vt* If someone **ill-treats** you, they treat you badly or cruelly. বাজে ব্যবহার করা

illusion (**illusions**) *n* An **illusion** is something that appears to exist or to be a particular thing but in reality does not exist or is something else. ভ্রান্তি

illustration (**illustrations**) *n* An **illustration** of something is a clear example of it. বিশদীকরণ

image (**images**) *n* If you have an **image** of someone or something, you have a picture or idea of them in your mind. প্রতিবিম্ব

imaginary *adj* An **imaginary** person, place, or thing exists only in your mind or in a story, and not in real life. কল্পিত

imagination (**imaginations**) *n* Your **imagination** is your ability to form pictures or ideas in your mind of new, exciting, or imaginary things. কল্পনা

imagine (**imagines, imagining, imagined**) *vt* If you **imagine** a situation, your mind forms a picture or idea of it. কল্পনা করা

imitate (**imitates, imitating, imitated**) *vt* If you **imitate** someone, you copy what they do or produce. নকল করা

imitation (**imitations**) *n* An **imitation** of something is a copy of it. নকল

immature *adj* Something that is **immature** is not yet fully developed. অপরিণত

immediate *adj* An **immediate** result, action, or reaction happens or is done without any delay. অবিলম্ব

immediately *adv* If something happens **immediately**, it happens without any delay. অবিলম্বে

immigrant (**immigrants**) *n* An **immigrant** is a person who has come to live in a country from another country. অভিবাসী

immigration *n* **Immigration** is the fact or process of people coming into a country in order to live and work there. অভিবাসন

immoral *adj* If you describe someone or their behaviour as **immoral**, you mean that their behaviour is bad or wrong. অনৈতিক

immune system (**immune systems**) *n* Your **immune system** consists of all the cells and processes in your body which protect you from illness and infection. রোগ প্রতিরোধ ক্ষমতা

impact (**impacts**) *n* The **impact** that something has on a situation, process, or person is a sudden and powerful effect that it has on them. প্রভাব

impartial *adj* If you are **impartial**, you are able to act fairly because you are not personally involved in a situation. নিরপেক্ষ

impatience *n* **Impatience** is annoyance caused by having to wait too long for something. ধৈর্যহীনতা

impatient *adj* If you are **impatient**, you are annoyed because you have had to wait too long for something. অধৈর্য

impatiently *adv* If you do something **impatiently**, you do it in an annoyed manner because you have had to wait too long for something. অধৈর্যভাবে

impersonal *adj* If you describe a place, organization, or activity as **impersonal**, you feel that the people there see you as unimportant or unwanted. নৈর্ব্যক্তিক

import (**imports, importing, imported**) *n* **Imports** are products or raw materials bought from another country for use in your own country. আমদানি ▷ *vt* When a country or organization **imports** a product, they buy it from another country for use in their own country. আমদানি করা

importance *n* The **importance** of something is its quality of being significant, valued, or necessary in a particular situation. গুরুত্ব

important *adj* If something is **important**, people care about it and think about it a lot. গুরুত্বপূর্ণ ▷ *adj* If someone is **important**, people pay a lot of attention to what they say and do. গণ্যমান্য

impossible *adj* Something that is **impossible** cannot be done or cannot happen. অসম্ভব

impractical *adj* If an idea or course of action is **impractical**, it is not sensible or practical. অবাস্তব

impress (**impresses, impressing, impressed**) *v* If someone or something **impresses** you, you feel great admiration for them. মন ভরিয়ে দেওয়া

impressed *adj* If you are **impressed** by something or someone, you feel great admiration for them. মুগ্ধ

impression (**impressions**) *n* Your **impression** of someone or something is what you think they are like. Your **impression** of a situation is what you think is going on. ধারণা

impressive *adj* **Impressive** is used to describe people or things which impress you. মনভরানো

improve (**improves, improving, improved**) *v* If something **improves**, or if you **improve** it, it gets better. উন্নতি করা

improvement (**improvements**) *n* If there is an **improvement** in something, it becomes better. If you make **improvements** to something, you make it better. উন্নতি

in *prep* **In** means not outside. মধ্যে *The juice is in the fridge.* ▷ *prep* You also use **in** to say when something happens. এ *He was born in winter.*

inaccurate *adj* If a statement or measurement is **inaccurate**, it is not accurate or correct. ক্রটিযুক্ত

inadequate *adj* If something is **inadequate**, there is not enough of it or it is not good enough. অপ্রতুল

inadvertently *adv* If you do something **inadvertently**, you do it without realizing what you are doing. অন্যমনস্কভাবে

inbox (**inboxes**) *n* On a computer, your **inbox** is the part of your mailbox which stores emails that have arrived for you. ইনবক্স

incentive (**incentives**) *n* An **incentive** is something that encourages you to do something. প্রণোদক

inch (**inches**) *n* An **inch** is a unit of length, equal to 2.54 centimetres. ইঞ্চি

incident (**incidents**) *n* An **incident** is an event, especially one involving something unpleasant. (*formal*) ঘটনা

include (**includes, including, included**) *vt* If something **includes** something else, it has it as one of its parts. অন্তর্ভুক্ত করা

included *adj* You use **included** to emphasize that a person or thing is part of the group of people or things that you are talking about. অন্তর্ভুক্ত

including *prep* You use **including** to talk about people or things that are part of a group. সহ *Nine people were hurt, including both drivers.*

inclusive *adj* If a price is **inclusive**, it includes all the charges connected with the goods or services offered. If a price is **inclusive** of postage and packing, it includes the charge for this. সমেত

income (**incomes**) *n* The **income** of a person or organization is the money that they earn or receive. আয়

income tax (**income taxes**) *n* **Income tax** is a part of your income that you have to pay regularly to the government. আয়কর

incompetent *adj* If you describe someone as **incompetent**, you are criticizing them because they cannot do their job or a task properly. অদক্ষ

incomplete *adj* Something that is **incomplete** is not yet finished, or does not have all the parts or details that it needs. অসম্পূর্ণ

inconsistent *adj* If you describe someone as **inconsistent**, you are criticizing them for not behaving in the same way every time a similar situation occurs. অসংগত

inconvenience (**inconveniences**) *n* If someone or something causes **inconvenience**, they cause problems or difficulties. অসুবিধা

inconvenient *adj* Something that is **inconvenient** causes problems or difficulties for someone. অসুবিধাজনক

incorrect *adj* Something that is **incorrect** is wrong or untrue. বেঠিক

increase (**increases, increasing, increased**) *n* If there is an **increase** in the number, level, or amount of something, it becomes greater. বৃদ্ধি ▷ *v* If something **increases** or you **increase** it, it becomes greater in number, level, or amount. বৃদ্ধি পাওয়া

increasingly *adv* You use **increasingly** to indicate that a situation or quality is becoming greater, stronger, or more common. অধিকতরভাবে

incredible *adj* If you describe someone or something as **incredible**, you like them very much or are impressed by them, because they are extremely or unusually good. আশ্চর্যজনক

indecisive *adj* If you are **indecisive**, you find it difficult to make decisions. দ্বিধাগ্রস্ত

indeed *adv* You use **indeed** to emphasize your agreement with something that has just been said. সত্যি

independence *n* A person's **independence** is their ability to do things without relying on other people. স্বাধীনতা

independent *adj* Someone who is **independent** does not rely on other people. স্বাধীন

index (**indices, indexes**) *n* An **index** is an alphabetical list at the back of a book saying

where particular things are mentioned in the book. সূচীপত্র ▷ *n* An **index** is a system by which changes in the value of something can be recorded, measured, or interpreted. সূচক সংখ্যা

index finger (**index fingers**) *n* Your **index finger** is the finger that is next to your thumb. তর্জনী

India *n* **India** is a republic in south Asia. ভারত

Indian (**Indians**) *adj* **Indian** means belonging or relating to India, or to its people or culture. ভারতীয় ▷ *n* An **Indian** is an Indian citizen, or a person of Indian origin. ভারতীয় নাগরিক

Indian Ocean *n* The **Indian Ocean** is an ocean bordered by Africa in the west, Asia in the north, and Australia in the east, and merging with the Antarctic Ocean in the south. ভারত মহাসাগর

indicate (**indicates, indicating, indicated**) *vt* If one thing **indicates** another, the first thing shows that the second is true or exists. চিহ্নিত করা

indicator (**indicators**) *n* An **indicator** is a measurement or value which gives you an idea of what something is like. সূচক

indigestion *n* If you have **indigestion**, you have pains in your stomach that are caused by difficulties in digesting food. বদহজম

indirect *adj* An **indirect** result or effect is not caused immediately and obviously by a thing or person, but happens because of something else that they have done. পরোক্ষ

indispensable *adj* If someone or something is **indispensable**, they are absolutely essential and other people or things cannot function without them. অপরিহার্য

individual *adj* **Individual** means relating to one person or thing, rather than to a large group. ব্যক্তিবিশেষ

Indonesia *n* **Indonesia** is a republic in south-east Asia. ইন্দোনেশিয়া

Indonesian (**Indonesians**) adj **Indonesian** means belonging or relating to Indonesia, or to its people or culture. ইন্দোনেশিয়া দেশীয় ▷ n An **Indonesian** is an Indonesian citizen, or a person of Indonesian origin. ইন্দোনেশিয়ার নাগরিক

indoor adj **Indoor** activities or things are ones that happen or are used inside a building, rather than outside. অন্তরঙ্গন

indoors adv If something happens **indoors**, it happens inside a building. গৃহাভ্যন্তর

industrial adj **Industrial** means relating to industry. শিল্প-সংক্রান্ত

industrial estate (**industrial estates**) n An **industrial estate** is an area which has been specially planned for a lot of factories. শিল্প এলাকা

industry n **Industry** is the work and processes involved in making things in factories. শিল্প

inefficient adj A person, organization, system, or machine that is **inefficient** does not work in the most economical way. অদক্ষ

inevitable adj If something is **inevitable**, it is certain to happen and cannot be prevented or avoided. অবশ্যম্ভাবী

inexpensive adj Something that is **inexpensive** does not cost much. সস্তা

inexperienced adj If you are **inexperienced**, you have little or no experience of a particular activity. অনভিজ্ঞ

infantry n The **infantry** are the soldiers in an army who fight on foot. পদাতিক সৈন্য

infant school (**infant schools**) n An **infant school** is a school for children between the ages of five and seven. শিশু-বিদ্যালয়

infection (**infections**) n An **infection** is a disease caused by germs. সংক্রমণ

infectious adj If you have an **infectious** disease, people near you can catch it from you. সংক্রামক

inferior (**inferiors**) adj Something that is **inferior** is not as good as something else. নিকৃষ্ট ▷ n If one person is regarded

as another person's **inferior**, they are considered to have less ability, status, or importance. অধস্তন

infertile adj Someone who is **infertile** is unable to produce babies. বন্ধ্যা

infinitive (**infinitives**) n The **infinitive** of a verb is its base form or simplest form, such as a 'do', 'take', and 'eat'. The **infinitive** is often used with 'to' in front of it. অপরিবর্তনশীল ক্রিয়া

infirmary (**infirmaries**) n Some hospitals are called **infirmaries**. চিকিৎসালয়

inflamed adj If part of your body is **inflamed**, it is red or swollen because of an infection or injury. জ্বালাযুক্ত

inflammation (**inflammations**) n An **inflammation** is a swelling in your body that results from an infection or injury. (formal) জ্বালা

inflatable adj An **inflatable** object is one that you fill with air when you want to use it. বাতাস ভরা

inflation n **Inflation** is a general increase in the prices of goods and services in a country. মূল্যবৃদ্ধি

inflexible adj Something or someone that is **inflexible** cannot or will not change or be altered, even if the situation changes. অনমনীয়

influence (**influences**, **influencing**, **influenced**) n **Influence** is the power to make other people agree with your opinions or make them do what you want. প্রভাব ▷ vt If you **influence** someone, you use your power to make them agree with you or do what you want. প্রভাবিত করা

influenza n **Influenza** is an illness caused by a virus. The symptoms are like those of a bad cold, but more serious. (formal) ইনফ্লুয়েঞ্জা

inform (**informs**, **informing**, **informed**) vt If you **inform** someone of something, you tell them about it. অবহিত করা

informal adj You use **informal** to describe behaviour, speech, or situations that are relaxed and casual rather than correct and serious. ঘরোয়া

information *n* If you have **information** about a particular thing, you know something about it. তথ্য

information office (**information offices**) *n* An **information office** is an office where you can go to get information. তথ্য কার্যালয়

informative *adj* Something that is **informative** gives you useful information. তথ্যভিত্তিক

infrastructure (**infrastructures**) *n* The **infrastructure** of a country or society consists of the basic facilities such as transport, communications, power supplies, and buildings, which enable it to function properly. পরিকাঠামো

infuriating *adj* Something that is **infuriating** annoys you very much. বিরক্তিকর

ingenious *adj* Something that is **ingenious** is very clever and involves new ideas or equipment. উদ্ভাবনশক্তিবিশিষ্ট

ingredient (**ingredients**) *n* **Ingredients** are the things that are used to make something, especially all the different foods you use when you are cooking a particular dish. উপকরণ

inhabitant (**inhabitants**) *n* The **inhabitants** of a place are the people who live there. বাসিন্দা

inhaler (**inhalers**) *n* An **inhaler** is a small device that helps you to breathe more easily if you have asthma or a bad cold. You put it in your mouth and breathe in deeply, and it sends a small amount of a drug into your lungs. ইনহেলার

inherit (**inherits, inheriting, inherited**) *vt* If you **inherit** money or property, you receive it from someone who has died. উত্তরাধিকার সূত্রে প্রাপ্ত

inheritance (**inheritances**) *n* An **inheritance** is money or property which you receive from someone who is dead. উত্তরাধিকার

inhibition (**inhibitions**) *n* **Inhibitions** are feelings of embarrassment that make it difficult for you to behave naturally. প্রবৃত্তি দমন

initial (**initials, initialling, initialled**) *adj* You use **initial** to describe something that happens at the beginning of a process. প্রারম্ভিক ▷ *vt* If someone **initials** an official document, they write their initials on it, for example to show that they have seen it or that they accept or agree with it. সই

initially *adv* **Initially** means in the early stages of a process or situation. শুরুতে

initials *npl* **Initials** are the capital letters which begin each word of a name. আদ্যক্ষর

initiative (**initiatives**) *n* An **initiative** is an important act intended to solve a problem. উদ্যোগ

inject (**injects, injecting, injected**) *vt* To **inject** someone with a substance such as a medicine, or to **inject** it into them, means to use a needle and a syringe to put it into their body. প্রবেশ করানো

injection (**injections**) *n* If you have an **injection**, someone puts a medicine into your body using a needle and a syringe. ইঞ্জেকশন

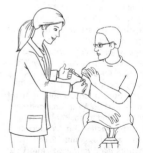

injure (**injures, injuring, injured**) *vt* If you **injure** a person or animal, you damage some part of their body. আঘাত করা

injured *adj* An **injured** person or animal has physical damage to part of their body, usually as a result of an accident or fighting. আহত

injury (injuries) *n* An **injury** is damage done to a person's body. আঘাত

injury time *n* **Injury time** is the period of time added to the end of a football game because play was stopped during the match when players were injured. ইনজুরি টাইম

injustice (injustices) *n* **Injustice** is unfairness in a situation. অবিচার

ink (inks) *n* **Ink** is the coloured liquid used for writing or printing. কালি

in-laws *npl* Your **in-laws** are the parents and close relatives of your husband or wife. শ্বশুরবাড়ি

inmate (inmates) *n* The **inmates** of a prison or a psychiatric hospital are the prisoners or patients who are living there. জেলের অধিবাসী

inn (inns) *n* An **inn** is a small hotel or a pub, usually an old one. (*old-fashioned*) সরাইখানা

inner *adj* The **inner** parts of something are the parts which are contained or enclosed inside the other parts, and which are closest to the centre. অন্তঃস্থিত

inner tube (inner tubes) *n* An **inner tube** is a rubber tube containing air which is inside a car tyre or a bicycle tyre. ইনার টিউব

innocent *adj* If someone is **innocent**, they did not commit a crime which they have been accused of. নির্দোষ

innovation (innovations) *n* An **innovation** is a new thing or new method of doing something. উদ্ভাবন

innovative *adj* Something that is **innovative** is new and original. উদ্ভাবনমূলক

inquest (inquests) *n* An **inquest** is an official inquiry into the cause of someone's death. তদন্ত

inquire (inquires, inquiring, inquired) *v* If you **inquire** about something, you ask for information about it. (*formal*) অনুসন্ধান করা

inquiries office (inquiries offices) *n* An **inquiries office** is an office where you

can go or call to get information. অনুসন্ধান কার্যালয়

inquiry (inquiries) *n* An **inquiry** is a question which you ask in order to get information. অনুসন্ধান

inquiry desk (enquiry desks) *n* The place in a hotel, hospital, airport, or other building where you obtain information is called the **inquiry desk**. অনুসন্ধান কক্ষ

inquisitive *adj* An **inquisitive** person likes finding out about things, especially secret things. কৌতূহলী

insane *adj* Someone who is **insane** has a mind that does not work in a normal way, with the result that their behaviour is very strange. অপ্রকৃতিস্থ

inscription (inscriptions) *n* An **inscription** is a piece of writing carved into a surface, or written on a book or photograph. খোদাই করা অক্ষর

insect (insects) *n* An **insect** is a small creature with six legs. Most insects have wings. পোকা

insecure *adj* If you feel **insecure**, you feel that you are not good enough or are not loved. অরক্ষিত

insensitive *adj* If you describe someone as **insensitive**, you mean that they are not aware of other people's feelings or problems. অনুভূতিহীন

inside (insides) *adv* **Inside** also means indoors. অভ্যন্তরে ▷ *n* The **inside** of something is the area that its sides surround. ভিতর ▷ *prep* If something is **inside** another thing, it is in it. ভেতরে *There was a letter inside the envelope.*

insincere *adj* If you say that someone is **insincere**, you are being critical of them because they say things they do not really mean, usually pleasant, admiring, or encouraging things. নিষ্ঠাহীন

insist (insists, insisting, insisted) *v* If you **insist** that something should be done, you say very firmly that it must be done. জোর করা

insomnia *n* Someone who suffers from **insomnia** finds it difficult to sleep. নিদ্রাহীনতা

inspect (**inspects, inspecting, inspected**) *vt* If you **inspect** something, you examine it or check it carefully. পরীক্ষা করা

inspector (**inspectors**) *n* An **inspector** is someone whose job is to inspect things. পরিদর্শক

instability (**instabilities**) *n* **Instability** is a lack of stability in a place, situation, or person. অস্থায়িত্ব

instalment (**instalments**) *n* If you pay for something in **instalments**, you pay small sums of money at regular intervals over a period of time. কিস্তি

instance (**instances**) *n* An **instance** is a particular example or occurrence of something. উদাহরণ

instant *adj* You use **instant** to describe something that happens immediately. অবিলম্ব

instantly *adv* If something happens **instantly**, it happens immediately. অবিলম্বে

instead *adv* If you do not do something, but do something else **instead**, you do the second thing and not the first thing. পরিবর্তে

instead of *prep* If you do one thing **instead** of another, you do the first thing and not the second thing. বদলে *Why don't they walk to work, instead of driving?*

instinct (**instincts**) *n* An **instinct** is the natural tendency that a person has to behave or react in a particular way. প্রবণতা

institute (**institutes**) *n* An **institute** is an organization or building where a particular type of work is done, especially research or teaching. প্রতিষ্ঠান

institution (**institutions**) *n* An **institution** is a large organization such as a parliament, a school, or a bank. সংস্থা

instruct (**instructs, instructing, instructed**) *vt* If you **instruct** someone to do something, you formally tell them to do it. (*formal*) নির্দেশ দেওয়া

instructions *npl* **Instructions** are clear and detailed information on how to do something. নির্দেশাবলী

instructor (**instructors**) *n* An **instructor** is a teacher, especially of driving, skiing, or swimming. নির্দেশক

instrument (**instruments**) *n* An **instrument** is a tool that you use to do something. যন্ত্র ▷ *n* An **instrument** is also something, for example a piano or a guitar, that you use to make music. বাদ্যযন্ত্র

insufficient *adj* Something that is **insufficient** is not enough for a particular purpose. (*formal*) অপ্রতুল

insulation *n* **Insulation** is a thick layer of material used to insulate something. ইন্সুলেশন

insulin *n* **Insulin** is a substance that most people produce naturally in their body and which controls the level of sugar in their blood. If your body does not produce enough insulin, then it develops a disease called diabetes. ইন্সুলিন

insult (**insults, insulting, insulted**) *n* An **insult** is a rude remark or action which offends someone. অবমাননা ▷ *vt* If you **insult** someone, you offend them by being rude to them. অপমান করা

insurance *n* **Insurance** is an arrangement in which you pay money regularly to a company, and they pay money to you if something unpleasant happens to you, for example if your property is stolen. বিমা

insurance certificate (**insurance certificates**) *n* An **insurance certificate** is a certificate that shows that a person or organization has insurance. বিমা সার্টিফিকেট

insurance policy (**insurance policies**) *n* An **insurance policy** is a written contract between a person and an insurance company. বিমা পলিসি

insure (**insures, insuring, insured**) *v* If you **insure** yourself or your property, you pay money to an insurance company so that if you become ill or your property is stolen, the company will pay you a sum of money. বিমা করা

insured *adj* If someone or their property is **insured**, they pay money to an insurance company so that, if they become ill or if their property is damaged or stolen, the company will pay them a sum of money. বিমাকৃত

intact *adj* Something that is **intact** is complete and has not been damaged or spoilt. অক্ষত

intellectual (intellectuals) *adj* **Intellectual** means involving a person's ability to think and to understand ideas and information. বুদ্ধি সম্পর্কিত ▷ *n* An **intellectual** is someone who spends a lot of time studying and thinking about complicated ideas. মেধাবী

intelligence *n* Your **intelligence** is your ability to understand and learn things. মেধা

intelligent *adj* An **intelligent** person has the ability to think, understand, and learn things quickly and well. বুদ্ধিমান

intend *v* If you **intend** to do something, you have decided or planned to do it. মনস্থ করা

intense *adj* Something that is **intense** is very great in strength or degree. প্রচণ্ড

intensive *adj* An **intensive** activity involves the concentration of energy or people on one particular task. ব্যাপক

intensive care unit (intensive care units) *n* The **intensive care unit** is the part of a hospital that provides continuous care and attention, often using special equipment, for people who are very seriously ill or injured. ইন্টেনসিভ কেয়ার ইউনিট

intention (intentions) *n* An **intention** is an idea or plan of what you are going to do. উদ্দেশ্য

intentional *adj* Something that is **intentional** is deliberate. ইচ্ছাকৃত

intercom (intercoms) *n* An **intercom** is a small box with a microphone which is connected to a loudspeaker in another

room. You use it to talk to the people in the other room. ইন্টারকম

interest (interests, interesting, interested) *n* If you have an **interest** in something, you want to learn or hear more about it. স্বার্থ ▷ *n* **Interest** is extra money that you receive if you have invested a sum of money. সুদ ▷ *vt* If something **interests** you, you want to learn more about it or to continue doing it. আগ্রহ জাগায়

interested *adj* If you are **interested** in something, you think it is important and you are keen to learn more about it or spend time doing it. আগ্রহী

interesting *adj* If you find something **interesting**, it attracts you or holds your attention. উৎসাহজনক

interest rate (interest rates) *n* The **interest rate** is the amount of interest that must be paid. It is expressed as a percentage of the amount that is borrowed or gained as profit. সুদের হার

interior (interiors) *n* The **interior** of something is the inside or central part of it. ভেতরের অংশ

interior designer (interior designers) *n* An **interior designer** is a person who is employed to design the decoration for the inside of people's houses. অন্দরসজ্জা বিশেষজ্ঞ

intermediate *adj* An **intermediate** stage or level is one that occurs between two other stages or levels. মধ্যবর্তী

internal *adj* You use **internal** to describe things that exist or happen inside a place or organization. অভ্যন্তরীণ

international *adj* **International** means between or involving different countries. আন্তর্জাতিক

Internet *n* **The Internet** is the computer network which allows computer users to connect with computers all over the world, and which carries email. ইন্টারনেট

Internet café (Internet cafés) *n* An **Internet café** is a café with computers where people can pay to use the Internet. ইন্টারনেট কাফে

Internet user (**Internet users**) *n* An **Internet user** is a person who uses the Internet. ইন্টারনেট ব্যবহারকারী

interpret (**interprets, interpreting, interpreted**) *vt* If you **interpret** something in a particular way, you decide that this is its meaning or significance. ব্যাখ্যা করা

interpreter (**interpreters**) *n* An **interpreter** is a person whose job is to translate what someone is saying into another language. দোভাষী

interrogate (**interrogates, interrogating, interrogated**) *vt* If someone, especially a police officer, **interrogates** someone, they question him or her for a long time, in order to get information from you. জিজ্ঞাসাবাদ করা

interrupt (**interrupts, interrupting, interrupted**) *v* If you **interrupt** someone who is speaking, you say or do something that causes them to stop. বাধা দেওয়া

interruption (**interruptions**) *n* An **interruption** is something such as an action, comment, or question, that causes someone or something to stop. বাধা

interval (**intervals**) *n* The **interval** between two events or dates is the period of time between them. বিরতি

interview (**interviews, interviewing, interviewed**) *n* An **interview** is a formal meeting at which someone is asked questions in order to find out if they are suitable for a job or a course of study. সাক্ষাৎকার ▷ *vt* If you **are interviewed** for a particular job or course of study, someone asks you questions about yourself to find out if you are suitable for it. সাক্ষাৎকার নেওয়া

interviewer (**interviewers**) *n* An **interviewer** is a person who is asking someone questions at an interview. সাক্ষাৎকার গ্রহণকারী

intimate *adj* If two people have an **intimate** friendship, they are very good friends. অন্তরঙ্গ

intimidate (**intimidates, intimidating, intimidated**) *vt* To **intimidate** someone means to frighten them, sometimes as a deliberate way of making them do something. ভয় দেখানো

into *prep* If you put one thing **into** another thing, you put the first thing inside the second thing. মধ্যে *Put the apples into a dish.* ▷ *prep* If you go **into** a place or a vehicle, you move from being outside it to being inside it. ভেতরে *He got into the car and started the engine.*

intolerant *adj* If you describe someone as **intolerant**, you disapprove of the fact that they do not accept behaviour and opinions that are different from their own. অনুদার

intranet (**intranets**) *n* An **intranet** is a network of computers, similar to the Internet, within a company or organization. ইন্ট্রানেট

introduce (**introduces, introducing, introduced**) *vt* To **introduce** something means to cause it to enter a place or exist in a system for the first time. পরিচয় করানো

introduction (**introductions**) *n* The **introduction** of something is the act of causing it to enter a place or exist in a system for the first time. পরিচয়

intruder (**intruders**) *n* An **intruder** is a person who enters a place without permission. অনধিকার প্রবেশকারী

intuition (**intuitions**) *n* Your **intuition** or your **intuitions** are feelings you have that something is true even when you have no evidence or proof of it. অন্তর্দৃষ্টি

invade (**invades, invading, invaded**) *v* To **invade** a country means to enter it by force with an army. আক্রমণ করা

invalid (**invalids**) *n* An **invalid** is someone who is very ill or disabled and needs to be cared for by someone else. অক্ষম

invent (**invents, inventing, invented**) *vt* If you **invent** something, you are the first person to think of it or make it. আবিষ্কার করা

invention (**inventions**) *n* An **invention** is a machine or system that has been invented by someone. আবিষ্কার

inventor (**inventors**) *n* An **inventor** is a person who has invented something, or whose job is to invent things. আবিষ্কারক

inventory (**inventories**) *n* An **inventory** is a written list of all the objects in a place. মালপত্রের তালিকা

inverted commas *npl* **Inverted commas** are the punctuation marks (' ') or (" ") which are used in writing to show where speech or a quotation begins and ends. ইনভার্টেড কমা

invest (**invests, investing, invested**) *v* If you **invest** in something, or if you **invest** a sum of money, you use your money in a way that you hope will increase its value, for example by buying shares or property. বিনিয়োগ করা

investigation (**investigations**) *n* An **investigation** is a careful search or examination in order to discover facts, etc. তদন্ত

investment *n* **Investment** is the activity of investing money. বিনিয়োগ

investor (**investors**) *n* An **investor** is a person or organization that buys stocks or shares, or pays money into a bank in order to receive a profit. বিনিয়োগকারী

invigilator (**invigilators**) *n* An **invigilator** supervises the people who are taking an examination in order to ensure that it starts and finishes at the correct time, and that there is no cheating. নজরদার

invisible *adj* If something is **invisible**, you cannot see it, because it is hidden or because it is very small or faint. অদৃশ্য

invitation (**invitations**) *n* An **invitation** is a written or spoken request to come to an event such as a party or a meeting. আমন্ত্রণ

invite (**invites, inviting, invited**) *vt* If you **invite** someone to something such as a party or a meal, you ask them to come to it. আমন্ত্রণ করা

invoice (**invoices, invoicing, invoiced**) *n* An **invoice** is an official document that lists goods or services that you have received and says how much money you owe for them. চালান ▷ *vt* If you **invoice** someone, you send them an invoice. চালান দেওয়া

involve (**involves, involving, involved**) *vt* If an activity **involves** something, that thing is a necessary part of it. জড়িয়ে থাকা

iPod® (**iPods**) *n* An **iPod** is a portable MP3 player that can play music downloaded from the Internet. আইপড

IQ (**IQs**) *abbr* Your **IQ** is your level of intelligence, as indicated by a special test. **IQ** is an abbreviation for 'Intelligence Quotient'. বুদ্ধ্যাঙ্ক

Iran *n* **Iran** is a republic in south-west Asia, between the Caspian Sea and the Persian Gulf. ইরান

Iranian (**Iranians**) *adj* **Iranian** means belonging or relating to Iran, or to its people or culture. ইরান দেশীয় ▷ *n* An **Iranian** is an Iranian citizen, or a person of Iranian origin. ইরানের নাগরিক

Iraq *n* **Iraq** is a republic in south-west Asia, on the Persian Gulf. ইরাক

Iraqi (**Iraqis**) *adj* **Iraqi** means belonging or relating to Iraq, or to its people or culture. ইরাক দেশীয় ▷ *n* An **Iraqi** is an Iraqi citizen, or a person of Iraqi origin. ইরাকের নাগরিক

Ireland *n* **Ireland** is an island off north-west Europe, to the west of Great Britain. আয়ার্ল্যান্ড

iris (**irises**) *n* The **iris** is the round coloured part of a person's eye. চোখের মণি

Irish *adj* **Irish** means belonging or relating to Ireland, or to its people, language, or culture. **Irish** sometimes refers to the whole of Ireland, and sometimes only to the Republic of Ireland. আয়ার্ল্যান্ড দেশীয় ▷ *n* **Irish** is a Celtic language spoken in Ireland. আয়ার্ল্যান্ডের ভাষা

Irishman (**Irishmen**) *n* An **Irishman** is a man who is an Irish citizen or is of Irish origin. আইরিস ভদ্রলোক

Irishwoman (**Irishwomen**) *n* An
Irishwoman is a woman who is an Irish
citizen or is of Irish origin. আইরিস ভদ্রমহিলা

iron (**irons, ironing, ironed**) *n* **Iron** is a
strong, hard, grey metal. লোহা ▷ *n* An **iron**
is a piece of equipment with a flat bottom
that gets hot. You move the bottom over
clothes to make them smooth. ইস্ত্রী ▷ *v* If
you **iron** clothes, you make them smooth
using an iron. ইস্ত্রি করা

ironic *adj* When you make an **ironic**
remark, you say something that you do not
mean, as a joke. বিদ্রূপনাময়

ironing *n* **Ironing** is the act of removing
the creases from clothes using an iron.
ইস্ত্রি করা

ironing board (**ironing boards**) *n* An
ironing board is a long narrow board
covered with cloth on which you iron
clothes. ইস্ত্রি করার বোর্ড

ironmonger (**ironmongers**) *n* An
ironmonger's or an **ironmonger's** is a shop
where articles for the house and garden
such as tools, nails, and building supplies
are sold. লোহার জিনিসের ব্যবসায়ী

irony *n* **Irony** is a form of humour which
involves saying things that you do not
mean. পরিহাস

irregular *adj* If events or actions occur
at **irregular** intervals, the periods of time
between them are of different lengths.
অনিয়মিত

irrelevant *adj* If you say that something
is **irrelevant**, you mean that it is not
important to or not connected with the
present situation or discussion. অপ্রাসঙ্গিক

irresponsible *adj* If you describe someone
as **irresponsible**, you are criticizing them
because they do things without properly
considering their possible consequences.
দায়িত্বজ্ঞানহীন

irritable *adj* If you are **irritable**, you are
easily annoyed. খিটখিটে

irritating *adj* Something that is **irritating**
keeps annoying you. বিরক্তিকর

Islam *n* **Islam** is the religion of the
Muslims, which teaches that there is only
one God and that Mohammed is His
prophet. ইসলাম ধর্ম

Islamic *adj* **Islamic** means belonging or
relating to Islam. ইসলাম ধর্ম সম্পর্কিত

island (**islands**) *n* An **island** is a piece
of land that is completely surrounded by
water. দ্বীপ

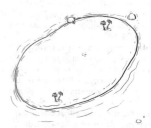

isolated *adj* If someone or something
is **isolated** they are separate from other
people or things of the same kind, either
physically or socially. বিচ্ছিন্ন

ISP (**ISPs**) *abbr* An **ISP** is a company that
provides Internet and email services. **ISP**
is an abbreviation for 'Internet service
provider'. "ইন্টারনেট সার্ভিস প্রোভাইডার" এর
সংক্ষিপ্তকরণ

Israel *n* **Israel** is a republic in south-west
Asia, on the Mediterranean Sea. ইস্রায়েল

Israeli (**Israelis**) *adj* **Israeli** means
belonging or relating to Israel, or to its
people or culture. ইস্রায়েল দেশীয় ▷ *n* An
Israeli is a person who comes from Israel.
ইস্রায়েলের নাগরিক

issue (**issues, issuing, issued**) *n* An **issue**
is an important subject that people are
arguing about or discussing. বিষয় ▷ *vt* If
someone **issues** a statement, they make it
formally or publicly. প্রেরণ করা

IT *abbr* **IT** is the theory and practice of
using computers to store and analyze

information. **IT** is an abbreviation for 'information technology'. তথ্যপ্রযুক্তি

it *pron* You use **it** to talk about a thing or an animal. এটি *This is a good book - have you read it?*

Italian (Italians) *adj* **Italian** means belonging or relating to Italy, or to its people, language, or culture. ইটালী দেশীয় ▷ *n* An **Italian** is a person who comes from Italy. ইটালীর নাগরিক ▷ *n* **Italian** is the language spoken in Italy, and in parts of Switzerland. ইটালিয়ান ভাষা

Italy *n* **Italy** is a republic in southern Europe. ইটালী

itch (itches, itching, itched) *vi* When a part of your body **itches**, you have an unpleasant feeling on your skin that makes you want to scratch. চুলকানি

itchy *adj* If a part of your body or something you are wearing is **itchy**, you have an unpleasant feeling on your skin that makes you want to scratch. (*informal*) চুলকানিযুক্ত

item (items) *n* An **item** is one of a collection or list of objects. তালিকাভুক্ত বিষয়

itinerary (itineraries) *n* An **itinerary** is a plan of a journey, including the route and the places that will be visited. সফরসূচি

its *det* You use **its** to say that something belongs to a thing or an animal. তার *The lion lifted its head.*

itself *pron* You use **itself** to talk about something that you have just talked about. নিজে থেকে *The kitten washed itself, then lay down by the fire.*

ivory (ivories) *n* **Ivory** is a valuable type of bone, which forms the tusks of an elephant. হাতির দাঁত

ivy *n* **Ivy** is an evergreen plant that grows up walls or along the ground. আইভিলতা

jab (jabs) *n* A **jab** is an injection to prevent illness. ইনজেকশন

jack (jacks) *n* A **jack** is a device for lifting a heavy object such as a car off the ground. জ্যাক

jacket (jackets) *n* A **jacket** is a short coat. জ্যাকেট

jacket potato (jacket potatoes) *n* A **jacket potato** is a large potato that has been baked with its skin on. খোসাসমেত স্যাঁকা আলু

jackpot (jackpots) *n* A **jackpot** is a large sum of money which is the most valuable prize in a game or lottery. লটারি

jail (jails, jailing, jailed) *n* A **jail** is a building where criminals are kept in order to punish them. কারাগার ▷ *vt* If someone **is jailed**, they are put in jail. কারাবাস করা

jam (**jams**) n **Jam** is a food that you spread on bread, made by cooking fruit with a large amount of sugar. জ্যাম

Jamaican (**Jamaicans**) adj **Jamaican** means belonging or relating to Jamaica or to its people or culture. জামাইকা দেশীয় ▷ n A **Jamaican** is a person who comes from Jamaica. জামাইকার মানুষ

jam jar (**jam jars**) n A **jam jar** is a glass container for jam, etc. জ্যাম রাখার জার

jammed adj If a place is **jammed**, a lot of people are packed tightly together there and can hardly move. গাদাগাদি করে ভরা

janitor (**janitors**) n A **janitor** is a person whose job is to look after a building. দ্বারপাল

January (**Januaries**) n **January** is the first month of the year in the Western calendar. জানুয়ারী

Japan n **Japan** is an archipelago and empire in east Asia, extending between the Sea of Japan and the Pacific. জাপান

Japanese (**japanese**) adj **Japanese** means belonging or relating to Japan, or to its people, language, or culture. জাপান দেশীয় ▷ n The **Japanese** are the people of Japan. জাপানী ▷ n **Japanese** is the language spoken in Japan. জাপানী

jar (**jars**) n A **jar** is a glass container with a lid, used for storing food. বয়াম

jaundice n **Jaundice** is an illness that makes your skin and eyes become yellow. জন্ডিস

javelin (**javelins**) n A **javelin** is a long spear that is thrown in sports competitions. বর্শা

jaw (**jaws**) n Your **jaw** is the part of your face below your mouth and cheeks. চোয়াল

jazz n **Jazz** is a style of music invented by black American musicians in the early part of the twentieth century. It has very strong rhythms and the musicians often improvise. জ্যাজ সংগীত

jealous adj If someone is **jealous**, they feel angry because they think that another person is trying to take away someone or something that they love. ঈর্ষাপরায়ণ

jeans npl **Jeans** are casual trousers that are usually made of strong blue denim. জিন্স

Jehovah's Witness (**Jehovah's Witnesses**) n A **Jehovah's Witness** is a member of a religious organization which accepts some Christian ideas and believes that the world is going to end very soon. জেহেবার সাক্ষী

jelly (**jellies**) n **Jelly** is a transparent food made from gelatine, fruit juice, and sugar, which is eaten as a dessert. জেলি

jellyfish (**jellyfish**) n A **jellyfish** is a sea creature that has a clear soft body and can sting you. জেলিফিস

jersey (**jerseys**) n A **jersey** is a knitted piece of clothing that covers the upper part of your body and your arms. (old-fashioned) জার্সি

Jesus n **Jesus** or **Jesus Christ** is the name of the man who Christians believe was the son of God, and whose teachings are the basis of Christianity. যীশু

jet (**jets**) n A **jet** is an aeroplane that is powered by jet engines. জেট

jetlag n If you are suffering from **jetlag**, you feel tired and slightly confused after a long journey by aeroplane. জেট-ল্যাগ

jetty (**jetties**) n A **jetty** is a wide stone wall or wooden platform where boats stop to let people get on and off, or to load or unload goods. জেটি

Jew (**Jews**) n A **Jew** is a person who believes in and practises the religion of Judaism. ইহুদী

jewel (**jewels**) n A **jewel** is a valuable stone, like a diamond. মণি ▷ n **Jewels** are things made with valuable stones, that you wear to decorate your body. গয়না

jeweller (**jewellers**) n A **jeweller** is a person who makes, sells, and repairs jewellery and watches. জহুরী ▷ n A **jeweller** or a **jeweller's** is a shop that sells jewellery and watches. জহুরীর দোকান

jewellery n **Jewellery** consists of ornaments that people wear such as rings and bracelets. গহনা

Jewish adj **Jewish** means belonging or relating to the religion of Judaism or to Jews. ইহুদী জাতীয়

jigsaw (**jigsaws**) n A **jigsaw** or **jigsaw puzzle** is a picture on cardboard or wood that has been cut up into odd shapes and which has to be put back together again. এক ধরনের ধাঁধা

job (**jobs**) n A **job** is the work that someone does to earn money. কাজ

job centre (**job centres**) n A **job centre** is a place where people who are looking for work can go to get advice on finding a job, and to look at advertisements placed by people who are looking for new employees. কাজ খোঁজার জায়গা

jobless adj Someone who is **jobless** does not have a job, but would like one. কর্মহীন

jockey (**jockeys**) n A **jockey** is someone who rides a horse in a race. ঘোড়সওয়ার

jog (**jogs, jogging, jogged**) vi If you **jog**, you run slowly, often as a form of exercise. জগিং

jogging n **Jogging** is the act of running at a slow regular pace as part of an exercise routine. জগিং করা

join (**joins, joining, joined**) v When things **join**, or you **join** them, they come together. যুক্ত করা ▷ v If you **join** a group of people, you become one of the group. যোগদান দেওয়া

joiner (**joiners**) n A **joiner** is a person who makes wooden window frames, door frames, doors, and cupboards. ছুতোর

joint (**joints**) adj **Joint** means shared by or belonging to two or more people. যৌথ ▷ n A **joint** is a place where two things meet or are fixed together. মিলনস্থল ▷ n A **joint** is a fairly large piece of meat which is suitable for roasting. বড় মাংসের টুকরো

joint account (**joint accounts**) n A **joint account** is a kind of bank account registered in the name of two or more people. যৌথ খাতা

joke (**jokes, joking, joked**) n A **joke** is something that is said or done to make you laugh, for example a funny story. কৌতুক ▷ vi If you **joke**, you tell funny stories or say amusing things. মজা করা

jolly (**jollier, jolliest**) adj A **jolly** person is happy and cheerful. হাসিখুশি

Jordan n **Jordan** is a kingdom in south-west Asia. জর্ডন

Jordanian (**Jordanians**) adj **Jordanian** means belonging or relating to the country of Jordan, or to its people or culture. জর্ডন দেশীয় ▷ n A **Jordanian** is a Jordanian citizen, or a person of Jordanian origin. জর্ডনের মানুষ

jot down v If you **jot** something **down**, you write it down in the form of a short informal note. নোট করা Keep a notebook nearby to jot down queries.

jotter (**jotters**) n A **jotter** is a small book for writing notes in. নোটবুক

journalism n **Journalism** is the job of collecting news and writing about it for newspapers, magazines, television, or radio. সাংবাদিকতা

journalist (**journalists**) n A **journalist** is a person whose job is to collect news, and write about it in newspapers or magazines or talk about it on television or radio. সাংবাদিক

journey (**journeys**) n When you make a **journey**, you travel from one place to another. যাত্রা

joy n **Joy** is a feeling of great happiness. আনন্দ

joystick (**joysticks**) n In some computer games, the **joystick** is the lever which the player uses in order to control the direction of the things on the screen. জয়স্টিক

judge (**judges, judging, judged**) n A **judge** is the person in a court of law who decides how the law should be applied, for example how criminals should be punished.

বিচারক ▷ vt If you **judge** a competition, you decide who or what is the winner. বিচার করা

judo n **Judo** is a sport or martial art in which two people wrestle and try to throw each other to the ground. জুডো

jug (**jugs**) n A **jug** is a container which is used for holding and pouring liquids. জগ

juggler (**jugglers**) n A **juggler** is someone who juggles in order to entertain people. জাদুকর

juice (**juices**) n **Juice** is the liquid that can be obtained from a fruit. রস

July (**Julys**) n **July** is the seventh month of the year in the Western calendar. জুলাই

jumbo jet (**jumbo jets**) n A **jumbo jet** or a **jumbo** is a very large jet aeroplane. বড় এরোপ্লেন

jump (**jumps, jumping, jumped**) v If you **jump**, you bend your knees, push against the ground with your feet, and move quickly upwards into the air. লাফানো

jumper (**jumpers**) n A **jumper** is a knitted piece of clothing which covers the upper part of your body and your arms. জাম্পার

jump leads npl **Jump leads** are two thick wires that can be used to start a car when its battery does not have enough power. The jump leads are used to connect the battery to the battery of another car that is working properly. জাম্প-লিডস

junction (**junctions**) n A **junction** is a place where roads or railway lines join. সংগম

June (**Junes**) n **June** is the sixth month of the year in the Western calendar. জুন

jungle (**jungles**) n A **jungle** is a forest in a tropical country where tall trees and other plants grow very closely together. জঙ্গল

junior adj A **junior** official or employee holds a low-ranking position in an organization or profession. কনিষ্ঠ

junk n **Junk** is an amount of old or useless things. আবর্জনা

junk mail n **Junk mail** is advertisements and publicity materials that you receive through the post or by email which you have not asked for and which you do not want. জাঙ্ক-মেল

jury (**juries**) n In a court of law, the **jury** is the group of people who have been chosen from the general public to listen to the facts about a crime and to decide whether the person accused is guilty or not. জুরি

just adv If you **just** did something, you did it a very short time ago. এইমাত্র

justice n **Justice** is fairness in the way that people are treated. সুবিচার

justify (**justifies, justifying, justified**) vt If someone or something **justifies** a particular decision, action, or idea, they show or prove that it is reasonable or necessary. যুক্তি দিয়ে বোঝানো

k

kangaroo (kangaroos) *n* A **kangaroo** is a large Australian animal. Female kangaroos carry their babies in a pocket on their stomachs. ক্যাঙ্গারু

karaoke *n* **Karaoke** is a form of entertainment in which a machine plays the tunes of songs, and people take it in turns to sing the words. কারাওকে

karate *n* **Karate** is a martial art in which people fight using their hands, elbows, feet, and legs. ক্যারাটে

Kazakhstan *n* **Kazakhstan** is a republic in central Asia. কাজাকস্তান

kebab (kebabs) *n* A **kebab** is pieces of meat or vegetables grilled on a long thin stick, or slices of grilled meat served in pitta bread. কাবাব

keen (keener, keenest) *adj* If you are **keen** on doing something, you very much want to do it. If you are **keen** that something should happen, you very much want it to happen. আগ্রহী

keep (keeps, keeping, kept) *v* If someone **keeps** still or warm, they stay like that. রাখা ▷ *vi* If someone **keeps** away from a place, they do not go near it. থাকা ▷ *vt* If you **keep** doing something, you do it many times or you do it some more. চালিয়ে যাওয়া ▷ *vt* When you **keep** something, you store it somewhere. রাখা

keep-fit *n* **Keep-fit** is the activity of keeping your body in good condition by doing special exercises. সুস্থ রাখা

keep out *v* If you **keep out** of something, you avoid getting involved in it. দূরে থাকা *They have kept out of the debate so far.*

keep up *v* If someone or something **keeps up** with another person or thing, the first one moves or progresses as fast as the second. পাল্লা দেওয়া *She shook her head and started to walk on. He kept up with her.*

kennel (kennels) *n* A **kennel** is a small hut made for a dog to sleep in. কুকুরের ঘর

Kenya *n* **Kenya** is a republic in East Africa, on the Indian Ocean. কেনিয়া

Kenyan (Kenyans) *adj* **Kenyan** means belonging or relating to Kenya, or to its people or culture. কেনিয়া দেশীয় ▷ *n* A **Kenyan** is a Kenyan citizen, or a person of Kenyan origin. কেনিয়ার নাগরিক

kerb (kerbs) *n* The **kerb** is the raised edge of a pavement which separates it from the road. রাস্তার ধার

kerosene *n* **Kerosene** is a strong-smelling liquid which is used as a fuel in heaters, lamps, and engines. (*US*) কেরোসিন

ketchup *n* **Ketchup** is a thick, cold sauce, usually made from tomatoes, that is sold in bottles. কেচাপ

kettle (kettles) *n* A **kettle** is a covered container that you use for boiling water. কেটলি

key (keys) *n* The **keys** on a computer or instrument are the buttons that you press on it. বোতাম ▷ *n* A **key** is a piece of metal that opens or closes a lock. চাবি

keyboard (keyboards) *n* The **keyboard** of a computer is the set of keys that you press in order to operate it. কী-বোর্ড

keyring (keyrings) *n* A **keyring** is a metal ring which you use to keep your keys together. You pass the ring through the holes in your keys. চাবির রিং

kick (kicks, kicking, kicked) *n* A **kick** is a forceful hit made with your foot. লাথি ▷ *v* If you **kick** someone or something, you hit them forcefully with your foot. লাথি মারা

kick off (**kick-offs**) v If an event, game, series, or discussion **kicks off**, or if someone **kicks it off**, it begins. শুরু করা *The Mayor kicked off the party.* ▷ n In football or rugby, **kick-off** is the time at which a particular match starts. শুরু করার সময়

kid (**kids, kidding, kidded**) n You can refer to a child as a **kid**. (*informal*) শিশু ▷ vi If you **are kidding**, you are saying something that is not really true, as a joke. (*informal*) তামাসা করা

kidnap (**kidnaps, kidnapping, kidnapped**) vt To **kidnap** someone is to take them away illegally and by force, and usually to hold them prisoner in order to demand something from their family, employer, or government. অপহরণ করা

kidney (**kidneys**) n Your **kidneys** are the two organs in your body that filter waste matter from your blood and send it out of your body in your urine. কিডনি

kill (**kills, killing, killed**) v If a person, animal, or other living thing **is killed**, something or someone causes them to die. মেরে ফেলা

killer (**killers**) n A **killer** is a person who has killed someone. ঘাতক

kilo (**kilos**) n A **kilo** is a metric unit of weight. One kilogram is a thousand grams, and is equal to 2.2 pounds. কিলো

kilometre (**kilometres**) n A **kilometre** is a metric unit of distance or length. One kilometre is a thousand metres, and is equal to 0.62 miles. কিলোমিটার

kilt (**kilts**) n A **kilt** is a skirt with a lot of vertical folds, traditionally worn by Scottish men. Kilts can also be worn by women and girls. ঘাঘরা

kind (**kinder, kindest, kinds**) adj Someone who is **kind** is friendly and helps you. দয়ালু ▷ n A **kind** of thing is a type or sort of that thing. ধরণ

kindly adv If you do something **kindly**, you do it in a gentle, caring and helpful way. দয়া করে

kindness n **Kindness** is the quality of being gentle, caring, and helpful. দয়া

king (**kings**) n A **king** is a man who is a member of the royal family of his country, and who is the head of state of that country. রাজা

kingdom (**kingdoms**) n A **kingdom** is a country or region that is ruled by a king or queen. রাজ্য

kingfisher (**kingfishers**) n A **kingfisher** is a brightly-coloured bird which lives near rivers and lakes and catches fish. মাছরাঙা

kiosk (**kiosks**) n A **kiosk** is a small shop in a public place such as a street or station. It sells things such as snacks or newspapers which you buy through a window. ছোট দোকান

kipper (**kippers**) n A **kipper** is a fish, usually a herring, which has been preserved by being hung in smoke. শুঁটকি মাছ

kiss (**kisses, kissing, kissed**) n A **kiss** is the act of touching somebody with your lips to show affection or to greet them. চুম্বন ▷ v If you **kiss** someone, you touch them with your lips to show affection, or to greet them or say goodbye. চুম্বন করা

kit (**kits**) n A **kit** is a group of items that are kept together because they are used for similar purposes. সাজসরঞ্জাম

kitchen (**kitchens**) n A **kitchen** is a room used for cooking and related jobs such as washing dishes. রান্নাঘর

kite (**kites**) n A **kite** is an object consisting of a light frame covered with paper or cloth, which you fly in the air at the end of a long string. ঘুড়ি

kitten (**kittens**) n A **kitten** is a very young cat. বেড়ালছানা

kiwi (**kiwis**) n A **kiwi**, or **kiwi fruit**, is a fruit with a brown hairy skin and green flesh. কিউই

km/h abbr **Km/h** is a written abbreviation for 'kilometres per hour'. কিমি/ঘণ্টা

knee (**knees**) n Your **knee** is the place where your leg bends. হাঁটু

kneecap (kneecaps) n Your **kneecaps** are the bones at the front of your knees. নি-ক্যাপ

kneel (kneels, kneeling, kneeled, knelt) vi When you **kneel**, you bend your legs so that your knees are touching the ground. হাঁটু-গাড়া

kneel down v When you **kneel down**, you bend your legs so that your knees are touching the ground. ভাঁজ করে বসা She kneeled down beside him.

knickers npl **Knickers** are a piece of underwear worn by women and girls which have holes for the legs and elastic around the top. মেয়েদের অন্তর্বাস

knife (knives) n A **knife** is a tool consisting of a sharp flat piece of metal attached to a handle, used to cut things or as a weapon. ছুরি

knit (knits, knitting, knitted) v When someone **knits** something, they make it from wool or a similar thread using knitting needles or a machine. বোনা

knitting n **Knitting** is something, such as an article of clothing, that is being knitted. কিছু বোনা

knitting needle (knitting needles) n **Knitting needles** are thin plastic or metal rods which you use when you are knitting. বোনার কাঁটা

knob (knobs) n A **knob** is a round handle or switch. হাতল

knock (knocks, knocking, knocked) n A **knock** is the act or sound of something being hit, such as a door or window, to attract someone's attention. ঠোকা মারার আওয়াজ ▷ vi If you **knock** on something such as a door or window, you hit it, usually several times, to attract someone's attention. ঠোকা মারা

knock down v To **knock down** a building or part of a building means to demolish or destroy it. ভেঙ্গে ফেলা Why doesn't he just knock the wall down?

knock out v To **knock** someone **out** means to cause them to become unconscious. অজ্ঞান করে দেওয়া I nearly knocked him out.

knot (knots) n If you tie a **knot** in a piece of string, rope, cloth, or other material, you pass one end or part of it through a loop and pull it tight. গিঁট

know (knows, knowing, knew, known) vt If you **know** something, you have that information in your mind. জানা ▷ vt If you **know** a person, you have met them and spoken to them. চেনা

know-all (know-alls) n If you say that someone is a **know-all**, you are critical of them because they think that they know a lot more than other people. (informal) সবজান্তা

know-how n **Know-how** is knowledge of the methods or techniques of doing something. (informal) কৌশল

knowledge n **Knowledge** is information and understanding about a subject, which someone has in their mind. জ্ঞান

knowledgeable adj A **knowledgeable** person knows a lot about many different things or a lot about a particular subject. জ্ঞানী

known adj You use **known** to describe someone or something that is clearly recognized by or familiar to all people, or to a particular group of people. পরিচিত

Koran n The **Koran** is the sacred book on which the religion of Islam is based. কোরান

Korea n **Korea** is a former country in East Asia, now divided into two separate countries, North Korea and South Korea. কোরিয়া

Korean (Koreans) adj **Korean** means belonging or relating to North or South Korea, or to their people, language, or culture. কোরিয়া দেশীয় ▷ n A **Korean** is a North or South Korean citizen, or a person of North or South Korean origin. কোরিয়ার মানুষ ▷ n **Korean** is the language spoken by people who live in North and South Korea. কোরিয়ার ভাষা

kosher adj Something, especially food, that is **kosher** is approved of or allowed by the laws of Judaism. ইহুদিদের ধর্মীয় খাবার

Kosovo *n* **Kosovo** is a disputed territory in south-east Europe. It is a self-declared independent state, but the Constitution of Serbia considers it to be an autonomous province of Serbia. কসোভো

Kuwait *n* **Kuwait** is a state on the north-west coast of the Persian Gulf. কুয়েত

Kuwaiti (**Kuwaitis**) *adj* **Kuwaiti** means belonging or relating to Kuwait, or to its people or culture. কুয়েত দেশীয় ▷ *n* A **Kuwaiti** is a Kuwaiti citizen, or a person of Kuwaiti origin. কুয়েতের নাগরিক

Kyrgyzstan *n* **Kyrgyzstan** is a republic in central Asia. কিরগিজস্তান

lab (**labs**) *n* A **lab** is a building or room when scientific experiments and research are performed. ল্যাব

label (**labels**) *n* A **label** is a piece of paper or plastic that is attached to an object in order to give information about it. লেবেল

laboratory (**laboratories**) *n* A **laboratory** is a building or room where scientific experiments and research are performed. ল্যাবরেটরী

labour *n* **Labour** is very hard work. শ্রম

labourer (**labourers**) *n* A **labourer** is a person who does a job which involves a lot of hard physical work. শ্রমিক

lace (**laces**) *n* **Lace** is a pretty cloth that has patterns of holes in it. লেস ▷ *n* **Laces** are like pieces of string for fastening shoes. ফিতে

lack n If there is a **lack** of something, there is not enough of it, or there is none at all. ঘাটতি

lacquer (**lacquers**) n **Lacquer** is a special type of liquid which is put on wood or metal to protect it and make it shiny. বার্নিশ

lad (**lads**) n A **lad** is a boy or young man. (*informal*) ছেলে

ladder (**ladders**) n A **ladder** is a piece of equipment used for climbing up something such as a wall. It consists of two long pieces of wood or metal with steps fixed between them. মই

ladies n Some people refer to a public toilet for women as the **ladies**. মহিলাদের

ladle (**ladles**) n A **ladle** is a large, round, deep spoon with a long handle, used for serving soup, stew, or sauce. হাতা

lady (**ladies**) n You can use **lady** when you are referring to a woman, especially when you are showing politeness or respect. ভদ্রমহিলা

ladybird (**ladybirds**) n A **ladybird** is a small round beetle that is red with black spots. এক ধরণের পোকা

lag behind vi If you **lag behind** someone or something, you make slower progress than them. পেছনে থাকা *He now lags 10 points behind the champion.*

lager (**lagers**) n **Lager** is a kind of pale beer. হালকা বিয়ার

lagoon (**lagoons**) n A **lagoon** is an area of calm sea water that is separated from the ocean by sand or rock. সমুদ্রের ধারে বালিয়াড়ি-ঘেরা লবনাক্ত জলের হ্রদ

laid-back adj If you describe someone as **laid-back**, you mean that they behave in a relaxed way as if nothing ever worries them. (*informal*) নিশ্চিন্ত

lake (**lakes**) n A **lake** is a large area of fresh water, surrounded by land. ঝিল

lamb (**lambs**) n A **lamb** is a young sheep. ভেড়া

lame (**lamer, lamest**) adj A **lame** person or animal cannot walk properly because an injury or illness has damaged one or both of their legs. খোঁড়া

lamp (**lamps**) n A **lamp** is a light that works by using electricity or by burning oil or gas. ল্যাম্প

lamppost (**lampposts**) n A **lamppost** is a tall metal or concrete pole that is fixed beside a road and has a light at the top. ল্যাম্প-পোস্ট

lampshade (**lampshades**) n A **lampshade** is a covering that is fitted round or over an electric light bulb in order to protect it or decorate it, or to make the light less harsh. ল্যাম্প-শেড

land (**lands, landing, landed**) n **Land** is an area of ground. জমি ▷ v When something **lands**, it comes down to the ground after moving through the air. নামা

landing (**landings**) n In a house or other building, the **landing** is the area at the top of the staircase which has rooms leading off it. চাতাল

landlady (**landladies**) n Someone's **landlady** is the woman who allows them to live or work in a building which she owns, in return for rent. বাড়িওয়ালি

landlord (**landlords**) n Someone's **landlord** is the man who allows them to live or work in a building which he owns, in return for rent. বাড়িওয়ালা

landmark (**landmarks**) n A **landmark** is a building or feature which is easily noticed and can be used to judge your position or the position of other buildings or features. দিকচিহ্ন

landowner (**landowners**) n A **landowner** is a person who owns land, especially a large amount of land. জমিদার

landscape (**landscapes**) n The **landscape** is everything that you can see when you look across an area of land, including hills, rivers, buildings, and trees. ভূদৃশ্য

landslide (**landslides**) n If an election is won by a **landslide**, it is won by a large number of votes. বিপুল ভোটে

lane (lanes) n A **lane** is a type of road, especially in the country. গলি

language (languages) n A **language** is a system of sounds and written symbols used by the people of a particular country, area, or tribe to communicate with each other. ভাষা

language laboratory (language laboratories) n A **language laboratory** is a classroom equipped with tape recorders or computers where people can practise listening to and talking foreign languages. বারবার অভ্যাসের দ্বারা বিদেশি ভাষা শেখার জন্যে টেপরেকর্ডার ইঃ যন্ত্রপাতিতে সজ্জিত ঘর

language school (language schools) n A **language school** is a private school where a foreign language is taught. ভাষা শেখার স্কুল

lanky (lankier, lankiest) adj If you describe someone as **lanky**, you mean that they are tall and thin and move rather awkwardly. ল্যাকপেকে

Laos n **Laos** is a republic in south-east Asia. লাওস

lap (laps) n Your **lap** is the flat area formed by your thighs when you are sitting down. কোল

laptop (laptops) n A **laptop** or a **laptop computer** is a small computer that you can carry around with you. ল্যাপটপ

larder (larders) n A **larder** is a room or large cupboard in a house, usually near the kitchen, in which food is kept. মিটসেফ

large (larger, largest) adj A **large** thing or person is big or bigger than usual. বড়

largely adv You use **largely** to say that a statement is mostly but not completely true. অধিকাংশ

laryngitis n **Laryngitis** is an infection of the throat in which your larynx becomes swollen and painful, making it difficult to speak. স্বরনালির প্রদাহ

laser (lasers) n A **laser** is a narrow beam of concentrated light produced by a special machine. লেসার

lass (lasses) n A **lass** is a young woman or girl. তরুণী

last (lasts, lasting, lasted) adj The **last** thing is the one before this one. গত ▷ adj The **last** thing or person comes after all the others. শেষ ▷ adv Something **last** happened on the most recent occasion on which it happened. শেষ ▷ v If an event or situation **lasts** for a particular length of time, it continues for that length of time. টিকে থাকা

lastly adv You use **lastly** when you want to make a final point that is connected with the ones you have already mentioned. সর্বশেষে

late (later, latest) adj **Late** means after the usual time that something happens. দেরীতে ▷ adj You use **late** when you are talking about someone who is dead. স্বর্গীয় ▷ adv **Late** also means after the proper time. দেরি ▷ adv **Late** means near the end of a period of time. শেষবেলা

lately adv **Lately** means recently. সাম্প্রতিককালে

later adv You use **later** to refer to a time or situation that is after the one that you have been talking about or after the present one. পরে

Latin n **Latin** is the language which the ancient Romans used to speak. ল্যাটিন

Latin America n You can use **Latin America** to refer to the countries of South America, Central America, and Mexico. ল্যাটিন আমেরিকা

Latin American adj **Latin American** means belonging or relating to the countries of South America, Central America, and Mexico. **Latin American** also means belonging or relating to the people or culture of these countries. ল্যাটিন আমেরিকীয়

latitude (latitudes) n The **latitude** of a place is its distance from the Equator. অক্ষাংশ

Latvia n **Latvia** is a republic in north-east Europe, on the Gulf of Riga and the Baltic Sea. ল্যাটভিয়া

Latvian (**Latvians**) *adj* **Latvian** means belonging to or relating to Latvia, its people, or their language. ল্যাটভিয়া সংক্রান্ত ▷ *n* A **Latvian** is a person from Latvia. ল্যাটভিয়ান ▷ *n* **Latvian** is the language spoken in Latvia. ল্যাটভিয়ান ভাষা

laugh (**laughs, laughing, laughed**) *n* A **laugh** is the act of making a sound while smiling and showing that you are happy or amused. হাসি ▷ *vi* When you **laugh**, you smile and make a sound because something is funny. হাসা

laughter *n* **Laughter** is the sound of people laughing. হাসির শব্দ

launch (**launches, launching, launched**) *vt* To **launch** a rocket, missile, or satellite means to send it into the air or into space. উৎক্ষেপণ

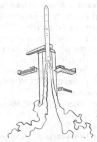

Launderette® (**Launderettes**) *n* A **Launderette** is a place where people can pay to use machines to wash and dry their clothes. লন্ডেরেট

laundry *n* **Laundry** is used to refer to clothes, sheets, and towels that are about to be washed, are being washed, or have just been washed. লন্ড্রি

lava *n* **Lava** is the very hot liquid rock that comes out of a volcano. লাভা

lavatory (**lavatories**) *n* A **lavatory** is a toilet. শৌচাগার

lavender *n* **Lavender** is a garden plant with sweet-smelling purple flowers. ল্যাভেন্ডার

law *n* **The law** is a system of rules that a society or government develops to deal with things like crime. আইন

lawn (**lawns**) *n* A **lawn** is an area of grass that is kept cut short and is usually part of a garden or park. লন

lawnmower (**lawnmowers**) *n* A **lawnmower** is a machine for cutting grass on lawns. ঘাস কাটার মেশিন

law school (**law schools**) *n* **Law school** is an institution that trains people to become lawyers. আইনের স্কুল

lawyer (**lawyers**) *n* A **lawyer** is a person who is qualified to advise people about the law and represent them in court. উকিল

laxative (**laxatives**) *n* A **laxative** is food or medicine that you take to make you go to the toilet. কোষ্ঠশোধক পদার্থ

lay (**lays, laying, laid**) *vt* When you **lay** something somewhere, you put it down so that it lies there. শোয়ানো ▷ *vt* When a bird **lays** an egg, it pushes an egg out of its body. ডিম পাড়া

layby (**laybys**) *n* A **layby** is a short strip of road by the side of a main road, where cars can stop for a while. রাস্তার ধারে গলি

layer (**layers**) *n* A **layer** of a material or substance is a quantity or flat piece of it that covers a surface or that is between two other things. স্তর

lay off *v* If workers **are laid off** by their employers, they are told to leave their jobs, usually because there is no more work for them to do. বরখাস্ত করা *They did not sell a single car for a month and had to lay off workers.*

layout (**layouts**) *n* The **layout** of a garden, building, or piece of writing is the way in which the parts of it are arranged. পরিকল্পনা

lazy (**lazier, laziest**) *adj* If someone is **lazy**, they do not want to work or make an effort. কুঁড়ে

lead (**leads, leading, led**) *n* The **lead** in a play, film, or show is the most important role in it. প্রধান ▷ *n* If you are in the **lead**

in a race or competition, you are winning. এগিয়ে থাকা ▷ *vt* If you **lead** someone to a place, you take them there. পথ দেখিয়ে নিয়ে যাওয়া

lead *n* **Lead** is a soft, grey, heavy metal. সীসা

leader (**leaders**) *n* The **leader** of an organization or a group of people is the person who is in charge of it. নেতা

lead-free *adj* Something such as petrol or paint which is **lead-free** is made without lead, or has no lead added to it. সীসা ছাড়া

lead singer (**lead singers**) *n* The **lead singer** of a pop group is the person who sings most of the songs. প্রধান গায়ক

leaf (**leaves**) *n* A **leaf** is one of the parts of a tree or plant that is flat, thin, and usually green. পাতা

leaflet (**leaflets**) *n* A **leaflet** is a little book or a piece of paper containing information about a particular subject. পুস্তিকা

league (**leagues**) *n* A **league** is a group of people, clubs, or countries that have joined together for a particular purpose. লীগ

leak (**leaks, leaking, leaked**) *n* A **leak** is a crack, hole, or other gap that a substance such as a liquid or gas can pass through. ফুটো ▷ *vi* If a container **leaks**, there is a hole or crack in it which lets a substance such as liquid or gas escape. You can also say that a container **leaks** a substance such as liquid or gas. ফুটো হয়ে যাওয়া

lean (**leans, leaning, leaned, leant**) *vi* When you **lean** in a particular direction, you bend your body in that direction. ঝুঁকে থাকা

lean forward *v* When you **lean forward**, you bend your body forwards. সামনে ঝোঁকা *He leaned forward to give her a kiss.*

lean on *v* If you **lean on** someone, you depend on them for support and help. ভরসায় থাকা *You can lean on me.*

lean out *v* When you **lean out**, you bend your body outwards. বাইরে ঝোঁকা *He opened the window and leaned out.*

leap (**leaps, leaping, leaped, leapt**) *vi* If you **leap**, you jump high in the air or jump a long distance. লাফানো

leap year (**leap years**) *n* A **leap year** is a year which has 366 days. The extra day is the 29th February. There is a leap year every four years in the Western calendar. অধিবর্ষ

learn (**learns, learning, learned, learnt**) *v* When you **learn**, you obtain knowledge or a skill through studying or training. শেখা

learner (**learners**) *n* A **learner** is someone who is learning about a particular subject or how to do something. শিক্ষার্থী

learner driver (**learner drivers**) *n* A **learner driver** is a person who is learning to drive a car. শিক্ষার্থী ড্রাইভার

lease (**leases, leasing, leased**) *n* A **lease** is a legal agreement under which someone pays money to another person in exchange for the use of a building or piece of land for a specified period of time. লিজ ▷ vt If you **lease** property or something such as a car, or if someone **leases** it to you, they allow you to use it in return for regular payments of money. লিজ দেওয়া

least adj You use **the least** to mean a smaller amount than any other thing or person, or the smallest amount possible. ন্যূনতম

leather (**leathers**) n **Leather** is treated animal skin which is used for making shoes, clothes, bags, and furniture. চামড়া

leave (**leaves, leaving, left**) n **Leave** is a period of time when you are not working at your job, because you are on holiday or vacation. ছুটি ▷ v When you **leave** a place, you go away from it. প্রস্থান করা ▷ vt If you **leave** something somewhere, you do not bring it with you. ছেড়ে আসা

leave out v If you **leave** someone or something **out** of something such as an activity or a collection, you do not include them in it. বাদ দেওয়া I never left him out of my team.

Lebanese (**Lebanese**) adj **Lebanese** means belonging or relating to Lebanon, or to its people or culture. লেবানন দেশীয় ▷ n A **Lebanese** is a Lebanese citizen, or a person of Lebanese origin. লেবাননের মানুষ

Lebanon n **Lebanon** is a republic in west Asia, on the Mediterranean. লেবানন

lecture (**lectures, lecturing, lectured**) n A **lecture** is a talk that someone gives in order to teach people about a particular subject, usually at a university. ভাষণ ▷ vi If you **lecture** on a particular subject, you give a lecture or a series of lectures about it. ভাষণ দেওয়া

lecturer (**lecturers**) n A **lecturer** is a teacher at university or college. অধ্যাপক

leek (**leeks**) n **Leeks** are long green and white vegetables which smell like onions. পেঁয়াজের মত সজ্জি

left adj If there is a certain amount of something **left**, it remains when the rest has gone or been used. বাকি

left adv If you are facing north and you turn **left**, you will be facing west. বাঁ-দিকে ▷ n The **left** is one side of something. For example, on a page, English writing begins on the left. বাঁ দিকে

left-hand adj **Left-hand** describes the position of something when it is on the left side. বাঁ-হাত

left-hand drive (**left-hand drives**) n A **left-hand drive** is a vehicle which has the steering wheel on the left side, and is designed to be used in countries where people drive on the right-hand side of the road. বাঁ-দিকে গাড়ি চালানো

left-handed adj Someone who is **left-handed** finds it easier to use their left hand rather than their right hand for activities such as writing and throwing a ball. বাঁ-হাতি

left luggage n **Left luggage** is used to refer to luggage that people leave at a special place in a railway station or an airport, and which they collect later. রেলওয়ে স্টেশন বা এয়ারপোর্টে পরে সংগ্রহ করা যায় এমন জিনিষপত্র রাখার জায়গা

left-luggage office (**left-luggage offices**) n A **left-luggage office** is a special place in a railway station or an airport, where you can leave luggage and collect it later. রেলওয়ে স্টেশন বা এয়ারপোর্টে অবস্থিত পরে সংগ্রহ করা যায় এমন জিনিষপত্র রাখার অফিস

leftovers npl You can refer to food that has not been eaten after a meal as **leftovers**. বেঁচে যাওয়া

left-wing adj **Left-wing** people have political ideas that are based on socialism. বামপন্থী

leg (**legs**) n A person's or animal's **legs** are the long parts of their body that they use for walking and standing. পা ▷ n The **legs** of a table or chair are the long parts that it stands on. পায়া

legal adj **Legal** is used to describe things that relate to the law. আইনী

legend (**legends**) n A **legend** is a very old and popular story that may be based on real events. উপকথা

leggings npl **Leggings** are tight trousers that are made out of a fabric which stretches easily. লেগিংস্

legible adj **Legible** writing is clear enough to read. স্পষ্ট

legislation n **Legislation** consists of a law or laws passed by a government. (*formal*) বিধান

leisure n **Leisure** is the time when you do not have to work and can do things that you enjoy. অবসর

leisure centre (**leisure centres**) n A **leisure centre** is a large public building containing different facilities for leisure activities, such as a sports hall, a swimming pool, and rooms for meetings. অবসর সময় কাটানোর জায়গা

lemon (**lemons**) n A **lemon** is a sour yellow citrus fruit. লেবু

lemonade (**lemonades**) n **Lemonade** is a clear, sweet, fizzy drink, or a drink that is made from lemons, sugar, and water. লেবুর সরবত

lend (**lends, lending, lent**) vt When people or organizations such as banks **lend** you money, they give it to you and you agree to pay it back at a future date, often with an extra amount as interest. ধার দেওয়া

length (**lengths**) n The **length** of something is the amount that it measures from one end to the other. দৈর্ঘ্য

lens (**lenses**) n A **lens** is a thin, curved piece of glass or plastic in something such as a camera or pair of glasses which makes things appear larger or clearer. লেস

Lent n **Lent** is the period of forty days before Easter, during which some Christians give up something that they enjoy. লেন্ট পর্ব

lentils npl **Lentils** are a type of dried seed used in cooking. শুঁটিজাতীয় গাছের বীজ

Leo n **Leo** is one of the twelve signs of the zodiac. Its symbol is a lion. People who are born between approximately the 23rd of July and the 22nd of August come under this sign. সিংহরাশি

leopard (**leopards**) n A **leopard** is a type of large wild cat from Africa or Asia. Leopards have yellow fur and black spots. চিতাবাঘ

leotard (**leotards**) n A **leotard** is a tight-fitting piece of clothing, covering the body but not the legs, that some people wear when they practise dancing or do exercise. ব্যালেনর্তকদের একধরনের আঁটোসাঁটো পোশাক

less adv You use **less** to talk about a smaller amount. অপেক্ষাকৃত কম ▷ pron You use **less** to talk about a smaller amount of something. কম *Borrowers are spending less and saving more.* ▷ adj **Less** means a smaller amount. কম

lesson (**lessons**) n A **lesson** is a fixed period of time during which people are taught something. পাঠ

let (**lets, letting**) vt If you **let** someone do something, you allow them to do it. হতে দেওয়া

let down v If you **let** someone **down**, you disappoint them, usually by not doing something that you said you would do. হতাশ করা *Don't worry, I won't let you down.*

let in v If an object **lets in** something such as air or water, it allows air or water to get into it or pass through it. প্রবেশ করতে দেওয়া *There is no glass in the front door to let in light.*

letter (**letters**) n **Letters** are written symbols that represent the sounds in a language. অক্ষর ▷ n A **letter** is a message on paper that you post to someone. চিঠি

letterbox (**letterboxes**) n A **letterbox** is a rectangular hole in a door through which letters are delivered. লেটারবক্স

lettuce (**lettuces**) n A **lettuce** is a plant with large green leaves that you eat in salads. লেটুস

leukaemia n **Leukaemia** is a serious disease of the blood. লিউকেমিয়া

level (levels) adj If one thing is **level** with another thing, it is at the same height. মুখোমুখি ▷ n A **level** is a point on a scale, for example a scale of amount, importance, or difficulty. মাত্রা

level crossing (level crossings) n A **level crossing** is a place where a railway line crosses a road. লেভেল ক্রসিং

lever (levers) n A **lever** is a handle or bar that you pull or push to operate a piece of machinery. লিভার

liar (liars) n A **liar** is someone who tells lies. মিথ্যাবাদী

liberal adj Someone who has **liberal** views believes people should have a lot of freedom in deciding how to behave and think. উদার

liberation n The **liberation** of a place or the people in it means the freeing of them from the political or military control of another country, area, or group of people. স্বাধীনতা

Liberia n **Liberia** is a republic in West Africa, on the Atlantic. লাইবেরিয়া

Liberian (Liberians) adj **Liberian** means belonging or relating to Liberia, its people, or its culture. লাইবেরিয়া দেশীয় ▷ n A **Liberian** is a person who comes from Liberia, or a person of Liberian origin. লাইবেরিয়ার মানুষ

Libra n **Libra** is one of the twelve signs of the zodiac. Its symbol is a pair of scales. People who are born between approximately the 23rd of September and the 22nd of October come under this sign. তুলা রাশি

librarian (librarians) n A **librarian** is a person who works in, or is in charge of a library. গ্রন্থাগারিক

library (libraries) n A public **library** is a building where things such as books, newspapers, videos, and music are kept for people to read, use, or borrow. গ্রন্থাগার

Libya n **Libya** is a republic in North Africa, on the Mediterranean. লিবিয়া

Libyan (Libyans) adj **Libyan** means belonging or relating to Libya, or to its people or culture. লিবিয়া দেশীয় ▷ n A **Libyan** is a Libyan citizen, or a person of Libyan origin. লিবিয়াবাসী

lice npl **Lice** are small insects that live on the bodies of people or animals. উকুন

licence (licences) n A **licence** is an official document which gives you permission to do, use, or own something. লাইসেন্স

lick (licks, licking, licked) vt When people or animals **lick** something, they move their tongue across its surface. চাটা

lid (lids) n A **lid** of a container is the top which you open to reach inside. ঢাকনা

lie (lies, lying, lay, lain) n A **lie** is something that you say that is not true. মিথ্যাকথা ▷ vi When you **lie** somewhere, your body is flat, and you are not standing or sitting. শুয়ে থাকা

Liechtenstein n **Liechtenstein** is a small mountainous country in central Europe on the Rhine. লিকটেন্সটাইন

lie-in (lie-ins) n If you have a **lie-in**, you rest by staying in bed later than usual in the morning. (informal) বিছানা ছেড়ে ওঠার সময় পার হয়ে যাওয়ার পরেও বিছানায় পড়ানো

lieutenant (lieutenants) n A **lieutenant** is a junior officer in the army, navy, or air force. লেফটেন্যান্ট

life (lives) n **Life** is the quality which people, animals, and plants have when they are not dead. জীবন

lifebelt (lifebelts) n A **lifebelt** is a large ring, usually made of a light substance such as cork, which someone who has fallen into deep water can use to float. লাইফবেল্ট

lifeboat (lifeboats) n A **lifeboat** is a boat used to rescue people who are in danger at sea. লাইফবোট

lifeguard (lifeguards) n A **lifeguard** is a person who works at a beach or swimming pool and rescues people when they are in danger of drowning. লাইফগার্ড

life jacket (**life jackets**) *n* A **life jacket** is a sleeveless jacket which keeps you floating in water. লাইফ জ্যাকেট

life-saving *adj* A **life-saving** drug, operation, or action is one that saves someone's life or is likely to save their life. জীবনদায়ক

lifestyle (**lifestyles**) *n* Your **lifestyle** is the way you live, for example the things you normally do. জীবনযাত্রার ধরণ

lift (**lifts, lifting, lifted**) *n* If you give someone a **lift**, you drive them from one place to another. গাড়িতে লিফ্ট ▷ *n* A **lift** is a device that carries people or goods up and down inside tall buildings. লিফ্ট দেওয়া ▷ *vt* If you **lift** something, you move it to another position, especially upwards. তুলে ধরা

light (**lighter, lightest, lights, lighting, lit, lighted**) *adj* Something that is **light** is not heavy. হাল্কা ▷ *adj* If a place is **light**, it is bright because of the sun or lamps. আলোকিত ▷ *n* **Light** is the bright energy that comes from the sun, that lets you see things. আলোক শক্তি ▷ *vt* When you **light** a fire, it starts burning. আলো জ্বালানো ▷ *n* A **light** is something, like a lamp, that allows you to see. বাতি ▷ *adj* A **light** colour is pale. উজ্জ্বল নয়

light bulb (**light bulbs**) *n* A **light bulb** is the round glass part of an electric light or lamp which light shines from. আলোর বাল্ব

lighter (**lighters**) *n* A **lighter** is a small device that produces a flame that is used to light cigarettes. লাইটার

lighthouse (**lighthouses**) *n* A **lighthouse** is a tower near or in the sea which contains a powerful flashing lamp to guide ships or to warn them of danger. লাইটহাউস

lighting *n* The **lighting** in a place is the way that it is lit. আলোকসজ্জা

lightning *n* **Lightning** is the bright flashes of light in the sky that you see during a thunderstorm. বজ্রপাত

like (**likes, liking, liked**) *prep* If things or people are **like** each other, they are almost the same. অনুরূপ *He's very funny, like my uncle.* ▷ *vt* If you **like** something, you think it is nice or interesting. পছন্দ করা ▷ *v* What something or someone is **like** is how they seem to you. সুন্দর

likely (**likelier, likeliest**) *adj* You use **likely** to indicate that something is probably true or will probably happen in a particular situation.

lilac (**lilacs, lilac**) *adj* Something that is **lilac** is pale pinkish-purple in colour. বেগুনি রঙের ▷ *n* A **lilac** is a small tree with pleasant-smelling purple, pink, or white flowers. এক ধরণের গাছ

lily (**lilies**) *n* A **lily** is a plant with large sweet-smelling flowers. লিলিফুল

lily of the valley (**lilies of the valley, lily of the valley**) *n* **Lily of the valley** are small plants with large leaves and small, white, bell-shaped flowers. এক ধরণের ফুলের গাছ

lime (**limes**) *n* A **lime** is a small, round citrus fruit with green skin. পাতিলেবু ▷ *n* **Lime** is a substance containing calcium. It is found in soil and water. চুন

limestone (**limestones**) *n* **Limestone** is a white rock which is used for building and making cement. চুনাপাথর

limit (**limits**) *n* A **limit** is the greatest amount, extent, or degree of something that is possible. সীমা

limousine (**limousines**) *n* A **limousine** is a large and very comfortable car. Limousines are usually driven by a chauffeur and are used by very rich or important people. লিমুজিন

limp (**limps, limping, limped**) *vi* If a person or animal **limps**, they walk with difficulty or in an uneven way because one of their legs or feet are hurt. খুঁড়িয়ে চলা

ine (lines) *n* A **line** is a long, thin mark or shape. লাইন

inen *n* **Linen** is a kind of cloth that is made from a plant called flax. শণের কাপড়

iner (liners) *n* A **liner** is a large passenger ship. যাত্রীবাহী জাহাজ

inguist (linguists) *n* A **linguist** is someone who is good at speaking or learning foreign languages. ভাষাতত্ত্ববিদ

inguistic *adj* **Linguistic** abilities or ideas relate to language. ভাষা সংক্রান্ত

ining (linings) *n* The **lining** of a piece of clothing or a curtain is a material attached to the inside of it in order to make it thicker or warmer. আস্তরণ

ink (links, linking, linked) *n* If there is a **link** between two things or situations, there is a relationship between them, for example because one thing causes or affects the other. সম্পর্ক ▷ *vt* If someone or something **links** two things or situations, there is a relationship between them, for example because one thing causes or affects the other. সংযোগ করা

ino *n* **Lino** is a floor covering which is made of cloth covered with a hard shiny substance. লাইনো

ion (lions) *n* A **lion** is a large wild member of the cat family that is found in Africa. Lions have yellowish fur, and male lions have long hair on their head and neck. সিংহ

ioness (lionesses) *n* A **lioness** is a female lion. সিংহী

ip (lips) *n* Your **lips** are the two outer parts of the edge of your mouth. ওষ্ঠযুগল

ip-read (lip-reads, lip-reading) *vi* If someone can **lip-read**, they are able to understand what someone else is saying by looking at the way the other person's lips move as they speak, without actually hearing any of the words. মুখ খুলে ধরতে পারা

ip salve (lip salves) *n* **Lip salve** is an oily substance that is put on cracked or dry lips to help them heal. ঠোঁটের মলম

lipstick (lipsticks) *n* **Lipstick** is a coloured substance which women put on their lips. লিপস্টিক

liqueur (liqueurs) *n* A **liqueur** is a strong sweet alcoholic drink. মদ

liquid (liquids) *n* A **liquid** is a substance such as water which is not solid and which can be poured. তরল

liquidizer (liquidizers) *n* A **liquidizer** is an electric machine that you use to turn solid food into liquid. তরল করবার মেশিন

list (lists, listing, listed) *n* A **list** is a set of things which all belong to a particular category, written down one below the other. তালিকা ▷ *vt* To **list** a set of things means to write them or say them one after another, usually in a particular order. তালিকাভুক্ত করা

listen (listens, listening, listened) *vi* If you **listen** to someone who is talking or to a sound, you give your attention to them. শোনা ▷ *vi* If you **listen** to someone, you do what they advise you to do, or you believe them. কোন কিছু শোনা

listener (listeners) *n* People who listen to the radio are often referred to as **listeners**. শ্রোতা

literally *adv* You can use **literally** to emphasize a statement. অক্ষরে অক্ষরে

literature *n* Novels, plays, and poetry are referred to as **literature**. সাহিত্য

Lithuania *n* **Lithuania** is a republic in north-east Europe, on the Baltic Sea. লিথুয়ানিয়া

Lithuanian (Lithuanians) *adj* **Lithuanian** means belonging or relating to Lithuania, or to its people, language, or culture. লিথুয়ানিয়া দেশীয় ▷ *n* A **Lithuanian** is a person who comes from Lithuania. লিথুয়ানিয়ার মানুষ ▷ *n* **Lithuanian** is the language spoken in Lithuania. লিথুয়ানিয়া ভাষা

litre (litres) *n* A **litre** is a metric unit of volume. It is equal to approximately 1.76 British pints or 2.11 American pints. লিটার

litter (litters) *n* **Litter** is rubbish which is left lying around outside. আজেবাজে জিনিষপত্র

▷ *n* A **litter** is a group of animals born to the same mother at the same time. একপাল

litter bin (**litter bins**) *n* A **litter bin** is a container, usually in a street, park, or public building, which people can put rubbish. জঞ্জাল ফেলার স্থান

little (**littler, littlest**) *adj* A person or thing that is **little** is small in size. ছোট

live (**lives, living, lived**) *adj* **Live** animals or plants are alive, rather than being dead or artificial. জীবন্ত ▷ *vi* You **live** in the place where your home is. বাস করা ▷ *vi* To **live** means to be alive. বেঁচে থাকা

lively (**livelier, liveliest**) *adj* You can describe someone as **lively** when they behave in an enthusiastic and cheerful way. প্রাণবন্ত

live on *v* If you **live on** a particular amount of money, or if you **live off** it, you have that amount of money to buy things. জীবনধারণ করা *Most students are unable to live on that amount of money.*

liver (**livers**) *n* Your **liver** is a large organ in your body which cleans your blood. লিভার

living *n* The work that you do for a **living** is the work that you do to earn the money that you need. জীবিকা

living room (**living rooms**) *n* The **living room** in a house is the room where people sit and relax. বসার ঘর

lizard (**lizards**) *n* A **lizard** is a reptile with short legs and a long tail. টিকটিকি

load (**loads, loading, loaded**) *n* A **load** is something, usually large or heavy, which is being carried. ভার ▷ *vt* If you **load** a vehicle, you put something on it. বোঝাই করা

loaf (**loaves**) *n* A **loaf** of bread is bread in a shape that can be cut into slices. পাউরুটি

loan (**loans, loaning, loaned**) *n* A **loan** is a sum of money that you borrow. ঋণ ▷ *vt* If you **loan** something to someone, you lend it to them. ধার দেওয়া

loathe (**loathes, loathing, loathed**) *vt* If you **loathe** something or someone, you dislike them very much. ঘৃণা করা

lobster (**lobsters**) *n* A **lobster** is a sea creature with a hard shell, two large claws, and eight legs. গলদা চিংড়ি

local *adj* **Local** means existing in or belonging to the area where you live, or to the area that you are talking about. স্থানীয়

local anaesthetic (**local anaesthetics**) *n* A **local anaesthetic** is a substance used by a doctor to stop you feeling pain, which affects only a small area of your body. অবশ করার ওষুধ

location (**locations**) *n* A **location** is a place, especially the place where something happens or is situated. অবস্থান

lock (**locks, locking, locked**) *n* The **lock** on something such as a door is the device which fastens it when you turn a key in it. তালা ▷ *n* A **lock** of hair is a small bunch of hairs on your head that grow together in the same direction. চুলের গোছা ▷ *vt* When you **lock** something, you fasten it by means of a key. তালা লাগানো

locker (**lockers**) *n* A **locker** is a small cupboard for someone's personal belongings, for example in a changing room. লকার

locket (**lockets**) *n* A **locket** is a piece of jewellery containing something such as a picture, which you wear on a chain around your neck. লকেট

lock out *v* If someone **locks** you **out** of a place, they prevent you entering it by locking the doors. বার করে দেওয়া *They had had a row, and she had locked him out of the apartment.*

ocksmith (locksmiths) *n* A **locksmith** is a person whose job is to make or repair locks. তালাওয়ালা

odger (lodgers) *n* A **lodger** is a person who pays money to live in someone else's house. অর্থের বিনিময়ে অন্যের বাড়িতে বাসকারী ব্যক্তি

oft (lofts) *n* A **loft** is the space inside the sloping roof of a building. চিলেকোঠা

og (logs) *n* A **log** is a thick piece of wood cut from a branch or trunk of a tree. কাঠের গুঁড়ি

ogical *adj* In a **logical** argument, each step or point must be true if the step before it is true. যুক্তিসংগত

og in *v* If you **log in** or **log on**, you type your name and a password so that you can start using a computer or a website. লগ-ইন করা *She turned on her computer and logged in.*

ogo (logos) *n* The **logo** of an organization is the special design that it puts on all its products. লোগো

og out *v* If you **log out** or **log off**, you stop using a computer or website by clicking on an instruction. লগ-আউট করা *I logged off and went out for a walk.*

ollipop (lollipops) *n* A **lollipop** is a sweet consisting of a hard disc or ball of a sugary substance on the end of a stick. ললিপপ

lolly (lollies) *n* A **lolly** is a sweet consisting of a hard disc or ball of a sugary substance on the end of a stick. লি

London *n* **London** is the capital city of the United Kingdom. লন্ডন

loneliness *n* **Loneliness** is the unhappiness that is felt by someone because they do not have any friends or do not have anyone to talk to. একাকিত্ব

lonely (lonelier, loneliest) *adj* A **lonely** person is unhappy because they are alone, or because they do not have any friends. একাকী

lonesome *adj* Someone who is **lonesome** is unhappy because they do not have any friends or do not have anyone to talk to. স্বজনহীন

long (longer, longest, longs, longing, longed) *adj* Something that is **long** takes a lot of time. দীর্ঘ ▷ *adj* Something that is **long** measures a great distance from one end to the other. লম্বা ▷ *adv* **Long** means a great amount of time. দীর্ঘ সময় ▷ *v* If you **long** for something, you want it very much. চাওয়া

longer *adv* **Longer** means for a greater amount of time. আরো কিছু সময়

longitude (longitudes) *n* The **longitude** of a place is its distance to the west or east of a line passing through Greenwich in England. দ্রাঘিমাংশ

long jump *n* **The long jump** is an athletics contest which involves jumping as far as you can from a marker which you run up to. লং জাম্প

loo (loos) *n* A **loo** is a toilet. (*informal*) শৌচালয়

look (looks, looking, looked) *n* A **look** is the act of directing your eyes so that you can see something. দৃষ্টিপাত ▷ *vi* When you **look** at something, you turn your eyes so that you can see it. দেখা ▷ *v* You use **look** when you describe how a person seems. দেখতে

look after *v* If you **look after** someone or something, you keep them healthy, safe, or in good condition. লক্ষ্য রাখা / *I love looking after the children.*

look at *vi* If you **look at** a book, newspaper, or magazine, you read it fairly quickly or read part of it. পড়া *You've just got to look at the last bit of Act Three.*

look for *v* If you **look for** something, for example something that you have lost, you try to find it. খোঁজা *I'm looking for my keys.*

look round *v* If you **look round** a place, or if you **look around** it, you walk round it and look at the different parts of it. চারিপাশে তাকানো *We went to look round the show homes.*

look up *v* If you **look up** a piece of information, you find it out by looking in a book or list. কিছুর মধ্যে খোঁজা *I looked your address up in your file.*

loose (**looser, loosest**) *adj* Something that is **loose** moves when it should not. আলগা ▷ *adj* **Loose** clothes are rather large and are not tight. ঢিলে

lorry (**lorries**) *n* A **lorry** is a large vehicle used to transport goods by road. লরি

lorry driver (**lorry drivers**) *n* A **lorry driver** is someone who drives a lorry as their job. লরিচালক

lose (**loses, losing, lost**) *v* If you **lose** a game, you do not win it. হেরে যাওয়া ▷ *vt* If you **lose** something, you do not know where it is. হারিয়ে যাওয়া

loser (**losers**) *n* The **losers** of a contest or struggle are the people who are defeated. পরাজিত

loss (**losses**) *n* **Loss** is the fact of no longer having something or of having less of it than before. ক্ষতি

lost *adj* If you are **lost**, you do not know where you are or you are unable to find your way. হারিয়ে যাওয়া

lot (**lots**) *n* A **lot** of something, or **lots** of something, is a large amount of it. প্রচুর

lotion (**lotions**) *n* A **lotion** is a liquid that you use to clean, improve, or protect your skin or hair. লোশন

lottery (**lotteries**) *n* A **lottery** is a type of gambling in which people bet on a number or a series of numbers being chosen as the winner. Lotteries usually offer large cash prizes and are often organized so that a percentage of the profits is donated to good causes. লটারি

loud (**louder, loudest**) *adj* If a noise is **loud**, the level of sound is very high and it can be easily heard. Someone or something that is **loud** produces a lot of noise. জোরালো

loudly *adv* If you do something **loudly**, you produce a lot of noise. উচ্চ আওয়াজে

loudspeaker (**loudspeakers**) *n* A **loudspeaker** is a piece of equipment, for example part of a radio, through which sound comes out. লাউডস্পিকার

lounge (**lounges**) *n* A **lounge** is a room in a house, or in a hotel, where people sit and relax. লাউঞ্জ

lousy (**lousier, lousiest**) *adj* If you describe something as **lousy**, you mean that it is of very bad quality. (*informal*) খারাপ

love (**loves, loving, loved**) *n* **Love** is the very strong warm feeling that you have when you care very much about someone, or you have strong romantic feelings for them. ভালবাসা ▷ *vt* If you **love** someone, you care very much about them. ভালোবাসা ▷ *vt* If you **love** something, you like it very much. পছন্দ করা

lovely (**lovelier, loveliest**) *adj* If you describe someone or something as **lovely**, you mean that they are very beautiful or that you like them very much. দারুণ সুন্দর

low (**lower, lowest**) *adj* Something that is **low** is close to the ground. নীচু ▷ *adj* A **low** number is a small number. কম ▷ *adv* If someone or something does something **low**, they do it close to the ground. নিচুভাবে

low-alcohol *adj* **Low-alcohol** beer or wine contains only a small amount of alcohol. কম-অ্যালকোহলযুক্ত

lower (**lowers, lowering, lowered**) *adj* You can use **lower** to refer to the bottom one of a pair of things. নিচের ▷ *vt* If you **lower** something, you move it slowly downwards. নিচু করা

low-fat *adj* **Low-fat** food and drinks contain only a very small amount of fat. কম ফ্যাটিযুক্ত

low season *n* **The low season** is the time of year when a place receives the fewest visitors, and fares and holiday accommodation are often cheaper. অসময়

loyalty (loyalties) *n* **Loyalty** is behaviour in which you stay firm in your friendship or support for someone or something. আনুগত্য

luck *n* **Luck** is success or good things that happen to you, which do not come from your own abilities or efforts. ভাগ্য

luckily *adv* You add **luckily** to your statement to indicate that you are glad that something happened or is the case. ভাগ্যবশতঃ

lucky (luckier, luckiest) *adj* If someone is **lucky**, they are in a very desirable situation. ভাগ্যবান

lucrative *adj* A **lucrative** business or activity earns you a lot of money. লোভনীয়

luggage *n* **Luggage** consists of the suitcases and bags that you take when you travel. তল্লিতল্লা

luggage rack (luggage racks) *n* A **luggage rack** is a shelf for putting luggage on, on a vehicle such as a train or bus. তল্লিতল্লা রাখার তাক

lukewarm *adj* **Lukewarm** water is only slightly warm. ঈষদুষ্ণ

lullaby (lullabies) *n* A **lullaby** is a quiet song which is intended to be sung to babies and young children to help them go to sleep. ঘুমপাড়ানি গান

lump (lumps) *n* A **lump** is a solid piece of something. ডেলা

lunatic (lunatics) *n* If you describe someone as a **lunatic**, you think they behave in a dangerous, stupid, or annoying way. (*informal*) উন্মাদ

lunch (lunches) *n* **Lunch** is a meal that you have in the middle of the day. মধ্যাহ্নভোজ

lunch break (lunch breaks) *n* Your **lunch break** is the period in the middle of the day when you stop work in order to have a meal. মধ্যাহ্নভোজ-বিরতি

lunchtime (lunchtimes) *n* **Lunchtime** is the period of the day when people have their lunch. মধ্যাহ্নভোজের নির্ধারিত সময়

lung (lungs) *n* Your **lungs** are the two organs inside your chest which you use for breathing. ফুসফুস

lush (lusher, lushest) *adj* **Lush** fields or gardens have a lot of very healthy grass or plants. ঘন শ্যামল

Luxembourg *n* **Luxembourg** is a small country in Western Europe. লুক্সেমবার্গ

luxurious *adj* Something that is **luxurious** is very comfortable and expensive. বিলাসবহুল

luxury *n* **Luxury** is very great comfort, especially among beautiful and expensive surroundings. বিলাস

lyrics *npl* The **lyrics** of a song are its words. গানের কথা

mac (macs) n A **mac** is a raincoat, especially one made from a particular kind of waterproof cloth. বর্ষাতি

macaroni npl **Macaroni** is a kind of pasta made in the shape of short hollow tubes. ম্যাকারনি

machine (machines) n A **machine** is a piece of equipment which uses electricity or an engine in order to do a particular kind of work. মেশিন

machine gun (machine guns) n A **machine gun** is a gun which fires a lot of bullets very quickly one after the other. মেশিন-গান

machinery n **Machinery** is machines in general, or machines that are used in a factory. যন্ত্রপাতি

machine washable adj **Machine washable** clothes are suitable for washing in a washing machine. মেশিনে ধোয়া যায় এমন

mackerel (mackerel) n A **mackerel** is a sea fish with a dark, patterned back. সামুদ্রিক মৎস্যবিশেষ

mad (madder, maddest) adj Someone who is **mad** has a mental illness which makes them behave in strange ways. পাগল ▷ adj You can say that someone is **mad** when they are very angry. (informal) ক্ষিপ্ত

Madagascar n **Madagascar** is an island republic in the Indian Ocean, off the east coast of Africa. মাদাগাসকার

madam n **Madam** is a formal and polite way of addressing a woman. মহোদয়া

madly adv If you do something **madly**, you do it in a fast, excited, or eager way. পাগলের মত

madman (madmen) n A **madman** is a man who is insane. পাগল লোক

madness n If you describe a decision or an action as **madness**, you think it is very foolish. পাগলামি

magazine (magazines) n A **magazine** is a weekly or monthly publication which contains articles, stories, photographs, and advertisements. পত্রিকা ▷ n In an automatic gun, the **magazine** is the part that contains the bullets. টোটা রাখার খোপ

maggot (maggots) n **Maggots** are tiny creatures that look like very small worms and turn into flies. পোকার ডিম

magic n **Magic** is the power to use supernatural forces to make impossible things happen, such as making people disappear or controlling events in nature. জাদুবিদ্যা ▷ adj You use **magic** to describe something that does things, or appears to do things, by magic. জাদু

magical adj Something that is **magical** seems to use magic or to be able to produce magic. জাদুবল

magician (magicians) n A **magician** is a person who entertains people by doing magic tricks. জাদুকর

magistrate (magistrates) n A **magistrate** is a person who is appointed to act as a judge in law courts which deal with minor crimes or disputes. বিচারক

magnet (magnets) n A **magnet** is a piece of iron which attracts iron or steel towards it. চুম্বক

magnetic *adj* If something is **magnetic**, it has the power of a magnet or functions like a magnet. চুম্বকীয়

magnificent *adj* Something or someone that is **magnificent** is extremely good, beautiful, or impressive. রাজসিক

magnifying glass (magnifying glasses) *n* A **magnifying glass** is a piece of glass which makes objects appear bigger than they actually are. আতস কাঁচ

magpie (magpies) *n* A **magpie** is a black and white bird with a long tail. ল্যাজঝোলা পাখি

mahogany *n* **Mahogany** is a dark reddish-brown wood that is used to make furniture. মেহগনি

maid (maids) *n* A **maid** is a woman who works as a servant in a hotel or private house. পরিচারিকা

maiden name (maiden names) *n* A married woman's **maiden name** is her parents' surname, which she used before she got married and started using her husband's surname. নারীর বিবাহপূর্ব নাম

mail (mails, mailing, mailed) *n* **Mail** is the letters and parcels that are delivered to you. চিঠি ▷ *vt* If you **mail** something, you post it. চিঠি পাঠানো

mailing list (mailing lists) *n* A **mailing list** is a list of names and addresses that a company or organization keeps, so that they can send people information or advertisements. ঠিকানার তালিকা

main *adj* The **main** thing is the most important one. মুখ্য

main course (main courses) *n* The **main course** is the most important dish of a meal. মূল খাবার

mainland *n* The **mainland** is the large main part of a country, in contrast to the islands around it. মূল ভূখন্ড

mainly *adv* You use **mainly** to say that a statement is true in most cases or to a large extent. প্রধানতঃ

main road (main roads) *n* A **main road** is an important road that leads from one town or city to another. মূল রাস্তা

maintain (maintains, maintaining, maintained) *vt* If you **maintain** something, you continue to have it, and do not let it stop or grow weaker. বজায় রাখা

maintenance *n* The **maintenance** of a building, road, vehicle, or machine is the process of keeping it in good condition. রক্ষণাবেক্ষণ

maize *n* **Maize** is a tall plant which produces corn. ভুট্টা

majesty (majesties) *n* You use majesty in expressions such as Your **Majesty** or Her **Majesty** when you are addressing or referring to a King or Queen. মহামান্য

major *adj* You use **major** to describe something that is more important, serious, or significant than other things. গুরুতর

majority *n* The **majority** of people or things in a group is more than half of them. অধিকাংশ

make (makes, making, made) *n* The **make** of a product is the name of the company that made it. নির্মাতা ▷ *vt* You can use **make** to show that a person does or says something. তৈরী করা ▷ *vt* If you **make** something, you put it together or build it from other things. তৈরী করা ▷ *vt* If you **make** a person do something, they must do it. বাধ্য করা

makeover (makeovers) *n* If a person or room is given a **makeover**, their appearance is improved, usually by an expert. রূপপরিবর্তন

maker (makers) *n* The **maker** of something is the person or company that makes it. নির্মাতা

make up *v* The people or things that **make up** something are the members or parts that form that thing. ভাগ *Women officers make up 13 per cent of the police force.* ▷ *n* **Make-up** consists of things such as lipstick or eye shadow which you can put on your face to make yourself look more attractive. অঙ্গসজ্জা

malaria *n* **Malaria** is a serious disease caught from mosquitoes. ম্যালেরিয়া

Malawi n **Malawi** is a republic in east central Africa. মালাউই

Malaysia n **Malaysia** is a federation in South-East Asia. মালয়েশিয়া

Malaysian (Malaysians) adj **Malaysian** means belonging or relating to Malaysia, or to its people or culture. মালয়েশিয়া দেশীয় ▷ n A **Malaysian** is a person who comes from Malaysia. মালয়েশিয়ার অধিবাসী

male (males) adj Someone who is **male** is a man or a boy. পুরুষ ▷ n Men and boys are sometimes referred to as **males** when they are being considered as a type. পুরুষ

malicious adj **Malicious** talk or behaviour is intended to harm people or their reputation, or to embarrass or upset them. কটূক্তি

malignant adj A **malignant** tumour or disease is serious, spreads rapidly to other parts of the body, and may cause death. প্রাণঘাতী

malnutrition n If someone is suffering from **malnutrition**, they are physically weak and extremely thin because they have not eaten enough food or had a balanced diet. অপুষ্টি

Malta n **Malta** is a republic occupying the islands of Malta, Gozo, and Comino, in the Mediterranean. মাল্টা

Maltese (Maltese) adj **Maltese** means belonging or relating to Malta, or to its people, language, or culture. মাল্টা দেশীয় ▷ n A **Maltese** is a person who comes from Malta. মাল্টার মানুষ ▷ n **Maltese** is a language spoken in Malta. মল্টিজ ভাষা

malt whisky (malt whiskies) n **Malt whisky** or **malt** is whisky that is made from malt. মল্ট হুইস্কি

mammal (mammals) n **Mammals** are animals such as dogs and humans that give birth to babies rather than laying eggs, and feed their young with milk. স্তন্যপায়ী

mammoth (mammoths) adj You can use **mammoth** to emphasize that a task is very great and needs a lot of effort to achieve.

বিরাট ▷ n A **mammoth** was a prehistoric animal like a large elephant with long curling tusks. হস্তিজাতীয় প্রাগঐতিহাসিক জন্তুবিশেষ

man (men) n A **man** is an adult male human. পুরুষ

manage (manages, managing, managed) vt If you **manage** an organization, business, or system, or the people who work in it, you are responsible for controlling them. পরিচালনা করা

manageable adj Something that is **manageable** is of a size, quantity, or level of difficulty that people are able to deal with. পরিচালনীয়

management (managements) n **Management** is the control and organizing of something. কর্তৃপক্ষ

manager (managers) n A **manager** is the person responsible for running part of or the whole of a business organization. পরিচালক

manageress (manageresses) n The **manageress** of a shop, restaurant, or other small business is the woman who is responsible for running it. পরিচালিকা

managing director (managing directors) n The **managing director** of a company is the senior working director, and is in charge of the way the company is managed. পরিচালন অধিকর্তা

mandarin (mandarins) n Journalists sometimes use **mandarin** to refer to someone who has an important job working for a government department. উচ্চপদস্থ কর্মচারী ▷ n A **mandarin** or a **mandarin orange** is a small orange whose skin comes off easily. কমলালেবু জাতীয় ফল

mangetout (mangetout, mangetouts) n **Mangetout** are a type of pea whose pods are eaten as well as the peas inside them. মটরশুঁটি

mango (mangoes, mangos) n A **mango** is a large, sweet yellowish fruit which grows in hot countries. আম

mania (manias) n If you say that a person or group has a **mania** for something, you mean that they enjoy it very much or devote a lot of time to it. প্রবল আকর্ষণ

maniac (maniacs) *n* A **maniac** is a mad person who is violent and dangerous. পাগল

manicure (manicures, manicuring, manicured) *n* A **manicure** is the cosmetic procedure of having the skin on your hands softened and your nails cut and polished. হাত ও নখের যত্ন ▷ *vt* If you **manicure** your hands or nails, you care for them by softening your skin and cutting and polishing your nails. হাত ও নখের যত্ন নেওয়া

manipulate (manipulates, manipulating, manipulated) *vt* If you say that someone **manipulates** people or events, you disapprove of them because they control or influence them to produce a particular result. কৌশলে চালনা করা

mankind *n* You can refer to all human beings as **mankind** when you are considering them as a group. মনুষ্যজাতি

man-made *adj* **Man-made** things are created or caused by people, rather than occurring naturally. মনুষ্যনির্মিত

manner *n* The **manner** in which you do something is the way that you do it. প্রকার

manners *npl* If someone has good **manners**, they are polite and observe social customs. If someone has bad **manners**, they are impolite and do not observe these customs. আচরণ

manpower *n* Workers are sometimes referred to as **manpower** when they are being considered as a part of the process of producing goods or providing services. লোকবল

mansion (mansions) *n* A **mansion** is a very large, expensive house. অট্টালিকা

mantelpiece (mantelpieces) *n* A **mantelpiece** is a shelf over a fireplace. ফায়ারপ্লেসের ওপরে অবস্থিত তাক

manual (manuals) *n* A **manual** is a book which tells you how to do something or how a piece of machinery works. নির্দেশগ্রন্থ

manufacture (manufactures, manufacturing, manufactured) *vt* To **manufacture** something means to make it in a factory, usually in large quantities. তৈরী করা

manufacturer (manufacturers) *n* A **manufacturer** is a business that makes goods in large quantities. নির্মাতা

manure *n* **Manure** is animal faeces that is spread on the ground in order to improve the growth of plants. সার

manuscript (manuscripts) *n* A **manuscript** is a handwritten or typed document, especially a writer's first version of a book before it is published. পাণ্ডুলিপি

many *det* If there are **many** people or things, there are a lot of them. অনেক *Does he have many friends?* ▷ *pron* **Many** is used to refer to a large number of people or things. খুব বেশি *We thought about the possibilities. There weren't many.*

Maori (Maoris) *adj* **Maori** means belonging to or relating to the race of people who have lived in New Zealand and the Cook Islands since before Europeans arrived. নিউজিল্যান্ডের আদিবাসী সংক্রান্ত ▷ *n* The **Maori** or the **Maoris** are people who are Maori. নিউজিল্যান্ডের আদিবাসী ▷ *n* **Maori** is the language spoken by the Maori people. মাওরি ভাষা

map (maps) *n* A **map** is a drawing of a particular area, showing its main features as they appear if you looked at them from above. মানচিত্র

maple (maples) n A **maple** is a tree with large leaves with five points. ম্যাপল

marathon (marathons) n A **marathon** is a race in which people run a distance of 26 miles (about 42 km). ম্যারাথন

marble n **Marble** is a very hard rock used, for example, to make statues and fireplaces. মার্বেল

march (marches, marching, marched) n A **march** is the action, by a group of soldiers, of walking somewhere with very regular steps, as a group. সৈন্যদলের চলন ▷ v When soldiers **march** somewhere, or when a commanding officer **marches** them somewhere, they walk there with very regular steps, as a group. মার্চ করা

March (Marches) n **March** is the third month of the year in the Western calendar. মার্চ মাস

mare (mares) n A **mare** is an adult female horse. ঘোটকী

margarine n **Margarine** is a substance similar to butter, made from vegetable oil and sometimes animal fats. মার্জারিন

margin (margins) n A **margin** is the difference between two amounts, especially the difference in the number of votes or points between the winner and the loser in a contest. ব্যবধান

marigold (marigolds) n A **marigold** is a type of yellow or orange flower. গাঁদাফুল

marina (marinas) n A **marina** is a small harbour for pleasure boats. প্রমোদতরণীর বন্দর

marinade (marinades, marinading, marinaded) n A **marinade** is a sauce of oil, vinegar, and spices, which you soak meat or fish in before cooking it, in order to flavour it. ম্যারিনেড ▷ v If you **marinade** meat or fish, you keep it in a mixture of oil, vinegar, spices, and herbs, before cooking it, so that it can develop a special flavour. ম্যারিনেড করা

marital status n Your **marital status** is whether you are married, single, or divorced. (formal) বৈবাহিক অবস্থা

maritime adj **Maritime** means relating to the sea and to ships. সমুদ্র সম্বন্ধীয়

marjoram n **Marjoram** is a kind of herb. মার্জোরাম

mark (marks, marking, marked) n A **mark** is a small dirty area on a surface. দাগ ▷ n A **mark** is a shape that you write or draw. চিহ্ন ▷ vt If you **mark** something, you write a word or symbol on it. চিহ্নিত করা ▷ vt When a teacher **marks** a student's work, the teacher corrects it or gives it a grade. নাম্বার দেওয়া

market (markets) n A **market** is a place where goods are bought and sold, usually in the open air. বাজার

marketing n **Marketing** is the organization of the sale of a product, for example, deciding on its price, the areas it should be supplied to, and how it should be advertised. বিপণন

marketplace (marketplaces) n In business, the **marketplace** refers to the activity of buying and selling products. বাজার

market research n **Market research** is the activity of collecting and studying information about what people want, need, and buy. মার্কেট রিসার্চ

marmalade (marmalades) n **Marmalade** is a food like jam made from oranges or lemons. কমলালেবুর জ্যাম

maroon adj Something that is **maroon** is dark reddish-purple in colour. বাদামী লাল

marriage (marriages) n A **marriage** is the relationship between a husband and wife, or the state of being married. বিবাহ

marriage certificate (marriage certificates) n A **marriage certificate** is a legal document that proves two people are married. বিবাহের সার্টিফিকেট

married adj If you are **married**, you have a husband or wife. বিবাহিত

marrow (marrows) n A **marrow** is a long, thick, green vegetable with soft white flesh that is eaten cooked. মজ্জা

marry (**marries, marrying, married**) v
When two people **get married** or **marry**,
they become each other's husband and
wife during a special ceremony. বিবাহ করা

marsh (**marshes**) n A **marsh** is a wet
muddy area of land. জলাভূমি

martyr (**martyrs**) n A **martyr** is someone
who is killed or made to suffer greatly
because of their religious or political beliefs.
শহীদ

marvellous adj If you describe someone
or something as **marvellous**, you are
emphasizing that they are very good. অপূর্ব

Marxism n **Marxism** is a political
philosophy based on the writings of Karl
Marx which stresses the importance of the
struggle between different social classes.
মার্কসবাদ

marzipan n **Marzipan** is a paste made
of almonds, sugar, and egg which is
sometimes put on top of cakes. মার্জিপান

mascara (**mascaras**) n **Mascara** is a
substance used to colour eyelashes. মাসকারা

masculine adj **Masculine** characteristics or
things relate to or are considered typical of
men, rather than women. পুরুষোচিত

mashed potatoes npl **Mashed potatoes**
are potatoes that have been boiled and
crushed into a soft mass, often with butter
and milk. আলুভাতে

mask (**masks**) n A **mask** is something
which you wear over your face for
protection or to disguise yourself. মুখোশ

masked adj Someone who is **masked** is
wearing a mask. মুখোশধারী

mass (**masses**) n A **mass** of something is a
large amount of it. অনেক

Mass (**masses**) n **Mass** is a Christian
church ceremony during which people
eat bread and drink wine in order to
remember the last meal of Jesus Christ.
গির্জার অনুষ্ঠান

massacre (**massacres**) n A **massacre** is the
killing of many people in a violent and cruel
way. বেপরোয়া হত্যাকান্ড

massive adj Something that is **massive** is
very large in size. বিশাল

mast (**masts**) n The **masts** of a boat are
the tall upright poles that support its sails.
মাস্তুল

master (**masters, mastering, mastered**)
n A servant's **master** is the man that he
or she works for. প্রভু ▷ vt If you **master**
something, you manage to learn how to
do it properly or understand it completely.
ওস্তাদি রপ্ত করা

masterpiece (**masterpieces**) n A
masterpiece is an extremely good painting,
novel, film, or other work of art. শ্রেষ্ঠ কৃতি

mat (**mats**) n A **mat** is a small piece of
material which you put on a table to protect
it from a hot plate or cup. মাদুর

match (**matches, matching, matched**)
n A **match** is a game of football, cricket,
or some other sport. ম্যাচ ▷ n If things or
people are a good **match**, they look good
together or go well together. সমকক্ষ ▷ v If
one thing **matches** another, they look good
together. মেলা ▷ n A **match** is a small, thin
stick that makes a flame when you rub it on
a rough surface. দেশলাই কাঠি

matching adj **Matching** is used to
describe things which are of the same
colour or design. সামঞ্জস্যপূর্ণ

mate (**mates**) n You can refer to someone's
friends as their **mates**. (informal) সঙ্গী

material (**materials**) n A **material** is what
something is made of, like rock, glass, or
plastic. উপাদান ▷ n **Material** is cloth. কাপড়

maternal adj **Maternal** feelings or actions
are typical of those of a mother towards her
child. মাতৃ সম্পর্কীয়

maternity hospital (**maternity hospitals**)
n A **maternity hospital** is a hospital that
provides help and medical care to women
when they are pregnant and when they
give birth. প্রসূতি হাসপাতাল

maternity leave n **Maternity leave** is
a period of paid absence from work, to
which a woman is legally entitled during

the months immediately before and after childbirth. প্রসূতি ছুটি

mathematical *adj* Something that is **mathematical** involves numbers and calculations. অঙ্কশাস্ত্র সম্বন্ধীয়

mathematics *npl* **Mathematics** is the study of numbers, quantities, or shapes. অঙ্কশাস্ত্র

maths *npl* Mathematics is usually referred to as **maths**. গণিত

matter (**matters, mattering, mattered**) *n* A **matter** is a task, situation, or event which you have to deal with or think about. ব্যাপার ▷ *v* If something **matters**, it is important because it has an effect on a situation. বড়ো বিষয়

mattress (**mattresses**) *n* A **mattress** is a large flat pad which is put on a bed to make it comfortable to sleep on. গদি

mature (**maturer, maturest**) *adj* A **mature** person or animal is fully grown. পরিণত

mature student (**mature students**) *n* A **mature student** is a person who begins their studies at university or college a number of years after leaving school, so that they are older than most of the people they are studying with. পরিণত ছাত্র

Mauritania *n* **Mauritania** is a republic in North-West Africa, on the Atlantic. মরিটানিয়া

Mauritius *n* **Mauritius** is an island and state in the Indian Ocean, east of Madagascar. মরিসাস

mauve *adj* Something that is **mauve** is of a pale purple colour. ফিকে লাল

maximum *adj* You use **maximum** to describe an amount which is the largest that is possible, allowed, or required. সর্বাধিক ▷ *n* A **maximum** is the greatest possible amount, degree, etc. সর্বোচ্চ

May (**Mays**) *n* **May** is the fifth month of the year in the Western calendar. মে মাস

may *v* If you **may** do something, it is possible that you will do it. হতে পারা *I may come back next year.* ▷ *v* If you **may** do something, you can do it because someone

allows you to do it. করতে পারা *Please may I leave the room?*

maybe *adv* You use **maybe** when you are not sure about something. সম্ভবতঃ

mayonnaise *n* **Mayonnaise** is a sauce made from egg yolks, oil, and vinegar, eaten cold. মেয়োনিজ

mayor (**mayors**) *n* The **mayor** of a town or city is the person who has been elected to represent it for a fixed period of time. মেয়র

maze (**mazes**) *n* A **maze** is a complex system of passages or paths separated by walls or hedges. গোলকধাঁধা

me *pron* You use **me** when you are talking about yourself. আমাকে *Can you hear me?*

meadow (**meadows**) *n* A **meadow** is a field with grass and flowers growing in it. তৃণভূমি

meal (**meals**) *n* A **meal** is an occasion when people eat. আহার

mealtime (**mealtimes**) *n* **Mealtimes** are occasions when you eat breakfast, lunch, or dinner. খাবার সময়

mean (**meaner, meanest, means, meaning, meant**) *adj* Someone who is **mean** is not nice to other people. নিকৃষ্ট ▷ *vt* If you ask what something **means**, you want to understand it. অর্থ ▷ *vt* If you **mean** what you are saying, it is not a joke. বলা ▷ *vt* If you **mean** to do something, it is not an accident. করতে চাওয়া

meaning (**meanings**) *n* The **meaning** of something such as a word, symbol, or gesture is the thing that it refers to or the message that it conveys. অর্থ

means *npl* You can refer to the money that someone has as their **means**. সংগতি

meantime *adv* **In the meantime** means in the period of time between two events, or while an event is happening. ইত্যবসরে

meanwhile *adv* **Meanwhile** means in the period of time between two events, or while an event is happening. এর মধ্যে

measles *npl* **Measles** is an infectious illness that gives you a high temperature and red spots. হাম

measure (measures, measuring, measured) *vt* If you **measure** something, you find out its size. পরিমাপ করা

measurements *npl* Your **measurements** are the size of your chest, waist, hips, and other parts of your body. পরিমাপ

meat (meats) *n* **Meat** is the flesh of a dead animal that people cook and eat. মাংস

meatball (meatballs) *n* **Meatballs** are small balls of chopped meat. They are usually eaten with a sauce. মাংসের ছোট ছোট বল

Mecca *n* **Mecca** is a city in Saudi Arabia, which is the holiest city in Islam because the Prophet Mohammed was born there. All Muslims face towards Mecca when they pray. মক্কা

mechanic (mechanics) *n* A **mechanic** is someone whose job is to repair and maintain machines and engines, especially car engines. মিস্ত্রি

mechanical *adj* A **mechanical** device has moving parts and uses power in order to do a particular task. যান্ত্রিক

mechanism (mechanisms) *n* A **mechanism** is a part of a machine that does a particular task. যন্ত্র কৌশল

medal (medals) *n* A **medal** is a small metal disc, given as an award for bravery or as a prize in a sporting event. পদক

medallion (medallions) *n* A **medallion** is a round metal disc which some people wear as an ornament, especially on a chain round their neck. লকেট

media *npl* You can refer to television, radio, and newspapers as the **media**. প্রচারমাধ্যম

mediaeval *adj* **Mediaeval** things relate to or date from the period in European history between about 500 AD and about 1500 AD. মধ্যযুগ

medical (medicals) *adj* **Medical** means relating to illness and injuries and to their treatment or prevention. চিকিৎসাবিদ্যা বিষয়ক ▷ *n* A **medical** is a thorough examination of your body by a doctor. শারীরিক পরীক্ষা

medical certificate (medical certificates) *n* A **medical certificate** is a document stating the result of a satisfactory medical examination. মেডিক্যাল সার্টিফিকেট

medicine *n* **Medicine** is the treatment of illness and injuries by doctors and nurses. ওষুধ

meditation *n* **Meditation** is the act of remaining in a silent and calm state for a period of time, as part of a religious training, or so that you are more able to deal with the problems of everyday life. ধ্যান

Mediterranean *n* The **Mediterranean** is the sea between southern Europe and North Africa. ভূমধ্যসাগর ▷ *adj* Something that is **Mediterranean** is characteristic of or belongs to the people or region around the Mediterranean Sea. ভূমধ্যসাগর সম্বন্ধীয়

medium *adj* You use **medium** to describe something which is average in size, degree, or amount, or approximately halfway along a scale between two extremes. মাঝারি

medium-sized *adj* **Medium-sized** means neither large nor small, but approximately halfway between the two. মাঝারি-মাপের

meet (meets, meeting, met) *vt* If you **meet** someone, you happen to be in the same place as them and start talking to them. You may know the other person, but be surprised to see them, or you may not know

m

them at all. সাক্ষাৎ করা ▷ vi If people **meet**, they happen to be in the same place and start talking to each other. They may know each other, but be surprised to see each other, or they may not know each other at all. সাক্ষাৎ করা

meeting (**meetings**) n A **meeting** is an event at which a group of people come together to discuss things or make decisions. বৈঠক

meet up v If two or more people **meet up**, they go to the same place, which they have earlier arranged to do, so that they can talk or do something together. একত্রিত হওয়া *We tend to meet up for lunch once a week.*

mega adj Young people sometimes use **mega** in front of nouns in order to emphasize that the thing they are talking about is very good, very large, or very impressive. (*informal*) বৃহৎ

melody (**melodies**) n A **melody** is a tune. (*formal*) মধুর সুর

melon (**melons**) n A **melon** is a large, sweet, juicy fruit with a thick green or yellow skin. তরমুজ

melt (**melts, melting, melted**) vt When you **melt** a solid substance, it changes to a liquid because of being heated. গলানো ▷ vi When a solid substance **melts**, it changes to a liquid because of being heated. গলা

member (**members**) n A **member** of a group or organization is one of the people, animals, or things belonging to it. সদস্য

membership n **Membership** is the fact or state of being a member of an organization. সদস্যতা

membership card (**membership cards**) n A **membership card** is a card that proves that you are a member of an organization. সদস্যপত্র

memento (**mementos** or **mementoes**) n A **memento** is an object which you keep because it reminds you of a person or a special occasion. স্মরণার্থ চিহ্ন

memo (**memos**) n A **memo** is an official note from one person to another within the same organization. স্মারকলিপি

memorial (**memorials**) n A **memorial** is a structure built in order to remind people of a famous person or event. স্মারণিক

memorize (**memorizes, memorizing, memorized**) vt If you **memorize** something, you learn it so that you can remember it exactly. মনে রাখা

memory (**memories**) n Your **memory** is your ability to remember things. স্মৃতিশক্তি ▷ n A **memory** is something you remember about the past. স্মৃতি

memory card (**memory cards**) n A **memory card** is a type of card containing computer memory that is used in digital cameras and other devices. মেমারী কার্ড

mend (**mends, mending, mended**) vt If you **mend** something that is damaged or broken, you repair it so that it works properly or can be used. মেরামত করা

meningitis n **Meningitis** is a serious infectious illness which affects your brain and spinal cord. মেনিনজাইটিস

menopause n The **menopause** is the time during which a woman stops menstruating, usually when she is about fifty. রজোনিবৃত্তি

menstruation n **Menstruation** is the approximate monthly discharge of blood and cellular debris from the uterus by nonpregnant women from puberty to the menopause. মাসিক

mental adj **Mental** means relating to the mind and the process of thinking. মানসিক

mental hospital (**mental hospitals**) n A **mental hospital** is a hospital for people who are suffering from mental illness. মানসিক চিকিৎসালয়

mentality (**mentalities**) n Your **mentality** is your attitudes or ways of thinking. মনোবৃত্তি

mention (**mentions, mentioning, mentioned**) vt If you **mention** something, you say something about it, usually briefly. উল্লেখ করা

menu (**menus**) n In a restaurant or café, the **menu** is a list of the available meals and drinks. খাদ্য তালিকা

merchant bank (**merchant banks**) n A **merchant bank** is a bank that deals mainly with firms, investment, and foreign trade, rather than with the public. ব্যবসায়িক ব্যাংক

mercury n **Mercury** is a silver-coloured liquid metal, used in thermometers. পারদ

mercy n If someone in authority shows **mercy**, they choose not to harm or punish someone they have power over. ক্ষমা

mere (**merest**) adj You use **mere** to say that something is small or not important. কেবল

merge (**merges, merging, merged**) v If one thing **merges** with another, or is **merged** with another, they combine or come together to make one whole thing. You can also say that two things **merge**, or **are merged**. মিলিত হওয়া

merger (**mergers**) n A **merger** is the joining together of two separate companies or organizations so that they become one. ব্যবসায়িক প্রতিষ্ঠান একত্রিত হওয়া

meringue (**meringues**) n A **Meringue** is a mixture of beaten egg whites and sugar which is baked in the oven. ডিমের শ্বেতাংশ ও চিনি দিয়া তৈরী কেক বিশেষ

mermaid (**mermaids**) n In fairy stories and legends, a **mermaid** is a woman with a fish's tail instead of legs, who lives in the sea. মৎস্যকন্যা

merry (**merrier, merriest**) adj **Merry** means happy and cheerful. (*old-fashioned*) আনন্দজনক

merry-go-round (**merry-go-rounds**) n A **merry-go-round** is a large circular platform at a fairground on which there are model animals or vehicles for people to sit on or in as it turns round. নাগরদোলা

mess n If something is a **mess** or in a **mess**, it is dirty or untidy. বিশৃঙ্খল

mess about v If you **mess about**, you spend time doing things without any particular purpose or without achieving anything. উদ্দেশ্যহীনভাবে কিছু করা The children scribbled with crayons at the table and messed about.

message (**messages**) n A **message** is a piece of information or a request that you send to someone or leave for someone when you cannot speak to them directly. বার্তা

messenger (**messengers**) n A **messenger** takes a message to someone, or takes messages regularly as their job. বার্তাবাহক

mess up v If someone **messes** something **up**, or if they **mess up**, they cause something to fail or be spoiled. (*informal*) বিশৃঙ্খল করা He had messed up his career.

messy (**messier, messiest**) adj A **messy** person or activity makes things dirty or untidy. নোংরা

metabolism (**metabolisms**) n Your **metabolism** is the way that chemical processes in your body cause food to be used in an efficient way, for example to give you energy. বিপাক

metal (**metals**) n **Metal** is a hard substance such as iron, steel, copper, or lead. ধাতু

meteorite (**meteorites**) n A **meteorite** is a large piece of rock or metal from space that has landed on Earth. উল্কাপিণ্ড

meter (**meters**) n A **meter** is a device that measures and records something such as the amount of gas or electricity that you have used. মিটার

method (**methods**) n A **method** is a particular way of doing something. পদ্ধতি

metre (**metres**) n A **metre** is a unit of length equal to 100 centimetres. মিটার

metric adj The **metric** system of measurement uses metres, grammes, and litres. দশমিক

Mexican (**Mexicans**) adj **Mexican** means belonging or relating to Mexico, or to its people or culture. মেক্সিকো সম্বন্ধীয় ▷ n A

m

Mexican is a Mexican citizen, or a person of Mexican origin. মেক্সিকান

Mexico n **Mexico** is a republic in North America, on the Gulf of Mexico and the Pacific. মেক্সিকো

microchip (**microchips**) n A **microchip** is a small piece of silicon inside a computer, on which electronic circuits are printed. মাইক্রোচিপ

microphone (**microphones**) n A **microphone** is a device used to record sounds or make them louder. মাইক্রোফোন

microscope (**microscopes**) n A **microscope** is an instrument which magnifies very small objects so that you can study them. অণুবীক্ষণ যন্ত্র

microwave (**microwaves**) n A **microwave** or a **microwave oven** is an oven which cooks food very quickly by a kind of radiation rather than by heat. মাইক্রোওয়েভ ওভেন

mid adj **Mid-** is used to form nouns or adjectives that refer to the middle part of a particular period of time, or the middle point of a particular place. মধ্য

midday n **Midday** is twelve o'clock in the middle of the day. মধ্যাহ্ন

middle (**middles**) n The **middle** of something is the part that is farthest from its edges, ends, or outside surface. মধ্যে

middle-aged adj **Middle-aged** people are between the ages of about 40 and 60. মধ্যবয়স্ক

Middle Ages npl In European history, the **Middle Ages** was the period between the end of the Roman Empire in 476 AD and about 1500 AD, especially the later part of this period. মধ্যযুগ

middle-class adj **Middle-class** people are the people in a society who are not working-class or upper-class, for example managers, doctors, and lawyers. মধ্যবিত্ত

Middle East n **The Middle East** is the area around the eastern Mediterranean that includes Iran and all the countries in Asia that are to the west and south-west of Iran. মধ্যপ্রাচ্য

midge (**midges**) n **Midges** are very small insects which bite. ডাঁশমাছি

midnight n **Midnight** is twelve o'clock in the middle of the night. মধ্যরাত্রি

midwife (**midwives**) n A **midwife** is a nurse who advises pregnant women and helps them to give birth. ধাত্রী

might v You use **might** when something is possible. সম্ভাব্য He might win the race.

migraine (**migraines**) n A **migraine** is a very severe headache. চরম মাথাব্যথা

migrant (**migrants**) n A **migrant** is a person who moves from one place to another, especially in order to find work. পরিযায়ী

migration (**migrations**) n **Migration** is the act of people moving from one place to another, especially in order to find work. পরিযাণ

mild (**milder, mildest**) adj Something that is **mild** is not very strong or severe. মৃদু

mile (**miles**) n A **mile** is a unit of distance equal to approximately 1.6 kilometres. মাইল

mileage (**mileages**) n **Mileage** refers to a distance that is travelled, measured in miles. মাইলেজ

mileometer (**mileometers**) n An **mileometer** is a device that records the number of miles that a bicycle or motor vehicle has travelled. মাইলোমিটার

military adj **Military** means relating to a country's armed forces. সামরিক

milk (**milks, milking, milked**) n **Milk** is the white liquid produced by cows and goats, which people drink and make into butter, cheese, and yoghurt. দুধ ▷ vt When someone **milks** a cow or goat, they get milk from it from an organ called the udder, which hangs beneath its body. দুধ দোওয়া

milk chocolate n **Milk chocolate** is chocolate that has been made with milk. It is lighter in colour and has a creamier taste than plain chocolate. দুধের চকোলেট

milkshake (milkshakes) *n* A **milkshake** is a cold drink made by mixing milk with a flavouring or fruit, and sometimes ice cream. দুধের সরবত

mill (mills) *n* A **mill** is a building where grain is crushed to make flour. পেষাইকল

millennium (millenniums or millennia) *n* A **millennium** is a thousand years. (*formal*) সহস্র বছর

millimetre (millimetres) *n* A **millimetre** is a metric unit of length equal to one tenth of a centimetre. মিলিমিটার

million (millions) *num* A **million** or one **million** is the number 1,000,000. দশলক্ষ

millionaire (millionaires) *n* A **millionaire** is someone who has money or property worth at least a million pounds or dollars. কোটিপতি

mimic (mimics, mimicking, mimicked) *vt* If you **mimic** someone's actions or voice, you imitate them in an amusing or entertaining way. নকল করা

mince *n* **Mince** is meat cut into very small pieces. কিমা

mind (minds, minding, minded) *n* Your **mind** is the part of your brain that thinks, understands, and remembers. মন ▷ *vt* If you **mind** something, it annoys you. মনে করা

mine (mines) *n* A **mine** is a deep hole or tunnel where people go to dig things like gold or diamonds out of rock. খনি ▷ *pron* **Mine** means belonging to me. আমার *That isn't your bag, it's mine.*

miner (miners) *n* A **miner** is a person who works underground in mines in order to obtain valuable minerals such as coal, diamonds, or gold. খনিজীবী

mineral (minerals) *adj* **Mineral** means of, relating to, or containing minerals. খনিজদ্রব্য ▷ *n* A **mineral** is a substance such as tin, salt, or coal that is formed naturally in rocks and in the earth. খনিজদ্রব্য

mineral water (mineral waters) *n* **Mineral water** is water that comes out

of the ground naturally and is considered healthy to drink. খনিজ মেশা প্রাকৃতিক জল

miniature (miniatures) *adj* **Miniature** things are much smaller than other things of the same kind. নিতান্ত ক্ষুদ্র ▷ *n* A **miniature** is a very small detailed painting, often of a person. ক্ষুদ্র নকল

minibus (minibuses) *n* A **minibus** is a large van which has seats in the back and windows along its sides. মিনিবাস

minicab (minicabs) *n* A **minicab** is a taxi which you have to arrange to pick you up by telephone. ছোট ট্যাক্সি

minimal *adj* Something that is **minimal** is very small in quantity or degree. যৎসামান্য

minimize (minimizes, minimizing, minimized) *vt* If you **minimize** a risk or problem, you reduce it to the lowest possible level. কম করা

minimum *adj* You use **minimum** to describe an amount which is the smallest that is possible, allowed, or required. অন্ততম ▷ *n* A **minimum** is the least possible amount, degree, or quantity. কমপক্ষে

mining *n* **Mining** is the industry and activities connected with getting valuable or useful minerals from the ground, for example coal, diamonds, or gold. খনি সম্বন্ধীয়

minister *n* A **minister** is a person who is in charge of a government department. মন্ত্রী

ministry (ministries) *n* A **ministry** is a government department. মন্ত্রক

mink (minks or mink) *n* A **mink** is a small furry animal with highly valued fur. বেজির মত দেখতে জলে বাসকারী জন্তু

minor (minors) *adj* You use **minor** to describe something that is less important, serious, or significant than other things in a group or situation. ক্ষুদ্র ▷ *n* A **minor** is a person who is still legally a child. In Britain, people are minors until they reach the age of eighteen. অপ্রাপ্তবয়স্ক

minority (minorities) *n* If you talk about a **minority** of people or things in a larger group, you are referring to a number of them that forms less than half of the larger group. সংখ্যালঘু

mint (**mints**) *n* The **mint** is the place where the official coins of a country are made. টাঁকশাল ▷ *n* **Mint** is a fresh-tasting herb. পুদিনা

minus *prep* You use **minus** when you take one number away from another number. বিয়োগ *Three minus two is one.*

minute (**minutest**, **minutes**) *adj* Something that is **minute** is very small. অতি ক্ষুদ্র ▷ *n* A **minute** is used for measuring time. There are sixty seconds in one **minute**. মিনিট

miracle (**miracles**) *n* If you say that an event or invention is a **miracle**, you mean that it is very surprising and fortunate. অঘটন

mirror (**mirrors**) *n* A **mirror** is an object made of glass in which you can see your reflection. আয়না

misbehave (**misbehaves**, **misbehaving**, **misbehaved**) *vi* If someone, especially a child, **misbehaves**, they behave in a way that is not acceptable to other people. অন্যায় আচরণ করা

miscarriage (**miscarriages**) *n* If a woman has a **miscarriage**, she gives birth to a foetus before it is properly formed and it dies. সন্তান প্রসবে ব্যর্থতা

miscellaneous *adj* A **miscellaneous** group consists of many different kinds of

things or people that are difficult to put into a particular category. বিবিধ

mischief *n* **Mischief** is playing harmless tricks on people or doing things you are not supposed to do. নষ্টামি

mischievous *adj* A **mischievous** person is eager to have fun by embarrassing people or by playing harmless tricks. অনিষ্টজনক

miser (**misers**) *n* If you say that someone is a **miser**, you disapprove of them because they seem to hate spending money, and to spend as little as possible. কৃপণ

miserable *adj* If you are **miserable**, you are very unhappy. শোচনীয়

misery (**miseries**) *n* **Misery** is great unhappiness. দুঃখ

misfortune (**misfortunes**) *n* A **misfortune** is something unpleasant or unlucky that happens to someone. দুর্ভাগ্য

mishap (**mishaps**) *n* A **mishap** is an unfortunate but not very serious event that happens to you. দুর্ঘটনা

misjudge (**misjudges**, **misjudging**, **misjudged**) *vt* If you say that someone **has misjudged** a person or situation, you mean that they have formed an incorrect idea or opinion about them, and often that they have made a wrong decision as a result of this. অন্যায় বিচার করা

mislay (**mislays**, **mislaying**, **mislaid**) *vt* If you **mislay** something, you put it somewhere and then forget where you have put it. ভুল স্থানে রাখা

misleading *adj* If you describe something as **misleading**, you mean that it gives you a wrong idea or impression. বিভ্রান্তিকর

misprint (**misprints**) *n* A **misprint** is a mistake in the way something is printed, for example a spelling mistake. ছাপার ভুল

miss (**misses**, **missing**, **missed**) *v* If you **miss** something that you are trying to hit or catch, you do not manage to hit it or catch it. ব্যর্থ হওয়া ▷ *vt* If you **miss** something, you do not notice it. লক্ষ্য না করা ▷ *vt* If you **miss** someone who is not with you, you feel sad that they are not there. অনুপস্থিতি বোধ করা

Miss (**Misses**) *n* You use **Miss** in front of the name of a girl or unmarried woman when you are speaking to her or referring to her. কুমারী

missile (**missiles**) *n* A **missile** is a tube-shaped weapon that moves long distances through the air and explodes when it reaches its target. ক্ষেপণাস্ত্র

missing *adj* If someone or something is **missing** or has **gone missing**, they are not where you expect them to be, and you cannot find them. অনুপস্থিত

mist (**mists**) *n* **Mist** consists of many tiny drops of water in the air, which make it difficult to see very far. কুয়াশা

mistake (**mistakes, mistaking, mistook, mistaken**) *n* A **mistake**, you do something which you did not intend to do, or which produces a result that you do not want. ভুল ▷ *vt* If you **mistake** one person or thing **for** another, you wrongly think that they are the other person or thing. ভুল করা

mistaken *adj* If you are **mistaken**, or if you have a **mistaken** belief, you are wrong about something. ভুল

mistakenly *adv* If you do or think something **mistakenly**, you do something which you did not intend to do, or you are wrong about something. ভুলভাবে

mistletoe *n* **Mistletoe** is a plant with pale berries that grows on the branches of some trees. মিসেলটো

misty *adj* If it is **misty**, there is a lot of mist in the air. কুয়াশাচ্ছন্ন

misunderstand (**misunderstands, misunderstanding, misunderstood**) *v* If you **misunderstand** someone or something, you do not understand them properly. ভুল বোঝা

misunderstanding (**misunderstandings**) *n* A **misunderstanding** is a failure to understand something such as a situation or a person's remarks. ভুল বোঝাবুঝি

mitten (**mittens**) *n* **Mittens** are gloves which have one section that covers your thumb and another section that covers your four fingers together. দস্তানা বিশেষ

mix (**mixes, mixing, mixed**) *n* A **mix** is a powder containing all the substances that you need in order to make something, to which you add liquid. মিশ্রণ ▷ *v* If two substances **mix**, or if you **mix** one substance with another, they combine to form a single substance. মিশ্রিত করা

mixed *adj* If you have **mixed** feelings about something or someone, you feel uncertain about them because you can see both good and bad points about them. মিশ্র

mixed salad (**mixed salads**) *n* A **mixed salad** is a mixture of raw or cold foods such as lettuce, cucumber, and tomatoes. মিশ্র স্যালাড

mixer (**mixers**) *n* A **mixer** is a machine used for mixing things together. মিক্সার

mixture *n* A **mixture** of things consists of several different things together. মিশ্রণ

mix up (**mix-ups**) *v* If you **mix up** two things or people, you confuse them, so that you think that one of them is the other one. তালগোল পাকিয়ে ফেলা / I mixed her up with someone else. ▷ *n* A **mix-up** is a mistake or a failure in the way that something has been planned. (*informal*) গুলিয়ে ফেলা

MMS *abbr* **MMS** is a method of sending messages over wireless networks, especially on mobile phones. **MMS** is an abbreviation of 'Multimedia Messaging Service'. এম এম এস

moan (**moans, moaning, moaned**) *vi* If you **moan**, you make a low sound, usually because you are unhappy or in pain. গোঙানি

moat (**moats**) *n* A **moat** is a deep, wide channel dug round a place such as a castle and filled with water, in order to protect the place from attack. দুর্গপরিখা

mobile *adj* Something or someone that is **mobile** is able to move or be moved easily. চলনশীল

mobile home (**mobile homes**) *n* A **mobile home** is a large caravan that people live in and that usually remains in the same place, but which can be pulled to another place using a car or van. চলমান বাড়ি

mobile number (**mobile numbers**) *n* Someone's **mobile number** is the series of numbers that you dial when you are making a telephone call to their mobile phone. মোবাইল নাম্বার

mobile phone (**mobile phones**) *n* A **mobile phone** is a small phone that you can take everywhere with you. মোবাইল ফোন

mock (**mocks, mocking, mocked**) *adj* You use **mock** to describe something which is not genuine, but which is intended to be very similar to the real thing. নকল ▷ *vt* If you **mock** someone, you laugh at them, tease them, or try to make them look foolish. কৌতুক করা

mod cons *npl* **Mod cons** are the modern facilities in a house that make it easy and pleasant to live in. (*informal*) আধুনিক সুবিধা

model (**models, modelling, modelled**) *adj* A **model** wife or a model teacher, for example, is an excellent wife or an excellent teacher. আদর্শ ▷ *n* A **model** is a small copy of something. ছাঁচ ▷ *vt* If one thing is **modelled** on another, the first thing is made so that it is like the second thing in some way. নকল করা ▷ *n* A **model** is a person whose job is to wear and show new clothes. মডেল

modem (**modems**) *n* A **modem** is a device which uses a telephone line to connect computers or computer systems. মডেম

moderate *adj* **Moderate** political opinions or policies are not extreme. মধ্যপন্থী

moderation *n* If someone's behaviour shows **moderation**, they act in a way that is reasonable and not extreme. সংযম

modern *adj* **Modern** means relating to the present time. আধুনিক

modernize (**modernizes, modernizing, modernized**) *vt* To **modernize** a system

means to replace old equipment or methods with new ones. আধুনিকীকরণ

modern languages *npl* **Modern languages** refers to the modern European languages, for example French, German, and Russian, which are studied at school or university. আধুনিক ভাষা

modest *adj* A **modest** house or other building is not large or expensive. পরিমিত

modification (**modifications**) *n* **Modification** is the act of changing something slightly in order to improve it. পরিবর্তন

modify (**modifies, modifying, modified**) *vt* If you **modify** something, you change it slightly in order to improve it. পরিবর্তন করা

module (**modules**) *n* A **module** is one of the units that some university or college courses are divided into. খণ্ডিত অংশ

moist (**moister, moistest**) *adj* Something that is **moist** is slightly wet. ভিজা

moisture *n* **Moisture** is tiny drops of water in the air or on a surface. আর্দ্রতা

moisturizer (**moisturizers**) *n* A **moisturizer** is a cream that you put on your skin to make it feel softer and smoother. ময়শ্চারাইজার

Moldova *n* **Moldova** is a republic in south-east Europe. মলডোভা

Moldovan (**Moldovans**) *adj* **Moldovan** means of or relating to Moldova or its inhabitants. মালডোভীয় ▷ *n* A **Moldovan** is a native or inhabitant of Moldova. মলডোভার মানুষ

mole (**moles**) *n* A **mole** is a small animal with black fur that lives under the ground. ছুঁচো ▷ *n* A **mole** is a person who works for an organization and gives secret information about it to other people or to its enemies. অনুপ্রবেশকারী ▷ *n* A **mole** is a natural dark spot on your skin. তিল

molecule (**molecules**) *n* A **molecule** is the smallest amount of a chemical substance which can exist. অণু

moment (moments) n A **moment** is a very short period of time. মুহূর্ত

momentarily adv **Momentarily** means for a short time. (written) ক্ষণিকের জন্য

momentary adj Something that is **momentary** lasts for only a very short time. ক্ষণিক

momentous adj A **momentous** event is very important. গুরুত্বপূর্ণ

Monaco n **Monaco** is a principality in south-west Europe, on the Mediterranean. মোনাকো

monarch (monarchs) n A **monarch** is a king or queen. রাজা

monarchy (monarchies) n A **monarchy** is a system in which a monarch rules over a country. রাজতন্ত্র

monastery (monasteries) n A **monastery** is a building in which monks live. মঠ

Monday (Mondays) n **Monday** is the day after Sunday and before Tuesday. সোমবার

monetary adj **Monetary** means relating to money, or to the money supply. আর্থিক

money n **Money** consists of the coins or banknotes that you can spend, or a sum that can be represented by these. টাকাপয়সা

Mongolia n **Mongolia** is a republic in east central Asia. মোঙ্গোলিয়া

Mongolian (Mongolians) adj **Mongolian** means belonging or relating to Mongolia, or to its people, language, or culture. মোঙ্গোলীয় ▷ n A **Mongolian** is a person who comes from Mongolia. মোঙ্গোলীয়বাসী ▷ n **Mongolian** is the language that is spoken in Mongolia. মোঙ্গোলিয়ান ভাষা

mongrel (mongrels) n A **mongrel** is a dog which is a mixture of different breeds. দোআঁশলা

monitor (monitors) n A **monitor** is a machine used to check or record things. মনিটর

monk (monks) n A **monk** is a member of a male religious community. সন্ন্যাসী

monkey (monkeys) n A **monkey** is an animal with a long tail which lives in hot countries and climbs trees. বাঁদর

monopoly (monopolies) n If a company, person, or state has a **monopoly** on something such as an industry, they have complete control over it. একচেটিয়া

monotonous adj Something that is **monotonous** is very boring because it has a regular repeated pattern which never changes. একঘেয়েমি

monsoon (monsoons) n The **monsoon** is the season of very heavy rain in Southern Asia. বর্ষাকাল

monster (monsters) n A **monster** is a large imaginary creature that is very frightening. দানব

month (months) n A **month** is one of the twelve periods of time that a year is divided into, for example January or February. মাস

monthly adj A **monthly** event or publication happens or appears every month. মাসিক

monument (monuments) n A **monument** is a large structure, usually made of stone, which is built to remind people of an event in history or of a famous person. স্মৃতিস্তম্ভ

mood (moods) n Your **mood** is the way you are feeling at a particular time. মেজাজ

moody (moodier, moodiest) adj A **moody** person often becomes depressed or angry without any warning. মেজাজি

moon n The **moon** is the object in the sky that goes round the Earth once every four weeks and that you can often see at night as a circle or part of a circle. চাঁদ

moor (moors, mooring, moored) n A **moor** is an area of high open ground covered mainly with rough grass and heather. বিস্তীর্ণ পতিত ভূমি ▷ v If you **moor** or **moor** a boat, you attach it to the land with a rope or cable so that it cannot drift away. জাহাজ নোঙর করা

m

mop (mops) n A **mop** consists of a sponge or many pieces of string attached to a long handle that is used for washing floors. ন্যাতা

moped (mopeds) n A **moped** is a kind of motorcycle with a very small engine. মোপেড

mop up v If you **mop up** a liquid, you clean it with a cloth so that the liquid is absorbed. ন্যাতা দেওয়া A waiter mopped up the mess.

moral (morals) adj **Moral** means relating to beliefs about what is right or wrong. নৈতিক

morale n **Morale** is the amount of confidence and optimism that people have. মনোবল

morals npl **Morals** are principles and beliefs concerning right and wrong behaviour. নীতি

more det You use **more** to talk about a greater amount of something. বেশি He has more chips than me. ▷ adv You can use **more** when something continues to happen for a further period of time. অধিক ▷ pron You use **more** to refer to an additional thing or amount. অধিকতর As the amount of work increased, workers ate more.

morgue (morgues) n A **morgue** is a building or room where dead bodies are kept before being cremated or buried. শবাগার

morning (mornings) n The **morning** is the part of a day between the time that people wake up and noon. সকাল

morning sickness n **Morning sickness** is a feeling of sickness that some women have, often in the morning, when they are pregnant. প্রাতঃকালীন বিবমিষা

Moroccan (Moroccans) adj **Moroccan** means belonging or relating to Morocco or to its people or culture. মরক্কো দেশীয় ▷ n A **Moroccan** is a person who comes from Morocco. মরক্কোবাসী

Morocco n **Morocco** is a kingdom in north-west Africa. মরক্কো

morphine n **Morphine** is a drug used to relieve pain. মরফিন

morse code n **Morse code** is a code used for sending messages. It represents each letter of the alphabet using short and long sounds or flashes of light, which can be written down as dots and dashes. সাংকেতিক লিখন পদ্ধতি

mortar (mortars) n A **mortar** is a short cannon which fires shells high into the air for a short distance. কামান ▷ n **Mortar** is a mixture of sand, water, and cement, which is put between bricks to make them stay firmly together. প্লাস্টার

mortgage (mortgages, mortgaging, mortgaged) n A **mortgage** is a loan of money which you get from a bank in order to buy a house. বন্ধক ▷ vt If you **mortgage** your house or land, you use it as a guarantee to a company in order to borrow money from them. বন্ধক দেওয়া

mosaic (mosaics) n A **mosaic** is a design made of small pieces of coloured stone or glass set in concrete or plaster. মোজাইক

Moslem (Moslems) adj **Moslem** means relating to Islam or Moslems. মুসলিম ▷ n A **Moslem** is someone who believes in Islam and lives according to its rules. মুসলমান

mosque (mosques) n A **mosque** is a building where Muslims go to worship. মসজিদ

mosquito (mosquitoes or **mosquitos)** n
Mosquitoes are small flying insects which
bite people in order to suck their blood. মশা

moss (mosses) n **Moss** is a very small, soft,
green plant which grows on damp soil, or
on wood or stone. শ্যাওলা

most adj You use **most** to talk about nearly
all the people or things in a group. বেশিরভাগ
▷ adv The **most** means the largest amount.
সর্বাধিক ▷ pron **Most** of a group of things or
people means nearly all of them. বেশিরভাগ
Most of the houses here are very old.

mostly adv You use **mostly** to indicate that
a statement is true about the majority of a
group of things or people, true most of the
time, or true in most respects. প্রধানত

MOT (MOTs) abbr In Britain, an **MOT** is a
test which, by law, must be made each year
on all road vehicles that are more than three
years old, in order to check that they are
safe to drive. মট

motel (motels) n A **motel** is a hotel intended
for people who are travelling by car. মোটেল

moth (moths) n A **moth** is an insect like
a butterfly, which usually flies about at
night. মথ

mother (mothers) n Your **mother** is your
female parent. মা

mother-in-law (mothers-in-law) n
Someone's **mother-in-law** is the mother of
their husband or wife. শাশুড়ী

mother tongue (mother tongues) n Your
mother tongue is the language that you
learn from your parents when you are a
baby. মাতৃভাষা

motionless adj Someone or something that
is **motionless** is not moving at all. নিশ্চল

motivated adj If you are **motivated**, you
feel enthusiastic and determined to achieve
success. অনুপ্রাণিত

motivation (motivations) n Your
motivation for doing something is what
causes you to want to do it. প্রেরণা

motive (motives) n Your **motive** for doing
something is your reason for doing it. উদ্দেশ্য

motor (motors) n A **motor** in a machine,
vehicle, or boat is the part that uses
electricity or fuel to produce movement,
so that the machine, vehicle, or boat can
work. মোটর

motorbike (motorbikes) n A **motorbike**
is a two-wheeled vehicle with an engine.
মোটরবাইক

motorboat (motorboats) n A **motorboat**
is a boat that is driven by an engine.
মোটরবোট

motorcycle (motorcycles) n A **motorcycle**
is a two-wheeled vehicle with an engine.
মোটরসাইকেল

motorcyclist (motorcyclists) n A
motorcyclist is someone who rides a
motorcycle. মোটরসাইকেল চালক

motorist (motorists) n A **motorist** is
someone who drives a car. গাড়ি চালক

motor mechanic (motor mechanics) n A
motor mechanic is someone whose job is
to repair and maintain car engines. মোটর
মিস্ত্রি

motor racing n **Motor racing** is the sport
of racing fast cars on a special track. মোটর
দৌড় প্রতিযোগিতা

motorway (motorways) n A **motorway**
is a wide road specially built for fast travel
over long distances. দ্রুতগামী গাড়ির জন্য রাস্তা

mould (moulds) n A **mould** is a container
used to make something into a particular
shape. ছাঁচ ▷ n **Mould** is a soft grey, green,
or blue substance that sometimes forms
in spots on old food or on damp walls or
clothes. ছাতা

mouldy adj Something that is **mouldy** is
covered with mould. ছাতা পড়া

mount (mounts, mounting, mounted) vt
To **mount** a campaign or event means to
organize it and make it take place. বন্দোবস্ত
করা

mountain (mountains) n A **mountain** is a
very high area of land with steep sides. পর্বত

mountain bike (mountain bikes) n A
mountain bike is a type of bicycle with a

strong frame and thick tyres. পাহাড়ে চড়ার বাইক

mountaineer (**mountaineers**) *n* A **mountaineer** is someone who climbs mountains as a hobby or sport. পর্বতারোহী

mountaineering *n* **Mountaineering** is the activity of climbing the steep sides of mountains as a hobby or sport. পর্বতারোহণ

mountainous *adj* A **mountainous** place has a lot of mountains. পর্বতময়

mount up *v* If something **mounts up**, it increases in quantity. বাড়া *Her medical bills mounted up.*

mourning *n* **Mourning** is behaviour in which you show sadness about a person's death. শোক

mouse (**mice**) *n* A **mouse** is a small animal with a long tail. ইঁদুর ▷ *n* You use a **mouse** to move things on a computer screen. মাউস

mouse mat (**mouse mats**) *n* A **mouse mat** is a flat piece of plastic or some other material that you rest the mouse on while using a computer. মাউস ম্যাট

mousse (**mousses**) *n* **Mousse** is a sweet light food made from eggs and cream. ডিম এবং ক্রীমের তৈরী খাবার

moustache (**moustaches**) *n* A man's **moustache** is the hair that grows on his upper lip. গোঁফ

mouth (**mouths**) *n* Your **mouth** is your lips, or the space behind your lips where your teeth and tongue are. মুখ

mouth organ (**mouth organs**) *n* A **mouth organ** is a small musical instrument. You play the harmonica by moving it across your lips and blowing and sucking air through it. মাউথ-অরগান

mouthwash (**mouthwashes**) *n* **Mouthwash** is a liquid that you put in your mouth and then spit out in order to clean your mouth and make your breath smell pleasant. মুখ ধোয়ার তরল প্রতিষেধক

move (**moves, moving, moved**) *n* A **move** is an action that you take. হস্তান্তর ▷ *vt* When you **move** something, you put it in a different place. সরানো ▷ *vi* If you **move**, you go to live in a different place. হস্তান্তরে যাওয়া

move back *v* If you **move back**, you change your position by going in a backward direction. পেছনে সরা *He moved back up the corridor.*

move forward *v* If you **move forward** an event, you arrange for it to take place at an earlier time than had been planned. সামনে যাওয়া *He had to move forward an 11 o'clock meeting.*

move in *v* If you **move in** somewhere, or if you **move into** a new house or place, you begin to live in a different house or place. প্রবেশ করা *A friend has moved in with me to rent my spare room.*

movement (**movements**) *n* **Movement** involves changing position or going from one place to another. আসা যাওয়া

movie (**movies**) *n* A **movie** is a motion picture. (*informal*) চলচ্চিত্র

moving *adj* If something is **moving**, it makes you feel a strong emotion such as pity. আবেগময়

mow (**mows, mowing, mowed, mown**) *v* If you **mow** an area of grass, you cut it using a lawnmower or a mower. কাস্তে বা মেশিন দিয়ে ঘাস কাটা

mower (**mowers**) *n* A **mower** is a machine for cutting grass, corn, or wheat. ঘাস কাটার যন্ত্র

Mozambique *n* **Mozambique** is a republic in south-east Africa. মোজাম্বিক

MP3 player (**MP3 players**) *n* An **MP3 player** is a machine on which you can play music downloaded from the Internet. এম পি থ্রি প্লেয়ার

MP4 player (**MP4 players**) *n* An **MP4 player** is a machine on which you can play music downloaded from the Internet. এম পি ফোর প্লেয়ার

mph *abbr* **mph** is written after a number to indicate the speed of something such as a vehicle. **mph** is an abbreviation for 'miles per hour'. এম পি এইচ

Mr *n* **Mr** is used before a man's name when you are speaking or referring to him. শ্রী

Mrs *n* **Mrs** is used before the name of a married woman when you are speaking or referring to her. শ্রীমতী

MS *abbr* **MS** is a serious disease of the nervous system, which gradually makes a person weaker, and sometimes affects their sight or speech. **MS** is an abbreviation for 'multiple sclerosis'. এম এস

Ms *n* **Ms** is used before a woman's name when you are speaking to her or referring to her. If you use **Ms**, you are not specifying if the woman is married or not. শ্রীযুক্তা

much *det* You use **much** to talk about a large amount of something. অনেক *We don't have much food.* ▷ *adv* You use **much** with 'so', 'too', and 'very' to mean a very large amount of something. খুব জোরে ▷ *pron* You use **much** to mean a large amount of something. অত্যধিক *I didn't think much about it then.*

mud *n* **Mud** is a sticky mixture of earth and water. কাদা

muddle (**muddles**) *n* A **muddle** is a confused state or situation. এলোমেলো অবস্থা

muddy (**muddier, muddiest**) *adj* Something that is **muddy** contains, or is covered in, mud. কর্দমাক্ত

mudguard (**mudguards**) *n* The **mudguards** of a bicycle or other vehicle are curved pieces of metal or plastic above the tyres, which stop mud getting on the rider or vehicle. মাড-গার্ড

muesli (**mueslis**) *n* **Muesli** is a breakfast cereal made from chopped nuts, dried fruit, and grains. মুয়েসলী

muffler (**mufflers**) *n* A **muffler** is a piece of cloth that you wear round your neck or head, usually to keep yourself warm. (*old-fashioned*) মাফলার

mug (**mugs, mugging, mugged**) *n* A **mug** is a large deep cup with straight sides. মগ ▷ *vt* If someone **mugs** you, they attack you in order to steal your money. ছিনতাই করা

mugger (**muggers**) *n* A **mugger** is a person who attacks someone violently in a street in order to steal money from them. ডাকাত

mugging (**muggings**) *n* A **mugging** is an attack on somebody in order to steal their money. ডাকাতি

mule (**mules**) *n* A **mule** is an animal whose parents are a horse and a donkey. খচ্চর

multinational (**multinationals**) *adj* A **multinational** company has branches or owns companies in many different countries. বহুজাতিক ▷ *n* A **multinational** is a company that has branches or owns companies in many different countries. বহুজাতিক

multiple sclerosis *n* **Multiple sclerosis** is a serious disease of the nervous system. The abbreviation 'MS' is also used. মাল্টিপল স্ক্লেরোসিস

multiplication *n* **Multiplication** is the process of increasing greatly in number or amount. গুণ

multiply (**multiplies, multiplying, multiplied**) *v* When something **multiplies**,

m

or when you **multiply** it, it increases greatly in number or amount. বাড়িয়ে তোলা

mum (**mums**) n Your **mum** is your mother. (informal) মা

mummy (**mummies**) n Some people, especially young children, call their mother **mummy**. (informal) মা ▷ n A **mummy** is a dead body which was preserved long ago by being rubbed with oils and wrapped in cloth. মমি

mumps n **Mumps** is a disease usually caught by children. It causes a mild fever and painful swelling of the glands in the neck. মাম্পস

murder (**murders, murdering, murdered**) n **Murder** is the crime of deliberately killing a person. খুন ▷ vt To **murder** someone means to commit the crime of killing them deliberately. খুন করা

murderer (**murderers**) n A **murderer** is a person who has murdered someone. খুনী

muscle (**muscles**) n Your **muscles** are the parts inside your body that connect your bones, and that help you to move. পেশী

muscular adj **Muscular** means involving or affecting your muscles. পেশীবহুল

museum (**museums**) n A **museum** is a public building where interesting and valuable objects are kept and displayed. জাদুঘর

mushroom (**mushrooms**) n **Mushrooms** are fungi with short stems and round tops. You can eat some kinds of mushrooms. ছত্রাক

music n **Music** is the pattern of sounds produced by people singing or playing instruments. সংগীত

musical (**musicals**) n A **musical** is a play or film that uses singing and dancing in the story. সংগীত ▷ adj **Musical** describes things that are concerned with playing or studying music. সংগীত-বিষয়ক

musical instrument (**musical instruments**) n A **musical instrument** is an object such as a piano, guitar, or violin which you play in order to produce music. বাদ্যযন্ত্র

musician (**musicians**) n A **musician** is a person who plays a musical instrument as their job or hobby. সংগীতকার

Muslim (**Muslims**) adj **Muslim** means relating to Islam or Muslims. মুসলিম ▷ n A **Muslim** is someone who believes in Islam and lives according to its rules. মুসলমান

mussel (**mussels**) n A **mussel** is a kind of shellfish. শুক্তিবিশেষ

must v You use **must** to show that you think something is very important. অবশ্যই You must tell the police all the facts.

mustard n **Mustard** is a yellow or brown paste made from seeds which tastes spicy. সরষে

mutter (**mutters, muttering, muttered**) v If you **mutter**, you speak very quietly so that you cannot easily be heard, often because you are complaining about something. বিড়বিড় করে কথা বলা

mutton n **Mutton** is meat from an adult sheep. ভেড়ার মাংস

mutual adj You use **mutual** to describe a situation, feeling, or action that is experienced, felt, or done by both of two people mentioned. পারস্পরিক

my det You use **my** to show that something belongs to you. আমার I went to sleep in my room.

Myanmar n **Myanmar** is a republic in south-east Asia. মায়ানমার

myself *pron* You use **myself** when you are talking about yourself. নিজে *I hurt myself when I fell down.*

mysterious *adj* Someone or something that is **mysterious** is strange, not known about, or not understood. রহস্যময়

mystery (**mysteries**) *n* A **mystery** is something that is not understood or known about. রহস্য

myth (**myths**) *n* A **myth** is an ancient story about gods and magic. পুরাণ

mythology *n* **Mythology** is a group of myths, especially those from a particular country, religion, or culture. পুরাণচর্চা

naff (**naffer, naffest**) *adj* If you say that something is **naff**, you mean it is very unfashionable or unsophisticated. (*informal*) অপরিমার্জিত

nag (**nags, nagging, nagged**) *v* If someone **nags** you, or if they **nag**, they keep asking you to do something you have not done yet or do not want to do. ঘ্যানঘ্যান করা

nail (**nails**) *n* A **nail** is a thin piece of metal. It is flat at one end and it has a point at the other end. পেরেক ▷ *n* Your **nails** are the thin hard parts that grow at the ends of your fingers and toes. নখ

nailbrush (**nailbrushes**) *n* A **nailbrush** is a small brush that you use to clean your nails when washing your hands. নখের ব্রাশ

nailfile (**nailfiles**) *n* A **nailfile** is a small strip of rough metal or card that you rub across the ends of your nails to shorten them or shape them. নেলফাইল

nail polish (**nail polishes**) *n* **Nail polish** is a thick liquid that women paint on their nails. নেলপালিশ

nail-polish remover (**nail-polish removers**) *n* **Nail-polish remover** is a solvent used to remove nail polish. নেলপালিশ-রিমুভার

nail scissors *npl* **Nail scissors** are small scissors that you use for cutting your nails. নখ কাটার কাঁচি

naive *adj* If you describe someone as **naive**, you think they lack experience, causing them to expect things to be uncomplicated or easy, or people to be honest or kind when they are not. সাধাসিধে

naked *adj* Someone who is **naked** is not wearing any clothes. উলঙ্গ

name (**names**) *n* The **name** of a person, thing, or place is the word or words that you use to identify them. নাম

nanny (**nannies**) *n* A **nanny** is a person who is paid by parents to look after their children. শিশু-পরিচর্যাকারী

nap (**naps**) *n* If you have a **nap**, you have a short sleep, usually during the day. স্বল্পসময়ের ঘুম

napkin (**napkins**) *n* A **napkin** is a small piece of cloth or paper used to protect your clothes when you are eating. রুমাল

nappy (**nappies**) *n* A **nappy** is a piece of thick cloth or paper which is fastened round a baby's bottom in order to absorb its waste. শিশুদের লেঙ্টি

narrow (**narrower, narrowest**) *adj* Something that is **narrow** measures a very small distance from one side to the other, especially compared to its length or height. সংকীর্ণ

narrow-minded *adj* If you describe someone as **narrow-minded**, you are criticizing them because they are unwilling to consider new ideas or other people's opinions. সংকীর্ণমনা

nasty (**nastier, nastiest**) *adj* Something that is **nasty** is very unpleasant or unattractive. জঘন্য

nation (**nations**) *n* A **nation** is an individual country considered together with its social and political structures. দেশ

national *adj* **National** means relating to the whole of a country, rather than to part of it or to other nations. জাতীয়

national anthem (**national anthems**) *n* A **national anthem** is a nation's official song. জাতীয় সঙ্গীত

nationalism *n* **Nationalism** is the desire for political independence of people who

feel they are historically or culturally a separate group within a country. জাতীয়তাবাদ

nationalist (**nationalists**) *n* A **nationalist** is someone who desires for the group of people to which they belong to gain political independence. জাতীয়তাবাদী

nationality (**nationalities**) *n* If you have the **nationality** of a particular country, you have the legal right to be a citizen of it. নাগরিকত্ব

nationalize (**nationalizes, nationalizing, nationalized**) *vt* If a government **nationalizes** a private industry, that industry becomes owned by the state and controlled by the government. জাতীয়করণ করা

national park (**national parks**) *n* A **national park** is a large area of natural land protected by the government because of its natural beauty, plants, or animals. রাষ্ট্রীয় পার্ক

native *adj* Your **native** country or area is the country or area where you were born and brought up. জন্মভূমি

native speaker (**native speakers**) *n* A **native speaker** of a language is someone who speaks that language as their first language rather than having learned it as a foreign language. মাতৃভাষা বক্তা

NATO *abbr* **NATO** is an international organization which consists of the USA, Canada, Britain, and other European countries, all of whom have agreed to support one another if they are attacked. **NATO** is an abbreviation for 'North Atlantic Treaty Organization'. ন্যাটো

natural *adj* If you say that it is **natural** for someone to act in a particular way, you mean that it is reasonable in the circumstances. স্বাভাবিক

natural gas *n* **Natural gas** is gas which is found underground or under the sea. It is collected and stored, and piped into people's homes to be used for cooking and heating. প্রাকৃতিক গ্যাস

naturalist (naturalists) *n* A **naturalist** is a person who studies plants, animals, and other living things. প্রকৃতিবিদ

naturally *adv* You use **naturally** to indicate that you think something is very obvious and not at all surprising in the circumstances. স্বাভাবিকভাবে

natural resources *npl* The **natural resources** of a place are all its land, forests, energy sources, and minerals which exist naturally there and can be used by people. প্রাকৃতিক সম্পদ

nature *n* **Nature** refers to all the animals, plants, and other things in the world that are not made by people, and all the events and processes that are not caused by people. প্রকৃতি

naughty (naughtier, naughtiest) *adj* You say that small children are **naughty** when they behave badly. দুষ্টু

nausea *n* **Nausea** is a feeling of sickness and dizziness. বমিভাব

naval *adj* **Naval** people and things belong to a country's navy. নৌ-বাহিনী সংক্রান্ত

navel (navels) *n* Your **navel** is the small hollow just below your waist at the front of your body. নাভি

navy (navies) *n* A country's **navy** is the part of its armed forces that fights at sea. নৌ-বাহিনী ▷ *adj* Something that is **navy** is very dark blue. গাঢ় নীল রং

NB *abbr* You write **NB** to draw someone's attention to what you are going to write next. পুনশ্চ

near (nearer, nearest) *adj* **Near** means at or in a place not far away. কাছে ▷ *adv* **Near** means at or to a place not far away. কাছাকাছি ▷ *prep* If something is **near** a place, thing, or person, it is not far away from them. কাছে *We are very near my house.*

nearby *adj* If something is **nearby**, it is only a short distance away. কাছেই ▷ *adv* If something is **nearby**, it is only a short distance away. নিকটবর্তী

nearly *adv* If something is **nearly** a quantity, it is very close to that quantity but slightly less than it. If something is **nearly** a certain state, it is very close to that state but has not quite reached it. প্রায়

near-sighted *adj* Someone who is **near-sighted** cannot see distant things clearly. (US) দূরের জিনিস যে দেখতে পায় না

neat (neater, neatest) *adj* A **neat** place, thing, or person is tidy, smart, and orderly. সুবিন্যস্ত

neatly *adv* **Neatly** means in a tidy or smart manner. সুবিন্যস্তভাবে

necessarily *adv* If you say that something is **not necessarily** true, you mean that it may not be true or is not always true. অবধারিতভাবে

necessary *adj* Something that is **necessary** is needed to get a particular result or effect. প্রয়োজন

necessity *n* **Necessity** is the need to do something. প্রয়োজনীয়তা

neck (necks) *n* Your **neck** is the part of your body which joins your head to the rest of your body. গলা

necklace (necklaces) *n* A **necklace** is a piece of jewellery such as a chain or string of beads, which someone wears round their neck. নেকলেস

nectarine (nectarines) *n* A **nectarine** is a fruit similar to a peach with a smooth skin. পীচ ফল

need (**needs, needing, needed**) *n* If you have a **need** for something, you cannot do what you want without it. চাহিদা ▷ *vt* If you **need** something, you believe that you must have it or do it. প্রয়োজন

needle (**needles**) *n* A **needle** is a small very thin piece of metal with a hole at one end and a sharp point at the other, which is used for sewing. সূচ

negative (**negatives**) *adj* A fact, situation, or experience that is **negative** is unpleasant, depressing, or harmful. নঞর্থক ▷ *n* A **negative** is a word, expression, or gesture that means 'no' or 'not'. নেতিবাচক

neglect (**neglects, neglecting, neglected**) *n* **Neglect** is the failure to look after someone or something properly. অবহেলা ▷ *vt* If you **neglect** someone or something, you fail to look after them properly. অবহেলা করা

neglected *adj* If someone is **neglected**, they have not been given enough love, attention or support. অবহেলিত

negotiate (**negotiates, negotiating, negotiated**) *v* If one person or group **negotiates** with another, they talk about a problem or a situation in order to solve the problem or complete the arrangement. রফা করা

negotiations *npl* **Negotiations** are discussions that take place between people with different interests, in which they try to reach an agreement. আপোস-আলোচনা

negotiator (**negotiators**) *n* **Negotiators** are people who take part in political or financial negotiations. আপোস-আলোচনায় অংশগ্রহণকারী ব্যক্তি

neighbour (**neighbours**) *n* Your **neighbours** are the people who live near you, especially the people who live in the house or flat which is next to yours. প্রতিবেশী

neighbourhood (**neighbourhoods**) *n* A **neighbourhood** is one of the parts of a town where people live. পাড়া

neither *conj* If you say that one person or thing does not do something and

neither does another, what you say is true of both the people or things that you are mentioning. কেউই নয় *I never learned to swim and neither did they.* ▷ *pron* You use **neither** to refer to each of two things or people, when you make a negative statement that includes both of them. উভয়েই নয় *They both smiled; neither seemed likely to be aware of my absence for long.* ▷ *adj* **Neither** means not one or the other of two things or people. দুটির মধ্যে কোনটি নয়

neither ... nor *conj* You use **neither ... nor** when you are talking about two or more things that are not true or that do not happen. কোনটিই নয় *The play was neither as funny nor as exciting as she said it was.*

neon *n* **Neon** is a gas which exists in very small amounts in the atmosphere. নিয়ন

Nepal *n* **Nepal** is a republic in South Asia. নেপাল

nephew (**nephews**) *n* Your **nephew** is the son of your sister or brother. ভাগ্নে/ভাইপো

nerve (**nerves**) *n* **Nerves** are long thin fibres that transmit messages between your brain and other parts of your body. স্নায়ু ▷ *n* **Nerve** is the courage you need to do something difficult or dangerous. সাহস

nerve-racking *adj* A **nerve-racking** situation or experience makes you feel very tense and worried. স্নায়ুর ওপর চাপসৃষ্টিকারী

nervous *adj* If you are **nervous**, you are worried and frightened, and show this in your behaviour. বিচলিত

nest (**nests**) *n* A **nest** is a place that birds, insects, and other animals make to lay eggs in or give birth to their young in. বাসা

net (**nets**) *n* A **net** is made from pieces of string or rope tied together with holes between them. It is for catching things like fish, or the ball in some sports. জাল

netball *n* **Netball** is a game played by two teams of seven players, usually women. Each team tries to score goals by throwing a ball through a net which is at the top of a pole at each end of the court. নেটবল

Netherlands *npl* **The Netherlands** is a kingdom in north-west Europe, on the North Sea. নেদারল্যান্ডস্

nettle (**nettles**) *n* A **nettle** is a wild plant with leaves that sting when you touch them. বিছুটি

network (**networks**) *n* A **network** of lines, roads, veins, or other long thin things is a large number of them which cross each other or meet at many points. নেটওয়ার্ক

neurotic *adj* If you say that someone is **neurotic**, you mean that they are always frightened or worried about things that you consider unimportant. বাতিকগ্রস্ত

neutral *adj* A **neutral** person or country does not support anyone in a disagreement, war, or contest. নিরপেক্ষ ▷ *n* **Neutral** is the position between the gears of a vehicle, in which the gears are not connected to the engine. নিউট্রাল

never *adv* **Never** means at no time in the past or future. কখনও নয়

nevertheless *adv* You use **nevertheless** when saying something that contrasts with what has just been said. (*formal*) তবুও

new (**newer, newest**) *adj* Something that is **new** was not there before. নতুন ▷ *adj* If something is **new**, nobody has used it before. নতুন ▷ *adj* A **new** thing or person is a different one from the one you had before. নতুন

newborn *adj* A **newborn** baby or animal is one that has just been born. নবজাত

newcomer (**newcomers**) *n* A **newcomer** is a person who has recently started a new activity, arrived in a place, or joined an organization. নবাগত

news *npl* **News** is information about a recently changed situation or a recent event. খবর

newsagent (**newsagents**) *n* A **newsagent** is the shopkeeper of a shop where newspapers, sweets, soft drinks, and stationery are sold. সংবাদকর্মী

newspaper (**newspapers**) *n* A **newspaper** is a publication consisting of large sheets of folded paper, on which news is printed. সংবাদপত্র

newsreader (**newsreaders**) *n* A **newsreader** is a person who reads the news on the radio or on television. সংবাদপাঠক

newt (**newts**) *n* A **newt** is a small creature that has four legs and a long tail and can live on land and in water. গোসাপ-জাতীয় প্রাণী

New Year *n* **New Year** or the **New Year** is the time when people celebrate the start of a year. নববর্ষ

New Zealand *n* **New Zealand** is an island country, with two main islands (the North Island and the South Island), in the south-east Pacific. নিউজিল্যান্ড

New Zealander (**New Zealanders**) *n* A **New Zealander** is a citizen of New Zealand, or a person of New Zealand origin. নিউজিল্যান্ডের অধিবাসী

next *adj* The **next** thing is the one that comes immediately after this one or after the last one. পরবর্তী ▷ *adv* The thing that happens **next** happens immediately after something else. এরপর

next of kin *n* Your **next of kin** is your closest relative, especially in official or legal documents. (*formal*) নিকটতম আত্মীয়

next to *prep* If one thing is **next to** another, it is at the side of it. পাশে *She sat down next to him on the sofa.*

Nicaragua *n* **Nicaragua** is a republic in Central America. নিকারাগুয়া

Nicaraguan (**Nicaraguans**) *adj* **Nicaraguan** means belonging or relating to Nicaragua, or to its people or culture. নিকারাগুয়া দেশীয় ▷ *n* A **Nicaraguan** is a person who comes from Nicaragua. নিকারাগুয়ার অধিবাসী

nice (**nicer, nicest**) *adj* If something is **nice**, you like it. সুন্দর

nickname (**nicknames**) *n* A **nickname** is an informal name for someone or something. ডাকনাম

nicotine *n* **Nicotine** is an addictive substance in tobacco. নিকোটিন

niece (**nieces**) *n* Your **niece** is the daughter of your sister or brother. ভাইঝি/ভাগ্নী

Niger *n* **Niger** is a landlocked republic in West Africa. নাইজার

Nigeria *n* **Nigeria** is a republic in West Africa, on the Gulf of Guinea. নাইজেরিয়া

Nigerian (**Nigerians**) *adj* **Nigerian** means belonging or relating to Nigeria, its people, or its culture. নাইজেরিয়া দেশীয় ▷ *n* A **Nigerian** is a Nigerian citizen, or a person of Nigerian origin. নাইজেরিয়ার অধিবাসী

night (**nights**) *n* The **night** is the part of each period of twenty-four hours when it is dark outside, especially the time when most people are sleeping. রাত

nightclub (**nightclubs**) *n* A **nightclub** is a place where people go late in the evening to dance. নাইটক্লাব

nightdress (**nightdresses**) *n* A **nightdress** is a sort of loose dress that a woman or girl wears in bed. রাতপোষাক

nightlife *n* The **nightlife** in a place is the entertainment and social activities that are available at night. নৈশ জীবন

nightmare (**nightmares**) *n* A **nightmare** is a very frightening dream. দুঃস্বপ্ন

night school (**night schools**) *n* Someone who goes to **night school** does an educational course in the evenings. নৈশ বিদ্যালয়

night shift (**night shifts**) *n* If a group of factory workers, nurses, or other people work the **night shift**, they work during the night before being replaced by another group, so that there is always a group working. রাতের শিফট

nil *n* **Nil** means the same as zero. It is often used in scores of sports games. শূন্য

nine *num* **Nine** is the number 9. নয়

nineteen (**nineteens**) *num* **Nineteen** is the number 19. উনবিংশ

nineteenth *adj* The **nineteenth** item in a series is the one that you count as number nineteen. উনবিংশতম

ninety *num* **Ninety** is the number 90. নব্বই

ninth (**ninths**) *adj* The **ninth** item in a series is the one that you count as number nine. নবম ▷ *n* A **ninth** is one of nine equal parts of something. নয় ভাগের এক ভাগ

nitrogen *n* **Nitrogen** is a colourless element that has no smell and is usually found as a gas. নাইট্রোজেন

no *det* You use **no** to mean not any or not one person or thing. না *He had no idea where to go.* ▷ *adv* You use **no** to mean not in any way. নয় ▷ *excl* You use **no!** to give a negative response to a question. না

nobody *n* **Nobody** means not one person. কোন ব্যক্তি নয়

nod (**nods, nodding, nodded**) *vi* If you **nod**, you move your head downwards and upwards to show that you are answering 'yes' to a question, or to show agreement, understanding, or approval. মাথা নেড়ে সম্মতি জানানো

noise *n* **Noise** is a loud or unpleasant sound. কোলাহল

noisy (**noisier, noisiest**) *adj* Someone or something that is **noisy** makes a lot of loud or unpleasant noise. কোলাহলপূর্ণ

nominate (**nominates, nominating, nominated**) *vt* If someone **is nominated** for a job, position, or prize, their name is formally suggested as a candidate for it. মনোনীত

nomination (**nominations**) *n* A **nomination** is an official suggestion of someone for a job, position, or prize. মনোনয়ন

none *pron* **None** means not one or not any. কিছু নয় *None of us knew her.*

nonsense *n* If you say that something spoken or written is **nonsense**, you mean that you consider it to be untrue or silly. বোকাবোকা

non-smoker (**non-smokers**) *n* A **non-smoker** is someone who does not smoke. অ-ধূমপায়ী

non-smoking *adj* A **non-smoking** area in a public place is an area in which people are not allowed to smoke. ধূমপান-বর্জিত

on-stop *adv* If you do something **non-stop**, you continue to do it without any pauses or breaks. বিরামহীন

noodles *npl* **Noodles** are long, thin pieces of pasta. নুডলস্

noon *n* **Noon** is twelve o'clock in the middle of the day. দ্বিপ্রহর

no one *pron* **No one** means not a single person, or not a single member of a particular group or set. কেউ নয় *No one can predict what will happen in the months ahead.*

nor *conj* You use **nor** after 'neither' to introduce the second of two things that are not true or that do not happen. ওটাও না *Neither her friends nor her family knew how old she was.*

normal *adj* Something that is **normal** is usual and ordinary, and in accordance with what people expect. স্বাভাবিক

normally *adv* If you say that something **normally** happens or that you **normally** do a particular thing, you mean that it is what usually happens or what you usually do. সাধারণতঃ

north *adj* The **north** edge, corner, or part of a place or country is the part which is towards the north. উত্তর ▷ *adv* If you go **north**, you travel towards the north. উত্তরদিক ▷ *n* The **north** is the direction on your left when you are looking towards the direction where the sun rises. সূর্যের দিকে মুখ করে তাকালে বাঁদিক

North Africa *n* **North Africa** is the part of Africa between the Mediterranean and the Sahara. উত্তর আফ্রিকা

North African (**North Africans**) *adj* **North African** means relating to North Africa or its inhabitants. উত্তর আফ্রিকা দেশীয় ▷ *n* A **North African** is a native or inhabitant of North Africa. উত্তর আফ্রিকার অধিবাসী

North America *n* **North America** is the third largest continent in the world, and

includes Greenland, Canada, the United States, Mexico, and Central America. উত্তর আমেরিকা

North American (**North Americans**) *adj* **North American** means relating to North America or its inhabitants. উত্তর আমেরিকা দেশীয় ▷ *n* A **North American** is a native or inhabitant of North America. উত্তর আমেরিকার অধিবাসী

northbound *adj* **Northbound** roads or vehicles lead or are travelling towards the north. উত্তরমুখী

northeast *n* The **northeast** is the direction which is halfway between north and east. উত্তরপূর্ব

northern *adj* **Northern** means in or from the north of a region or country. উত্তরাঞ্চল

Northern Ireland *n* **Northern Ireland** is that part of the United Kingdom occupying the north-east part of Ireland. আয়ার্ল্যান্ডের উত্তরপূর্ব অঞ্চল

North Korea *n* **North Korea** is a republic in North-East Asia. উত্তর কোরিয়া

North Pole *n* The **North Pole** is the place on the surface of the earth which is farthest towards the north. উত্তর মেরু

North Sea *n* The **North Sea** is the part of the Atlantic between Great Britain and the North European mainland. উত্তর সাগর

northwest *n* The **northwest** is the direction which is halfway between north and west. উত্তরপশ্চিম

Norway *n* **Norway** is a kingdom in north-west Europe. নরওয়ে

Norwegian (**Norwegians**) *adj* **Norwegian** means belonging or relating to Norway, or to its people, language, or culture. নরওয়ে দেশীয় ▷ *n* A **Norwegian** is a person who comes from Norway. নরওয়ের অধিবাসী ▷ *n* **Norwegian** is the language spoken in Norway. নরওয়ের ভাষা

nose (**noses**) *n* Your **nose** is the part of your face which sticks out above your mouth. You use it for smelling and breathing. নাক

n

nosebleed (nosebleeds) n If someone has a **nosebleed**, blood comes out from inside their nose. নাক থেকে রক্তক্ষরণ

nostril (nostrils) n Your **nostrils** are the two openings at the end of your nose. নাসারন্ধ্র

nosy (nosier, nosiest) adj If you describe someone as **nosy**, you mean that they are interested in things which do not concern them. (informal) কৌতূহলী

not adv You use **not** or **n't** to show that something is the opposite of true. না

note (notes) n A **note** is one musical sound. ধ্বনি ⊳ n A **note** is a piece of paper money. ব্যাঙ্কের টাকা ⊳ n A **note** is a short letter or message. স্মারকলিপি

notebook (notebooks) n A **notebook** is a small book for writing notes in. নোটবুক

note down v When you **note** something **down**, you write it down so that you have a record of it. টুকে রাখা She noted down the names.

notepad (notepads) n A **notepad** is a pad of paper that you use for writing notes or letters on. নোটপ্যাড

notepaper n **Notepaper** is paper that you use for writing letters on. নোটপেপার

nothing n **Nothing** means not anything. কিছু না

notice (notices, noticing, noticed) n A **notice** is a sign that gives information or instructions. সূচনা ⊳ n **Notice** is advance warning about something. নোটিশ ⊳ vt If you **notice** something, you suddenly see or hear it. দেখতে পাওয়া

noticeable adj Something that is **noticeable** is very obvious, so that it is easy to see or recognize. লক্ষণীয়

noticeboard (noticeboards) n A **noticeboard** is a board which is usually attached to a wall in order to display notices giving information about something. নোটিশবোর্ড

notify (notifies, notifying, notified) vt If you **notify** someone of something, you officially inform them of it. (formal) জানানো

nought (noughts) n **Nought** is the number 0. শূন্য সংখ্যা

noun (nouns) n A **noun** is a word such as 'car', 'love', or 'man' which is used to refer to person or thing. বিশেষ্য পদ

novel (novels) n A **novel** is a book containing a long story about imaginary people and events. উপন্যাস

novelist (novelists) n A **novelist** is a person who writes novels. ঔপন্যাসিক

November (Novembers) n **November** is the eleventh month of the year in the Western calendar. নভেম্বর মাস

now adv You use **now** to talk about the present time. এখন

nowadays adv **Nowadays** means at the present time, in contrast with the past. আজকাল

nowhere adv You use **nowhere** to emphasize that a place has more of a particular quality than any other places, or that it is the only place where something happens or exists. কোথাও না

nuclear adj **Nuclear** means relating to the nuclei of atoms, or to the energy produced when these nuclei are split or combined. পারমাণবিক

nude (nudes) adj A **nude** person is not wearing any clothes. নগ্ন ⊳ n A **nude** is a picture or statue of a person who is not wearing any clothes. নগ্ন অবস্থা

nuisance (nuisances) n If you say that someone or something is a **nuisance**, you mean that they annoy you or cause you problems. আপদ

numb adj If a part of your body is **numb**, you cannot feel anything there. অসাড়

number (numbers) n A **number** is a word such as 'two', 'nine', or 'twelve', or a symbol such as 1, 3, or 47, which is used in counting something. সংখ্যা

number plate (number plates) n A **number plate** is a sign on the front and back of a vehicle that shows its registration number. নম্বরপ্লেট

numerous *adj* If people or things are **numerous**, they exist or are present in large numbers. প্রচুরসংখ্যক

nun (**nuns**) *n* A **nun** is a member of a female religious community. সন্ন্যাসিনী

nurse (**nurses**) *n* A **nurse** is a person whose job is to care for people who are ill. সেবিকা

nursery (**nurseries**) *n* A **nursery** is a place where children who are not old enough to go to school are looked after. শিশু-আলয়

nursery rhyme (**nursery rhymes**) *n* A **nursery rhyme** is a traditional poem or song for young children. শিশু ছড়া

nursery school (**nursery schools**) *n* A **nursery school** is a school for very young children. শিশু বিদ্যালয়

nursing home (**nursing homes**) *n* A **nursing home** is a private hospital for old people. আরোগ্য-নিকেতন

nut (**nuts**) *n* A **nut** is a small piece of metal with a hole through which you put a bolt. Nuts and bolts are used to hold things together such as pieces of machinery. নাট
▷ *n* The firm shelled fruit of some trees and bushes are called **nuts**. বাদাম

or come into contact with nuts. বাদামের অ্যালার্জি

nutmeg *n* **Nutmeg** is a spice made from the seed of a tree that grows in hot countries. Nutmeg is usually used to flavour sweet food. জায়ফল

nutrient (**nutrients**) *n* **Nutrients** are chemical substances that people and animals need from food and plants need from soil. পুষ্টিদায়ক

nutrition *n* **Nutrition** is the process of taking and absorbing nutrients from food. পুষ্টি

nutritious *adj* **Nutritious** food contains the proteins, vitamins, and minerals which help your body to be healthy. পুষ্টিকর

nutter (**nutters**) *n* If you refer to someone as a **nutter**, you mean that they are mad or that their behaviour is very strange. (*informal*) উন্মত্ত

nylon *n* **Nylon** is a strong, flexible, artificial material. নাইলন

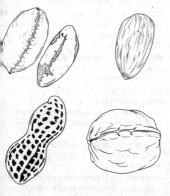

nut allergy (**nut allergies**) *n* If you have a **nut allergy**, you become ill if you eat nuts

O

oak (oaks) n An oak is a large tree with strong, hard wood. ওক গাছ

oar (oars) n Oars are long poles with flat ends which are used for rowing a boat. বৈঠা

oasis (oases) n An oasis is a small area in a desert where water and plants are found. মরুদ্যান

oath (oaths) n An oath is a formal promise. শপথ

oatmeal n Oatmeal is a kind of flour made by crushing oats. ওটমিল

oats npl Oats are a cereal crop or its grains, used for making porridge or feeding animals. জই

obedient adj An obedient person or animal does what they are told to do. বাধ্য

obese adj Someone who is obese is extremely fat. স্থূল

obey (obeys, obeying, obeyed) v If you obey a rule, instruction, or person, you do what you are told to do. মান্য করা

obituary (obituaries) n Someone's obituary is an account of their character and achievements which is published shortly after they have died. শোকসংবাদ

object (objects) n An object is anything that has a fixed shape or form and that is not alive. বস্তু

objection (objections) n If you make an objection to something, you say that you do not like it or agree with it. আপত্তি

objective (objectives) n Your objective is what you are trying to achieve. উদ্দেশ্য

oblong (oblongs) adj An oblong is a shape which has two long sides and two short sides and in which all the angles are right angles. আয়তাকার

obnoxious adj If you describe someone as obnoxious, you think that they are very unpleasant. জঘন্য

oboe (oboes) n An oboe is a musical instrument shaped like a tube which you play by blowing through a double reed in the top end. একপ্রকার বাদ্যযন্ত্র

observant adj Someone who is observant pays a lot of attention to things and notices more about them than most people do. পর্যবেক্ষণশীল

observatory (observatories) n An observatory is a building with a large telescope from which scientists study the stars and planets. পর্যবেক্ষণাগার

observe (observes, observing, observed) vt If you observe someone or something, you watch them carefully. নজর করা

observer (observers) n An observer is someone who sees or notices something. পর্যবেক্ষক

obsessed adj If someone is obsessed with a person or thing, they keep thinking about them and find it difficult to think about anything else. জর্জরিত

obsession (obsessions) *n* If you say that someone has an **obsession** with someone or something, you feel they are spending too much of their time thinking about that person or thing. আবেশ

obsolete *adj* Something that is **obsolete** is no longer needed because a better thing now exists. অচল

obstacle (obstacles) *n* An **obstacle** is something which makes it difficult for you to go forward or do something. বাধা

obstinate *adj* If you describe someone as **obstinate**, you are critical of them because they are very determined to do what they want, and refuse to be persuaded to do something else. জেদি

obstruct (obstructs, obstructing, obstructed) *vt* To **obstruct** someone or something means to block their path, making it difficult for them to move forward. বাধার সৃষ্টি করা

obtain (obtains, obtaining, obtained) *vt* To **obtain** something means to get it or achieve it. (*formal*) জোগাড় করা

obvious *adj* If something is **obvious**, it is easy to see or understand. সুস্পষ্ট

obviously *adv* You use **obviously** when you are stating something that you expect your listener to know already. সুস্পষ্টই

occasion (occasions) *n* An **occasion** is a time when something happens. ঘটনাকাল

occasional *adj* **Occasional** means happening sometimes, but not regularly or often. কখনও সখনও

occasionally *adv* **Occasionally** means from time to time. মাঝে মধ্যে

occupation (occupations) *n* Your **occupation** is your job or profession. পেশা ⊳ *n* The **occupation** of a country is its invasion and control by a foreign army. শক্তিবলে এলাকা দখল

occupy (occupies, occupying, occupied) *vt* The people who **occupy** a building or place are the people who live or work there. বাস করা

occur (occurs, occurring, occurred) *vi* When an event **occurs**, it happens. ঘটা

occurrence (occurrences) *n* An **occurrence** is something that happens. (*formal*) ঘটনা

ocean (oceans) *n* The **ocean** is the sea. মহাসমুদ্র

Oceania *n* **Oceania** is the islands of the central and South Pacific, including Melanesia, Micronesia, and Polynesia. ওশেনিয়া

October (Octobers) *n* **October** is the tenth month of the year in the Western calendar. অক্টোবর মাস

octopus (octopuses) *n* An **octopus** is a sea creature with eight tentacles. অক্টোপাস

odd (odder, oddest) *adj* If something is **odd**, it is strange or unusual. অস্বাভাবিক ⊳ *adj* You say that two things are **odd** when they do not belong to the same set or pair. বিজোড় ⊳ *adj* **Odd** numbers, such as three and seventeen, are numbers that cannot be divided by the number two. বিজোড়

odour (odours) *n* An **odour** is a smell, especially one that is unpleasant. দুর্গন্ধ

of *prep* You use **of** to show that one thing belongs to another. এর …*the holiday homes of the rich.* ⊳ *prep* You use **of** to talk about amounts. পরিমাণ *A glass of milk.* ⊳ *prep* You use **of** to mean **about**. সম্বন্ধে *He was dreaming of her.*

off *prep* If you take something **off** another thing, it is no longer on it. বিছিন্ন করা *He took his feet off the desk.* ⊳ *adv* When something

O

that uses electricity is **off**, it is not using electricity. বন্ধ করা

offence (**offences**) *n* An **offence** is a crime. অপরাধ

offend (**offends, offending, offended**) *vt* If you **offend** someone, you upset or embarrass them. অস্বস্তিতে ফেলা

offensive *adj* Something that is **offensive** upsets or embarrasses people because it is rude or insulting. অস্বস্তিকর

offer (**offers, offering, offered**) *n* An **offer** is something that someone says they will give you or do for you. প্রস্তাব ▷ *vt* If you **offer** something to someone, you ask them if they would like to have it or to use it. প্রস্তাব দেওয়া

office (**offices**) *n* An **office** is a room or a part of a building where people work sitting at desks. অফিস

office hours *npl* **Office hours** are the times when an office or similar place is open for business. অফিসের সময়

officer (**officers**) *n* In the armed forces, an **officer** is a person in a position of authority. অফিসার

official *adj* Something that is **official** is approved by the government or by someone else in authority. অফিস-সংক্রান্ত

off-peak *adv* If things are available **off-peak**, they are available at a time when there is less demand for them, so they are cheaper than usual. মন্দার সময়

off-season *adj* If something is **off-season** it relates to the time of the year when not many people go on vacation and when things such as hotels and plane tickets are often cheaper. মন্দার সময় ▷ If something happens **off-season** it happens at the time of the year when not many people go on vacation and when things such as hotels and plane tickets are often cheaper. মন্দার সময় *Visiting hours are more flexible off-season.*

offside *adj* In games such as football or hockey, when an attacking player is **offside**,

they have broken the rules by being nearer to the goal than a defending player when the ball is passed to them. অফসাইড

often *adv* If something happens **often**, it happens many times or much of the time. প্রায়ই

oil (**oils, oiling, oiled**) *n* Oil is a smooth thick liquid used as a fuel and for lubricating machines. Oil is found underground. তেল ▷ *vt* If you **oil** something, you put oil onto it or into it in order to make it work smoothly or to protect it. তেল দেওয়া

oil refinery (**oil refineries**) *n* An **oil refinery** is a factory where oil is refined. তৈল শোধনাগার

oil rig (**oil rigs**) *n* An **oil rig** is a structure on land or in the sea that is used when getting oil from the ground. তেল তোলবার পাটাতন ও যন্ত্রপাতি

oil slick (**oil slicks**) *n* An **oil slick** is a layer of oil that floats on the sea or on a lake. It is formed when oil accidentally spills out of a ship or container. ভাসমান তেলের আস্তরণ

oil well (**oil wells**) *n* An **oil well** is a deep hole which is made in order to get oil out of the ground. তৈলকূপ

ointment (**ointments**) *n* An **ointment** is a smooth thick substance that is put on sore skin or a wound to help it heal. মলম

OK! *excl* You can say '**OK!**' to show that you agree to something. ঠিক আছে

okay *adj* If you say that something is **okay**, you find it satisfactory or acceptable. (*informal*) ঠিকঠাক ▷ *excl* You can say '**Okay!**' to show that you agree to something. সম্মতিদান

old (**older, oldest**) *adj* An **old** person is someone who has lived for a long time. বয়স্ক ▷ *adj* An **old** thing is something that somebody made a long time ago. পুরানো

old-age pensioner (**old-age pensioners**) *n* An **old-age pensioner** is a person who is old enough to receive a pension from their employer or the government. পেনশনভোগী

old-fashioned adj Something that is **old-fashioned** is no longer used, done, or believed by most people, because it has been replaced by something that is more modern. পুরানো আমলের

olive (**olives**) n **Olives** are small green or black fruit with a bitter taste. অলিভ ▷ n An **olive** or an **olive tree** is a tree on which olives grow. অলিভ গাছ

olive oil (**olive oils**) n **Olive oil** is edible oil obtained by pressing olives. অলিভ তেল

Oman n **Oman** is a country in south-east Arabia, on the Gulf of Oman and the Arabian Sea. ওমান

omelette (**omelettes**) n An **omelette** is a food made by beating eggs and cooking them in a flat pan. ওমলেট

on adv When something that uses electricity is **on**, it is using electricity. চালু ▷ prep If someone or something is **on** a surface, it is resting there. ওপরে There was a large box on the table.

on behalf of n If you do something **on behalf of** someone, you do it for that person as their representative. কারোর পক্ষে

once adv If something happens **once**, it happens one time only. একবার

one num **One** is the number 1. এক ▷ pron You can use **one** to refer to the first of two or more things. আরেকজন One of the twins was thinner than the other.

one-off (**one-offs**) n A **one-off** is something that is made or happens only once. একবারের জন্য

one's det You use **one's** to show that something belongs to people in general. কারোর নিজের It is natural to want to care for one's family and children.

oneself pron Speakers or writers use **oneself** to say things about themselves and about other people. নিজের To work, one must have time to oneself.

onion (**onions**) n An **onion** is a small round vegetable. It is white with a brown skin, and has a strong smell and taste. পিঁয়াজ

online adj If you are **online**, your computer is connected to the Internet. অনলাইন ▷ adv If you do something **online**, you do it while connected to a computer or the Internet. অনলাইনে

onlooker (**onlookers**) n An **onlooker** is someone who watches an event take place but does not take part in it. দর্শক

only adj If you talk about the **only** thing or person, you mean that there are no others. কেবলমাত্র ▷ adv You use **only** when you are saying how small or short something is. কেবলমাত্র ▷ adj If you are an **only** child, you have no brothers or sisters. একমাত্র

on time adj If you are **on time**, you are not late. সময়ে

onto prep If something moves **onto** a surface, it moves to a place on that surface. কিছুর ওপরে The cat climbed onto her lap. ▷ prep When you get **onto** a bus, train, or plane, you enter it. কিছুর মধ্যে He got onto the plane.

open (**opens, opening, opened**) adj You use **open** to describe something which has been opened. উন্মুক্ত ▷ v When you **open** something, or when it **opens**, you move it or it moves so that it is no longer closed. খোলা ▷ v When a shop or office **opens**, people are able to go in. খোলা

opening hours npl **Opening hours** are the times during which a shop, bank, library, or bar is open for business. খোলা থাকার সময়

opera (**operas**) n An **opera** is a musical entertainment. It is like a play, but most of the words are sung. অপেরা

operate (**operates, operating, operated**) v If you **operate** a business or organization, you work to keep it running properly. If a business or organization **operates**, it carries out its work. চালনা করা ▷ vi When surgeons **operate** on a patient, they cut open the patient's body in order to remove, replace, or repair a diseased or damaged part. অস্ত্রোপচার করা

operating theatre (operating theatres)
n An **operating theatre** is a room in
a hospital where surgeons carry out
operations. অস্ত্রোপচার কক্ষ

operation (operations) n An **operation**
is a highly organized activity that involves
many people doing different things. উদ্যোগ
▷ n If a patient has an **operation**, a surgeon
cuts open their body in order to remove,
replace, or repair a diseased or damaged
part. অস্ত্রোপচার

operator (operators) n An **operator** is a
person who works at a telephone exchange
or on the switchboard of an office or hotel.
অপারেটর

opinion (opinions) n Your **opinion** about
something is what you think or believe
about it. মতামত

opinion poll (opinion polls) n An **opinion
poll** involves asking people for their
opinion on a particular subject, especially
one concerning politics. জনসমীক্ষা

opponent (opponents) n A politician's
opponents are other politicians who
belong to a different party or have different
aims or policies. বিরোধী পক্ষ

opportunity (opportunities) n An
opportunity is a situation in which it is
possible for you to do something that you
want to do. সুযোগ

oppose (opposes, opposing, opposed)
vt If you **oppose** someone or their plans or
ideas, you disagree with what they want to
do and try to prevent them from doing it.
বিরোধিতা করা

opposed adj If you are **opposed** to
something, you disagree with it or
disapprove of it. বিরোধী

opposing adj **Opposing** ideas or
tendencies are totally different from each
other. বিরোধিতামূলক

opposite adj The **opposite** side or part of
something is the side or part that is furthest
away from you. বিপরীত ▷ adv If one thing
is **opposite** another, it is facing it. মুখোমুখি

▷ prep If one thing is **opposite** another, it
is across from it. সামনাসামনি ▷ adj If things
are **opposite**, they are as different as they
can be. বিপরীত

opposition n **Opposition** is strong, angry,
or violent disagreement and disapproval.
বিরোধিতা

optician (opticians) n An **optician** is
someone whose job involves testing
people's eyesight and making and selling
glasses and contact lenses. চশমা-বিক্রেতা

optimism n **Optimism** is the feeling of
being hopeful about the future or about the
success of something. আশাবাদ

optimist (optimists) n An **optimist** is
someone who is hopeful about the future.
আশাবাদী

optimistic adj Someone who is **optimistic**
is hopeful about the future or about the
success of something. আশাপ্রদ

option (options) n An **option** is one of
two or more things that you can choose
between. বিকল্প

optional adj If something is **optional**, you
can choose whether or not you do it or have
it. ঐচ্ছিক

opt out v If you **opt out** of something, you
choose not to be involved in it. স্বেচ্ছায় সরে
আসা More and more people are opting out of
the urban lifestyle.

or conj You use **or** to show what you can
choose or what is possible. অথবা You can
have tea or coffee.

oral (orals) adj **Oral** is used to describe
things that involve speaking rather than
writing. মৌখিক ▷ n An **oral** is an examination,
especially in a foreign language, that is
spoken rather than written. মৌখিক

orange (oranges) n **Orange** is a colour
between red and yellow. কমলারঙ ▷ n An
orange is a round fruit with a thick skin and
lots of juice. কমলালেবু

orange juice (orange juices) n **Orange
juice** is the liquid that can be obtained from
an orange and drunk. কমলালেবুর রস

orchard (**orchards**) *n* An **orchard** is an area of land on which fruit trees are grown. ফলের বাগান

orchestra (**orchestras**) *n* An **orchestra** is a large group of musicians who play a variety of different instruments together. অর্কেস্ট্রা

orchid (**orchids**) *n* An **orchid** is a plant with brightly coloured, unusually shaped flowers. অর্কিড

ordeal (**ordeals**) *n* An **ordeal** is an extremely unpleasant and difficult experience. কঠিন পরীক্ষা

order (**orders, ordering, ordered**) *n* If someone gives you an **order**, they tell you to do something. আদেশ ▷ *vt* If you **order** someone to do something, you tell them to do it. আদেশ দেওয়া

order form (**order forms**) *n* An **order form** is a document filled in by customers when ordering goods. অর্ডার ফর্ম

ordinary *adj* **Ordinary** people or things are not special or different in any way. সাধারণ

oregano *n* **Oregano** is a herb that is used in cooking. ওরেগ্যানো

organ (**organs**) *n* An **organ** is a large musical instrument with pipes of different lengths through which air is forced. It has keys and pedals rather like a piano, and is often found in a church. অর্গান ▷ *n* An **organ** is a part of your body that has a particular purpose or function, for example your heart or your lungs. অঙ্গ

organic *adj* **Organic** food is grown without using chemicals. জৈব

organism (**organisms**) *n* An **organism** is a living thing. ক্ষুদ্রাতিক্ষুদ্র প্রাণী

organization (**organizations**) *n* An **organization** is an official group of people, for example a business or a club. সংস্থা

organize (**organizes, organizing, organized**) *vt* If you **organize** an activity or event, you make all the arrangements for it. আয়োজন করা

Orient *n* The eastern part of Asia is sometimes referred to as the **Orient**. (*literary, old-fashioned*) পূর্ব এশিয়া

oriental *adj* You use **oriental** to talk about things that come from places in eastern Asia. পূর্ব এশিয়া সম্পর্কিত

origin (**origins**) *n* You can refer to the beginning, cause, or source of something as its **origin** or its **origins**. উদ্ভব

original *adj* You use **original** to refer to something that existed at the beginning of a process or activity, or the characteristics that something had when it first existed. মৌলিক

originally *adv* When you say what happened or was the case **originally**, you are saying what happened or was the case when something began or came into existence, often to contrast it with what happened later. গোড়াতে

ornament (**ornaments**) *n* An **ornament** is an attractive object that you display in your home or garden. অলংকার

orphan (**orphans**) *n* An **orphan** is a child whose parents are dead. অনাথ

ostrich (**ostriches**) *n* An **ostrich** is a very large, long-necked African bird that cannot fly. উটপাখি

other *adj* **Other** people or things are different people or things. অন্যান্য

otherwise *adv* You use **otherwise** when stating the general condition or quality of something, when you are also mentioning an exception to this. অন্যভাবে ▷ *conj* You use **otherwise** after stating a situation or fact, to say what the result or consequence would be if this situation or fact was not the case. না হলে *I'm lucky that I'm interested in school work; otherwise I'd go mad.* ▷ *adv* You use **otherwise** to say what the result would be if things were different. অন্যথায়

otter (otters) *n* An **otter** is a small animal with brown fur, short legs, and a long tail. Otters swim well and eat fish. ভোঁদড়

ought *vt* If someone **ought to** do something, it is the right thing to do. উচিত

ounce (ounces) *n* An **ounce** is a unit of weight. There are sixteen ounces in a pound and one ounce is equal to 28.35 grams. আউন্স

our *det* You use **our** to show that something belongs to you and one or more other people. আমাদের *Our house is near the school.*

ours *pron* You use **ours** when you are talking about something that belongs to you and one or more other people. আমাদের *That car is ours.*

ourselves *pron* You use **ourselves** when you are talking about yourself and one or more other people. আমাদের নিজেদের *We sat by the fire to keep ourselves warm.* ▷ *pron* 'We did it **ourselves**' means that you and one or more other people did it without anymore help. আমরা নিজেরা *We built the house ourselves.*

out *adj* If a light is **out**, it is no longer shining. চলে যাওয়া ▷ *adv* If you are **out**, you are not at home. বাইরে ▷ *prep* If you go **out** of a place, you leave it. বাইরে বেরিয়ে আসা *She ran out of the house.*

outbreak (outbreaks) *n* An **outbreak** of something unpleasant is a sudden occurrence of it. প্রকোপ

outcome (outcomes) *n* The **outcome** of an action or process is the result of it. ফলাফল

outdoor *adj* **Outdoor** activities or things take place or are used outside, rather than in a building. বহিঃস্থ

outdoors *adv* If something happens **outdoors**, it happens outside in the fresh air rather than in a building. বহিরঙ্গনে

outfit (outfits) *n* An **outfit** is a set of clothes. পোষাক

outgoing *adj* **Outgoing** things such as planes, mail, and passengers are leaving or being sent somewhere. বহিৰ্গামী

outing (outings) *n* An **outing** is a short enjoyable trip, usually with a group of people, away from your home, school, or place of work. আনন্দভ্ৰমণ

outline (outlines) *n* An **outline** is a general explanation or description of something. প্রান্তরেখা

outlook (outlooks) *n* Your **outlook** is your general attitude towards life. দৃষ্টিভঙ্গি

out of date *adj* Something that is **out of date** is old-fashioned and no longer useful. পুরানো

out-of-doors *adv* When you are **out-of-doors**, you are not inside a building, but in the open air. রাস্তায়

outrageous *adj* If you describe something as **outrageous**, you are emphasizing that it is unacceptable or very shocking. সাংঘাতিক

outset *n* If something happens at the **outset** of an event, process, or period of time, it happens at the beginning of it. If something happens from the **outset**, it happens from the beginning and continues to happen. প্রারম্ভ

outside (outsides) *adj* An **outside** thing surrounds another thing. বাইরের ▷ *adv* If you are **outside**, you are not in a building. বাইরে ▷ *n* The **outside** of something is the part that covers the rest of it. বাইরের দিক ▷ *prep* If you are **outside** something or somewhere, you are not inside it. বাইরের দিক *The man was waiting outside a shop.*

outsize adj **Outsize** or **outsized** things are much larger than usual or much larger than you would expect. বেঢপ

outskirts npl **The outskirts** of a city or town are the parts that are farthest from its centre. শহরতলি

outspoken adj If you are **outspoken**, you give your opinions about things openly, even if they shock people. স্পষ্টভাষী

outstanding adj If you describe a person or their work as **outstanding**, you think that they are remarkable and impressive. অসামান্য

oval adj **Oval** things have a shape that is like a circle but is wider in one direction than the other. ডিম্বাকৃতি

ovary (**ovaries**) n A woman's **ovaries** are the two organs in her body that produce eggs. ডিম্বাশয়

oven (**ovens**) n An **oven** is a cooker or part of a cooker that is like a box with a door. You cook food inside an oven. আভেন

oven glove (**oven gloves**) n An **oven glove** is a glove made of thick material, used for holding hot dishes from an oven. আভেন-দস্তানা

ovenproof adj An **ovenproof** dish is one that has been specially made to be used in an oven without being damaged by the heat. আভেন-নিরোধী

over adj If something is **over**, it has finished. শেষ ▷ prep If one thing is **over** another thing, the first thing is above or higher than the second thing. ওপরে *There was a lamp over the table.*

overall adv You use **overall** to indicate that you are talking about a situation in general or about the whole of something. সামগ্রিক

overalls npl **Overalls** consist of a single piece of clothing that combines trousers and a jacket. You wear overalls over your clothes in order to protect them while you are working. ডাংরি জাতীয় পোশাক

overcast adj If it is **overcast**, or if the sky or the day is **overcast**, the sky is completely covered with cloud and there is not much light. মেঘাচ্ছন্ন

overcharge (**overcharges**, **overcharging**, **overcharged**) vt If someone **overcharges** you, they charge you too much for their goods or services. বেশি পয়সা নেওয়া

overcoat (**overcoats**) n An **overcoat** is a thick warm coat. ওভারকোট

overcome (**overcomes**, **overcoming**, **overcame**) vt If you **overcome** a problem or a feeling, you successfully deal with it and control it. পরাজিত করা

overdone adj If food is **overdone**, it has been spoiled by being cooked for too long. বেশি করে ফেলা

overdraft (**overdrafts**) n If you have an **overdraft**, you have spent more money than you have in your bank account. গচ্ছিত টাকার পরিমাণের থেকে বেশি টাকা তোলা

overdrawn adj If you are **overdrawn** or if your bank account is **overdrawn**, you have spent more money than you have in your account, and so you are in debt to the bank. গচ্ছিত টাকার পরিমাণের থেকে বেশি টাকা তোলা

overdue adj If you say that a change or an event is **overdue**, you mean that it should have happened before now. বিলম্বিত

overestimate (**overestimates**, **overestimating**, **overestimated**) vt If you **overestimate** someone or something, you think that they are better, bigger, or more important than they really are. অতি মূল্যায়ন করা

overhead projector (**overhead projectors**) n An **overhead projector** is a machine that has a light inside it and makes the writing or pictures on a sheet of plastic appear on a screen or wall. The abbreviation 'OHP' is also used. ওভারহেড প্রোজেক্টর

overheads npl The **overheads** of a business are its regular and essential expenses. স্থির ব্যয়

overlook (**overlooks**, **overlooking**, **overlooked**) vt If a building or window **overlooks** a place, you can see the place from the building or window. উঁচু থেকে কোন কিছু দেখা

overrule (**overrules, overruling, overruled**) *vt* If someone in authority **overrules** a person or their decision, they officially decide that the decision is incorrect or not valid. খারিজ করা

overseas *adv* If something happens or exists **overseas**, it happens or exists abroad. বিদেশ

oversight (**oversights**) *n* In business, **oversight** of a system or process is the responsibility for making sure that it works efficiently and correctly. তত্ত্বাবধান ▷ *n* If there has been an **oversight**, someone has forgotten to do something which they should have done. অনিচ্ছাকৃত ভুল

oversleep (**oversleeps, oversleeping, overslept**) *vi* If you **oversleep**, you sleep longer than you should have done. বেশি সময় ধরে ঘুমানো

overtake (**overtakes, overtaking, overtook, overtaken**) *v* If you **overtake** or **overtake** a moving vehicle or person, you pass them because you are moving faster than they are. ওভারটেক

overtime *n* **Overtime** is time that you spend doing your job in addition to your normal working hours. বাড়তি সময়

overweight *adj* Someone who is **overweight** weighs more than is considered healthy or attractive. বাড়তি ওজন

owe (**owes, owing, owed**) *vt* If you **owe** money to someone, they have lent it to you and you have not yet paid it back. ধার করা

owing to *prep* If something is **owing to** another thing, it is a result of that thing. কারণে *He was out of work owing to an injury.*

owl (**owls**) *n* An **owl** is a bird with large eyes which hunts small animals at night. পেঁচা

own (**owns, owning, owned**) *adj* You use **own** to say that something belongs to you. নিজের ▷ *vt* If you **own** something, it is your property. মালিকানা লাভ করা

owner (**owners**) *n* The **owner** of something is the person to whom it belongs. মালিক

own up *v* If you **own up** to something wrong that you have done, you admit that you did it. স্বীকার করা *Own up to your failure, but don't dwell on it.*

oxygen *n* **Oxygen** is a colourless gas in the air which is needed by all plants and animals. অক্সিজেন

oyster (**oysters**) *n* An **oyster** is a large flat shellfish which produces pearls. অয়েস্টার

ozone *n* **Ozone** is a form of oxygen. There is a layer of ozone high above the earth's surface. ওজোন

ozone layer *n* **The ozone layer** is the area high above the Earth's surface that protects living things from the harmful effects of the sun. ওজোনের স্তর

p

PA (PAs) *abbr* A **PA** is a person who does office work and administrative work for someone. **PA** is an abbreviation for 'personal assistant'. পি এ

pace (paces) *n* The **pace** of something is the speed at which it happens or is done. গতি

pacemaker (pacemakers) *n* A **pacemaker** is a device that is placed inside someone's body in order to help their heart beat in the right way. পেসমেকার

Pacific Ocean *n* **The Pacific Ocean** is a very large sea to the west of North and South America, and to the east of Asia and Australia. প্রশান্ত মহাসাগর

pack (packs, packing, packed) *n* A **pack** of things is a collection of them that is sold or given together in a box or bag. প্যাক ▷ *vt* When you **pack** a bag, you put clothes and other things into it, because you are leaving a place or going on holiday. ছোট প্যাকেট

package (packages) *n* A **package** is a small parcel. বান্ডিল

packaging *n* **Packaging** is the container or wrappings that something is sold in. মোড়ক

packed *adj* A place that is **packed** is very crowded. ভিড়ে ঠাসা

packed lunch (packed lunches) *n* A **packed lunch** is food, for example, sandwiches, which you take to work, to school, or on a trip and eat as your lunch. প্যাক করা খাবার

packet (packets) *n* A **packet** is a small box, bag, or envelope in which a quantity of something is sold. মোড়ক

pad (pads) *n* A **pad** is a thick flat piece of a material such as cloth or foam rubber. প্যাড

paddle (paddles, paddling, paddled) *n* A **paddle** is a short oar. You use it to move a small boat through water. দাঁড় ▷ *vt* If someone **paddles** a boat, they move it using a paddle. দাঁড় চালানো ▷ *vi* If you **paddle**, you walk in shallow water. অগভীর জলে চলা

paddling pool (paddling pools) *n* A **paddling pool** is a shallow artificial pool for children to paddle in. প্যাডেলিং পুল

padlock (padlocks) *n* A **padlock** is a lock which is used for fastening two things together. তালা

page (pages, paging, paged) *n* A **page** is a side of one of the pieces of paper in a book, magazine, or newspaper. পৃষ্ঠা ▷ *v* If someone **is paged**, they receive a message over a speaker that someone is trying to contact them. পেজ করা

pager (pagers) *n* A **pager** is a small electronic device which gives you a message when someone is trying to contact you. পেজার

paid *adj* **Paid** means to do with the money a worker receives from his or her employer. You can say, for example, that someone is well **paid** when they receive a lot of money for the work that they do. সবেতন

pail (**pails**) *n* A **pail** is a bucket, usually made of metal or wood. (*old-fashioned*) হাতওয়ালা বালতি

pain (**pains**) *n* If you feel **pain**, or if you are in **pain**, you feel great discomfort in a part of your body, because of illness or an injury. ব্যথা

painful *adj* If a part of your body is **painful**, it hurts. বেদনাদায়ক

painkiller (**painkillers**) *n* A **painkiller** is a drug which reduces or stops physical pain. বেদনা উপশমকারী

paint (**paints, painting, painted**) *n* **Paint** is a liquid used to decorate buildings, or to make a picture. রঙ ▷ *v* If you **paint** a wall or a door, you cover it with **paint**. রঙ করা ▷ *v* If you **paint** something on a piece of paper or cloth, you make a picture of it using **paint**. রঙ করা

paintbrush (**paintbrushes**) *n* A **paintbrush** is a brush which you use for painting. রঙ করার তুলি

painter (**painters**) *n* A **painter** is an artist who paints pictures. চিত্রকর

painting (**paintings**) *n* A **painting** is a picture which someone has painted. চিত্র

pair (**pairs**) *n* A **pair** of things are two things of the same size and shape that are intended to be used together. জোড়া

Pakistan *n* **Pakistan** is a republic in South Asia, on the Arabian Sea. পাকিস্তান

Pakistani (**Pakistanis**) *adj* **Pakistani** means belonging or relating to Pakistan, or to its people or culture. পাকিস্তান দেশীয় ▷ *n* A **Pakistani** is a Pakistani citizen, or a person of Pakistani origin. পাকিস্তানী

pal (**pals**) *n* Your **pals** are your friends. (*informal, old-fashioned*) বন্ধু

palace (**palaces**) *n* A **palace** is a very large splendid house, especially the home of a king, queen, or president. প্রাসাদ

pale (**paler, palest**) *adj* Something that is **pale** is not strong or bright in colour. ফ্যাকাসে

Palestine *n* **Palestine** is an area between the Jordan River and the Mediterranean Sea. প্যালেস্টাইন

Palestinian (**Palestinians**) *adj* **Palestinian** means belonging or relating to the region between the River Jordan and the Mediterranean Sea. প্যালেস্টাইন দেশীয় ▷ *n* A **Palestinian** is an Arab who comes from the region that used to be called Palestine. প্যালেস্টাইনের নাগরিক

palm (**palms**) *n* The **palm** of your hand is the inside part of your hand, between your fingers and your wrist. তালু ▷ n A **palm** or a **palm tree** is a tree that grows in hot countries. It has long leaves at the top, and no branches. তালগাছ

pamphlet (pamphlets) n A **pamphlet** is a very thin book with a paper cover, which gives information about something. পুস্তিকা

pan (pans) n A **pan** is a round metal container with a handle, which is used for cooking things, usually on top of a cooker. পাত্র

Panama n **Panama** is a republic in Central America. পানামা

pancake (pancakes) n A **pancake** is a thin, flat, circular piece of cooked batter that is eaten hot, often with a sweet or savoury filling. প্যানকেক

panda (pandas) n A **panda** is a large animal with black and white fur which lives in China. পান্ডা

panic (panics, panicking, panicked) n **Panic** is a strong feeling of anxiety or fear that makes you act without thinking carefully. আতঙ্ক ▷ v If you **panic**, or if someone or something **panics** you, you become anxious or afraid, and act without thinking carefully. আতঙ্কিত হওয়া

panther (panthers) n A **panther** is a large wild animal that belongs to the cat family. Panthers are usually black. চিতাবাঘ

pantomime (pantomimes) n A **pantomime** is a funny musical play for children, usually performed at Christmas. নির্বাক নাটক

pants npl **Pants** are a piece of underwear with two holes to put your legs through and elastic round the top. অন্তর্বাস

paper (papers) n **Paper** is a material that you write on or wrap things with. কাগজ ▷ n A **paper** is a newspaper. খবরের কাগজ

paperback (paperbacks) n A **paperback** is a book with a paper cover. মলাট দেওয়া বই

paperclip (paperclips) n A **paperclip** is a small piece of bent wire that is used to fasten papers together. পেপারক্লিপ

paper round (paper rounds) n A **paper round** is a job of delivering newspapers to houses along a particular route. সংবাদপত্র বিলি

paperweight (paperweights) n A **paperweight** is a small heavy object which you place on papers to prevent them from being disturbed or blown away. পেপারওয়েট

paperwork n **Paperwork** consists of the letters, reports, and records which have to be dealt with as the routine part of a job. লেখার কাজ

paprika n **Paprika** is a red powder used for flavouring meat and other food. লঙ্কাগুঁড়ো

parachute (parachutes) n A **parachute** is a device which enables a person to jump from an aircraft and float safely to the ground. It consists of a large piece of thin cloth attached to your body by strings. প্যারাসুট

parade (parades) n A **parade** is a line of people or vehicles moving together through a public place in order to celebrate an important day or event. কুচকাওয়াজ

paradise n According to some religions, **paradise** is a wonderful place where people go after they die, if they have led good lives. স্বর্গ

paraffin n **Paraffin** is a strong-smelling liquid which is used as a fuel in heaters, lamps, and engines. প্যারাফিন

paragraph (paragraphs) n A **paragraph** is a section of a piece of writing. A paragraph always begins on a new line and contains at least one sentence. অনুচ্ছেদ

Paraguay n **Paraguay** is an inland republic in South America. প্যারাগুয়ে

Paraguayan (Paraguayans) adj **Paraguayan** means of or relating to Paraguay, its people, or its culture. প্যারাগুয়ে

p

দেশীয় ▷ *n* A **Paraguayan** is a citizen of Paraguay, or a person of Paraguayan origin. প্যারাগুয়ের মানুষ

parallel *adj* **Parallel** events or situations happen at the same time as one another, or are similar to one another. সমান্তরাল

paralysed *adj* If someone or part of their body is **paralysed**, they have no feeling in their body, or in part of their body, and are unable to move. অবশ

paramedic (**paramedics**) *n* A **paramedic** is a person whose training is similar to that of a nurse and who helps to do medical work. চিকিৎসাকার্যের সহায়ক

parcel (**parcels**) *n* A **parcel** is something wrapped in paper, usually so that it can be sent to someone by post. মোড়ক

pardon (**pardons**) *excl* You say '**Pardon?**' when you want someone to repeat what they have just said because you have not heard or understood it. আরেকবার যদি বলেন ▷ *n* If someone who has been found guilty of a crime is given a **pardon**, they are officially allowed to go free and are not punished. ক্ষমা করা

parent (**parents**) *n* A **parent** is a father or mother. পিতা বা মাতা

park (**parks, parking, parked**) *n* A **park** is a place with grass and trees. People go to **parks** to take exercise or play games. পার্ক ▷ *v* When someone **parks** a car, they leave it somewhere. গাড়ি পার্ক করা

parking *n* **Parking** is the action of moving a vehicle into a place in a car park or by the side of the road where it can be left. পার্কিং

parking meter (**parking meters**) *n* A **parking meter** is a device which you have to put money into when you park in a parking space. পার্কিং মিটার

parking ticket (**parking tickets**) *n* A **parking ticket** is a piece of paper with instructions to pay a fine, and is put on your car when you have parked it somewhere illegally. পার্কিং টিকিট

parliament (**parliaments**) *n* The **parliament** of a country is the group of people who make or change its laws. সংসদ

parole *n* If a prisoner is given **parole**, he or she is released before the official end of their prison sentence and has to promise to behave well. শর্তাধীনে ছাড়া পাওয়া

parrot (**parrots**) *n* A **parrot** is a tropical bird with a curved beak and brightly coloured or grey feathers. Parrots can be kept as pets. টিয়াপাখি

parsley *n* **Parsley** is a small plant with curly leaves used for flavouring or decorating savoury food. পার্সলে

parsnip (**parsnips**) *n* A **parsnip** is a root vegetable similar in shape to a carrot. গাজর প্রজাতির সজি

part (**parts**) *n* **Part** of something is a piece or a section of it. অংশ

partial *adj* You use **partial** to refer to something that is true or exists to some extent, but is not complete or total. আংশিক

participate (**participates, participating, participated**) *vi* If you **participate** in an activity, you are involved in it with other people. অংশগ্রহণ করা

particular *adj* You use **particular** to emphasize that you are talking about one thing or one kind of thing rather than other similar ones. নির্দিষ্ট

particularly *adv* You use **particularly** to indicate that what you are saying applies especially to one thing or situation. বিশেষত

parting (**partings**) *n* **Parting** is the act of leaving a particular person or place. ছেড়ে যাওয়া

partly *adv* You use **partly** to indicate that something is true or exists to some extent, but not completely. আংশিক

partner (**partners**) *n* Your **partner** is the person you are married to or are having a long-term romantic relationship with. অংশীদার

partridge (partridges) *n* A **partridge** is a wild bird with brown feathers, a round body, and a short tail. তিতির

part-time *adj* If someone is a **part-time** worker or has a **part-time** job, they work for only part of each day or week. কিছু সময় ▷ *adv* If someone works **part-time**, they work for only part of each day or week. খণ্ডকাল

part with *v* If you **part with** something that you would prefer to keep, you give it or sell it to someone else. হাত-ছাড়া করা *Think carefully before parting with money.*

party (parties, partying, partied) *n* A **party** is a social event at which people enjoy themselves doing things such as eating or dancing. পার্টি ▷ *n* A **party** of people is a group of them doing something together, for example travelling. দল ▷ *vi* If you **party**, you enjoy yourself doing things with other people such as eating and dancing. পার্টিতে মজা করা

pass (passes, passing, passed) *n* A **pass** is a document that allows you to do something. অনুমতিপত্র ▷ *n* A **pass** is a narrow way between two mountains. সরু গিরিপথ ▷ *n* A **pass** in an examination, test, or course is a successful result in it. উত্তীর্ণ ▷ *vt* If you **pass** something to someone, you give it to them. হস্তান্তরিত করা ▷ *vt* When you **pass** someone, you go by them. অতিক্রম করা ▷ *v* If you **pass** a test, you do well. সাফল্যলাভ করা

passage (passages) *n* A **passage** is a long, narrow space between walls or fences connecting one room or place with another. বারান্দা ▷ *n* A **passage** in a book, speech, or piece of music is a section of it. রচনাংশ

passenger (passengers) *n* A **passenger** in a bus, boat, or plane is a person who is travelling in it, but who is not driving or working on it. যাত্রী

passion fruit (passion fruit) *n* A **passion fruit** is a small, round, brown fruit that is produced by certain types of tropical flower. প্যাশন ফ্রুট

passive *adj* If you describe someone as **passive**, you mean they do not take action but instead let things happen to them. নিষ্ক্রিয়

pass out *v* If you **pass out**, you faint or collapse. জ্ঞান হারানো *He felt sick and dizzy and then passed out.*

Passover *n* **Passover** is a Jewish festival beginning in March or April and lasting for seven or eight days. ইহুদিদের বাৎসরিক অনুষ্ঠান

passport (passports) *n* Your **passport** is an official document which you need to show when you enter or leave a country. পাসপোর্ট

password (passwords) *n* A **password** is a secret word or phrase that enables you to enter a place or use a computer system. পাসওয়ার্ড

past *adj* **Past** events and things happened or existed before the present time. বিগত ▷ *n* The **past** is the period of time before now. অতীত ▷ *prep* You use **past** when you are telling the time. অতিবাহিত *It was ten past eleven.* ▷ *prep* Something that is **past** a place is on the other side of it. পরে *It's just past the school there.*

pasta *n* **Pasta** is a type of food made from a mixture of flour, eggs, and water that is formed into different shapes. Spaghetti and macaroni are types of pasta. পাস্তা

paste (pastes, pasting, pasted) *n* **Paste** is a soft, wet mixture, which you can spread easily. লেই ▷ *vt* If you **paste** something on to a surface, you stick it with glue. সেঁটে দেওয়া ▷ *vt* If you **paste** words or pictures on a computer, you copy them from one place and put them somewhere new. পেস্ট

pasteurized *adj* **Pasteurized** milk, cream, or cheese has had bacteria removed from it by a special heating process to make it safer to eat or drink. পাস্তুরীকরণ

pastime (**pastimes**) *n* A **pastime** is something that you enjoy doing in your spare time. অবসর বিনোদন

pastry *n* **Pastry** is a food made of flour, fat, and water that is used for making pies and flans. কেক

patch (**patches**) *n* A **patch** on a surface is a part of it which is different in appearance from the area around it. আলাদা অংশ

patched *adj* Something that is **patched** has been mended by having a piece of material fastened over a hole. জোড়াতালি দেওয়া

paternity leave *n* If a man has **paternity leave**, his employer allows him some time off work because his child has just been born. পিতৃত্ব লাভের জন্য প্রাপ্ত ছুটি

path (**paths**) *n* A **path** is a strip of ground that people walk along. পথ

pathetic *adj* If you describe a person or animal as **pathetic**, you mean that they are sad and weak or helpless, and they make you feel very sorry for them. করুণ

patience *n* If you have **patience**, you are able to stay calm and not get annoyed, for example when something takes a long time. ধৈর্য

patient (**patients**) *adj* If you are **patient**, you don't get angry quickly. ধৈর্যশীল ▷ *n* A **patient** is someone that a nurse or a doctor is looking after. রোগী

patio (**patios**) *n* A **patio** is a paved area in a garden, where people can sit to eat or relax. বাগানে বসার স্থান

patriotic *adj* Someone who is **patriotic** loves their country and feels very loyal towards it. দেশভক্তি

patrol (**patrols**) *n* **Patrol** is the action of moving round an area or building in order to make sure that there is no trouble there. টহল দল

patrol car (**patrol cars**) *n* A **patrol car** is a police car used for patrolling streets and roads. পুলিশের গাড়ি

pattern (**patterns**) *n* A **pattern** is a particular way in which something is usually or repeatedly done. ধরণ

pause (**pauses**) *n* A **pause** is a short period when something stops before it continues again. থামা

pavement (**pavements**) *n* A **pavement** is a path with a hard surface by the side of a road. ফুটপাথ

pavilion (**pavilions**) *n* A **pavilion** is a building on the edge of a sports field where players can change their clothes and wash. খেলয়াড়দের ঘর

paw (**paws**) *n* The **paws** of an animal such as a cat, dog, or bear are its feet. থাবা

pawnbroker (**pawnbrokers**) *n* A **pawnbroker** is a person who will lend you money if you give them something that you own. The pawnbroker can sell that thing if you do not pay back the money before a certain time. বন্ধকি মহাজন

pay (**pays, paying, paid**) *n* Your **pay** is the money that you get from your employer as wages or salary. বেতন ▷ *v* When you **pay** an amount of money to someone, you give it to them because you are buying something from them or because you owe it to them. টাকা দেওয়া

payable *adj* If an amount of money is **payable**, it has to be paid or it can be paid. পরিশোধনীয়

pay back *v* If you **pay back** money that you have borrowed from someone, you give them an equal amount at a later time. টাকা ফেরত দেওয়া *He will have to pay back everything he has stolen.*

payment (**payments**) *n* **Payment** is the act of paying money to someone or of being paid. পেমেন্ট

payphone (**payphones**) *n* A **payphone** is a telephone which you need to put coins or a card in before you can make a call. Payphones are usually in public places. পেফোন

PC (**PCs**) *n* A **PC** is a computer that is used by one person at a time in a business, a school, or at home. **PC** is an abbreviation for 'personal computer'. পি সি

PDF (**PDFs**) *n* **PDF** files are computer documents which look exactly like the original documents, regardless of which software or operating system was used to create them. **PDF** is an abbreviation for 'Portable Document Format'. পি ডি এফ

peace *n* When there is **peace** in a country, it is not involved in a war. শান্তি

peaceful *adj* **Peaceful** means not involving war or violence. শান্তিপূর্ণ

peach (**peaches**) *n* A **peach** is a soft, round, juicy fruit with sweet yellow flesh and pinky-yellow skin. পীচফল

peacock (**peacocks**) *n* A **peacock** is a large bird. The male has a very large tail covered with blue and green spots, which it can spread out like a fan. ময়ূর

peak (**peaks**) *n* The **peak** of a process or activity is the point at which it is at its strongest, most successful, or most fully developed. শীর্ষ

peak hours *npl* **Peak hours** are the busiest hours, for example in traffic. অফিসের সময়

peanut (**peanuts**) *n* **Peanuts** are small nuts often eaten as a snack. চীনেবাদাম

peanut allergy (**peanut allergies**) *n* If you have a **peanut allergy**, you become ill if you eat peanuts or peanut butter, or come into contact with peanuts or peanut butter. চীনেবাদামে অ্যালার্জি

peanut butter *n* **Peanut butter** is a brown paste made out of crushed peanuts which you can spread on bread and eat. চীনেবাদাম মাখা

pear (**pears**) *n* A **pear** is a juicy fruit which is narrow at the top and wider at the bottom. It has white flesh and green or yellow skin. নাসপাতি

pearl (**pearls**) *n* A **pearl** is a hard, shiny, white, ball-shaped object which grows inside the shell of an oyster. Pearls are used for making jewellery. মুক্ত

peas *npl* **Peas** are small, round, green seeds eaten as a vegetable. মটর

peat *n* **Peat** is dark decaying plant material which is found in some cool wet regions. It can be burned as a fuel or used as compost. জলাভূমির উত্তিজ্ঞ পদার্থ

pebble (**pebbles**) *n* A **pebble** is a small stone. নুড়ি

peculiar *adj* If you describe someone or something as **peculiar**, you think that they are strange or unusual, often in an unpleasant way. বৈশিষ্ট্যসূচক

pedal (**pedals**) *n* The **pedals** on a bicycle are the two parts that you push with your feet in order to make the bicycle move. প্যাডেল

pedestrian (**pedestrians**) *n* A **pedestrian** is a person who is walking, especially in a town. পদযাত্রী

pedestrian crossing (**pedestrian crossings**) *n* A **pedestrian crossing** is a place where pedestrians can cross a street and where motorists must stop to let them cross. পথচারীদের যাওয়ার স্থান

pedestrianized *adj* A **pedestrianized** area has been made into an area that is intended for pedestrians, not vehicles. শুধু পথচারীদের জন্য করা স্থান

pedestrian precinct (**pedestrian precincts**) *n* A **pedestrian precinct** is a street or part of a town where vehicles are not allowed. শুধু পথচারীদের জন্য স্থান

pedigree *adj* A **pedigree** animal is descended from animals which have all been of a particular breed, and is therefore considered to be of good quality. উচ্চজাতের

peel (**peels, peeling, peeled**) *n* The **peel** of a fruit such as a lemon or apple is its skin. খোসা ▷ *vt* When you **peel** fruit or vegetables, you remove their skins. খোসা ছাড়ানো

peg (**pegs**) *n* A **peg** is a small hook or knob on a wall or door which is used for hanging things on. পেগ

Pekinese (**Pekineses**) *n* A **Pekinese** is a type of small dog with long hair, short legs, and a short, flat nose. ছোট্ট চীনা কুকুর

pelican (**pelicans**) *n* A **pelican** is a type of large water bird. It catches fish and keeps them in the bottom part of its beak which is shaped like a large bag. পেলিকান পাখি

pelican crossing (**pelican crossings**) *n* A **pelican crossing** is a place pedestrians can cross a busy road. They press a button at the side of the road, which operates traffic lights to stop the traffic. পেলিকান ক্রসিং

pellet (**pellets**) *n* A **pellet** is a small ball of paper, mud, lead, or other material. ক্ষুদ্র দলা

pelvis (**pelvises**) *n* Your **pelvis** is the wide curved group of bones at the level of your hips. শ্রোণী

pen (**pens**) *n* A **pen** is a writing instrument, which you use to write in ink. কলম

penalize (**penalizes, penalizing, penalized**) *vt* If someone **is penalized** for something, they are made to suffer some disadvantage because of it. দণ্ডিত করা

penalty (**penalties**) *n* A **penalty** is a punishment for doing something which is against a law or rule. সাজা

pencil (**pencils**) *n* A **pencil** is a thin wooden rod with graphite down the centre which is used for writing or drawing. পেনসিল

pencil case (**pencil cases**) *n* A **pencil case** is a small bag, etc. for holding pencils and pens. পেনসিল কেস

pencil sharpener (**pencil sharpeners**) *n* A **pencil sharpener** is a small device with a blade inside, used for making pencils sharp. পেনসিল কাটার কল

pendant (**pendants**) *n* A **pendant** is an ornament on a chain that you wear round your neck. পেনডেন্ট

penfriend (**penfriends**) *n* A **penfriend** is someone you write friendly letters to and receive letters from, although the two of you may never have met. পত্রবন্ধু

penguin (**penguins**) *n* A **penguin** is a black and white sea bird found mainly in the South Pole. Penguins cannot fly. পেঙ্গুইন

penicillin *n* **Penicillin** is a drug that kills bacteria and is used to treat infections. পেনিসিলিন

peninsula (**peninsulas**) *n* A **peninsula** is a long narrow piece of land that is joined at one part to the mainland and is almost completely surrounded by water. উপদ্বীপ

penknife (**penknives**) *n* A **penknife** is a small knife with a blade that folds back into the handle. পকেট ছুরি

penny (**pennies, pence**) *n* In Britain, a **penny** is a coin or an amount which is worth one hundredth of a pound. বৃটেনের মুদ্রা

pension (**pensions**) *n* A **pension** is a sum of money which a retired, widowed, or disabled person regularly receives from the state or from a former employer. পেনশন

pensioner (**pensioners**) *n* A **pensioner** is a person who receives a pension. পেনশনভোগী

pentathlon (**pentathlons**) *n* A **pentathlon** is an athletics competition in which each person must compete in five different events. প্রতিযোগিতাবিশেষ

penultimate *adj* The **penultimate** thing in a series is the one before the last. (*formal*) শেষের আগেরটা

people npl **People** are men, women, and children. জনগণ

pepper (**peppers**) n **Pepper** is a spice with a hot taste which you put on food. গোলমরিচ
▷ n A **pepper** is a green, red, or yellow vegetable with seeds inside it. লঙ্কা

peppermill (**peppermills**) n A **peppermill** is a machine for grinding pepper into powder. গোলমরিচ পেষার যন্ত্র

peppermint n **Peppermint** is a strong fresh-tasting flavouring that is obtained from a plant or made artificially. মেনথল

per prep You use **per** to talk about each one of something. For example, if a vehicle is travelling at 40 miles **per** hour, it travels 40 miles each hour. প্রতি Buses use much less fuel per person than cars.

per cent adv You use **per cent** to talk about amounts. For example, if an amount is 10 per cent (10%) of a larger amount, it is equal to 10 hundredths of the larger amount. শতকরা

percentage (**percentages**) n A **percentage** is a fraction of an amount expressed as a particular number of hundredths. শতাংশ

percussion n **Percussion** instruments are musical instruments that you hit, such as drums. পারকাসন

perfect adj Something that is **perfect** is as good as it can possibly be. নিখুঁত

perfection n **Perfection** is the quality of being perfect. ক্রটিহীনতা

perfectly adv You can use **perfectly** to emphasize an adjective or adverb, especially when you think the person you are talking to might doubt what you are saying. নিখুঁতভাবে

perform (**performs, performing, performed**) vt When you **perform** a task or action, you complete it. সম্পাদন করা

performance (**performances**) n A **performance** involves entertaining an audience by singing, dancing, or acting. সম্পাদিত কার্য

perfume (**perfumes**) n **Perfume** is a pleasant-smelling liquid which women put on their necks and wrists to make themselves smell nice. সুগন্ধী

perhaps adv You use **perhaps** when you are not sure about something. হয়ত

period (**periods**) n A particular **period** is a particular length of time. পর্ব

perjury n If someone who is giving evidence in a court of law commits **perjury**, they lie. মিথ্যা সাক্ষী

perm (**perms**) n If you have a **perm**, your hair is curled and treated with chemicals so that it stays curly for several months. পার্ম

permanent adj **Permanent** means lasting for ever or occurring all the time. স্থায়ী

permanently adv If something lasts or occurs **permanently**, it lasts for ever or occurs all the time. স্থায়ীভাবে

permission n If you give someone **permission** to do something, you tell them that they can do it. অনুমতি

permit (**permits**) n A **permit** is an official document allowing you to do something. অনুমতিপত্র

persecute (**persecutes, persecuting, persecuted**) vt If someone is **persecuted**, they are treated cruelly and unfairly, often because of their race or beliefs. নির্যাতন করা

persevere (**perseveres, persevering, persevered**) vi If you **persevere** with something difficult, you continue doing it and do not give up. অধ্যবসায়ী হওয়া

Persian adj Something that is **Persian** belongs to or relates to the ancient kingdom of Persia, or sometimes to the modern state of Iran. পারস্যের

persistent adj If something bad is **persistent**, it continues to exist or happen for a long time. অটল

person (**people** or **persons**) n A **person** is a man, woman, or child. ব্যক্তি

personal adj A **personal** opinion, quality, or thing belongs or relates to a particular person. ব্যক্তিগত

personal assistant (personal assistants)
n A **personal assistant** is a person who
does office work and administrative work
for someone. The abbreviation 'PA' is also
used. ব্যক্তিগত সহায়ক

personality (personalities) *n* Your
personality is your whole character and
nature. ব্যক্তিত্ব

personally *adv* You use **personally** to
emphasize that you are giving your own
opinion. ব্যক্তিগতভাবে

**personal organizer (personal
organizers)** *n* A **personal organizer** is
a book containing personal or business
information, which you can add pages to or
remove pages from to keep the information
up to date. Small computers with a
similar function are also called **personal
organizers**. পার্সোনাল অর্গানাইজার

personal stereo (personal stereos) *n* A
personal stereo is a small cassette or CD
player with very light headphones, which
people carry round so that they can listen
to music while doing something else.
ব্যক্তিগত স্টিরিও

personnel *npl* The **personnel** of an
organization are the people who work for it.
সংস্থার কর্মীবৃন্দ

perspective (perspectives) *n* A
perspective is a particular way of thinking
about something. পরিপ্রেক্ষিত

perspiration *n* **Perspiration** is the liquid
that appears on your skin when you are hot
or frightened. (*formal*) ঘাম

**persuade (persuades, persuading,
persuaded)** *vt* If you **persuade** someone
to do a particular thing, you get them to
do it, usually by convincing them that it is a
good idea. জোর করা

persuasive *adj* Someone or something
that is **persuasive** is likely to persuade
you to do or believe a particular thing.
বিশ্বাস-উৎপাদক

Peru *n* **Peru** is a republic in western South
America, on the Pacific. পেরু

Peruvian (Peruvians) *adj* **Peruvian**
means belonging or related to Peru, or
to its people or culture. পেরু দেশীয় ▷ *n* A
Peruvian is a citizen of Peru, or a person of
Peruvian origin. পেরুর অধিবাসী

pessimist (pessimists) *n* A **pessimist** is
someone who thinks that bad things are
going to happen. নৈরাশ্যবাদী

pessimistic *adj* Someone who is
pessimistic thinks that bad things are
going to happen. হতাশাবাদ সংক্রান্ত

pest (pests) *n* A **pest** is an insect or small
animal which damages crops or food
supplies. পোকা

pester (pesters, pestering, pestered) *vt*
If you say that someone **is pestering** you,
you mean that they keep asking you to do
something, or keep talking to you, and you
find this annoying. জ্বালাতন করা

pesticide (pesticides) *n* **Pesticides** are
chemicals which farmers put on their crops
to kill harmful insects. পোকানাশক ওষুধ

pet (pets) *n* A **pet** is an animal that you
keep in your home to give you company
and pleasure. পোষ্য

petition (petitions) *n* A **petition** is a
document signed by a lot of people which
asks for some official action to be taken.
আর্জি

petrified *adj* If you are **petrified**, you are
extremely frightened. অত্যন্ত ভয়ার্ত

petrol *n* **Petrol** is a liquid used as a fuel for
motor vehicles. পেট্রল

petrol station (petrol stations) *n* A **petrol
station** is a garage by the side of the road
where petrol is sold and put into vehicles.
পেট্রল স্টেশন

petrol tank (petrol tanks) *n* The **petrol
tank** in a motor vehicle is the container for
petrol. পেট্রল ট্যাঙ্ক

pewter *n* **Pewter** is a grey metal made by
mixing tin and lead. মিশ্রিত দস্তা

pharmacist (pharmacists) *n* A
pharmacist is a person who is qualified to
prepare and sell medicines. ঔষধ প্রস্তুতকারক

pharmacy (**pharmacies**) n A **pharmacy** is a place where medicines are sold or given out. ঔষধালয়

PhD (**PhDs**) n A **PhD** is a degree awarded to people who have done advanced research. **PhD** is an abbreviation for 'Doctor of Philosophy'. পি এইচ ডি

pheasant (**pheasants, pheasant**) n A **pheasant** is a bird with a long tail. পক্ষীবিশেষ

philosophy n **Philosophy** is the study or creation of theories about basic things such as the nature of existence or how people should live. দর্শনশাস্ত্র

phobia (**phobias**) n A **phobia** is an unreasonably strong fear of something. ভীতি

phone (**phones, phoning, phoned**) n A **phone** is a piece of equipment that you use to talk to someone in another place. ফোন ▷ v When you **phone** someone, you dial their phone number and speak to them by phone. ফোন করা

phone back v If you **phone** someone **back**, you telephone them again or in return for a telephone call that they have made to you. ফোনের জবাবী ফোন I'll phone you back later.

phone bill (**phone bills**) n A **phone bill** is an account or bill for the charges for a telephone and line and for calls made from it. ফোনের বিল

phonebook (**phonebooks**) n A **phonebook** is a book that contains an alphabetical list of the names, addresses, and telephone numbers of the people in a town or area. ফোনে নামের তালিকা

phonebox (**phoneboxes**) n A **phonebox** is a small shelter outdoors or in a building in which there is a public telephone. ফোনবক্স

phone call (**phone calls**) n If you make a **phone call**, you dial someone's phone number and speak to them by phone. ফোনকল

phonecard (**phonecards**) n A **phonecard** is a plastic card that you can use instead of money in some public telephones. ফোনকার্ড

phone number (**phone numbers**) n Your **phone number** is the number that other people dial when they want to talk to you on the telephone. ফোন নম্বর

photo (**photos**) n A **photo** is a picture that is made using a camera. ফটো

photo album (**photo albums**) n A **photo album** is a book in which you keep photographs that you have collected. ফটো অ্যালবাম

photocopier (**photocopiers**) n A **photocopier** is a machine which quickly copies documents by photographing them. ফটোকপির যন্ত্র

photocopy (**photocopies, photocopying, photocopied**) n A **photocopy** is a document made by a photocopier. ফটোকপি ▷ vt If you **photocopy** a document, you make a copy of it with a photocopier. ফটোকপি করা

photograph (**photographs, photographing, photographed**) n A **photograph** is a picture that is made using a camera. ছবি ▷ vt When you **photograph** someone or something, you use a camera to obtain a picture of them. ছবি তোলা

photographer (**photographers**) n A **photographer** is someone who takes photographs, especially as their job. চিত্রগ্রাহক

photography n **Photography** is the skill, job, or process of producing photographs. আলোকচিত্র বিদ্যা

phrase (**phrases**) n A **phrase** is a short group of words that are used as a unit and whose meaning is not always obvious from the words contained in it. বাগধারা

phrasebook (**phrasebooks**) n A **phrasebook** is a book used by people travelling to a foreign country. It has lists of useful words and expressions, together with the translation of each word or expression in the language of that country. শব্দানুবাদ সম্বলিত বই

p

physical (physicals) *adj* **Physical** means connected with a person's body, rather than with their mind. শারীরিক ▷ *n* A **physical** is a medical examination of the body to diagnose disease or verify fitness. দেহের ডাক্তারি পরীক্ষা

physicist (physicists) *n* A **physicist** is a person who studies physics. পদার্থবিদ

physics *n* **Physics** is the scientific study of forces such as heat, light, sound, pressure, gravity, and electricity. পদার্থবিদ্যা

physiotherapist (physiotherapists) *n* A **physiotherapist** is a person whose job is using physiotherapy to treat people. ফিজিওথেরাপিস্ট

physiotherapy *n* **Physiotherapy** is medical treatment given to people who cannot move a part of their body and involves exercise, massage, or heat treatment. ফিজিওথেরাপি

pianist (pianists) *n* A **pianist** is a person who plays the piano. পিয়ানোবাদক

piano (pianos) *n* A **piano** is a large musical instrument with a row of black and white keys, which you strike with your fingers. পিয়ানো

pick (picks, picking, picked) *n* The best things or people in a particular group are the **pick** of that group. শ্রেষ্ঠ ব্যক্তি বা বস্তু ▷ *vt* If you **pick** someone, you choose them. বাছাই করা ▷ *vt* When you **pick** flowers, fruit, or leaves, you take them from a plant or tree. তোলা

pick on *v* If someone **picks on** you, they repeatedly criticize or attack you unfairly. (*informal*) হয়রান করা *They were always picking on her.*

pick out *v* If you can **pick out** something or someone, you recognize them when it is difficult to see them. নির্ণয় করা *With my binoculars, I pick out a figure a mile or so away.*

pickpocket (pickpockets) *n* A **pickpocket** is a person who steals things from people's pockets or bags in public places. পকেটমার

pick up *v* If you **pick** something **up**, you lift it upwards from a surface using your fingers. উঠিয়ে নেওয়া *Ridley picked up the pencil.*

picnic (picnics) *n* When people have a **picnic**, they eat a meal out of doors. পিকনিক

picture (pictures) *n* A **picture** consists of lines and shapes which are drawn, painted, or printed on a surface and show a person, thing, or scene. চিত্র

picture frame (picture frames) *n* A **picture frame** is the wood, metal, or plastic that is fitted around a picture, especially when it is displayed or hung on a wall. ছবির কাঠামো

picturesque *adj* A **picturesque** place is attractive, interesting, and unspoiled. ছবির মত সুন্দর

pie (pies) *n* A **pie** consists of meat, vegetables, or fruit, baked in pastry. পাই

piece (pieces) *n* A **piece** of something is a portion, part, or section of it that has been removed, broken off, or cut off. টুকরো

pie chart (pie charts) *n* A **pie chart** is a circle divided into sections to show the relative proportions of a set of things. পাই চার্ট

pier (piers) *n* A **pier** is a large platform which sticks out into the sea and which people can walk along. জেটি

pierce (pierces, piercing, pierced) *vt* If a sharp object **pierces** something, or if you **pierce** something with a sharp object, the object goes into it and makes a hole in it. ফুটো করা

pierced *adj* If your ears or some other part of your body is **pierced**, you have a small hole made through them so that you can wear a piece of jewellery in them. বেঁধানো

piercing (piercings) *n* A **piercing** is a hole that has been made in part of someone's body that they can put jewellery in. ছিদ্র

pig (pigs) *n* A **pig** is a farm animal with a pink, white, or black skin. Pigs are kept for their meat, which is called pork, ham, or bacon. শূয়রের

pigeon (pigeons) *n* A **pigeon** is a grey bird which is often seen in towns. পায়রা

piggybank (piggybanks) *n* A **piggybank** is a small container shaped like a pig, with a narrow hole in the top through which to put coins. Children often use piggybanks to save money. কয়েন রাখবার কৌটো

pigtail (pigtails) *n* If someone has a **pigtail** or **pigtails**, their hair is plaited or braided into one or two lengths. শূয়োরের লেজ

pile (piles) *n* A **pile** of things is a quantity of them lying on top of one another. স্তূপ

piles *npl* **Piles** are painful swellings that can appear in the veins inside a person's anus. অর্শ

pile-up (pile-ups) *n* A **pile-up** is a road accident in which a lot of vehicles crash into each other. বহু গাড়ীর মধ্যে পথ দুর্ঘটনা

pilgrim (pilgrims) *n* A **pilgrim** is a person who makes a journey to a holy place. তীর্থযাত্রী

pilgrimage (pilgrimages) *n* If someone makes a **pilgrimage** to a place, they make a journey there because the place is holy according to their religion, or very important to them personally. তীর্থস্থান

pill (pills) *n* **Pills** are small solid round masses of medicine or vitamins that you swallow. বড়ি

pillar (pillars) *n* A **pillar** is a tall solid structure which is usually used to support part of a building. স্তম্ভ

pillow (pillows) *n* A **pillow** is a rectangular cushion which you rest your head on when you are in bed. বালিশ

pillowcase (pillowcases) *n* A **pillowcase** is a cover for a pillow, which can be removed and washed. বালিশের ঢাকা

pilot (pilots) *n* A **pilot** is a person who is trained to fly an aircraft. বিমানচালক

pilot light (pilot lights) *n* A **pilot light** is a small gas flame in a cooker, stove, boiler, or fire. It burns all the time and lights the main

large flame when the gas is turned fully on. পাইলট লাইট

pimple (pimples) *n* **Pimples** are small raised spots, especially on the face. ব্রণ

PIN *n* Someone's **PIN** or **PIN number** is a secret number which they can use, for example, with a bank card to withdraw money from a cash machine. **PIN** is an abbreviation for 'personal identification number'. পিন নম্বর

pin (pins) *n* **Pins** are very small thin pieces of metal with points at one end, which are used to fasten things together. পিন

pinafore (pinafores) *n* A **pinafore** or a **pinafore dress** is a sleeveless dress. It is worn over a blouse or sweater. টিলা পোশাক

pinch (pinches, pinching, pinched) *vt* If you **pinch** a part of someone's body, you take a piece of their skin between your thumb and first finger and give it a short squeeze. চিমটি কাটা

pine (pines) *n* A **pine** or a **pine tree** is a tall tree with long thin leaves which it keeps all year round. পাইন গাছ

pineapple (pineapples) *n* A **pineapple** is a large oval fruit with sweet, juicy, yellow flesh and thick, brown skin. আনারস

pink (pinker, pinkest) *adj* Something that is **pink** is the colour between red and white. গোলাপী

pint (pints) *n* A **pint** is a unit of measurement for liquids. In Britain, it is equal to 568 cubic centimetres or one eighth of an imperial gallon. In America, it is equal to 473 cubic centimetres or one eighth of an American gallon. পাঁইট

pip (**pips**) *n* Pips are the small hard seeds in a fruit such as an apple or orange. ছোট বীজ

pipe (**pipes**) *n* A pipe is a long, round, hollow object through which a liquid or gas can flow. পাইপ

pipeline (**pipelines**) *n* A pipeline is a large pipe used for carrying oil or gas over a long distance. পাইপলাইন

pirate (**pirates**) *n* Pirates are sailors who attack other ships and steal property from them. জলদস্যু

Pisces *n* Pisces is one of the twelve signs of the zodiac. Its symbol is two fish. People who are born approximately between the 19th of February and the 20th of March come under this sign. মীনরাশি

pistol (**pistols**) *n* A pistol is a small handgun. পিস্তল

piston (**pistons**) *n* A piston is a cylinder or metal disc that is part of an engine. পিস্টন

pitch (**pitches, pitching, pitched**) *n* A pitch is an area of ground that is marked out and used for playing a game such as football, cricket, or hockey. খেলার জন্য জায়গা ▷ *n* The pitch of a sound is how high or low it is. আওয়াজ ▷ *vt* If you pitch something somewhere, you throw it forcefully while aiming carefully. জোরে ছোঁড়া

pity (**pities, pitying, pitied**) *n* If you feel pity for someone, you feel very sorry for them. করুণা ▷ *vt* If you pity someone, you feel very sorry for them. করুণা করা

pixel (**pixels**) *n* A pixel is the smallest area on a computer screen which can be given a separate colour by the computer. পিক্সেল

pizza (**pizzas**) *n* A pizza is a flat piece of dough covered with tomatoes, cheese, and other savoury food, which is baked in an oven. পিৎজা

place (**places, placing, placed**) *n* A place is a building, area, town, or country. স্থান ▷ *vt* If you place something somewhere, you put it in a particular position. স্থাপন করা ▷ *n* A place is where something belongs. অবস্থান

placement *n* The placement of something is the act of putting it in a particular place. স্থাপন

place of birth (**places of birth**) *n* Your place of birth is the place where you were born. জন্মস্থান

plain (**plainer, plainest, plains**) *adj* A plain object, surface, or fabric is entirely in one colour and has no pattern, design, or writing on it. সাদামাটা ▷ *n* A plain is a large, flat area of land with very few trees on it. সমতলভূমি

plain chocolate *n* Plain chocolate is dark-brown chocolate that has a stronger and less sweet taste than milk chocolate. সাধারণ চকোলেট

plait (**plaits**) *n* A plait is a length of hair that has been twisted over and under two other lengths of hair to make one thick length of hair. বিনুনি

plan (**plans, planning, planned**) *n* A plan is a method of achieving something that you have worked out in detail beforehand. পরিকল্পনা ▷ *v* If you plan what you are going to do, you decide in detail what you are going to do, and you intend to do it. পরিকল্পনা

plane (**planes**) *n* A plane is a vehicle with wings and one or more engines which can fly. বিমান ▷ *n* A plane is a flat level surface which may be sloping at a particular angle. তল ▷ *n* A plane is a tool that has a flat bottom with a sharp blade in it, used for shaping wood. একটি যন্ত্রবিশেষ

planet (**planets**) *n* A planet is a large, round object in space that moves around a star. The Earth is a planet. গ্রহ

planning *n* Planning is the process of deciding in detail how to do something before you actually start to do it. পরিকল্পনা

plant (**plants, planting, planted**) *n* A plant is a factory or a place where power is produced. কারখানা ▷ *n* A plant is a living thing that grows in earth and has a stem, leaves, and roots. উদ্ভিদ ▷ *vt* When you

plant a seed, plant, or young tree, you put it into earth so that it will grow. রোপণ করা

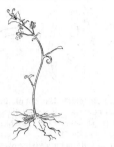

plant pot (**plant pots**) n A **plant pot** is a container that is used for growing plants. গাছের টব

plaque (**plaques**) n A **plaque** is a flat piece of metal or wood, which is fixed to a wall or monument in memory of a person or event. স্মৃতিফলক

plasma screen (**plasma screens**) n A **plasma screen** is a type of thin television screen or computer screen that produces high-quality images. প্লাজমা স্ক্রীণ

plasma TV (**plasma TVs**) n A **plasma TV** is a type of television set with a thin screen that produces high-quality images. প্লাজমা টিভি

plaster (**plasters**) n **Plaster** is a paste which people put on walls and ceilings so that they are smooth. পলেস্তারা ▷ n A **plaster** is a strip of material with a soft part in the middle. You can cover a cut on your body with a **plaster**. প্লাস্টার

plastic (**plastics**) n **Plastic** is a light but strong material produced by a chemical process. প্লাস্টিক

plastic bag (**plastic bags**) n A **plastic bag** is a bag made from a very thin flexible plastic. প্লাস্টিক ব্যাগ

plastic surgery n **Plastic surgery** is the practice of performing operations to repair or replace skin which has been damaged, or to improve people's appearance. প্লাস্টিক সার্জারি

plate (**plates**) n A **plate** is a round or oval flat dish used to hold food. প্লেট

platform (**platforms**) n A **platform** is a flat raised structure or area on which someone or something can stand. পাটাতন

platinum n **Platinum** is a very valuable silvery-grey metal. প্ল্যাটিনাম

play (**plays, playing, played**) n A **play** is a piece of writing performed in a theatre, on the radio, or on television. নাটক ▷ vi When you **play**, you spend time using toys and taking part in games. খেলা করা ▷ vt If you **play** an instrument, you make music with it. বাজানো

player (**players**) n A **player** in a sport or game is a person who takes part. খেলোয়াড় ▷ n You can use **player** to refer to a musician. বাদক

playful adj A **playful** gesture is friendly and cheerful. খেলাসুলভ

playground (**playgrounds**) n A **playground** is a piece of land where children can play. খেলার মাঠ

playgroup (**playgroups**) n A **playgroup** is an informal kind of school for very young children where they learn by playing. শিশু বিদ্যালয়

playing card (**playing cards**) n **Playing cards** are thin pieces of card with numbers and pictures on them, which are used to play games. তাস

playing field (**playing fields**) n A **playing field** is a large area of grass where people play sports. খেলার মাঠ

PlayStation® (**PlayStations**) n A **PlayStation** is a type of games console. প্লে-স্টেশন

playtime n In a school for young children, **playtime** is the period of time between lessons when they can play outside. খেলার সময়

play truant v If children **play truant**, they stay away from school without permission. স্কুল পালানো

p

playwright (**playwrights**) *n* A **playwright** is a person who writes plays. নাট্যকার

pleasant (**pleasanter, pleasantest**) *adj* Something that is **pleasant** is enjoyable or attractive. মনোরম

please! *excl* You say **please!** when you are politely asking or inviting someone to do something. অনুগ্রহ করে

pleased *adj* If you are **pleased**, you are happy about something or satisfied with it. আনন্দিত

pleasure *n* If something gives you **pleasure**, you get a feeling of happiness, satisfaction, or enjoyment from it. আনন্দ

plenty *n* If there is **plenty** of something, there is a lot of it. প্রচুর

pliers *npl* **Pliers** are a tool with two handles at one end and two hard, flat, metal parts at the other. **Pliers** are used to hold or pull out things such as nails. একপ্রকার যন্ত্র

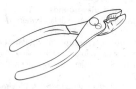

plot (**plots, plotting, plotted**) *n* A **plot** is a small piece of land, especially one that is intended for a purpose such as building houses or growing vegetables. জমি ▷ *n* A **plot** is a secret plan to do something that is illegal or wrong. ষড়যন্ত্র করা

plough (**ploughs, ploughing, ploughed**) *n* A **plough** is a large farming tool with sharp blades, which is attached to a tractor or an animal and used to turn over the soil before planting. লাঙল ▷ *vt* When a farmer **ploughs** an area of land, they turn over the soil using a plough. হলকর্ষণ করা

plug (**plugs**) *n* A **plug** on a piece of electrical equipment is a small plastic object

with two or three metal pins which fit into the holes of an electric socket. প্লাগ

plughole (**plugholes**) *n* A **plughole** is a small hole in a bath or sink which allows the water to flow away and into which you can put a plug. প্লাগের গর্ত

plug in *v* If you **plug** a piece of electrical equipment **in**, you push its plug into an electric socket so that it can work. প্লাগ ঢোকানো *I filled the kettle and plugged it in.*

plum (**plums**) *n* A **plum** is a small sweet fruit with a smooth red or yellow skin and a stone in the middle. আলুবখরা

plumber (**plumbers**) *n* A **plumber** is a person whose job is to connect and repair things such as water and drainage pipes, baths, and toilets. নলের মিস্ত্রি

plumbing *n* The **plumbing** in a building consists of the water and drainage pipes, baths, and toilets in it. জল, নলের সংযোগ করা

plump (**plumper, plumpest**) *adj* A **plump** person is rather fat. মোটাসোটা

plunge (**plunges, plunging, plunged**) *vi* If something or someone **plunges** in a particular direction, especially into water, they fall, rush, or throw themselves in that direction. ডুবে যাওয়া

plural (**plurals**) *n* The **plural** of a noun is the form of it that is used to refer to more than one person or thing. বহুবচন

plus *prep* You use **plus** to show that one number or quantity is being added to another. যুক্ত হওয়া *Two plus two equals four.*

plywood *n* **Plywood** is wood that consists of thin layers of wood stuck together. প্লাইউড

p.m. *abbr* **p.m.** is used after a number to show that you are referring to a particular time between noon and midnight. p.m. is an abbreviation for 'post meridiem'. দুপুর এবং মধ্যরাত্রির মধ্যবর্তী সময়

pneumatic drill (**pneumatic drills**) *n* A **pneumatic drill** is operated by air under pressure and is very powerful. Pneumatic drills are often used for digging up roads. হাওয়াভরা ড্রিল

pneumonia *n* **Pneumonia** is a serious disease which affects your lungs and makes breathing difficult. নিউমোনিয়া

poached *adj* If fish, animals, or birds are **poached**, someone has caught them illegally on someone else's property. অবৈধ শিকার ▷ *adj* **Poached** eggs, fish, or other food is cooked gently in boiling water, milk, or other liquid. অল্প আঁচে সিদ্ধ

pocket (**pockets**) *n* A **pocket** is a small bag or pouch that forms part of a piece of clothing. পকেট

pocket calculator (**pocket calculators**) *n* A **pocket calculator** is a very small electronic device that you use for making mathematical calculations. পকেটে রাখবার ক্যালকুলেটর

pocket money *n* **Pocket money** is a small amount of money given regularly to children by their parents. হাতখরচ

podcast (**podcasts**) *n* A **podcast** is an audio file that can be downloaded and listened to on a computer or iPod. পডকাস্ট

poem (**poems**) *n* A **poem** is a piece of writing in which the words are chosen for their beauty and sound and are carefully arranged, often in short lines. কবিতা

poet (**poets**) *n* A **poet** is a person who writes poems. কবি

poetry *n* Poems, considered as a form of literature, are referred to as **poetry**. কবিতা

point (**points, pointing, pointed**) *n* A **point** is an idea or a fact. মতামত ▷ *n* A **point** is a mark that you win in a game or a sport. পয়েন্ট ▷ *vi* If you **point** at something,

you stick out your finger to show where it is. উদ্দেশ্য করা ▷ *n* The **point** of something is its thin, sharp end. Needles and knives have **points**. ডগা

pointless *adj* Something that is **pointless** has no purpose. উদ্দেশ্যহীন

point out *v* If you **point out** an object or place to someone, you direct their attention to it. সূচিত করা *Now and then they would stop to point things out to each other.*

poison (**poisons, poisoning, poisoned**) *n* **Poison** is a substance that harms or kills people or animals if they swallow or absorb it. বিষ ▷ *vt* To **poison** someone or something means to give poison to them or to add poison to them, causing them harm. বিষ দেওয়া

poisonous *adj* Something that is **poisonous** will kill you or harm you if you swallow or absorb it. বিষাক্ত

poke (**pokes, poking, poked**) *vt* If you **poke** someone or something, you quickly push them with your finger or with a sharp object. ঠেলে দেওয়া

poker *n* **Poker** is a card game that people usually play in order to win money. পোকার

Poland *n* **Poland** is a republic in central Europe, on the Baltic. পোল্যান্ড

polar *adj* **Polar** refers to the area around the North and South Poles. মেরুদেশীয়

polar bear (**polar bears**) *n* A **polar bear** is a large white bear which is found near the North Pole. শ্বেতভাল্লুক

p

Pole (Poles) *n* A **Pole** is a citizen of Poland, or a person of Polish origin. পোল্যান্ডের নাগরিক

pole (poles) *n* A **pole** is a long, thin piece of wood or metal, used especially for supporting things. খুঁটি

pole vault *n* **The pole vault** is an athletics event in which athletes jump over a high bar, using a long flexible pole to help lift themselves up. পোল ভল্ট

police *n* The **police** are the official organization that is responsible for making sure that people obey the law. পুলিশ

policeman (policemen) *n* A **policeman** is a man who is a member of the police force. পুরুষ-পুলিশ

police officer (police officers) *n* A **police officer** is a member of the police force. পুলিশ অফিসার

police station (police stations) *n* A **police station** is the local office of a police force in a particular area. পুলিশ স্টেশন

policewoman (policewomen) *n* A **policewoman** is a woman who is a member of the police force. মহিলা পুলিশ

polio *n* **Polio** is a serious infectious disease which can cause paralysis. পোলিও

Polish *adj* **Polish** means belonging or relating to Poland, or to its people, language, or culture. পোল্যান্ডের ▷ *n* **Polish** is the language spoken by people in Poland. পোলিশ ভাষা

polish (polishes, polishing, polished) *n* **Polish** is a substance that you put on the surface of an object in order to clean it, protect it, and make it shine. পালিশ ▷ *vt* If you **polish** something, you put polish on it or rub it with a cloth to make it shine. পালিশ করা

polite (politer, politest) *adj* A **polite** person has good manners and is not rude to other people. নম্র

politely *adv* If you do something **politely**, you do it with good manners and without being rude to other people. নম্রভাবে

politeness *n* **Politeness** is good manners in front of other people. নম্রতা

political *adj* **Political** means relating to the way power is achieved and used in a country or society. রাজনৈতিক

politician (politicians) *n* A **politician** is a person whose job is in politics, especially a member of parliament. রাজনীতিক

politics *npl* **Politics** is the actions or activities concerned with achieving and using power in a country or organization. রাজনীতি

poll (polls) *n* A **poll** is a survey in which people are asked their opinions about something. সমীক্ষা

pollen *n* **Pollen** is a powder produced by flowers in order to fertilize other flowers. পরাগরেণু

pollute (pollutes, polluting, polluted) *vt* To **pollute** water, air, or land means to make it dirty and dangerous to live in or to use, especially with poisonous chemicals or sewage. দূষিত করা

polluted *adj* If water, air, or land is **polluted**, it has been made dirty by poisonous substances. দূষিত

pollution *n* **Pollution** is poisonous substances that are polluting water, air, or land. দূষণ

polo-necked sweater (**polo-necked sweaters**) *n* A polo-necked sweater is a sweater with a high neck which folds over. পোলো নেকড সোয়েটার

polo shirt (polo shirts) *n* A **polo shirt** is a soft short-sleeved piece of clothing with a collar, which you put on over your head. পোলো শার্ট

Polynesia *n* **Polynesia** is the division of islands in the Pacific which includes

Samoa, Tonga, the Cook Islands, and Tuvalu. পলিনেশিয়া

Polynesian (**Polynesians**) *adj* **Polynesian** means relating to Polynesia, its people, or any of their languages. পলিনেশিয়া দেশীয় ▷ *n* A **Polynesian** is a person who lives in Polynesia, or a person of Polynesian origin. পলিনেশিয়ার অধিবাসী ▷ *n* **Polynesian** is a branch of languages, which includes Māori, Hawaiian, and other languages of the South and central Pacific. পলিনেশিয়া ভাষা

polythene bag (**polythene bags**) *n* A **polythene bag** is a bag made of thin plastic, especially one used to store or protect food or household articles. পলিথিনের ব্যাগ

pomegranate (**pomegranates**) *n* A **pomegranate** is a round fruit with a thick reddish skin. It contains lots of small seeds with juicy flesh around them. বেদানা

pond (**ponds**) *n* A **pond** is a small, usually man-made, area of water. পুকুর

pony (**ponies**) *n* A **pony** is a type of small horse. টাট্টু ঘোড়া

ponytail (**ponytails**) *n* If someone has their hair in a **ponytail**, it is tied up at the back so that it hangs down like a tail. পনিটেল

pony trekking *n* **Pony trekking** is the act of riding ponies cross-country, especially as a pastime. টাট্টু ঘোড়ায় ভ্রমণ

poodle (**poodles**) *n* A **poodle** is a type of dog with thick curly hair. একজাতীয় কুকুর

pool (**pools**) *n* A **pool** of people, money, or things is a quantity or number of them that is available for use. বহুলোকের সমষ্টি ▷ *n* A **pool** is a small area of still water. স্থির জলের পুকুর

poor (**poorer, poorest**) *adj* Someone who is **poor** has very little money and few possessions. দরিদ্র

poorly *adj* If someone is **poorly**, they are ill. দুর্বল

popcorn *n* **Popcorn** is a snack which consists of grains of maize that have been heated until they have burst and become large and light. পপকর্ণ

pope (**popes**) *n* The **pope** is the head of the Roman Catholic Church. পোপ

poplar (**poplars**) *n* A **poplar** or a **poplar tree** is a type of tall thin tree. উঁচু গাছবিশেষ

poppy (**poppies**) *n* A **poppy** is a plant with large, delicate, red flowers. আফিম গাছ

popular *adj* Someone or something that is **popular** is liked by a lot of people. জনপ্রিয়

popularity *n* The **popularity** of someone or something is the degree to which they are liked by other people. জনপ্রিয়তা

population (**populations**) *n* The **population** of a place is the people who live there, or the number of people living there. জনসংখ্যা

pop-up (**pop-ups**) *n* On a computer screen, a **pop-up** is a small window that appears on the screen when you perform particular operations. A **pop-up** may contain items such as a menu or advertisement. পপ-আপ

porch (**porches**) *n* A **porch** is a sheltered area at the entrance to a building. It has a roof and sometimes walls. গাড়ি-বারান্দা

porridge *n* **Porridge** is a thick sticky food made from oats cooked in water or milk and eaten hot, especially for breakfast. যবের পায়েস

port (**ports**) *n* **Port** is a type of strong, sweet red wine. মদ্যবিশেষ ▷ *n* A **port** is a town or a harbour area with docks and warehouses, where ships load or unload goods or passengers. বন্দর

portable *adj* A **portable** machine or device is designed to be easily carried or moved. বহনযোগ্য

porter (**porters**) *n* A **porter** is a person whose job is to be in charge of the entrance of a building such as a hotel. কুলি

portfolio (**portfolios**) *n* A **portfolio** is a set of pictures or photographs of someone's work, which they show to potential employers. পোর্টফোলিও

p

portion (**portions**) *n* A **portion of** something is a part of it. অংশ

portrait (**portraits**) *n* A **portrait** is a painting, drawing, or photograph of a person. প্রতিকৃতি

Portugal *n* **Portugal** is a republic in south-west Europe, on the Atlantic. পর্তুগাল

Portuguese (**Portuguese**) *adj* **Portuguese** means belonging or relating to Portugal, or its people, language, or culture. পর্তুগাল দেশীয় ▷ *n* The **Portuguese** are the people of Portugal. পর্তুগীজ ▷ *n* **Portuguese** is the language spoken in Portugal, Brazil, Angola, and Mozambique. পর্তুগীজ ভাষা

position (**positions**) *n* The **position** of someone or something is the place where they are. অবস্থা

positive *adj* If you are **positive**, you are hopeful and confident, and think of the good aspects of a situation rather than the bad ones. আশাবাদী

possess (**possesses, possessing, possessed**) *vt* If you **possess** something, you have it or own it. ভোগদখল করা

possession *n* If you are in **possession** of something, you have it, because you have obtained it or because it belongs to you. (*formal*) ভোগদখল

possibility (**possibilities**) *n* If you say there is a **possibility** that something is the case or that something will happen, you mean that it might be the case or it might happen. সম্ভাবনা

possible *adj* If it is **possible** to do something, it can be done. সম্ভব

possibly *adv* You use **possibly** to indicate that you are not sure whether something is true or will happen. সম্ভবতঃ

post (**posts, posting, posted**) *n* A **post** is a strong upright pole fixed into the ground. খুঁটি ▷ *n* A **post** is a job or official position in a company or organization. পদমর্যাদা ▷ *n* The **post** is a system for collecting and delivering letters and parcels. ডাক ▷ *vt* If

you **post** a letter, you put a stamp on it and send it to someone. প্রেরণ করা

postage *n* **Postage** is the money that you pay for sending letters and parcels by post. ডাকমূল্য

postal order (**postal orders**) *n* A **postal order** is a piece of paper representing a sum of money which you can buy at a post office and send to someone as a way of sending them money by post. পোস্টাল অর্ডার

postbox (**postboxes**) *n* A **postbox** is a metal box in a public place, where you put letters and packets to be collected. They are then sorted and delivered. ডাকবাক্স

postcard (**postcards**) *n* A **postcard** is a piece of card, often with a picture on one side, which you can write on and post to someone without using an envelope. পোস্টকার্ড

postcode (**postcodes**) *n* Your **postcode** is a short sequence of numbers and letters at the end of your address. পোস্ট কোড

poster (**posters**) *n* A **poster** is a large notice, advertisement, or picture that you stick on a wall. পোস্টার

postgraduate (**postgraduates**) *n* A **postgraduate** is a student with a first degree from a university who is studying or doing research at a more advanced level. স্নাতকোত্তর ছাত্র

postman (**postmen**) *n* A **postman** is a man whose job is to collect and deliver letters and parcels that are sent by post. ডাকবিলি কর্মী

postmark (**postmarks**) *n* A **postmark** is a mark which is printed on letters and packages at a post office. It shows the time and place at which something was posted. ডাকচিহ্ন

post office (**post offices**) *n* A **post office** is a building where you can buy stamps, post letters, and parcels, and use other services provided by the national postal service. পোস্ট অফিস

postpone (postpones, postponing, postponed) vt If you postpone an event, you arrange for it to take place at a later time than was originally planned. স্থগিত রাখা

postwoman (postwomen) n A postwoman is a woman whose job is to collect and deliver letters, etc. ডাকবিলি মহিলা কর্মী

pot (pots) n A pot is a deep round container for cooking food. পাত্র

potato (potatoes) n Potatoes are vegetables with brown or red skins and white insides. আলু

potato peeler (potato peelers) n A potato peeler is a special tool used for removing the skin from potatoes. আলুর খোসা ছাড়াবার যন্ত্র

potential adj You use potential to say that someone or something is capable of developing into the particular kind of person or thing. সম্ভাব্য ▷ n If something has potential, it is capable of being useful or successful in the future. সম্ভাবনা

pothole (potholes) n A pothole is a large hole in the surface of a road, caused by traffic and bad weather. গর্ত

pot plant (pot plants) n A pot plant is a plant which is grown in a container, especially indoors. টবের গাছ

pottery n Pottery is objects made from clay. চীনামাটির তৈরী দ্রব্য

potty (potties) n A potty is a deep bowl which a small child uses as a toilet. পটি

pound (pounds) n The pound is the unit of money which is used in Britain. It is represented by the symbol £. Some other countries, for example, Egypt, also have a unit of money called a pound. পাউন্ড

pound sterling (pounds sterling) n Pound sterling is the official name for the standard monetary unit of Britain. পাউন্ড স্টার্লিং

pour (pours, pouring, poured) vt If you pour a liquid, you make it flow steadily out of a container by holding the container at an angle. ঢালা

poverty n Poverty is the state of being very poor. দারিদ্র্য

powder (powders) n Powder consists of many tiny particles of a solid substance. পাউডার

power n If someone has power, they have control over people. ক্ষমতা ▷ n The power of something is its strength. শক্তি

power cut (power cuts) n A power cut is a period of time when the electricity supply to a particular building or area is stopped, sometimes deliberately. বিদ্যুৎ সরবরাহে ঘাটতি

powerful adj A powerful person or organization is able to control or influence people and events. শক্তিশালী

practical adj Practical means involving real situations, rather than ideas and theories. বাস্তব

practically adv Practically means almost. প্রায়

practice (practices) n You can refer to something that people do regularly as a practice. অভ্যাস

practise (practises, practising, practised) vt If you practise something, you keep doing it regularly in order to do it better. অভ্যাস করা

praise (**praises, praising, praised**) vt If you **praise** someone or something, you express approval for their achievements or qualities. প্রশংসা করা

pram (**prams**) n A **pram** is like a baby's cot on wheels, which you can push along when you want to take the baby somewhere. প্যারামবুলেটর

prank (**pranks**) n A **prank** is a childish trick. (old-fashioned) দুষ্টুমিভরা কৌতুক

prawn (**prawns**) n A **prawn** is a small edible shellfish, similar to a shrimp. চিংড়িমাছ

pray (**prays, praying, prayed**) v When people **pray**, they speak to God in order to give thanks or to ask for help. প্রার্থনা করা

prayer (**prayers**) n **Prayer** is the activity of speaking to God. প্রার্থনা

precaution (**precautions**) n A **precaution** is an action that is intended to prevent something dangerous or unpleasant from happening. সতর্কতা

preceding adj You refer to the period of time or the thing immediately before the one that you are talking about as the **preceding** one. পূর্ববর্তী

precinct (**precincts**) n A shopping **precinct** is an area in the centre of a town in which cars are not allowed. পরিপার্শ্ব

precious adj If you say that something such as a resource is **precious**, you mean that it is valuable and should not be wasted or used badly. মূল্যবান

precise adj You use **precise** to emphasize that you are referring to an exact thing, rather than something vague. সঠিক

precisely adv **Precisely** means accurately and exactly. সঠিকভাবে

predecessor (**predecessors**) n Your **predecessor** is the person who had your job before you. পূর্বসূরী

predict (**predicts, predicting, predicted**) vt If you **predict** an event, you say that it will happen. ভবিষ্যদ্বাণী করা

predictable adj Something that is **predictable** is obvious in advance and will happen. অনুমানসাপেক্ষ

prefect (**prefects**) n In some schools, especially in Britain, a **prefect** is an older pupil who does special duties and helps the teachers to control the younger pupils. প্রিফেক্ট

prefer (**prefers, preferring, preferred**) vt If you **prefer** someone or something, you like that person or thing better than another. পছন্দ করা

preferably adv You use **preferably** to show that something is more desirable or suitable. আরো ভাল করে

preference (**preferences**) n If you have a **preference** for something, you would like to have or do that thing rather than something else. পছন্দ

pregnancy n **Pregnancy** is the condition of being pregnant or the period of time during which a female is pregnant. গর্ভাবস্থা

pregnant adj If a woman or female animal is **pregnant**, she has a baby or babies developing in her body. গর্ভবতী

prehistoric adj **Prehistoric** people and things existed at a time before information was written down. প্রাগৈতিহাসিক

prejudice (**prejudices**) n **Prejudice** is an unreasonable dislike of someone or something, or an unreasonable preference for one group over another. পূর্বকল্পিত ধারণা

prejudiced adj If someone is **prejudiced** against a particular group, they have an unreasonable dislike of them. পূর্বকল্পিত ধারণার বশবর্তী

premature adj Something that is **premature** happens too early or earlier than expected. অকাল

premiere (**premieres**) n The **premiere** of a new play or film is the first public performance of a new another. প্রিমিয়ার

premises npl The **premises** of a business or an institution are all the buildings and land that it occupies. প্রাঙ্গণ

premonition (**premonitions**) *n* If you have a **premonition**, you have a feeling that something is going to happen, often something unpleasant. পূর্বাশঙ্কা

preoccupied *adj* If you are **preoccupied**, you are thinking a lot about something or someone, and so you hardly notice other things. পূর্বব্যস্ত

prepaid *adj* **Prepaid** items are paid for in advance, before the time when you would normally pay for them. পূর্বপ্রদত্ত

preparation *n* **Preparation** is the process of getting something ready for use or for a particular purpose. প্রস্তুতি

prepare (**prepares, preparing, prepared**) *vt* If you **prepare** something, you make it ready for something that is going to happen. প্রস্তত হওয়া

prepared *adj* If you are **prepared** to do something, you are willing to do it. প্রস্তুত

prescribe (**prescribes, prescribing, prescribed**) *vt* If a doctor **prescribes** treatment, he or she states what medicine or treatment a patient should have. ঔষধ ব্যবহারের নির্দেশ দেওয়া

prescription (**prescriptions**) *n* A **prescription** is a medicine which a doctor has told you to take, or the form on which the doctor has written the details of that medicine. ঔষধ ব্যবহারের নির্দেশিকা

presence *n* Someone's **presence** in a place is the fact that they are there. উপস্থিতি

present (**presents, presenting, presented**) *adj* If someone is **present** somewhere, they are there উপস্থিত ▷ *n* A **present** is something that you give to someone for them to keep. উপহার ▷ *n* The **present** is the period of time that is taking place now. বর্তমান ▷ *vt* If you **present** someone with a prize or with information, you give it to them. পুরস্কার দেওয়া

presentation (**presentations**) *n* A **presentation** is the act of formally giving something such as a prize or document. উপস্থাপনা

presenter (**presenters**) *n* A radio or television **presenter** is a person who introduces the items in a particular programme. উপস্থাপক

presently *adv* If you say that something is **presently** happening, you mean that it is happening now. বর্তমানে

preservative (**preservatives**) *n* A **preservative** is a chemical that is added to substances to prevent them from decaying. সংরক্ষক

president (**presidents**) *n* The **president** of a country that has no king or queen is the person who is the head of state of that country. রাষ্ট্রপতি

press (**presses, pressing, pressed**) *n* The **press** refers to newspapers and the journalists who write them. সংবাদপত্র ▷ *vt* If you **press** something somewhere, you push it firmly against something else. চাপ দেওয়া

press conference (**press conferences**) *n* A **press conference** is a meeting held by a famous or important person in which they answer journalists' questions. সংবাদ-সম্মেলন

press-up (**press-ups**) *n* **Press-ups** are exercises that you do by lying with your face towards the floor and pushing with your hands to raise your body until your arms are straight. প্রেস-আপ

pressure (**pressures, pressuring, pressured**) *n* **Pressure** is the force produced when you press hard on something. চাপ ▷ *vt* If you **pressure** someone to do something, you try forcefully to persuade them to do it. চাপ সৃষ্টি করা

prestige *n* If a person, a country, or an organization has **prestige**, they are admired and respected because they are important or successful. মর্যাদা

prestigious *adj* A **prestigious** institution or activity is respected and admired by people. মর্যাদাপূর্ণ

presumably *adv* If you say that something is **presumably** the case, you mean that you think it is true, although you are not certain. সম্ভবতঃ

presume (**presumes, presuming, presumed**) *vt* If you **presume** that something is the case, you think that it is true, although you are not certain. সাময়িকভাবে ধরে নেওয়া

pretend (**pretends, pretending, pretended**) *vt* If you **pretend** that something is true, you try to make people believe that it is true, although it is not. ভান করা

pretext (**pretexts**) *n* A **pretext** is a reason which you pretend has caused you to do something. ছুতো

prettily *adv* If something is done or carried out **prettily** it is done or carried out in an attractive or pleasant manner. বেশ ভালভাবে

pretty (**prettier, prettiest**) *adj* If you describe someone, especially a girl, as **pretty**, you mean that they look nice and are attractive in a delicate way. মিষ্টি ▷ *adv* You can use **pretty** before an adjective or adverb to mean 'quite' or 'rather'. বেশ ভাল

prevent (**prevents, preventing, prevented**) *vt* If you **prevent** something, you stop it happening or being done. প্রতিরোধ করা

prevention *n* **Prevention** is the act of stopping something happening or being done. নিবারণ

previous *adj* A **previous** event or thing is one that occurred before the one you are talking about. প্রাক্তন

previously *adv* **Previously** means at some time before the period that you are talking about. পূর্বে

prey *n* A creature's **prey** are the creatures that it hunts and eats in order to live. শিকার

price (**prices**) *n* The **price** of something is the amount of money that you must pay to buy it. মূল্য

price list (**price lists**) *n* A **price list** is a list of the prices of a good or service. মূল্যের তালিকা

prick (**pricks, pricking, pricked**) *vt* If you **prick** something, you make small holes in it with a sharp object such as a pin. ফুটো করা

pride *n* **Pride** is a feeling of satisfaction which you have because you or people close to you have done something good or possess something good. গর্ব

primarily *adv* You use **primarily** to say what is mainly true in a particular situation. প্রাথমিকভাবে

primary *adj* You use **primary** to describe something that is extremely important or most important for someone or something. (*formal*) মুখ্য

primary school (**primary schools**) *n* A **primary school** is a school for children between the ages of 5 and 11. প্রাথমিক স্কুল

prime minister (**prime ministers**) *n* The leader of the government in some countries is called the **prime minister**. প্রধান মন্ত্রী

primitive *adj* **Primitive** means belonging to a society in which people live in a very simple way, usually without industries or a writing system. আদিম

primrose (**primroses**) *n* A **primrose** is a wild plant with pale yellow flowers. হলদে ফুলবিশেষ

prince (**princes**) *n* A **prince** is a male member of a royal family, especially the son of the king or queen of a country. রাজকুমার

princess (**princesses**) *n* A **princess** is a female member of a royal family, usually the daughter of a king or queen or the wife of a prince. রাজকুমারী

principal (**principals**) *adj* **Principal** means first in order of importance. মুখ্য ▷ *n* The **principal** of a school or college is the person in charge of it. প্রধানশিক্ষক

principle (**principles**) *n* A **principle** is a belief that you have about the way you should behave. নীতি

print (**prints, printing, printed**) *n* **Print** is all the letters and numbers in a printed document. মুদ্রণ ▷ v If you **print** something, you use a machine to put words or pictures on paper. ছাপা ▷ v If you **print** when you are writing, you do not join the letters together. খোদাই করা

printer (**printers**) n A **printer** is a person or firm whose job is printing books, leaflets, or similar material. মুদ্রাকর ▷ n A **printer** is a machine that can be connected to a computer in order to make copies on paper of information held by the computer. মুদ্রণযন্ত্র

printout (**printouts**) n A **printout** is a piece of paper on which information from a computer has been printed. কম্পিউটারে ছাপা কাগজ

priority (**priorities**) n If something is a **priority**, it is the most important thing you have to achieve or deal with before everything else. অগ্রাধিকার

prison (**prisons**) n A **prison** is a building where criminals are kept. কারাগার

prisoner (**prisoners**) n A **prisoner** is a person who is kept in a prison as a punishment or because they have been captured by an enemy. কয়েদী

prison officer (**prison officers**) n A **prison officer** is someone who works as a guard at a prison. কারাগারের কর্মকর্তা

privacy n **Privacy** is the fact of being alone so that you can do things without being seen or disturbed. গোপনীয়তা

private adj **Private** industries and services are owned and controlled by an individual person or group, rather than by the state. বেসরকারি

private property n **Private property** is land or belongings owned by a person or group and kept for their exclusive use. ব্যক্তিগত সম্পত্তি

privatize (**privatizes, privatizing, privatized**) vt If an organization that is owned by the state **is privatized**, the government sells it to one or more private companies. বেসরকারিকরণ

privilege (**privileges**) n A **privilege** is a special right or advantage that only one person or group has. সুযোগ

prize (**prizes**) n A **prize** is something valuable, such as money or a trophy, that is given to the winner of a game or competition. পুরস্কার

prize-giving (**prize-givings**) n A **prize-giving** is a ceremony where prizes are awarded to people who have produced a very high standard of work. পুরস্কার প্রদান

prizewinner (**prizewinners**) n A **prizewinner** is a person, animal, or thing that wins a prize. পুরস্কার প্রাপক

probability (**probabilities**) n The **probability** of something happening is how likely it is to happen, sometimes expressed as a fraction or a percentage. সম্ভাবনা

probable adj Something that is **probable** is likely to be true or likely to happen. সম্ভব

probably adv If you say that something is **probably** true, you think that it is likely to be true, although you are not sure. সম্ভবতঃ

problem (**problems**) n A **problem** is an unsatisfactory situation that causes difficulties for people. সমস্যা

proceedings npl Legal **proceedings** are legal action taken against someone. (formal) কার্যকলাপ

proceeds npl The **proceeds** of an event or activity are the money that has been obtained from it. অর্থসংগ্রহ

process (**processes**) n A **process** is a series of actions or events which have a particular result. প্রক্রিয়া

procession (**processions**) n A **procession** is a group of people who are walking, riding, or driving in a line as part of a public event. মিছিল

produce (**produces, producing, produced**) vt To **produce** something means to cause it to happen. উৎপন্ন করা

p

producer (producers) *n* A **producer** is a person whose job is to produce plays, films, programmes, or CDs. প্রযোজক

product (products) *n* A **product** is something that is produced and sold in large quantities. উৎপাদিত দ্রব্য

production *n* **Production** is the process of manufacturing or growing something in large quantities, or the amount of goods manufactured or grown. উৎপাদন

productivity *n* **Productivity** is the rate at which goods are produced. উৎপাদনশীলতা

profession (professions) *n* A **profession** is a ty pe of job that requires advanced education or training. পেশা

professional (professionals) **Professional** means relating to a person's work, especially work that requires special training. পেশাগত *His professional career started in a city law firm* ▷ *n* A **professional** is a person who belongs to or engages in one of the professions. পেশাদার

professionally *adv* If someone is **professionally** trained or qualified it means they have received special training that relates to their job. পেশাগতভাবে

professor (professors) *n* A **professor** in a British university is the most senior teacher in a department. অধ্যাপক

profit (profits) *n* A **profit** is an amount of money that you gain when you are paid more for something than it cost you. লাভ

profitable *adj* A **profitable** activity or organization makes a profit. লাভজনক

program (programs, programming, programmed) *n* A **program** is a set of instructions that a computer follows in order to perform a particular task. প্রোগ্রাম ▷ *vt* When you **program** a computer, you give it a set of instructions to make it able to perform a particular task. প্রোগ্রাম করা

programme (programmes) *n* A **programme** of actions or events is a series of actions or events that are planned to be done. কার্যক্রম

programmer (programmers) *n* A computer **programmer** is a person whose job involves writing programs for computers. প্রোগ্রামার

programming *n* **Programming** is the process of giving a set of instructions to a computer to make it able to perform a particular task. প্রোগ্রামিং

progress *n* **Progress** is the process of gradually improving or getting nearer to achieving or completing something. উন্নতি

prohibit (prohibits, prohibiting, prohibited) *vt* If someone **prohibits** something, they forbid it or make it illegal. *(formal)* নিষেধ করে

prohibited *adj* If something is **prohibited**, law or someone in authority forbids it or makes it illegal. নিষিদ্ধ

project (projects) *n* A **project** is a carefully planned task that requires a lot of time and effort. প্রকল্প

projector (projectors) *n* A **projector** is a machine that projects films or slides onto a screen or wall. প্রোজেক্টর

promenade (promenades) *n* In a seaside town, the **promenade** is the road by the sea where people go for a walk. সাগরতীরের রাস্তা

promise (promises, promising, promised) *n* A **promise** is a statement which you make to a person in which you say that you will definitely do something or give them something. প্রতিজ্ঞা ▷ *vt* If you **promise** that you will do something, you say to someone that you will definitely do it. প্রতিজ্ঞা করা

promising *adj* Someone or something that is **promising** seems likely to be very good or successful. সম্ভাবনাময়

promote (promotes, promoting, promoted) *vt* If people **promote** something, they help to make it happen, increase, or become more popular. প্রচার করা

promotion (**promotions**) *n* A **promotion** is a means of making something happen, increase or become more popular. প্রচার

prompt *adj* A **prompt** action is done without any delay. তুরিত

promptly *adv* If you do something **promptly**, you do it immediately. তাড়াতাড়ি

pronoun (**pronouns**) *n* A **pronoun** is a word which is used instead of a noun group to refer to someone or something. 'He', 'she', 'them', and 'something' are pronouns. সর্বনাম

pronounce (**pronounces**, **pronouncing**, **pronounced**) *vt* To **pronounce** a word means to say it. উচ্চারণ করা

pronunciation (**pronunciations**) *n* The **pronunciation** of words is the way they are pronounced. উচ্চারণ

proof (**proofs**) *n* **Proof** is a fact or a piece of evidence which shows that something is true or exists. প্রমাণ ▷ *n* In publishing, the **proofs** of a book, magazine, or article are a first copy of it that is printed so that mistakes can be corrected before more copies are printed and published. প্রুফ সংশোধন

propaganda *n* **Propaganda** is information, often inaccurate information, which an organization publishes or broadcasts in order to influence people. প্রচার

proper *adj* You use **proper** to describe things that you consider to be real or satisfactory. সঠিক

properly *adv* If something is done **properly**, it is done in a correct and satisfactory way. সঠিকভাবে

property *n* Someone's **property** consists of all the things that belong to them, or something that belongs to them. (*formal*) সম্পদ

proportion (**proportions**) *n* A **proportion** of an amount or group is a part of it. (*formal*) অনুপাত

proportional *adj* If one amount is **proportional** to another, the two amounts increase and decrease at the same rate so there is always the same relationship between them. (*formal*) আনুপাতিক

proposal (**proposals**) *n* A **proposal** is a suggestion or plan, often a formal or written one. প্রস্তাব

propose (**proposes**, **proposing**, **proposed**) *vt* If you **propose** a plan or idea, you suggest it. প্রস্তাব করা

prosecute (**prosecutes**, **prosecuting**, **prosecuted**) *v* If the authorities **prosecute** someone, they charge them with a crime and put them on trial. অভিযুক্ত করা

prospect (**prospects**) *n* A **prospect** is a possibility or a possible event. সম্ভাবনা

prospectus (**prospectuses**) *n* A **prospectus** is a document produced by a college, school, or company which gives details about it. প্রসপেকটাস

prosperity *n* **Prosperity** is a condition in which a person or community is being financially successful. আর্থিক উন্নতি

protect (**protects**, **protecting**, **protected**) *vt* To **protect** someone or something means to prevent them from being harmed or damaged. রক্ষা করা

protection *n* If something gives **protection** against something unpleasant, it prevents people or things from being harmed or damaged by it. সুরক্ষা

protein (**proteins**) *n* **Protein** is a substance which the body needs and which is found in meat, eggs, and milk. প্রোটিন

protest (**protests**, **protesting**, **protested**) *n* A **protest** is the act of saying or showing publicly that you do not approve of something. প্রতিবাদ ▷ *v* To **protest** means to say or show publicly that you do not agree with something. প্রতিবাদ করা

proud (**prouder**, **proudest**) *adj* If you feel **proud**, you feel pleasure and satisfaction at something that you own, have done, or are connected with. গর্বিত

prove (**proves**, **proving**, **proved**, **proven**) *v* If something **proves** to be true or to have a particular quality, it becomes clear after a period of time that it is true or has that quality. প্রমাণ করা

proverb (**proverbs**) *n* A **proverb** is a short sentence that people often quote, which gives advice or tells you something about life. For example, 'A bird in the hand is worth two in the bush.' প্রবাদ

provide (**provides, providing, provided**) *vt* If you **provide** something that someone needs or wants, you give it to them or make it available to them. দেওয়া

provided *conj* If something will happen **provided** that another thing happens, the first thing will happen only if the second thing also happens. এই শর্তে *He can go running, provided that he wears the right kind of shoes.*

provide for *v* If you **provide for** someone, you support them financially and make sure that they have the things that they need. আর্থিকভাবে সাহায্য করা *She won't let him provide for her.*

provisional *adj* You use **provisional** to describe something that has been arranged or appointed for the present, but may be changed soon. শর্তাধীন

proximity *n* **Proximity** to a place or person is the fact of being near to them. (*formal*) নিকটত্ব

prune (**prunes**) *n* A **prune** is a dried plum. শুকনো খেজুর

pry (**pries, prying, pried**) *vi* If you say that someone is **prying**, you disapprove of them because they are trying to find out about someone else's private affairs. উঁকি মারা

pseudonym (**pseudonyms**) *n* A **pseudonym** is a name which someone, usually a writer, uses instead of his or her real name. ছদ্মনাম

psychiatric *adj* **Psychiatric** means relating to psychiatry. মনোরোগ সংক্রান্ত

psychiatrist (**psychiatrists**) *n* A **psychiatrist** is a doctor who treats people suffering from mental illness. মনোচিকিৎসক

psychological *adj* **Psychological** means concerned with a person's mind and thoughts. মানসিক

psychologist (**psychologists**) *n* A **psychologist** is a person who studies the human mind and tries to explain why people behave in the way that they do. মনোবিদ

psychology *n* **Psychology** is the scientific study of the human mind and the reasons for people's behaviour. মনোবিজ্ঞান

psychotherapy *n* **Psychotherapy** is the use of psychological methods to treat people who are mentally ill. সাইকোথেরাপি

PTO *abbr* **PTO** is a written abbreviation for 'please turn over'. You write it at the bottom of a page to indicate that there is more writing on the other side. পরের পৃষ্ঠায় দেখুন

public *adj* **Public** means relating to all the people in a country or community. জনগণ ▷ *n* You can refer to people in general as **the public**. জনগণ

publication (**publications**) *n* The **publication** of a book or magazine is the act of printing it and making it available. প্রকাশনা

public holiday (**public holidays**) *n* A **public holiday** is a holiday observed over the whole country. গণছুটি

publicity *n* **Publicity** is advertising, information, or actions intended to attract the public's attention to someone or something. প্রচার

public opinion *n* **Public opinion** is the opinion or attitude of the public regarding a particular matter. জনমত

public relations *npl* **Public relations** are the state of the relationship between an organization and the public. জনসম্পর্ক

public school (**public schools**) *n* In Britain, a **public school** is a private school that provides secondary education which parents have to pay for. পাবলিক স্কুল

public transport *n* **Public transport** is a system of buses, trains, etc, running on fixed routes, on which the public may travel. জনগণের ব্যবহৃত যানবাহন

publish (publishes, publishing, published) *vt* When a company **publishes** a book or magazine, it prints copies of it, which are sent to shops and sold. প্রকাশনা করে

publisher (publishers) *n* A **publisher** is a person or company that publishes books, newspapers, or magazines. প্রকাশক

pudding (puddings) *n* A **pudding** is a cooked sweet food made with flour, fat, and eggs, and usually served hot. পুডিং

puddle (puddles) *n* A **puddle** is a small shallow pool of rain or other liquid on the ground. কাদামাখা ডোবা

Puerto Rico *n* **Puerto Rico** is an autonomous commonwealth in the Caribbean. পোর্টো রিকো

puff pastry *n* **Puff pastry** is a type of pastry which is very light and consists of a lot of thin layers. পাফ পেস্ট্রি

pull (pulls, pulling, pulled) *vt* When you **pull** something, you hold it and move it towards you. টানা

pull down *v* To **pull down** a building or statue means to deliberately destroy it. ধুলিস্মাৎ করে দেওয়া *They pulled the offices down, leaving a large open space.*

pull out *v* When a vehicle or driver **pulls out**, the vehicle moves out into the road or nearer the centre of the road. টেনে বার করা *She pulled out into the street.*

pullover (pullovers) *n* A **pullover** is a woollen piece of clothing that covers the upper part of your body and your arms. পুলওভার

pull up *v* When a vehicle or driver **pulls up**, the vehicle slows down and stops. টেনে ধরা *The car pulled up and the driver jumped out.*

pulse (pulses) *n* Your **pulse** is the regular beating of blood through your body, which you can feel, for example, at your wrist or neck. স্পন্দন

pulses *npl* Some large dried seeds which can be cooked and eaten are called **pulses**, for example the seeds of peas, beans, and lentils. ডাল

pump (pumps, pumping, pumped) *n* A **pump** is a machine that is used to force a liquid or gas to flow in strong regular movements in a particular direction. পাম্প ▷ *vt* To **pump** a liquid or gas in a certain direction means to force it to flow in that direction, using a pump. পাম্প করা

pumpkin (pumpkins) *n* A **pumpkin** is a large, round, orange-coloured vegetable with a thick skin. কুমড়ো

pump up *v* If you **pump up** something such as a tyre, you fill it with air, using a pump. হাওয়া ভর্তি করা *Pump all the tyres up.*

punch (punches, punching, punched) *n* A **punch** is a blow with the fist. ঘুঁষি ▷ *n* **Punch** is a drink usually made from wine or spirits mixed with sugar, fruit, and spices. মদ দিয়ে বানানো পানীয় ▷ *vt* If you **punch** someone or something, you hit them hard with your fist. ঘুঁষি মারা

punctual *adj* Someone who is **punctual** arrives somewhere or does something at the right time and is not late. সময়ানুবর্তী

punctuation *n* **Punctuation** is the system of signs such as full stops, commas, and question marks that you use in writing to divide words into sentences and clauses. ছেদযতি চিহ্ন

puncture (**punctures**) *n* A **puncture** is a small hole in a car or bicycle tyre that has been made by a sharp object. গাড়ীর চাকায় ফুটো

punish (**punishes, punishing, punished**) *vt* To **punish** someone means to make them suffer in some way because they have done something wrong. শাস্তি দেওয়া

punishment *n* **Punishment** is the act of punishing someone or being punished. শাস্তি

punk *n* **Punk** or **punk rock** is rock music that is played in a fast, loud, and aggressive way. Punk rock was particularly popular in the late 1970s. পাঙ্ক মিউজিক

pupil (**pupils**) *n* The **pupils** of a school are the children who go to it. ছাত্রছাত্রী ▷ *n* The **pupils** of your eyes are the small, round, black holes in the centre of them. চোখের মণি

puppet (**puppets**) *n* A **puppet** is a doll that you can move, either by pulling strings which are attached to it, or by putting your hand inside its body and moving your fingers. পুতুলনাচ

puppy (**puppies**) *n* A **puppy** is a young dog. কুকুরছানা

purchase (**purchases, purchasing, purchased**) *vt* When you **purchase** something, you buy it. (*formal*) ক্রয় করা

pure (**purer, purest**) *adj* **Pure** means not mixed with anything else. আসল

purple *adj* Something that is **purple** is reddish-blue in colour. বেগুনী

purpose (**purposes**) *n* The **purpose** of something is the reason for which it is made or done. উদ্দেশ্য

purr (**purrs, purring, purred**) *vi* When a cat **purrs**, it makes a low vibrating sound with its throat. গরগর আওয়াজ করা

purse (**purses**) *n* A **purse** is a very small bag that people, especially women, keep their money in. টাকার ব্যাগ

pursue (**pursues, pursuing, pursued**) *vt* If you **pursue** a particular aim or result, you make efforts to achieve it or to progress in it. (*formal*) অনুসরণ করা

pursuit *n* Your **pursuit** of something that you want consists of your attempts at achieving it. অনুসরণ

pus *n* **Pus** is a thick yellowish liquid that forms in wounds when they are infected. পুঁজ

push (**pushes, pushing, pushed**) *v* When you **push** something, you press it in order to move it away from you পিছনে ঠেলা

pushchair (**pushchairs**) *n* A **pushchair** is a small chair on wheels, in which a small child can sit and be wheeled around. পুশ-চেয়ার

push-up (**push-ups**) *n* **Push-ups** are exercises to strengthen your arms and chest muscles. They are done by lying with your face towards the floor and pushing with your hands to raise your body until your arms are straight. (US) পুশ-আপ

put (**puts, putting**) *vt* When you **put** something somewhere, you move it there. রাখা

put aside *v* If you **put** something **aside**, you keep it to be dealt with or used at a later time. সরিয়ে রাখা *I put money aside each month because I'm saving for a holiday.*

put away *v* If you **put** something **away**, you put it into the place where it is normally kept when it is not being used. ঠিক জায়গায় রাখা *Put your maths books away, it's time for your history lesson.*

put back *v* To **put** something **back** means to delay it or postpone it. স্থগিত রাখা *The trip has been put back to April.*

put forward *v* If you **put forward** a plan, proposal, or name, you suggest that it should be considered for a particular purpose or job. সামনে রাখা *I asked my boss to put my name forward for the job in head office.*

put in *v* If you **put in** an amount of time or effort doing something, you spend that time or effort doing it. সময় দেওয়া *We put in three hours' work every evening.*

put off *v* If you **put** something **off**, you delay doing it. দেরী করা *She put off telling him until the last moment.*

put up *v* If people **put up** a wall, building, tent, or other structure, they construct it. নির্মাণ করা *They put up their tents and settled down for the night.*

puzzle (**puzzles**) *n* A **puzzle** is a question, game, or toy which you have to think about carefully in order to answer it correctly or put it together properly. ধাঁধা

puzzled *adj* Someone who is **puzzled** is confused because they do not understand something. হতবুদ্ধি হওয়া

puzzling *adj* If something is **puzzling**, it is confusing or difficult to understand. হতবুদ্ধিকর

pyjamas *npl* A pair of **pyjamas** consists of loose trousers and a loose jacket that are worn in bed. পায়জামা

pylon (**pylons**) *n* **Pylons** are very tall metal structures which hold electric cables high above the ground so that electricity can be transmitted over long distances. উঁচু ইলেকট্রিক খুঁটি

pyramid (**pyramids**) *n* A **pyramid** is a three-dimensional shape with a flat base and flat triangular sides which slope upwards to a point. পিরামিড

q

Qatar *n* **Qatar** is a state in east Arabia, in the Persian Gulf. কাতার

quail (**quails, quail**) *n* A **quail** is a small bird which is often shot and eaten. কোয়েল

quaint (**quainter, quaintest**) *adj* Something that is **quaint** is attractive because it is unusual and rather old-fashioned. মনোরম

qualification (**qualifications**) *n* Your **qualifications** are the examinations that you have passed. যোগ্যতা

qualified *adj* If you give someone or something **qualified** support or approval, you give support or approval that is not total and suggests that you have some doubts. সীমিত সমর্থন

qualify (**qualifies, qualifying, qualified**) *v* When someone **qualifies**, they pass the examinations that they need to pass in order to work in a particular profession. যোগ্যতা অর্জন করা

quality (**qualities**) *n* The **quality** of something is how good or bad it is. গুণমান

quantify (**quantifies, quantifying, quantified**) *v* If you try to **quantify** something, you try to calculate how much of it there is. পরিমাণ নির্ণয় করা

quantity (**quantities**) *n* A **quantity** is an amount that you can measure or count. পরিমাণ

quarantine *n* If a person or animal is in **quarantine**, they are kept separate from other people or animals in case they have an infectious disease. সঙ্গরোধ

quarrel (**quarrels, quarrelling, quarrelled**) *n* A **quarrel** is an angry argument between two or more friends or family members. ঝগড়া ▷ *vi* When two or more people **quarrel**, they have an angry argument. ঝগড়া করা

quarry (**quarries**) *n* A **quarry** is an area that is dug out from a piece of land or mountainside in order to extract stone, slate, or minerals. খাদান

quarter (**quarters**) *n* A **quarter** is one of four equal parts of something. এক-চতুর্থাংশ

quarter final (**quarter finals**) *n* A **quarter final** is one of the four matches in a competition which decides which four players or teams will compete in the semi-final. কোয়ার্টার ফাইনাল

quartet (**quartets**) *n* A **quartet** is a group of four people who play musical instruments or sing together. চার গায়ক

quay (**quays**) *n* A **quay** is a long platform beside the sea or a river where boats are tied. নৌকা বাঁধার পাটাতন

queen (**queens**) *n* A **queen** is a woman who rules a country as its monarch. রাণী

query (**queries, querying, queried**) *n* A **query** is a question about a particular point. প্রশ্ন ▷ *vt* If you **query** something, you check it by asking about it because you are not sure if it is correct. প্রশ্ন করা

question (**questions, questioning, questioned**) *n* A **question** is something which you say or write in order to ask about a particular matter. প্রশ্ন ▷ *vt* If you **question** someone, you ask them questions about something. জিজ্ঞাসা করা

question mark (**question marks**) *n* A **question mark** is the punctuation mark (?) which is used in writing at the end of a question. জিজ্ঞাসা চিহ্ন

questionnaire (**questionnaires**) *n* A **questionnaire** is a written list of questions which are answered by a number of people in order to provide information for a report or survey. সমীক্ষার প্রশ্নাবলী

queue (**queues, queuing, queued**) *n* A **queue** is a line of people or vehicles that are waiting for something. লাইন ▷ *vi* When people **queue**, they stand in a line waiting for something. লাইনে দাঁড়ানো

quick (**quicker, quickest**) *adj* Someone or something that is **quick** moves or does things with great speed. তাড়াতাড়ি

quickly *adv* If someone or something moves or does something **quickly** they move or do something with great speed. তাড়াতাড়ি করে

quiet (**quieter, quietest**) *adj* Something or someone that is **quiet** makes only a small amount of noise. শান্ত

quietly *adv* If someone or something does something **quietly** they do it with only a small amount of noise. নিঃশব্দে

quilt (**quilts**) *n* A **quilt** is a bed-cover filled with warm soft material, which is often decorated with lines of stitching. লেপ

quit (**quits, quitting, quit**) *vt* If you **quit** your job, you choose to leave it. (*informal*) ছেড়ে দেওয়া

quite *adv* **Quite** means a bit but not a lot. বেশ

quiz (**quizzes**) *n* A **quiz** is a game or competition in which someone tests your knowledge by asking you questions. কুইজ

quota (**quotas**) *n* A **quota** is the limited number or quantity which is officially allowed. কোটা

quotation (**quotations**) *n* A **quotation** is a sentence or phrase taken from a book, poem, or play. উদ্ধৃতি

quotation marks *npl* **Quotation marks** are punctuation marks used in writing to show where speech or a quotation begins and ends. They are usually written or printed as (' ') and (" "). উদ্ধৃতি চিহ্ন

quote (**quotes, quoting, quoted**) *n* A **quote** from a book, poem, or play is a sentence or phrase from it. উদ্ধৃতি দেওয়া ▷ *vt* If you **quote** something, you repeat what someone has written or said. If you **quote** someone as saying something, you repeat what they have written or said. উদ্ধৃতি দেওয়া

rabbit (**rabbits**) *n* A **rabbit** is a small furry animal with long ears which is often kept as a pet. খরগোশ

rabies *n* **Rabies** is a serious infectious disease which humans can get from the bite of an animal such as a dog which has the disease. জলাতঙ্ক রোগ

race (**races, racing, raced**) *n* A **race** is a competition to see who is the fastest, for example in running or driving. দৌড় প্রতিযোগিতা ▷ *n* A **race** is one of the major groups which human beings can be divided into according to their physical features, such as their skin colour. জাতি ▷ *v* If you **race**, you take part in a race. দৌড় প্রতিযোগিতায় অংশগ্রহণ করা

racecourse (**racecourses**) *n* A **racecourse** is a track on which horses race. ঘোড়দৌড়ের মাঠ

racehorse (**racehorses**) *n* A **racehorse** is a horse that is trained to run in races. রেসের ঘোড়া

racer (**racers**) *n* A **racer** is a person or animal that takes part in races. দৌড় প্রতিযোগী

racetrack (**racetracks**) *n* A **racetrack** is a piece of ground that is used for races between runners, horses, dogs, cars, or motorcycles. (*US*) দৌড় প্রতিযোগিতার ট্র্যাক

racial *adj* **Racial** describes things relating to people's race. জাতিগত

racing car (**racing cars**) *n* A **racing car** is a car that has been specially designed for motor racing. রেসিং কার

racing driver (**racing drivers**) n A **racing driver** is a person who takes part in motor racing. মোটরগাড়ি রেসের চালক

racism n **Racism** is the belief that people of some races are inferior to others. জাতিবিদ্বেষ

racist (**racists**) adj If you describe people, things, or behaviour as **racist**, you mean that they are influenced by the belief that some people are inferior because they belong to a particular race. জাতিবিদ্বেষী ▷ n A **racist**, or a person with **racist** views, believes that people of some races are inferior to others. জাতিবিদ্বেষী

rack (**racks**) n A **rack** is a piece of equipment used for holding things or for hanging things on. তাক

racket (**rackets**) n A **racket** is a loud unpleasant noise. কোলাহলপূর্ণ আওয়াজ

racoon (**racoons**) n A **racoon** is a small animal that has dark-coloured fur with white stripes on its face and on its long tail. Racoons live in forests in North and Central America and the West Indies. র‍্যাকুন

racquet (**racquets**) n A **racquet** is an oval-shaped bat with strings across it. Racquets are used in tennis, squash, and badminton. ব্যাকেট (টেনিসের ব্যাট)

radar n **Radar** is a way of discovering the position or speed of objects such as aircraft or ships by using radio signals. র‍্যাডার

radiation n **Radiation** is very small particles of a radioactive substance. Large amounts of radiation can cause illness and death. বিকিরণ

radiator (**radiators**) n A **radiator** is a hollow metal device which is connected to a central heating system and used to heat a room. রেডিয়েটর

radio n **Radio** is the broadcasting of programmes for the public to listen to. বেতার

radioactive adj Something that is **radioactive** contains a substance that produces energy in the form of powerful rays which are harmful in large doses. তেজস্ক্রিয়

radio-controlled adj A **radio-controlled** device works by receiving radio signals which operate it. রেডিয়ো নিয়ন্ত্রিত

radio station (**radio stations**) n A **radio station** is an installation consisting of one or more transmitters or receivers, etc, used for radiocommunications. বেতারকেন্দ্র

radish (**radishes**) n **Radishes** are small red or white vegetables that are the roots of a plant. They are eaten raw in salads. মূলো

raffle (**raffles**) n A **raffle** is a competition in which you buy numbered tickets. Afterwards some numbers are chosen and if your ticket has one of these numbers on it, you win a prize. লটারি

raft (**rafts**) n A **raft** is a floating platform made from large pieces of wood tied together. ভেলা

rag (**rags**) n A **rag** is a piece of old cloth which you can use to clean or wipe things. ন্যাকড়া

rage (**rages**) n **Rage** is strong, uncontrollable anger. প্রচণ্ড রাগ

raid (**raids, raiding, raided**) n A **raid** is a sudden surprise attack. আচমকা হামলা ▷ vt When soldiers **raid** a place, they make a sudden armed attack against it, with the aim of causing damage rather than occupying any of the enemy's land. আচমকা হামলা করা

rail (**rails**) n A **rail** is a horizontal bar which is fixed to something and used as a fence or a support, or to hang things on. হাতল

railcard (**railcards**) n A **railcard** is an identity card that allows people to buy train tickets cheaply. রেলকার্ড

railings npl A fence made from metal bars is called a **railing** or **railings**. রেলিং

railway (**railways**) n A **railway** is a route between two places along which trains travel on steel rails. রেলওয়ে

railway station (**railway stations**) n A **railway station** is a building by a railway line where trains stop so that people can get on or off. রেলওয়ে স্টেশন

rain (**rains, raining, rained**) *n* Rain is water that falls from the clouds in small drops. বৃষ্টি ▷ *vi* When rain falls, you can say that it **is raining.** বৃষ্টি পড়া

rainbow (**rainbows**) *n* A **rainbow** is the arch of different colours that you sometimes see in the sky when it is raining. রামধনু

raincoat (**raincoats**) *n* A **raincoat** is a waterproof coat. বর্ষাতি

rainforest (**rainforests**) *n* A **rainforest** is a thick forest of tall trees found in tropical areas where there is a lot of rain. রেনফরেস্ট

rainy (**rainier, rainiest**) *adj* If it is **rainy**, it is raining a lot. বর্ষণময়

raise (**raises, raising, raised**) *vt* If you **raise** something, you move it to a higher position. ওঠানো

raisin (**raisins**) *n* **Raisins** are dried grapes. কিসমিস্

rake (**rakes**) *n* A **rake** is a garden tool consisting of a row of metal teeth attached to a long handle. বাগান করবার যন্ত্র

rally (**rallies**) *n* A **rally** is a large public meeting held in support of something such as a political party. সমাবেশ

ram (**rams, ramming, rammed**) *n* A **ram** is an adult male sheep. পুরুষ ভেড়া ▷ *vt* If one

vehicle **rams** another, it crashes into it with a lot of force. প্রচণ্ড জোরে ধাক্কা মারা

Ramadan *n* **Ramadan** is the ninth month of the Muslim year, when Muslims do not eat between the rising and setting of the sun. During Ramadan, Muslims celebrate the fact that it was in this month that God first revealed the words of the Quran to Mohammed. রমজান

rambler (**ramblers**) *n* A **rambler** is a person whose hobby is going on long walks in the countryside, often as part of an organized group. এদিক-ওদিক বিচরণকারী ব্যক্তি

ramp (**ramps**) *n* A **ramp** is a sloping surface between two places that are at different levels. র্যাম্প

random *adj* A **random** sample or method is one in which all the people or things involved have an equal chance of being chosen. এলোমেলো

range (**ranges, ranging, ranged**) *n* The **range** of something is the maximum area within which it can reach things or detect things. সীমা ▷ *n* A **range** of mountains or hills is a line of them. পর্বতমালা ▷ *vi* If things **range** between two points or **range** from one point to another, they vary within these points on a scale of measurement or quality. প্রসার

rank (**ranks, ranking, ranked**) *n* Someone's **rank** is their position in an organization, or in society. পদমর্যাদা ▷ *n* A **rank** of people or things is a row of them. সারি ▷ *v* When someone or something **is ranked** a particular position, they are at that position on a scale. স্থান

ransom (**ransoms**) *n* A **ransom** is money that is demanded as payment for the return of someone who has been kidnapped. মুক্তিপণ

rape (**rapes, raping, raped**) *n* Rape is the crime of forcing someone to have sex. ধর্ষণ ▷ *n* **Rape** is a plant with yellow flowers which is grown as a crop. Its seeds are

crushed to make cooking oil. সর্ষেজাতীয় গাছ ▷ vt If someone **is raped**, they are forced to have sex, usually by violence or threats of violence. ধর্ষিত হওয়া

rapids npl **Rapids** are a section of a river where the water moves very fast. খর

rapist (rapists) n A **rapist** is a man who has raped someone. ধর্ষণকারী

rare (rarer, rarest) adj If something is **rare**, it is not common, and is therefore interesting, valuable, or unusual. দুর্লভ ▷ adj Meat that is **rare** is cooked very lightly so that the inside is still red. আধসিদ্ধ

rarely adv **Rarely** means not very often. কখনও সখনও

rash (rashes) n A **rash** is an area of red spots on your skin which appear when you are ill or have an allergy. ফুসকুড়ি

raspberry (raspberries) n A **raspberry** is a small, soft, red fruit that grows on bushes. রাস্পবেরি ফল

rat (rats) n A **rat** is an animal which has a long tail and looks like a large mouse. ধেড়ে ইঁদুর

rate (rates, rating, rated) n The **rate** at which something happens is the speed or frequency with which it happens. গতি ▷ vt If you **rate** someone or something as good or bad, you consider them to be good or bad. মূল্যায়ন করা

rate of exchange (rates of exchange) n The **rate of exchange** of a country's unit of currency is the amount of another currency that you get in exchange for it. মুদ্রার বিনিময় হার

rather adv You use **rather** to mean 'a little bit'. বরং

ratio (ratios) n The **ratio** of something is the relationship between two things expressed in numbers or amounts, to show how much greater one is than the other. অনুপাত

rational adj **Rational** decisions and thoughts are based on reason rather than on emotion. যুক্তিবুদ্ধিসম্পন্ন

rattle (rattles) n A **rattle** is a rapid succession of short sharp sounds. ঠকঠক আওয়াজ

rattlesnake (rattlesnakes) n A **rattlesnake** is a poisonous American snake which can make a rattling noise with its tail. একধরনের বিষাক্ত সাপ

rave (raves, raving, raved) n A **rave** or a **rave** review is a very enthusiastic review. উচ্ছ্বসময় ▷ v If someone **raves**, they talk in an excited and uncontrolled way. উচ্ছ্বসিত হয়ে কথা বলা

raven (ravens) n A **raven** is a large bird with shiny black feathers and a deep harsh call. দাঁড়কাক

ravenous adj If you are **ravenous**, you are extremely hungry. প্রচন্ড ক্ষুধার্ত

ravine (ravines) n A **ravine** is a very deep, narrow valley with steep sides. সংকীর্ণ গিরিখাত

raw (rawer, rawest) adj A **raw** substance is in its natural state before being processed. কাঁচা

razor (razors) n A **razor** is a tool that people use for shaving. রেজর

razor blade (razor blades) n A **razor blade** is a small flat piece of metal with a very sharp edge which is put into a razor and used for shaving. রেজর ব্লেড

reach (reaches, reaching, reached) vt When you **reach** a place, you arrive there. পৌঁছানো ▷ vi If you **reach** somewhere, you move your arm and hand to take or touch something. নাগাল পাওয়া

react (**reacts, reacting, reacted**) *vi* When you **react** to something that has happened to you, you behave in a particular way because of it. প্রতিক্রিয়া জানানো

reaction (**reactions**) *n* Your **reaction** to something that has happened or something that you have experienced is what you feel, say, or do because of it. প্রতিক্রিয়া

reactor (**reactors**) *n* A **reactor** is a device which produces nuclear energy. পারমাণবিক চুল্লি

read (**reads, reading**) *v* When you **read** something such as a book or article, you look at and understand the words that are written there. পড়া

reader (**readers**) *n* The **readers** of a book, newspaper, or magazine are the people who read it. পাঠক

readily *adv* If you do something **readily**, you do it willingly. সাগ্রহে

reading *n* **Reading** is the activity of reading books. পঠন

read out *v* If you **read** something **out**, you say the words aloud, especially in a loud, clear voice. জোরে জোরে পড়া *We read plays out in class.*

ready (**readier, readiest**) *adj* If someone or something is **ready**, they have reached the required stage for something or they are properly prepared for action or use. প্রস্তুত

ready-cooked *adj* If food that you buy is **ready-cooked**, you only have to heat it before eating it because it has already been cooked. চটজলদি তৈরী

real *adj* Something that is **real** is true and is not imagined. প্রকৃত ▷ *adj* If something is **real**, it is not a copy. খাঁটি

realistic *adj* If you are **realistic** about a situation, you recognize and accept its true nature and try to deal with it practically. বাস্তবধর্মী

reality *n* You use **reality** to refer to real things or the real nature of things rather than imagined, invented, or theoretical ideas. বাস্তবতা

reality TV *n* **Reality TV** is a type of television which aims to show how ordinary people behave in everyday life, or in situations, often created by the programme makers, which are intended to represent everyday life. রিয়ালিটি টিভি

realize (**realizes, realizing, realized**) *v* If you **realize** that something is true, you become aware of that fact or understand it. উপলব্ধি করা

really *adv* You say **really** to show how much you mean something. (*spoken*) প্রকৃতপক্ষে ▷ *adv* You say **really** to show that what you are saying is true. সত্যসত্যই

rear *adj* **Rear** means situated in the back part of something or refers to the back part of something. পশ্চাৎ ▷ *n* The **rear** of something is the back part of it. পিছনের

rear-view mirror (**rear-view mirrors**) *n* Inside a car, the **rear-view mirror** is the mirror that enables you to see the traffic behind when you are driving. পশ্চাৎ দর্শনযোগ্য আয়না

reason (**reasons**) *n* The **reason** for something is a fact or situation which explains why it happens. কারণ

reasonable *adj* If you think that someone is fair and sensible you can say they are **reasonable**. যুক্তিসম্পন্ন

reasonably *adv* If someone behaves or acts **reasonably** they behave or act fairly and sensibly. যুক্তিসম্পন্নভাবে

reassure (**reassures, reassuring, reassured**) *vt* If you **reassure** someone, you say or do things to make them stop worrying about something. দুশ্চিন্তামুক্ত করা

reassuring *adj* If you find someone's words or actions **reassuring**, they make you feel less worried. দুশ্চিন্তামুক্তকর

rebate (**rebates**) *n* A **rebate** is an amount of money which is paid to you when you have paid more tax, rent, or rates than you needed to. ছাড়

rebellious adj A **rebellious** person behaves in an unacceptable way and does not do what they are told. অবাধ্য

rebuild (rebuilds, rebuilding, rebuilt) vt When people **rebuild** something such as a building, they build it again after it has been damaged or destroyed. পুনর্নির্মাণ

receipt (receipts) n A **receipt** is a piece of paper that you get from someone as confirmation that they have received money or goods from you. রসিদ

receive (receives, receiving, received) vt When you **receive** something, you get it after someone gives it to you or sends it to you. পাওয়া

receiver (receivers) n A telephone **receiver** is the part that you hold near to your ear and speak into. ফোনের রিসিভার
▷ n A **receiver** is someone who is officially appointed to manage the affairs of a business, usually when it is facing financial failure. প্রাপক

recent adj A **recent** event or period of time happened only a short while ago. সাম্প্রতিক

recently adv If you have done something **recently** or if something happened **recently**, it happened only a short time ago. সাম্প্রতিককালে

reception (receptions) n In a hotel, office, or hospital the **reception** is the place where people are received and their reservations, appointments, and inquiries are dealt with. রিসেপশন

receptionist (receptionists) n In a hotel, office, or hospital, the **receptionist** is the person whose job is to answer the telephone, arrange reservations or appointments, and deal with people when they first arrive. রিসেপশনিস্ট

recession (recessions) n A **recession** is a period when the economy of a country is not very successful. আর্থিক মন্দা

recharge (recharges, recharging, recharged) vt If you **recharge** a battery, you put an electrical charge back into the battery by connecting it to a machine that draws power from another source of electricity such as the mains. রিচার্জ করা

recipe (recipes) n A **recipe** is a list of ingredients and a set of instructions that tell you how to cook something. রন্ধনপ্রণালী

recipient (recipients) n The **recipient** of something is the person who receives it. (formal) গ্রহীতা

reckon (reckons, reckoning, reckoned) vt If you **reckon** that something is true, you think that it is true. (informal) চিন্তা করা

reclining adj A **reclining** seat has a back that you can lower so that it is more comfortable to sit in. হেলানো

recognizable adj Something that is **recognizable** is easy to recognize or identify. চেনার মত

recognize (recognizes, recognizing, recognized) vt If you **recognize** someone or something, you know who or what they are, because you have seen or heard them before or because they have been described to you. চিনতে পারা

recommend (recommends, recommending, recommended) vt If someone **recommends** something or someone to you, they suggest that you would find them good or useful. সুপারিশ করা

recommendation (recommendations) n The **recommendations** of a person or a committee are their suggestions or advice on what is the best thing to do. সুপারিশ

reconsider (reconsiders, reconsidering, reconsidered) v If you **reconsider** a decision or method, you think about it and try to decide whether it should be changed. পুনর্বিবেচনা

record (records, recording, recorded) n If you keep a **record** of something, you keep a written account or photographs of it so that it can be looked at later. লিখিত বিবরণ ▷ vt If you **record** a piece of information or an event, you write it down or photograph it so that in the future people can look at it. লিখিত বিবরণ রাখা ▷ n A **record** is the best result ever. রেকর্ড ▷ vt If you **record** something like a TV programme, you make a copy of it so that you can watch it later. রেকর্ড করা

recorded delivery n If you send a letter or parcel **recorded delivery**, you send it using a Post Office service which gives you an official record of the fact that it has been posted and delivered. রেকর্ডকৃত ডেলিভারি

recorder (**recorders**) n A **recorder** is a hollow musical instrument that you play by blowing down one end and covering a series of holes with your fingers. বাঁশরি ▷ n A **recorder** is a machine or instrument that keeps a record of something, for example, in an experiment or on a vehicle. রেকর্ডার

recording (**recordings**) n A **recording** of something such as moving pictures and sounds is a computer file or a disk on which they are stored. রেকর্ডিং

recover (**recovers, recovering, recovered**) vi When you **recover** from an illness or an injury, you become well again. আরোগ্য লাভ করা

recovery (**recoveries**) n If a sick person makes a **recovery**, he or she becomes well again. আরোগ্য লাভ

recruitment n The **recruitment** of workers, soldiers, or members is the act or process of selecting them for an organization or army and persuading them to join. নিয়োগ

rectangle (**rectangles**) n A **rectangle** is a shape with four sides whose angles are all right angles. Each side of a rectangle is the same length as the one opposite to it. আয়তক্ষেত্র

rectangular adj Something that is **rectangular** is shaped like a rectangle. আয়তকার

rectify (**rectifies, rectifying, rectified**) vt If you **rectify** something that is wrong, you change it so that it becomes correct or satisfactory. শুধরানো

recurring adj Something that is **recurring** happens more than once. পৌনঃপুনিক

recycle (**recycles, recycling, recycled**) vt If you **recycle** things that have already been used, such as bottles or sheets of paper, you process them so that they can be used again. পুনর্ব্যবহারযোগ্য করে তোলা

recycling n **Recycling** is the means by which things that have already been used, such as bottles or sheets of paper, are processed so that they can be used again. পুনর্ব্যবহারযোগ্য

red (**redder, reddest**) adj Something that is **red** is the colour of blood or tomatoes. লাল

Red Cross n The **Red Cross** is an international organization that helps people who are suffering, for example, as a result of war, floods, or disease. রেড ক্রশ

redcurrant (**redcurrants**) n **Redcurrants** are very small, bright red berries that grow in bunches on a bush and can be eaten as a fruit or cooked to make a sauce for meat. লাল বেরী জাতীয় ফল

redecorate (**redecorates, redecorating, redecorated**) v If you **redecorate** a room or a building, you put new paint or wallpaper on it. পুনঃসজ্জিত করা

red-haired adj A **red-haired** person is a person whose hair is red and brown in colour. লাল চুলওয়ালা লোক

redhead (**redheads**) n A **redhead** is person, especially a woman, whose hair is a colour that is between red and brown. লাল চুলওয়ালা মহিলা

red meat (**red meats**) n **Red meat** is meat such as beef or lamb, which is dark brown

r

in colour after it has been cooked. গরু, ভেড়া-ছাগলের মাংস

redo (**redoes, redoing, redid, redone**) vt If you **redo** a piece of work, you do it again in order to improve it or change it. পুনর্গঠন করা

Red Sea n The **Red Sea** is a long narrow sea between Arabia and north-east Africa. রেড সী

reduce (**reduces, reducing, reduced**) vt If you **reduce** something, you make it smaller. হ্রাস করা

reduction (**reductions**) n When there is a **reduction** in something, it is made smaller. হ্রাস

redundancy (**redundancies**) n If there are **redundancies** within an organization, some of its employees are dismissed because their jobs are no longer necessary or because the organization can no longer afford to pay them. ছাঁটাই

redundant adj If you are made **redundant**, you lose your job because it is no longer necessary or because your employer cannot afford to keep paying you. ছাঁটাই হওয়া

red wine (**red wines**) n **Red wine** is wine that gets its red colour from the skins of the grapes. রেড ওয়াইন

reed (**reeds**) n **Reeds** are tall plants that grow in shallow water or wet ground. নলখাগড়া

reel (**reels**) n A **reel** is a cylinder-shaped object around which you wrap something such as thread or cinema film. রীল

refer (**refers, referring, referred**) vi If you **refer** to a particular subject or person, you mention them. প্রসঙ্গ উল্লেখ করা

referee (**referees**) n The **referee** is the official who controls a sports match. রেফারি

reference (**references**) n **Reference** to someone or something is the act of talking about them or mentioning them. A **reference** is a particular example of this. প্রসঙ্গ

reference number (**reference numbers**) n A **reference number** is a number that tells you where you can obtain the information you want. রেফারেন্স নম্বর

refill (**refills, refilling, refilled**) vt If you **refill** something, you fill it again after it has been emptied. পুনরায় ভর্তি করা

refinery (**refineries**) n A **refinery** is a factory which refines a substance such as oil or sugar. শোধনাগার

reflect (**reflects, reflecting, reflected**) vt If something **reflects** an attitude or situation, it shows that the attitude or situation exists. প্রতিফলিত হওয়া

reflection (**reflections**) n A **reflection** is an image that you can see in a mirror or in water. প্রতিফলন

reflex (**reflexes**) n A **reflex** or a **reflex action** is a normal uncontrollable reaction of your body to something that you feel, see, or experience. প্রতিবর্ত ক্রিয়া

refresher course (**refresher courses**) n A **refresher course** is a training course in which people improve their knowledge or skills and learn about new developments that are related to the job that they do. কোন বিষয় সম্বন্ধে সাম্প্রতিক জ্ঞান প্রদানের জন্য প্রশিক্ষণ ব্যবস্থা

refreshing adj A **refreshing** bath or drink makes you feel energetic or cool again after you have been tired or hot. তরতাজা

refreshments npl **Refreshments** are drinks and small amounts of food that are provided, for example, during a meeting or journey. জলখাবার

refrigerator (**refrigerators**) n A **refrigerator** is a large container which is kept cool inside, usually by electricity, so that the food and drink in it stays fresh. রেফ্রিজারেটর

refuel (**refuels, refuelling, refuelled**) v When an aircraft or other vehicle **refuels**, it is filled with more fuel so that it can continue its journey. পুনরায় তেল নেওয়া

refuge n If you take **refuge** somewhere, you try to protect yourself from physical harm by going there. আশ্রয়

refugee (**refugees**) *n* **Refugees** are people who have been forced to leave their country because there is a war there or because of their political or religious beliefs. উদ্বাস্তু

refund (**refunds, refunding, refunded**) *n* A **refund** is a sum of money which is returned to you, for example because you have returned goods to a shop. ফেরত মূল্য ▷ *vt* If someone **refunds** your money, they return it to you. মূল্য ফেরত দেওয়া

refusal (**refusals**) *n* A **refusal** is the fact of firmly saying or showing that you will not do, allow, or accept something. প্রত্যাখ্যান

refuse (**refuses, refusing, refused**) *n* **Refuse** consists of the rubbish and unwanted things in a house, shop, or factory that are regularly thrown away. আবর্জনা ▷ *v* If you **refuse** to do something, you deliberately do not do it, or say firmly that you will not do it. প্রত্যাখ্যান করা

regain (**regains, regaining, regained**) *vt* If you **regain** something that you have lost, you get it back again. পুনরায় লাভ করা

regard (**regards, regarding, regarded**) *n* If you have a high **regard** for someone, you have a lot of respect for them. শ্রদ্ধা ▷ *vt* If you **regard** someone or something in a particular way, you think of them in that way, or have that opinion of them. বিবেচনা করা

regarding *prep* You can use **regarding** to say what people are talking or writing about. সম্পর্কে *They refused to give any information regarding the accident.*

regiment (**regiments**) *n* A **regiment** is a large group of soldiers commanded by a colonel. রেজিমেন্ট

region (**regions**) *n* A **region** is an area of a country or of the world. অঞ্চল

regional *adj* **Regional** is used to describe things which relate to a particular area of a country or of the world. আঞ্চলিক

register (**registers, registering, registered**) *n* A **register** is an official list or record.

নিবন্ধগ্রহ ▷ *vi* If you **register** for something, you put your name on an official list. নিবন্ধিত করা

registered *adj* A **registered** letter or parcel is sent by a special postal service, for which you pay extra money for insurance in case it gets lost. নিবন্ধিত

registration *n* The **registration** of something is the recording of it in an official list. তালিকাভুক্তকরণ

registry office (**registry offices**) *n* A **registry office** is a place where births, marriages, and deaths are officially recorded, and where people can get married without a religious ceremony. নিবন্ধীকরণ কার্যালয়

regret (**regrets, regretting, regretted**) *n* **Regret** is a feeling of sadness or disappointment. অনুশোচনা ▷ *vt* If you **regret** something that you have done, you wish that you had not done it. অনুশোচনা করা

regular *adj* **Regular** things happen at equal intervals, or involve things happening at equal intervals. নিয়মিত

regularly *adv* If you do something **regularly** or something happens **regularly**, you do it or it happens at equal intervals. নিয়মিতভাবে

regulation *n* **Regulation** is the controlling of an activity or process, usually by means of rules. বিধিনিয়ম

rehearsal (**rehearsals**) *n* A **rehearsal** of a play, dance, or piece of music is the time when those taking part practise it. অনুষ্ঠানের মহড়া

rehearse (**rehearses, rehearsing, rehearsed**) *v* When people **rehearse** a play, dance, or piece of music, they practise it. অনুষ্ঠানের মহড়া দেওয়া

reimburse (**reimburses, reimbursing, reimbursed**) *vt* If you **reimburse** someone for something, you pay them back the money that they have spent or lost because of it. (*formal*) শোধ করে দেওয়া

reindeer (**reindeer**) *n* A **reindeer** is a type of deer that lives in northern areas of Europe, Asia, and America. বল্গা হরিণ

reins *npl* **Reins** are the long leather straps attached to a horse's head which are used to make it go faster or stop. লাগাম

reject (**rejects, rejecting, rejected**) *vt* If you **reject** something such as a proposal or request, you do not accept it or agree to it. বাতিল করা

relapse (**relapses**) *n* If someone has a **relapse** or if there is a **relapse** then that person starts to behave in a particular way again or a situation returns to how it was before. পুনরাক্রমণ

related *adj* If two or more things are **related**, there is a connection between them. সম্পর্কিত

relation (**relations**) *n* **Relations** between people, groups, or countries are contacts between them and the way they behave towards each other. সম্পর্ক

relationship (**relationships**) *n* The **relationship** between two people or groups is the way they feel and behave towards each other. সম্পর্ক

relative (**relatives**) *n* Your **relatives** are the members of your family. আত্মীয়

relatively *adv* **Relatively** means to a certain degree, especially when compared with other things of the same kind. তুলনামূলকভাবে

relax (**relaxes, relaxing, relaxed**) *v* If you **relax**, or if something **relaxes** you, you feel calmer and less worried or tense. বিশ্রাম নেওয়া

relaxation *n* **Relaxation** is a way of spending time in which you rest and feel comfortable. বিশ্রাম

relaxed *adj* If you are **relaxed**, you are calm and not worried or tense. নিশ্চিত

relaxing *adj* Something that is **relaxing** is pleasant and helps you to relax. নিরুদ্বেগজনিত

relay (**relays**) *n* A **relay** or a **relay race** is a race between two or more teams in which each member of the team runs or swims one section of the race. রিলে রেস

release (**releases, releasing, released**) *n* When someone is released, you refer to their **release**. মুক্তি ▷ *vt* If a person or animal **is released** from somewhere where they have been locked up or looked after, they are set free or allowed to go. মুক্ত হওয়া

relegate (**relegates, relegating, relegated**) *vt* If a team that competes in a league **is relegated**, it is moved to a lower division because it finished at or near the bottom of its division at the end of a season. বহিষ্কার করা

relevant *adj* If something is **relevant** to a situation or person, it is important or significant in that situation or to that person. প্রাসঙ্গিক

reliable *adj* **Reliable** people or things can be trusted to work well or to behave in the way that you want them to. বিশ্বাসী

relief *n* If you feel a sense of **relief**, you feel glad because something unpleasant has not happened or is no longer happening. স্বস্তি

relieve (**relieves, relieving, relieved**) *vt* If something **relieves** an unpleasant feeling or situation, it makes it less unpleasant or causes it to disappear completely. স্বস্তি পাওয়া

relieved *adj* If you are **relieved**, you feel glad because something unpleasant has not happened or is no longer happening. উদ্বেগমুক্ত

religion n **Religion** is belief in a god or gods. ধর্ম

religious adj **Religious** means connected with religion or with one particular religion. ধার্মিক

reluctant adj If you are **reluctant** to do something, you do not really want to do it. অনিচ্ছুক

reluctantly adv If you do something **reluctantly** you do not really want to do it. অনিচ্ছুকভাবে

rely on v If you **rely on** someone or something, you need them and depend on them in order to live or work properly. কাউকে বিশ্বাস করা *The country relies heavily on tourism.*

remain (**remains, remaining, remained**) v To **remain** in a particular state means to stay in that state and not change. থেকে যাওয়া

remaining adj The **remaining** things or people out of a group are the things or people that still exist, are still present, or have not yet been dealt with. অবশিষ্টাংশ

remains npl The **remains** of something are the parts of it that are left after most of it has been taken away or destroyed. অবশিষ্ট

remake (**remakes**) n A **remake** is a film that has the same story, and often the same title, as a film that was made earlier. পুনর্গঠন

remark (**remarks**) n If you make a **remark** about something, you say something about it. মন্তব্য

remarkable adj Someone or something that is **remarkable** is very impressive or unusual. স্মরণীয়

remarkably adv **Remarkably** means impressively or unusually. স্মরণীয়ভাবে

remarry (**remarries, remarrying, remarried**) vi If someone **remarries**, they marry again after they have obtained a divorce from their previous husband or wife, or after their previous husband or wife has died. পুনর্বিবাহ

remedy (**remedies**) n A **remedy** is a successful way of dealing with a problem. প্রতিকার

remember (**remembers, remembering, remembered**) v If you **remember** people or events from the past, you still have an idea of them in your mind and you are able to think about them. স্মরণ করা

remind (**reminds, reminding, reminded**) vt If someone **reminds** you of a fact or event that you already know about, they say something which makes you think about it. মনে করানো

reminder (**reminders**) n If one thing is a **reminder** of another, the first thing makes you think about the second. (*written*) স্মরণচিহ্ন

remorse n **Remorse** is a strong feeling of guilt and regret about something wrong that you have done. প্রবল অনুশোচনা

remote (**remoter, remotest**) adj **Remote** areas are far away from places where most people live. সুদূর

remote control n **Remote control** is a system of controlling a machine or vehicle from a distance by using radio or electronic signals. দূরনিয়ন্ত্রণ

remotely adv You use **remotely** to emphasize a negative statement. ক্ষীণভাবে

removable adj A **removable** part of something is a part that can easily be moved from its place or position. অপসারণযোগ্য

removal n The **removal** of something is the act of removing it. অপসারণ

removal van (**removal vans**) n A **removal van** is a large vehicle that is used to transport furniture or equipment from one building to another. মালপত্র বহনের ভ্যান

remove (**removes, removing, removed**) vt If you **remove** something from a place, you take it away. (*written*) অপসারণ করা

rendezvous (**rendezvous**) n A **rendezvous** is a meeting, often a secret one, that you have arranged with someone for a particular time and place. পূর্বনির্দিষ্ট সাক্ষাত

renew (renews, renewing, renewed) *vt* If you **renew** an activity or a relationship, you begin it again. পুননবীকরণ করা

renewable *adj* **Renewable** resources are ones such as wind, water, and sunlight, which are constantly replacing themselves and therefore do not become used up. নবীকরণযোগ্য

renovate (renovates, renovating, renovated) *vt* If someone **renovates** an old building or machine, they repair it and get it back into good condition. মেরামত করা

renowned *adj* A person or place that is **renowned** for something, usually something good, is well known because of it. বিখ্যাত

rent (rents, renting, rented) *n* **Rent** is the amount of money that you pay regularly to use a house, flat, or piece of land. ভাড়া ▷ *vt* If you **rent** something, you regularly pay its owner in order to have it and use it yourself. ভাড়া দেওয়া

rental (rentals) *n* The **rental** of something such as a car or television is the fact of paying an amount of money in order to have and use it. ভাড়ার অর্থ

reorganize (reorganizes, reorganizing, reorganized) *vt* To **reorganize** something means to change the way in which it is organized or done. পুনর্গঠন করা

rep (reps) *n* A **rep** is a person who travels round selling their company's products or services to other companies. ভ্রাম্যমাণ বিক্রেতা

repair (repairs, repairing, repaired) *n* A **repair** is something that you do to mend something that has been damaged. মেরামত ▷ *vt* If you **repair** something that has been damaged or is not working properly, you mend it. মেরামত করা

repair kit (repair kits) *n* A **repair kit** is a group of items that you keep together, usually in the same container, in case you need to repair something. মেরামতির কিট

repay (repays, repaying, repaid) *vt* If you **repay** a debt, you pay back the money you owe to somebody. পরিশোধ করা

repayment (repayments) *n* A **repayment** is an amount of money paid at regular intervals in order to repay a debt. পরিশোধ

repeat (repeats, repeating, repeated) *n* If there is a **repeat** of an event, usually an undesirable event, it happens again. পুনরাবৃত্তি ▷ *vt* If you **repeat** something, you say or write it again. পুনরাবৃত্তি করা

repeatedly *adv* If you do something **repeatedly**, you do it many times. বারবার

repellent *adj* If you think that something is horrible and disgusting, you can say it is **repellent**. (*formal*) নিবারক

repercussions *npl* If an action or event has **repercussions**, it causes unpleasant things to happen some time after the original action or event. (*formal*) গভীর প্রতিক্রিয়া

repetitive *adj* **Repetitive** actions are repeated many times and are therefore boring. পুনরাবৃত্তিমূলক

replace (replaces, replacing, replaced) *vt* To **replace** a person or thing means to put another person or thing in their place. বদল করা

replacement *n* If you refer to the **replacement** of one thing by another, you mean that the second thing takes the place of the first. পরিবর্তন

replay (replays, replaying, replayed) *n* A **replay** is a showing again of a sequence of action, esp of part of a sporting contest immediately after it happens. পুনঃপ্রদর্শন ▷ *vt* If a match between two sports teams **is replayed**, the two teams play it again, because neither team won the first time, or because the match was stopped because of bad weather. পুনঃপ্রদর্শন করা

replica (replicas) *n* A **replica** of something such as a statue, machine, or weapon is an accurate copy of it. প্রতিরূপ

reply (replies, replying, replied) *n* A **reply** is something that you say or write when you answer someone or answer a letter or advertisement. উত্তর ▷ *vi* When you **reply** to something that someone has said or written to you, you say or write an answer to them. উত্তর দেওয়া

report (reports, reporting, reported) *n* A **report** is a news article or broadcast which gives information about something that has just happened. প্রতিবেদন ▷ *vt* If you **report** something that has happened, you tell people about it. প্রতিবেদন করা ▷ *n* A **report** is an official written account of how well or how badly a pupil has done during the term or year that has just finished. পরীক্ষার ফলাফল

reporter (reporters) *n* A **reporter** is someone who writes news articles or broadcasts news reports. প্রতিবেদক

represent (represents, representing, represented) *vt* If someone **represents** you, they act on your behalf. প্রতিনিধিত্ব করা

representative *adj* A **representative** group acts on behalf of a larger group. প্রতিনিধি

reproduction (reproductions) *n* A **reproduction** is a copy of something such as an antique or a painting. অনুকরণ

reptile (reptiles) *n* **Reptiles** are a group of animals which have scales on their skin and lay eggs. Snakes and crocodiles are reptiles. সরীসৃপ

republic (republics) *n* A **republic** is a country that has a president or whose system of government is based on the idea that every citizen has equal status. প্রজাতন্ত্র

repulsive *adj* **Repulsive** means horrible and disgusting. জঘন্য

reputable *adj* A **reputable** company or person is reliable and trustworthy. বিশ্বাসযোগ্য

reputation (reputations) *n* To have a **reputation** for something means to be known or remembered for it. নামডাক

request (requests, requesting, requested) *n* If you make a **request**, you politely ask for something or ask someone to do something. (*formal*) অনুরোধ ▷ *vt* If you **request** something, you ask for it politely or formally. (*formal*) অনুরোধ করা

require (requires, requiring, required) *vt* To **require** something means to need it. (*formal*) দরকার হওয়া

requirement (requirements) *n* A **requirement** is a quality or qualification that you must have in order to be allowed to do something or to be suitable for something. চাহিদা

rescue (rescues, rescuing, rescued) *n* A **rescue** is an attempt to save someone from a dangerous or unpleasant situation. উদ্ধার ▷ *vt* If you **rescue** someone, you get them out of a dangerous or unpleasant situation. উদ্ধার করা

research *n* **Research** is work that involves studying something and trying to discover facts about it. গবেষণা

resemblance (resemblances) *n* If there is a **resemblance** between two people or things, they are similar to each other. সাদৃশ্য

resemble (resembles, resembling, resembled) *vt* If one thing or person **resembles** another, they are similar to that thing or person. সদৃশ হওয়া

resent (resents, resenting, resented) *vt* If you **resent** someone or something, you feel bitter and angry about them. ক্রুদ্ধ হওয়া

resentful *adj* If you are **resentful**, you feel resentment. ক্রুদ্ধ

reservation (reservations) *n* If you have **reservations** about something, you are not sure that it is entirely good or right. সংরক্ষণ

r

reserve (**reserves, reserving, reserved**) n A **reserve** is a supply of something that is available for use when needed. মজুত ▷ n A nature **reserve** is an area of land where animals, birds, and plants are officially protected. অভয়ারণ্য ▷ vt If something **is reserved** for a particular person or purpose, it is kept specially for that person or purpose. সংরক্ষিত রাখা

reserved adj Someone who is **reserved** keeps their feelings hidden. গম্ভীর

reservoir (**reservoirs**) n A **reservoir** is a lake used for storing water before it is supplied to people. জলাধার

resident (**residents**) n The **residents** of a house or area are the people who live there. আবাসিক

residential adj A **residential** area contains houses rather than offices or factories. বসবাসের জন্য নির্দিষ্ট

resign (**resigns, resigning, resigned**) vi If you **resign** from a job or position, you formally announce that you are leaving it. পদত্যাগ করা

resin (**resins**) n **Resin** is a sticky substance produced by some trees. গঁদের আঠা

resist (**resists, resisting, resisted**) vt If you **resist** a change, you refuse to accept it and try to prevent it. বাধা দেওয়া

resistance n **Resistance** to a change or a new idea is a refusal to accept it. বাধা

resit (**resits, resitting, resat**) v If someone **resits** a test or examination, they take it again, usually because they failed the first time. পুনরায় পরীক্ষা দেওয়া

resolution (**resolutions**) n A **resolution** is a formal decision taken at a meeting by means of a vote. প্রস্তাব

resort (**resorts**) n A holiday **resort** is a place where people can spend their holidays. অবসর-নিবাস

resort to v If you **resort to** a course of action that you do not really approve of, you adopt it because you cannot see any other way of achieving what you want.

পন্থা নেওয়া Some schools have resorted to recruiting teachers from overseas.

resource (**resources**) n The **resources** of a country, organization, or person are the materials, money, and other things they have and can use. সম্পদ

respect (**respects, respecting, respected**) n If you have **respect** for someone, you have a good opinion of them. শ্রদ্ধা ▷ vt If you **respect** someone, you have a good opinion of their character or ideas. শ্রদ্ধা করা

respectable adj Someone or something that is **respectable** is approved of by society and considered to be morally correct. শ্রদ্ধেয়

respectively adv **Respectively** means in the same order as the items you have just mentioned. যথাক্রমে

respond (**responds, responding, responded**) vi When you **respond** to something that is done or said, you react by doing or saying something. জবাব দেওয়া

response (**responses**) n Your **response** to an event or to something that is said is your reply or reaction to it. জবাব

responsibility (**responsibilities**) n If you have **responsibility** for something or someone, it is your job or duty to deal with them. দায়িত্ব

responsible adj If you are **responsible** for something bad that has happened, it is your fault. দায়িত্বশীল

rest (**rests, resting, rested**) n The **rest** is the parts of something that are left. বাকি ▷ v If you **rest** or if you **rest** your body, you sit or lie down and do not do anything active for a while. বিশ্রাম নেওয়া

restaurant (**restaurants**) n A **restaurant** is a place where you can buy and eat a meal. রেস্তোঁরা

restful adj Something that is **restful** helps you to feel calm and relaxed. বিশ্রামপূর্ণ

restless adj If you are **restless**, you are bored or dissatisfied, and want to do something else. বিশ্রামহীন

restore (**restores, restoring, restored**) *vt*
To **restore** something means to cause it to
exist again. পুনরুদ্ধার করা

restrict (**restricts, restricting, restricted**)
vt If you **restrict** something, you put a
limit on it to stop it becoming too large.
নিষেধ করা

restructure (**restructures,
restructuring, restructured**) *vt* To
restructure an organization or system
means to change the way it is organized,
usually in order to make it work more
effectively. পুনর্গঠন করা

result (**results, resulting, resulted**) *n*
A **result** is something that happens or
exists because of something else that has
happened. ঘটনার পরিণাম ▷ *vi* If something
results in a particular situation or event, it
causes that situation or event to happen.
পরিণতি হওয়া

resume (**resumes, resuming, resumed**) *v*
If you **resume** an activity, it begins again.
(*formal*) পুনরারম্ভ করা

retail (**retails, retailing, retailed**) *n* Retail
is the activity of selling goods direct to the
public. খুচরো বিক্রি ▷ *vi* If an item in a shop
retails at or for a particular price, it is for
sale at that price. খুচরো বিক্রি করা

retailer (**retailers**) *n* A **retailer** is a person
or business that sells goods to the public.
খুচরো বিক্রেতা

retail price (**retail prices**) *n* The **retail
price** of something is the price it is on sale
for in a shop. খুচরো বিক্রির দাম

retire (**retires, retiring, retired**) *vi* When
older people **retire**, they leave their job and
stop working. অবসর গ্রহণ করা

retired *adj* A **retired** person is an older
person who has left his or her job and
has usually stopped working completely.
অবসরপ্রাপ্ত

retirement *n* **Retirement** is the time when
a worker retires. অবসরগ্রহণ

retrace (**retraces, retracing, retraced**) *vt* If
you **retrace** your steps, you return to where

you started from, using the same route.
পূর্বপথ অনুসরণ করা

return (**returns, returning, returned**) *n*
Your **return** is when you arrive back at a
place where you were before. ফেরত ▷ *n*
The **return** on an investment is the amount
of money you gain from it. মুনাফা ▷ *vt* If you
return something to someone, you give it
back to them. ফিরিয়ে দেওয়া ▷ *vi* When you
return to a place, you go back to it after you
have been away. ফিরে যাওয়া ▷ *n* A **return**
or a **return ticket** is a ticket that allows you
to travel to a place and then back again.
রিটার্ন টিকিট

reunion (**reunions**) *n* A **reunion** is a party
or occasion when people who have not
seen each other for a long time meet again.
পুনর্মিলন উৎসব

reuse (**reuses, reusing, reused**) *vt*
When you **reuse** something, you use
it again instead of throwing it away.
পুনর্ব্যবহার

reveal (**reveals, revealing, revealed**) *vt* To
reveal something means to make people
aware of it. প্রকাশ করা

revenge *n* **Revenge** involves hurting
someone who has hurt you. প্রতিশোধ

revenue *n* **Revenue** is money that a
company, organization, or government
receives from people. রাজস্ব

reverse (**reverses, reversing, reversed**) *n*
If your car is in **reverse**, you have changed
gear so that you can drive it backwards.
উল্টো ▷ *vt* To **reverse** a process, decision,
or policy means to change it to its opposite.
উল্টো করা

review (**reviews**) *n* A **review** of a situation
or system is its formal examination by
people in authority. This is usually done in
order to see whether it can be improved or
corrected. পর্যালোচনা

revise (**revises, revising, revised**) *vt* If you
revise something, you alter it in order to
make it better or more accurate. পরিমার্জনা
করা

revision (**revisions**) *n* To make a **revision** of something that is written or something that has been decided means to make changes to it in order to improve it, make it more modern, or make it more suitable for a particular purpose. পরিমার্জনা

revive (**revives, reviving, revived**) *v* When something such as a feeling or a practice **revives** or **is revived**, it becomes active or successful again. পুনরায় প্রাণসঞ্চার করা

revolting *adj* **Revolting** means horrible and disgusting. বিরক্তিকর

revolution (**revolutions**) *n* A **revolution** is a successful attempt by a large group of people to change their country's political system, using force. বিপ্লব

revolutionary *adj* **Revolutionary** activities, organizations, or people have the aim of causing a political revolution. বৈপ্লবিক

revolver (**revolvers**) *n* A **revolver** is a kind of hand gun. রিভলবার

reward (**rewards**) *n* A **reward** is something that you are given because you have behaved well, worked hard, or provided a service to the community. পুরস্কার

rewarding *adj* Something that is **rewarding** gives you satisfaction or brings you benefits. সুফলদায়ক

rewind (**rewinds, rewinding, rewound**) *v* When a recording on a tape, computer file, or disk **rewinds** or when you **rewind** it, the recording goes backwards so that you can play it again. পিছনে ঘোরানো

rheumatism *n* **Rheumatism** is an illness that makes your joints or muscles stiff and painful. Older people, especially, suffer from rheumatism. বাত

rhubarb *n* **Rhubarb** is a plant with large leaves and long red stems. লম্বা বৃত্তওয়ালা গাছ

rhythm (**rhythms**) *n* A **rhythm** is a regular series of sounds, movements, or actions. ছন্দ

rib (**ribs**) *n* Your **ribs** are the curved bones that go from your backbone around your chest. পাঁজর

ribbon (**ribbons**) *n* A **ribbon** is a long, narrow piece of cloth used as a fastening or decoration, for example on a birthday present. ফিতে

rice *n* **Rice** consists of white or brown grains taken from a cereal plant. চাল

rich (**richer, richest**) *adj* A **rich** person has a lot of money or valuable possessions. ধনী

ride (**rides, riding, rode, ridden**) *n* A **ride** is a journey on a horse or bicycle, or in a vehicle. আরোহণ ▷ *v* If you **ride** a horse, you sit on it and control its movements. আরোহণ করা

rider (**riders**) *n* A **rider** is someone who rides a horse, bicycle, or motorcycle. আরোহী

ridiculous *adj* If you say that something or someone is **ridiculous**, you mean that they are very foolish. হাস্যকর

riding *n* **Riding** is the activity or sport of riding horses. আরোহণ

rifle (**rifles**) *n* A **rifle** is a gun with a long barrel. রাইফেল

rig (**rigs**) *n* A **rig** is a large structure that is used for extracting oil or gas from the ground or the sea bed. রিগ

right *adj* If something is **right**, it is correct and there have been no mistakes. ঠিক ▷ *adj* The **right** side is the side that is towards the east when you look north. ডান ▷ *adv* If someone is **right** about something, they are correct. যথার্থ ▷ *n* **Right** is used to talk about actions that are good and acceptable. ন্যায়সঙ্গত

right angle (**right angles**) *n* A **right angle** is an angle of ninety degrees. সমকোণ

right-hand *adj* If something is on the **right-hand** side of something, it is positioned on the right of it. ডানদিকে

right-hand drive *n* In a motor vehicle, **right-hand drive** is a driving system in which the steering wheel is on the right side. Cars with **right-hand drive** are designed to be driven in countries where people drive on the left side of the road. গাড়ির ডানদিকে স্টিয়ারিং

right-handed *adj* Someone who is **right-handed** uses their right hand rather than their left hand for activities such as writing and sports, and for picking things up. ডানহাতি

rightly *adv* If you do something **rightly** you do it in accordance with the facts or correctly. সঠিকভাবে

right of way (**rights of way**) *n* A **right of way** is a public path across private land. সরকারি পথ

right-wing *adj* A **right-wing** person or group has conservative or capitalist views. দক্ষিণ-পন্থী

rim (**rims**) *n* The **rim** of a container or a circular object is the edge which goes all the way round the top or round the outside. বেড়

ring (**rings, ringing, rang, rung**) *n* A **ring** is a round piece of metal that you wear on a finger. আংটি ▷ *vt* When you **ring** someone, you telephone them. ফোন করা ▷ *v* When a bell **rings**, or when you **ring** it, it makes a clear, loud sound. বাজা

ring back *v* If you **ring** someone **back**, you phone them, either because they phoned you earlier and you were out or because you did not finish an earlier conversation. ফোনের জবাবে ফোন করা *Tell her I'll ring back in a few minutes.*

ring binder (**ring binders**) *n* A **ring binder** is a file with hard covers, which you can

insert pages into. The pages are held in by metal rings on a bar attached to the inside of the file. একধরণের ফাইল

ring road (**ring roads**) *n* A **ring road** is a road that goes round the edge of a town so that traffic does not have to go through the town centre. রিং রোড

ringtone (**ringtones**) *n* A **ringtone** is a musical tune played by a mobile phone when a call is received. রিং টোন

ring up *v* When you **ring** someone **up** you telephone them. ফোন করা *He rang up and invited us over for dinner.*

rink (**rinks**) *n* A **rink** is a large area where people go to skate. স্কেটিং এর স্থান

rinse (**rinses, rinsing, rinsed**) *n* When you give something a **rinse**, you wash it in clean water in order to remove dirt or soap from it. ধৌতকরণ ▷ *vt* When you **rinse** something, you wash it in clean water in order to remove dirt or soap from it. ধুয়ে ফেলা

riot (**riots, rioting, rioted**) *n* When there is a **riot**, a crowd of people behave violently in a public place, for example they fight, throw stones, or damage buildings and vehicles. দাঙ্গা ▷ *vi* If people **riot**, they behave violently in a public place. দাঙ্গা লাগা

rip (**rips, ripping, ripped**) *v* If you **rip** something, you tear it forcefully with your hands or with a tool such as a knife. If something rips, it is torn forcefully. জোর করে ছেঁড়া

ripe (**riper, ripest**) *adj* **Ripe** fruit or grain is fully grown and ready to be harvested or eaten. পাকা

rip off (**rip-offs**) *v* If someone **rips** you **off**, they cheat you by charging too much for goods or services. (*informal*) প্রতারণা *People are buying these products and getting ripped off.* ▷ *n* If you say that something that you bought was a **rip-off**, you mean that you were charged too much money or that it was of very poor quality. (*informal*) প্রবঞ্চনা

rip up v If you **rip** something **up**, you tear it into small pieces. কুটিকুটি করে ছেঁড়া *He ripped up the letter.*

rise (**rises, rising, rose, risen**) n If there is a **rise** in an amount, the amount increases. বৃদ্ধি ▷ vi If something **rises** or **rises up**, it moves upwards. ওঠা

risk (**risks, risking, risked**) n If there is a **risk** of something unpleasant, there is a possibility that it will happen. ঝুঁকি ▷ vt If you **risk** something unpleasant, you do something knowing that the unpleasant thing might happen as a result. ঝুঁকি নেওয়া

risky (**riskier, riskiest**) adj If an activity or action is **risky**, it is dangerous or could fail. ঝুঁকিপ্রবণ

ritual (**rituals**) adj **Ritual** activities happen as part of a ritual or tradition. আনুষ্ঠানিক ▷ n A **ritual** is a religious service or other ceremony which involves a series of actions performed in a fixed order. আনুষ্ঠানিক ক্রিয়াকর্ম

rival (**rivals**) adj **Rival** groups are groups of people that compete against each other. প্রতিদ্বন্দ্বী দল ▷ n Your **rival** is a person, business, or organization who you are competing or fighting against in the same area or for the same things. প্রতিদ্বন্দ্বী

rivalry (**rivalries**) n **Rivalry** is competition or conflict between people or groups. প্রতিদ্বন্দ্বিতা

river (**rivers**) n A **river** is a large amount of fresh water flowing continuously in a long line across land, such as the Amazon or the Nile. নদী

road (**roads**) n A **road** is a long piece of hard ground built between two places so that people can drive or ride easily from one to the other. রাস্তা

roadblock (**roadblocks**) n When the police or the army put a **roadblock** across a road, they stop all the traffic going through, for example because they are looking for a criminal. রাস্তা বন্ধ

road map (**road maps**) n A **road map** is a map which shows the roads in a particular area in detail. রাস্তার ম্যাপ

road rage n **Road rage** is an angry or violent reaction by a driver towards another road user. রাস্তায় চালকের ক্রোধ

road sign (**road signs**) n A road sign is a sign near a road giving information or instructions to drivers. পথনির্দেশমূলক চিহ্ন

road tax n **Road tax** is a tax paid every year by the owners of every motor vehicle which is being used on the roads. পথকর

roadworks npl **Roadworks** are repairs or other work being done on a road. রাস্তা সারাই

roast adj **Roast** meat has been roasted. ঝলসানো

rob (**robs, robbing, robbed**) vt If a person or place **is robbed**, money or property is stolen from them, often using force. ডাকাতি করা

robber (**robbers**) n A **robber** is someone who steals money or property from a bank, a shop, or a vehicle, often by using force or threats. ডাকাত

robbery (**robberies**) n **Robbery** is the crime of stealing money or property, often using force. ডাকাতি

robin (**robins**) n A **robin** is a small brown bird with a red breast. রবিন পাখি

robot (**robots**) n A **robot** is a machine which moves and performs certain tasks automatically. রোবট

rock (**rocks, rocking, rocked**) n **Rock** is the hard material that is in the ground and in mountains. পাথর ▷ v If something **rocks**, it moves from side to side. দোল খাওয়া ▷ n A **rock** is a piece of this material. শিলার টুকরো

rock climbing n **Rock climbing** is the activity of climbing cliffs or large rocks, as a hobby or sport. পাহাড়ে চড়া

rocket (**rockets**) n A **rocket** is a space vehicle shaped like a long tube. রকেট

rocking chair (**rocking chairs**) n A **rocking chair** is a chair that is built on two curved pieces of wood so that you can rock yourself backwards and forwards when you are sitting in it. রকিং চেয়ার

rocking horse (rocking horses) *n* A **rocking horse** is a toy horse which a child can sit on and which can be made to rock backwards and forwards. খেলনা ঘোড়া

rod (rods) *n* A **rod** is a long thin bar made of metal or wood. দণ্ড

rodent (rodents) *n* **Rodents** are small mammals, for example rats and squirrels, with sharp front teeth. তীক্ষ্ণদন্তী প্রাণীবিশেষ

role (roles) *n* The **role** of someone or something in a situation is their function or position in it. ভূমিকা

roll (rolls, rolling, rolled) *n* A **roll** of paper, plastic, cloth, or wire is a long piece of it that has been wrapped many times around itself or around a tube. পাকানো বস্তু ▷ *v* If something **rolls** or if you **roll** it, it moves along a surface, turning over many times. গড়িয়ে দেওয়া

roll call (roll calls) *n* If you take a **roll call**, you check which of the members of a group are present by reading their names out. নামডাকা

roller (rollers) *n* A **roller** is a cylinder that turns round in a machine or device. রোলার

rollercoaster (rollercoasters) *n* A **rollercoaster** is a small railway at a fair that goes up and down steep slopes fast and that people ride on for pleasure or excitement. রোলার কোস্টার

rollerskates *npl* **Rollerskates** are shoes with four small wheels on the bottom. স্কেটিং এর জুতো

rollerskating *n* **Rollerskating** is the activity of moving over a flat surface wearing rollerskates. স্কেটিং এর জুতো পরে স্কেটিং করা

rolling pin (rolling pins) *n* A **rolling pin** is a cylinder that you roll backwards and forwards over uncooked pastry in order to make the pastry flat. রোলিং পিন

Roman *adj* **Roman** means related to or connected with ancient Rome and its empire. রোম দেশীয়

romance (romances) *n* A **romance** is a relationship between two people who are in love with each other but who are not married to each other. প্রেম

Romanesque *adj* **Romanesque** architecture is in the style that was common in western Europe around the eleventh century. It is characterized by rounded arches and thick pillars. প্রাচীন ইউরোপিয়ান স্থাপত্যকলা

Romania *n* **Romania** is a republic in south-east Europe. রোমানিয়া

Romanian (Romanians) *adj* **Romanian** means belonging or relating to Romania, or to its people, language, or culture. রোমানিয়া দেশীয় ▷ *n* A **Romanian** is a person who comes from Romania. রোমানিয়ার অধিবাসী ▷ *n* **Romanian** is the language spoken in Romania. রোমানিয়া ভাষা

romantic *adj* Someone who is **romantic** or does **romantic** things says and does things that make their partner feel special and loved. কল্পনাময়

roof (roofs) *n* The **roof** of a building or car is the covering on top of it. ছাদ

room (rooms) *n* A **room** is a part of a building that has its own walls. ঘর ▷ *n* If there is **room** somewhere, there is enough empty space. জায়গা

roommate (roommates) *n* Your **roommate** is the person you share an apartment or house with. সহবাসী

room service *n* **Room service** is a service in a hotel by which meals or drinks are provided for guests in their rooms. ঘরে পরিষেবা

root (roots) *n* The **roots** of a plant are the parts that grow underground. মূল

rope (ropes) *n* A **rope** is a very thick cord, made by twisting together several thinner cords. দড়ি

rope in *v* If you say that you **were roped in** to do a particular task, you mean that someone persuaded you to help them do that task. (*informal*) টেনে আনা *Visitors were roped in to help pick tomatoes.*

rose (roses) *n* A **rose** is a flower which has a pleasant smell and grows on a bush with thorns. গোলাপ ফুল

rosemary *n* **Rosemary** is a herb used in cooking. It comes from an evergreen plant with small narrow leaves. রোজমেরি

rosé (rosés) *n* **Rosé** is wine which is pink in colour. একপ্রকার মদ্য

rot (rots, rotting, rotted) *v* When food, wood, or other substances **rot**, or when something **rots** them, they decay and fall apart. পচে যাওয়া

rotten *adj* If food, wood, or another substance is **rotten**, it has decayed and can no longer be used. পচা

rough (rougher, roughest) *adj* If something is **rough**, it is not smooth or even. রুক্ষ ▷ *adj* If you are **rough**, you are not being careful or gentle. অভদ্য

roughly *adv* If you do something **roughly** you do it with too much force. জোরসহকারে

roulette *n* **Roulette** is a gambling game in which a ball is dropped onto a revolving wheel with numbered holes in it. The players bet on which hole the ball will end up in. একধরণের জুয়াখেলা

round (rounder, roundest, rounds) *adj* Something **round** is in the shape of a ball or a circle. গোল ▷ *n* A **round** of events is a series of similar events, especially one which comes after or before a similar series. রাউন্ড ▷ *n* A **round** is a circular shape. চক্র ▷ *prep* **Round** a place or object means on all sides of it. চক্রাকারে *They were sitting round the kitchen table.*

roundabout (roundabouts) *n* A **roundabout** is a circle at a place where several roads meet. রাস্তার মোড়

round trip (round trips) *n* If you make a **round trip**, you travel to a place and then back again. যাতায়াত

round up *v* If people or animals **are rounded up**, someone gathers them together. একত্রীকরণ *He had sought work as a cowboy, rounding up cattle.*

route (routes) *n* A **route** is a way from one place to another. রুট

routine (routines) *n* A **routine** is the usual series of things that you do at a particular time in a particular order. দৈনন্দিন কার্যসূচী

row (rows, rowing, rowed) *n* A **row** is a line of things or people. সারি ▷ *n* A **row** is a serious disagreement or noisy argument. তর্কবিতর্ক ▷ *v* When you **row**, or when you **row** a boat, you make it move through the water by using oars. দাঁড় বাওয়া ▷ *vi* If two people **row**, they have a noisy argument. তর্কবিতর্ক করা

rowing *n* **Rowing** is a sport in which people or teams race against each other in boats with oars. নৌকা বাওয়া

rowing boat (rowing boats) *n* A **rowing boat** is a small boat that you move through the water by using oars. বাইচের নৌকা

royal *adj* **Royal** means related to or belonging to a king, queen, or emperor, or to a member of their family. রাজকীয়

rub (rubs, rubbing, rubbed) *vt* If you **rub** something, you move your hand or a cloth backwards and forwards over it while pressing firmly. ঘষা

rubber (rubbers) *n* **Rubber** is a strong material that stretches. **Rubber** is used to make things like tyres and boots for wet weather. রবার ▷ *n* A **rubber** is a small piece of rubber used to remove pencil mistakes. রবার

rubber band (rubber bands) *n* A **rubber band** is a thin circle of very elastic rubber. You put it around things such as papers in order to keep them together. রবার ব্যান্ড

ubber gloves npl **Rubber gloves** are gloves made of rubber that you wear to protect your hands, for example when you are washing up or gardening. রবার দস্তানা

ubbish adj If you think that someone is not very good at something, you can say that they are **rubbish** at it. (informal) অকর্মের ঢেঁকি ▷ n **Rubbish** consists of unwanted things or waste material such as old food. আবর্জনা

ubbish dump (**rubbish dumps**) n A **rubbish dump** is a place where rubbish is left, for example on open ground outside a town. আবর্জনা জড়ো করবার জায়গা

ucksack (**rucksacks**) n A **rucksack** is a bag, often on a frame, used for carrying things on your back. পিঠে নেওয়ার ব্যাগ

ude (**ruder, rudest**) adj If someone is **rude**, they behave in a way that is not polite. রূঢ়

ug (**rugs**) n A **rug** is a piece of thick material that you put on the floor and use like a carpet. শতরঞ্জি

ugby n **Rugby** is a game played by two teams, who try to get an oval ball past a line at their opponents' end of the pitch. রাগবি

uin (**ruins, ruining, ruined**) n **Ruin** is the state of no longer having any money. কর্পদকহীন ▷ vt To **ruin** something means to severely harm, damage, or spoil it. ক্ষয় করা

ule (**rules, ruling, ruled**) n **Rules** are instructions that tell you what you must do or must not do. নিয়ম ▷ v Someone who **rules** a country controls it. রাজত্ব করা

ule out v If you **rule out** an idea or course of action, you reject it because it is impossible or unsuitable. বাতিল করা The Prime Minister is believed to have ruled out cuts in child benefit or pensions.

uler (**rulers**) n A **ruler** is also a person who rules a country. শাসক ▷ n A **ruler** is a long, flat piece of wood or plastic with straight edges. You use a **ruler** for measuring things or drawing straight lines. রুলার

rum (**rums**) n **Rum** is an alcoholic drink made from sugar cane juice. একপ্রকার মদ্য

rumour (**rumours**) n A **rumour** is a piece of information that may or may not be true, but that people are talking about. গুজব

run (**runs, running, ran, run**) n A **run** is a journey you make by running. দৌড় ▷ vi You say that something long, such as a road, **runs** in a particular direction when you are describing its course or position. দৌড়ানো ▷ vi When you **run**, you move very quickly on your legs. দৌড়ানো

run away v If you **run away** from a place, you secretly leave it. পলায়ন করা I ran away from home when I was sixteen.

runner (**runners**) n A **runner** is a person who runs, especially for sport or pleasure. দৌড়বীর

runner bean (**runner beans**) n **Runner beans** are long green beans that are eaten as a vegetable. লম্বাজাতের বীন

runner-up (**runners-up**) n A **runner-up** is someone who finishes in second place in a race or competition. দ্বিতীয় বিজেতা

running n **Running** is the activity of moving fast on foot, especially as a sport. দৌড়

run out v If you **run out** of something, you have no more of it left. নিঃশেষিত হওয়া By now the plane was running out of fuel.

run over v If a vehicle **runs over** someone or something, it knocks them down. চাপা দেওয়া He ran over an elderly man.

runway (**runways**) n At an airport, the **runway** is the long strip of ground with a hard surface which an aeroplane takes off from or lands on. রানওয়ে

rural adj **Rural** means relating to country areas as opposed to large towns. গ্রামীণ

rush (**rushes, rushing, rushed**) n A **rush** is a situation in which you need to go somewhere or do something very quickly. দ্রুত ধাবন ▷ vi If you **rush** somewhere, you go there quickly. দ্রুত ধাবিত হওয়া

r

rush hour (**rush hours**) *n* The **rush hour** is one of the periods of the day when most people are travelling to or from work. তাড়াহুড়োর সময়

rusk (**rusks**) *n* **Rusks** are hard, dry biscuits that are given to babies and young children. কড়া পাউরুটি

Russia *n* **Russia** is the largest country in the world, covering north Eurasia. **Russia** borders on the Pacific and Arctic Oceans, and the Baltic, Black, and Caspian Seas. রাশিয়া

Russian (**Russians**) *adj* **Russian** means belonging or relating to Russia, or to its people, language, or culture. রাশিয়া দেশীয় ▷ *n* A **Russian** is a person who comes from Russia. রাশিয়ার অধিবাসী ▷ *n* **Russian** is the language spoken in Russia, and other countries such as Belarus, Kazakhstan, and Kyrgyzstan. রুশ ভাষা

rust *n* **Rust** is a brown substance that forms on iron or steel when it comes into contact with water. মরচে

rusty (**rustier, rustiest**) *adj* A **rusty** metal object has a lot of rust on it. মরচে ধরা

ruthless *adj* Someone who is **ruthless** is very harsh or determined, and will do anything that is necessary to achieve their aim. নিষ্ঠুর

rye *n* **Rye** is a cereal grown in cold countries. Its grains can be used to make flour, bread, or other foods. দানাশস্য

S

sabotage (**sabotages, sabotaging, sabotaged**) *n* **Sabotage** is the deliberate destruction, disruption, or damage of equipment, a public service, etc, as by enemy agents, dissatisfied employees, etc. নাশকতা ▷ *vt* If a machine, railway line, or bridge is **sabotaged**, it is deliberately damaged or destroyed, for example in a war or as a protest. নষ্ট করা

sachet (**sachets**) *n* A **sachet** is a small closed plastic or paper bag, containing a small quantity of something. পুরিয়া

sack (**sacks, sacking, sacked**) *n* A **sack** is a large bag made of rough woven material. বস্তা ▷ *n* If your employers give you the **sack**, they tell you that you can no longer work for them. বরখাস্ত ▷ *vt* If your employers **sack** you, they tell you that you can no longer work for them because you have done something that they did not like or because your work was not good enough. বরখাস্ত করা

sacred *adj* Something that is **sacred** is believed to be holy. পবিত্র

sacrifice (**sacrifices**) *n* To offer an animal as a **sacrifice**, means to kill it in a special religious ceremony. বলিদান

sad (**sadder, saddest**) *adj* If you are **sad**, you feel unhappy. দুঃখিত

saddle (**saddles**) *n* A **saddle** is a leather seat that you put on the back of an animal so that you can ride the animal. ঘোড়ার জিন

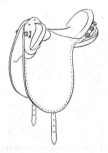

saddlebag (saddlebags) *n* A **saddlebag** is a bag fastened to the saddle of a bicycle or motorcycle, or the saddle of a horse. স্যাডল্ থলে

sadly *adv* If you feel or do something **sadly**, you feel or do it unhappily. দুঃখিত হয়ে

safari (safaris) *n* A **safari** is an expedition for hunting or observing wild animals, especially in East Africa. শিকার যাত্রা

safe (safer, safest, safes) *adj* Something that is **safe** does not cause physical harm or danger. নিরাপদ ▷ *n* A **safe** is a strong metal cupboard with special locks, in which you keep money, jewellery, or other valuable things. সিন্দুক

safety *n* **Safety** is the state of being safe from harm or danger. নিরাপত্তা

safety belt (safety belts) *n* A **safety belt** is a strap that you fasten across your body for safety when travelling in a car or aeroplane. নিরাপত্তা পেটি

safety pin (safety pins) *n* A **safety pin** is a bent metal pin used for fastening things together. The point of the pin has a cover so that when the pin is closed it cannot hurt anyone. সেফটি পিন

saffron *n* **Saffron** is a yellowish-orange powder obtained from a flower and used to give flavour and colouring to some foods. জাফরান

Sagittarius *n* **Sagittarius** is one of the twelve signs of the zodiac. Its symbol is a creature that is half horse, half man, shooting an arrow. People who are born approximately between the 22nd of November and the 21st of December come under this sign. ধনুরাশি

Sahara *n* The **Sahara** is a desert in North Africa, extending from the Atlantic to the Red Sea and from the Mediterranean to central Mali, Niger, Chad, and the Sudan. সাহারা মরুভূমি

sail (sails, sailing, sailed) *n* **Sails** are large pieces of material attached to the mast of a boat. পাল ▷ *v* If you **sail** a boat, or if a boat **sails**, it moves across water using its sails. নৌকো করে পাড়ি দেওয়া

sailing (sailings) *n* A **sailing** is a voyage made by a ship carrying passengers. জাহাজযাত্রা

sailing boat (sailing boats) *n* A **sailing boat** is a boat with sails. পাল তোলা নৌকে

sailor (sailors) *n* A **sailor** is a person who works on a ship as a member of its crew. নাবিক

saint (saints) *n* A **saint** is someone who has died and been officially recognized and honoured by the Christian church because his or her life was a perfect example of the way Christians should live. সন্ত

salad (salads) *n* A **salad** is a mixture of uncooked vegetables, eaten as part of a meal. স্যালাড

salad dressing (salad dressings) *n* **Salad dressing** is a mixture of oil, vinegar, herbs, and other flavourings, which you pour over a salad. স্যালাডের মশলা

salami (salamis) *n* **Salami** is a type of strong-flavoured sausage. It is usually thinly sliced and eaten cold. স্যালামী

salary (salaries) *n* Your **salary** is the money that you are paid each month by your employer. বেতন

S

sale n The **sale** of goods is the selling of them for money. বিক্রি

sales assistant (sales assistants) n A **sales assistant** is a person who works in a shop selling things to customers. বিক্রি সহায়ক

salesman (salesmen) n A **salesman** is a man whose job is selling things to people. বিক্রেতা (পুরুষ)

salesperson (salespeople, salespersons) n A **salesperson** is a person whose job is selling things to people. বিক্রেতা

sales rep (sales reps) n A **sales rep** is an employee of a company who travels around a particular area selling the company's goods to shops, etc. বিক্রি প্রতিনিধি

saleswoman (saleswomen) n A **saleswoman** is a woman who sells things, either in a shop or directly to customers on behalf of a company. বিক্রেতা (মহিলা)

saliva n **Saliva** is the watery liquid that forms in your mouth. লালা

salmon (salmon) n A **salmon** is a large edible silver-coloured fish with pink flesh. স্যামন মাছ

saloon (saloons) n A **saloon** or a **saloon car** is a car with seats for four or more people, a fixed roof, and a boot that is separated from the rear seats. গাড়ি

salt n **Salt** is a substance in the form of white powder or crystals, used to improve the flavour of food or to preserve it. Salt occurs naturally in sea water. নুন

saltwater adj **Saltwater** fish live in water which is salty. **Saltwater** lakes contain salty water. নোনাজল

salty (saltier, saltiest) adj **Salty** things contain salt or taste of salt. নোনতা

salute (salutes, saluting, saluted) v If you **salute** someone, you greet them or show your respect with a formal sign. Soldiers usually salute officers by raising their right hand so that their fingers touch their forehead. অভিবাদন করা

same adj If two things are the **same**, they are like one another. এক রকম

sample (samples) n A **sample** of a substance or product is a small quantity of it, showing you what it is like. নমুনা

sand n **Sand** is a powder that consists of extremely small pieces of stone. বালু

sandal (sandals) n **Sandals** are light shoes that have straps instead of a solid part over the top of your foot. চপ্পল

sandcastle (sandcastles) n A **sandcastle** is a pile of sand made to look like a castle, usually by a child on a beach. সৈকতে শিশুদের বানানো বালির ঘর

sand dune (sand dunes) n A **sand dune** is a hill of sand near the sea or in a sand desert. বালির পাহাড়

sandpaper n **Sandpaper** is strong paper that has a coating of sand on it. It is used for rubbing wood or metal surfaces to make them smoother. শিরিষ কাগজ

sandpit (sandpits) n A **sandpit** is a shallow hole or box in the ground with sand in it where small children can play. বালি ভরা গর্ত

sandstone n **Sandstone** is a type of rock which contains a lot of sand. এক ধরনের পাথর

sandwich (sandwiches) n A **sandwich** consists of two slices of bread with a layer of food between them. স্যান্ডুইচ

sanitary towel (**sanitary towels**) *n* A **sanitary towel** is a pad of thick soft material which women wear to absorb the blood during menstruation. স্যানিটারি টাওয়েল

San Marino *n* **San Marino** is a republic in south central Europe in the Apennines, forming an enclave in Italy. স্যান ম্যারিনো দেশ

sapphire (**sapphires**) *n* A **sapphire** is a precious stone which is blue in colour. নীলা

sarcastic *adj* Someone who is **sarcastic** says the opposite of what they really mean in order to mock or insult someone. বাঁকা

sardine (**sardines**) *n* **Sardines** are a kind of small sea fish, often eaten as food. সারডিন মাছ

satchel (**satchels**) *n* A **satchel** is a bag with a long strap that schoolchildren use for carrying books. থলে

satellite (**satellites**) *n* A **satellite** is an object which has been sent into space in order to collect information or to be part of a communications system. উপগ্রহ

satellite dish (**satellite dishes**) *n* A **satellite dish** is a piece of equipment which receives satellite television signals. উপগ্রহ ডিশ

satisfaction *n* **Satisfaction** is the pleasure you feel when you do something you wanted or needed to do. সন্তুষ্টি

satisfactory *adj* If something is **satisfactory**, it is acceptable to you or fulfils a particular need or purpose. সন্তোষজনক

satisfied *adj* If you are **satisfied** with something, you are pleased because you have got what you wanted. সন্তুষ্ট

satnav *n* **Satnav** is a system that uses information from satellites to find the best way of getting to a place. It is often found in cars. **Satnav** is an abbreviation for 'satellite navigation'. উপগ্রহ ভিত্তিক পথ নির্দেশিকা

Saturday (**Saturdays**) *n* **Saturday** is the day after Friday and before Sunday. শনি বার

sauce (**sauces**) *n* A **sauce** is a thick liquid which is served with other food. সস (খাদ্য দ্রব্য)

saucepan (**saucepans**) *n* A **saucepan** is a deep metal cooking pot, usually with a long handle and a lid. সসপ্যান (পাত্র)

saucer (**saucers**) *n* A **saucer** is a small curved plate on which you stand a cup. চায়ের প্লেট

Saudi (**Saudis**) *adj* **Saudi** or **Saudi Arabian** means belonging or relating to Saudi Arabia or to its people, language, or culture. সৌদি আরবীয় ▷ *n* The **Saudis** or **Saudi Arabians** are the people who come from Saudi Arabia. সৌদি আরবের মানুষ

Saudi Arabia *n* **Saudi Arabia** is a kingdom in south-west Asia, occupying most of the Arabian peninsula between the Persian Gulf and the Red Sea. সৌদি আরব

Saudi Arabian (**Saudi Arabians**) *adj* **Saudi** or **Saudi Arabian** means belonging or relating to Saudi Arabia or to its people, language, or culture. সৌদি আরবীয় ▷ *n* The **Saudi Arabians** or **Saudis** are the people who come from Saudi Arabia. সৌদি আরবের মানুষ

sauna (**saunas**) *n* A **sauna** is a hot steam bath. সওনা এক ধরনের বাষ্পস্নান

sausage (**sausages**) *n* A **sausage** consists of minced meat, mixed with other ingredients, inside a long thin skin. সসেজ (মাংস জাতীয় খাবার)

save (**saves, saving, saved**) *vt* If you **save** someone or something, you help them to escape from danger. বাঁচানো ▷ *vt* If you **save** something, you keep it because you will need it later. বাঁচিয়ে রাখা

save up *v* If you **save up**, you gradually collect money by spending less than you

S

get, usually in order to buy something that you want. সাশ্রয় *She is saving up to buy a car.*

savings npl Your **savings** are the money that you have saved, especially in a bank or a building society. সঞ্চয়

savoury adj **Savoury** food has a salty or spicy flavour rather than a sweet one. নোনতা খাবার

saw (saws) n A **saw** is a tool for cutting wood, which has a blade with sharp teeth along one edge. করাত

sawdust n **Sawdust** is the very fine fragments of wood which are produced when you saw wood. কাঠের গুঁড়ো

saxophone (saxophones) n A **saxophone** is a musical wind instrument in the shape of a curved metal tube with keys and a curved mouthpiece. স্যাক্সোফোন (বাদ্য যন্ত্র)

say (says, saying, said) vt When you **say** something, you talk. বলা

saying (sayings) n A **saying** is a traditional sentence that people often say and that gives advice or information about life. বাণী

scaffolding n **Scaffolding** is a temporary framework of poles and boards that is used by workmen to stand on while they are working on the outside structure of a building. ভারা

scale (scales) n A **scale** is a set of levels or numbers which are used in a particular system of measuring things or comparing things. মানদণ্ড ▷ n The **scales** of a fish or reptile are the small, flat pieces of hard skin that cover its body. আঁশ

scales npl **Scales** are a piece of equipment for weighing things or people. দাঁড়িপাল্লা

scallop (scallops) n **Scallops** are large shellfish with two flat fan-shaped shells. Scallops can be eaten. এক ধরনের শামুক

scam (scams) n A **scam** is an illegal trick, usually with the purpose of getting money from people or avoiding paying tax. (*informal*) কেলেঙ্কারী

scampi npl **Scampi** are large prawns, often served fried in breadcrumbs. বাগদা চিংড়ি

scan (scans, scanning, scanned) n A **scan** is a medical test in which a machine sends a beam of X-rays over a part of your body in order to check whether your organs are healthy. স্ক্যান (ডাক্তারী পরীক্ষা) ▷ vt When you **scan** an area, a group of things, or a piece of writing, you look at it carefully, usually because you are looking for something in particular. সযত্নে পরীক্ষা করা

scandal (scandals) n A **scandal** is a situation, event, or someone's behaviour that shocks a lot of people because they think it is immoral. কেলেঙ্কারী

Scandinavia n **Scandinavia** is the peninsula of north Europe occupied by Norway and Sweden. স্ক্যান্ডিনেভিয়া (স্থানের নাম)

Scandinavian adj **Scandinavian** means belonging or relating to a group of northern European countries that includes Denmark, Norway, and Sweden, or to the people, languages, or culture of those countries. স্ক্যান্ডেনেভিয়

scanner (scanners) n A **scanner** is a machine which is used to examine, identify, or record things, for example by moving a beam of light, sound, or X-rays over them. স্ক্যানার যন্ত্র

scar (scars) n A **scar** is a mark on the skin which is left after a wound has healed. ক্ষত চিহ্ন

scarce (scarcer, scarcest) adj If something is **scarce**, there is not enough of it. স্বল্প

scarcely *adv* You use **scarcely** to emphasize that something is only just true or only just the case. বড়জোর

scare (**scares, scaring, scared**) *n* If someone or something gives you a **scare**, they frighten you. ভয় ▷ *vt* If something **scares** you, it frightens or worries you. ভয় দেখানো

scarecrow (**scarecrows**) *n* A **scarecrow** is an object in the shape of a person, which is put in a field where crops are growing in order to frighten birds away. কাকতাড়ুয়া

scared *adj* If you are **scared** of someone or something, you are frightened of them. ভীত

scarf (**scarfs, scarves**) *n* A **scarf** is a piece of cloth that you wear round your neck or head, usually to keep yourself warm. মাফলার

scarlet *adj* Something that is **scarlet** is bright red. রক্তিম

scary (**scarier, scariest**) *adj* Something that is **scary** is rather frightening. ভয় পাওয়ার মত

scene (**scenes**) *n* A **scene** in a play, film, or book is part of it in which a series of events happen in the same place. দৃশ্য

scenery *n* The **scenery** in a country area is the land, water, or plants that you can see around you. প্রাকৃতিক দৃশ্য

scent (**scents**) *n* The **scent** of something is the pleasant smell that it has. সুগন্ধী

sceptical *adj* If you are **sceptical** about something, you have doubts about it. সন্দেহ বাতিক

schedule (**schedules**) *n* A **schedule** is a plan that gives a list of events or tasks and the times at which each one should happen or be done. নির্ঘণ্ট

scheme (**schemes**) *n* A **scheme** is a plan or arrangement, especially one produced by a government or other organization. কর্মসূচী

schizophrenic *adj* Someone who is **schizophrenic** is suffering from schizophrenia. স্কিজোফ্রেনিয়ার রোগী

scholarship (**scholarships**) *n* If you get a **scholarship** to a school or university, your studies are paid for by the school or university, or by some other organization. বৃত্তি

school (**schools**) *n* A **school** is a place where children are educated. You usually refer to this place as **school** when you are talking about the time that children spend there. বিদ্যালয়

schoolbag (**schoolbags**) *n* A **schoolbag** is a bag that children use to carry books and other things to and from school. স্কুলের ব্যাগ

schoolbook (**schoolbooks**) *n* **Schoolbooks** are books giving information about a particular subject, which children use at school. স্কুলের বই

schoolboy (**schoolboys**) *n* A **schoolboy** is a boy who goes to school. স্কুলের ছাত্র

schoolchildren *npl* **Schoolchildren** are children who go to school. স্কুলের বাচ্চা

schoolgirl (**schoolgirls**) *n* A **schoolgirl** is a girl who goes to school. স্কুলের মেয়ে

schoolteacher (**schoolteachers**) *n* A **schoolteacher** is a teacher in a school. স্কুল শিক্ষক

school uniform (**school uniforms**) *n* A **school uniform** is a special set of clothes which some children wear at school. স্কুলের পোশাক

science *n* **Science** is the study of the nature and behaviour of natural things and the knowledge that we obtain about them. বিজ্ঞান

science fiction *n* **Science fiction** consists of stories and films about events that take place in the future or in other parts of the universe. কল্পবিজ্ঞান

scientific *adj* **Scientific** is used to describe things that relate to science or to a particular science. বিজ্ঞানসম্মত

scientist (**scientists**) *n* A **scientist** is someone who has studied science and whose job is to teach or to do research in science. বিজ্ঞানী

sci-fi *n* **Sci-fi** consists of stories in books, magazines, and films about events that take place in the future or in other parts of the universe. **Sci-fi** is short for 'science fiction'. (*informal*) কল্পবিজ্ঞান

scissors *npl* **Scissors** are a small tool with two sharp blades which are screwed together. You use scissors for cutting things such as paper and cloth. কাঁচি

scoff (**scoffs, scoffing, scoffed**) *vi* If you **scoff**, you speak in a ridiculing way about something. ব্যঙ্গ করা

scold (**scolds, scolding, scolded**) *vt* If you **scold** someone, you speak angrily to them because they have done something wrong. (*formal*) বকাঝকা করা

scooter (**scooters**) *n* A **scooter** is a small lightweight motorcycle. স্কুটার

score (**scores, scoring, scored**) *n* The **score** in a game is the number of points that each team or player has. স্কোর (খেলার ফলাফল) ▷ *n* The **score** of a piece of music is the written version of it. স্বরলিপি ▷ *v* If you **score** in a game, you get a goal, run, or point. স্কোর করা

Scorpio *n* **Scorpio** is one of the twelve signs of the zodiac. Its symbol is a scorpion. People who are born approximately between the 23rd of October and the 21st of November come under this sign. বৃশ্চিকরাশি

scorpion (**scorpions**) *n* A **scorpion** is a small creature which looks like a large

insect. Scorpions have a long curved tail, and some of them are poisonous. বিছে

Scot (**Scots**) *n* A **Scot** is a person of Scottish origin. স্কটিশ বংশোদ্ভূত

Scotland *n* **Scotland** is a country that is part of the United Kingdom, occupying the north of Great Britain. স্কটল্যান্ড (দেশ)

Scots *adj* **Scots** means belonging or relating to Scotland, its people, language, or culture. স্কটল্যান্ড দেশীয়

Scotsman (**Scotsmen**) *n* A **Scotsman** is a man of Scottish origin. স্কটল্যান্ডের পুরুষ

Scotswoman (**Scotswomen**) *n* A **Scotswoman** is a woman of Scottish origin. স্কটল্যান্ডের মহিলা

Scottish *adj* **Scottish** means belonging or relating to Scotland, its people, language, or culture. স্কটল্যান্ড দেশীয়

scout (**scouts**) *n* A **scout** is someone who is sent to an area of countryside to find out the position of an enemy army. গোয়েন্দা

scrambled eggs *npl* **Scrambled eggs** are eggs that have been broken, mixed together, and then heated and stirred in a pan. ডিমের ঝুরি

scrap (**scraps, scrapping, scrapped**) *n* A **scrap** of something is a very small piece or amount of it. টুকরো ▷ *n* You can refer to a fight or a argument as a **scrap**. ঝগড়া ▷ *vt* If you **scrap** something, you get rid of it or cancel it. বাতিল করা

scrapbook (**scrapbooks**) *n* A **scrapbook** is a book with empty pages on which you can stick things such as pictures or newspaper articles in order to keep them. স্ক্র্যাপ বই

scrap paper *n* **Scrap paper** is loose pieces of paper used for writing notes on. আলাদা কাগজ

scratch (**scratches, scratching, scratched**) *n* **Scratches** on someone or something are small cuts. আঁচড় ▷ *v* If you **scratch** part of your body, you rub your nails against your skin. চুলকানো ▷ *vt* If a sharp thing **scratches** someone or something, it makes small cuts on their skin or on its surface. আঁচড়ে যাওয়া

scream (screams, screaming, screamed) *n* A **scream** is a sharp piercing cry or sound, esp one denoting fear or pain. ভয়ার্ত চিৎকার ▷ *vi* When someone **screams**, they make a very loud, high-pitched cry, for example because they are in pain or are very frightened. ভয়ে চিৎকার করা

screen (screens, screening, screened) *n* A **screen** is the flat vertical surface on which pictures or words are shown on a television, on a computer, or in a cinema. পর্দা ▷ *vt* When a film or a television programme **is screened**, it is shown in the cinema or broadcast on television. ছবি দেখান

screensaver (screensavers) *n* A **screensaver** is a moving picture which appears on a computer screen when the computer is not being used. কম্পিউটারের স্ক্রীনসেভার

screw (screws) *n* A **screw** is a small metal device for fixing things together. It has a wide top, a pointed end, and a groove along its length. স্ক্রু

screwdriver (screwdrivers) *n* A **screwdriver** is a tool for fixing screws into place. স্ক্রুড্রাইভার

scribble (scribbles, scribbling, scribbled) *v* If you **scribble** or **scribble** something, you write it quickly and untidily. হাতে লেখা

scrub (scrubs, scrubbing, scrubbed) *vt* If you **scrub** something, you rub it hard in order to clean it, using a stiff brush and water. ঘসে ঘসে মোছা

scuba diving *n* **Scuba diving** is the activity of swimming underwater using special breathing equipment. The equipment consists of cylinders of air which you carry on your back and which are connected to your mouth by rubber tubes. ডুব সাঁতার

sculptor (sculptors) *n* A **sculptor** is someone who creates sculptures. ভাস্কর

sculpture (sculptures) *n* A **sculpture** is a work of art that is produced by carving or shaping materials such as stone or clay. ভাস্কর্য

sea *n* The **sea** is the salty water that covers much of the earth's surface. সমুদ্র

seafood *n* **Seafood** refers to shellfish and other sea creatures that you can eat. সামুদ্রিক খাবার

seagull (seagulls) *n* A **seagull** is a type of bird that lives near the sea. সিগাল

seal (seals, sealing, sealed) *n* A **seal** is an animal which eats fish and lives partly on land and partly in the sea. সীল (জলজ প্রাণী) ▷ *n* A **seal** is an official stamp on a document. সীলমোহর ▷ *vt* When you **seal** an envelope, you close it by folding part of it and sticking it down. বন্ধ করা

sea level *n* If you are at **sea level**, you are at the same level as the surface of the sea. সমুদ্রপৃষ্ঠ

seam (seams) *n* A **seam** is a line of stitches joining two pieces of cloth together. সেলাই করা

seaman (seamen) *n* A **seaman** is a sailor. নাবিক

search (searches, searching, searched) *n* A **search** is an attempt to find something by looking for it carefully. তল্লাসী ▷ *v* If you **search for** something or someone, you look carefully for them. If you **search** a place, you look carefully for something there. সন্ধান করা

search engine (search engines) *n* A **search engine** is a computer program that

S

searches for documents on the Internet.
কম্পিউটারের সার্চ ইঞ্জিন

search party (**search parties**) *n* A **search party** is an organized group of people who are searching for someone who is missing. তল্লাসী দল

seashore (**seashores**) *n* The **seashore** is the part of a coast where the land slopes down into the sea. সমুদ্র তীর

seasick *adj* If someone is **seasick** when they are travelling in a boat, they vomit or feel sick because of the way the boat is moving. সমুদ্র ভ্রমণের ফলে অসুস্থ

seaside *n* You can refer to an area that is close to the sea, especially where people go for their holidays, as the **seaside**. সমুদ্রতীরে

season (**seasons**) *n* The **seasons** are the periods into which a year is divided and which each have their own typical weather conditions. ঋতু

seasonal *adj* **Seasonal** means happening during one particular time of the year. মৌসুমী

seasoning *n* **Seasoning** is salt, pepper, or spices that are added to food to improve its flavour. সুস্বাদু করে তোলা

season ticket (**season tickets**) *n* A **season ticket** is a ticket for a series of events, such as football matches, or a number of journeys, that you usually buy at a reduced rate. সিজন টিকিট

seat (**seats**) *n* A **seat** is an object that you can sit on, for example a chair. আসন ▷ *n* When someone is elected to parliament, you can say that they or their party have won a **seat**. আসন

seatbelt (**seatbelts**) *n* A **seatbelt** is a strap that you fasten across your body for safety when travelling in a car or aeroplane. সুরক্ষা-বন্ধনী

sea water *n* **Sea water** is salt water from the sea. সমুদ্রের জল

seaweed (**seaweeds**) *n* **Seaweed** is a plant that grows in the sea. সামুদ্রিক উদ্ভিদ

second (**seconds**) *adj* The **second** thing in a number of things is the one that you count as number two. দ্বিতীয় ▷ *n* A **second** is an amount of time. There are sixty seconds in one minute. সেকেন্ড

secondary school (**secondary schools**) *n* A **secondary school** is a school for pupils between the ages of 11 or 12 and 17 or 18. মাধ্যমিক বিদ্যালয়

second class *n* **Second class** is accommodations on a train or ship which are cheaper and less comfortable than the first class accommodations. দ্বিতীয় শ্রেণী ▷ *adj* **Second-class** things are regarded as less valuable or less important than others of the same kind. অপেক্ষাকৃত খারাপ

secondhand *adj* **Secondhand** things are not new and have been owned by someone else. ব্যবহার করা

secondly *adv* You say **secondly** when you want to make a second point or give a second reason for something. দ্বিতীয়তঃ

second-rate *adj* If you describe something as **second-rate**, you mean that it is of poor quality. খারাপ

secret (**secrets**) *adj* If something is **secret**, it is known about by only a small number of people, and is not told or shown to anyone else. গোপন ▷ *n* A **secret** is a fact that is known by only a small number of people, and is not told to anyone else. গোপনীয়

secretary (**secretaries**) *n* A **secretary** is a person who is employed to do office work, such as typing letters or answering phone calls. সচিব

secretly *adv* If you do something **secretly**, it is known about by only a small number of people. গোপনভাবে

secret service (**secret services**) *n* A country's **secret service** is a government department whose job is to find out enemy secrets and to prevent its own government's secrets from being discovered. গোয়েন্দা বিভাগ

sect (**sects**) *n* A **sect** is a group of people that has separated from a larger group and has a particular set of religious or political beliefs. সম্প্রদায়

section (**sections**) *n* A **section** of something is one of the parts that it is divided into. বিভাগ

sector (**sectors**) *n* A **sector** of something, especially a country's economy, is a particular part of it. ক্ষেত্র

secure *adj* If something such as a job or institution is **secure**, it is safe and reliable, and unlikely to be lost or fail. নিরাপদ

security *n* **Security** refers to all the precautions that are taken to protect a place. নিরাপত্তা

security guard (**security guards**) *n* A **security guard** is someone whose job is to protect a building or to collect and deliver large amounts of money. নিরাপত্তা রক্ষী

sedative (**sedatives**) *n* A **sedative** is a drug that calms you or makes you sleep. শান্তকারী

see (**sees, seeing, saw, seen**) *v* If you **see** something, you are looking at it or you notice it. দেখা ▷ *vt* If you **see** someone, you meet them. সাক্ষাৎ করা

seed (**seeds**) *n* A **seed** is one of the small hard parts of a plant from which a new plant grows. বীজ

seek (**seeks, seeking, sought**) *vt* If you **seek** something, you try to find it or obtain it. (*formal*) চাওয়া

seem (**seems, seeming, seemed**) *v* You use **seem** to say that someone or something gives the impression of having a particular quality, or that something gives the impression of happening in the way you describe. মনে হওয়া

seesaw (**seesaws**) *n* A **seesaw** is a long board which is balanced on a fixed part in the middle. To play on it, a child sits on each end, and when one end goes up, the other goes down. টেকি

see-through *adj* **See-through** clothes are made of thin cloth, so that you can see a person's body or underwear through them. ফিনফিনে

seize (**seizes, seizing, seized**) *vt* If you **seize** something, you take hold of it quickly and firmly. আটক করা

seizure (**seizures**) *n* If someone has a **seizure**, they have a heart attack or an epileptic fit. ফিট হওয়া

seldom *adv* If something **seldom** happens, it does not happen often. কদাচিৎ

select (**selects, selecting, selected**) *vt* If you **select** something, you choose it from a number of things of the same kind. নির্বাচন করা

selection *n* **Selection** is the act of selecting one or more people or things from a group. নির্বাচন

self-assured *adj* Someone who is **self-assured** shows confidence in what they say and do because they are sure of their own abilities. স্ব-আশ্বাযুক্ত

self-catering *n* If you go on a **self-catering** holiday or you stay in **self-catering** accommodation, you stay in a place where you have to make your own meals. স্ব-ব্যবস্থাপনা

self-centred *adj* Someone who is **self-centred** is only concerned with their own wants and needs and never thinks about other people. আত্ম-কেন্দ্রিক

self-conscious *adj* Someone who is **self-conscious** is easily embarrassed and nervous about the way they look or appear. আত্ম সচেতন

self-contained *adj* You can describe someone as **self-contained** when they do not need help or resources from other people. আত্ম-নির্ভর

self-control *n* Your **self-control** is your ability to control your feelings and appear calm. আত্ম-নিয়ন্ত্রণ

self-defence *n* **Self-defence** is the use of force to protect yourself against someone who is attacking you. আত্ম-রক্ষা

S

self-discipline n **Self-discipline** is the ability to control yourself and to make yourself work hard or behave in a particular way without needing anyone else to tell you what to do. আত্ম-শৃংখলা

self-employed adj If you are **self-employed**, you organize your own work and taxes and are paid by people for a service you provide, rather than being paid a regular salary by a person or a firm. স্ব-নিযুক্ত

selfish adj If you say that someone is **selfish**, you disapprove of them because they care only about themselves, and not about other people. স্বার্থপর

self-service adj A **self-service** shop, restaurant, or garage is one where you get things for yourself rather than being served by another person. স্বপরিবেশন

sell (**sells, selling, sold**) vt If you **sell** something that you own, you let someone have it in return for money. বিক্রি করা

sell-by date (**sell-by dates**) n The **sell-by date** on a food container is the date by which the food should be eaten or eaten before it starts to decay. তারিখের মধ্যে বিক্রি করা

selling price (**selling prices**) n The **selling price** of something is the price for which it is sold. বিক্রয় মূল্য

sell off v If you **sell** something **off**, you sell it because you need the money. বিক্রি করে দেওয়া *The company is selling off some sites and concentrating on cutting debts.*

Sellotape® n **Sellotape** is a clear sticky tape that you use to stick paper or card together or onto a wall. সেলোটেপ

sell out v If a shop **sells out** of something, it sells all its stocks of it. বিক্রি হয়ে যাওয়া *The supermarket sold out of flour in a single day.*

semester (**semesters**) n In colleges and universities in the United States and some other countries, a **semester** is one of two

periods into which the year is divided. সেমিস্টার

semicircle (**semicircles**) n A **semicircle** is one half of a circle, or something having the shape of half a circle. অর্ধ গোলাকার

semi-colon (**semi-colons**) n A **semi-colon** is the punctuation mark ; which is used to indicate a pause intermediate in value or length between that of a comma and that of a full stop. সেমি কোলন/অর্ধ বিরাম

semi-detached house (**semi-detached houses**) n A **semi-detached house** is a house that is joined to another house on one side by a shared wall. এক দেওয়ালের বাড়ি

semifinal (**semifinals**) n A **semifinal** is one of the two matches or races in a competition that are held to decide who will compete in the final. সেমিফাইনাল

semi-skimmed milk n **Semi-skimmed milk** or **semi-skimmed** is milk from which some of the cream has been removed. মাঠা তোলা দুধ

send (**sends, sending, sent**) vt When you **send** someone something, you arrange for them to receive it, for example by post. পাঠানো

send back v When you **send** something **back**, you arrange for it to be taken and delivered to the person who sent it to you, for example by post. ফেরত পাঠানো *The camera was damaged, so I sent it back to the manufacturer.*

sender (**senders**) n The **sender** of a letter, package, or radio message is the person who sent it. প্রেরক

send off v If you **send off** a letter or parcel, you send it somewhere by post. পাঠিয়ে দেওয়া *He sent off copies to various people.*

send out v If you **send out** things such as leaflets or bills, you send them to a large number of people at the same time. বিতরণ করা *She sent out four hundred invitations to the party.*

Senegal n **Senegal** is a republic in West Africa, on the Atlantic. সেনেগাল দেশ

Senegalese (**Senegalese**) adj **Senegalese** means belonging or relating to Senegal, or to its people or culture. সেনেগালীয় ▷ n A **Senegalese** is a Senegalese citizen, or a person of Senegalese origin. সেনেগালের নাগরিক

senior adj The **senior** people in an organization have the highest and most important jobs in it. বরিষ্ঠ

senior citizen (**senior citizens**) n A **senior citizen** is a person who is old enough to receive an old-age pension. বরিষ্ঠ নাগরিক

sensational adj A **sensational** event or situation is so remarkable that it causes great excitement and interest. চাঞ্চল্যসৃষ্টিকারী

sense (**senses**) n Your **senses** are the physical abilities of sight, smell, hearing, touch, and taste. বোধ

senseless adj A **senseless** action seems to have no meaning or purpose. কান্ডজ্ঞানহীন

sense of humour Someone's **sense of humour** is the fact that they find certain things amusing. কৌতুক বোধ

sensible adj A **sensible** person is able to make good decisions and judgements based on reason. বিচারবুদ্ধি সম্পন্ন

sensitive adj If you are **sensitive** to other people's problems and feelings, you understand and are aware of them. সংবেদনশীল

sensuous adj **Sensuous** things give pleasure to the mind or body through the senses. ভাবময়

sentence (**sentences, sentencing, sentenced**) n A **sentence** is a group of words which, when they are written down, begin with a capital letter and end with a full stop, question mark, or exclamation mark. Most sentences contain a subject and a verb. বাক্য ▷ n In a law court, a **sentence** is the punishment that a person receives after they have been found guilty of a

crime. রায় ▷ vt When a judge **sentences** someone, he or she states in court what their punishment will be. শাস্তি প্রদান

sentimental adj A **sentimental** person or thing feels or makes you feel emotions such as tenderness, affection, or sadness, sometimes in a way that is exaggerated or foolish. আবেগপ্রবণ

separate (**separates, separating, separated**) adj If one thing is **separate** from another, the two things are apart and are not connected. পৃথক ▷ v If you **separate** people or things that are together, or if they **separate**, they move apart. আলাদা করা

separately adv If people or things are dealt with **separately** or do something **separately**, they are dealt with or do something at different times or places, rather than together. আলাদাভাবে

separation (**separations**) n The **separation** of two or more things or groups is the fact that they are separate or become separate, and are not linked. বিচ্ছেদ

September (**Septembers**) n **September** is the ninth month of the year in the Western calendar. সেপ্টেম্বর মাস

septic tank (**septic tanks**) n A **septic tank** is an underground tank where faeces, urine, and other waste matter is made harmless using bacteria. সেপ্টিক ট্যাংক

sequel (**sequels**) n The **sequel** to a book or film is another book or film which continues the story. ধারাবাহিক

sequence (**sequences**) n A **sequence** of things is a number of them that come one after another in a particular order. ক্রম

Serbia n **Serbia** is a republic in south-east Europe. সার্বিয়া

Serbian (**Serbians**) adj **Serbian** means of, relating to, or characteristic of Serbia, its people, or their language (formerly regarded as a dialect of Serbo-Croat). সার্বিয় ▷ n A **Serbian** is a native or inhabitant of

S

Serbia. সার্বিয়ার নাগরিক ▷ n **Serbian** is the language spoken in Serbia. সার্বিয়ার ভাষা

sergeant (**sergeants**) n A **sergeant** is a non-commissioned officer of middle rank in the army, marines, or air force. সার্জেন্ট

serial (**serials**) n A **serial** is a story which is broadcast or published in a number of parts over a period of time. ধারাবাহিক

series (**series**) n A **series** of things or events is a number of them that come one after the other. সিরিজ

serious adj **Serious** problems or situations are very bad and cause people to be worried or afraid. গুরুতর

seriously adv **Seriously** means that something is done in a serious manner or to a serious degree. গুরুতরভাবে

servant (**servants**) n A **servant** is someone who is employed to work in another person's house, for example to cook or clean. চাকর

serve (**serves, serving, served**) n A **serve** is when you hit a ball or a shuttlecock in a game of tennis or badminton in order to start the game. সার্ভ (খেলার ক্ষেত্রে) ▷ vt If you **serve** your country, an organization, or a person, you do useful work for them. সেবা করা

server (**servers**) n A **server** is part of a computer network which does a particular task, for example storing or processing information, for all or part of the network. কম্পিউটার সার্ভার ▷ n In tennis and badminton, the **server** is the player whose turn it is to hit the ball or shuttlecock to start play. খেলোয়ার যে সার্ভ করে

service (**services, servicing, serviced**) n A **service** is an organization or system that provides something for the public. পরিষেবা ▷ vt If you have a vehicle or machine **serviced**, you arrange for someone to examine, adjust, and clean it so that it will keep working efficiently and safely. মেরামত করান

service area (**service areas**) n A **service area** is a place beside a motorway where

you can buy petrol and other things, or have a meal. সার্ভিস এলাকা

service charge (**service charges**) n A **service charge** is an amount that is added to your bill in a restaurant to pay for the work of the person who comes and serves you. পরিষেবা শুল্ক

serviceman (**servicemen**) n A **serviceman** is a man who is in the army, navy, or air force. সৈনিক

service station (**service stations**) n A **service station** is a place that sells things such as petrol, oil, and spare parts. Service stations often sell food, drink, and other goods. পেট্রোল পাম্প

servicewoman (**servicewomen**) n A **servicewoman** is a woman who is in the army, navy, or air force. মহিলা সৈনিক

serviette (**serviettes**) n A **serviette** is a square of cloth or paper that you use to protect your clothes or to wipe your mouth when you are eating. ন্যাপকিন

session (**sessions**) n A **session** is a meeting or series of meetings of a court, parliament, or other official group. অধিবেশন

set (**sets, setting**) n A **set** of things is a number of things that belong together. গুচ্ছ ▷ vt If you **set** something somewhere, you put it there. বসান

setback (**setbacks**) n A **setback** is an event that delays your progress or reverses some of the progress that you have made. বাধা

set off v When you **set off**, you start a journey. রওনা দেওয়া He set off for the station.

set out v When you **set out**, you start a journey. যাত্রা শুরু করা I set out for the cottage.

settee (**settees**) n A **settee** is a long comfortable seat with a back and arms, for two or three people. সেটি, বসার আসন

settle (**settles, settling, settled**) vt If two people **settle** an argument or problem, or if someone or something **settles** it, they solve it by making a decision about who is right or about what to do. নিষ্পত্তি করা

settle down *v* When someone **settles down**, they start living a quiet life in one place, especially when they get married or buy a house. থিতু হওয়া *One day I'll settle down and have a family.*

seven *num* **Seven** is the number 7. সাত

seventeen *num* **Seventeen** is the number 17. সতেরো

seventeenth *adj* The **seventeenth** item in a series is the one that you count as number seventeen. সপ্তদশ

seventh (**sevenths**) *adj* The **seventh** item in a series is the one that you count as number seven. সপ্তম ▷ *n* A **seventh** is one of seven equal parts of something. সাত ভাগের এক ভাগ

seventy *num* **Seventy** is the number 70. সত্তর

several *det* **Several** is used to talk about a number of people or things that is not large but is greater than two. বেশ কিছু *Several hundred students gathered on campus.* ▷ *pron* **Several** means a small number of people or things that is greater than two. বেশ কিছু *You may have to try several before you find the right treatment.* ▷ *adj* You use **several** for talking about a number of people or things that is not large but is greater than two. অনেক

sew (**sews, sewing, sewed, sewn**) *v* When you **sew** something such as clothes, you make them or repair them by joining pieces of cloth together by passing thread through them with a needle. সেলাই করা

sewer (**sewers**) *n* A **sewer** is a large underground channel that carries waste matter and rainwater away. পয়ঃপ্রণালী

sewing *n* **Sewing** is the activity of making or mending clothes or other things using a needle and thread. সেলাই এর কাজ

sewing machine (**sewing machines**) *n* A **sewing machine** is a machine that you use for sewing. সেলাই মেসিন

sew up *v* If you **sew up** pieces of cloth or tears in cloth or skin, you join them together using a needle and thread. সেলাই করা *Next day, Miss Stone decided to sew up the rip.*

sex (**sexes**) *n* The **sexes** are the two groups, male and female, into which people and animals are divided. লিঙ্গ

sexism *n* **Sexism** is the belief that the members of one sex, usually women, are less intelligent or less capable than those of the other sex and need not be treated equally. স্ত্রী-পুরুষবাদ

sexist *adj* If you describe people or their behaviour as **sexist**, you mean that they are influenced by the belief that the members of one sex, usually women, are less intelligent or less capable than those of the other sex and need not be treated equally. স্ত্রী-পুরুষবাদী

shabby (**shabbier, shabbiest**) *adj* **Shabby** things or places look old and in bad condition. খারাপ

shade *n* **Shade** is a cool area of darkness where the sun does not reach. ছায়ার নিচে

shadow (**shadows**) *n* A **shadow** is a dark shape on a surface that is made when something stands between a light and the surface. ছায়া

shake (**shakes, shaking, shook, shaken**) *vt* If you **shake** something, you hold it and move it quickly up and down. ঝাঁকানো ▷ *v* If someone or something **shakes**, they move quickly backwards and forwards or up and down. কাঁপা

shaken *adj* If you are **shaken**, you are upset and unable to think calmly. অস্থির

shaky (**shakier, shakiest**) *adj* If your body or your voice is **shaky**, you cannot control it properly and it trembles, for example because you are ill or nervous. দুর্বল

shall *v* You use **shall**, usually with 'I' and 'we', when you are talking about something that will happen in the future. ভবিষ্যতে করা হবে *I shall know more tomorrow.*

shallow (**shallower, shallowest**) *adj* A **shallow** hole, container, or layer of water measures only a short distance from the top to the bottom. অগভীর

shambles *npl* If a place, event, or situation is a **shambles**, everything is in disorder. বিশৃঙ্খল

shame *n* **Shame** is an uncomfortable feeling that you have when you know that you have done something wrong or embarrassing, or when someone close to you has. লজ্জা

shampoo (**shampoos**) *n* **Shampoo** is a liquid that you use for washing your hair. স্যাম্পু

shape (**shapes**) *n* The **shape** of an object, a person, or an area is the form or pattern of its outline. আকার

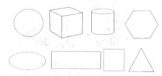

share (**shares, sharing, shared**) *n* If you have or do your **share** of something, you have or do the amount that is reasonable or fair. অংশ ▷ *vt* If you **share** something with another person, you both have it, use it, do it, or experience it. ভাগ করে নেওয়া

shareholder (**shareholders**) *n* A **shareholder** is a person who owns shares in a company. শেয়ার ধারক

share out *v* If you **share** something **out**, you give each person in a group an equal or fair part of it. সমানভাবে ভাগ করে দেওয়া *The funding will be shared out between universities, hospitals, and research bodies.*

shark (**sharks**) *n* **Sharks** are very large fish with sharp teeth. হাঙর মাছ

sharp (**sharper, sharpest**) *adj* A **sharp** point or edge is very thin and can cut through things quickly. ধারালো ▷ *adj* A **sharp** feeling is sudden and is very big or strong. তীক্ষ্ণ

shave (**shaves, shaving, shaved**) *v* When a man **shaves**, he removes the hair from his face using a razor or shaver so that his face is smooth. দাড়ি কামানো

shaver (**shavers**) *n* A **shaver** is an electric device used for shaving hair from the face and body. দাড়ি কামানোর মেশিন

shaving cream (**shaving creams**) *n* **Shaving cream** is a soft soapy substance which men put on their face before they shave. দাড়ি কামানোর ক্রীম

shaving foam (**shaving foams**) *n* **Shaving foam** is a soft soapy substance which men put on their face before they shave. দাড়ি কামানোর ফোম

shawl (**shawls**) *n* A **shawl** is a large piece of woollen cloth worn over a woman's shoulders or head, or wrapped around a baby to keep it warm. শাল

she *pron* You use **she** to talk about a woman, a girl, or a female animal. সে (মেয়ে) *She's seventeen years old.*

shed (**sheds**) *n* A **shed** is a small building used for storing things such as garden tools. শেড

sheep (**sheep**) *n* A **sheep** is a farm animal with a thick woolly coat. মেষ

sheepdog (**sheepdogs**) *n* A **sheepdog** is a breed of dog. Some sheepdogs are used for controlling sheep. কুকুর

sheepskin (sheepskins) n **Sheepskin** is the skin of a sheep with the wool still attached to it, used especially for making coats and rugs. ভেড়ার ছাল

sheer (sheerer, sheerest) adj You can use **sheer** to emphasize that a state or situation is complete and does not involve anything else. নিছক

sheet (sheets) n A **sheet** is a large piece of cloth that you sleep on or cover yourself with in bed. চাদর ▷ n A **sheet** is a piece of paper, glass, plastic, or metal. পাত

shelf (shelves) n A **shelf** is a flat piece of wood, metal, or glass which is attached to a wall or to the sides of a cupboard. তাক

shell (shells) n The **shell** of an egg or nut is its hard part. খোলা ▷ n The **shell** of an animal such as a snail is the hard part that covers its back and protects it. খোলস

shellfish (shellfish) n A **shellfish** is a small creature with a shell that lives in the sea. খোসওয়ালা জলজ প্রাণী

shell suit (shell suits) n A **shell suit** is a casual suit which is made of thin nylon. পাতলা স্যুট

shelter (shelters) n A **shelter** is a small building or covered place which is made to protect people from bad weather or danger. আশ্রয়

shepherd (shepherds) n A **shepherd** is a person whose job is to look after sheep. মেষ পালক

sherry (sherries) n **Sherry** is a type of strong wine that is made in south-western Spain. শেরী মদ

shield (shields) n A **shield** is a large piece of metal or leather which soldiers used to carry to protect their bodies while they were fighting. ঢাল

shift (shifts, shifting, shifted) n If someone's opinion, a situation, or a policy changes slightly, the change is called a **shift**. পরিবর্তন ▷ v If you **shift** something, or if it **shifts**, it moves slightly. সরানো

shifty adj Someone who looks **shifty** gives the impression of being dishonest. (informal) অসৎ

shin (shins) n Your **shin** is the front part of your leg between your knee and ankle. জাং

shine (shines, shining, shined, shone) vi When the sun or a light **shines**, it gives out bright light. উজ্জ্বল হওয়া

shiny (shinier, shiniest) adj **Shiny** things are bright and reflect light. উজ্জ্বল

ship (ships) n A **ship** is a large boat which carries passengers or cargo. জাহাজ

shipbuilding n **Shipbuilding** is the industry of building ships. জাহাজ নির্মান

shipment (shipments) n A **shipment** is an amount of a particular kind of cargo that is sent to another country on a ship, train, aeroplane, or other vehicle. চালান

shipwreck (shipwrecks) n When there is a **shipwreck**, a ship is destroyed in an accident at sea. জাহাজ দুর্ঘটনা

shipwrecked adj If someone is **shipwrecked**, their ship is destroyed in an accident at sea but they survive and manage to reach land. জাহাজ দুর্ঘটনা থেকে বেঁচে যাওয়া

shipyard (shipyards) n A **shipyard** is a place where ships are built and repaired. জাহাজঘাটি

shirt (shirts) n A **shirt** is a piece of clothing worn on the upper part of your body with a collar, sleeves, and buttons down the front. জামা

shiver (shivers, shivering, shivered) vi When you **shiver**, your body shakes slightly because you are cold or frightened. ঠান্ডায় কাঁপা

shock (shocks, shocking, shocked) n If you have a **shock**, you suddenly have an unpleasant or surprising experience. হতবাক ▷ vt If something **shocks** you, it makes you feel very upset. হতবাক হওয়া

shocking adj You can say that something is **shocking** if you think that it is very bad. (informal) ভয়ানক

shoe (**shoes**) n **Shoes** are objects worn on your feet. Shoes cover most of your foot but not your ankle. জুতো

shoelace (**shoelaces**) n **Shoelaces** are long, narrow pieces of material like pieces of string that you use to fasten your shoes. জুতোর ফিতে

shoe polish (**shoe polishes**) n **Shoe polish** is a substance that you put on your shoes in order to clean them, protect them, and make them shine. জুতোর পালিশ

shoe shop (**shoe shops**) n A **shoe shop** is a shop that sells shoes. জুতোর দোকান

shoot (**shoots, shooting, shot**) vt To **shoot** a person or animal means to kill or injure them by firing a gun at them. গুলি করা

shooting (**shootings**) n A **shooting** is an occasion when someone is killed or injured by being shot with a gun. গুলি করার ঘটনা

shop (**shops**) n A **shop** is a building or part of a building where things are sold. দোকান

shop assistant (**shop assistants**) n A **shop assistant** is a person who works in a shop selling things to customers. দোকান সহায়ক

shopkeeper (**shopkeepers**) n A **shopkeeper** is a person who owns a small shop. দোকানদার

shoplifting n **Shoplifting** is stealing from a shop by hiding things in a bag or in your clothes. দোকান থেকে চুরি করা

shopping n When you do the **shopping**, you go to shops and buy things. কেনাকাটা

shopping bag (**shopping bags**) n A **shopping bag** is a strong container with one or two handles, used to carry things in when you go shopping. থলে

shopping centre (**shopping centres**) n A **shopping centre** is an area in a town where a lot of shops have been built close together. কেনাকাটার স্থান

shopping trolley (**shopping trolleys**) n A **shopping trolley** is a large metal basket on wheels which is provided by shops such as supermarkets for customers to use while they are in the shop. জিনিসপত্র রাখার ট্রলি

shop window (**shop windows**) n A **shop window** is a large piece of glass along the front of a shop, behind which some of the goods that the shop sells are displayed. দোকানের প্রদর্শনী

shore (**shores**) n The **shores** or the **shore** of a sea, lake, or wide river is the land along the edge of it. Someone who is **on shore** is on the land rather than on a ship. তীর

short (**shorter, shortest**) adj If something is **short**, it does not last very long. স্বল্পমেয়াদী ▷ adj A **short** thing is small in length, distance, or height. ছোট

shortage (**shortages**) n If there is a **shortage** of something, there is not enough of it. ঘাটতি

shortcoming (**shortcomings**) n The **shortcomings** of a person or thing are their faults or weaknesses. ক্রটি

shortcrust pastry n **Shortcrust pastry** is a basic type of pastry that is made with half the quantity of fat to flour, and has a crisp but crumbly texture. পেস্ট্রি

shortcut (**shortcuts**) n A **shortcut** is a quicker way of getting somewhere than the usual route. ছোট রাস্তা

shortfall (**shortfalls**) n If there is a **shortfall** in something, there is not enough of it. কম হওয়া

shorthand n **Shorthand** is a quick way of writing which uses signs to represent words or syllables. শর্টহ্যান্ড লেখা

shortlist (**shortlists**) n A **shortlist** is a list of people or things which have been chosen from a larger group, for example for a job or a prize. The successful person or thing is then chosen from the small group. বাছাই

shortly adv If something happens **shortly** after or before something else, it happens a short amount of time after or before it. তাড়াতাড়ি

shorts npl **Shorts** are trousers with short legs. হাফ প্যান্ট

short-sighted adj If you are **short-sighted**, you cannot see things properly when they are far away, because there is something wrong with your eyes. অদূরদর্শী

short-sleeved adj A **short-sleeved** shirt, dress, or other item of clothing has sleeves that cover the top part of your arms. হাফ হাতা জামা

short story (**short stories**) n A **short story** is a written story about imaginary events that is only a few pages long. ছোট গল্প

shot (**shots**) n If you fire a **shot**, you fire a gun once. গুলি চালনা

shotgun (**shotguns**) n A **shotgun** is a gun which fires a lot of small metal balls at one time. বন্দুক

should v You use **should** when you are saying what is the right thing to do. উচিত *He should tell us what happened.*

shoulder (**shoulders**) n Your **shoulders** are the parts of your body between your neck and the tops of your arms. কাঁধ

shoulder blade (**shoulder blades**) n Your **shoulder blades** are the two large, flat, triangular bones that you have in the upper part of your back, below your shoulders. কাঁধের পিছন দিক

shout (**shouts, shouting, shouted**) n A **shout** is the noise made when someone speaks very loudly. চিৎকার ▷ v If you **shout**, you say something very loudly, usually

because you want people a long distance away to hear you or because you are angry. চিৎকার করা

shovel (**shovels**) n A **shovel** is a tool like a spade, used for lifting and moving earth, coal, or snow. বেলচা

show (**shows, showing, showed, shown**) n A **show** of a feeling is an attempt by someone to make it clear that they have that feeling. লোককে দেখানো ▷ vt If information or a fact **shows** that a situation exists, it proves it. দেখানো ▷ v If you **show** someone something, you let them see it. দেখানো ▷ vt If you **show** someone how to do something, you teach them how to do it. প্রদর্শন করা

show business n **Show business** is the entertainment industry. বিনোদন শিল্প

shower (**showers**) n A **shower** is a thing that you stand under, that covers you with water so you can wash yourself. শাওয়ার ▷ n A **shower** is a short period of rain. একপশলা বৃষ্টি

shower cap (**shower caps**) n A **shower cap** is a waterproof cap that you wear in the shower to keep your hair dry. স্নানের সময় পরবার টুপি

shower gel (**shower gels**) n **Shower gel** is liquid soap you use in the shower. স্নানের তরল সাবান

showerproof adj If a garment etc is **showerproof**, it is resistant to or partly impervious to rain. বৃষ্টিনিরোধী

S

showing (**showings**) *n* A **showing** is a presentation, exhibition, or display. প্রদর্শনী

show jumping *n* **Show jumping** is a sport in which horses are ridden in competitions to demonstrate their skill in jumping over fences and walls. শো জাম্পিং

show off (**show-offs**) *v* If you say that someone **is showing off**, you are criticizing them for trying to impress people by showing in a very obvious way what they can do or what they own. লোক দেখানো *All right, there's no need to show off.* ▷ *n* If you say that someone is a **show-off**, you are criticizing them for trying to impress people by showing in a very obvious way what they can do or what they own. (*informal*) লোক দেখানো

show up *v* If a person you are expecting to meet does not **show up**, they do not arrive at the place where you expect to meet them. উপস্থিত হওয়া *We waited until five o'clock, but he did not show up.*

shriek (**shrieks, shrieking, shrieked**) *vi* When someone **shrieks**, they make a short, very loud cry, for example, because they are suddenly surprised, are in pain, or are laughing. চিৎকার

shrimp (**shrimps, shrimp**) *n* **Shrimps** are small shellfish with long tails and many legs. চিংড়িমাছ

shrine (**shrines**) *n* A **shrine** is a holy place associated with a sacred person or object. প্রার্থনা স্থল

shrink (**shrinks, shrinking, shrank, shrunk**) *v* If something **shrinks** or you **shrink** it, it becomes smaller. ছোট হয়ে যাওয়া

shrub (**shrubs**) *n* **Shrubs** are low plants like small trees with several stems instead of a trunk. ঝোপ

shrug (**shrugs, shrugging, shrugged**) *vi* If you **shrug**, you raise your shoulders to show that you are not interested in something or that you do not know or care about something. অনিচ্ছার ভঙ্গী

shrunken *adj* Someone or something that is **shrunken** has become smaller than they used to be. খাটো

shudder (**shudders, shuddering, shuddered**) *vi* If you **shudder**, you shake with fear, horror, or disgust, or because you are cold. ভয় পাওয়া

shuffle (**shuffles, shuffling, shuffled**) *vi* If you **shuffle** somewhere, you walk there without lifting your feet properly off the ground. ঘসটে চলা

shut (**shuts, shutting, shut**) *v* If you **shut** something such as a door or if it **shuts**, it moves so that it fills a hole or a space. বন্ধ করা

shut down *v* If a factory or business **is shut down**, it is closed permanently. বন্ধ করে দেওয়া, পাট তুলে নেওয়া *Smaller contractors were forced to shut down.*

shutters *npl* **Shutters** are wooden or metal covers fitted on the outside of a window. They can be opened to let in the light, or closed to keep out the sun or the cold. জানালা দরজার শাটার

shuttle (**shuttles**) *n* A **shuttle** is a spacecraft that is designed to travel into space and back to earth several times. ফেরি যান

shuttlecock (**shuttlecocks**) *n* A **shuttlecock** is the small object that you hit over the net in a game of badminton. শাটলকক

shut up *v* If you **shut up**, you stop talking. If you say **'shut up'** to someone, you are rudely telling them to stop talking. চুপ করা *He wished she would shut up.*

shy (**shyer, shyest**) *adj* A **shy** person is nervous and uncomfortable in the company of other people. লাজুক

Siberia *n* **Siberia** is a vast region of Russia and north Kazakhstan. সাইবেরিয়া

siblings *npl* Your **siblings** are your brothers and sisters. (*formal*) ভাইবোন

sick (**sicker, sickest**) *adj* If you are **sick**, you are ill. **Sick** usually means physically ill, but it can sometimes be used to mean mentally ill. অসুস্থ

sickening adj You describe something as **sickening** when it gives you feelings of horror or disgust, or makes you feel sick in your stomach. অসুস্থ করে তোলার মত

sick leave n **Sick leave** is the time that a person spends away from work because of illness or injury. অসুস্থতার জন্য ছুটি

sickness n **Sickness** is the state of being ill or unhealthy. অসুস্থতা

sick note (**sick notes**) n A **sick note** is an official note signed by a doctor which states that someone is ill and needs to stay off work for a particular period of time. অসুস্থতার প্রমাণ পত্র

sick pay n When you are ill and unable to work, **sick pay** is the money that you get from your employer instead of your normal wages. অসুস্থ থাকাকালীন বেতন

side (**sides**) n The **side** of something is a place to the left or right of it. পাশ ▷ n The **side** of something is also its edge. দিক ▷ n The different **sides** in a game are the groups of people who are playing against each other. দল

sideboard (**sideboards**) n A **sideboard** is a long cupboard which is about the same height as a table. Sideboards are usually kept in dining rooms to put plates and glasses in. সাইড বোর্ড, আলমারী

side effect (**side effects**) n The **side effects** of a drug are the effects, usually bad ones, that the drug has on you in addition to its function of curing illness or pain. পার্শ্ব প্রতিক্রিয়া

sidelight (**sidelights**) n The **sidelights** on a vehicle are the small lights at the front that help other drivers to notice the vehicle and to judge its width. গাড়ির আলো

side street (**side streets**) n A **side street** is a quiet, often narrow street which leads off a busier street. পার্শ্ব রাস্তা

sideways adv **Sideways** means from or towards the side of something or someone. পাশ দিয়ে

sieve (**sieves**) n A **sieve** is a tool consisting of a metal or plastic ring with a fine wire net

attached. It is used for separating liquids from solids or larger pieces of something from smaller pieces. ছাঁকনী

sigh (**sighs, sighing, sighed**) n When you let out a **sigh**, you let out a deep breath. দীর্ঘশ্বাস ছাড়া ▷ vi When you **sigh**, you let out a deep breath, as a way of expressing feelings such as disappointment, tiredness, or pleasure. দীর্ঘশ্বাস ছেড়ে বাঁচা

sight (**sights**) n Your **sight** is your ability to see. দৃষ্টি

sightseeing n **Sightseeing** is the activity of visiting the interesting places that tourists usually visit. দর্শনীয় স্থান দেখে বেড়ানো

sign (**signs, signing, signed**) n A **sign** is a mark or a shape that has a special meaning. চিহ্ন ▷ v When you **sign** a document, you write your name on it. স্বাক্ষর করা ▷ n You can make a **sign** to somebody by moving something. সংকেত

signal (**signals, signalling, signalled**) n A **signal** is a sound or action which is intended to send a particular message. সংকেত ▷ v If you **signal** something, or if you **signal** to someone, you make a gesture or sound in order to give someone a particular message. সংকেত দেওয়া

signature (**signatures**) n Your **signature** is your name, written in your own characteristic way. স্বাক্ষর

significance n The **significance** of something is its importance. গুরুত্ব

significant adj A **significant** amount of something is large enough to be important or noticeable. গুরুত্বপূর্ণ

sign language (**sign languages**) n **Sign language** is movements of your hands and arms used to communicate. There are several official systems of sign language, used, for example, by deaf people. ইশারা ভাষা

sign on v In the UK, when an unemployed person **signs on**, they officially inform the authorities that they are unemployed, so that they can receive money from the government in order to live. ভাতার জন্য আবেদন *He has signed on at the job centre.*

signpost (**signposts**) *n* A **signpost** is a sign where roads meet that tells you which direction to go in to reach a particular place or different places. পথ নির্দেশ

Sikh (**Sikhs**) *n* A **Sikh** is a member of an Indian religion which separated from Hinduism in the sixteenth century and which teaches that there is only one God. শিখ ▷ *adj* **Sikh** means of or relating to Sikhs or their religious beliefs and customs. শিখ সম্প্রদায়ের

silence (**silences**) *n* If there is **silence**, it is completely quiet. চুপচাপ

silencer (**silencers**) *n* A **silencer** is a device that is fitted onto a gun to make it very quiet when it is fired. যাতে শব্দ হয় না

silent *adj* If something is **silent**, it is quiet, with no sound at all. নিস্তব্ধ ▷ *adj* If you are **silent**, you are not talking. চুপচাপ

silicon chip (**silicon chips**) *n* A **silicon chip** is a very small piece of silicon inside a computer. It has electronic circuits on it and can hold large quantities of information or perform mathematical or logical operations. সিলিকন চিপ

silk (**silks**) *n* **Silk** is a very smooth, fine cloth made from a substance produced by a kind of moth. রেশম

silly (**sillier, silliest**) *adj* Someone who is being **silly** is behaving in a foolish or childish way. বোকা

silver *n* **Silver** is a valuable greyish-white metal used for making jewellery and ornaments. রূপো

similar *adj* If one thing is **similar to** another, or if a number of things are **similar**, they have features that are the same. অনুরূপ

similarity (**similarities**) *n* If there is a **similarity** between two or more things, they share some features that are the same. সাদৃশ্য

simmer (**simmers, simmering, simmered**) *v* When you **simmer** food, you cook it gently at just below boiling point. হালকা আঁচে রান্না করা

simple (**simpler, simplest**) *adj* If something is **simple**, it is not complicated, and is therefore easy to understand or do. সরল

simplify (**simplifies, simplifying, simplified**) *vt* If you **simplify** something, you make it easier to understand. সরলীকরণ

simply *adv* **Simply** means in a simple and uncomplicated manner. সরলভাবে

simultaneous *adj* Things which are **simultaneous** happen or exist at the same time. এক সঙ্গে

simultaneously *adv* If things happen or exist **simultaneously** they happen or exist at the same time. এক সঙ্গে

since *adv* You use **since** when you are talking about something that started in the past, and that has not stopped from then until now. থেকে ▷ *conj* You use **since** when you are talking about something that started in the past, and that has not stopped from then until now. যখন থেকে *I've lived here since I was six years old.* ▷ *prep* You use **since** when you are talking about something that started in the past, and that has not stopped from then until now. থেকে *I've not seen her since my birthday.*

sincere *adj* If you say that someone is **sincere**, you approve of them because they really mean the things they say. নিষ্ঠাবান

sincerely *adv* If you say or feel something **sincerely**, you really mean it or feel it. নিষ্ঠার সঙ্গে

sing (**sings, singing, sang, sung**) *v* If you **sing**, you make musical sounds with your voice, usually producing words that fit a tune. গান করা

singer (**singers**) *n* A **singer** is a person who sings, especially as a job. গায়ক

singing n **Singing** is the activity of making musical sounds with your voice. গান গাওয়া

single (singles) adj You use **single** to emphasize that you are referring to one thing, and no more than one thing. একটি

single parent (single parents) n A **single parent** is someone who is bringing up a child or children on their own, because the other parent is not living with them. একলা মা বা বাবা

singles npl **Singles** is a game of tennis or badminton in which one player plays another. The plural **singles** can be used to refer to one or more of these matches. এক জন করে খেলা, সিংগলস

single ticket (single tickets) n A **single ticket** is a ticket for a journey from one place to another but not back again. একদিকের টিকিট

singular n The **singular** of a noun is the form of it that is used to refer to one person or thing. একক

sinister adj Someone or something that is **sinister** seems evil or harmful. ক্ষতিকর

sink (sinks, sinking, sank, sunk) n A **sink** is a basin with taps that supply water. জলের সিংক ▷ v If a boat **sinks**, or if something **sinks** it, it disappears below the surface of a mass of water. ডুবে যাওয়া

sinus (sinuses) n Your **sinuses** are the spaces in the bone behind your nose. নাকের হাড়

sir (sirs) n People sometimes say **sir** as a polite way of addressing a man whose name they do not know or a man of superior rank. 'Dear Sir' is used at the beginning of official letters addressed to men. মহাশয়

siren (sirens) n A **siren** is a warning device which makes a long, loud, wailing noise. Most fire engines, ambulances, and police cars have sirens. সাইরেন

sister (sisters) n Your **sister** is a girl or woman who has the same parents as you. বোন

sister-in-law (sisters-in-law) n Your **sister-in-law** is the sister of your husband or wife, or the woman who is married to your brother. ননদ, শ্যালিকা, বৌদি

sit (sits, sitting, sat) vi If you **are sitting** somewhere, for example in a chair, your weight is supported by your buttocks rather than your feet. বসা

sitcom (sitcoms) n A **sitcom** is an amusing television drama series about a set of characters. **Sitcom** is an abbreviation for 'situation comedy'. হাস্যরসাত্মক নাটক

sit down v When you **sit down** somewhere, you lower your body until you are sitting on something. বসুন I sat down, stunned.

site (sites) n A **site** is a piece of ground that is used for a particular purpose or where a particular thing happens or is situated. স্থল

sitting room (sitting rooms) n A **sitting room** is a room in a house where people sit and relax. বসার ঘর

situated adj If something is **situated** somewhere, it is in a particular place or position. অবস্থিত

situation (situations) n You use **situation** to refer generally to what is happening at a particular place and time, or to refer to what is happening to you. পরিস্থিতি

six num **Six** is the number 6. ছয়

sixteen num **Sixteen** is the number 16. ষোল

sixteenth adj The **sixteenth** item in a series is the one that you count as number sixteen. ষোড়শ

sixth adj The **sixth** item in a series is the one that you count as number six. ষষ্ঠ

sixty num **Sixty** is the number 60. ষাট

size (sizes) n The **size** of something is how big or small it is. আকার

skate (skates, skating, skated) vi If you **skate**, you move about wearing ice-skates or roller-skates. স্কেট করা

skateboard (skateboards) n A **skateboard** is a narrow board with wheels at each end, which people stand on and ride for pleasure. স্কেট বোর্ড

skateboarding n **Skateboarding** is the activity of riding on a skateboard. স্কেট বোর্ডে চড়া

skates npl **Skates** are boots with a thin metal blade underneath that people wear to move quickly on ice. স্কেট করার জুতো

skating n **Skating** is the act or process of moving about wearing ice-skates or roller-skates. স্কেটিং করা

skating rink (**skating rinks**) n A **skating rink** is a large area covered with ice where people go to ice-skate, or a large area of concrete where people go to roller-skate. স্কেটিং করার স্থান

skeleton (**skeletons**) n Your **skeleton** is the framework of bones in your body. কংকাল

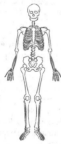

sketch (**sketches, sketching, sketched**) n A **sketch** is a drawing that is done quickly without a lot of details. প্রাথমিক চিত্রাঙ্কন ▷ v If you **sketch** something, you make a quick rough drawing of it. তাড়াতাড়ি চিত্র আঁকা

skewer (**skewers**) n A **skewer** is a long metal which is used to hold pieces of food together during cooking. শিক

ski (**skis, skiing, skied**) n **Skis** are long, flat, narrow pieces of wood, metal, or plastic that are fastened to boots so that you can move easily over snow. স্কি, (বরফের খেলার উপকরণ) ▷ vi When people **ski**, they move over snow on skis. স্কি খেলা

skid (**skids, skidding, skidded**) vi If a vehicle **skids**, it slides sideways or forwards while moving, for example when you are trying to stop it suddenly on a wet road. পিছলে যাওয়া

skier (**skiers**) n A **skier** is a person who moves over snow on skis. স্কি খেলে যে ব্যক্তি

skiing n **Skiing** is the act or process of moving over snow on skis. স্কি খেলা

skilful adj Someone who is **skilful** at something does it very well. দক্ষ

ski lift (**ski lifts**) n A **ski lift** is a machine for taking people to the top of a slope so that they can ski down it. It consists of a series of seats hanging down from a moving wire. স্কি খেলতে উচু স্থানে নিয়ে যাবার লিফট

skill (**skills**) n A **skill** is a type of activity or work which requires special training or knowledge. দক্ষতা

skilled adj Someone who is **skilled** has the knowledge and ability to do something well. দক্ষতাসম্পন্ন

skimmed milk n **Skimmed milk** is milk from which the cream has been removed. মাখন তোলা দুধ

skimpy (**skimpier, skimpiest**) adj **Skimpy** means too small in size or quantity. খুব ছোট

skin (**skins**) n Your **skin** covers your whole body. চামড়া ▷ n The **skin** of a fruit or vegetable covers the outside of it. খোসা

skinhead (**skinheads**) n A **skinhead** is a young person whose hair is shaved or cut very short. Skinheads are usually regarded as violent and aggressive. নেড়ামাথা

skinny (**skinnier, skinniest**) adj If you say that someone is **skinny**, you mean that they are very thin in a way you find unattractive. (informal) খুব রোগা

skin-tight adj **Skin-tight** clothes fit very tightly so that they show the shape of your body. খুব আঁটো, চামড়ার সাথে লেগে থাকে

skip (**skips, skipping, skipped**) vi If you **skip** along, you move along jumping from one foot to the other. লাফিয়ে চলা ▷ *vt* If you **skip** something, you decide not to do it. ছেড়ে দেওয়া

skirt (**skirts**) *n* A **skirt** is a piece of clothing worn by women and girls. It fastens at the waist and hangs down around the legs. স্কার্ট

skirting board (**skirting boards**) *n* **Skirting board** or **skirting** is a narrow length of wood which goes along the bottom of a wall in a room and makes a border between the walls and the floor. চৌকাঠ

skive (**skives, skiving, skived**) *v* If you **skive**, you avoid working, especially by staying away from the place where you should be working. (*informal*) কাজে ফাঁকি দেওয়া

skull (**skulls**) *n* Your **skull** is the bony part of your head which holds your brain. মাথার খুলি

sky (**skies**) *n* The **sky** is the space around the earth which you can see when you stand outside and look upwards. আকাশ

skyscraper (**skyscrapers**) *n* A **skyscraper** is a very tall building in a city. গগনচুম্বী ভবন

slack (**slacker, slackest**) *adj* Something that is **slack** is loose and not tightly stretched. ঢিলে

slag off *v* To **slag** someone **off** means to criticize them in an unpleasant way. (*informal*) সমালোচনা করা *All bands slag off their record companies. It's just the way it is.*

slam (**slams, slamming, slammed**) *v* If you **slam** a door or window, or if it **slams**, it shuts noisily and with great force. সজোরে বন্ধ করা

slang *n* **Slang** is words, expressions, and meanings that are informal and are used by people who know each other very well or who have the same interests. গালিগালাজের ভাষা

slap (**slaps, slapping, slapped**) *vt* If you **slap** someone, you hit them with the palm of your hand. চড় মারা

slate *n* **Slate** is a dark grey rock that can be easily split into thin layers. স্লেট পাথর

slave (**slaves, slaving, slaved**) *n* A **slave** is a person who is owned by another person and has to work for that person without pay. কৃতদাস ▷ *vi* If you say that a person **is slaving over** something or **is slaving for** something, you mean that they are working very hard. খুব কষ্টে কাজ করা

sledge (**sledges**) *n* A **sledge** is an object used for travelling over snow. It consists of a framework which slides on two strips of wood or metal. বরফে চলার গাড়ি

sledging *n* **Sledging** is the activity of riding over snow on a sledge. স্লেজ গাড়িতে চড়া

sleep (**sleeps, sleeping, slept**) *n* **Sleep** is the natural state of rest in which your eyes are closed, your body is inactive, and your mind does not think. ঘুম ▷ *vi* When you **sleep**, you rest with your eyes closed and your mind and body inactive. ঘুমোন

sleep in *v* If you **sleep in**, you sleep longer than usual. অনেকক্ষণ ধরে ঘুমোন *Yesterday, few players turned up because most slept in.*

sleeping bag (**sleeping bags**) *n* A **sleeping bag** is a large warm bag for sleeping in, especially when you are camping. স্লিপিং ব্যাগ

sleeping car (**sleeping cars**) *n* A **sleeping car** is a railway carriage containing beds for passengers to sleep in at night. ঘুমোনোর ব্যবস্থা সহ রেলের কামরা

sleeping pill (**sleeping pills**) *n* A **sleeping pill** is a pill that you can take to help you sleep. ঘুমের বড়ি

sleepwalk (**sleepwalks, sleepwalking, sleepwalked**) *vi* If someone **sleepwalks**, they walk around while they are asleep. ঘুমিয়ে হাঁটা

sleepy (**sleepier, sleepiest**) *adj* If you feel **sleepy**, you feel tired and ready to go to sleep. ঘুম চোখ

sleet (**sleets, sleeting, sleeted**) *n* **Sleet** is rain that is partly frozen. হিমেল বৃষ্টি ▷ *v*

S

When partly melted snow or hail, or partly frozen rain, falls from the clouds, you can say that it is **sleeting**. হিমেল বৃষ্টি হওয়া

sleeve (**sleeves**) n The **sleeves** of a coat, shirt, or other item of clothing are the parts that cover your arms. হাতা

sleeveless adj A **sleeveless** dress, top, or other item of clothing has no sleeves. হাতা কাটা

slender adj A **slender** person is thin and graceful in an attractive way. (written) আকর্ষণীয়

slice (**slices, slicing, sliced**) n A **slice** of bread, meat, fruit, or other food is a thin piece that has been cut from a larger piece. টুকরো ▷ vt If you **slice** food, you cut it into thin pieces. টুকরো করে কাটা

slide (**slides, sliding, slid**) n A **slide** in a playground is a structure that has a steep slope for children to slide down. স্লাইড (বাচ্চাদের খেলার উপকরণ) ▷ v When something **slides** somewhere, or when you **slide** it somewhere, it moves there smoothly over or against something else. গড়িয়ে পড়া

slight (**slighter, slightest**) adj Something that is **slight** is very small in degree or quantity. সামান্য

slightly adv **Slightly** means to some degree but not much. আরো কিছুটা

slim (**slimmer, slimmest**) adj A **slim** person has a thin nicely shaped body. তন্বী

sling (**slings**) n A **sling** is an object made of ropes, straps, or cloth that is used for carrying things. দোলনা

slip (**slips, slipping, slipped**) n A **slip** is a small or unimportant mistake. ক্রটি ▷ n A **slip** of paper is a small piece of paper. চিরকূট ▷ n A **slip** is a thin piece of clothing that a woman wears under her dress or skirt. অন্তর্বাস ▷ vi If you **slip**, you accidentally slide and lose your balance. পিছলে পড়া

slipped disc (**slipped discs**) n If you have a **slipped disc**, you have a bad back because one of the discs in your spine has moved out of its proper position. পিঠের হাড় সরে যাওয়া অবস্থা

slipper (**slippers**) n **Slippers** are loose soft shoes that you wear in the house. চপ্পল

slippery adj Something that is **slippery** is smooth, wet, or greasy, making it difficult to walk on or to hold. পিচ্ছিল

slip road (**slip roads**) n A **slip road** is a road which cars use to drive on and off a motorway. গাড়ি চলাচলের ছোট রাস্তা

slip up (**slip-ups**) v If you **slip up**, you make a small or unimportant mistake. ভুল করা We slipped up a few times. ▷ n A **slip-up** is a small or unimportant mistake. (informal) ছোট্ট ভুল

slope (**slopes**) n A **slope** is a surface that is at an angle, so that one end is higher than the other. ঢালু স্থান

sloppy (**sloppier, sloppiest**) *adj* Work that is **sloppy** is messy and careless. খারাপ

slot (**slots**) *n* A **slot** is a narrow opening in a machine or container, for example a hole that you put coins in to make a machine work. নির্দিষ্ট স্থান

slot machine (**slot machines**) *n* A **slot machine** is a machine from which you can get food or cigarettes or on which you can gamble. You make it work by putting coins into a slot. স্লট মেসিন

Slovak (**Slovaks**) *adj* **Slovak** means of, relating to, or characteristic of Slovakia, its people, or their language. স্লোভাকিয় ▷ *n* **Slovak** is the official language of Slovakia, belonging to the West Slavonic branch of the Indo-European family. Slovak is closely related to Czech, they are mutually intelligible. স্লোভাক ভাষা ▷ *n* A **Slovak** is a native or inhabitant of Slovakia. স্লোভাকিয়ার নাগরিক

Slovakia *n* **Slovakia** is a country in central Europe. স্লোভাকিয়া (দেশ)

Slovenia *n* **Slovenia** is a republic in south central Europe. স্লোভেনিয়া (দেশ)

Slovenian (**Slovenians**) *adj* **Slovenian** means belonging or relating to Slovenia, or to its people, language, or culture. স্লোভেনিয়া দেশীয় ▷ *n* A **Slovenian** is a person of Slovenian origin. স্লোভেনিয়ার মানুষ ▷ *n* **Slovenian** is the language spoken in Slovenia. স্লোভেনিয় ভাষা

slow (**slower, slowest**) *adj* Something that is **slow** moves, happens, or is done without much speed. ধীরগতি

slow down *v* If something **slows down**, or if you **slow** it **down**, it starts to move or happen more slowly. গতি কম করা *The car slowed down.*

slowly *adv* If something happens or is done **slowly**, it happens or is done without much speed. ধীরে ধীরে

slug (**slugs**) *n* A **slug** is a small slow-moving creature, with a long slippery body, like a snail without a shell. খোলসহীন পোকা

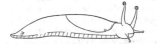

slum (**slums**) *n* A **slum** is an area of a city where living conditions are very bad. বস্তি

slush *n* **Slush** is snow that has begun to melt and is therefore very wet and dirty. কাদা

sly *adj* A **sly** look, expression, or remark shows that you know something that other people do not know. চতুর চাহনি

smack (**smacks, smacking, smacked**) *vt* If you **smack** someone, you hit them with your hand. চড় মারা

small (**smaller, smallest**) *adj* If something is **small**, it is not large in size or amount. ছোট

small ads *npl* The **small ads** in a newspaper are short advertisements in which you can advertise something such as an object for sale or a room to let. ছোট বিজ্ঞাপন

smart (**smarter, smartest**) *adj* **Smart** people and things are pleasantly neat and clean in appearance. সৌম্য দর্শন

smart phone (**smart phones**) *n* A **smart phone** is a type of cellphone that can perform many of the operations that a computer does, such as accessing the Internet. স্মার্ট ফোন

smash (**smashes, smashing, smashed**) *v* If something **smashes**, or if you **smash** it, it breaks into many pieces, for example when it is hit or dropped. ভেঙে টুকরো টুকরো হওয়া

smashing *adj* If you describe something or someone as **smashing**, you mean that you like them very much. (*informal*) আকর্ষণীয়

smear (**smears**) *n* A **smear** or a **smear test** is a medical test in which a few cells are taken from a woman's cervix and examined to see if any cancer cells are present. স্মিয়ার পরীক্ষা

smell (**smells, smelling, smelled, smelt**) n The **smell** of something is a quality it has which you become aware of through your nose. গন্ধ ▷ vt If you **smell** something, you become aware of it through your nose. গন্ধ পাওয়া ▷ vi If something **smells** of a particular thing, it has a particular quality which you become aware of through your nose. গন্ধ ছাড়া

smelly (**smellier, smelliest**) adj Something that is **smelly** has an unpleasant smell. দুর্গন্ধযুক্ত

smile (**smiles, smiling, smiled**) n A **smile** is the expression that you have on your face when you smile. হাসি ▷ vi When you **smile**, the corners of your mouth curve up and you sometimes show your teeth. People smile when they are pleased or amused, or when they are being friendly. হাসা

smiley (**smileys**) n A **smiley** is a symbol used in email to show how someone is feeling. :-) is a smiley showing happiness. (informal) কম্পিউটারে ব্যবহৃত স্মাইলি

smoke (**smokes, smoking, smoked**) n **Smoke** consists of gas and small bits of solid material that are sent into the air when something burns. ধোঁয়া ▷ vi If something **is smoking**, smoke is coming from it. ধোঁয়া বার হওয়া

smoke alarm (**smoke alarms**) n A **smoke alarm** or a **smoke detector** is a device fixed to the ceiling of a room which makes a loud noise if there is smoke in the air, to warn people. ধোঁয়ার সতর্কতা

smoked adj **Smoked** glass has been made darker by being treated with smoke. ধোঁয়াচ্ছন্ন

smoker (**smoker**) n A **smoker** is a person who habitually smokes tobacco. ধূমপায়ী

smoking n **Smoking** is the act or habit of smoking cigarettes, cigars, or a pipe. ধূমপান

smooth (**smoother, smoothest**) adj A **smooth** surface has no roughness or holes. মসৃণ

SMS n **SMS** is a way of sending short written messages from one mobile phone to another. **SMS** is an abbreviation for 'short message system'. এস এম এস (মোবাইলে বার্তা পাঠানো)

smudge (**smudges**) n A **smudge** is a dirty, blurred mark. দাগ

smug adj If you say that someone is **smug**, you are criticizing the fact they seem very pleased with how good, clever, or fortunate they are. আত্মসন্তুষ্ট

smuggle (**smuggles, smuggling, smuggled**) vt If someone **smuggles** things or people into a place or out of it, they take them there illegally or secretly. পাচার করা

smuggler (**smugglers**) n **Smugglers** are people who take goods into or out of a country illegally. পাচারকারী

smuggling n **Smuggling** is the act of taking things or people into a place or out of it, illegally or secretly. পাচার

snack (**snacks**) n A **snack** is a small, quick meal, or something eaten between meals. জলখাবার

snack bar (**snack bars**) n A **snack bar** is a place where you can buy drinks and simple meals such as sandwiches. জলযোগের দোকান

snail (**snails**) n A **snail** is a small animal that has a spiral shell. It moves slowly, leaving behind a trail of slime. শামুক

snake (**snakes**) n A **snake** is a long, thin reptile with no legs. সাপ

snap (**snaps, snapping, snapped**) v If something **snaps** or if you **snap** it, it breaks

suddenly, usually with a sharp cracking
noise. ভেঙে যাওয়া

snapshot (**snapshots**) *n* A **snapshot** is
a photograph that is taken quickly and
casually. ফোটো

snarl (**snarls, snarling, snarled**) *vi* When an
animal **snarls**, it makes a fierce, rough sound
in its throat while showing its teeth. গর্জন করা

snatch (**snatches, snatching, snatched**) *v*
If you **snatch** something, or if you **snatch at**
it, you take it or pull it away quickly. ছিনিয়ে
নেওয়া

sneeze (**sneezes, sneezing, sneezed**) *vi*
When you **sneeze**, you suddenly take in
your breath and then blow it down your
nose noisily without being able to stop
yourself, for example because you have a
cold. হাঁচি

sniff (**sniffs, sniffing, sniffed**) *v* When you
sniff, you breathe in air through your nose
hard enough to make a sound, for example
when you are trying not to cry, or in order
to show disapproval. শব্দ করে নাক টানা

snigger (**sniggers, sniggering, sniggered**)
vi If someone **sniggers**, they laugh quietly
in a disrespectful way, for example at
something rude or unkind. আড়িছলের হাসা

snob (**snobs**) *n* If you call someone a
snob, you disapprove of them because
they admire upper-class people and dislike
lower-class people. নাকউঁচু লোক

snooker *n* **Snooker** is a game involving balls
on a large table. The players use long sticks
called cues to hit a white ball, and score points
by knocking coloured balls into the pockets at
the sides of the table. স্নুকার খেলা

snooze (**snoozes, snoozing, snoozed**) *n*
A **snooze** is a short, light sleep, especially
during the day. (*informal*) দিবানিদ্রা ▷ *vi* If
you **snooze**, you sleep lightly for a short
period of time. (*informal*) হাল্কা ঘুমোন

snore (**snores, snoring, snored**) *vi* When
someone who is asleep **snores**, they make
a loud noise each time they breathe. নাক
ডাকা

snorkel (**snorkels**) *n* A **snorkel** is a tube
through which a person swimming just
under the surface of the sea can breathe.
ডুবসাতারুর নিঃশ্বাস নেবার নল

snow (**snows, snowing, snowed**) *n* **Snow**
is the soft white bits of frozen water that
fall from the sky in cold weather. বরফ ▷ *vi*
When it **snows**, snow falls from the sky.
বরফ পড়া

snowball (**snowballs**) *n* A **snowball** is a
ball of snow. বরফের গোলা

snowflake (**snowflakes**) *n* A **snowflake** is
one of the soft, white bits of frozen water
that fall as snow. বরফের কুঁচি

snowman (**snowmen**) *n* A **snowman** is
a large shape which is made out of snow,
especially by children, and is supposed to
look like a person. বরফের মনুষ্যাকৃতি

snowplough (**snowploughs**) *n* A
snowplough is a vehicle which is used to
push snow off roads or railway lines. বরফ
সরানোর যন্ত্র

snowstorm (**snowstorms**) *n* A **snowstorm**
is a very heavy fall of snow, usually when
there is also a strong wind blowing at the
same time. তুষার ঝড়

so *adv* You use **so** to talk about something
without repeating the same words. তাই
▷ *conj* You use **so** and **so that** to talk about
the reason for doing something. যাতে

S

They went outside so that nobody would hear them. ▷ *adv* You can use **so** in front of adjectives and adverbs to make them stronger. ভীষণ

soak (**soaks, soaking, soaked**) *v* When you **soak** something, or when you leave it to **soak**, you put it into a liquid and leave it there. ভিজিয়ে রাখা

soaked *adj* If someone or something gets **soaked** or **soaked through**, water or some other liquid makes them extremely wet. ভেজা

soap (**soaps**) *n* **Soap** is a substance that you use with water for washing yourself or sometimes for washing clothes. সাবান

soap dish (**soap dishes**) *n* A **soap dish** is a shallow container with a wide uncovered top, used in a bathroom for holding soap. সাবানদানি

soap opera (**soap operas**) *n* A **soap opera** is a television drama serial about the daily lives of a group of people. টেলিভিশনের ধারাবাহিক

soap powder (**soap powders**) *n* **Soap powder** is a powder made from soap and other substances that you use for washing your clothes, especially in a machine. সাবানের গুঁড়ো

sob (**sobs, sobbing, sobbed**) *vi* When someone **sobs**, they cry in a noisy way, breathing in short breaths. কাঁদা

sober *adj* When you are **sober**, you are not drunk. ভদ্র

sociable *adj* **Sociable** people enjoy meeting and talking to other people. সামাজিক

social *adj* **Social** means relating to society. সামাজিক

socialism *n* **Socialism** is a set of left-wing political principles whose general aim is to create a system in which everyone has an equal opportunity to benefit from a country's wealth. Under socialism, the country's main industries are usually owned by the state. সমাজবাদ

socialist (**socialists**) *adj* **Socialist** means based on socialism or relating to socialism. সমাজবাদী ▷ *n* A **socialist** is a person who believes in socialism or who is a member of a socialist party. সমাজবাদী

social security *n* **Social security** is money that is paid by the government to people who are unemployed, poor, or ill. সামাজিক নিরাপত্তা

social services *npl* **Social services** are services provided by the local authority to help people who have serious family problems or financial problems. সমাজ সেবা

social worker (**social workers**) *n* A **social worker** is a person whose job is to do social work. সমাজসেবী

society (**societies**) *n* **Society** consists of all the people in a country or region, considered as a group. সমাজ

sociology *n* **Sociology** is the study of society or of the way society is organized. সমাজ বিজ্ঞান

sock (**socks**) *n* **Socks** are pieces of clothing which cover your foot and ankle and are worn inside shoes. মোজা

socket (**sockets**) *n* A **socket** is a device on a piece of electrical equipment into which you can put a plug or bulb. সকেট (সরঞ্জাম)

sofa (**sofas**) *n* A **sofa** is a long, comfortable seat with a back and arms, which two or three people can sit on. সোফা (আসবাব পত্র)

sofa bed (**sofa beds**) *n* A **sofa bed** is a type of sofa whose seat folds out so that it can also be used as a bed. সোফা তথা বিছানা

soft (**softer, softest**) *adj* Something that is **soft** is nice to touch, and not rough or hard. নরম ▷ *adj* A **soft** sound or light is very gentle. কোমল

soft drink (**soft drinks**) *n* A **soft drink** is a cold, non-alcoholic drink such as lemonade. হাল্কা পানীয়

software *n* Computer programs are referred to as **software**. কম্পিউটারের সফটওয়্যার

soggy (**soggier, soggiest**) *adj* Something that is **soggy** is unpleasantly wet. ভিজে ন্যাতানো

soil *n* **Soil** is the substance on the surface of the earth in which plants grow. মাটি

solar *adj* **Solar** is used to describe things relating to the sun. সৌর

solar power *n* **Solar power** is heat radiation from the sun converted into electrical power. সৌর শক্তি

solar system (**solar systems**) *n* The **solar system** is the sun and all the planets that go round it. সৌর জগৎ

soldier (**soldiers**) *n* A **soldier** is a person who works in an army. সৈনিক

sold out *adj* If a performance, sports event, or other entertainment is **sold out**, all the tickets for it have been sold. বিক্রি শেষ

solicitor (**solicitors**) *n* In Britain, a **solicitor** is a lawyer who gives legal advice, prepares legal documents and cases, and represents clients in the lower courts of law. উকিল

solid *adj* Something that is **solid** stays the same shape whether it is in a container or not. কঠিন ▷ *adj* Something that is **solid** is not hollow. নিরেট

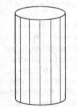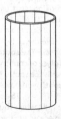

solo (**solos**) *n* A **solo** is a piece of music or a dance performed by one person. একক

soloist (**soloists**) *n* A **soloist** is a person who performs a solo, usually a piece of music. একক শিল্পী

soluble *adj* A substance that is **soluble** will dissolve in a liquid. গলে যায়

solution (**solutions**) *n* A **solution** to a problem is a way of dealing with it so that the difficulty is removed. সমাধান

solve (**solves, solving, solved**) *vt* If you **solve** a problem or a question, you find a solution or an answer to it. সমাধান করা

solvent (**solvents**) *n* A **solvent** is a liquid that can dissolve other substances. যা অন্য উপাদানকে গলায়

Somali (**Somalis**) *adj* **Somali** means of, relating to, or characteristic of Somalia, the Somalis, or their language. সোমালীয় ▷ *n* A **Somali** is a member of a tall dark-skinned people inhabiting Somalia. সোমালিয়ার নাগরিক ▷ *n* **Somali** is the language spoken by the Somali people. সোমালী ভাষা

Somalia *n* **Somalia** is a republic in north-east Africa, on the Indian Ocean and the Gulf of Aden. সোমালিয়া (দেশ)

some *det* You use **some** to talk about an amount of something. কিছুটা *Can I have some orange juice, please?* ▷ *pron* **Some** means a quantity of something or a number of people or things. সে গুলির কিছু *The apples are ripe and we are going to pick some.*

somebody *pron* You use **somebody** to talk about a person without saying who you mean. কেউ

somehow *adv* You use **somehow** when you cannot say how somebody did something, or how somebody will do something. যে কোন রকমে

someone *pron* You use **someone** to talk about a person without saying who you mean. কোন একজন *I need someone to help me.*

someplace *adv* You use **someplace** to talk about a place without saying where you mean. কোন এক স্থান

something *pron* You use **something** to talk about a thing without saying what it is. কিছু জিনিস *He knew that there was something wrong.*

sometime *adv* You use **sometime** to talk about a time in the future or the past that is not known. কখনো

sometimes *adv* You use **sometimes** to talk about things that do not take place all the time. কখনো কখনো

somewhere *adv* You use **somewhere** to talk about a place without saying where you mean. কোনখানে

son (**sons**) *n* A person's **son** is their male child. পুত্র

song (**songs**) *n* A **song** is a piece of music with words and music sung together. গান

son-in-law (**sons-in-law**) *n* A person's **son-in-law** is the husband of their daughter. জামাতা

soon *adv* If something is going to happen **soon**, it will happen after a short time. শীঘ্র

soot *n* **Soot** is black powder which rises in the smoke from a fire and collects on the inside of chimneys. ধোঁয়ার কালি

sophisticated *adj* A **sophisticated** person is comfortable in social situations and knows about culture, fashion, and other matters that are considered socially important. অত্যাধুনিক

soppy (**soppier, soppiest**) *adj* If you describe someone or something as **soppy**, you mean that they are foolishly sentimental. আবেগপ্রবন

soprano (**sopranos**) *n* A **soprano** is a woman, girl, or boy with a high singing voice. মুখ্যগায়ক/গায়িকা

sorbet (**sorbets**) *n* **Sorbet** is a frozen dessert made with fruit juice, sugar, and water. সরবত

sorcerer (**sorcerers**) *n* In fairy stories, a **sorcerer** is a person who performs magic by using the power of evil spirits. জাদুকর

sore (**sorer, sorest, sores**) *adj* If part of your body is **sore**, it causes you pain and discomfort. ব্যথা ▷ *n* A **sore** is a painful spot on your body where the skin is infected. ঘা

sorry *excl* You say '**Sorry!**' as a way of apologizing to someone for something that you have done which has upset them or caused them difficulties, or when you bump into them accidentally. দুঃখিত ▷ *adj* If you are **sorry** about something, you feel sad about it. দুঃখিত ▷ *adj* If you feel **sorry** for someone, you feel sad for them. দুঃখিত

sort (**sorts**) *n* A particular **sort** of something is one of its different kinds or types. ধরণ

sort out *v* If you **sort out** a group of things, you organize or tidy them. বাছাই *We try to sort out the truth from the lies.*

SOS *n* An **SOS** is a signal which indicates to other people that you are in danger and need help quickly. সতর্ক বার্তা

so-so *adv* **So-so** means in an average or indifferent manner. (*informal*) মোটামুটি

soul (**souls**) *n* A person's **soul** is the spiritual part of them which some people believe continues existing after their body is dead. আত্মা

sound (**sounder, soundest, sounds**) *adj* If something is **sound**, it is in good condition or healthy. মজবুত ▷ *n* A **sound** is something that you hear. শব্দ

soundtrack (**soundtracks**) *n* The **soundtrack** of a film is its sound, speech, and especially the music. আওয়াজ, সঙ্গীত

soup (**soups**) *n* **Soup** is liquid food made by cooking meat, fish, or vegetables in water. সুপ, ঝোল

sour *adj* Something that is **sour** has a sharp taste like the taste of a lemon. টক

south *adj* The **south** edge, corner, or part of a place or country is the part which is towards the south. দক্ষিণ ▷ *adv* If you go **south**, you travel towards the south. দক্ষিণদিকে ▷ *n* **The south** is the direction on your right when you are looking towards the place where the sun rises. দক্ষিণদিক

South Africa *n* **South Africa** is a republic occupying the southernmost part of the African continent. দক্ষিণ আফ্রিকা

South African (**South Africans**) *adj* **South African** means of or relating to the Republic of South Africa, its inhabitants, or any of their languages. দক্ষিণ আফ্রিকা দেশীয় ▷ n A **South African** is a native or inhabitant of the Republic of South Africa. দক্ষন আফিকার নাগরিক

South America n **South America** is the fourth largest of the continents, bordering on the Caribbean in the north, the Pacific in the west, and the Atlantic in the east and joined to Central America by the Isthmus of Panama. দক্ষিন আমেরিকা

South American (**South Americans**) adj **South American** means of or relating to the continent of South America or its inhabitants. দক্ষিণ আমেরিকার ▷ n A **South American** is a native or inhabitant of South America. দক্ষিণ আমেরিকার মানুষ

southbound adj **Southbound** roads or vehicles lead or are travelling towards the south. দক্ষিণ মুখী

southeast n The **southeast** is the direction which is halfway between south and east. দক্ষিণপূর্ব

southern adj **Southern** means in or from the south of a region or country. দক্ষিণাঞ্চলীয়

South Korea n **South Korea** is a republic in north-east Asia. দক্ষিণ কোরিয়া

South Pole n The **South Pole** is the place on the surface of the earth which is farthest towards the south. দক্ষিণ মেরু

southwest n The **southwest** is the direction which is halfway between south and west. দক্ষিণপশ্চিম

souvenir (**souvenirs**) n A **souvenir** is something which you buy or keep to remind you of a holiday, place, or event. স্মরণিকা

soya n **Soya** flour, butter, or other food is made from soya beans. সয়া

soy sauce n **Soy sauce** is a dark brown liquid made from soya beans and used as a flavouring, especially in Chinese cooking. সয়া সস

spa (**spas**) n A **spa** is a place where water with minerals in it bubbles out of the ground. স্পা

space (**spaces**) n You use **space** to talk about an area that is empty. জায়গা ▷ n **Space** is the area past the Earth, where the stars and planets are. মহাকাশ

spacecraft (**spacecraft**) n A **spacecraft** is a rocket or other vehicle that can travel in space. মহাকাশযান

spade (**spades**) n A **spade** is a tool used for digging, with a flat metal blade and a long handle. কোদাল

spaghetti n **Spaghetti** is a type of pasta which looks like long pieces of string. এক ধরণের পাস্তা

Spain n **Spain** is a kingdom of south-west Europe, occupying the Iberian peninsula between the Mediterranean and the Atlantic. স্পেন

spam (**spams**) n **Spam** is unwanted email that is sent to a large number of people, usually as advertising. অপ্রয়োজনীয় ই-মেল

Spaniard (**Spaniards**) n A **Spaniard** is a Spanish citizen, or a person of Spanish origin. স্পেনের বংশোদ্ভুত

spaniel (**spaniels**) n A **spaniel** is a type of dog with long ears that hang down. কুকুরের প্রজাতি

Spanish adj **Spanish** means belonging or relating to Spain, or to its people, language, or culture. স্পেনীয় বা স্পেনের ▷ n **Spanish** is the main language spoken in Spain, and in many countries in South and Central America. স্পেনের ভাষা

spank (**spanks, spanking, spanked**) vt If someone **spanks** a child, they punish them by hitting them on the bottom several times. পাছায় চাটি মারা

spanner (**spanners**) n A **spanner** is a metal tool used for tightening a nut. স্প্যানার

spare (**spares, sparing, spared**) adj You use **spare** to describe something that is the same as things that you are already using, but that you do not need yet and are keeping ready in case another one is needed. বাড়তি ▷ vi If you have something such as time, money, or space to **spare**, you have some extra time, money, or space that you have not used or which you do not need. বাড়তি থাকা

spare part (spare parts) *n* **Spare parts** are parts that you can buy separately to replace old or broken parts in a piece of equipment. যন্ত্রাংশ

spare room (spare rooms) *n* A **spare room** is a bedroom which is kept especially for visitors to sleep in. অতিথি কক্ষ

spare time *n* Your **spare time** is the time during which you do not have to work and you can do whatever you like. খালি সময়

spare tyre (spare tyres) *n* A **spare tyre** is a wheel with a tyre on it that you keep in your car in case you get a flat tyre and need to replace one of your wheels. অতিরিক্ত টায়ার

spare wheel (spare wheels) *n* A **spare wheel** is a wheel with a tyre on it that you keep in your car in case you get a flat tyre and need to replace one of your wheels. অতিরিক্ত চাকা

spark (sparks) *n* A **spark** is a tiny bright piece of burning material that flies up from something that is burning. স্ফুলিংগ

sparkling water (sparkling waters) *n* **Sparkling water** is slightly fizzy water. টল টলে জল

spark plug (spark plugs) *n* A **spark plug** is a device in the engine of a motor vehicle, which produces electric sparks to make the petrol burn. স্পার্ক প্লাগ, গাড়ির যন্ত্রাংশ

sparrow (sparrows) *n* A **sparrow** is a small brown bird that is common in Britain. চড়াই পাখি

spasm (spasms) *n* A **spasm** is a sudden tightening of your muscles, which you cannot control. খিঁচুনি

spatula (spatulas) *n* A **spatula** is an object like a knife with a wide, flat blade. Spatulas are used in cooking. রান্নার খুন্তি

speak (speaks, speaking, spoke, spoken) *v* When you **speak**, you use your voice in order to say something. বলা

speaker (speakers) *n* A **speaker** at a meeting, conference, or other gathering is a person who is making a speech or giving a talk. বক্তা

speak up *v* If you ask someone to **speak up**, you are asking them to speak more loudly. জোরে বলা *I'm quite deaf – you'll have to speak up.*

special *adj* Someone or something that is **special** is different from normal, often in a way that makes them better or more important than other people or things. বিশেষ

specialist (specialists) *n* A **specialist** is a person who has a particular skill or knows a lot about a particular subject. বিশেষজ্ঞ

speciality (specialities) *n* Someone's **speciality** is the kind of work they do best or the subject they know most about. বৈশিষ্ট্য

specialize (specializes, specializing, specialized) *vi* If you **specialize in** an area of study or a type of work, you know a lot about it and spend a lot of your time and attention on it. বিশেষ জ্ঞান লাভ করা

specially *adv* If something has been done **specially** for a particular person or purpose, it has been done only for that person or purpose. বিশেষ করে

special offer (special offers) *n* A **special offer** is a product, service, or programme that is offered at reduced prices or rates. বিশেষ সুবিধা

species (species) *n* A **species** is a class of plants or animals whose members have the same characteristics and are able to breed with each other. প্রজাতি

specific *adj* You use **specific** to emphasize that you are talking about a particular thing or subject. সুনির্দিষ্ট

specifically *adv* You use **specifically** to emphasize that a subject is being considered separately from other subjects. সুনির্দিষ্টভাবে

specify (specifies, specifying, specified)
vt If you **specify** something, you state it
precisely. সুনির্দিষ্ট করা

spectacles npl **Spectacles** are two lenses
in a frame that some people wear in front of
their eyes in order to help them see better.
(formal) চশমা

spectacular adj Something that is
spectacular is very impressive or dramatic.
নয়নাভিরাম

spectator (spectators) n A **spectator**
is someone who watches something,
especially a sporting event. দর্শক

**speculate (speculates, speculating,
speculated)** v If you **speculate** about
something, you guess about its nature
or identity, or about what might happen.
অনুমান করা

speech n **Speech** is the ability to speak or
the act of speaking. বাক্

speechless adj If you are **speechless**, you
are temporarily unable to speak, usually
because something has shocked you.
হতবাক

speed (speeds) n The **speed** of something
is the rate at which it moves, happens, or is
done. গতি

speedboat (speedboats) n A **speedboat**
is a boat that can go very fast because it has
a powerful engine. স্পীডবোট

speeding n **Speeding** means the act or
process of moving or travelling quickly.
দ্রুত গতি

speed limit (speed limits) n The **speed
limit** on a road is the maximum speed at
which you are legally allowed to drive.
গতিসীমা

speedometer (speedometers) n A
speedometer is the instrument in a vehicle
which shows how fast the vehicle is moving.
গতি পরিমাপক

speed up v When something **speeds up**,
it moves, happens, or is done more quickly.
গতি বাড়ানো Try to speed up your breathing
and stretch your legs.

spell (spells, spelling, spelled, spelt) n
A **spell** of a particular type of weather or
a particular activity is a short period of
time during which this type of weather
or activity occurs. সময় ▷ n A **spell** is a
situation in which events are controlled by a
magical power. জাদুমন্ত্র ▷ vt When you **spell**
a word, you write or speak each letter in the
word in the correct order. বানান করা

spellchecker (spellcheckers) n A
spellchecker is a special program on a
computer which you can use to check for
spelling mistakes. বানান পরীক্ষক

spelling (spellings) n The **spelling** of a
word is the correct sequence of letters in
it. বানান

spend (spends, spending, spent) vt When
you **spend** money, you buy things with it.
ব্যয় করা ▷ vt To **spend** time or energy is to
use it doing something. অতিবাহিত করা

sperm (sperms or **sperm)** n A **sperm** is a
cell produced in the sex organs of a male
animal which can enter a female animal's
egg and fertilize it. শুক্রাণু

spice (spices) n A **spice** is a part of a
plant, or a powder made from that part,
which you put in food to give it flavour.
মশলা

spicy (spicier, spiciest) adj **Spicy** food is
strongly flavoured with spices. মশলাযুক্ত

spider (spiders) n A **spider** is a small
creature with eight legs. মাকড়সা

spill (spills, spilling, spilled, spilt) v If a
liquid **spills** or if you **spill** it, it accidentally
flows over the edge of a container. ছড়িয়ে
পড়া

spinach n **Spinach** is a vegetable with
large green leaves. পালংশাক

spinal cord (spinal cords) n Your **spinal
cord** is a thick cord of nerves inside your
spine which connects your brain to nerves
in all parts of your body. মেরুদণ্ড

spin drier (spin driers) n A **spin drier** is a
machine that partly dries clothes that you
have washed by turning them round and

S

round very fast to remove the water. কাপড় শুকোনোর যন্ত্র

spine (**spines**) n Your **spine** is the row of bones down your back. শিরদাঁড়া

spinster (**spinsters**) n A **spinster** is a woman who has never been married; used especially when talking about an old or middle-aged woman. (*old-fashioned*) অবিবাহিতা মহিলা

spire (**spires**) n The **spire** of a church is a tall cone-shaped structure on top of a tower. শিখর

spirit n Your **spirit** is the part of you that is not physical and that is connected with your deepest thoughts and feelings. আত্মশক্তি

spirits npl You can refer to your **spirits** when saying how happy or unhappy you are. For example, if your spirits are high, you are happy. ভেতরের শক্তি

spiritual adj **Spiritual** means relating to people's deepest thoughts and beliefs, rather than to their bodies and physical surroundings. আধ্যাত্মিক

spit (**spits, spitting, spat**) n **Spit** is the watery liquid produced in your mouth. থুথু ▷ v If someone **spits**, they force an amount of spit out of their mouth. If you **spit** liquid or food somewhere, you force a small amount of it out of your mouth. থুথু ফেলা

spite n If you do something cruel out of **spite**, you do it because you want to hurt or upset someone. দ্বেষ ▷ vt If you do something cruel to **spite** someone, you do it in order to hurt or upset them. শত্রুতা করা

spiteful adj Someone who is **spiteful** does cruel things to hurt people they dislike. বিদ্বেষী

splash (**splashes, splashing, splashed**) vi If you **splash** about or **splash** around in water, you hit or disturb the water in a noisy way, causing some of it to fly up into the air. জল ছিটান

splendid adj If you say that something is **splendid**, you mean that it is very good. চমৎকার

splint (**splints**) n A **splint** is a long piece of wood or metal that is fastened to a broken arm, leg, or back to keep it still. সহায়ক দন্ড

splinter (**splinters**) n A **splinter** is a very thin sharp piece of wood or glass which has broken off from a larger piece. ধারালো টুকরো

split (**splits, splitting**) v If something **splits**, or if you **split** it, it is divided into two or more parts. দ্বিখন্ড হওয়া

split up v If two people **split up**, they end their relationship or marriage. সম্পর্ক ছিন্ন করা I split up with my boyfriend.

spoil (**spoils, spoiling, spoiled, spoilt**) vt If you **spoil** something, you damage it or stop it from working as it should. নষ্ট করা ▷ vt If you **spoil** children, you give them everything they want or ask for. নষ্ট করে দেওয়া

spoilsport (**spoilsports**) n If you say that someone is a **spoilsport**, you mean that they are behaving in a way that ruins other people's pleasure or enjoyment. (*informal*) বেরসিক

spoilt adj A **spoilt** child is a child who has been given everything he wants which has a bad effect on his character. বখাটে

spoke (**spokes**) n The **spokes** of a wheel are the bars that join the outer ring to the centre. চাকার স্পোক

spokesman (**spokesmen**) n A **spokesman** is a male spokesperson. মুখপাত্র (পুরুষ)

spokesperson (**spokespersons, spokespeople**) n A **spokesperson** is a person who speaks as the representative of a group or organization. মুখপাত্র

spokeswoman (**spokeswomen**) n A **spokeswoman** is a female spokesperson. মুখপাত্র (মহিলা)

sponge (sponges) n A **sponge** is a piece of sponge that you use for washing yourself or for cleaning things. স্পঞ্জ ▷ n A **sponge** is a light cake or pudding made from flour, eggs, sugar, and sometimes fat. কেক (মিষ্টিদ্রব্য)

sponge bag (sponge bags) n A **sponge bag** is a small bag in which you keep things such as soap and a toothbrush when you are travelling. সেভিং ব্যাগ

sponsor (sponsors, sponsoring, sponsored) n A **sponsor** is a person or organization that sponsors something or someone. আয়োজক ▷ vt If an organization **sponsors** something such as an event, it pays some or all of the expenses connected with it, often in order to get publicity for itself. আয়োজন করা

sponsorship n **Sponsorship** is financial support given by a sponsor. আর্থিক সহায়তা

spontaneous adj **Spontaneous** acts are not planned or arranged, but are done because someone suddenly wants to do them. স্বতঃস্ফূর্ত

spooky (spookier, spookiest) adj If something is **spooky**, it has a frightening and unnatural atmosphere. (informal) ভয়াল

spoon (spoons) n A **spoon** is a tool used for eating, stirring, and serving food. It is shaped like a small shallow bowl with a long handle. চামচ

spoonful (spoonfuls) n You can refer to an amount of food resting on a spoon as a **spoonful** of food. চামচ ভর্তি

sport (sports) n **Sports** are games and other competitive activities which need physical effort and skill. ক্রীড়া

sportsman (sportsmen) n A **sportsman** is a man who takes part in sports. ক্রীড়াবিদ

sportswear n **Sportswear** is the special clothing worn for playing sports or for informal leisure activities. খেলার পোশাক

sportswoman (sportswomen) n A **sportswoman** is a woman who takes part in sports. মহিলা খেলোয়াড়

sporty (sportier, sportiest) adj A **sporty** person enjoys playing sport. খেলোয়াড় সুলভ

spot (spots, spotting, spotted) n **Spots** are small, round, coloured areas on a surface. দাগ ▷ n You can refer to a particular place as a **spot**. স্থান ▷ vt If you **spot** something or someone, you notice them. খুঁজে পাওয়া

spotless adj Something that is **spotless** is completely clean. তকতকে

spotlight (spotlights) n A **spotlight** is a powerful light, used for example in a theatre, which can be directed so that it lights up a small area. স্পটলাইট

spotty (spottier, spottiest) adj Someone who is **spotty** has spots on their face. মুখে দাগ আছে যার

spouse (spouses) n Someone's **spouse** is the person they are married to. স্বামী বা স্ত্রী

sprain (sprains, spraining, sprained) n A **sprain** is the injury caused by spraining a joint. মচকানো ▷ vt If you **sprain** your ankle or wrist, you accidentally damage it by twisting it, for example, when you fall. মচকে যাওয়া

spray (sprays, spraying, sprayed) n **Spray** consists of a lot of small drops of water which are being splashed or forced into the air. ছড়ানো ▷ v If you **spray** drops of a liquid or small pieces of something somewhere, or if they **spray** somewhere, they cover a place or shower someone. ছড়িয়ে দেওয়া

spread (spreads, spreading, spread) n A **spread** is a soft food which you put on bread. মাখন জাতীয় খাবার ▷ *vt* If you **spread** something somewhere, you open it out. ছড়িয়ে দেওয়া ▷ *vt* If you **spread** something on a surface, you put it all over the surface. ছড়িয়ে দেওয়া ▷ *vi* If something **spreads**, it reaches a larger area. ছড়িয়ে যাওয়া

spread out *v* If people, animals, or vehicles **spread out**, they move apart from each other. ছড়িয়ে যাওয়া *They spread out to search the area.*

spreadsheet (spreadsheets) *n* A **spreadsheet** is a computer program that is used for displaying and dealing with numbers. Spreadsheets are used mainly for financial planning. স্প্রেডশীট কম্পিউটার প্রোগ্রাম

spring (springs) *n* **Spring** is the season between winter and summer when the weather becomes warmer and plants start to grow again. বসন্তকাল ▷ *n* A **spring** is a long piece of metal that goes round and round, It goes back to the same shape after you pull it. স্প্রিং

spring-cleaning *n* **Spring-cleaning** is the process of thoroughly cleaning a place, especially your home. You can also say that you give a place a **spring-cleaning**. ব্যাপক পরিষ্কার করা

spring onion (spring onions) *n* **Spring onions** are small onions with long green leaves. They are often eaten raw in salads. পেঁয়াজকলি

springtime *n* **Springtime** is the period of time during which spring lasts. বসন্ত কালের সময়

sprinkler (sprinklers) *n* A **sprinkler** is a device used to spray water. Sprinklers are used to water plants or grass, or to put out fires in buildings. স্প্রিংকলার

sprint (sprints, sprinting, sprinted) *n* A **sprint** is a short fast race. দৌড় প্রতিযোগিতা ▷ *vi* If you **sprint**, you run or ride as fast as you can over a short distance. দ্রুত দৌড়ন

sprinter (sprinters) *n* A **sprinter** is a person who takes part in short, fast races. ধাবক

sprouts *npl* **Sprouts** are vegetables that look like tiny cabbages. সজি

spy (spies, spying, spied) *n* A **spy** is a person whose job is to find out secret information about another country or organization. গুপ্তচর ▷ *vi* Someone who **spies** for a country or organization tries to find out secret information for them about other countries or organizations. গুপ্তচরের কাজ করা

spying *n* **Spying** is the act or process of finding out secret information for a country or organization about other countries or organizations. চরবৃত্তি

squabble (squabbles, squabbling, squabbled) *vi* When people **squabble**, they quarrel about something that is not really important. ঝগড়া করা

squander (squanders, squandering, squandered) *vt* If you **squander** money, resources, or opportunities, you waste them. নষ্ট করা

square (squares) *adj* If something is **square**, it has a shape similar to a square. বর্গাকার ▷ *n* A **square** is a shape with four sides of the same length and four corners that are all right angles. বর্গক্ষেত্র

squash (squashes, squashing, squashed) *n* **Squash** is a game in which two players hit a small rubber ball against the walls of a court using rackets. স্কোয়াশ খেলা ▷ *vt* If someone or something **is squashed**, they are pressed or crushed with such force that they become injured or lose their shape. চেপে যাওয়া

squeak (squeaks, squeaking, squeaked) *vi* If something or someone **squeaks**, they make a short, high-pitched sound. আওয়াজ করা

squeeze (squeezes, squeezing, squeezed) *vt* If you **squeeze** something, you press it firmly, usually with your hands. চেপা

squeeze in *v* If you **squeeze** a person or thing **in** somewhere or if they **squeeze in** there, they manage to get through or into a small space. গাদাগাদি করে *They went down in the lift, squeezing in with half a dozen guests.*

squid (squids or **squid)** *n* A **squid** is a sea creature with a long soft body and many tentacles. স্কুইড

squint (squints, squinting, squinted) *vi* If you **squint** at something, you look at it with your eyes partly closed. ট্যারা

squirrel (squirrels) *n* A **squirrel** is a small furry wild animal with a long bushy tail. কাঠবিড়ালী

Sri Lanka *n* **Sri Lanka** is a republic in South Asia, occupying the island of Ceylon. শ্রীলংকা (দেশ)

stab (stabs, stabbing, stabbed) *vt* If someone **stabs** another person, they push a knife into their body. ছুরিকাঘাত

stability *n* **Stability** is the quality of being stable. স্থিতিশীলতা

stable (stabler, stablest, stables) *adj* If something is **stable**, it is not likely to change or come to an end suddenly. স্থিতিশীল ▷ *n* A **stable** or **stables** is a building in which horses are kept. আস্তাবল

stack (stacks) *n* A **stack** of things is a neat pile of them. গাদা

stadium (stadiums, stadia) *n* A **stadium** is a large sports ground with rows of seats all round it. ক্রীড়াছল

staff (staffs) *npl* The **staff** of an organization are the people who work for it. কর্মচারী ▷ *n* A **staff** is a stout rod or stick. ছড়ি

staffroom (staffrooms) *n* The **staffroom** is a room that an organization provides for the use of the people who work for it. কর্মীদের বিশ্রাম ঘর

stage (stages) *n* A **stage** of an activity, process, or period is one part of it. পর্যায়

stagger (staggers, staggering, staggered) *vi* If you **stagger**, you walk very unsteadily,

for example because you are ill or drunk. টলমল করা

stag night (stag nights) *n* A **stag night** is a party for a man who is getting married very soon, to which only men are invited. পুরুষদের নৈশ ভোজ

stain (stains, staining, stained) *n* A **stain** is a mark on something that is difficult to remove. দাগ ▷ *vt* If a liquid **stains** something, the thing becomes coloured or marked by the liquid. দাগ লাগা

stained glass *n* **Stained glass** consists of pieces of glass of different colours used to make decorative windows or other objects. রঙিন কাঁচ

stainless steel *n* **Stainless steel** is a metal which does not rust, made from steel and chromium. মরচে পরে না এমন ধাতু

stain remover (stain removers) *n* **Stain remover** is a substance that you use for removing an unwanted stain from a surface. দাগ ওঠানোর উপাদান

staircase (staircases) *n* A **staircase** is a set of stairs inside a house. সিঁড়ি

stairs *npl* **Stairs** are a set of steps inside a building which go from one floor to another. সিঁড়ি

stale (staler, stalest) *adj* **Stale** food or air is no longer fresh. বাসি

stalemate (stalemates) *n* **Stalemate** is a situation in which neither side in an argument or contest can make progress. অচলাবস্থা

stall (stalls) *n* A **stall** is a large table on which you put goods that you want to sell, or information that you want to give people. দোকান

stamina *n* **Stamina** is the physical or mental energy needed to do a tiring activity for a long time. শারীরিক শক্তি

stammer (stammers, stammering, stammered) *v* If you **stammer**, you speak with difficulty, hesitating and repeating words or sounds. তোতলানো

stamp (stamps, stamping, stamped) *n* A **stamp** or a **postage stamp** is a small piece

S

of paper which you stick on an envelope or parcel, to show that you have paid the cost of posting it. ডাকটিকিট ▷ *vt* If you **stamp** a mark or word on an object, you press the mark or word onto the object, using a stamp. সীলমোহর লাগান

stand (**stands, standing, stood**) *vi* When you **are standing**, you are on your feet. দাঁড়ান ▷ *n* A **stand** at a sports ground is where people sit or stand to watch. বসার স্থান

standard (**standards**) *adj* **Standard** means usual and normal. সাধারণ ▷ *n* A **standard** is a level of quality or achievement, especially a level that is thought to be acceptable. গুনমানের মাপকাঠি

standard of living (**standards of living**) *n* Your **standard of living** is the level of comfort and wealth which you have. জীবনধারনের মান

stand for *v* If letters **stand for** particular words, they are an abbreviation for those words. অর্থাৎ *CCTV stands for Closed Circuit Television.*

standing order (**standing orders**) *n* A **standing order** is an instruction to your bank to pay a fixed amount of money to someone at regular times. স্থায়ী আদেশ

stand out *v* If something **stands out**, it can be clearly noticed or is clearly better or more important than other similar things. বিশিষ্ট হওয়া *The dark shape of the castle stands out clearly on the skyline.*

standpoint (**standpoints**) *n* If you look at an event, situation, or idea from a particular **standpoint**, you look at it in a particular way. দৃষ্টিভঙ্গী

stand up *v* When you are **standing up**, your body is upright, your legs are straight, and your weight is supported by your feet. উঠে দাঁড়ান *Shop assistants have to stand up all day.*

staple (**staples, stapling, stapled**) *n* **Staples** are small pieces of bent wire that are used mainly for holding sheets of paper together firmly. You put the staples into the paper using a device called a stapler. স্টেপল ▷ *n* A **staple** is a food, product, or activity that is basic and important in people's everyday lives. প্রধান পণ্য ▷ *vt* If you **staple** something, you fasten it to something else or fix it in place using staples. বাঁধা

stapler (**staplers**) *n* A **stapler** is a device used for putting staples into sheets of paper. স্টেপলার

star (**stars, starring, starred**) *n* A **star** is a large ball of burning gas in space. Stars look like small points of light in the sky. নক্ষত্র ▷ *n* A **star** is somebody who is famous for doing something, for example acting or singing. তারকা ▷ *v* If an actor or actress **stars** in a play or film, he or she has one of the most important parts in it. You can also say that a play or film stars a famous actor or actress. অভিনয় করা ▷ *n* A **star** is a shape that has four, five, or more points sticking out of it in a pattern. তারকা চিহ্ন

starch (**starches**) *n* **Starch** is a carbohydrate found in foods such as bread, potatoes, and rice. শ্বেতসার

stare (**stares, staring, stared**) *vi* If you **stare** at someone or something, you look at them for a long time. এক দৃষ্টে তাকানো

stark (**starker, starkest**) *adj* **Stark** choices or statements are harsh and unpleasant. কঠিন

start (**starts, starting, started**) *n* If you make a **start** on doing something, you begin to do it. সূচনা ▷ *vt* If you **start** to do something, you begin to do it. শুরু করা

▷ *v* When something **starts**, it begins. শুরু হওয়া

starter (**starters**) *n* A **starter** is a small quantity of food served as the first course of a meal. আহারের প্রথম পদ

startle (**startles, startling, startled**) *vt* If something sudden and unexpected **startles** you, it surprises you and frightens you slightly. বিস্মিত করা

start off *v* If you **start off** by doing something, you do it as the first part of an activity. চালু করা *I started off by setting out the facts.*

starve (**starves, starving, starved**) *vi* If people **starve**, they suffer greatly and may die from lack of food. না খেয়ে থাকা

state (**states, stating, stated**) *n* You can refer to countries as **states**, particularly when you are discussing politics. দেশ ▷ *vt* If you **state** something, you say or write it in a formal or definite way. বলা

stately home (**stately homes**) *n* A **stately home** is a very large old house, especially one that people can pay to visit. পুরোনো বড় বাড়ি

statement (**statements**) *n* A **statement** is something that you say or write which gives information in a formal or definite way. বিবৃতি

station (**stations**) *n* A **station** is a building by a railway line where a train stops. রেল স্টেশন

stationer (**stationers**) *n* A **stationer** or a **stationer's** is a shop that sells paper, envelopes, and other materials or equipment used for writing. স্টেশনারী দোকান

stationery *n* **Stationery** is paper, envelopes, and writing equipment. খাতাপত্র-কাগজকলন

statistics *npl* **Statistics** are facts obtained from analyzing information that is expressed in numbers. পরিসংখ্যান

statue (**statues**) *n* A **statue** is a large sculpture of a person or an animal, made of stone, bronze, or some other hard material. মূর্তি

status quo *n* The **status quo** is the situation that exists at a particular time. স্থিতাবস্থা

stay (**stays, staying, stayed**) *n* The time you spend in a place is your **stay** there. অবস্থান কাল ▷ *vi* If you **stay** in a place, you do not move away from it. থাকা ▷ *vi* If you **stay** somewhere, you live there for a short time. কোথাও থাকা

stay in *v* If you **stay in**, you remain at home during the evening and do not go out. বাড়িতে থাকা *We decided to stay in and have dinner at home.*

stay up *v* If you **stay up**, you remain out of bed at a later time than normal. বেশিক্ষণ জেগে থাকা *I used to stay up late with my mum and watch movies.*

steady (**steadier, steadiest**) *adj* Something that is **steady** continues or develops gradually without any interruptions and is unlikely to change suddenly. ক্রমাগত

steak (**steaks**) *n* **Steak** is beef without much fat on it. মাংসের ফালি

steal (**steals, stealing, stole, stolen**) *v* If you **steal** something from someone, you take it away from them without their permission and without intending to return it. চুরি করা

S

steam *n* **Steam** is the hot mist that forms when water boils. **Steam** vehicles and machines are powered by steam. বাষ্প

steel *n* **Steel** is a very strong metal made mainly from iron. ইস্পাত

steep (**steeper, steepest**) *adj* A **steep** slope rises at a very sharp angle and is difficult to go up. খাড়া

steeple (**steeples**) *n* A **steeple** is a tall pointed structure on top of the tower of a church. চূড়া

steering *n* The **steering** in a car or other vehicle is the mechanical parts of it which make it possible to steer. গাড়ির স্টিয়ারিং

steering wheel (**steering wheels**) *n* The **steering wheel** in a vehicle is the wheel which the driver holds to steer the vehicle. স্টিয়ারিং চাকা

step (**steps**) *n* If you take a **step**, you lift your foot and put it down in a different place. ধাপ ▷ *n* A **step** is a flat surface that you put your feet on to walk up or down to somewhere. পদক্ষেপ ফেলা

stepbrother (**stepbrothers**) *n* Someone's **stepbrother** is the son of their stepfather or stepmother. সৎ ভাই

stepdaughter (**stepdaughters**) *n* Someone's **stepdaughter** is a daughter that was born to their husband or wife during a previous relationship. সৎ মেয়ে

stepfather (**stepfathers**) *n* Your **stepfather** is the man who has married your mother after the death of your father or divorce of your parents. সৎ বাবা

stepladder (**stepladders**) *n* A **stepladder** is a portable ladder that is made of two sloping parts that are hinged together at the top so that it will stand up on its own. মই বা সিঁড়ি

stepmother (**stepmothers**) *n* Your **stepmother** is the woman who has married your father after the death of your mother or divorce of your parents. সৎ মা

stepsister (**stepsisters**) *n* Someone's **stepsister** is the daughter of their stepfather or stepmother. সৎ বোন

stepson (**stepsons**) *n* Someone's **stepson** is a son born to their husband or wife during a previous relationship. সৎ ছেলে

stereo (**stereos**) *n* A **stereo** is a record player with two speakers. স্টিরিও

stereotype (**stereotypes**) *n* A **stereotype** is a fixed general image or set of characteristics representing a particular type of person or thing, but which may not be true in reality. একই রকম

sterile *adj* Something that is **sterile** is completely clean and free of germs. বিশুদ্ধ

sterilize (**sterilizes, sterilizing, sterilized**) *vt* If you **sterilize** a thing or place, you make it completely clean and free from germs. জীবাণুমুক্ত করা

sterling *n* **Sterling** is the money system of Great Britain. ব্রিটেনের মুদ্রা

steroid (**steroids**) *n* A **steroid** is a type of chemical substance which occurs naturally in the body, and can also be made artificially. রাসায়নিক উপাদান

stew (**stews**) *n* A **stew** is a meal made by cooking meat and vegetables in liquid at a low temperature. স্টিউ

steward (**stewards**) *n* A **steward** is a man whose job is to look after passengers on a ship, plane, or train. যাত্রীদের পরিচারক

stick (**sticks, sticking, stuck**) *n* A **stick** is a long, thin piece of wood. লাঠি ▷ *vt* If you **stick** one thing to another, you join them together using glue. আটকানো

sticker (**stickers**) *n* A **sticker** is a small piece of paper or plastic with writing or a picture on it, that you can stick onto a surface. স্টিকার

stick insect (**stick insects**) *n* A **stick insect** is an insect with a long thin body and legs. পোকা

stick out *v* If something **sticks out**, or if you **stick** it **out**, it extends beyond something else. বেরিয়ে থাকা *A newspaper was sticking out of his back pocket.*

sticky (stickier, stickiest) *adj* A **sticky** substance can stick to other things. **Sticky** things are covered with a sticky substance. আঠালো

stiff (stiffer, stiffest) *adj* Something that is **stiff** is firm and does not bend easily. শক্ত

stifling *adj* **Stifling** heat is so hot that it makes you feel uncomfortable. প্রচণ্ড

still (stiller, stillest) *adj* If you are **still**, you are not moving. নিশ্চল ▷ *adv* If a situation **still** exists, it has continued and exists now. এখনো

sting (stings, stinging, stung) *n* The **sting** of an insect is the part that stings you. হুল ▷ *v* If an insect or plant **stings** you, it pricks your skin, usually with poison, so that you feel a sharp pain. হুল ফোটান

stingy (stingier, stingiest) *adj* If you describe someone as **stingy**, you are criticizing them for being unwilling to spend money. *(informal)* কৃপণ

stink (stinks, stinking, stank, stunk) *n* A **stink** is a strong foul smell or stench. দুর্গন্ধ ▷ *vi* To **stink** means to smell extremely unpleasant. দুর্গন্ধ ছড়ানো

stir (stirs, stirring, stirred) *vt* When you **stir** a liquid, you mix it inside a container using something such as a spoon. নাড়ান

stitch (stitches, stitching, stitched) *n* **Stitches** are the pieces of thread that have been sewn in a piece of cloth. সেলাই ▷ *vt* If you **stitch** cloth, you use a needle and thread to join two pieces together or to make a decoration. সেলাই করা

stock (stocks, stocking, stocked) *n* **Stocks** are shares in the ownership of a company. A company's **stock** consists of all the shares that people have bought in it. কোম্পানীর শেয়ার ▷ *vt* A shop that **stocks** particular goods keeps a supply of them to sell. মজুত রাখা

stockbroker (stockbrokers) *n* A **stockbroker** is someone whose profession is buying and

selling stocks and shares for clients. শেয়ার দালাল

stock cube (stock cubes) *n* A **stock cube** is a solid cube made from dried meat or vegetable juices and other flavourings. **Stock cubes** are used to add flavour to dishes such as stews and soups. গুকনো খাবার

stock exchange (stock exchanges) *n* A **stock exchange** is a place where people buy and sell stocks and shares. শেয়ার বিনিময় কেন্দ্র

stock market (stock markets) *n* **The stock market** consists of the activity of buying stocks and shares, and the people and institutions that organize it. শেয়ার বাজার

stock up *v* If you **stock up** with something or **stock up** on it, you buy a lot of it, in case you cannot get it later. প্রচুর পরিমানে মজুত করা *People are stocking up on fuel.*

stomach (stomachs) *n* Your **stomach** is the organ inside your body where food is digested. পাকস্হলী

stomachache (stomachaches) *n* If you have a **stomachache**, you have a pain in your stomach. পেটের ব্যথা

stone (stones) *n* **Stone** is a hard solid material that is found in the ground. It is often used for building. পাথর ▷ *n* A **stone** is a small piece of rock that is found on the ground. কাঁকর

stool (stools) *n* A **stool** is a seat with legs but no support for your back or arms. বসার টুল

stop (stops, stopping, stopped) *n* If something that is moving comes to a **stop**, it slows down and no longer moves. থামা ▷ *v* If you **stop** doing something, you do not do it any more. থামানো ▷ *vi* If something **stops**, it does not do what it did any more. বন্ধ হওয়া

stopover (stopovers) *n* A **stopover** is a short stay in a place in between parts of a journey. স্বল্প কালের জন্য থামা

stopwatch (stopwatches) *n* A **stopwatch** is a watch with buttons which you press at the beginning and end of an event, so that you can measure exactly how long it takes. স্টপ ওয়াচ

storage *n* **Storage** is the process of keeping something in a particular place until it is needed. গুদামে রাখা

store (**stores, storing, stored**) *n* A **store** is a shop. **Store** is used mainly to refer to a large shop selling a variety of goods, but in American English, a **store** can be any shop. গুদাম ▷ *vt* When you **store** things, you put them in a container or other place and leave them there until they are needed. গুদামজাত করা

storm (**storms**) *n* A **storm** is very bad weather, with heavy rain, strong winds, and often thunder and lightning. ঝড়

stormy (**stormier, stormiest**) *adj* If there is **stormy** weather, there is a strong wind and heavy rain. ঝোড়ো

story (**stories**) *n* A **story** is a description of imaginary people and events, which is written or told in order to entertain. গল্প

stove (**stoves**) *n* A **stove** is a piece of equipment for heating a room or cooking. স্টোভ

straight (**straighter, straightest**) *adj* A **straight** line or edge continues in the same direction and does not bend or curve. সোজা

straighteners *npl* **Straighteners** are a heated device that you use to make your hair straight. চুল সোজা করার সরঞ্জাম

straightforward *adj* If something is **straightforward**, it is not complicated to do or understand. স্পষ্টভাষী

straight on *adv* You use **straight on** to indicate that the way from one place to another is forward. সোজাভাবে

strain (**strains, straining, strained**) *n* If **strain** is put on a person or organization, they have to do more than they are really able to do. চাপ ▷ *vt* To **strain** something means to make it do more than it is really able to do. চাপ দেওয়া

strained *adj* If someone's appearance, voice, or behaviour is **strained**, they seem worried and nervous. ক্লান্ত

stranded *adj* If you are **stranded**, you are prevented from leaving a place, for example because of bad weather. আটকে পড়া

strange (**stranger, strangest**) *adj* **Strange** means unusual or unexpected. অদ্ভুত

stranger (**strangers**) *n* A **stranger** is someone you have not met before or do not know at all. If two people are **strangers**, they have never met or do not know each other at all. আগন্তুক

strangle (**strangles, strangling, strangled**) *vt* To **strangle** someone means to kill them by tightly squeezing their throat. গলা টিপে মারা

strap (**straps**) *n* A **strap** is a narrow piece of leather, cloth, or other material. Straps are used to carry things or hold them in place. ফিতা

strategic *adj* **Strategic** means relating to the most important, general aspects of something such as a military operation or political policy. রণনীতি বিষয়ক

strategy (**strategies**) *n* A **strategy** is a general plan or set of plans intended to achieve something, especially over a long period. নীতিকৌশল

straw (**straws**) *n* **Straw** is the dry, yellow stems of crops. খড় ▷ *n* A **straw** is a thin tube that you use to suck a drink into your mouth. সরু নল

strawberry (**strawberries**) *n* A **strawberry** is a small red fruit with tiny seeds in its skin. স্ট্রবেরি ফল

stray (**strays**) *n* A **stray** is a domestic animal, fowl, etc, that has wandered away from its place of keeping and is lost. হারিয়ে যাওয়া গৃহপালিত জন্তু

stream (**streams**) *n* A **stream** is a small narrow river. জল স্রোত

street (**streets**) *n* A **street** is a road in a town or village, usually with houses along it. রাস্তা

streetlamp (**streetlamps**) *n* A **streetlamp** is a tall post with a light at the top, which stands by the side of the road to light it up, usually in a town. রাস্তার আলো

street map (**street maps**) *n* A **street map** is a map of a town or city, showing the positions and names of all the streets. রাস্তার মানচিত্র

streetwise *adj* Someone who is **streetwise** knows how to deal with difficult or dangerous situations in big cities. (*informal*) অভিজ্ঞ

strength *n* Your **strength** is the physical energy that you have, which gives you the ability to do things such as lift heavy objects. শক্তি

strengthen (**strengthens, strengthening, strengthened**) *vt* To **strengthen** something means to make it stronger. মজবুত করা

stress (**stresses, stressing, stressed**) *n* If you lay **stress** on a point, you emphasize it because you think it is important. চাপ ▷ *vt* If you **stress** a point in a discussion, you put extra emphasis on it because you think it is important. চাপ সৃষ্টি করা

stressed *adj* If you feel **stressed**, you feel tension and anxiety because of difficulties in your life. চাপে পড়া

stressful *adj* A **stressful** situation or experience causes someone to feel stress. কষ্টকর

stretch (**stretches, stretching, stretched**) *vi* Something that **stretches** over an area covers all of it. প্রসারিত হওয়া ▷ *vi* When you **stretch**, you hold out part of your body as far as you can. ছড়িয়ে দেওয়া

stretcher (**stretchers**) *n* A **stretcher** is a long piece of canvas with a pole along each side, which is used to carry an injured person. স্ট্রেচার

stretchy (**stretchier, stretchiest**) *adj* **Stretchy** material is slightly elastic and stretches easily. টানলে বড় হয়

strict (**stricter, strictest**) *adj* A **strict** rule or order is very precise or severe and must be obeyed absolutely. কঠোর

strictly *adv* If something is done **strictly** it is done severely and must be obeyed absolutely. কঠোর ভাবে

strike (**strikes, striking, struck, stricken**) *n* When there is a **strike**, workers stop doing their work for a period of time, usually in order to try to get better pay or conditions for themselves. ধর্মঘট ▷ *vt* If you **strike** someone or something, you deliberately hit them. আঘাত করা ▷ *vi* When workers **strike**, they stop working for a period of time, usually to try to get better pay or conditions. ধর্মঘট পালন করা ▷ *v* To **strike** someone or something means to attack them or to affect them, quickly and violently. আক্রমণ করা

striker (**strikers**) *n* A **striker** is a person who is on strike. ধর্মঘটী

striking *adj* Something that is **striking** is very noticeable or unusual. লক্ষণীয়

string (**strings**) *n* **String** is thin rope that is made of twisted threads. সরু দড়ি ▷ *n* The **strings** on an instrument are the thin pieces of wire that are stretched across it and that make sounds when the instrument is played. তার

strip (**strips, stripping, stripped**) *n* A **strip** of something is a long narrow piece of it. লম্বা লম্বা ফালি ▷ *v* If you **strip**, or if someone **strips** you, your clothes are removed from your body. জামা কাপড় খোলা

stripe (**stripes**) *n* A **stripe** is a long line which is a different colour from the areas next to it. সরু সরু রেখা

striped *adj* Something that is **striped** has stripes on it. ডোরা কাটা

S

stripy adj Something that is **stripy** has stripes on it. (*informal*) ডোরা কাটা

stroke (**strokes, stroking, stroked**) n If someone has a **stroke**, a blood vessel in their brain bursts or gets blocked, which may kill them or cause one side of their body to be paralysed. স্ট্রোক (অসুখ) ▷ vt If you **stroke** someone or something, you move your hand slowly and gently over them. টোকা মারা

stroll (**strolls**) n A **stroll** is a leisurely walk. ঘুরে বেড়ান

strong (**stronger, strongest**) adj Someone who is **strong** is healthy with good muscles. সবল ▷ adj **Strong** things are not easy to break. শক্ত

strongly adv If something is built **strongly**, it means it is not easily broken. মজবুতভাবে

structure (**structures**) n The **structure** of something is the way in which it is made, built, or organized. কাঠামো

struggle (**struggles, struggling, struggled**) n A **struggle** is an attempt to obtain something or to defeat someone who is denying you something. সংগ্রাম ▷ v If you **struggle** or **struggle** to do something difficult, you try hard to do it. সংগ্রাম করা

stub (**stubs**) n The **stub** of a cigarette or a pencil is the short piece which remains when the rest has been used. বর্জিতাংশ

stubborn adj A **stubborn** person is determined to do what they want and refuses to change their mind. একগুঁয়ে

stub out v When someone **stubs out** a cigarette, they put it out by pressing it against something hard. টিপে নেবানো *A sign told visitors to stub out their cigarettes.*

stuck adj If something is **stuck** in a place, it cannot move. দাঁড়িয়ে যাওয়া ▷ adj If you get **stuck**, you can't go on doing something because it is too difficult. আটকে যাওয়া

stuck-up adj If you say that someone is **stuck-up**, you mean that are very proud

and unfriendly because they think they are very important. (*informal*) অহংকার

stud (**studs**) n **Studs** are small pieces of metal which are attached to a surface for decoration. পেরেকের মাথা

student (**students**) n A **student** is a person who is studying at a university, college, or school. ছাত্র-ছাত্রী

student discount (**student discounts**) n A **student discount** is a reduction in the usual price of something that students are allowed to pay. ছাত্রছাত্রীর জন্য ছাড়

studio (**studios**) n A **studio** is a room where a designer, painter, or photographer works. স্টুডিও

studio flat (**studio flats**) n A **studio flat** is a small flat with one room for living and sleeping in, a kitchen, and a bathroom. You can also talk about a studio. ছোট ফ্ল্যাটবাড়ি

study (**studies, studying, studied**) v If you **study**, you spend time learning about a particular subject or subjects. লেখা পড়া করা

stuff n You can use **stuff** to refer to things in a general way, without mentioning the things themselves by name. (*informal*) বস্তু

stuffy (**stuffier, stuffiest**) adj If you describe a person or institution as **stuffy**, you are criticizing them for being formal and old-fashioned. পুরোন ধাঁচের

stumble (**stumbles, stumbling, stumbled**) vi If you **stumble**, you nearly fall while walking or running. হোঁচট খাওয়া

stunned adj **Stunned** means shocked or astonished. বিস্মিত

stunning adj A **stunning** person or thing is extremely beautiful or impressive. আকর্ষক

stunt (**stunts**) n A **stunt** is something interesting that someone does to get attention or publicity. লোক দেখানো

stuntman (**stuntmen**) n A **stuntman** is a man whose job is to do dangerous things, either for publicity, or in a film instead of an actor so that the actor does not risk being injured. বিপজ্জনক দৃশ্যের নেপথ্য অভিনেতা

stupid (**stupider, stupidest**) *adj* If you say that someone or something is **stupid**, you mean that they show a lack of good judgement or intelligence and they are not at all sensible. বোকা

stutter (**stutters, stuttering, stuttered**) *vi* If someone **stutters**, they have difficulty speaking because they find it hard to say the first sound of a word. তোতলানো

style (**styles**) *n* The **style** of something is the general way it is done or presented. শৈলী

stylist (**stylists**) *n* A **stylist** is a person whose job is to cut and arrange people's hair. চুল কাটেন এবং স্টাইল করেন যিনি

subject (**subjects**) *n* The **subject** of a conversation, letter, or book is the person or thing that is being discussed or written about. বিষয়

submarine (**submarines**) *n* A **submarine** is a ship that can travel below the surface of the sea. ডুবোজাহাজ

subscription (**subscriptions**) *n* A **subscription** is an amount of money that you pay regularly to receive a service or magazine, or to belong to or support an organization. চাঁদা

subsidiary (**subsidiaries**) *n* A **subsidiary** is a company which is part of a larger and more important company. অধীনস্থ সংস্থা

subsidize (**subsidizes, subsidizing, subsidized**) *vt* If an authority **subsidizes** something, they pay part of the cost of it. ভর্তুকি দেওয়া

subsidy (**subsidies**) *n* A **subsidy** is money paid by an authority in order to help an industry or business, or to pay for a public service. ভর্তুকি

substance (**substances**) *n* A **substance** is a solid, powder, liquid, or gas. পদার্থ

substitute (**substitutes, substituting, substituted**) *n* A **substitute** is something or someone that you use instead of something or someone else. পরিবর্ত ▷ *v* If

you **substitute** one thing for another, you use it instead of the other thing. বদলান

subtitled *adj* If a foreign film is **subtitled**, a printed translation of the words is shown at the bottom of the picture. ছবির কথা অনুবাদ করে নিচে লেখা

subtitles *npl* **Subtitles** are a printed translation of the words of a foreign film that are shown at the bottom of the picture. ছবির কথা অনুবাদ করে নিচে লেখা হয়

subtle (**subtler, subtlest**) *adj* Something **subtle** is not immediately obvious or noticeable. সূক্ষ্ম

subtract (**subtracts, subtracting, subtracted**) *vt* If you **subtract** one number from another, you take the first number away from the second. বিয়োগ করা

suburb (**suburbs**) *n* The **suburbs** of a city are the areas on the edge of it where people live. শহরতলী

suburban *adj* **Suburban** means relating to a suburb. শহরতলী সংক্রান্ত

subway (**subways**) *n* A **subway** is a passage for pedestrians underneath a busy road. ভূগর্ভস্থ পায়ে হাঁটার পথ

succeed (**succeeds, succeeding, succeeded**) *vi* To **succeed** means to achieve the result that you wanted or to perform in a satisfactory way. সফল হওয়া

success *n* **Success** is the achievement of something you have wanted to achieve. সাফল্য

successful *adj* Someone or something that is **successful** achieves a desired result or performs in a satisfactory way. সফল

successfully *adv* If something happens or is carried out successfully, it achieves a desired result or performs in a satisfactory way. সফলভাবে

successive *adj* **Successive** means happening or existing one after another without a break. ধারাবাহিক, পরপর

successor (**successors**) *n* Someone's **successor** is the person who takes their job after they have left. উত্তরাধিকারী

S

such det You use **such** to refer back to the thing or person that you have just mentioned, or a thing or person like the one that you have just mentioned. এই রকম *We regard such methods as entirely unacceptable.* ▷ det You use **such** in front of an adjective followed by a noun to make the adjective stronger. ভীষণ *They're such good friends.* ▷ det **Such** means like this or like that. এইরকম *How could you do such a thing?* ▷ det You use **such a** or **such an** in front of an adjective followed by a noun to make the adjective stronger. কি ভীষণ *It's such an ugly building.*

suck (**sucks, sucking, sucked**) v If you **suck** something, you hold it in your mouth and pull at it with the muscles in your cheeks and tongue, for example in order to get liquid out of it. চোষা

Sudan n **Sudan** is a republic in north-east Africa, on the Red Sea. সুদান

Sudanese (**Sudanese**) adj **Sudanese** means belonging or relating to Sudan, or to its people or culture. সুদান দেশীয় ▷ npl The **Sudanese** are the people of Sudan. সুদানের নাগরিক

sudden adj Something that is **sudden** happens quickly and unexpectedly. হঠাৎ

suddenly adv If something happens **suddenly**, it happens quickly and unexpectedly. হঠাৎকরে

sue (**sues, suing, sued**) v If you **sue** someone, you start a legal case against them to claim money from them because they have harmed you in some way. মামলা করা

suede n **Suede** is thin soft leather with a slightly rough surface. চামড়া

suffer (**suffers, suffering, suffered**) v If you **suffer** pain or an illness, or if you **suffer from** a pain or illness, you are badly affected by it. কষ্ট পাওয়া

suffocate (**suffocates, suffocating, suffocated**) vi If someone **suffocates**, they die because there is no air for them to breathe. দম বন্ধ হয়ে আসা

sugar n **Sugar** is a sweet substance, often in the form of white or brown crystals, used to sweeten food and drink. চিনি

sugar-free adj **Sugar-free** drinks do not contain any sugar. চিনি-বিহীন

suggest (**suggests, suggesting, suggested**) vt If you **suggest** something, you put forward a plan or idea for someone to consider. পরামর্শ দেওয়া

suggestion (**suggestions**) n If you make a **suggestion**, you put forward an idea or plan for someone to think about. পরামর্শ

suicide (**suicides**) n People who commit **suicide** deliberately kill themselves. আত্মহত্যা

suicide bomber (**suicide bombers**) n A **suicide bomber** is a terrorist who carries out a bomb attack, knowing that he or she will be killed in the explosion. আত্মঘাতী বোমাবাজ

suit (**suits, suiting, suited**) n A **suit** is a matching jacket and trousers, or a matching jacket and skirt. পরিধানের স্যুট ▷ vt If a piece of clothing or a particular style or colour **suits** you, it makes you look attractive. উপযুক্ত হওয়া

suitable adj Someone or something that is **suitable** for a particular purpose or occasion is right or acceptable for it. উপযুক্ত

suitcase (**suitcases**) n A **suitcase** is a case for carrying clothes when you are travelling. সুটকেস

suite (**suites**) n A **suite** is a set of rooms in a hotel or other building. হোটেলের সুইট

sulk (**sulks, sulking, sulked**) vi If you **sulk**, you are silent and bad-tempered for a while because you are annoyed about something. চাপা রাগে চুপ থাকা

sulky adj Someone who is **sulky** is sulking or is unwilling to enjoy themselves. গোমড়ামুখো

sultana (**sultanas**) n **Sultanas** are dried white grapes. কিশমিশ

sum (**sums**) n A **sum** of money is an amount of money. টাকার পরিমাণ ▷ n In maths, a **sum** is a problem you work out using numbers. অঙ্ক

summarize (**summarizes, summarizing, summarized**) v If you **summarize** something, you give a brief description of its main points. সারসংক্ষেপ করা

summary (**summaries**) n A **summary** is a short account of something giving the main points but not the details. সারাংশ

summer (**summers**) n **Summer** is the season between spring and autumn. In summer the weather is usually warm or hot. গ্রীষ্মকাল

summer holidays npl Your **summer holidays** are a period of time in the summer during which you relax and enjoy yourself away from home. গরমের ছুটি

summertime n **Summertime** is the period of time during which summer lasts. গরমের দিন

summit (**summits**) n A **summit** is a meeting between the leaders of two or more countries to discuss important matters. শিখর সম্মেলন

sum up v If you **sum up** or **sum** something **up**, you briefly describe the main features of something. যোগ করা *Well, to sum up, what is the message that you are trying to communicate?*

sun n The **sun** is the ball of fire in the sky that the Earth goes round, and that gives us heat and light. সূর্য

sunbathe (**sunbathes, sunbathing, sunbathed**) vi When people **sunbathe**, they sit or lie in a place where the sun shines on them, in order to get a suntan. রৌদ্রস্নান

sunbed (**sunbeds**) n A **sunbed** is a piece of equipment with ultraviolet lights. You lie on it to make your skin browner. সানবেড

sunblock (**sunblocks**) n **Sunblock** is a cream which you put on your skin to protect it completely from the sun. সানব্লক ক্রীম

sunburn (**sunburns**) n If someone has **sunburn**, their skin is red and sore because they have spent too much time in the sun. রোদে পোড়া

sunburnt adj Someone who is **sunburnt** has sore bright pink skin because they have spent too much time in hot sunshine. রোদে পুড়ে যাওয়া

suncream (**suncreams**) n **Suncream** is a cream that protects your skin from the sun's rays, especially in hot weather. সান ক্রীম

Sunday (**Sundays**) n **Sunday** is the day after Saturday and before Monday. রবিবার

sunflower (**sunflowers**) n A **sunflower** is a tall plant with large yellow flowers. সূর্যমুখী

sunglasses npl **Sunglasses** are spectacles with dark lenses to protect your eyes from bright sunlight. রোদ চসমা

sunlight n **Sunlight** is the light that comes from the sun. সূর্যরশ্মি

sunny (**sunnier, sunniest**) adj When it is **sunny**, the sun is shining brightly. রৌদ্রোজ্জ্বল

sunrise n **Sunrise** is the time in the morning when the sun first appears. সূর্য ওঠা

sunroof (**sunroofs**) n A **sunroof** is a panel in the roof of a car that opens to let sunshine and air enter the car. সান রুফ, গাড়িতে আলো বাতাস আসার স্থান

sunscreen (**sunscreens**) n A **sunscreen** is a cream that protects your skin from the sun's rays in hot weather. রোধনিরোধী ক্রিম

sunset n **Sunset** is the time in the evening when the sun disappears. সূর্যাস্ত

sunshine n **Sunshine** is the light and heat that comes from the sun. সূর্যকিরণ

sunstroke n **Sunstroke** is an illness caused by spending too much time in hot sunshine. সর্দিগর্মি

suntan (**suntans**) n If you have a **suntan**, the sun has turned your skin a brown colour. রোদে বিবর্ণ

suntan lotion (**suntan lotions**) n **Suntan lotion** protects your skin from the sun. রোদ থেকে সুরক্ষার লোশন

suntan oil (**suntan oils**) *n* **Suntan oil** protects your skin from the sun. রোদ থেকে সুরক্ষার তেল

super *adj* **Super** means very nice or good. (*informal, old-fashioned*) খুব ভাল

superb *adj* If something is **superb**, it is very good indeed. অত্যন্ত ভাল

superficial *adj* If you describe someone as **superficial**, you disapprove of them because they do not think deeply, and have little understanding of anything serious or important. ওপর-ওপর

superior (**superiors**) *adj* You use **superior** to describe someone or something that is better than other similar people or things. উন্নততর ▷ *n* Your **superior** in an organization that you work for is a person who has a higher rank than you. ঊর্ধ্বতন

supermarket (**supermarkets**) *n* A **supermarket** is a large shop which sells all kinds of food and some household goods. বড়দোকান

supernatural *adj* **Supernatural** creatures, forces, and events are believed by some people to exist or happen, although they are impossible according to scientific laws. অতিপ্রাকৃতিক

superstitious *adj* People who are **superstitious** believe in things that are not real or possible, for example magic. কুসংস্কারাচ্ছন্ন

supervise (**supervises, supervising, supervised**) *vt* If you **supervise** an activity or a person, you make sure that the activity is done correctly or that the person is behaving correctly. তদারক করা

supervisor (**supervisors**) *n* A **supervisor** is a person who supervises activities or people, especially workers or students. তদারককারী

supper (**suppers**) *n* Some people refer to the main meal eaten in the early part of the evening as **supper**. নৈশভোজ

supplement (**supplements**) *n* A **supplement** is something which is added to another thing in order to improve it. অতিরিক্ত

supplier (**suppliers**) *n* A **supplier** is a person or company that provides you with goods or equipment. সরবরাহকারী

supplies *npl* You can use **supplies** to refer to food, equipment, and other essential things that people need, especially when these are provided in large quantities. যোগান

supply (**supplies, supplying, supplied**) *n* A **supply** of something is an amount of it which is available for use. If something is in short **supply**, there is very little of it available. সরবরাহ ▷ *vt* If you **supply** someone with something, you provide them with it. সরবরাহ করা

supply teacher (**supply teachers**) *n* A **supply teacher** is a teacher whose job is to take the place of other teachers at different schools when they are unable to be there. অস্থায়ী শিক্ষক

support (**supports, supporting, supported**) *n* If you give someone your **support**, you agree with them, and perhaps try to help them because you want them to succeed. সমর্থন ▷ *vt* If you **support** someone or their ideas or aims, you agree with them, and perhaps help them because you want them to succeed. সমর্থন করা

supporter (**supporters**) *n* **Supporters** are people who support someone or something, for example a political leader or a sports team. সমর্থক

suppose (**supposes, supposing, supposed**) *vt* You use **suppose** or **supposing** when you are considering a possible situation or action and trying to think what effects it would have. মনে করা

supposedly *adv* **Supposedly** means that the following word or description is misleading and is not definitely known to be true. আনুমানিকভাবে

supposing *conj* You say **supposing** to ask someone to pretend that something is true or to imagine that something will happen. ধরে নেওয়া যাক *Supposing he sees us?*

surcharge (**surcharges**) *n* A **surcharge** is an extra payment of money in addition to the usual payment for something. It is added for a specific reason, for example by a company because costs have risen or by a government as a tax. শুল্ক

sure (**surer, surest**) *adj* If you are **sure** that something is true, you are certain that it is true. If you are not **sure** about something, you do not know for certain what the true situation is. নিশ্চিত

surely *adv* You use **surely** to emphasize that you think something should be true, and you would be surprised if it was not true. নিশ্চিতভাবে

surf (**surfs, surfing, surfed**) *n* **Surf** is the mass of white foam formed by waves as they fall on the shore. ফেনার ঢেউ ▷ *vi* If you **surf**, you ride on big waves on a special board. সামুদ্রিক ক্রীড়া

surface (**surfaces**) *n* The **surface** of something is the top part of it or the outside of it. উপরিভাগ

surfboard (**surfboards**) *n* A **surfboard** is a long narrow board that is used for surfing. সার্ফবোর্ড

surfer (**surfers**) *n* A **surfer** rides on big waves on a special board. যে সার্ফিং করে

surfing *n* **Surfing** is the sport of riding on the top of a wave while standing or lying on a special board. সমুদ্রের ঢেউয়ে খেলা

surge (**surges**) *n* A **surge** is a sudden large increase in something that has previously been steady, or has only increased or developed slowly. হঠাৎ বৃদ্ধি পাওয়া

surgeon (**surgeons**) *n* A **surgeon** is a doctor who performs surgery. শল্যচিকিৎসক

surgery (**surgeries**) *n* **Surgery** is medical treatment which involves cutting open a person's body in order to repair or remove a diseased or damaged part. অস্ত্রোপচার ▷ *n* A **surgery** is the room or house where a doctor or dentist works. ডাক্তারখানা

surname (**surnames**) *n* Your **surname** is the name that you share with other members of your family. পদবী

surplus (**surpluses**) *adj* **Surplus** is used to describe something that is extra or that is more than is needed. বেশি ▷ *n* If there is a **surplus** of something, there is more than is needed. অতিরিক্ত

surprise (**surprises**) *n* A **surprise** is an unexpected event, fact, or piece of news. বিস্ময়

surprised *adj* If you are **surprised** at something, you have a feeling of surprise, because it is unexpected or unusual. বিস্মিত

surprising *adj* Something that is **surprising** is unexpected or unusual and makes you feel surprised. বিস্ময়কর

surprisingly *adv* **Surprisingly** means unexpectedly or unusually. বিস্ময়করভাবে

surrender (**surrenders, surrendering, surrendered**) *vi* If you **surrender**, you stop fighting or resisting someone and agree that you have been beaten. আত্মসমর্পণ

surrogate mother (**surrogate mothers**) *n* A **surrogate mother** is a woman who has agreed to give birth to a baby on behalf of another woman. অন্যমহিলার বাচ্চার জন্মদাত্রী

surround (**surrounds, surrounding, surrounded**) *vt* If something or someone **is surrounded** by something, that thing is situated all around them. ঘিরে ফেলা

surroundings *npl* The place where someone or something is can be referred to as their **surroundings**. পরিবেশ

survey (**surveys**) *n* If you carry out a **survey**, you try to find out detailed information about a lot of different people or things, usually by asking people a series of questions. সমীক্ষা

surveyor (**surveyors**) *n* A **surveyor** is a person whose job is to survey land. সমীক্ষক

survival n **Survival** is the fact of continuing to live or exist in spite of great danger or difficulty. জীবিত থাকা

survive (**survives, surviving, survived**) v If someone **survives** in a dangerous situation, they do not die. বেঁচে থাকা

survivor (**survivors**) n A **survivor** of a disaster, accident, or illness is someone who continues to live afterwards in spite of coming close to death. জীবিত ব্যক্তি

suspect (**suspects, suspecting, suspected**) n A **suspect** is a person who the police think may be guilty of a crime. সন্দেহভাজন ▷ vt If you say that you **suspect** that something is true, you mean that you believe it is probably true, but you want to make it sound less strong or direct. সন্দেহ করা

suspend (**suspends, suspending, suspended**) vt If you **suspend** something, you delay or stop it for a while. নিলম্বিত করা

suspense n **Suspense** is a state of excitement or anxiety about something that is going to happen very soon. ধিধা

suspension n The **suspension** of something is the act of delaying or stopping it for a while. নিলম্বন

suspension bridge (**suspension bridges**) n A **suspension bridge** is a type of bridge that is supported from above by cables. টানা সেতু

suspicious adj If you are **suspicious** of someone or something, you do not trust them. সন্দেহবাতিক

swallow (**swallows, swallowing, swallowed**) n When you take a **swallow**, you cause something to go from your mouth down into your stomach. গলাধঃকরণ ▷ vt If you **swallow** something, you cause it to go from your mouth down into your stomach. গিলে নেওয়া ▷ vi When you **swallow**, you cause something to go from your mouth down into your stomach. গিলে খাওয়া

swamp (**swamps**) n A **swamp** is an area of wet land with wild plants growing in it. জলাভূমি

swan (**swans**) n A **swan** is a large white bird with a long neck that lives on rivers and lakes. রাজহংস

swap (**swaps, swapping, swapped**) v If you **swap** something with someone, you give it to them and receive a different thing in exchange. বিনিময়

swat (**swats, swatting, swatted**) vt If you **swat** an insect, you hit it with a quick, swinging movement. দ্রুতগতিতে মারা

sway (**sways, swaying, swayed**) vi When people or things **sway**, they lean or swing slowly from one side to the other. দোল খাওয়া

Swaziland n **Swaziland** is a kingdom in southern Africa. সোয়াজিল্যান্ড

swear (**swears, swearing, swore, sworn**) vi If someone **swears**, they use language that is considered to be rude or offensive. গালি দেওয়া

swearword (**swearwords**) n A **swearword** is a word which is considered to be rude or offensive. Swearwords are usually used when people are angry. কটুক্তি

sweat (**sweats, sweating, sweated**) n **Sweat** is the salty colourless liquid which comes through your skin when you are hot, ill, or afraid. ঘাম ▷ vi.When you **sweat**, sweat comes through your skin. ঘামা

sweater (**sweaters**) n A **sweater** is a warm knitted piece of clothing which covers the upper part of your body and your arms. শীত বস্ত্র

sweatshirt (**sweatshirts**) n A **sweatshirt** is a loose warm piece of casual clothing, usually made of thick cotton, which covers the upper part of your body and your arms. ঢিলে ঢালা শার্ট

sweaty (**sweatier, sweatiest**) adj If your clothing or body is **sweaty**, it is soaked or covered with sweat. ঘর্মাক্ত

Swede (**Swedes**) *n* A **Swede** is a person who comes from Sweden. সুইডেনের লোক

swede (**swedes**) *n* A **swede** is a round yellow root vegetable with a brown or purple skin. শালগম

Sweden *n* **Sweden** is a kingdom in north-west Europe, occupying the eastern part of the Scandinavian Peninsula, on the Gulf of Bothnia and the Baltic. সুইডেন

Swedish *adj* **Swedish** means belonging or relating to Sweden, or to its people, language, or culture. সুইডেন দেশীয় ▷ *n* **Swedish** is the language spoken in Sweden. সুইডেনের ভাষা

sweep (**sweeps, sweeping, swept**) *vt* If you **sweep** an area of ground, you push dirt or rubbish off it with a broom. ঝাড়ু দেওয়া

sweet (**sweeter, sweetest, sweets**) *adj* **Sweet** food or drink contains a lot of sugar. মিষ্টি ▷ *adj* If you describe something as **sweet**, you mean that it gives you great pleasure and satisfaction. আনন্দদায়ক ▷ *n* A **sweet** is something sweet, such as fruit or a pudding, that you eat at the end of a meal. মিষ্টদ্রব্য

sweetcorn *n* **Sweetcorn** consists of the yellow seeds of the maize plant, which are eaten as a vegetable. ভুট্টা

sweetener (**sweeteners**) *n* A **sweetener** is an artificial substance that can be used instead of sugar. চিনির পরিবর্ত

sweets *npl* **Sweets** are small sweet things such as toffees, chocolates, and mints. মিষ্টদ্রব্য

sweltering *adj* If the weather is **sweltering**, it is very hot. গরম

swerve (**swerves, swerving, swerved**) *v* If a vehicle or other moving thing **swerves**, it suddenly changes direction, often in order to avoid hitting something. ঘুরিয়ে নেওয়া

swim (**swims, swimming, swam, swum**) *vi* When you **swim**, you move through water by making movements with your arms and legs. সাঁতার কাটা

swimmer (**swimmers**) *n* A **swimmer** is a person who swims, especially for sport or pleasure, or a person who is swimming. সাঁতারু

swimming *n* **Swimming** is the activity of swimming, especially as a sport or for pleasure. সাঁতার

swimming costume (**swimming costumes**) *n* A **swimming costume** is a piece of clothing that is worn for swimming, especially by women and girls. সাঁতারের পোশাক

swimming pool (**swimming pools**) *n* A **swimming pool** is a place that has been built for people to swim in. It consists of a large hole that has been tiled and filled with water. সাঁতার কাটার জলাশয়

swimming trunks *npl* **Swimming trunks** are the shorts that a man wears when he goes swimming. সাঁতারের প্যান্ট

swimsuit (**swimsuits**) *n* A **swimsuit** is a piece of clothing that is worn for swimming, especially by women and girls. মেয়েদের সাঁতারের পোশাক

swing (**swings, swinging, swung**) *n* A **swing** is the act or manner of swinging or the distance covered while swinging. দোলা ▷ *v* If something **swings** or if you **swing** it, it moves repeatedly backwards and forwards or from side to side from a fixed point. দোল খাওয়া

Swiss *adj* **Swiss** means belonging or relating to Switzerland, or to its people or culture. সুইৎজারল্যান্ডের ▷ *npl* The **Swiss** are the people of Switzerland. সুইৎজারল্যান্ডের নাগরিক

switch (**switches, switching, switched**) *n* A **switch** is a small control for an electrical device which you use to turn the device on or off. বিদ্যুতের সুইচ ▷ *vi* If you **switch** to something different, for example to a different system, task, or subject of conversation, you change to it from what

S

you were doing or saying before. পরিবর্তন করা

switchboard (**switchboards**) n A **switchboard** is a place in a large office or business where all the telephone calls are connected. সুইচ বোর্ড

switch off v If you **switch off** an electrical device, you stop it working by operating a switch. বন্ধ করা *The driver switched off the headlights.*

switch on v If you **switch on** an electrical device, you make it start working by operating a switch. চালু করা *We switched on the radio.*

Switzerland n **Switzerland** is a federal republic in west central Europe. সুইৎজারল্যান্ড, (দেশ)

swollen adj If a part of your body is **swollen**, it is larger and rounder than normal, usually as a result of injury or illness. ফোলা

sword (**swords**) n A **sword** is a weapon with a handle and a long blade. অসি

swordfish (**swordfish**) n A **swordfish** is a large sea fish with a very long upper jaw. সামুদ্রিক মাছ

swot (**swots, swotting, swotted**) vi If you **swot**, you study very hard, especially when you are preparing for an examination. (*informal*) পরীক্ষার পড়া

syllable (**syllables**) n A **syllable** is a part of a word that contains a single vowel sound and that is pronounced as a unit. For example, 'book' has one syllable, and 'reading' has two syllables. বর্ণ বিভাজন

syllabus (**syllabuses**) n You can refer to the subjects that are studied in a particular course as the **syllabus**. পাঠ্যক্রম

symbol (**symbols**) n A **symbol** of something such as an idea is a shape or design that is used to represent it. প্রতীক

symmetrical adj If something is **symmetrical**, it has two halves which are exactly the same, except that one half is the mirror image of the other. সদৃশ

sympathetic adj If you are **sympathetic** to someone who has had a misfortune, you are kind to them and show that you understand how they are feeling. সহানুভূতিশীল

sympathize (**sympathizes, sympathizing, sympathized**) vi If you **sympathize** with someone who has had a misfortune, you show that you are sorry for them. সহানুভূতি প্রদর্শন

sympathy (**sympathies**) n If you have **sympathy** for someone who has had a misfortune, you are sorry for them, and show this in the way you behave towards them. সহানুভূতি

symphony (**symphonies**) n A **symphony** is a piece of music written to be played by an orchestra, usually in four parts. সঙ্গীত

symptom (**symptoms**) n A **symptom** of an illness is something wrong with your body that is a sign of the illness. লক্ষণ

synagogue (**synagogues**) n A **synagogue** is a building where Jewish people worship. ইহুদীদের পূজাস্থল

Syria n **Syria** is a republic in West Asia, on the Mediterranean. সিরিয়া (দেশ)

Syrian (**Syrians**) adj **Syrian** means belonging or relating to Syria, or to its people or culture. সিরিয়া দেশীয় ▷ n A **Syrian** is a Syrian citizen, or a person of Syrian origin. সিরিয়ার নাগরিক

syringe (**syringes**) n A **syringe** is a small tube with a fine hollow needle, used for injecting drugs or for taking blood from someone's body. সিরিঞ্জ

syrup (**syrups**) n **Syrup** is a sweet liquid made by cooking sugar with water or fruit juice. চিনির শিরা

system (**systems**) n A **system** is a way of working, organizing, or doing something which follows a fixed plan or set of rules. ব্যবস্থা

systematic *adj* Something that is done in a **systematic** way is done according to a fixed plan, in a thorough and efficient way. সুপরিকল্পিত

systems analyst (**systems analysts**) *n* A **systems analyst** is someone whose job is to decide what computer equipment and software a company needs, and to provide it. সিস্টেম এ্যানালিস্ট

t

table (**tables**) *n* A **table** is a piece of furniture with a flat top that you put things on or sit at. টেবিল ▷ *n* A **table** is a set of facts or figures arranged in columns and rows. সারণী

tablecloth (**tablecloths**) *n* A **tablecloth** is a large piece of material used to cover a table, especially during a meal. টেবিল ক্লথ

tablespoon (**tablespoons**) *n* A **tablespoon** is a fairly large spoon used for serving food and in cookery. টেবিলচামচ

tablet (**tablets**) *n* A **tablet** is a small, solid, round mass of medicine which you swallow. ট্যাবলেট

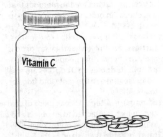

table tennis *n* **Table tennis** is a game played inside by two or four people. The players stand at each end of a table which has a low net across the middle and hit a small light ball over the net, using small bats. টেবিল টেনিস

table wine (**table wines**) *n* **Table wine** is fairly cheap wine that is drunk with meals. টেবিল ওয়াইন

taboo (**taboos**) *adj* If a subject or activity is **taboo**, it is a social custom to avoid doing that activity or talking about that subject, because people find it embarrassing or offensive. নিষিদ্ধ ▷ *n* If there is a **taboo** on a subject or activity, it is a social custom to avoid doing that activity or talking about that subject, because people find it embarrassing or offensive. নিষিদ্ধ

tackle (**tackles, tackling, tackled**) *n* A **tackle** is when you try to take the ball away from someone in a game such as football. সামলানো ▷ *vt* If you **tackle** a difficult task, you start dealing with it in a determined way. সামলে রাখা

tact *n* **Tact** is the ability to avoid upsetting or offending people by being careful not to say or do things that would hurt their feelings. বিচক্ষণতা

tactful *adj* If you describe someone as **tactful**, you approve of them because they are careful not to say or do anything that would offend or upset other people. কৌশলী

tactics *npl* **Tactics** are the methods that you choose in order to achieve what you want. কৌশল

tactless *adj* If you describe someone as **tactless**, you think what they say or do is likely to offend other people. কাণ্ডজ্ঞানহীন

tadpole (**tadpoles**) *n* **Tadpoles** are small water creatures which grow into frogs or toads. ব্যাঙাচি

tag (**tags**) *n* A **tag** is a small piece of card or cloth which is attached to an object and has information about that object on it. টিকলি

Tahiti *n* **Tahiti** is an island in the South Pacific, in the Windward group of the Society Islands. তাহিতি

tail (**tails**) *n* The **tail** of an animal is the part extending beyond the end of its body. লেজ

tailor (**tailors**) *n* A **tailor** is a person who makes clothes, especially for men. দর্জি

Taiwan *n* **Taiwan** is an island in south-east Asia between the East China Sea and the South China Sea, off the south-east coast of the People's Republic of China. তাইওয়ান

Taiwanese (**Taiwanese**) *adj* **Taiwanese** means of or relating to Taiwan or its inhabitants. তাইওয়ান দেশীয় ▷ *n* A **Taiwanese** is a native or inhabitant of Taiwan. তাইওয়ানের বসবাসকারী

Tajikistan *n* **Tajikistan** is a republic in central Asia. তাজিকিস্তান

take (**takes, taking, took, taken**) *vt* If you **take** a vehicle, you ride in it from one place to another. যানবাহনে চড়া ▷ *vt* If you **take** something, you move it or carry it. নেওয়া ▷ *vt* If you **take** something that does not belong to you, you steal it. হস্তগত করা

take after *v* If you **take after** a member of your family, you look or behave like them. সদৃশ হওয়া *He takes after his dad.*

take apart *v* If you **take** something **apart**, you separate it into its different parts. আলাদা করা *When the clock stopped, he took it apart.*

take away (**takeaways**) *v* If you **take** something **away** from someone, you remove it from them. সরিয়ে নেওয়া *If you don't like it, we'll take it away for free.* ▷ *n* A **takeaway** is a shop or restaurant which sells hot food to be eaten elsewhere. A meal that you buy there is also called a **takeaway**. দোকানের বাইরে নিয়ে যাওয়ার খাবার

take back *v* If you **take** something **back**, you return it. ফেরত নেওয়া *I once took back a pair of shoes that fell apart after a week.*

take off (**takeoffs**) *v* When an aircraft **takes off**, it leaves the ground and starts flying. বিমান ওড়া *We took off at 11 o'clock.* ▷ *n* **Takeoff** is the beginning of a flight, when an aircraft leaves the ground. বিমানের আকাশ আরোহন

take over (**takeovers**) *v* To **take over** something such as a company or country means to gain control of it. দখল নেওয়া *The company has been taken over by a multinational corporation.* ▷ n A **takeover** is the act of gaining control of a company by buying a majority of its shares. অধিগ্রহণ

takings npl The **takings** of a business such as a shop or cinema consist of the amount of money it gets from selling its goods or tickets during a certain period. বিক্রয় মারফত টাকা পাওয়া

talcum powder n **Talcum powder** is fine powder with a pleasant smell which people put on their bodies after they have had a bath or a shower. ট্যালকম পাউডার

tale (tales) n A **tale** is a story, especially one involving adventure or magic. কাহিনী

talent (talents) n **Talent** is the natural ability to do something well. প্রতিভা

talented adj Someone who is **talented** has a natural ability to do something well. প্রতিভাবান

talk (talks, talking, talked) n **Talk** is the things you say to someone when you talk. কথা ▷ vi When you **talk**, you use spoken language to express your thoughts, ideas, or feelings. কথা বলা

talkative adj Someone who is **talkative** talks a lot. বাচাল

talk to v If you **talk to** someone, you have a conversation with them. কথোপকথন করা *I talked to him yesterday.*

tall (taller, tallest) adj Someone or something that is **tall** is above average height. লম্বা

tame (tamer, tamest) adj A **tame** animal or bird is not afraid of humans. গৃহপালিত

tampon (tampons) n A **tampon** is a firm piece of cotton wool that a woman puts inside her vagina when she is menstruating, in order to absorb the blood. রজঃস্রাবে ব্যবহৃত ন্যাপকিন

tan (tans) n If you have a **tan**, your skin has become darker than usual because you have been in the sun. তামাটে

tandem (tandems) n A **tandem** is a bicycle designed for two riders. একপ্রকার সাইকেল

tangerine (tangerines) n A **tangerine** is a small sweet orange. একপ্রকার কমলালেবু

tank (tanks) n A **tank** is a large container for holding liquid or gas. বড় আধার ▷ n A **tank** is a military vehicle covered with armour and equipped with guns or rockets. যুদ্ধের ট্যাঙ্ক

tanker (tankers) n A **tanker** is a ship or lorry used for transporting large quantities of gas or liquid, especially oil. ট্যাঙ্কার জাহাজ

tanned adj If someone is **tanned**, his or her skin is darker because of the time he or she has spent in the sun. পিঙ্গল

tantrum (tantrums) n If a child has a **tantrum**, it suddenly loses its temper in a noisy and uncontrolled way. রাগারাগি

Tanzania n **Tanzania** is a republic in East Africa, on the Indian Ocean. তানজানিয়া

Tanzanian (Tanzanians) adj **Tanzanian** means of or relating to Tanzania or its inhabitants. তানজানিয়া দেশীয় ▷ n A **Tanzanian** is a native or inhabitant of Tanzania. তানজানিয়ার অধিবাসী

tap (taps) n A **tap** is a device that controls the flow of a liquid or gas from a pipe or container. জলের কল

tap-dancing n **Tap-dancing** is a style of dancing in which the dancers wear special shoes with pieces of metal on the heels and toes. The shoes make loud sharp sounds as the dancers move their feet. ট্যাপ নৃত্য

tape (tapes, taping, taped) n **Tape** is a narrow plastic strip covered with a magnetic substance. It is used to record sounds, pictures, and computer information. ফিতা ▷ vt If you **tape** music, sounds, or television pictures, you record them using a tape recorder or a video recorder. টেপ করা

tape measure (tape measures) n A **tape measure** is a strip of metal, plastic, or cloth with marks on it, used for measuring, especially for clothes and DIY. টেপ পরিমাপক

tape recorder (**tape recorders**) n A **tape recorder** is a machine used for recording and playing music, speech, or other sounds. টেপ রেকর্ডার

target (**targets**) n A **target** is something that someone is trying to hit with a weapon or other object. লক্ষ্য

tariff (**tariffs**) n A **tariff** is a tax on goods coming into a country. শুল্ক

tarmac n **Tarmac** is a material used for making road surfaces, consisting of crushed stones mixed with tar. **Tarmac** is a trademark. রাস্তার পিচ

tarpaulin n **Tarpaulin** is a fabric made of canvas or similar material coated with tar, wax, paint, or some other waterproof substance. টারপুলিন

tarragon n **Tarragon** is a European herb with narrow leaves which are used to add flavour to food. ট্যারাগন

tart (**tarts**) n A **tart** is a shallow pastry case with a filling of sweet food or fruit. পেস্ট্রি

tartan adj **Tartan** cloth, which traditionally comes from Scotland, has different coloured stripes crossing each other. পশমের বস্ত্র

task (**tasks**) n A **task** is an activity or piece of work which you have to do. কাজ

Tasmania n **Tasmania** is an island in the South Pacific, south of mainland Australia. তাসমানিয়া

taste (**tastes, tasting, tasted**) n Your sense of **taste** is your ability to recognize the flavour of things with your tongue. স্বাদ ▷ vi If food or drink **tastes** of something, it has that particular flavour. স্বাদ নেওয়া

tasteful adj If you describe something as **tasteful**, you mean that it is attractive and elegant. মার্জিত

tasteless adj If you describe something as **tasteless**, you mean that it is vulgar and unattractive. স্বাদহীন

tasty (**tastier, tastiest**) adj If you say that food, especially savoury food, is **tasty**, you mean that it has a pleasant and fairly strong flavour which makes it good to eat. সুস্বাদু

tattoo (**tattoos**) n A **tattoo** is a design on someone's skin, made by pricking little holes and filling them with coloured dye. উল্কি

Taurus n **Taurus** is one of the twelve signs of the zodiac. Its symbol is a bull. People who are born approximately between the 20th of April and the 20th of May come under this sign. বৃষরাশি

tax (**taxes**) n A **Tax** is an amount of money that you have to pay to the government so that it can pay for public services. কর

taxi (**taxis**) n A **taxi** is a car driven by a person whose job is to take people where they want to go in return for money. ট্যাক্সি

taxi driver (**taxi drivers**) n A **taxi driver** is a person whose job is to take people in a car to the place they want to go to in return for money. ট্যাক্সি চালক

taxpayer (**taxpayers**) n **Taxpayers** are people who pay a percentage of their income to the government as tax. করদাতা

tax return (**tax returns**) n A **tax return** is an official form that you fill in with details about your income and personal situation, so that the tax you owe can be calculated. ট্যাক্স রিটার্ন

TB n **TB** is a very serious infectious disease that affects someone's lungs and other parts of their body. **TB** is an abbreviation for 'tuberculosis'. যক্ষ্মা

tea (**teas**) n **Tea** is a drink. You make it by pouring hot water on to the dry leaves of a plant called the tea bush. চা ▷ n **Tea** is a meal that you eat in the afternoon or the early evening. চা-পান

tea bag (**tea bags**) n **Tea bags** are small paper bags with tea leaves in them. You put them into hot water to make tea. চা ব্যাগ

teach (**teaches, teaching, taught**) vt If you **teach** someone something, you give them instructions so that they know about it or know how to do it. পড়ানো

teacher (**teachers**) *n* A **teacher** is a person who teaches, usually as a job at a school or similar institution. শিক্ষক

teaching *n* **Teaching** is the work that a teacher does in helping students to learn. শিক্ষকতা

teacup (**teacups**) *n* A **teacup** is a cup that you use for drinking tea. চায়ের কাপ

team (**teams**) *n* A **team** is a group of people who play together against another group in a sport or game. দল

teapot (**teapots**) *n* A **teapot** is a container with a lid, a handle, and a spout, used for making and serving tea. চায়ের কেটলি

tear (**tears, tearing, tore, torn**) *n* **Tears** are the liquid that comes out of your eyes when you cry. অশ্রু ▷ *n* A **tear** in something is a hole that has been made in it. ছেঁড়া ▷ *vt* If you **tear** something, you pull it into pieces or make a hole in it. ছিঁড়ে ফেলা

tear gas *n* **Tear gas** is a gas that causes your eyes to sting and fill with tears so that you cannot see. It is sometimes used by the police or army to control crowds. কাঁদানে গ্যাস

tear up *v* If you **tear up** a piece of paper, you tear it into a lot of small pieces. টুকরো করে ছিঁড়ে ফেলা *Don't you dare tear up her ticket.*

tease (**teases, teasing, teased**) *vt* To **tease** someone means to laugh at them or make jokes about them in order to embarrass, annoy, or upset them. উত্যক্ত করা

teaspoon (**teaspoons**) *n* A **teaspoon** is a small spoon that you use to put sugar into tea or coffee. চা-চামচ

teatime (**teatimes**) *n* **Teatime** is the period of the day when people have their tea. It can be eaten in the late afternoon or in the early part of the evening. চা খাবার সময়

tea towel (**tea towels**) *n* A **tea towel** is a cloth used to dry dishes after they have been washed. টি টাওয়েল

technical *adj* **Technical** means involving the sorts of machines, processes, and materials used in industry, transport, and communications. প্রায়োগিক

technician (**technicians**) *n* A **technician** is someone whose job involves skilled practical work with scientific equipment, for example in a laboratory. যন্ত্রকুশলী

technique (**techniques**) *n* A **technique** is a particular method of doing an activity, usually a method that involves practical skills. কৌশল

techno *n* **Techno** is a form of modern electronic music with a very fast beat. টেকনো

technological *adj* **Technological** means relating to or associated with technology. প্রযুক্তিগত

technology (**technologies**) *n* **Technology** refers to things which are the result of scientific knowledge being used for practical purposes. প্রযুক্তি

teddy bear (**teddy bears**) *n* A **teddy bear** or a **teddy** is a soft toy that looks like a bear. টেডি বিয়ার

tee (**tees**) *n* In golf, a **tee** is a small piece of wood or plastic which is used to support the ball before it is hit at the start of each hole. গলফের শুরুর স্থান

teenager (**teenagers**) *n* A **teenager** is someone between 13 and 19 years of age. কিশোর বা কিশোরী

teens *npl* If you are in your **teens**, you are between 13 and 19 years old. কৈশোর

tee-shirt (**tee-shirts**) *n* A **tee-shirt** is a cotton shirt with short sleeves and no collar or buttons. টি-শার্ট

teethe (**teethes, teething, teethed**) *vi* When babies **are teething**, their teeth are starting to appear through their gums. দুধের দাঁত পড়া

teetotal *adj* Someone who is **teetotal** does not drink alcohol. মদ্যপানে অনিচ্ছুক

telecommunications *npl* **Telecommunications** is the technology of sending signals and messages over long distances using electronic equipment, for example by radio and telephone. বৈদ্যুতিন যোগাযোগব্যবস্থা

telegram (telegrams) n A **telegram** is a message that is sent by electricity or radio and then printed and delivered to someone's home or office. তার

telephone (telephones) n The **telephone** is an electrical system used to talk to someone in another place by dialling a number on a piece of equipment and speaking into it. টেলিফোন

telephone directory (telephone directories) n The **telephone directory** is a book that contains an alphabetical list of the names, addresses, and telephone numbers of the people in a particular area. টেলিফোনের তথ্যসম্বলিত তালিকা

telesales n **Telesales** is a method of selling in which someone employed by a company telephones people to try to persuade them to buy the company's products or services. টেলিফোনের মাধ্যমে বিক্রয়

telescope (telescopes) n A **telescope** is an instrument shaped like a tube. It has lenses inside it that make distant things seem larger and nearer when you look through it. টেলিস্কোপ

television (televisions) n A **television** or a **television set** is a piece of electrical equipment consisting of a box with a screen on which you can watch programmes with pictures and sounds. টেলিভিশন

tell (tells, telling, told) vt If you **tell** someone something, you let them know about it. বলা ▷ vt If you **tell** someone to do something, you say that they must do it. বলা ▷ vt If you can **tell** something, you know it. বলতে পারা

teller (tellers) n A **teller** is someone who works in a bank and who customers pay money to or get money from. খাজাঞ্চি

tell off v If you **tell** someone **off**, you speak to them angrily or seriously because they have done something wrong. তিরস্কার করা *I'm always getting told off for being late.*

telly (tellies) n A **telly** is a piece of equipment consisting of a box with a glass screen on it on which you can watch programmes with pictures and sounds. *(informal)* টেলিভিশন

temp (temps) n A **temp** is a person who is employed by an agency that sends them to work in different offices for short periods of time, for example to replace someone who is ill or on holiday. অস্থায়ী কর্মী

temper (tempers) n If you say that someone has a **temper**, you mean that they become angry very easily. মেজাজ

temperature (temperatures) n The **temperature** of something is how hot or cold it is. তাপমাত্রা

temple (temples) n A **temple** is a building used for the worship of a god or gods, especially in the Buddhist and Hindu religions. মন্দির

temporary adj Something that is **temporary** lasts for only a limited time. অস্থায়ী

tempt (tempts, tempting, tempted) v Something that **tempts** you attracts you and makes you want it, even though it may be wrong or harmful. প্রলুব্ধ করা

temptation (temptations) n **Temptation** is the state you are in when you want to do or have something, although you know it might be wrong or harmful. প্রলোভন

tempting *adj* If something is **tempting**, it makes you want to do it or have it. প্রলুব্ধকর

ten *num* **Ten** is the number 10. দশ

tenant (tenants) *n* A **tenant** is someone who pays rent for the place they live in, or for land or buildings that they use. ভাড়াটে

tend (tends, tending, tended) *vi* If something **tends** to happen, it usually happens or it happens often. ঝোঁক থাকা

tendency (tendencies) *n* A **tendency** is a worrying or unpleasant habit or action that keeps occurring. প্রবণতা

tender (tenderer, tenderest) *adj* Someone or something that is **tender** is kind and gentle. নরম

tendon (tendons) *n* A **tendon** is a strong cord of tissue in your body joining a muscle to a bone. কণ্ডরা

tennis *n* **Tennis** is a game played by two or four players on a rectangular court with a net across the middle. The players use rackets to hit a ball over the net. টেনিস

tennis court (tennis courts) *n* A **tennis court** is an area in which you play the game of tennis. টেনিস কোর্ট

tennis player (tennis players) *n* A **tennis player** is a person who plays tennis, either as a job or for fun. টেনিস খেলোয়াড়

tennis racket (tennis rackets) *n* A **tennis racket** is the racket that you use when you play tennis. টেনিস ব্যাট

tenor (tenors) *n* A **tenor** is a male singer with a fairly high voice. উচ্চ আওয়াজসম্পন্ন পুরুষ গায়ক

tenpin bowling *n* **Tenpin bowling** is a game in which you try to knock down ten objects shaped like bottles by rolling a heavy ball towards them. It is usually played in a place called a bowling alley. টেনপিন বোলিং

tense (tenser, tensest, tenses) *adj* If you are **tense**, you are worried and nervous, and

cannot relax. স্নায়ুচাপে পীড়িত ▷ *n* The **tense** of a verb group is its form, which usually shows whether you are referring to past, present, or future time. ক্রিয়ার কাল

tension (tensions) *n* **Tension** is a feeling of fear or nervousness produced before a difficult, dangerous, or important event. স্নায়ুচাপ পীড়ন

tent (tents) *n* A **tent** is a shelter made of canvas or nylon and held up by poles and ropes, used mainly by people who are camping. তাঁবু

tenth (tenths) *adj* The **tenth** item in a series is the one that you count as number ten. দশম ▷ *n* A **tenth** is one of ten equal parts of something. এক-দশমাংশ

term (terms) *n* A **term** is a word or expression with a specific meaning. শব্দ ▷ *n* A **term** is one of the periods of time that a school, college, or university year is divided into. শিক্ষাবর্ষের ভাগ

terminal (terminals) *adj* A **terminal** illness or disease cannot be cured and eventually causes death. অন্তিম ▷ *n* A **terminal** is a place where vehicles, passengers, or goods begin or end a journey. প্রান্ত

terminally *adv* If someone is **terminally** ill, it means that they will die of an illness or disease that cannot be cured. চূড়ান্তভাবে

terrace (terraces) *n* A **terrace** is a row of similar houses joined together by their side walls. ছাদ

terraced *adj* A **terraced** slope or side of a hill has flat areas like steps cut into it, where crops or other plants can be grown. ধাপ কাটা

terrible *adj* **Terrible** means extremely bad. সাংঘাতিক

terribly *adv* **Terribly** means in an extremely bad manner. সাংঘাতিকভাবে

terrier (terriers) *n* A **terrier** is a small breed of dog. There are many different types of terrier. টেরিয়ার

terrific *adj* If you describe something or someone as **terrific**, you are very pleased with them or very impressed by them. (*informal*) দারুণ

terrified *adj* If you are **terrified**, you are extremely frightened. সন্ত্রস্ত

terrify (terrifies, terrifying, terrified) *vt* If something **terrifies** you, it makes you feel extremely frightened. সন্ত্রস্ত হওয়া

territory (territories) *n* **Territory** is land which is controlled by a particular country or ruler. শাসিত অঞ্চল

terrorism *n* **Terrorism** is the use of violence in order to achieve political aims or to force a government to do something. উগ্রপন্থা

terrorist (terrorists) *n* A **terrorist** is a person who uses violence in order to achieve political aims. উগ্রপন্থী

terrorist attack (terrorist attacks) *n* A **terrorist attack** is a violent incident, usually involving murder and bombing, carried out by people who are trying to achieve political aims. উগ্রপন্থী হামলা

test (tests, testing, tested) *n* A **test** is an action or experiment to find out how well something works. পরীক্ষা ▷ *vt* If you **test** something, you try it to see what it is like, or how it works. পরীক্ষা করা ▷ *n* A **test** is something you do to show how much you know or what you can do. পরীক্ষা

testicle (testicles) *n* A man's **testicles** are the two sex glands that produce sperm. অন্ডকোষ

test tube (test tubes) *n* A **test tube** is a small tube-shaped container made from glass. Test tubes are used in laboratories. পরীক্ষার নল

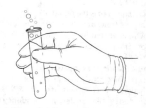

tetanus *n* **Tetanus** is a serious painful disease caused by bacteria getting into wounds. It makes your muscles, especially your jaw muscles, go stiff. ধনুষ্টংকার

text (texts, texting, texted) *n* **Text** is any written material. লিখিত বস্তু ▷ *vt* If you **text** someone, you send them a text message on a mobile phone. বার্তা পাঠানো

textbook (textbooks) *n* A **textbook** is a book about a particular subject that is intended for students. পাঠ্যবই

textile (textiles) *n* **Textiles** are types of woven cloth. বস্ত্র

text message (text messages) *n* A **text message** is a message that you send using a mobile phone. বার্তা

Thai (Thais) *adj* **Thai** means belonging or relating to Thailand, or to its people, language, or culture. থাইল্যান্ড দেশীয় ▷ *n* A **Thai** is a person who comes from Thailand. থাইল্যান্ডের নাগরিক ▷ *n* **Thai** is the language spoken in Thailand. থাইল্যান্ডের ভাষা

Thailand *n* **Thailand** is a kingdom in south-east Asia, on the Andaman Sea and the Gulf of Thailand. থাইল্যান্ড

than *prep* You use **than** when you are talking about the difference between two people or things. অপেক্ষা *Children learn faster than adults.*

thank (thanks, thanking, thanked) *vt* When you **thank** someone for something,

you express your gratitude to them for it.
ধন্যবাদ দেওয়া

thanks! *excl* You can say '**thanks!**' to
show that you are grateful to someone for
something they have done. ধন্যবাদ

that *det* You use **that** to talk about
something that you have mentioned before.
তাহা *For that reason the claims procedure
is as simple and helpful as possible.* ▷ *conj*
You use **that** to join two different things
you are saying. যেটা *I felt sad that he was
leaving.* ▷ *pron* You use **that** to talk about
something that you have mentioned before.
তাহা *They said you wanted to talk to me. Why
was that?* ▷ *det* You use **that** to talk about
somebody or something a distance away
from you. ওই *Look at that car over there.*
❑ *Who's that beautiful girl?* ▷ *pron* You use
that to talk about somebody or something
a distance away from you. ওই *Who's that?*
▷ *pron* You use **that** to show which person
or thing you are talking about. ওই *There's
the girl that I told you about.*

thatched *adj* A **thatched** house has a roof
made of straw or reeds. খড় ছাওয়া চাল

the *det* You use **the** before a noun when
it is clear which person or thing you are
talking about. টি *It's always hard to think
about the future.* ▷ *det* You use **the** before
a noun to talk about things of that type in
general. এই *The computer has developed
very quickly in recent years.*

theatre (**theatres**) *n* A **theatre** is a
building with a stage on which plays and
other entertainments are performed.
রঙ্গমঞ্চ

theft (**thefts**) *n* **Theft** is the criminal act of
stealing. চুরি

their *det* You use **their** to say that something
belongs to a group of people, animals, or
things. তাদের *They took off their coats.*

theirs *pron* You use **theirs** to say that
something belongs to a group of people,
animals, or things. কেবলমাত্র তাদের *The house
next to theirs was empty.*

them *pron* You use **them** to talk about
more than one person, animal, or thing.
তাদেরকে *I've lost my keys. Have you seen them?*

theme (**themes**) *n* A **theme** in a piece of
writing, a discussion, or a work of art is an
important idea or subject in it. বিষয়বস্তু

theme park (**theme parks**) *n* A **theme park**
is a large outdoor area where people pay
to go to enjoy themselves. All the different
activities in a theme park are usually based
on a particular idea or theme. থিম পার্ক

themselves *pron* You use **themselves** to
talk about people, animals, or things that
you have just talked about. তারা নিজেরা *They
all seemed to be enjoying themselves.*

then *adv* **Then** means at that time. তখন
▷ *conj* You also use **then** to say that one
thing happens after another. (*informal*)
তারপর *She said good night, then went to bed.*

theology *n* **Theology** is the study of
religion. ধর্মতত্ত্ব

theory (**theories**) *n* A **theory** is a formal
idea or set of ideas intended to explain
something. তত্ত্ব

therapy *n* **Therapy** is the treatment of
mental or physical illness without the use of
drugs or operations. ঔষধবর্জিত চিকিৎসা

there *adv* **There** also means to a place, or
at a place. সেখানে ▷ *pron* You use **there**
to say that something is in a place or is
happening, or to make someone notice it.
কোন জায়গায় *There are flowers on the table.*

therefore *adv* You use **therefore** when you
are talking about the result of something.
সুতরাং

thermometer (**thermometers**) *n* A
thermometer is an instrument for
measuring the temperature of a room or of
a person's body. থার্মোমিটার

t

Thermos® (**Thermoses**) *n* A **Thermos** or **Thermos flask** is a container which is used to keep hot drinks hot or cold drinks cold. It has two thin shiny glass walls with no air between them. থার্মোস

thermostat (**thermostats**) *n* A **thermostat** is a device that switches a system or motor on or off according to the temperature. Thermostats are used, for example, in central heating systems and fridges. থার্মোস্ট্যাট

these *det* You use **these** to talk about someone or something that you have already mentioned. এইগুলি *These people need more support.* ▷ *pron* You use **these** to talk about people or things that are near you. এইগুলি *I like these, on this table.* ▷ *det* You use **these** to talk about people or things that are near you. এইগুলি *These bags are very heavy.* ▷ *det* You use **these** to introduce people or things that you are going to talk about. এইগুলি *If you're looking for a builder, these phone numbers will be useful.*

they *pron* You use **they** when you are talking about more than one person, animal, or thing. তাহারা *They are all in the same class.*

thick (**thicker, thickest**) *adj* If something is **thick**, it is deep or wide between one side and the other. পুরু ▷ *adj* If a liquid is **thick**, it flows slowly. ঘন

thickness (**thicknesses**) *n* The **thickness** of something is the distance between its two opposite surfaces. পুরুত্ব

thief (**thieves**) *n* A **thief** is a person who steals something from another person. চোর

thigh (**thighs**) *n* Your **thighs** are the top parts of your legs, between your knees and your hips. ঊরু

thin (**thinner, thinnest**) *adj* If something is **thin**, it is narrow between one side and the other. পাতলা ▷ *adj* If a person or animal is **thin**, they are not fat and they do not weigh much. রোগা

thing (**things**) *n* You use **thing** as a substitute for another word when you are unable to be more precise, or you do not need or want to be more precise. জিনিস

think (**thinks, thinking, thought**) *v* If you **think** something, you believe that it is true. মনে করা ▷ *vi* When you **think**, you use your mind. চিন্তা করা

third (**thirds**) *adj* The **third** item in a series is the one that you count as number three. তৃতীয় ▷ *n* A **third** is one of three equal parts of something. এক তৃতীয়াংশ

thirdly *adv* You use **thirdly** when you are about to mention the third thing in a series of items. তৃতীয়তঃ

third-party insurance *n* **Third-party insurance** is insurance that covers you if you injure someone or damage someone's property. থার্ড পার্টি ইন্সিওরেন্স

thirst (**thirsts**) *n* **Thirst** is the feeling that you need to drink something. তৃষ্ণা

thirsty (**thirstier, thirstiest**) *adj* If you are **thirsty**, you feel a need to drink something. তৃষ্ণার্ত

thirteen *num* **Thirteen** is the number 13. ত্রয়োদশ

thirteenth *adj* The **thirteenth** item in a series is the one that you count as number thirteen. ত্রয়োদশতম

thirty *num* **Thirty** is the number 30. ত্রিশ

this *det* You use **this** to talk about someone or something that you have already mentioned. এই *How can we resolve this problem?* ▷ *pron* You use **this** to talk about somebody or something near you. এইখানি *'Would you like a different one?'—'No, this is great.'* ▷ *det* You use **this** followed by a noun, or followed by an adjective and a noun, to talk about somebody or something that is near you. এই *I like this room much better than the other one.* ▷ *pron* You use **this** to introduce someone or something that you are going to talk about. এইটি *This is what I will do. I will call her and explain.*

thistle (**thistles**) *n* A **thistle** is a wild plant which has leaves with sharp points and purple flowers. কাঁটাছবিশেষ

thorn (**thorns**) *n* **Thorns** are the sharp points on some plants and trees such as roses and holly. কাঁটা

thorough *adj* A **thorough** action is done very carefully and methodically. পুঙ্খানুপুঙ্খ

thoroughly *adv* If somebody does something **thoroughly**, they do it with great care. পুঙ্খানুপুঙ্খরূপে

those *det* You use **those** to talk about people or things that have already been mentioned. ওইগুলি *I don't know any of those people you mentioned.* ▷ *pron* You use **those** to talk about people or things a distance away from you. ওইগুলি *Those are nice shoes.* ▷ *det* You use **those** to talk about people or things a distance away from you. ওইগুলি *What are those buildings?*

though *adv* You use **though** when talking about an idea that is not what you would expect. যদিও ▷ *conj* You use **though** to add information that changes what you have already said. তবুও *They went to the same school, though they never met there.* ▷ *conj* You use **though** to start talking about an idea that is not what you would expect. যদিও *He plays in adult tennis games even though he is only 15.*

thought (**thoughts**) *n* A **thought** is an idea or opinion. মনন

thoughtful *adj* If you are **thoughtful**, you are quiet and serious because you are thinking about something. মননশীল

thoughtless *adj* If you describe someone as **thoughtless**, you are critical of them because they forget or ignore other people's wants, needs, or feelings. মননহীন

thousand *num* A **thousand** or one **thousand** is the number 1,000. সহস্র

thousandth (**thousandths**) *adj* The **thousandth** item in a series is the one you count as number one thousand. সহস্রতম ▷ *n* A **thousandth** is one of a thousand equal parts of something. এক-সহস্রাংশ

thread (**threads**) *n* **Thread** or a **thread** is a long very thin piece of a material such as cotton, nylon, or silk, especially one that is used in sewing. সুতো

threat (**threats**) *n* A **threat** to someone or something is a danger that something unpleasant might happen to them. হুমকি

threaten (**threatens, threatening, threatened**) *vt* If someone **threatens** to do something unpleasant to you, or if they **threaten** you, they say or imply that they will do something unpleasant to you, especially if you do not do what they want. হুমকি দেওয়া

threatening *adj* You can describe someone's behaviour as **threatening** when you think that they are trying to harm you. ভীতিজনক

three *num* **Three** is the number 3. তিন

three-dimensional *adj* A **three-dimensional** object is solid rather than flat, because it can be measured in three dimensions, usually the height, length, and width. ত্রিমাত্রিক

thrifty (**thriftier, thriftiest**) *adj* If you say that someone is **thrifty**, you are praising them for saving money, not buying unnecessary things, and not wasting things. হিসাবী

thrill (**thrills**) *n* If something gives you a **thrill**, it gives you a sudden feeling of great excitement, pleasure, or fear. রোমাঞ্চ

thrilled *adj* If you are **thrilled** about something, you are pleased and excited about it. রোমাঞ্চিত

thriller (**thrillers**) *n* A **thriller** is a book, film, or play that tells an exciting story about something such as criminal activities or spying. রোমাঞ্চকর কাহিনী

thrilling *adj* Something that is **thrilling** is very exciting and enjoyable. রোমাঞ্চকর

throat (**throats**) *n* Your **throat** is the back part of your mouth that you use to swallow and to breathe. গলা ▷ *n* Your **throat** is the front part of your neck. টুঁটি

throb (**throbs, throbbing, throbbed**) *vi* If part of your body **throbs**, you feel a series of strong and usually painful beats there. স্পন্দিত হওয়া

throne (**thrones**) *n* A **throne** is an ornate chair used by a king, queen, or emperor on important occasions. সিংহাসন

through *prep* **Through** means going all the way from one side of something to the other side. মধ্যে *We walked through the forest.*

throughout *prep* If something happens **throughout** a period of time, it happens for all of that period. সম্পূর্ণরূপে *It rained heavily throughout the game.*

throw (**throws, throwing, threw, thrown**) *vt* If you **throw** an object that you are holding, you move your hand quickly and let go of the object, so that it moves through the air. ছোঁড়া

throw away *v* If you **throw away** or **throw out** something you do not want, you get rid of it. ফেলা দেওয়া *I never throw anything away.*

throw out *v* When you **throw out** something that you do not want, you get rid of it. ফেলা দেওয়া

throw up *v* To **throw up** means to vomit. (*informal*) বমি করা *She threw up after reading reports of the trial.*

thrush (**thrushes**) *n* A **thrush** is a small brown bird with small marks on its chest. গায়ক পক্ষী

thug (**thugs**) *n* If you refer to someone as a **thug**, you think they are violent or a criminal. খুনে

thumb (**thumbs**) *n* Your **thumb** is the short, thick digit on the side of your hand next to your first finger. বুড়ো আঙুল

thumbtack (**thumbtacks**) *n* A **thumbtack** is a short pin with a broad flat top which is used for fastening papers or pictures to a board, wall, or other surface. (*US*) ছোট মাথাওয়ালা পেরেক

thump (**thumps, thumping, thumped**) *v* If you **thump** something, you hit it hard, usually with your fist. ঘুসি মারা

thunder *n* **Thunder** is the loud noise that you hear from the sky after a flash of lightning, especially during a storm. বজ্র

thunderstorm (**thunderstorms**) *n* A **thunderstorm** is a storm in which there is thunder, lightning, and heavy rain. বজ্রবিদ্যুৎসহ ঝোড়ো বৃষ্টি

thundery *adj* When the weather is **thundery**, there is a lot of thunder, or there are heavy clouds which make you think that there will be thunder soon. বজ্রপাতযুক্ত

Thursday (**Thursdays**) *n* **Thursday** is the day after Wednesday and before Friday. বৃহস্পতিবার

thyme *n* **Thyme** is a type of herb. একপ্রকার সুগন্ধি লতা

Tibet *n* **Tibet** is an autonomous region of south-west China. তিব্বত

Tibetan (**Tibetans**) *adj* **Tibetan** means of, relating to, or characteristic of Tibet, its people, or their language. তিব্বত দেশীয় ▷ *n* A **Tibetan** is a native or inhabitant of Tibet. তিব্বতী ▷ *n* **Tibetan** is a language spoken by people who live in Tibet. তিব্বতী ভাষা

tick (**ticks, ticking, ticked**) *n* A **tick** is a written mark like a V with the right side extended. You use it to show that something is correct or has been dealt with. টিক চিহ্ন ▷ *vt* If you **tick** something that is written on a piece of paper, you put a tick next to it. চিহ্নিত করা

ticket (**tickets**) *n* A **ticket** is an official piece of paper or card which shows that you have paid for a journey or have paid to enter a place of entertainment. টিকিট

ticket machine (**ticket machines**) *n* A **ticket machine** is a machine, for example in a railway station, from which you can get tickets by putting in money and pressing a button. টিকিট কাটার মেশিন

ticket office (**ticket offices**) *n* A **ticket office** is a place, for example at a theatre, cinema, or railway station, where tickets are sold. টিকিট বিক্রির অফিস

tickle (**tickles, tickling, tickled**) *vt* When you **tickle** someone, you move your fingers lightly over their body, often in order to make them laugh. কাতুকুতু দেওয়া

ticklish *adj* A **ticklish** problem, situation, or task is difficult and needs to be dealt with carefully. কষ্টসাধ্য,সহজে কাতুকুতু লাগে এমন

tick off *v* If you **tick off** an item on a list, you put a tick by it to show that it has been dealt with. দাগ দিয়ে রাখা *He ticked off my name on a piece of paper.*

tide (**tides**) *n* The **tide** is the regular change in the level of the sea on the shore. জোয়ার-ভাটা

tidy (**tidier, tidiest, tidies, tidying, tidied**) *adj* Something that is **tidy** is neat and arranged in an orderly way. পরিষ্কার পরিচ্ছন্ন ▷ *vt* When you **tidy** a place, you make it neat by putting things in their proper places. পরিষ্কার পরিচ্ছন্ন করা

tidy up *v* When you **tidy up** or **tidy** a place **up**, you put things back in their proper places so that everything is neat. গোছগাছ করা *She spent an hour tidying up the shop.*

tie (**ties, tying, tied**) *n* A **tie** is a long, narrow piece of cloth that you tie in a knot in and wear around your neck with a shirt. টাই ▷ *vt* If you **tie** something, you fasten it with string or a rope. বাঁধা

tie up *v* When you **tie** something **up**, you fasten string or rope round it so that it is firm or secure. শক্ত করে বাঁধা *He tied up the bag and took it outside.*

tiger (**tigers**) *n* A **tiger** is a large fierce animal belonging to the cat family. Tigers are orange with black stripes. বাঘ

tight (**tighter, tightest**) *adj* If clothes are **tight**, they are so small that they fit very close to your body. আঁটসাঁট ▷ *adj* Something that is **tight** is fastened so that it is not easy to move it. বাঁধা

tighten (**tightens, tightening, tightened**) *v* If you **tighten** your grip on something,

or if your grip on something **tightens**, you hold it more firmly or securely. আঁটা

tights *npl* **Tights** are a piece of clothing made of thin material such as nylon which covers your hips and each of your legs and feet separately. একপ্রকার আঁটসাঁট পোশাক

tile (**tiles**) *n* **Tiles** are flat square pieces of baked clay, carpet, cork, or other substance, which are fixed as a covering onto a floor, wall, or roof. টালি

tiled *adj* A **tiled** surface is covered with tiles. টালি দ্বারা বাঁধানো

till (**tills**) *conj* If something happens **till** something else happens, the first thing happens before the other thing and stops when the other thing happens. (*informal*) যতক্ষণ পর্যন্ত *They slept till the alarm woke them.* ▷ *n* In a shop, a **till** is a cash register where money is kept, and where customers pay for what they have bought. টাকা রাখবার কাউন্টার ▷ *prep* If something happens **till** a time, it happens before that time and stops at that time. (*informal*) যতক্ষণ পর্যন্ত *She lived there till last year.* ▷ *prep* If something does not happen **till** a time, it does not happen before that time and only starts happening at that time. (*informal*) পর্যন্ত *The shop doesn't open till half past nine.*

timber *n* **Timber** is wood used for building houses and making furniture. কাঠ

time *n* **Time** is how long something takes to happen. We measure **time** in minutes, hours, days, weeks, months, and years. সময় ▷ *n* The **time** is a moment in the day that you describe in hours and minutes. সময়

time bomb (**time bombs**) *n* A **time bomb** is a bomb with a mechanism that causes it to explode at a particular time. টাইম বম্ব

time off *n* If you have **time off**, you do not go to work or school, for example, because you are ill or it is a day when you do not usually work. ছুটি

timer (**timers**) *n* A **timer** is a device that measures time, especially one that is part of a machine and causes it to start or stop working at specific times. সময়-পরিমাপক যন্ত্র

timetable (**timetables**) n A **timetable** is a plan of the times when particular events are to take place. সময় সারণী

time zone (**time zones**) n A **time zone** is one of the areas into which the world is divided where the time is calculated as being a particular number of hours behind or ahead of GMT. সময়-মান মণ্ডল

tin (**tins**) n **Tin** is a kind of soft, pale grey metal. টিন ▷ n A **tin** is a metal container for food. ধাতুর কৌটো

tinfoil n **Tinfoil** consists of shiny metal in the form of a thin sheet which is used for wrapping food. টিন ফয়েল

tinned adj **Tinned** food has been preserved by being sealed in a tin. কৌটোয় সংরক্ষিত

tin opener (**tin openers**) n A **tin opener** is a tool that is used for opening tins of food. কৌটো খোলার যন্ত্র

tinsel n **Tinsel** consists of small strips of shiny paper attached to long pieces of thread. People use tinsel as a decoration. চকচকে কাগজ

tinted adj If something is **tinted**, it has a small amount of a particular colour or dye in it. আবছা

tiny (**tinier, tiniest**) adj Someone or something that is **tiny** is extremely small. ক্ষুদ্র

tip (**tips, tipping, tipped**) n The **tip** of something long and narrow is the end of it. প্রান্ত ▷ n If you give someone such as a waiter a **tip**, you give them some money for their services. বকশিস ▷ n A **tip** is a useful piece of advice. পরামর্শ ▷ v If an object or part of your body **tips**, or if you **tip** it, it moves into a sloping position with one end or side higher than the other. মাথা হেলানো ▷ vt If you **tip** someone such as a waiter, you give them some money for their services. বকশিশ দেওয়া

tipsy adj If someone is **tipsy**, they are slightly drunk. নেশাগ্রস্ত

tired adj If you are **tired**, you feel that you want to rest or sleep. ক্লান্ত

tiring adj If you describe something as **tiring**, you mean that it makes you tired so that you want to rest or sleep. ক্লান্তিকর

tissue (**tissues**) n In animals and plants, **tissue** consists of cells that are similar in appearance and function. টিস্যু

title (**titles**) n The **title** of a book, play, film, or piece of music is its name. শিরোনাম

to prep You use **to** when you are talking about the position or direction of something. প্রতি She went to the window and looked out. ▷ You use **to** before the infinitive (= the simple form of a verb). এর It was time to leave.

toad (**toads**) n A **toad** is an animal like a frog, but with a drier skin. ব্যাঙ

toadstool (**toadstools**) n A **toadstool** is a fungus that you cannot eat because it is poisonous. বিষাক্ত ছত্রাক

toast (**toasts**) n **Toast** is slices of bread heated until they are brown and crisp. টোস্ট ▷ n When you drink a **toast** to someone, you wish them success or good health, and then drink some alcoholic drink. শুভেচ্ছা

toaster (**toasters**) n A **toaster** is a piece of electric equipment used to toast bread. টোস্ট বানানোর যন্ত্র

tobacco (**tobaccos**) n **Tobacco** is the dried leaves of a plant which people smoke in pipes, cigars, and cigarettes. তামাক

tobacconist (**tobbaconists**) n A **tobacconist** or a **tobacconist's** is a shop that sells cigarettes, tobacco, etc. তামাক বিক্রির দোকান

toboggan (**toboggans**) n A **toboggan** is a light wooden board with a curved front, used for travelling down hills on snow or ice. হাল্কা কাঠের বোর্ড

tobogganing n **Tobogganing** is the activity of travelling down a slope on snow or ice using a toboggan. বরফের ওপর খেলা

today adv You use **today** to refer to the day on which you are speaking or writing. আজ

toddler (toddlers) n A **toddler** is a young child who has only just learnt to walk. বাচ্চা

toe (toes) n Your **toes** are the five movable parts at the end of each foot. পায়ের আঙুল

toffee (toffees) n A **toffee** is a sweet made by boiling sugar and butter together with water. টফি

together adv If people do something **together**, they do it with each other. একসাথে

Togo n **Togo** is a republic in West Africa, on the Gulf of Guinea. টোগো (দেশ)

toilet (toilets) n A **toilet** is a large bowl connected to the drains which you use when you want to get rid of urine or faeces from your body. শৌচাগার

toilet bag (toilet bags) n A **toilet bag** is a small bag in which you keep things such as soap, a flannel, and a toothbrush when you are travelling. প্রসাধনী থলে

toilet paper n **Toilet paper** is paper that you use to clean yourself after getting rid of urine or faeces from your body. শৌচাগারে ব্যবহৃত কাগজ

toiletries npl **Toiletries** are products such as soap and toothpaste that you use when cleaning or taking care of your body. প্রসাধনী সামগ্রী

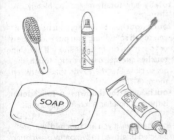

toilet roll (toilet rolls) n A **toilet roll** is a long narrow strip of toilet paper that is wound around a small cardboard tube. শৌচাগারে ব্যবহৃত কাগজের বান্ডিল

token (tokens) n A **token** is a piece of paper, plastic, or metal which can be used instead of money. টোকন

tolerant adj If you are **tolerant**, you let other people say and do what they like, even if you do not agree with it or approve of it. সহিষ্ণু

toll (tolls) n A **toll** is a sum of money that you have to pay in order to use a particular bridge or road. পথ কর

tomato (tomatoes) n A **tomato** is a small, soft, red fruit that is used in cooking as a vegetable or eaten raw in salads. টমেটো

tomato sauce n **Tomato sauce** is a thick sauce made with tomatoes and often served with pasta. টমেটো সস

tomb (tombs) n A **tomb** is a stone structure containing the body of a dead person. সমাধি সৌধ

tomboy (tomboys) n If you say that a girl is a **tomboy**, you mean that she likes playing rough or noisy games, or doing things that were traditionally considered to be things that boys enjoy. পুরুষালী মেয়ে

tomorrow adv You use **tomorrow** to refer to the day after today. আগামী কাল

ton (tons) n A non-metric **ton** is a unit of weight equal to 2,240 pounds in Britain and 2,000 pounds in the United States. টন (পরিমাপ)

tongue (tongues) n Your **tongue** is the soft movable part inside your mouth that you use for tasting, licking, and speaking. জিভ

tonic (tonics) n **Tonic** or **tonic water** is a colourless, fizzy drink that has a slightly bitter flavour. টনিক

tonight adv **Tonight** is used to refer to the evening of today or the night that follows today. আজ রাত

tonsillitis n **Tonsillitis** is a painful swelling of your tonsils caused by an infection. টনসিলের অসুখ

tonsils *npl* Your **tonsils** are the two small soft lumps in your throat at the back of your mouth. টনসিল

too *adv* **Too** means also. এছাড়া ▷ *adv* You also use **too** to mean more than you want or need. খুব বেশি

tool (**tools**) *n* A **tool** is any instrument or simple piece of equipment, for example, a hammer or a knife, that you hold in your hands and use to do a particular kind of work. হাতিয়ার

tooth (**teeth**) *n* Your **teeth** are the hard, white things in your mouth that you use to bite and chew food. দাঁত ▷ The **teeth** of a comb, a saw, or a zip are the parts that are in a row along its edge. ধারাল দাঁত

toothache *n* **Toothache** is pain in one of your teeth. দাঁতব্যথা

toothbrush (**toothbrushes**) *n* A **toothbrush** is a small brush used for cleaning your teeth. দাঁত মাজার ব্রাশ

toothpaste (**toothpastes**) *n* **Toothpaste** is a thick substance which you use to clean your teeth. দাঁতের মাজন

toothpick (**toothpicks**) *n* A **toothpick** is a small stick which you use to remove food from between your teeth. দাঁত কাঠি

top (**tops**) *n* The **top** thing is the highest one. শীর্ষস্থান ▷ *n* The **top** of something is the highest part of it. উঁচু অংশ ▷ *n* The **top** of something is the part that fits over the end of it. ওপরের অংশ

topic (**topics**) *n* A **topic** is a particular subject that you write about or discuss. প্রসঙ্গ

topical *adj* **Topical** means relating to events that are happening at the time when you are speaking or writing. ঘটনা অনুযায়ী

top-secret *adj* **Top-secret** information or activity is intended to be kept completely secret. অতি গোপন

top-up card (**top-up cards**) *n* A **top-up card** is a card bought by a mobile-phone user entitling him or her to a stipulated amount of credit for future calls. মোবাইলে ব্যবহৃত কার্ড

torch (**torches**) *n* A **torch** is a small, battery-powered electric light which you carry in your hand. টর্চ

tornado (**tornadoes, tornados**) *n* A **tornado** is a violent storm with strong circular winds. ঘূর্ণিঝড়

tortoise (**tortoises**) *n* A **tortoise** is a slow-moving animal with a shell into which it can pull its head and legs for protection. কচ্ছপ

torture (**tortures, torturing, tortured**) *n* If someone is subjected to **torture**, another person deliberately causes them great pain, in order to punish them or make them reveal information. নির্যাতন ▷ *vt* If someone **is tortured**, another person deliberately causes them great pain over a period of time, in order to punish them or to make them reveal information. নির্যাতন করা

toss (**tosses, tossing, tossed**) *vt* If you **toss** something somewhere, you throw it there lightly and carelessly. নিক্ষেপ করা

total (**totals**) *adj* The **total** number or cost of something is the number or cost that you get when you add together or count all the parts in it. মোট ▷ *n* A **total** is the number that you get when you add several numbers together or when you count how many things there are in a group. যোগফল

totally *adv* **Totally** means completely. সম্পূর্ণরূপে

touch (**touches, touching, touched**) *vt* If you **touch** something, you put your fingers or your hand on it. স্পর্শ করা ▷ *v* If one thing **touches** another, or two things **touch**, they are so close that there is no space between them. ছোঁয়া

touchdown (**touchdowns**) *n* **Touchdown** is the landing of an aircraft or spacecraft. অবতরণ

touched *adj* If you are **touched**, you are affected or moved to sympathy or emotion. অভিভূত

touching *adj* If something is **touching**, it causes feelings of sadness or sympathy. হৃদয়স্পর্শী

touchline n In sports such as rugby and football, the **touchline** is one of the two lines which mark the side of the playing area. পার্শ্ব রেখা

touch pad (touch pads) n A **touch pad** is a flat pad on some computers that you slide your finger over in order to move the cursor. টাচপ্যাড

touchy (touchier, touchiest) adj **Touchy** people are easily upset or irritated. স্পর্শ কাতর

tough (tougher, toughest) adj A **tough** person has a strong character and can tolerate difficulty or hardship. কষ্টসহিষ্ণু

toupee (toupees) n A **toupee** is a piece of artificial hair worn by a man to cover a patch on his head where he has lost his hair. পরচুল

tour (tours, touring, toured) n A **tour** is an organized trip that people such as musicians, politicians, or theatre companies go on to several different places, stopping to meet people or perform. ভ্রমণ ▷ v When people such as musicians, politicians, or theatre companies **tour**, they go on a tour, for example in order to perform or to meet people. ভ্রমণ করা

tour guide (tour guides) n A **tour guide** is someone who helps tourists who are on holiday or shows them round a place. ভ্রমণ নির্দেশক

tourism n **Tourism** is the business of providing services for people on holiday. পর্যটন

tourist (tourists) n A **tourist** is a person who is visiting a place for pleasure, especially when they are on holiday. পর্যটক

tourist office (tourist offices) n A **tourist office** is a place where tourists can go to get information, to make bookings, etc. পর্যটন দপ্তর

tournament (tournaments) n A **tournament** is a sports competition in which players who win a match continue to play further matches until just one person or team is left. প্রতিযোগিতা

towards prep **Towards** means in the direction of something. অভিমুখে He moved towards the door.

tow away v If one vehicle **tows away** another, it removes it by pulling it along behind it. টেনে নিয়ে যাওয়া They threatened to tow away my car.

towel (towels) n A **towel** is a piece of thick, soft cloth that you use to dry yourself with. তোয়ালে

tower (towers) n A **tower** is a tall narrow structure that is often part of a castle. চূড়া

town (towns) n A **town** is a place with many streets and buildings where people live and work. শহর

town centre (town centres) n The **town centre** is the main part of a town, where the shops are. শহরের কেন্দ্রস্থল

town hall (town halls) n The **town hall** in a town is a large building owned and used by the town council, often as its headquarters. টাউন হল

town planning n **Town planning** is the planning and design of all the new buildings, roads, and parks in a place in order to make them attractive and convenient for the people who live there. নগর পরিকল্পনা

toxic adj A **toxic** substance is poisonous. বিষাক্ত

toy (toys) n A **toy** is an object that children play with, for example, a doll or a model car. খেলনা

trace (traces) n A **trace** of something is a very small amount of it. অবশিষ্টাংশ

tracing paper n **Tracing paper** is transparent paper which you put over a picture so that you can draw over its lines in order to produce a copy of it. স্বচ্ছ কাগজ

track (tracks) n A **track** is a narrow road or path. সরু পথ

track down v If you **track down** someone or something, you find them after a long and difficult search. খোঁজ পাওয়া *It took two years to track him down.*

tracksuit (tracksuits) *n* A **tracksuit** is a loose, warm suit consisting of trousers and a top, worn mainly when exercising. ট্রাক স্যুট

tractor (tractors) *n* A **tractor** is a farm vehicle that is used for pulling farm machinery. ট্রাক্টর

trade (trades) *n* **Trade** is the activity of buying, selling, or exchanging goods or services between people, firms, or countries. ব্যবসা

trademark (trademarks) *n* A **trademark** is a name or symbol that a company uses on its products and that cannot legally be used by another company. মার্কা

trade union (trade unions) *n* A **trade union** is an organization formed by workers in order to represent their rights and interests to their employers. শ্রমিক সংঘ

trade unionist (trade unionists) *n* A **trade unionist** is an active member of a trade union. শ্রমিক নেতা

tradition (traditions) *n* A **tradition** is a custom or belief that has existed for a long time. ঐতিহ্য

traditional *adj* **Traditional** customs, · beliefs, or methods are ones that have existed for a long time without changing. চিরাচরিত

traffic *n* **Traffic** refers to all the vehicles that are moving along the roads in an area. যানবাহন

traffic jam (traffic jams) *n* A **traffic jam** is a long line of vehicles that cannot move because there is too much traffic, or because the road is blocked. যানজট

traffic lights *npl* **Traffic lights** are the coloured lights at road junctions which control the flow of traffic. ট্রাফিক লাইট

traffic warden (traffic wardens) *n* A **traffic warden** is a person whose job is to make sure that cars are not parked illegally. যান নিয়ন্ত্রক

tragedy (tragedies) *n* A **tragedy** is an extremely sad event or situation. বিয়োগান্তক

tragic *adj* Something that is **tragic** is extremely sad, usually because it involves suffering. মর্মস্পর্শী

trailer (trailers) *n* A **trailer** is a vehicle without an engine which is pulled by a car or lorry. ট্রেইলার

train (trains, training, trained) *n* A **train** is a long vehicle that is pulled by an engine along a railway line. ট্রেন ▷ *vt* If you **train** to do something, you learn the skills that you need in order to do it. প্রশিক্ষণ দেওয়া

trained *adj* A person who is **trained** in a particular kind of work has learned the skills that you need in order to do it. প্রশিক্ষণ প্রাপ্ত

trainee (trainees) *n* A **trainee** is a junior employee who is being taught how to do a job. শিক্ষানবিশ

trainer (trainers) *n* A **trainer** is someone who teaches you the skills you need to be able to do something. প্রশিক্ষক

trainers *npl* **Trainers** are shoes that people wear, especially for running and other sports. খেলার জুতো

training *n* **Training** is the process of learning the skills that you need for a particular job or activity. প্রশিক্ষণ

training course (training courses) *n* A **training course** is a series of lessons or lectures teaching the skills that you need for a particular job or activity. প্রশিক্ষণ পাঠ্যসূচী

tram (trams) *n* A **tram** is a public transport vehicle, usually powered by electricity, which travels along rails laid in the surface of a street. ট্রাম গাড়ি

tramp (tramps) *n* A **tramp** is a person with no home or job who travels around and gets money by doing occasional work or by begging. ভবঘুরে ▷ *n* A **tramp** is a difficult and long walk. কষ্টকর দীর্ঘপথ

trampoline (trampolines) *n* A **trampoline** is a piece of equipment on which you jump up and down as a sport. It consists of a large piece of strong cloth held by springs in a frame. ট্রাম্পোলিন (খেলার সামগ্রী)

tranquillizer (tranquillizers) n A **tranquillizer** is a drug that is used to make people or animals become sleepy or unconscious. ঘুমপাড়ানি ওষুধ

transaction (transactions) n A **transaction** is a business deal. (formal) লেনদেন

transcript (transcripts) n A **transcript** of something that is spoken is a written copy of it. প্রতিলিপি

transfer (transfers) n The **transfer** of something or someone is the act of transferring them. হস্তান্তর, বদলী

transform (transforms, transforming, transformed) vt To **transform** someone or something means to change them completely. রূপান্তর করা

transfusion (transfusions) n A blood **transfusion** is a process in which blood is injected into the body of a person who is badly injured or ill. শরীরে ঢোকান

transistor (transistors) n A **transistor** is a small electronic component in something such as a television or radio, which is used to amplify or control electronic signals. ট্রানজিস্টার

transit n Transit is the carrying of goods or people by vehicle from one place to another. স্থানান্তরণ

transition (transitions) n Transition is the process in which something changes from one state to another. রূপান্তর

translate (translates, translating, translated) vt If something that someone has said or written **is translated**, it is said or written again in a different language. অনুবাদ করা

translation (translations) n A **translation** is a piece of writing or speech that has been translated from a different language. অনুবাদ

translator (translators) n A **translator** is a person whose job is translating writing

or speech from one language to another. অনুবাদক

transparent adj If an object or substance is **transparent**, you can see through it. স্বচ্ছ

transplant (transplants) n A **transplant** is a surgical operation in which a part of a person's body is replaced because it is diseased. প্রতিস্থাপন

transport (transports, transporting, transported) n Transport refers to any type of vehicle that you can travel in. পরিবহন ▷ vt When goods or people **are transported** from one place to another, they are moved there. পরিবহন করা

transvestite (transvestites) n A **transvestite** is a person, usually a man, who enjoys wearing clothes normally worn by people of the opposite sex. যে অন্য লিঙ্গের পোশাক পড়ে

trap (traps) n A **trap** is a device which is placed somewhere or a hole which is dug somewhere in order to catch animals or birds. ফাঁদ

traumatic adj A **traumatic** experience is very shocking or upsetting, and may cause psychological damage. বেদনাবহ

travel (travels, travelling, travelled) n Travel is the act of travelling. ভ্রমণ ▷ vi If you **travel**, you go from one place to another, often to a place that is far away. ভ্রমণ করা

travel agency (travel agencies) n A **travel agency** is a business which makes arrangements for people's holidays and journeys. ভ্রমণ সংস্থা

travel agent (travel agents) n A **travel agent** is a person who arranges people's holidays and journeys. ভ্রমণ ব্যবস্থার দোকান

travel insurance n Travel insurance is an arrangement in which you pay money to a company, and they pay money to you if your property is stolen or damaged, or if you get a serious illness. ভ্রমণবীমা

traveller (travellers) n A **traveller** is a person who is making a journey or who travels a lot. ভ্রমণকারী

traveller's cheque (traveller's cheques)
n **Traveller's cheques** are special cheques
that you can exchange for local currency
when you are abroad. ট্রভেলার্র চেক

travelling n **Travelling** is the process of
going from one place to another, often one
that is far away. ভ্রমণ

tray (trays) n A **tray** is a flat piece of
wood, plastic, or metal that has raised
edges and that is used for carrying food
or drinks. পাত্র

treacle n **Treacle** is a thick, sweet, sticky
liquid that is obtained when sugar is
processed. It is used in making cakes and
puddings. চটচটে আঠালো মিষ্টি পদার্থ

tread (treads, treading, trod, trodden) vi
If you **tread on** something, you put your
foot on it when you are walking or standing.
পা রাখা

treasure n In children's stories, **treasure**
is a collection of valuable old objects,
such as gold coins and jewels. (literary)
ধনসম্পত্তি

treasurer (treasurers) n The **treasurer** of
a society or organization is the person in
charge of its finances. কোষাধ্যক্ষ

treat (treats, treating, treated) n If you
give someone a **treat**, you buy or arrange
something special for them which they will
enjoy. উপহার ▷ vt If you **treat** someone or
something in a particular way, you behave
towards them in that way. পণ্য করা

treatment (treatments) n **Treatment** is
medical attention given to a sick or injured
person or animal. চিকিৎসা

treaty (treaties) n A **treaty** is a written
agreement between countries. চুক্তি

treble (trebles, trebling, trebled) v If
something **trebles**, or if you **treble** it, it
becomes three times greater in number or
amount. তিনগুণ করা

tree (trees) n A **tree** is a tall plant with a
hard trunk, branches, and leaves. গাছ

trek (treks, trekking, trekked) n A **trek**
is a long and often difficult journey. কঠিন

দীর্ঘযাত্রা ▷ vi If you **trek** somewhere, you go
on a journey across difficult country, usually
on foot. কঠিন পথে চলা

tremble (trembles, trembling, trembled)
vi If you **tremble**, you shake slightly, usually
because you are frightened or cold. কাঁপা

tremendous adj You use **tremendous** to
emphasize how strong a feeling or quality
is, or how large an amount is. দারুণ

trench (trenches) n A **trench** is a long
narrow channel dug in the ground. সুড়ঙ্গ

trend (trends) n A **trend** is a change
towards something different. প্রবণতা

trendy (trendier, trendiest) adj If you say
that something or someone is **trendy**, you
mean that they are very fashionable and
modern. (informal) আধুনিক

trial (trials) n A **trial** is a formal meeting in
a law court, at which a judge and jury listen
to evidence and decide whether a person is
guilty of a crime. বিচার

trial period (trial periods) n If you are
on a **trial period** for a job, you do the job
for a short period of time to see if you are
suitable for it. পরীক্ষামূলক সময়

triangle (triangles) n A **triangle** is a shape
with three straight sides. ত্রিভুজ ▷ n A
triangle is an instrument made of metal in
the shape of a **triangle** that you hit with a
stick to make music. ধাতুর বাদ্যযন্ত্র

tribe (tribes) n **Tribe** is sometimes used
to refer to a group of people of the same
race, language, and customs, especially in a
developing country. উপজাতি

tribunal (tribunals) n A **tribunal** is
a special court or committee that is
appointed to deal with particular problems.
বিশেষ আদালত

trick (tricks, tricking, tricked) n A **trick**
is an action that is intended to deceive
someone. কৌশল ▷ vt If someone **tricks**
you, they deceive you, often in order to
make you do something. প্রতারণা করা

tricky (trickier, trickiest) adj A **tricky** task
or problem is difficult to deal with. কঠিন

tricycle (tricycles) *n* A **tricycle** is a cycle with three wheels, two at the back and one at the front. Tricycles are usually ridden by children. তিন চাকার সাইকেল

trifle (trifles) *n* **Trifles** are things that are not considered important. নগণ্য

trim (trims, trimming, trimmed) *vt* If you **trim** something, for example, someone's hair, you cut off small amounts of it in order to make it look neater and tidier. ছাঁটা

Trinidad and Tobago *n* **Trinidad and Tobago** is an independent republic in the Caribbean. ত্রিনিদাদ এন্ড টোবাগো, (দেশ)

trip (trips, tripping, tripped) *n* A **trip** is a journey that you make to a place and back again. ভ্রমণ ▷ *vi* If you **trip** when you are walking, you knock your foot against something and fall or nearly fall. হোঁচট খাওয়া

triple *adj* **Triple** means consisting of three things or parts. তিনটি অংশ

triplets *npl* **Triplets** are three children born at the same time to the same mother. ত্রয়ী

triumph (triumphs, triumphing, triumphed) *n* A **triumph** is a great success or achievement. বিজয় ▷ *vi* If you **triumph**, you win a victory or succeed in overcoming something. বিজয়প্রাপ্ত হওয়া

trivial *adj* If you describe something as **trivial**, you think that it is unimportant and not serious. তুচ্ছ

trolley (trolleys) *n* A **trolley** is a small cart on wheels that you use to carry things such as shopping or luggage. ট্রলি

trombone (trombones) *n* A **trombone** is a long brass musical instrument which you play by blowing into it and sliding part of it backwards and forwards. পেতলের বাদ্য যন্ত্র

troops *npl* **Troops** are soldiers. সৈন্য

trophy (trophies) *n* A **trophy** is a prize such as a cup, given to the winner of a competition. ট্রফি

tropical *adj* **Tropical** means belonging to or typical of the tropics. গ্রীষ্মপ্রধান স্থান

trot (trots, trotting, trotted) *vi* If you **trot** somewhere, you move fairly fast at a speed between walking and running, taking small quick steps. দ্রুত বেগে চলা

trouble (troubles) *n* You can refer to problems or difficulties as **trouble**. সমস্যা

troublemaker (troublemakers) *n* A **troublemaker** is someone who causes trouble. সমস্যা সৃষ্টিকারী

trough (troughs) *n* A **trough** is a long container from which farm animals drink or eat. জল পানের লম্বা পাত্র

trousers *npl* **Trousers** are a piece of clothing that you wear over your body from the waist downwards, and that cover each leg separately. You can also say a pair of trousers. পাতলুন

trout (trout, trouts) *n* A **trout** is a kind of fish that lives in rivers and streams. মাছ

trowel (trowels) *n* A **trowel** is a small garden tool which you use for digging small holes or removing weeds. খুরপী

truce (truces) *n* A **truce** is an agreement between two people or groups to stop fighting or quarrelling for a short time. সংঘর্ষ বিরতি

truck (trucks) *n* A **truck** is a large vehicle that is used to transport goods by road. *(US)* ট্রাক

truck driver (truck drivers) *n* A **truck driver** is someone who drives a truck as their job. *(US)* ট্রাক চালক

true (truer, truest) *adj* If a story is **true**, it really happened. সত্য ▷ *adj* If something is **true**, it is right or correct. সঠিক

truly *adv* **Truly** means completely and genuinely. যথাযথ

trumpet (trumpets) *n* A **trumpet** is a brass wind instrument. বাদ্য যন্ত্র

trunk (trunks) *n* A **trunk** is the thick stem of a tree. The branches and roots grow from the **trunk**. গাছের গুঁড়ি ▷ *n* An elephant's **trunk** is its long nose. Elephants use their **trunks** to suck up water and to lift things. গুঁড় ▷ *n* A **trunk** is a large, strong box that you use to keep things in. টিনের বাক্স

t

trunks npl **Trunks** are shorts that a man wears when he goes swimming. হাফ প্যান্ট

trust (**trusts, trusting, trusted**) n Your **trust** in someone is your belief that they are honest and sincere and will not deliberately do anything to harm you. বিশ্বাস ▷ vt If you **trust** someone, you believe that they are honest and sincere and will not deliberately do anything to harm you. বিশ্বাস করা

trusting adj A **trusting** person believes that people are honest and sincere and do not intend to harm him or her. আস্থাশীল

truth n The **truth** about something is all the facts about it, rather than things that are imagined or invented. সত্য

truthful adj If a person or their comments are **truthful**, they are honest and do not tell any lies. সত্যবাদী

try (**tries, trying, tried**) n If you have a **try** at doing something, you make an effort to do it. চেষ্টা ▷ vi If you **try** to do something, you do it as well as you can. চেষ্টা করা ▷ vt If you **try** something, you test it to see what it is like or how it works. পরীক্ষা করা

try on v If you **try on** a piece of clothing, you put it on to see if it fits you or if it looks nice. যাচাই করা Try on clothing and shoes to make sure they fit.

try out v If you **try** something **out**, you test it in order to find out how useful or effective it is. ব্যবহারিক প্রমানের পরিক্ষা The company hopes to try out the system in September.

T-shirt (**T-shirts**) n A **T-shirt** is a cotton shirt with short sleeves and no collar or buttons. টি শার্ট

tsunami (**tsunamis**) n A **tsunami** is a very large wave, often caused by an earthquake, that flows onto the land and destroys things. সুনামি

tube (**tubes**) n A **tube** is a long, round, hollow piece of metal, rubber, or plastic. নল ▷ n A **tube** is a soft metal or plastic container that you press to make what is in it come out. টিউব

tuberculosis n **Tuberculosis**, or **TB**, is a serious infectious disease that affects the lungs. যক্ষ্মা

Tuesday (**Tuesdays**) n **Tuesday** is the day after Monday and before Wednesday. মঙ্গলবার

tug-of-war (**tugs-of-war**) n A **tug-of-war** is a sports event in which two teams test their strength by pulling against each other on opposite ends of a rope. টানাটানি

tuition n If you are given **tuition** in a particular subject, you are taught about that subject, especially on your own or in a small group. গৃহশিক্ষা

tuition fees npl **Tuition fees** are the money that you pay to be taught, especially in a college or university. শিক্ষার বেতন

tulip (**tulips**) n **Tulips** are garden flowers that grow in the spring. টিউলিপ ফুল

tumble dryer (**tumble dryers**) n A **tumble dryer** is an electric machine which dries washing by turning it over and over and blowing warm air onto it. কাপড় শুকোনোর ড্রায়ার

tummy (**tummies**) n Your **tummy** is your stomach. উদর

tumour (**tumours**) n A **tumour** is a mass of diseased or abnormal cells that has grown in someone's body. টিউমার

tuna (**tuna, tunas**) n A **tuna** or a **tuna fish** is a large fish that lives in warm seas. টুনা মাছ

tune (**tunes**) n A **tune** is a series of musical notes that is pleasant to listen to. সুর

Tunisia n **Tunisia** is a republic in North Africa, on the Mediterranean. টিউনিশিয়া

Tunisian (**Tunisians**) adj **Tunisian** means belonging to or relating to Tunisia, or to its people or culture. টিউনেশিয় ▷ n A **Tunisian** is a person who comes from Tunisia. টিউনেশিয়ার নাগরিক

tunnel (**tunnels**) n A **tunnel** is a long passage which has been made under the ground, usually through a hill or under the sea. সুড়ঙ্গ

turbulence n **Turbulence** is a state of confusion and disorganized change. উত্তাল

Turk (Turks) *n* A **Turk** is a person who comes from Turkey. তুরস্কের লোক

Turkey *n* **Turkey** is a Eurasian republic in western Asia and south-eastern Europe. তুরস্ক (দেশ)

turkey (turkeys) *n* A **turkey** is a large bird that is kept on a farm for its meat. বড় পাখি

Turkish *adj* **Turkish** means belonging or relating to Turkey, or to its people, language, or culture. তুরস্ক দেশীয় ▷ *n* **Turkish** is the main language spoken in Turkey. তুর্কী ভাষা

turn (turns, turning, turned) *n* A **turn** is a change of direction. দিক পরিবর্তন ▷ *v* When you **turn**, you move in a different direction. অন্যদিকে ফেরা ▷ *v* When something **turns**, it moves around in a circle. ঘুরে যাওয়া ▷ *vi* If one thing **turns** into another thing, it becomes that thing. পরিণত হওয়া

turn around *v* To **turn around** means to move in a different direction or to move into a different position. বিভিন্ন দিশায় ঘোরা *She turned around to see a woman standing there.* ❑ *I felt a tapping on my shoulder and I turned around.*

turn back *v* If you **turn back**, or if someone **turns** you **back** when you are going somewhere, you change direction and go towards where you started from. পেছন ফেরা *Police attempted to turn back protesters.*

turn down *v* If you **turn down** a person or their request or offer, you refuse their request or offer. নাকচ করা *After careful consideration I turned the invitation down.*

turning (turnings) *n* If you take a particular **turning**, you go along a road which leads away from the side of another road. দিক পরিবর্তন

turnip (turnips) *n* A **turnip** is a round vegetable with a green and white skin. শালগম

turn off *v* If you **turn off** the road or path you are going along, you start going along a different road or path which leads away from it. রাস্তাবদল করা *Turn off at the bridge.*

turn on *v* When you **turn on** a piece of equipment or a supply of something, you cause heat, sound, or water to be produced by adjusting the controls. চালু করা *She asked them why they hadn't turned the lights on.*

turn out *v* If something **turns out** a particular way, it happens in that way or has the result or degree of success indicated. প্রতীয়মান হওয়া *I was positive things were going to turn out fine.*

turnover *n* The **turnover** of a company is the value of goods or services sold during a particular period of time. মোট লেনদেন

turn up *v* If you say that someone or something **turns up**, you mean that they arrive, often unexpectedly, or after you have been waiting for a long time. হাজির হওয়া *We waited for the bus, but it never turned up.*

turquoise *adj* **Turquoise** is used to describe things that are of a light greenish-blue colour. ভুতে

turtle (turtles) *n* A **turtle** is a large reptile with a thick shell which lives in the sea. কচ্ছপ

tutor (tutors) *n* A **tutor** is a teacher at a British university or college. গৃহশিক্ষক

tutorial (tutorials) *n* In a British university or college, a **tutorial** is a regular meeting between a tutor and one or several students for discussion of a subject that is being studied. শিক্ষাস্থল

tuxedo (tuxedos) *n* A **tuxedo** is a black or white jacket worn by men for formal social events. জ্যাকেট

TV (TVs) *n* A **TV** is a piece of electrical equipment with a glass screen on which you can watch programmes with pictures and sounds. **TV** is an abbreviation for 'television'. টিভি

tweezers *npl* **Tweezers** are a small tool that you use for tasks such as picking up small objects or pulling out hairs. Tweezers consist of two strips of metal or plastic joined together at one end. চিমটি

twelfth *adj* The **twelfth** item in a series is the one that you count as number twelve. দ্বাদশ

twelve *num* **Twelve** is the number 12. বারো

twentieth *adj* The **twentieth** item in a series is the one that you count as number twenty. বিংশতি

twenty *num* **Twenty** is the number 20. কুড়ি

twice *adv* If something happens **twice**, it happens two times. দুবার

twin (**twins**) *n* If two people are **twins**, they have the same mother and were born on the same day. যমজ

twin beds *npl* **Twin beds** are two single beds in one bedroom. দুই শয্যার ঘর

twinned *adj* When a place or organization in one country is **twinned** with a place or organization in another country, a special relationship is formally established between them. সংলগ্ন

twist (**twists, twisting, twisted**) *vt* If you **twist** something, you turn it to make a spiral shape, for example by turning the two ends of it in opposite directions. মোচড়ান

twit (**twits**) *n* If you call someone a **twit**, you are insulting them and saying that they are silly or stupid. (*informal*) অবমাননাকর সম্বোধন

two *num* **Two** is the number 2. দুই

type (**types, typing, typed**) *n* A **type** of something is the kind of thing that it is. প্রকার ▷ *v* If you **type** something, you write it with a machine, for example a computer. টাইপ করা

typewriter (**typewriters**) *n* A **typewriter** is a machine with keys which are pressed in order to print letters, numbers, or other characters onto paper. টাইপ করার যন্ত্র

typhoid *n* **Typhoid** or **typhoid fever** is a serious infectious disease that produces fever and diarrhoea and can cause death. It is spread by dirty water or food. টাইফয়েড

typical *adj* You use **typical** to describe someone or something that shows the most usual characteristics of a particular type of person or thing, and is therefore a good example of that type. বিশেষ ধরণের

typist (**typists**) *n* A **typist** is someone who works in an office typing letters and other documents. টাইপ করে যে

tyre (**tyres**) *n* A **tyre** is a thick ring of rubber filled with air and fitted round the wheel of a vehicle. টায়ার

u

UFO (UFOs) *abbr* A **UFO** is an object seen in the sky or landing on Earth which cannot be identified and which is often believed to be from another planet. **UFO** is an abbreviation for 'unidentified flying object'. ইউ এফ ও

Uganda *n* **Uganda** is a republic in East Africa. উগান্ডা

Ugandan (Ugandans) *adj* **Ugandan** means belonging or relating to Uganda or to its people or culture. উগান্ডা দেশীয় ▷ *n* A **Ugandan** is a Ugandan citizen, or a person of Ugandan origin. উগান্ডার নাগরিক

ugh! *excl* **Ugh!** is used in writing to represent the sound that people make if they think something is unpleasant, horrible, or disgusting. বিরক্তিকর।

ugly (uglier, ugliest) *adj* If you say that someone or something is **ugly**, you mean that they are unattractive and unpleasant to look at. কুৎসিত

UHT milk *n* **UHT milk** is milk which has been treated at a very high temperature so that it can be kept for a long time if the container is not opened. **UHT** is an abbreviation for 'ultra-heat-treated'. আল্ট্রা হিট ট্রিটেড দুধ

UK *n* The **UK** is Great Britain and Northern Ireland. **UK** is an abbreviation for 'United Kingdom'. ইউনাইটেড কিংডম এর সংক্ষিপ্তকরণ

Ukraine *n* **Ukraine** is a republic in south-east Europe, on the Black Sea and the Sea of Azov. ইউক্রেন

Ukrainian (Ukrainians) *adj* **Ukrainian** means of or relating to Ukraine, its people, or their language. ইউক্রেন দেশীয় ▷ *n* A **Ukrainian** is a Ukrainian citizen, or a person of Ukrainian origin. ইউক্রেনের নাগরিক ▷ *n* **Ukrainian** is the official language of Ukraine. It is an East Slavonic language closely related to Russian. ইউক্রেনের ভাষা

ulcer (ulcers) *n* An **ulcer** is a sore area on or inside a part of your body which is very painful and may bleed. নালি ঘা

Ulster *n* **Ulster** is a province and former kingdom of Northern Ireland. আলস্টার

ultimate *adj* You use **ultimate** to describe the final result or the original cause of a long series of events. চূড়ান্ত

ultimately *adv* **Ultimately** means finally, after a long series of events. পরিশেষে

ultimatum (ultimatums, ultimata) *n* An **ultimatum** is a warning that unless someone acts in a particular way within a particular time limit, action will be taken against them. শেষ প্রস্তাব

ultrasound *n* **Ultrasound** refers to sound waves which travel at such a high frequency that they cannot be heard by humans. আল্ট্রাসাউন্ড

umbrella (umbrellas) *n* An **umbrella** is an object which you use to protect yourself from the rain. It consists of a long stick with a folding frame covered in cloth. ছাতা

umpire (**umpires**) n An **umpire** is a person whose job is to make sure that a sports match or contest is played fairly and that the rules are not broken. আম্পায়ার

UN abbr The **UN** is an organization which most countries belong to. Its role is to encourage international peace, co-operation, and friendship. **UN** is an abbreviation for 'United Nations'. ইউনাইটেড নেশনস এর সংক্ষিপ্তকরণ

unable adj If you are **unable** to do something, it is impossible for you to do it. অক্ষম

unacceptable adj If you describe something as **unacceptable**, you strongly disapprove of it or object to it and feel that it should not be allowed to happen or continue. অগ্রহণযোগ্য

unanimous adj When a group of people or their opinion is **unanimous**, they all agree about something. সর্বসম্মত

unattended adj When people or things are left **unattended**, they are not being watched or looked after. একলা

unavoidable adj If something bad is **unavoidable**, it cannot be avoided or prevented. অনিবার্য

unbearable adj If you describe something as **unbearable**, you mean that it is so unpleasant, painful, or upsetting that you feel unable to accept it or deal with it. অসহনীয়

unbeatable adj If you describe something as **unbeatable**, you mean that it is the best thing of its kind. অপরাজিত

unbelievable adj If you say that something is **unbelievable**, you are emphasizing that it is very extreme, impressive, or shocking. অবিশ্বাস্য

unbreakable adj **Unbreakable** objects cannot be broken, usually because they are made of a very strong material. অভঙ্গুর

uncanny adj If something is **uncanny**, it is strange and difficult to explain. অস্বাভাবিক

uncertain adj If you are **uncertain** about something, you do not know what to do. অনিশ্চিত

uncertainty (**uncertainties**) n **Uncertainty** is a state of doubt about the future or about what is the right thing to do. অনিশ্চয়তা

unchanged adj Something that is **unchanged** has stayed the same during a period of time. অপরিবর্তিত

uncivilized adj If you describe someone's behaviour as **uncivilized**, you find it unacceptable, for example because it is very cruel or very rude. অসভ্য

uncle (**uncles**) n Your **uncle** is the brother of your mother or father, or the husband of your aunt. আংকল

unclear adj If something is **unclear**, it is not known or not certain. অস্পষ্ট

uncomfortable adj If you are **uncomfortable**, you are not physically relaxed, and feel slight pain or discomfort. অস্বস্তি কর

unconditional adj Something that is **unconditional** is done or given to someone freely, without anything being required in return. শর্তহীন

unconscious adj Someone who is **unconscious** is in a state similar to sleep, as a result of a shock, accident, or injury. অজ্ঞান

uncontrollable adj If something such as an emotion is **uncontrollable**, you can do nothing to prevent it or control it. অদম্য

unconventional adj If someone is **unconventional**, they do not behave in the same way as most other people in their society. প্রথাবিহির্ভূত

undecided adj If you are **undecided** about something, you have not yet made a decision about it. অনিশ্চিত

undeniable adj If something is **undeniable**, it is definitely true or definitely exists. অস্বীকার্য

under prep If one thing is **under** another thing, it is lower down than it, or the second thing covers the first thing. নিচে *There was a dog under the table.* ❑ *He was standing under a large painting.*

underage *adj* Someone who is **underage** is not legally old enough to do something. নাবালক

underestimate (**underestimates, underestimating, underestimated**) *vt* If you **underestimate** something, you do not realize how large it is or will be. অবমূল্যায়ন করা

undergo (**undergoes, undergoing, underwent, undergone**) *vt* If you **undergo** something necessary or unpleasant, it happens to you. অতিক্রম করা

undergraduate (**undergraduates**) *n* An **undergraduate** is a student at a university or college who is studying for his or her first degree. স্নাতক পাঠরত

underground *adv* Something that is **underground** is below the surface of the ground. ভূগর্ভস্থ ▷ *n* The **underground** in a city is the railway system in which electric trains travel below the ground in tunnels. ভূগর্ভ

underground station (**underground stations**) *n* An **underground station** is a station of an underground railway system. ভূগর্ভস্থ স্টেশন

underline (**underlines, underlining, underlined**) *vt* If a person or event **underlines** something, they draw attention to it and emphasize its importance. গুরুত্ব আরোপ করা

underneath *adv* If one thing is **underneath** another thing, the second thing covers the first thing. তলায় ▷ *prep* If one thing is **underneath** another thing, the second thing covers the first thing. কোন কিছুর নিচে *The ring was underneath the sofa.*

underpaid *adj* People who are **underpaid** are not paid enough money for the job that they do. কম মূল্য প্রাপ্তি

underpants *npl* **Underpants** are a piece of underwear with two holes for your legs and

elastic around the waist. **Underpants** refers only to men's underwear. অন্তর্বাস

underpass (**underpasses**) *n* An **underpass** is a road or path that goes underneath a railway or another road. ভূগর্ভস্থ পথ

underskirt (**underskirts**) *n* An **underskirt** is any skirtlike garment worn under a skirt. স্কার্টের নিচে পরবার পোষাক

understand (**understands, understanding, understood**) *vt* If you **understand** someone, or if you **understand** what they are saying, you know what they mean. বুঝতে পারা

understandable *adj* If you describe someone's behaviour or feelings as **understandable**, you mean that they have reacted to a situation in a natural way or in the way you would expect. বোধগম্য

understanding *adj* If you are **understanding** towards someone, you are kind and forgiving. বুঝদার

undertaker (**undertakers**) *n* An **undertaker** is a person whose job is to deal with the bodies of people who have died and to arrange funerals. শবদেহ সংৎকারকারী

underwater *adv* Something that exists or happens **underwater** exists or happens below the surface of the sea, a river, or a lake. জলের নীচে

underwear *n* **Underwear** is clothing which you wear next to your skin under your other clothes, such as a bra, a vest, and underpants. অন্তর্বাস

undisputed *adj* If you describe something as **undisputed**, you mean that everyone accepts that it exists or is true. তর্কাতীত

undo (**undoes, undoing, undid, undone**) *vt* If you **undo** something, you unfasten, loosen, or untie it. আলগা করা

undoubtedly *adv* **Undoubtedly** means certainly, definitely or unquestionably. নিঃসন্দেহে

u

undress (undresses, undressing, undressed) v When you **undress**, you take off your clothes. If you **undress** someone, you take off their clothes. পোষাক খোলা

unemployed adj Someone who is **unemployed** does not have a job. বেকার

unemployment n **Unemployment** is the fact that people who want jobs cannot get them. বেকারত্ব

unexpected adj Something that is **unexpected** surprises you because you did not think it was likely to happen. অপ্রত্যাশিত

unexpectedly adv **Unexpectedly** means surprisingly. অপ্রত্যাশিতভাবে

unfair adj Something that is **unfair** is not right or not just. অন্যায়িত

unfaithful adj If someone is **unfaithful** to their lover or to the person they are married to, they have a sexual relationship with someone else. অবিশ্বাসী

unfamiliar adj If something is **unfamiliar** to you, or if you are **unfamiliar** with it, you know very little about it and have not seen or experienced it before. অপরিচিত

unfashionable adj If something is **unfashionable**, it is not approved of or done by most people. প্রচলিত ফ্যাশন বহির্ভূত

unfavourable adj **Unfavourable** conditions or circumstances cause problems and reduce the chance of success. অসন্তোষজনক

unfit adj If you are **unfit**, your body is not in good condition because you have not been taking regular exercise. অশক্ত

unforgettable adj If something is **unforgettable**, it is so impressive that you are likely to remember it for a long time. অবিস্মরণীয়

unfortunately adv You can use **unfortunately** to express regret about what you are saying. দুর্ভাগ্যবশতঃ

unfriendly adj If you describe someone as **unfriendly**, you mean that they behave in an unkind or hostile way. অবন্ধুজনোচিত

ungrateful adj If you describe someone as **ungrateful**, you are criticizing them for not showing thanks or for being unkind to someone who has helped them or done them a favour. অকৃতজ্ঞ

unhappy (unhappier, unhappiest) adj If you are **unhappy**, you are sad and depressed. অসুখী

unhealthy (unhealthier, unhealthiest) adj Something that is **unhealthy** is likely to cause illness or poor health. অস্বাস্থ্যকর

unhelpful adj If you say that someone or something is **unhelpful**, you mean that they do not help you or improve a situation, and may even make things worse. অসহায়তাকর

uni (unis) n A **uni** is an institution where students study for degrees and where academic research is done. **Uni** is short for 'university'. (informal) বিশ্ববিদ্যালয়

unidentified adj If you describe someone or something as **unidentified**, you mean that nobody knows who or what they are. অসনাক্ত

uniform (uniforms) n A **uniform** is a special set of clothes which some people wear to work in, and which some children wear at school. ইউনিফর্ম

unimportant adj If you describe something or someone as **unimportant**, you mean that they do not have much effect or value, and are therefore not worth considering. গুরুত্বহীন

uninhabited adj An **uninhabited** place is one where nobody lives. বসতিহীন

unintentional adj Something that is **unintentional** is not done deliberately, but happens by accident. অনিচ্ছাকৃত

union (unions) n A **union** is an organization that has been formed by workers in order to represent their rights and interests to their employers, for example in order to improve working conditions or wages. ইউনিয়ন

unique adj Something that is **unique** is the only one of its kind. অনন্য

unit (**units**) *n* If you consider something as a **unit**, you consider it as a single complete thing. ইউনিট

unite (**unites, uniting, united**) *v* If a group of people or things **unite**, they join together and act as a group. ঐক্যবদ্ধ হওয়া

United Arab Emirates *npl* The **United Arab Emirates** are a group of seven emirates in south-west Asia, on the Persian Gulf, consisting of Abu Dhabi, Dubai, Sharjah, Ajman, Umm al Qaiwain, Ras el Khaimah, and Fujairah. সংযুক্ত আরব আমিরশাহী

United Kingdom *n* The **United Kingdom** is the official name for the country consisting of Great Britain and Northern Ireland. যুক্তরাজ্য

United Nations *n* The **United Nations** is a worldwide organization which most countries belong to. Its role is to encourage international peace, cooperation, and friendship. রাষ্ট্রসংঘ

United States *n* **The United States of America** is the official name for the country in North America that consists of fifty states and the District of Columbia. It is bordered by Canada in the north and Mexico in the south. The form **United States** is also used. মার্কিন যুক্তরাষ্ট্র

universe *n* The **universe** is the whole of space, and all the stars, planets, and other forms of matter and energy in it. বিশ্বব্রহ্মাণ্ড

university (**universities**) *n* A **university** is an institution where students study for degrees and where academic research is done. বিশ্ববিদ্যালয়

unknown *adj* If something is **unknown** to you, you have no knowledge of it. অজানা

unleaded *n* Unleaded fuels contain a reduced amount of lead in order to reduce the pollution caused when they are burned. You can refer to such fuels as **unleaded**. কম লীডযুক্ত

unleaded petrol *n* **Unleaded petrol** contains a smaller amount of lead than most fuels so that it produces fewer harmful substances when it is burned. কম লীডযুক্ত পেট্রল

unless *conj* **Unless** means if the thing you are talking about does not happen. যদি না *He says he won't go to the party, unless I go too.*

unlike *prep* If one thing is **unlike** another thing, the two things are different. অন্যরকম *You're so unlike your father!*

unlikely (**unlikelier, unlikeliest**) *adj* If you say that something is **unlikely** to happen or **unlikely** to be true, you believe that it will not happen or that it is not true, although you are not completely sure. কম সম্ভাবনাযুক্ত

unlisted *adj* If a person or their telephone number is **unlisted**, the number is not listed in the telephone book, and the telephone company will refuse to give it to people who ask for it. তালিকাভুক্ত নয়

unload (**unloads, unloading, unloaded**) *vt* If you **unload** goods from a vehicle, you remove the goods from the vehicle. খালাস করা

unlock (**unlocks, unlocking, unlocked**) *vt* If you **unlock** something such as a door, a room, or a container, you open it using a key. তালা খোলা

unlucky (**unluckier, unluckiest**) *adj* If you are **unlucky**, you have bad luck. ভাগ্যহীন

unmarried *adj* Someone who is **unmarried** is not married. অবিবাহিত

unnecessary *adj* If you describe something as **unnecessary**, you mean that it is not needed or does not have to be done. অপ্রয়োজনীয়

unofficial *adj* An **unofficial** action is not authorized, approved, or organized by a person in authority. বেসরকারী

unpack (**unpacks, unpacking, unpacked**) *v* When you **unpack** a suitcase, box, or bag, you take the things out of it. জিনিসপত্র বার করা

unpaid *adj* If you do **unpaid** work, you do a job without receiving any money for it. বেতনবিহীন

u

unpleasant adj If something is **unpleasant**, it gives you bad feelings, for example by making you feel upset or uncomfortable. অমনোরম

unplug (**unplugs, unplugging, unplugged**) vt If you **unplug** a piece of electrical equipment, you take its plug out of the socket. প্লাগ খুলে ফেলা

unpopular adj If something or someone is **unpopular**, most people do not like them. অজনপ্রিয়

unprecedented adj If something is **unprecedented**, it has never happened before. অভূতপূর্ব

unpredictable adj If someone or something is **unpredictable**, you cannot tell what they are going to do or how they are going to behave. অনিশ্চিত

unreal adj If you say that a situation is **unreal**, you mean that it is so strange that you find it difficult to believe it is happening. অসত্য

unrealistic adj If you say that someone is being **unrealistic**, you mean that they do not recognize the truth about a situation, especially about the difficulties involved. অবাস্তব

unreasonable adj If you say that someone is being **unreasonable**, you mean that they are behaving in a way that is not fair or sensible. অযৌক্তিক

unreliable adj If you describe a person, machine, or method as **unreliable**, you mean that you cannot trust them to do or provide what you want. অবিশ্বাসযোগ্য

unroll (**unrolls, unrolling, unrolled**) v If you **unroll** something such as a sheet of paper or cloth, it opens up and becomes flat when it was previously rolled in a cylindrical shape. খুলে ফেলা

unsatisfactory adj If you describe something as **unsatisfactory**, you mean that it is not as good as it should be, and cannot be considered acceptable. অসন্তোষজনক

unscrew (**unscrews, unscrewing, unscrewed**) v If you **unscrew** something such as a lid, or if it **unscrews**, you keep turning it until you can remove it. ঘুরিয়ে খোলা

unshaven adj If a man is **unshaven**, he has not shaved recently and there are short hairs on his face and chin. দাড়ি না কামানো

unskilled adj People who are **unskilled** do not have any special training for a job. অদক্ষ

unstable adj You can describe something as **unstable** if it is likely to change suddenly, especially if this creates difficulty. অস্থির

unsteady adj If you are **unsteady**, you have difficulty doing something because you cannot completely control your body. কম্পমান

unsuccessful adj Something that is **unsuccessful** does not achieve what it was intended to achieve. অসফল

unsuitable adj Someone or something that is **unsuitable** for a particular purpose or situation does not have the right qualities for it. অযোগ্য

unsure adj If you are **unsure** of yourself, you don't have much confidence. অনিশ্চিত

untidy adj Something that is **untidy** is messy, and not neatly arranged. অপরিষ্কার

untie (**unties, untying, untied**) vt If you **untie** something that is tied to another thing, or if you **untie** two things that are tied together, you remove the string or rope that holds them. বাঁধন খোলা

until conj **Until** a particular time means during the period before that time. না পর্যন্ত *I waited until it got dark.* ▷ prep If something happens **until** a time, it happens before that time and then stops at that time. পর্যন্ত *Wait here until I come back.*

unusual adj If something is **unusual**, it does not happen very often or you do not see it or hear it very often. অস্বাভাবিক

unwell adj If you are **unwell**, you are ill. অসুস্থ

unwind (**unwinds, unwinding, unwound**) *vi* When you **unwind** after working hard, you relax. বিশ্রাম নেওয়া

unwise *adj* Something that is **unwise** is foolish. অবিবেচক

unwrap (**unwraps, unwrapping, unwrapped**) *vt* When you **unwrap** something, you take off the paper or covering that is around it. মোড়ক খোলা

unzip (**unzips, unzipping, unzipped**) *vt* To **unzip** an item of clothing or a bag means to unfasten its zip. চেন খোলা

up *adv* When something moves **up**, it moves from a lower place to a higher place. ওপরে

upbringing *n* Your **upbringing** is the way your parents treat you and the things that they teach you when you are growing up. পালন

update (**updates, updating, updated**) *vt* If you **update** something, you make it more modern, usually by adding newer parts to it. আপডেট করা

uphill *adv* If something or someone is **uphill** or is moving **uphill**, they are near the top of a hill or are going up a slope. পাহাড়ে চড়া

upon *prep* **Upon** means the same as **on**. ওপরে *He stood upon the bridge.*

upper *adj* You use **upper** to describe something that is above something else. ওপরের

upright *adj* If you are sitting or standing **upright**, you have your back straight and are not bending or lying down. সোজা

upset (**upsets, upsetting, upset**) *adj* If you are **upset**, you are unhappy or disappointed because something unpleasant has happened. বিচলিত ▷ *vt* If something **upsets** you, it makes you feel worried or unhappy. বিচলিত করা

upside down *adv* If you hang **upside down**, your head is below your feet. ওপরের অংশ নিচের দিকে করা ▷ *adj* If something is **upside down**, the part that is usually at the bottom is at the top. নিচের অংশ ওপরের দিকে করা

upstairs *adv* If you go **upstairs** in a building, you go up a staircase towards a higher floor. ওপরতলা

uptight *adj* If someone is **uptight**, they are very tense, because they are worried or annoyed about something. (*informal*) স্নায়ুচাপগ্রস্ত

up-to-date *adj* If something is **up-to-date**, it is the newest thing of its kind. আধুনিক

upwards *adv* If someone moves or looks **upwards**, they move or look up towards a higher place. ওপরদিকে

uranium *n* **Uranium** is a radioactive metal that is used to produce nuclear energy and weapons. ইউরেনিয়াম

urgency *n* **Urgency** is the quality of being urgent or pressing. জরুরী অবস্থা

urgent *adj* If something is **urgent**, it needs to be dealt with as soon as possible. জরুরী

urine *n* **Urine** is the liquid that you get rid of from your body when you go to the toilet. প্রস্রাব

URL (**URLs**) *n* A **URL** is an address that shows where a particular page can be found on the World Wide Web. **URL** is an abbreviation for 'Uniform Resource Locator'. ওয়েব অ্যাড্রেস

Uruguay *n* **Uruguay** is a republic in South America, on the Atlantic. উরুগুয়ে

Uruguayan (**Uruguayans**) *adj* **Uruguayan** means of or relating to Uruguay or its inhabitants. উরুগুয়ে সম্পর্কিত ▷ *n* A **Uruguayan** is a native or inhabitant of Uruguay. উরুগুয়ের বসবাসকারী

US *n* The **US** is an abbreviation for 'the United States'. মার্কিন যুক্তরাষ্ট্র

us *pron* You use **us** to talk about yourself and the person or people with you. আমাদের *He has invited us to a party.*

USA *n* The **USA** is an abbreviation for 'the United States of America'. মার্কিন যুক্তরাষ্ট্র

use (**uses, using, used**) *n* Your **use** of something is the action or fact of your using it. ব্যবহার ▷ *vt* If you **use** something, you do something with it. ব্যবহার করা

used *adj* A **used** handkerchief, glass, or other object is dirty or spoiled because it has been used. ব্যবহৃত ▷ *v* You use **used to** to talk about something that was true in the past but is not true now. অতীতে করা হত

useful *adj* If something is **useful**, you can use it to do something or to help you. দরকারী

useless *adj* If something is **useless**, you cannot use it. অদরকারী

user (**users**) *n* The **users** of a product, machine, service, or place are the people who use it. ব্যবহারকারী

user-friendly *adj* If you describe something such as a machine or system as **user-friendly**, you mean that it is well designed and easy to use. ব্যবহারকারী-সহায়ক

use up *v* If you **use up** a supply of something, you finish it so that none of it is left. নিঃশেষ করে ফেলা *Did you use up the milk?*

usual *adj* **Usual** is used to describe what happens or what is done most often in a particular situation. প্রচলিত

usually *adv* If something **usually** happens, it is the thing that most often happens in a particular situation. সাধারণতঃ

utility room (**utility rooms**) *n* A **utility room** is a room in a house which is usually connected to the kitchen and which contains things such as a washing machine, sink, and cleaning equipment. নিত্য-ব্যবহার্য জিনিসপত্র রাখার ঘর

U-turn (**U-turns**) *n* If you make a **U-turn** when you are driving or cycling, you turn in a half circle in one movement, so that you are then going in the opposite direction. উলটো দিকে ঘোরা

Uzbekistan *n* **Uzbekistan** is a republic in central Asia. উজবেকিস্তান

vacancy (**vacancies**) *n* A **vacancy** is a job or position which has not been filled. শূন্যপদ

vacant *adj* If something is **vacant**, it is not being used by anyone. খালি

vacate (**vacates, vacating, vacated**) *vt* If you **vacate** a place or a job, you leave it and make it available for other people. (*formal*) খালি করা

vaccinate (**vaccinates, vaccinating, vaccinated**) *vt* If a person or animal **is vaccinated**, they are given, usually by injection, a substance containing a harmless form of a disease, to prevent them from getting that disease. টিকা দেওয়া

vaccination (**vaccinations**) *n* **Vaccination** is the process of giving a person or animal, usually by injection, a substance containing a harmless form of a disease, to prevent them from getting that disease. টিকাদান

vacuum (**vacuums, vacuuming, vacuumed**) *v* If you **vacuum** something, you clean it using a vacuum cleaner. ভ্যাকুয়াম ক্লিনার দিয়ে পরিষ্কার করা

vacuum cleaner (**vacuum cleaners**) *n* A **vacuum cleaner** or a **vacuum** is an electric machine which sucks up dust and dirt from carpets. ভ্যাকুয়াম ক্লিনার

vague (**vaguer, vaguest**) *adj* If something is **vague**, it is not clear, distinct, or definite. অস্পষ্ট

vain (**vainer, vainest**) *adj* A **vain** attempt or action is one that fails to achieve what was intended. নিষ্ফল

Valentine's Day *n* On **Valentine's Day**, the 14th of February, people send a greetings card to someone that they are in love with or are attracted to, usually without signing their name. ভ্যালেন্টাইনস দিবস

valid *adj* A **valid** reason or argument is logical and reasonable, and therefore worth taking seriously. বৈধ

valley (**valleys**) *n* A **valley** is a low area of land between hills, often with a river flowing through it. উপত্যকা

valuable *adj* Something that is **valuable** is very useful. মূল্যবান

valuables *npl* **Valuables** are things that you own that are worth a lot of money, especially small objects such as jewellery. দামী জিনিস

value *n* The **value** of something such as a quality or a method is its importance or usefulness. মূল্য

vampire (**vampires**) *n* In horror stories, **vampires** are creatures who come out of their graves at night and suck the blood of living people. বাদুড়

van (**vans**) *n* A **van** is a medium-sized road vehicle that is used for carrying goods. ভ্যান গাড়ি

vandal (**vandals**) *n* A **vandal** is someone who deliberately damages things, especially public property. তছনছকারী ব্যক্তি

vandalism *n* **Vandalism** is the deliberate damaging of things, especially public property. তছনছ করা

vandalize (**vandalizes, vandalizing, vandalized**) *v* If something **is vandalized** by someone, they deliberately damage it. তছনছ হয়ে যাওয়া

vanilla *n* **Vanilla** is a flavouring used in ice cream and other sweet food. ভ্যানিলা

vanish (**vanishes, vanishing, vanished**) *vi* If someone or something **vanishes**, they disappear suddenly or cease to exist altogether. উধাও হয়ে যাওয়া

variable *adj* Something that is **variable** is likely to change at any time. পরিবর্তনযোগ্য

varied *adj* Something that is **varied** consists of things of different types, sizes, or qualities. পরিবর্তিত হওয়া

variety (**varieties**) *n* If something has **variety**, it consists of things which are different from each other. বৈচিত্র্য

various *adj* If you say that there are **various** things, you mean there are several different things of the type mentioned. বিভিন্ন

varnish (**varnishes, varnishing, varnished**) *n* **Varnish** is an oily liquid which is painted onto wood to give it a hard, clear, shiny surface. বার্নিশ ▷ *vt* If you **varnish** something, you paint it with varnish. বার্নিশ করা

vary (**varies, varying, varied**) *vi* If things **vary**, they are different in size, amount, or degree. আলাদা হওয়া

vase (**vases**) *n* A **vase** is a jar used for holding cut flowers or as an ornament. ফুলদানি

VAT *abbr* **VAT** is a tax that is added to the price of goods or services. **VAT** is an abbreviation for 'value added tax'. মূল্য সংযোজিত কর

Vatican *n* **The Vatican** is the city state in Rome ruled by the pope which is the centre of the Roman Catholic Church. ভ্যাটিকান

veal *n* **Veal** is meat from a calf. কচি বাছুর

vegan (**vegans**) *n* A **vegan** is someone who never eats meat or any animal products such as milk, butter, or cheese. নিরামিষে আসক্ত ব্যক্তি

vegetable (**vegetables**) *n* **Vegetables** are edible plants such as cabbages, potatoes, and onions. সবজি

vegetarian (**vegetarians**) *adj* Someone who is **vegetarian** never eats meat or fish.

V

নিরামিষাশী ▷ *n* A **vegetarian** is someone who does not eat meat or fish. নিরামিষাশী

vegetation *n* **Vegetation** is plants, trees, and flowers. (*formal*) উদ্ভিদসমূহ

vehicle (**vehicles**) *n* A **vehicle** is a machine with an engine, for example a car, that carries people or things from place to place. বাহন

veil (**veils**) *n* A **veil** is a piece of thin soft cloth that women sometimes wear over their heads and which can also cover their face. ওড়না

vein (**veins**) *n* Your **veins** are the tubes in your body through which your blood flows towards your heart. শিরা

Velcro® *n* **Velcro** is a material consisting of two strips of nylon fabric which you press together to close things such as pockets and bags. ভেলক্রো®

velvet *n* **Velvet** is a soft fabric with a thick layer of short cut threads on one side. মখমল

vending machine (**vending machines**) *n* A **vending machine** is a machine from which you can get things such as cigarettes, chocolate, or coffee by putting in money and pressing a button. ভেন্ডিং মেশিন

vendor (**vendors**) *n* A **vendor** is someone who sells things such as newspapers or hamburgers from a small stall or cart. ছোট বিক্রেতা

Venetian blind (**Venetian blinds**) *n* A **Venetian blind** is a window blind made of thin horizontal strips which can be adjusted to let in more or less light. ভেনেশিয়ান ব্লাইন্ড

Venezuela *n* **Venezuela** is a republic in South America, on the Caribbean. ভেনিজুয়েলা

Venezuelan (**Venezuelans**) *adj* **Venezuelan** means of or relating to Venezuela or its inhabitants. ভেনিজুয়েলা দেশীয় ▷ *n* A **Venezuelan** is a native or inhabitant of Venezuela. ভেনিজুয়েলার বসবাসকারী

venison *n* **Venison** is the meat of a deer. হরিণের মাংস

venom *n* **Venom** is a feeling of great bitterness or anger towards someone. কারোর প্রতি বিতৃষ্ণা

ventilation *n* **Ventilation** is the act or process of allowing fresh air to get into a room or building. বায়ু-চলাচল

venue (**venues**) *n* The **venue** for an event or activity is the place where it will happen. স্থান

verb (**verbs**) *n* A **verb** is a word such as 'sing' or 'feel' which is used to say what someone or something does or what happens to them, or to give information about them. ক্রিয়া

verdict (**verdicts**) *n* In a law court, a **verdict** is the decision that is given by the jury or judge at the end of a trial. রায়

versatile *adj* If you say that a person is **versatile**, you approve of them because they have many different skills. বহুমুখী দক্ষতার অধিকারী

version (**versions**) *n* A **version** of something is a form of it in which some details are different from earlier or later forms. সংস্করণ

versus *prep* **Versus** is used for showing that two teams or people are on different sides in a game. বনাম *It will be the US versus Belgium in tomorrow's game.*

vertical *adj* Something that is **vertical** stands or points straight upwards. উলম্ব

vertigo *n* If you get **vertigo** when you look down from a high place, you feel unsteady and sick. ভার্টিগো

very *adv* **Very** is used before a word to make it stronger. খুব

vest (**vests**) *n* A **vest** is a piece of underwear which is worn to keep the top part of your body warm. দেহের উপরিভাগের অন্তর্বাস

vet (**vets**) *n* A **vet** is someone who is qualified to treat sick or injured animals. পশু-চিকিৎসক

veteran (**veterans**) *adj* A **veteran** campaigner, actor, or other person is someone who has been involved in their particular activity for a long time. অভিজ্ঞ ও প্রবীণ ▷ n A **veteran** is someone who has served in the armed forces of their country, especially during a war. সশস্ত্র সেনাবাহিনীর প্রাক্তন কর্মী

veto (**vetoes**) n If someone in authority puts a **veto** on something, they forbid it, or stop it being put into action. ভেটো

via prep If you go somewhere **via** a place, you go through that place on the way. হয়ে *We're flying from London to Australia via Hong Kong.*

vice (**vices**) n A **vice** is a habit which is regarded as a weakness in someone's character, but not usually as a serious fault. দুর্বলতা

vice versa adv **Vice versa** is used to indicate that the reverse of what you have said is also true. For example, 'Women may bring their husbands with them, and vice versa' means that men may also bring their wives with them. বিপরীতভাবে

vicinity n If something is in the **vicinity** of a place, it is in the nearby area. (formal) প্রতিবেশী অঞ্চল

vicious adj A **vicious** person is violent and cruel. উগ্র

victim (**victims**) n A **victim** is someone who has been hurt or killed by someone or something. শিকার

victory (**victories**) n A **victory** is a success in a war or a competition. বিজয়

video (**videos**) n A **video** is a film or television programme recorded on magnetic tape. ভিডিও

video camera (**video cameras**) n A **video camera** is a camera that you use to record something that is happening so that you can watch it later. ভিডিও ক্যামেরা

videophone (**videophones**) n A **videophone** is a telephone which has a camera and screen so that people who are using the phone can see and hear each other. ভিডিও ফোন

Vietnam n **Vietnam** is a republic in south-east Asia. ভিয়েতনাম

Vietnamese (**Vietnamese**) adj **Vietnamese** means of, relating to, or characteristic of Vietnam, its people, or their language. ভিয়েতনাম দেশীয় ▷ n A **Vietnamese** is a native or inhabitant of Vietnam. ভিয়েতনামের নাগরিক ▷ n **Vietnamese** is the language spoken in Vietnam. ভিয়েতনামের ভাষা

view (**views**) n Your **views** on something are the opinions or beliefs that you have about it. মতামত

viewer (**viewers**) n **Viewers** are people who watch television. দর্শক

viewpoint (**viewpoints**) n Someone's **viewpoint** is the way they think about things in general or about a particular thing. দৃষ্টিকোণ

vile (**viler**, **vilest**) adj If you say that someone or something is **vile**, you mean that they are extremely unpleasant. বিশ্রী

villa (**villas**) n A **villa** is a fairly large house, especially one that is used for holidays in Mediterranean countries. বড় বাড়ী

village (**villages**) n A **village** consists of a group of houses, together with other buildings such as a school, in a country area. গ্রাম

villain (**villains**) n A **villain** is someone who deliberately harms other people or breaks the law in order to get what he or she wants. খলনায়ক

vinaigrette (**vinaigrettes**) n **Vinaigrette** is a dressing made by mixing oil, vinegar, salt, pepper, and herbs, which is put on salad. ভিনিগার মাখানো খাবার

vine (**vines**) n A **vine** is a climbing or trailing plant, especially one which produces grapes. দ্রাক্ষালতা

vinegar n **Vinegar** is a sharp-tasting liquid, usually made from sour wine or malt, which is used to make things such as salad dressing. ভিনিগার

V

vineyard (**vineyards**) *n* A **vineyard** is an area of land where grapevines are grown in order to produce wine. আঙুরের ক্ষেত

viola (**violas**) *n* A **viola** is a musical instrument which looks like a violin but is slightly larger. ভায়োলা

violence *n* **Violence** is behaviour which is intended to hurt or kill people. হিংসা

violent *adj* If someone is **violent**, or if they do something which is **violent**, they use physical force or weapons to hurt other people. হিংসাত্মক

violin (**violins**) *n* A **violin** is a musical instrument with four strings stretched over a shaped hollow box. You hold a violin under your chin and play it with a bow. বেহালা

violinist (**violinists**) *n* A **violinist** is someone who plays the violin. বেহালাবাদক

virgin (**virgins**) *n* A **virgin** is someone who has never had sex. কুমারী

Virgo *n* **Virgo** is one of the twelve signs of the zodiac. Its symbol is a young woman. People who are born approximately between the 23rd of August and the 22nd of September come under this sign. কন্যা রাশি

virtual *adj* You can use **virtual** to indicate that something is so nearly true that for most purposes it can be regarded as being true. প্রকৃত

virtual reality *n* **Virtual reality** is an environment which is produced by a computer and seems very like reality to the person experiencing it. কম্পিউটার উৎপাদিত পরিবেশ

virus (**viruses**) *n* A **virus** is a kind of germ that can cause disease. ভাইরাস

visa (**visas**) *n* A **visa** is an official document or a stamp put in your passport which allows you to enter or leave a particular country. ভিসা

visibility *n* **Visibility** is how far or how clearly you can see in particular weather conditions. দৃষ্টিগোচরতা

visible *adj* If an object is **visible**, it can be seen. দৃষ্টিগোচর

visit (**visits, visiting, visited**) *n* If you pay someone a **visit**, you go to see them and spend time with them. সাক্ষাৎ ▷ *vt* If you **visit** someone, you go to see them and spend time with them. সাক্ষাৎ করা

visiting hours *npl* In an institution such as a hospital or prison, **visiting hours** are the times during which people from outside the institution are officially allowed to visit people who are staying at the institution. সাক্ষাতের সময়

visitor (**visitors**) *n* A **visitor** is someone who is visiting a person or place. সাক্ষাৎকারী

visitor centre (**visitor centres**) *n* A **visitor centre** at a place of interest is a building or group of buildings that provides information, often with video displays and exhibitions. ভিজিটর কেন্দ্র

visual *adj* **Visual** means relating to sight, or to things that you can see. দর্শনকেন্দ্রিক

visualize (**visualizes, visualizing, visualized**) *vt* If you **visualize** something, you imagine what it is like by forming a mental picture of it. মনশ্চক্ষুতে দেখা

vital *adj* If something is **vital**, it is necessary or very important. খুব গুরুত্বপূর্ণ

vitamin (**vitamins**) *n* **Vitamins** are organic substances in food which you need in order to remain healthy. ভিটামিন

vivid *adj* **Vivid** memories and descriptions are very clear and detailed. উজ্জ্বল

vocabulary (**vocabularies**) *n* Your **vocabulary** is the total number of words you know in a particular language. শব্দভাণ্ডার

vocational *adj* **Vocational** training and skills are the training and skills needed for a particular job or profession. বৃত্তিমূলক

vodka (**vodkas**) *n* **Vodka** is a strong, clear, alcoholic drink. ভডকা

voice (**voices**) *n* When someone speaks or sings, you hear their **voice**. কণ্ঠস্বর

voicemail *n* **Voicemail** is an electronic system which can store telephone messages, so that someone can listen to them later. ভয়েসমেল

void (**voids**) adj Something that is **void** is officially considered to have no value or authority. বাতিল ▷ n If you describe a situation or a feeling as a **void**, you mean that it seems empty because there is nothing interesting or worthwhile about it. শূন্যতা

volcano (**volcanoes**) n A **volcano** is a mountain from which hot melted rock, gas, steam, and ash sometimes burst. আগ্নেয়গিরি

volleyball n **Volleyball** is a sport in which two teams use their hands to hit a large ball over a high net. ভলিবল

volt (**volts**) n A **volt** is a unit used to measure the force of an electric current. ভোল্ট

voltage (**voltages**) n The **voltage** of an electrical current is its force measured in volts. ভোল্টেজ

volume (**volumes**) n The **volume** of something is the amount of it that there is. পরিমাণ

voluntarily adv If something is done **voluntarily**, it is done because you choose to do it and not because you have to do it. স্বেচ্ছায়

voluntary adj **Voluntary** is used to describe actions and activities that you

do because you choose them, rather than because you have to do them. স্বেচ্ছাপ্রণোদিত

volunteer (**volunteers, volunteering, volunteered**) n A **volunteer** is someone who does work without being paid for it, especially for an organization such as a charity. স্বেচ্ছাসেবী ▷ v If you **volunteer** to do something, you offer to do it without being forced to do it. স্বেচ্ছাপ্রম করা

vomit (**vomits, vomiting, vomited**) vi If you **vomit**, food and drink comes back up from your stomach and out through your mouth. বমি করা

vote (**votes, voting, voted**) n A **vote** is a choice made by a particular person or group in a meeting or an election. নির্বাচন ▷ v When you **vote**, you indicate your choice officially at a meeting or in an election, for example, by raising your hand or writing on a piece of paper. নির্বাচন করা

voucher (**vouchers**) n A **voucher** is a piece of paper that can be used instead of money to pay for something. রসিদ

vowel (**vowels**) n A **vowel** is a sound such as the ones represented in writing by the letters 'a', 'e', 'i', 'o', and 'u', which you pronounce with your mouth open, allowing the air to flow through it. স্বরবর্ণ

vulgar adj If you describe something as **vulgar**, you think it is in bad taste or of poor artistic quality. স্থূল কারুকার্যময়

vulnerable adj If someone or something is **vulnerable** to something, they have some weakness or disadvantage which makes them more likely to be harmed or affected by that thing. অরক্ষিত

vulture (**vultures**) n A **vulture** is a large bird which lives in hot countries and eats the flesh of dead animals. শকুনি

V

wafer (**wafers**) *n* A **wafer** is a thin crisp biscuit, often eaten with ice cream. ওয়েফার

waffle (**waffles, waffling, waffled**) *n* If someone talks or writes a lot without saying anything clear or important, you can call what they say or write **waffle**. (*informal*) বকবকানি ▷ *vi* If you say that someone **waffles**, you are critical of them because they talk or write a lot without actually making any clear or important points. (*informal*) বকবক করা

wage (**wages**) *n* Someone's **wages** are the amount of money that is regularly paid to them for the work that they do. মজুরী

waist (**waists**) *n* Your **waist** is the middle part of your body, above your hips. কোমর

waistcoat (**waistcoats**) *n* A **waistcoat** is a sleeveless piece of clothing with buttons, usually worn over a shirt. ওয়েস্টকোট

wait (**waits, waiting, waited**) *vi* If you say that something can **wait**, you mean that it is not important, so you will do it later. প্রতীক্ষা করা

waiter (**waiters**) *n* A **waiter** is a man who serves food and drink in a restaurant. হোটেলের পরিচারক

waiting list (**waiting lists**) *n* A **waiting list** is a list of people who have asked for something which they cannot receive immediately, for example medical treatment or housing, and so who must wait until it is available. প্রতীক্ষা তালিকা

waiting room (**waiting rooms**) *n* A **waiting room** is a room in a place such as a railway station or a clinic, where people can sit down while they wait. প্রতীক্ষালয়

waitress (**waitresses**) *n* A **waitress** is a woman who serves food and drink in a restaurant. হোটেলের মহিলা পরিচারক

wait up *v* If you **wait up**, you deliberately do not go to bed, especially because you are expecting someone to return home late at night. কারোর জন্য প্রতীক্ষা করা *I hope he doesn't expect you to wait up for him.*

waive (**waives, waiving, waived**) *vt* If you **waive** your right to something, for example legal representation, or if someone else **waives** it, you no longer have the right to receive it. ছেড়ে দেওয়া

wake up *v* When you **wake up**, you become conscious again after being asleep. জেগে ওঠা *It's lovely to wake up every morning and see a blue sky.*

Wales *n* **Wales** is a principality that is part of the United Kingdom, in the west of Great Britain. রাজকুমার পরিচালিত রাজ্য

walk (**walks, walking, walked**) *n* A **walk** is a journey that you make by walking. পায়ে হাঁটা ▷ *vi* When you **walk**, you move along by putting one foot in front of the other. হাঁটা

walkie-talkie (**walkie-talkies**) *n* A **walkie-talkie** is a small portable radio which you can talk into and hear messages through so that you can communicate with someone far away. ওয়াকি-টকি

walking *n* **Walking** is the activity of going for walks in the country. হাঁটা

walking stick (**walking sticks**) *n* A **walking stick** is a long wooden stick which a person can lean on while walking. হাঁটার লাঠি

walkway (**walkways**) *n* A **walkway** is a path or passage for pedestrians, especially one which is raised above the ground. হেঁটে বেড়াবার স্থান

wall (**walls**) *n* A **wall** is one of the vertical sides of a building or room. দেওয়াল

wallet (**wallets**) *n* A **wallet** is a small flat folded case where you can keep banknotes and credit cards. পয়সা রাখার ব্যাগ

wallpaper (**wallpapers**) *n* **Wallpaper** is thick coloured or patterned paper that is used to decorate the walls of rooms. ওয়ালপেপার

walnut (**walnuts**) *n* **Walnuts** are light brown edible nuts which have a wrinkled shape and a very hard round shell. আখরোট

walrus (**walruses**) *n* A **walrus** is a large, fat animal which lives in the sea. It has two long teeth called tusks that point downwards. সিন্ধুঘোটক

waltz (**waltzes, waltzing, waltzed**) *n* A **waltz** is a piece of music with a rhythm of three beats in each bar, which people can dance to. তিনতালের নৃত্য ▷ *vi* If you **waltz** with someone, you dance a waltz with them. তিনতালে নৃত্য করা

wander (**wanders, wandering, wandered**) *vi* If you **wander** in a place, you walk around there in a casual way, often without intending to go in any particular direction. ঘুরে বেড়ানো

want (**wants, wanting, wanted**) *vt* If you **want** something, you would like to have it. চাওয়া

war (**wars**) *n* A **war** is a period of fighting between countries. যুদ্ধ

ward (**wards**) *n* A **ward** is a room in a hospital which has beds for many people, often people who need similar treatment. হাসপাতালের ঘর ▷ *n* A **ward** is a district which forms part of a political constituency or local council. অঞ্চল

warden (**wardens**) *n* A **warden** is an official who is responsible for a particular place or thing, and for making sure that certain laws are obeyed. ওয়ার্ডের প্রহরী

wardrobe (**wardrobes**) *n* A **wardrobe** is a tall cupboard in which you hang your clothes. পোশাকের আলমারি

warehouse (**warehouses**) *n* A **warehouse** is a large building where raw materials or manufactured goods are stored before they are taken to a shop. গুদামঘর

warm (**warmer, warmest**) *adj* Something that is **warm** has some heat but not enough to be hot. উষ্ণ

warm up *v* If you **warm** something **up**, or if it **warms up**, it gets hotter. গরম করা *Have you warmed the milk up, Mum?*

warn (**warns, warning, warned**) *v* If you **warn** someone about a possible danger or problem, you tell them about it so that they are aware of it. সতর্ক করা

warning (**warnings**) *n* A **warning** is something which is said or written to tell people of a possible danger, problem, or other unpleasant thing that might happen. সতর্কতা

warranty (**warranties**) *n* A **warranty** is a written guarantee which enables you to get a product repaired or replaced free of charge within a certain period of time. ওয়ারান্টি

wart (**warts**) *n* A **wart** is a small lump which grows on your skin and which is usually caused by a virus. আব

wash (**washes, washing, washed**) *vt* If you **wash** something, you clean it using water and usually a substance such as soap or detergent. ধোওয়া

washbasin (**washbasins**) *n* A **washbasin** is a large bowl for washing your hands and face. It is usually fixed to a wall, with taps for hot and cold water. মুখ ধোওয়ার বেসিন

washing *n* **Washing** is clothes, sheets, and other things that need to be washed, are being washed, or have just been washed. কাপড় ধোওয়া

washing line (**washing lines**) *n* A **washing line** is a strong cord which you can hang wet clothes on while they dry. কাপড় শুকোবার দড়ি

washing machine (**washing machines**) *n* A **washing machine** is a machine that you use to wash clothes in. কাপড় ধোওয়ার মেশিন

W

washing powder (**washing powders**) n
Washing powder is a powder that you use
with water to wash clothes. কাপড় ধোওয়ার
পাউডার

washing-up n To do the **washing-up**
means to wash the pans, plates, cups, and
cutlery which have been used in cooking
and eating a meal. ধৌতকরণ

washing-up liquid (**washing-up liquids**)
n **Washing-up liquid** is a thick soapy liquid
which you add to hot water to clean dirty
dishes. তরল সাবান

wash up v If you **wash up**, you wash the
pans, plates, cups, and cutlery which have
been used in cooking and eating a meal.
পরিষ্কার করা I made breakfast and then washed
up the plates.

wasp (**wasps**) n A **wasp** is a small insect
with a painful sting. It has yellow and black
stripes across its body. বোলতা

waste (**wastes, wasting, wasted**) n If
you waste something such as time,
money, or energy, you use too much of it
doing something that is not important or
necessary, or is unlikely to succeed. You
can say that doing this is a **waste** of time,
money, or energy. অপচয় ▷ vt If you **waste**
something such as time, money, or energy,
you use too much of it doing something
that is not important or necessary, or is
unlikely to succeed. অপচয় করা

wastepaper basket (**wastepaper baskets**)
n A **wastepaper basket** is a container for
rubbish, especially paper, which is usually
placed on the floor in the corner of a room
or next to a desk. নোংরা ফেলবার ঝুড়ি

watch (**watches, watching, watched**) n
A **watch** is a small clock that you wear
on your wrist. হাতঘড়ি ▷ v If you **watch**
something, you look at it for a period of
time. লক্ষ্য করা

watch out v If you tell someone to **watch
out**, you are warning them to be careful,
because something unpleasant might
happen to them or they might get into

difficulties. সতর্ক হওয়া You have to watch out
– there are dangers everywhere.

watch strap (**watch straps**) n A **watch
strap** is a strap of leather, cloth, etc,
attached to a watch for fastening it round
the wrist. হাতঘড়ির ব্যান্ড

water (**waters, watering, watered**) n
Water is a clear thin liquid that has no
colour or taste when it is pure. It falls from
clouds as rain. জল ▷ vt If you **water** plants,
you pour water over them in order to help
them to grow. জল

watercolour (**watercolours**) n
Watercolours are coloured paints, used
for painting pictures, which you apply
with a wet brush or dissolve in water first.
জলরং

watercress n **Watercress** is a small plant
with white flowers which grows in streams
and pools. Its leaves taste hot and are eaten
raw in salads. হালিম শাক

waterfall (**waterfalls**) n A **waterfall** is a
place where water flows over the edge of
a steep cliff or rocks and falls into a pool
below, such as Niagara Falls and Victoria
Falls. ঝরণা

watering can (**watering cans**) n A
watering can is a container with a long
spout which is used to water plants. ঝারি

watermelon (**watermelons**) n A
watermelon is a large, round fruit with
green skin, pink flesh, and black seeds.
তরমুজ

waterproof adj Something that is
waterproof does not let water pass
through it. জলনিরোধী

water-skiing n **Water-skiing** is the act of
standing on skis in the water while being
pulled along by a boat. ওয়াটার-স্কি

wave (**waves, waving, waved**) n If you
give a **wave**, you move your hand from
side to side in the air, usually to say hello or
goodbye to someone. হাত নাড়া ▷ v If you
wave your hand, you move it from side to
side, usually to say hello or goodbye. হাত

নাড়ানো ▷ *n* **Waves** on the surface of the sea are the parts that move up and down. ঢেউ

wavelength (**wavelengths**) *n* A **wavelength** is the distance between the same point on two waves of energy such as light or sound that are next to each other. তরঙ্গদৈর্ঘ্য

wavy (**wavier, waviest**) *adj* **Wavy** hair is not straight or curly, but curves slightly. ঢেউখেলানো

wax *n* **Wax** is a solid, slightly shiny substance made of fat or oil which is used to make candles and polish. মোম

way (**ways**) *n* A **way** of doing something is how you do it. উপায় ▷ *n* The **way** to a place is how you get there. রাস্তা

way in (**ways in**) *n* The **way in** is the point where you enter a place, for example, a door or gate. ঢোকার রাস্তা

way out (**ways out**) *n* The **way out** is the point where you leave a place, for example, a door or gate. বেরোবার রাস্তা

we *pron* You use **we** to talk about yourself and one or more other people as a group. আমরা *We said we would always be friends.*

weak (**weaker, weakest**) *adj* If someone is **weak**, they do not have very much strength or energy. দুর্বল

weakness (**weaknesses**) *n* **Weakness** is the state or quality of having little strength or energy. দুর্বলতা

wealth *n* **Wealth** is a large amount of money or property owned by someone, or the possession of it. সম্পদ

wealthy (**wealthier, wealthiest**) *adj* Someone who is **wealthy** has a large amount of money, property, or valuable possessions. সম্পদশালী

weapon (**weapons**) *n* A **weapon** is an object such as a gun, knife, or missile. অস্ত্রশস্ত্র

wear (**wears, wearing, wore, worn**) *vt* When you **wear** clothes, shoes, or jewellery, you have them on your body. পরা

weasel (**weasels**) *n* A **weasel** is a small wild animal with a long thin body, a tail, short legs, and reddish-brown fur. বেজি

weather *n* The **weather** is the condition of the atmosphere in an area at a particular time, for example, if it is raining, hot, or windy. আবহাওয়া

weather forecast (**weather forecasts**) *n* A **weather forecast** is a statement saying what the weather will be like the next day or for the next few days. আবহাওয়ার পূর্বাভাস

web (**webs**) *n* A **web** is the thin net made by a spider from a string that comes out of its body. মাকড়সার জাল

w

Web *n* The **Web** is made up of a very large number of websites all joined together. You can use it anywhere in the world to search for information. Web is short for World Wide Web. ওয়েব

Web 2.0 *n* **Web 2.0** is the Internet viewed as a medium in which interactive experience, in the form of blogs, wikis, forums, etc, plays a more important role than simply accessing information. ওয়েব ২.০

web address (**web addresses**) *n* A **web address** is a website's location on the Internet. ওয়েব অ্যাড্রেস

web browser (**web browsers**) *n* A **web browser** is a piece of computer software that you use to search for information on the Internet, especially on the World Wide Web. ওয়েব ব্রাউজার

webcam (**webcams**) *n* A **webcam** is a video camera that takes pictures which can be viewed on a website. The pictures are often of something that is happening while you watch. ওয়েবক্যাম

webmaster (**webmasters**) *n* A **webmaster** is someone who is in charge of a website, especially someone who does that as their job. ওয়েবমাস্টার

website (**websites**) *n* A **website** is a set of data and information about a particular subject which is available on the Internet. ওয়েবসাইট

webzine (**webzines**) *n* A **webzine** is a website which contains the kind of articles, pictures, and advertisements that you would find in a magazine. ওয়েবজিন

wedding (**weddings**) *n* A **wedding** is a marriage ceremony and the celebration that often takes place afterwards. বিবাহ

wedding anniversary (**wedding anniversaries**) *n* Your **wedding anniversary** is a date that you remember or celebrate because you got married on that date in a previous year. বিবাহবার্ষিকী

wedding dress (**wedding dresses**) *n* A **wedding dress** is a special dress that a woman wears at her wedding. বিবাহের পোষাক

wedding ring (**wedding rings**) *n* A **wedding ring** is a ring that you wear to show that you are married. বিবাহের আংটি

Wednesday (**Wednesdays**) *n* **Wednesday** is the day after Tuesday and before Thursday. বুধবার

weed (**weeds**) *n* A **weed** is a wild plant growing where it is not wanted, for example in a garden. আগাছা

weedkiller (**weedkillers**) *n* **Weedkiller** is a substance you put on your garden to kill weeds. আগাছানাশক

week (**weeks**) *n* A **week** is a period of seven days, which is often considered to start on Monday and end on Sunday. সপ্তাহ

weekday (**weekdays**) *n* A **weekday** is any day of the week except Saturday and Sunday. সপ্তাহের কাজের দিন

weekend (**weekends**) *n* A **weekend** is Saturday and Sunday. সপ্তাহান্ত

weep (**weeps, weeping, wept**) *v* If someone **weeps**, they cry. (*literary*) ফুঁপিয়ে কাঁদা

weigh (**weighs, weighing, weighed**) *vt* If someone or something **weighs** a particular amount, that is how heavy they are. ওজন করা

weight (**weights**) *n* The **weight** of a person or thing is how heavy they are, measured in units such as kilos or pounds. ওজন

weightlifter (**weightlifters**) *n* A **weightlifter** is a person who does weightlifting. ভারোত্তোলক

weightlifting *n* **Weightlifting** is a sport in which the competitor who can lift the heaviest weight wins. ভারোত্তোলন

weird (**weirder, weirdest**) *adj* **Weird** means strange and peculiar. (*informal*) অদ্ভু

welcome! (**welcomes, welcoming, welcomed**) *excl* You say '**Welcome!**' when you are greeting someone who has just arrived somewhere. স্বাগত-সম্ভাষণ ▷ *n* If you give someone a **welcome**, you greet them in a friendly way when they arrive. স্বাগত ▷ *vt* If you **welcome** someone, you greet them in a friendly way when they arrive somewhere. স্বাগত জানানো

well (**better, best, wells**) *adj* If you are **well**, you are healthy and not ill. সুস্থ ▷ *adv* If you do something **well**, you do it in a good way. ভাল ▷ *n* A **well** is a deep hole in the ground from which people take water, oil, or gas. কুয়ো

well-behaved *adj* If you describe someone, especially a child, as **well-behaved**, you mean that they behave in a way that adults generally like and think is correct. সুন্দর আচরণবিশিষ্ট

well done! *excl* You say '**Well done!**' to indicate that you are pleased that someone has done something good. সাবাস

wellingtons *npl* **Wellingtons** are long rubber boots which you wear to keep your feet dry. লম্বা রাবারের জুতো

well-known *adj* Something or someone that is **well-known** is famous or familiar. সুপরিচিত

well-off *adj* Someone who is **well-off** is rich enough to be able to do and buy most of the things that they want. (*informal*) বড়লোক

well-paid *adj* If you say that a person or their job is **well-paid**, you mean that they receive a lot of money for the work that they do. মোটা বেতন প্রাপ্ত

Welsh *adj* **Welsh** means belonging or relating to Wales, or to its people, language, or culture. ওয়েলস দেশীয় ▷ *n* **Welsh** is a language of Wales. ওয়েলস ভাষা

west *adj* The **west** part of a place, country, or region is the part which is towards the west. পশ্চিমাংশ ▷ *adv* If you go **west**, you travel towards the west. পশ্চিম দিকে ▷ *n* The **west** is the direction in which you look to see the sun set. পশ্চিম

westbound *adj* **Westbound** roads or vehicles lead to or are travelling towards the west. পশ্চিমদিকে

western (**westerns**) *adj* **Western** means in or from the west of a region or country. পশ্চিমাঞ্চল ▷ *n* A **western** is a film or book about the life of cowboys. গোপালকের জীবনকাহিনী

West Indian (**West Indians**) *adj* **West Indian** means belonging or relating to the West Indies, or to its people or culture. ওয়েস্ট ইন্ডিয়া দেশীয় ▷ *n* A **West Indian** is a person who comes from the West Indies. ওয়েস্ট ইন্ডিয়ার নাগরিক

West Indies *npl* The **West Indies** is an archipelago off Central America, extending over 2400 km (1500 miles) in an arc from the peninsula of Florida to Venezuela, separating the Caribbean Sea from the Atlantic Ocean. ওয়েস্ট ইন্ডিজ

wet (**wetter, wettest**) *adj* If something is **wet**, it is covered in water or another liquid. ভিজে

wetsuit (**wetsuits**) *n* A **wetsuit** is a close-fitting rubber suit which an underwater swimmer wears in order to keep their body warm. সাঁতারুর পোষাক

whale (**whales**) *n* A **whale** is a very large sea mammal. তিমি

what *det* You use **what** with a noun, when you ask for information. কি বোঝাতে ব্যবহৃত হয় *What time is it?* ▷ *pron* You use **what** in questions when you ask for information. কি? *What do you want?*

whatever *conj* You use **whatever** to talk about anything or everything of a type. যা কিছু *We can do whatever you want.*

wheat *n* **Wheat** is a cereal crop grown for its grain, which is ground into flour to make bread. গম

wheat intolerance *n* If you have a **wheat intolerance**, you become ill if you eat food containing wheat. গমে অ্যালার্জি

wheel (**wheels**) *n* A **wheel** is a circular object which turns round on a rod attached to its centre. Wheels are fixed underneath vehicles so that they can move along. চাকা

wheelbarrow (**wheelbarrows**) *n* A **wheelbarrow** is a small open cart with one

W

wheel and handles that is used for carrying things, for example in the garden. হুইলব্যারো

wheelchair (**wheelchairs**) n A **wheelchair** is a chair with wheels that sick or disabled people use in order to move about. হুইলচেয়ার

when adv You use **when** to ask what time something happened or will happen. কখন? ▷ conj You use **when** to talk about the time at which something happens. যখন I asked him when he'd be back.

whenever conj You use **whenever** to talk about any time or every time that something happens. যখনই Whenever I talked to him, he seemed quite nice.

where adv You use **where** to ask questions about the place something is in. কোথায়? ▷ conj You use **where** to talk about the place in which something is situated or happens. কোথা থেকে People were wondering where the noise was coming from.

whether conj You use **whether** when you are talking about a choice between two or more things. কিনা They now have two weeks to decide whether or not to buy the house.

which det You use **which** when you want help to choose between things. কোন? Which shoes should I put on? ▷ pron You use **which** to ask questions when there are two or more possible answers. কোনটা Which is your room?

whichever det **Whichever** means any person or thing. যা কিছু Whichever way we do this, it isn't going to work.

while conj If one thing happens **while** another thing is happening, the two things are happening at the same time. যখন She goes to work while her children are at school. ▷ n A **while** is a period of time. কিছুক্ষণ

whip (**whips**) n A **whip** is a long thin piece of leather or rope fastened to a handle. It is used for hitting animals or people. চাবুক

whipped cream n **Whipped cream** is cream that has been stirred very fast until it is thick or stiff. ফেটানো ক্রিম

whisk (**whisks**) n A **whisk** is a kitchen tool used for whisking eggs or cream. ফেটানোর মেশিন

whiskers npl The **whiskers** of an animal such as a cat or a mouse are the long stiff hairs that grow near its mouth. গোঁফ

whisky (**whiskies**) n **Whisky** is a strong alcoholic drink made, especially in Scotland, from grain such as barley or rye. মদ্যবিশেষ

whisper (**whispers, whispering, whispered**) v When you **whisper**, you say something very quietly, using your breath rather than your throat, so that only one person can hear you. ফিসফিস করা

whistle (**whistles, whistling, whistled**) n A **whistle** is a small metal tube which you blow in order to produce a loud sound and attract someone's attention. বাঁশি ▷ v When you **whistle**, you make sounds by forcing your breath out between your lips or teeth. শিস দেওয়া

hite (whiter, whitest) adj Something that
s white is the colour of snow or milk. সাদা

hiteboard (whiteboards) n A
whiteboard is a shiny white board on
which people draw or write using special
pens. Whiteboards are often used for
teaching or giving talks. হোয়াইট বোর্ড

**hitewash (whitewashes, whitewashing,
whitewashed)** v Whitewash is a mixture
of lime or chalk and water used for painting
walls white. চুনকাম করা

hiting (whitings, whiting) n A whiting
s a black and silver fish that lives in the sea.
সামুদ্রিক মৎসবিশেষ

ho pron You use **who** in questions when
you ask about someone's name. কে Who
won the quiz?

hoever conj You use **whoever** to talk
about somebody when you do not know
who they are. যে কেউ Whoever wins the prize
s going to be famous for life.

hole adj The **whole** of something is all of
t. গোটা ▷ n A **whole** is a single thing which
contains several different parts. সম্পূর্ণ

holefoods npl **Wholefoods** are foods
which have not been processed much and
which have not had artificial ingredients
added. অপরিশীলিত খাদ্য

holemeal adj **Wholemeal** flour is made
from the complete grain of the wheat plant,
including the outer part. **Wholemeal** bread
or pasta is made from wholemeal flour. আটা

holesale adj **Wholesale** goods are
bought cheaply in large quantities and
then sold again to shops. পাইকারি ▷ n
Wholesale is the activity of buying and
selling goods in large quantities and
therefore at cheaper prices, usually to
shopkeepers who then sell them to the
public. পাইকারি হারে ক্রয়বিক্রয়

hom pron **Whom** is used in formal
or written English instead of 'who' when
somebody does something to somebody.
formal) যাকে The book is about her husband,
whom she married ten years ago.

whose det You use **whose** to ask who
something belongs to. কার Whose bag is
this? ▷ pron You use **whose** to explain who
something belongs to. যার He shouted at the
driver whose car was blocking the street.

why adv You use **why** when you are asking
about the reason for something. কেন

wicked adj You use **wicked** to describe
someone or something that is very bad in a
way that is deliberately harmful to people.
মন্দ

wide (wider, widest) adj Something that is
wide is a large distance from one side to the
other. চওড়া ▷ adv If you open something
wide, you open it fully. চওড়াভাবে

widespread adj Something that is
widespread exists or happens over a large
area or to a very great extent. ব্যাপক

widow (widows) n A **widow** is a woman
whose husband has died. বিধবা

widower (widowers) n A **widower** is a
man whose wife has died. বিপত্নীক

width (widths) n The **width** of something
is the distance that it measures from one
side to the other. বহর

wife (wives) n A man's **wife** is the woman
he is married to. স্ত্রী

Wi-Fi n **Wi-Fi** is a system for using
the Internet from laptop computers
with wireless connections. **Wi-Fi** is an
abbreviation of 'wireless fidelity'. ওয়াই-ফাই

wig (wigs) n A **wig** is a mass of false hair
which is worn on your head. পরচুলা

wild (wilder, wildest) adj **Wild** animals
and plants live or grow in natural
surroundings and are not looked after by
people. বন্য

wildlife n You can use **wildlife** to refer to
animals and other living things that live in
the wild. বন্যজীবন

will (wills) n **Will** is the determination
to do something. ইচ্ছা ▷ n A **will** is a
legal document stating what you want to
happen to your money when you die. দলিল
▷ v You use **will** to talk about things that

W

are going to happen in the future. হবে *Mum will be angry.*

willing *adj* If someone is **willing** to do something, they do not mind doing it or have no objection to doing it. ইচ্ছুক

willingly *adv* If someone does something **willingly**, they have no objection to doing it. ইচ্ছাকৃতভাবে

willow (**willows**) *n* A **willow** is a tree with long narrow leaves and branches that hang down. উইলো গাছ

willpower *n* **Willpower** is a very strong determination to do something. ইচ্ছাশক্তি

wilt (**wilts, wilting, wilted**) *vi* If a plant **wilts**, it gradually bends downwards and becomes weak, because it needs more water or is dying. শুকিয়ে যাওয়া

win (**wins, winning, won**) *v* If you **win** something such as a competition, battle, or argument, you defeat those people who are competing or fighting against, or you do better than everyone else involved. জেতা

wind (**winds, winding, winded, wound**) *n* **Wind** is air that moves. বাতাস ▷ *vt* If you are **winded** by something, you have difficulty breathing for a short time. দম ফুরানো ▷ *vi* If a road or river **winds**, it twists and turns. ঘুরে যাওয়া ▷ *vt* When you **wind** something long around something, you wrap it around several times. ঘুরিয়ে বাঁধা

windmill (**windmills**) *n* A **windmill** is a tall building with sails which turn as the wind blows. Windmills are used to grind grain or pump water. হাওয়া কল

window (**windows**) *n* A **window** is a space in the wall of a building or in the side of a vehicle, which has glass in it so that light can pass through and people can see in or out. জানালা

window pane (**window panes**) *n* A **window pane** is a piece of glass in the window of a building. জানালার কাঁচ

window seat (**window seats**) *n* A **window seat** is a seat which is fixed to the wall

underneath a window in a room. জানালার ধারের সীট

windowsill (**windowsills**) *n* A **windowsill** is a shelf along the bottom of a window, either inside or outside a building. গোবরাট

windscreen (**windscreens**) *n* The **windscreen** of a car or other vehicle is the glass window at the front through which the driver looks. গাড়ির সামনের কাঁচ

windscreen wiper (**windscreen wipers**) *n* A **windscreen wiper** is a device that wipes rain from a vehicle's windscreen. গাড়ির সামনের কাঁচ পরিষ্কার করবার ওয়াইপার

windsurfing *n* **Windsurfing** is a sport in which you move along the surface of the sea or a lake on a long narrow board with a sail on it. একটি জলের ক্রীড়া

windy (**windier, windiest**) *adj* If it is **windy** the wind is blowing a lot. বাতাসযুক্ত

wine (**wines**) *n* **Wine** is an alcoholic drink, usually made from grapes. মদ্যবিশেষ

wineglass (**wineglasses**) *n* A **wineglass** is a glass drinking vessel, typically having a small bowl on a stem, with a flared foot. ওয়াইনের গ্লাস

wine list (**wine lists**) *n* A restaurant's **wine list** is a list of all the wines that it has available. ওয়াইনের তালিকা

wing (**wings**) *n* The **wings** of a bird or insect are the parts of its body that it uses for flying. ডানা

wing mirror (**wing mirrors**) *n* The **wing mirrors** on a car are the mirrors on each side of the car on the outside. গাড়ির দুধারে লাগানো আয়না

wink (**winks, winking, winked**) *vi* When you **wink** at someone, you look towards them and close one eye very briefly, usually as a signal that something is a joke or a secret. চোখ টিপে ইশারা করা

winner (**winners**) *n* The **winner** of a prize, race, or competition is the person, animal, or thing that wins it. বিজয়ী

winning *adj* You can use **winning** to describe a person or thing that wins something such as a competition, game, or election. জয়ী

winter (winters) n Winter is the season between autumn and spring. In winter the weather is usually cold. শীতকাল

winter sports npl Winter sports are sports that take place on ice or snow, for example skating and skiing. শীতকালের খেলা

wipe (wipes, wiping, wiped) vt If you wipe something, you rub its surface to remove dirt or liquid from it. মোছা

wipe up v If you wipe up dirt or liquid from something, you remove it using a cloth. মুছে ফেলা Wipe up spills immediately.

wire (wires) n A wire is a long thin piece of metal that is used to fasten things or to carry electric current. তার

wisdom n Wisdom is the ability to use your experience and knowledge to make sensible decisions and judgments. জ্ঞান

wisdom tooth (wisdom teeth) n Your wisdom teeth are the four large teeth at the back of your mouth which usually grow much later than your other teeth. আক্কেল দাঁত

wise (wiser, wisest) adj A wise person is able to use their experience and knowledge to make sensible decisions and judgments. জ্ঞানী

wish (wishes, wishing, wished) n A wish is a desire for something. মনোবাসনা ▷ vt If you wish to do something, you want to do it. ইচ্ছা করা

wit n Wit is the ability to use words or ideas in an amusing and clever way. রসিকতা

witch (witches) n A witch is a woman who is believed to have magic powers, especially evil ones. ডাইনি

with prep If one person is with another, they are together in one place. সঙ্গে He's watching a film with his friends. ▷ prep You use with to say that someone has something. সহ My daughter is the girl with brown hair.

withdraw (withdraws, withdrawing, withdrew, withdrawn) vt If you withdraw

something from a place, you remove it or take it away. (formal) প্রত্যাহার করা

withdrawal (withdrawals) n The withdrawal of something is the act or process of removing it or ending it. (formal) প্রত্যাহার

within prep If something is within a place, area, or object, it is inside it or surrounded by it. (formal) মধ্যে The sports fields must be within the city.

without prep If you do something without someone, they are not in the same place as you are, or they are not doing the same thing as you. ছাড়া He went without me.

witness (witnesses) n A witness to an event such as an accident or crime is a person who saw it. সাক্ষী

witty (wittier, wittiest) adj Someone or something that is witty is amusing in a clever way. রসময়

wolf (wolves) n A wolf is a wild animal that looks like a large dog. নেকড়ে

woman (women) n A woman is an adult female human being. মহিলা

wonder (wonders, wondering, wondered) vt If you wonder about something, you think about it and try to guess or understand more about it. অবাক হওয়া

wonderful adj If you describe something or someone as wonderful, you think they are extremely good. দারুণ

wood (woods) n Wood is the hard material that trees are made of. কাঠ ▷ n A wood is a large area of trees growing near each other. জঙ্গল

wooden adj A wooden object is made of wood. কাঠনির্মিত

woodwind adj Woodwind instruments are musical instruments such as flutes, clarinets, and recorders that you play by blowing into them. বায়ুচালিত বাদ্যযন্ত্র

woodwork n You can refer to the doors and other wooden parts of a house as the woodwork. কাঠের কাজ

wool n Wool is the hair that grows on sheep and on some other animals. পশম

woollen *adj* **Woollen** clothes are made from wool. পশমনির্মিত

woollens *npl* **Woollens** are clothes, especially sweaters, that are made of wool. উলনির্মিত

word (**words**) *n* **Words** are things that you say or write. শব্দ

work (**works, working, worked**) *n* People who have **work** have a job. কাজ ▷ *vi* When you **work**, you do something that uses a lot of your time or effort. কাজ করা ▷ *vi* If a machine **works**, it does its job. ঠিকঠাক চলা

worker (**workers**) *n* **Workers** are people who are employed in industry or business and who are not managers. কর্মী

work experience *n* **Work experience** is a period of time that a young person, especially a student, spends working in a company as a form of training. কর্ম অভিজ্ঞতা

workforce (**workforces**) *n* The **workforce** is the total number of people in a country or region who are physically able to do a job and are available for work. কর্মীবাহিনী

working-class *adj* If you are **working-class**, you are a member of the group of people in a society who do not own much property, who have low social status, and who do jobs which involve using physical skills rather than intellectual skills. শ্রমিকশ্রেণী

workman (**workmen**) *n* A **workman** is a man who works with his hands, for example a builder or plumber. মজুর

work of art (**works of art**) *n* A **work of art** is a painting or piece of sculpture of high quality. শিল্পকর্ম

work out *v* If you **work out** a solution to a problem or mystery, you find the solution by thinking or talking about it. সমাধান খোঁজা *They are planning to meet later today to work out a solution.*

work permit (**work permits**) *n* A **work permit** is an official document that someone needs in order to work in a particular foreign country. কাজের অনুমতিপত্র

workplace (**workplaces**) *n* Your **workplace** is the place where you work. কর্মক্ষেত্র

workshop (**workshops**) *n* A **workshop** is a room or building containing tools or machinery for making or repairing things. কারখানা

workspace *n* A person's **workspace** is the area, especially in an office, that is allocated for them to work in. কাজ করার জায়গা

workstation (**workstations**) *n* A **workstation** is a computer. কম্পিউটার

world *n* The **world** is the planet that we live on. পৃথিবী

World Cup *n* The **World Cup** is an international competition held between national teams in various sports, most notably association football. বিশ্বকাপ

worm (**worms**) *n* A **worm** is a small thin animal without bones or legs which lives in the soil. কেঁচো

worn *adj* **Worn** things are damaged or thin because they are old and have been used a lot. জরাজীর্ণ

worried *adj* When you are **worried**, you are unhappy because you keep thinking about problems that you have or about unpleasant things that might happen in the future. চিন্তিত

worry (**worries, worrying, worried**) *vi* If you **worry**, you keep thinking about a problem or about something unpleasant that might happen. চিন্তা করা

worrying *adj* If something is **worrying**, it causes people to worry. চিন্তার বিষয়

worse *adj* **Worse** is the comparative of **bad** and **badly**. It means more bad. আরো খারাপ ▷ *adv* **Worse** is the comparative of **badly**. It means more badly. অধিকতর খারাপ

worsen (**worsens, worsening, worsened**) *v* If a situation **worsens**, it becomes more difficult, unpleasant, or unacceptable. আরো খারাপ করা

worship (**worships, worshipping, worshipped**) *v* If you **worship** a god, you show your respect to the god, for example by saying prayers. পূজা করা

worst adj **Worst** is the superlative of **bad**. It means most bad. সবথেকে খারাপ

worth n Someone's **worth** is their value, usefulness, or importance. মূল্য

worthless adj Something that is **worthless** is of no real use or value. মূল্যহীন

would v You use **would** to say that someone agreed to do something. হবে *They said they would come to my party.*

wound (**wounds, wounding, wounded**) n A **wound** is a part of your body that you have hurt with something like a knife or a gun. আঘাত ▷ vt If somebody or something **wounds** you, they hurt you. আঘাত লাগা

wrap (**wraps, wrapping, wrapped**) vt When you **wrap** something, you fold paper or cloth tightly round it to cover it completely, for example in order to protect it or so that you can give it to someone as a present. মোড়া

wrapping paper (**wrapping papers**) n **Wrapping paper** is special paper which is used for wrapping presents. মোড়ার কাগজ

wrap up v If you **wrap** something **up**, you fold paper or cloth tightly round it to cover it. গুটিয়ে ফেলা *I'll take the opportunity to wrap up some presents.*

wreck (**wrecks, wrecking, wrecked**) n A **wreck** is something such as ship, car, plane, or building which has been destroyed, usually in an accident. ধ্বংস ▷ vt To **wreck** something means to completely destroy or ruin it. ধ্বংস করা

wreckage n When a plane, car, or building has been destroyed, you can refer to what remains as the **wreckage**. ধ্বংসাবশেষ

wren (**wrens**) n A **wren** is a very small brown bird. পঙ্কীবিশেষ

wrench (**wrenches, wrenching, wrenched**) n If you say that leaving someone or something is a **wrench**, you feel very sad about it. কষ্টকর ▷ vt If you **wrench** something, usually something that is in a fixed position, you pull or twist it violently. হ্যাঁচকা মারা

wrestler (**wrestlers**) n A **wrestler** is someone who wrestles as a sport. কুস্তিগির

wrestling n **Wrestling** is a sport in which two people wrestle and try to throw each other to the ground. কুস্তি

wrinkle (**wrinkles**) n **Wrinkles** are lines which form on someone's face as they grow old. বলিরেখা

wrinkled adj Someone who has **wrinkled** skin has a lot of wrinkles. বলিরেখাযুক্ত

wrist (**wrists**) n Your **wrist** is the part of your body between your hand and arm which bends when you move your hand. কব্জি

write (**writes, writing, wrote, written**) v When you **write** something on a surface, you use something such as a pen or pencil to produce words, letters, or numbers on it. লেখা

write down v When you **write** something **down**, you record it on a piece of paper using a pen or pencil. লিখে রাখা *I wrote down exactly what I thought.*

writer (**writers**) n A **writer** is a person whose job is writing books, stories, or articles. লেখক

writing n **Writing** is something that has been written or printed. লেখা

writing paper (**writing papers**) n **Writing paper** is paper for writing letters on. It is usually of good, smooth quality. লেখার কাগজ

wrong adj If there is something **wrong**, there is something that is not as it should be. ভুল ▷ adj If you say that an answer is **wrong**, you mean that it is not right. ভুল ▷ adj If you say that something someone does is **wrong**, you mean that it is bad. অন্যায়

wrong number (**wrong numbers**) n A **wrong number** is a telephone number dialled in error. ভুল নম্বর

X y

Xmas (**Xmases**) *n* **Xmas** is used in written English to represent the word Christmas. (*informal*) বড়দিন

X-ray (**X-rays, X-raying, X-rayed**) *n* An **X-ray** is a type of radiation that can pass through most solid materials. X-rays are used by doctors to examine the bones or organs inside your body, and at airports to see inside people's luggage. এক্স-রে ▷ *vt* If someone or something **is X-rayed**, an X-ray picture is taken of them. এক্স-রে করা

xylophone (**xylophones**) *n* A **xylophone** is a musical instrument which consists of a row of wooden bars of different lengths. You play the xylophone by hitting the bars with special hammers. জাইলোফোন

yacht (**yachts**) *n* A **yacht** is a large boat with sails or a motor, used for racing or for pleasure trips. প্রমোদতরণী

yard (**yards**) *n* A **yard** is a unit of length equal to 36 inches or approximately 91.4 centimetres. গজ ▷ *n* A **yard** is a flat area of concrete or stone that is next to a building and often has a wall around it. আঙ্গিনা

yawn (**yawns, yawning, yawned**) *vi* If you **yawn**, you open your mouth very wide and breathe in more air than usual, often when you are tired or when you are not interested in something. হাই তোলা

year (**years**) *n* A **year** is a period of twelve months, beginning on the first of January and ending on the thirty-first of December. বৎসর

yearly *adj* A **yearly** event happens once a year or every year. বাৎসরিক ▷ *adv* If something happens **yearly**, it happens once a year or every year. বার্ষিক

yeast (**yeasts**) *n* **Yeast** is a kind of fungus which is used to make bread rise, and in making alcoholic drinks such as beer. ঈস্ট

yell (**yells, yelling, yelled**) *v* If you **yell**, you shout loudly, usually because you are excited, angry, or in pain. চিৎকার করা

yellow *adj* Something that is **yellow** is the colour of lemons, butter, or the middle part of an egg. হলুদ

Yellow Pages® *n* **Yellow Pages** is a book that contains advertisements and telephone numbers for businesses and organizations in a particular area, grouped according to the type of business they do. ইয়েলো পেজ

Yemen n **Yemen** is a republic in south-west Arabia, on the Red Sea and the Gulf of Aden. ইয়েমেন

yes! excl You say '**yes!**' to give a positive response to a question. হ্যাঁ!

yesterday adv You use **yesterday** to refer to the day before today. গতকাল

yet adv You use **yet** when you expect something to happen, but it hasn't happened. এখনও

yew (yews) n A **yew** or a **yew tree** is an evergreen tree. It has sharp leaves which are broad and flat, and red berries. একধরণের চিরসবুজ গাছ

yield (yields, yielding, yielded) vi If you **yield** to someone or something, you stop resisting them. (formal) মেনে নেওয়া

yoga n **Yoga** is a type of exercise in which you move your body into various positions in order to become more fit or flexible, and to improve your breathing, and to relax your mind. যোগব্যায়াম

yoghurt (yoghurts) n **Yoghurt** is a slightly sour thick liquid made by adding bacteria to milk. দই

yolk (yolks) n The **yolk** of an egg is the yellow part in the middle. ডিমের কুসুম

you pron **You** means the person or people that someone is talking or writing to. তুমি Can I help you?

young (younger, youngest) adj A **young** person, animal, or plant has not lived for very long. অল্পবয়সী

younger adj A **younger** person or animal has lived for a shorter time than another. অপেক্ষাকৃত ছোট

youngest adj The **youngest** person or animal of a group has lived for the shortest time of all of them. সবথেকে ছোট

your det You use **your** to show that something belongs to the people that you are talking to. আপনার/তোমার I do like your name.

yours pron **Yours** refers to something belonging to the people that you are talking to. আপনার His hair is longer than yours.

yourself pron **Yourself** means you alone. আপনি/তুমি নিজে You'll hurt yourself.

yourselves pron A speaker or writer uses **yourselves** to refer to the people that they are talking or writing to. **Yourselves** is used when the object of a verb or preposition refers to the same people as the subject of the verb. আপনাদের নিজেদের Treat yourselves to an ice cream.

youth n Someone's **youth** is the period of their life when they are a child, before they are a fully mature adult. যৌবন

youth club (youth clubs) n A **youth club** is a club where young people can go to meet each other and take part in various leisure activities. Youth clubs are often run by a church or local authority. যুব সঙ্ঘ

youth hostel (youth hostels) n A **youth hostel** is a place where people can stay cheaply when they are travelling. ইউথ হোস্টেল

y

Z

Zambia n **Zambia** is a republic in southern Africa. জাম্বিয়া

Zambian (**Zambians**) adj **Zambian** means of or relating to Zambia or its inhabitants. জাম্বিয়া দেশীয় ▷ n A **Zambian** is a native or inhabitant of Zambia. জাম্বিয়ার বসবাসকারী

zebra (**zebras, zebra**) n A **zebra** is an African wild horse which has black and white stripes. জেব্রা

zebra crossing (**zebra crossings**) n In Britain, a **zebra crossing** is a place on the road that is marked with black and white stripes, where vehicles are supposed to stop so that people can walk across. জেব্রা ক্রসিং

zero (**zeros, zeroes**) n **Zero** is freezing point on the Centigrade scale. It is often written as 0°C. শূন্য

zest n **Zest** is a feeling of pleasure and enthusiasm. উদ্দীপনা ▷ n The **zest** of a lemon, orange, or lime is the outer skin when it is used to give flavour to something such as a cake or drink. পাতিলেবুর খোসা

Zimbabwe n **Zimbabwe** is a country in south-east Africa. জিম্বাবোয়ে

Zimbabwean (**Zimbabweans**) adj **Zimbabwean** means of or relating to Zimbabwe or its inhabitants. জিম্বাবোয়ে দেশীয় ▷ n A **Zimbabwean** is a native or inhabitant of Zimbabwe. জিম্বাবোয়ের বসবাসকারী

Zimmer® frame (**Zimmer frames**) n A **Zimmer frame** or a **Zimmer** is a frame that old or ill people sometimes use to help them walk. বয়স্কদের হাঁটার সহায়ক

zinc n **Zinc** is a bluish-white metal which is used to make other metals such as brass, or to cover other metals such as iron to stop them rusting. দস্তা

zip (**zips, zipping, zipped**) n A **zip** is a device used to open and close parts of clothes and bags. It consists of two rows of metal or plastic teeth which separate or fasten together as you pull a small tag along them. চেন ▷ vt When you **zip** something, you fasten it using a zip. চেন টানা

zit (**zits**) n **Zits** are spots on someone's skin, especially a young person's. (informal) ত্বকে দাগ

zodiac n The **zodiac** is a diagram used by astrologers to represent the positions of the planets and stars. It is divided into twelve sections, each with a special name and symbol. রাশিচক্র

zone (**zones**) n A **zone** is an area that has particular features or characteristics. অঞ্চল

zoo (**zoos**) n A **zoo** is a park where live animals are kept so that people can look at them. চিড়িয়াখানা

zoology n **Zoology** is the scientific study of animals. প্রাণীতত্ত্ব

zoom lens (**zoom lenses**) n A **zoom lens** is a lens that you can attach to a camera, which allows you to make the details larger or smaller while always keeping the picture clear. জুম লেন্স

Index

অনুমতিপত্র pass, permit
অনুমান assume
অনুমান করা expect, speculate
অনুমানসাপেক্ষ predictable
অনুমোদন approval, authorize
অনুমোদন করা approve
অনুরাগী fan
অনুরূপ similar
অনুরূপ like
অনুরোধ request
অনুরোধ করা request
অনুলিপি copy
অনুশাসন discipline
অনুশীলন exercise
অনুশোচনা regret
অনুশোচনা করা regret
অনুষ্ঠান-পরিচালক compere
অনুষ্ঠানের মহড়া rehearsal
অনুষ্ঠানের মহড়া দেওয়া rehearse
অনুসন্ধান enquiry, inquiry
অনুসন্ধান কক্ষ inquiry desk
অনুসন্ধান করা inquire
অনুসন্ধানকারী explorer
অনুসন্ধান কার্যালয় inquiries office
অনুসরণ pursuit
অনুসরণ করা follow, pursue
অনুসারে according to
অনেক many, mass, much, several
অনেকক্ষণ ধরে ঘুমোন sleep in
অনেকগুলি either
অনৈতিক immoral
অন্ডকোষ testicle
অন্তঃস্থিত inner
অন্তরঙ্গ intimate
অন্তরঙ্গ indoor
অন্তর্দৃষ্টি intuition
অন্তর্ধান disappearance
অন্তর্বাস pants, slip, underpants, underwear
অন্তর্ভুক্ত করা include
অন্তর্হিত হওয়া disappear
অন্তিম final, terminal
অন্তিম তারিখ expiry date
অন্ত্যেষ্টি funeral
অন্ত্যেষ্টিক্রিয়া সম্পূর্ণ করবার স্থান funeral parlour
অন্ত্র bowels
অন্দরসজ্জা বিশেষজ্ঞ interior designer
অন্ধ blind
অন্ধকার dark
অন্ধকারাচ্ছন্ন gloomy
অন্ধকূপ dungeon
অন্ধ ভক্ত fanatic
অন্য একটি another

অন্যত্র elsewhere
অন্যথায় otherwise
অন্যদিকে ফেরা turn
অন্যভাবে otherwise
অন্যমনস্কভাবে inadvertently
অনামহিলার বাচ্চার জন্মদাত্রী surrogate mother
অন্যরকম unlike
অন্যান্য other
অন্যায় wrong
অন্যায় আচরণ করা misbehave
অন্যায় বিচার করা misjudge
অন্যের পরিচয়-তথ্য চুরি করা identity theft
অপচয় waste
অপচয় করা waste
অপছন্দ করা dislike
অপমান করা insult
অপরাজিত unbeatable
অপরাধ crime, offence
অপরাধপ্রবণ ব্যক্তি crook
অপরাধবোধ guilt
অপরাধ-সম্পর্কিত criminal
অপরাধী convict, criminal
অপরাধীদের দল gang
অপরাধীদের সদস্য gangster
অপরাহ্ন afternoon
অপরিচিত unfamiliar
অপরিণত immature
অপরিবর্তনশীল ক্রিয়া infinitive
অপরিবর্তিত unchanged
অপরিমার্জিত naff
অপরিষ্কার untidy
অপরিহার্য indispensable
অপসারণ removal
অপসারণ করা remove
অপসারণযোগ্য removable
অপহরণ করা abduct, hijack, kidnap
অপহরণকারী hijacker
অপুষ্টি malnutrition
অপূর্ব marvellous
অপেক্ষা than
অপেক্ষা করা hang on
অপেক্ষা করিয়ে রাখা hold up
অপেক্ষাকৃত কম fewer, less
অপেক্ষাকৃত খারাপ second class
অপেক্ষাকৃত ছোট younger
অপেশাদার amateur
অপ্রকৃতিস্থ insane
অপ্রতুল inadequate, insufficient
অপ্রত্যাশিত unexpected
অপ্রত্যাশিতভাবে unexpectedly
অপ্রয়োজনীয় unnecessary
অপ্রয়োজনীয় ই-মেল spam

অপ্রাপ্তবয়স্ক minor
অপ্রাসঙ্গিক irrelevant
অফিস office
অফিস-সংক্রান্ত official
অফিসার officer
অফিসের সময় office hours, peak hours
অবতরণ touchdown
অবদান contribution
অবদান রাখা contribute
অবধারিতভাবে necessarily
অবজ্ঞানোচিত unfriendly
অবমাননা contempt, insult
অবমাননাকার সম্বোধন twit
অবমূল্যায়ন করা underestimate
অবরোহণ করা descend
অবশ paralysed
অবশ করার ওষুধ local anaesthetic
অবশিষ্ট remains
অবশিষ্টাংশ remaining, trace
অবশেষ finally
অবশ্যম্ভাবী inevitable
অবসর leisure
অবসরগ্রহণ retirement
অবসর গ্রহণ করা retire
অবসর-নিবাস resort
অবসরপ্রাপ্ত retired
অবসর বিনোদন pastime
অবসর সময় কাটানোর জায়গা leisure centre
অবসাদ-প্রতিরোধক antidepressant
অবস্থা condition, position
অবস্থান location, place
অবস্থান কাল stay
অবস্থিত situated
অবহিত করা inform
অবহেলা neglect
অবহেলা করা ignore, neglect
অবহেলিত neglected
অবাক হওয়া wonder
অবাধ্য disobedient, rebellious
অবাস্তব impractical, unrealistic
অবিচলিত consistent
অবিচার injustice
অবিবাহিত bachelor, unmarried
অবিবাহিত মহিলা spinster
অবিবেচক unwise
অবিরতভাবে constantly
অবিরাম endless
অবিলম্ব immediate, instant
অবিলম্বে immediately, instantly
অবিশ্বাসযোগ্য unreliable
অবিশ্বাসী unfaithful
অবিশ্বাস্য unbelievable
অবিস্মরণীয় unforgettable

অবৈদ্যুতিক acoustic

অবৈধ illegal

অবৈধ শিকার poached

অব্যাহতি পাওয়া get away

অভঙ্গুর unbreakable

অভদ্র rough

অভব্যতা reserve

অভিজ্ঞ experienced, streetwise

অভিজ্ঞ ও প্রবীণ veteran

অভিজ্ঞতা experience

অভিধান dictionary

অভিনন্দিত করা congratulate

অভিনয় acting

অভিনয় করা act, star

অভিনেতা actor

অভিনেত্রী actress

অভিবাদন করা salute

অভিবাসন immigration

অভিবাসী immigrant

অভিভাবকত্ব custody

অভিভূত touched

অভিমুখে towards

অভিযান. adventure

অভিযান campaign, expedition

অভিযুক্ত accused

অভিযুক্ত করা prosecute

অভিযোগ complaint, grouse

অভিযোগ করা complain

অভিযোগে charge

অভিযোগে দায়ী করা charge

অভিযোজন adjust, adjustment

অভিযোজনযোগ্য adjustable

অভিশাপ curse

অভূতপূর্ব unprecedented

অভ্যন্তরীণ internal

অভ্যন্তরে inside

অভ্যাস habit, practice

অভ্যাস করা practise

অমনোযোগী absent-minded

অমনোযোগী করা distract

অমনোরম unpleasant

অমান্য করা disobey

অমীমাংসিত থাকা draw

অম্ল acid

অম্লবর্ষণ acid rain

অযোগ্য unsuitable

অযৌক্তিক unreasonable

অরক্ষিত insecure, vulnerable

অরণ্য forest

অর্জন করা achieve

অর্থ mean, meaning

অর্থ নির্ধারণ করা define

অর্থনীতিবিদ economist

অর্থনৈতিক economic

অর্থবিনিয়োগ finance

অর্থব্যবস্থা economy

অর্থশাস্ত্র economics

অর্থসংগ্রহ proceeds

অর্থসংস্থান finance

অর্থাৎ e.g., stand for

অর্ধ গোলাকার semicircle

অর্ধেক half

অর্ধেক দাম half-price

অর্ধেক দামে half-price

অর্ধেকভাবে fifty-fifty

অর্শ piles

অলংকার ornament

অলস easy-going

অলিভ গাছ olive

অলিভ তেল olive oil

অল্প bit

অল্প আঁচে সিদ্ধ poached

অল্প কয়েকটি few

অল্পতম minimum

অল্পবয়সী young

অল্পবিস্তর বাধা hitch

অশক্ত unfit

অশিক্ষিত illiterate

অশিষ্ট দেওয়ালিলখন graffiti

অশোধিত crude

অশোভন blatant

অশ্রু tear

অষ্টম eighth

অষ্টাদশীয় eighteenth

অসংযত extravagant

অসচ্ছল hard up

অসৎ dishonest, shifty

অসতর্ক careless

অসত্য false, unreal

অসনাক্ত unidentified

অসন্তুষ্ট dissatisfied

অসন্তোষজনক unfavourable, unsatisfactory

অসফল disappointment, flop, unsuccessful

অসফল হওয়া backfire

অসভ্য uncivilized

অসমঞ্জস inconsistent

অসময় low season

অসম্পূর্ণ incomplete

অসম্ভব impossible

অসম্মত হওয়া disagree

অসম্মতি disagreement

অসহনীয় unbearable

অসহায়তাকর unhelpful

অসহ্য ঠান্ডা chilly

অসাড় numb

অসাধারণ excellent, exceptional, extraordinary

অসাধু bent

অসামরিক চাকুরে civil servant

অসামরিক ব্যক্তি civilian

অসামান্য outstanding

অসি sword

অসুখী unhappy

অসুখে পড়া catch

অসুবিধা difficulty, disadvantage, drawback, inconvenience

অসুবিধাজনক inconvenient

অসুস্থ ill, sick, unwell

অসুস্থ করে তোলার মত sickening

অসুস্থতা illness, sickness

অসুস্থতার জন্য ছুটি sick leave

অসুস্থতার প্রমাণ পত্র sick note

অসুস্থ থাকাকালীন বেতন sick pay

অস্ট্রিয়া-বাসী Austrian

অস্ট্রিয়া সম্পর্কিত Austrian

অস্ট্রেলিয়া-বাসী Australian

অস্ট্রেলিয়া সম্পর্কিত Australian

অস্তিত্ব exist

অস্ত্রশস্ত্র weapon

অস্ত্রোপচার operation, surgery

অস্ত্রোপচার কক্ষ operating theatre

অস্ত্রোপচার করা operate

অস্থায়িত্ব instability

অস্থায়ী temporary

অস্থায়ী কর্মী temp

অস্থায়ী শিক্ষক supply teacher

অস্থিভঙ্গ fracture

অস্থির shaken, unstable

অস্পষ্ট dim, unclear, vague

অস্বস্তিকর embarrassing, offensive, uncomfortable

অস্বস্তিতে ফেলা offend

অস্বাভাবিক abnormal, odd, uncanny, unusual

অস্বাস্থ্যকর unhealthy

অস্বীকার করা deny

অস্বীকার্য undeniable

অহংকার stuck-up

আকাউন্ট নম্বর account number

আকোয়ারিয়াম aquarium

আঙ্গোলা-বাসী Angolan

আঙ্গোলা সম্পর্কিত Angolan

আডাপ্টর adaptor

আড্রিয়াটিক সাগর Adriatic Sea

আড্রিয়াটিক সাগরের সাথে সম্পর্কযুক্ত Adriatic

আনোরেক্সিয়া একটি রোগ anorexia

আনোরেক্সিয়া রোগী anorexic

আন্টার্কটিকা মহাদেশ Antarctica

আপস্ট্রফি, একটি চিহ্ন apostrophe

আপিন্ডিসাইটিস appendicitis

আম্প amp

আয়রোবিক ব্যায়াম aerobics

অ্যালার্জি allergy
অ্যালার্জির ওষুধ antihistamine
আলার্ম ঘড়ি alarm clock
আস্পারাগাস asparagus
আইন law
আইনী legal
আইনের বসড়া bill
আইনের স্কুল law school
আইবুড়োভাত hen night
আইভিলতা ivy
আইরিস ভদ্রমহিলা Irishwoman
আইরিস ভদ্রলোক Irishman
আইসক্রিম dessert
আইসক্রিম খাওয়ার চামচ
   dessert spoon
আইসল্যান্ড দেশীয় Icelandic
আইসল্যান্ডের ভাষা Icelandic
আইসিং সুগার icing sugar
আওয়াজ pitch
আওয়াজ করা click, squeak
আওয়াজ পরিবর্ধক amplifier
আওয়াজ, সঙ্গীত soundtrack
আংকল uncle
আংটা buckle, clasp
আংটি ring
আংশিক partial, partly
আঁকড়া hook
আঁকড়ে ধরা grasp
আঁকা draw
আঁকাবাঁকা পথ detour
আঁচড় scratch
চুলকানো scratch
আঁচড়ে যাওয়া scratch
আঁটসাঁট tight
আঁটা tighten
আঁধার darkness
আঁশ scale
আকর্ষ stunning
আকর্ষণ attraction
আকর্ষণ করা attract
আকর্ষণীয় attractive
আকর্ষণীয় slender, smashing
আকস্মিক abrupt
আকস্মিকভাবে abruptly
আকাঙ্ক্ষা desire
আকাঙ্ক্ষিত হওয়া desire
আকার shape, size
আকাশ sky
আকৃতি figure
আক্কেল দাঁত wisdom tooth
আক্রমণ attack, blow
আক্রমণ করা attack, invade, strike
আক্রমণাত্মক aggressive
আখরোট walnut
আগন্তুক stranger

আগমন arrival
আগস্ট মাস August
আগাছা weed
আগাছানাশক weedkiller
আগাম advance
আগামী future
আগামী কাল tomorrow
আগুন fire
আগে ago, before, early
আগে নিয়ে যাওয়া bring forward
আগের দিন eve
আগ্নেয়গিরি volcano
আগ্রহ enthusiasm
আগ্রহ জাগায় interest
আগ্রহী interested, keen
আঘাত hit, hurt, injury, wound
আঘাত করা hit, hurt, injure, strike
আঘাত লাগা wound
আঙিনা yard
আঙুর grape
আঙুরের ক্ষেত vineyard
আঙুল finger
আঙুলের ছাপ fingerprint
আঙুলের নখ fingernail
আচমকা তীব্র আওয়াজ crash
আচমকা বিপর্যয় catastrophe
আচমকা হামলা raid
আচমকা হামলা করা raid
আচরণ behaviour, manners
আচরণ করা behave
আছে have
আজ today
আজকাল nowadays
আজ রাত tonight
আজারবাইজান-বাসী Azerbaijani
আজারবাইজান সম্পর্কিত Azerbaijani
আজেবাজে জিনিষপত্র litter
আঞ্চলিক regional
আট eight
আটক blockage, capture, detention
আটক করা seize
আটকানো glue, stick
আটকে থাকার অনুভূতি হয় যার
   claustrophobic
আটকে পড়া stranded
আটকে যাওয়া stuck
আটলান্টিক মহাসমুদ্র Atlantic Ocean
আটা wholemeal
আঠা glue
আঠারো eighteen
আঠালো sticky
আড়ি পেতে শোনা পেতে শোনা bugged
আতঙ্ক panic
আতঙ্কিত হওয়া panic

আতশ কাঁচ magnifying glass
আতসবাজি fireworks
আতিথেয়তা hospitality
আত্ম-কেন্দ্রিক self-centred
আত্মঘাতী বোমাবাজ suicide bomber
আত্মজীবনী autobiography
আত্ম-নিয়ন্ত্রণ self-control
আত্ম-নির্ভর self-contained
আত্ম-রক্ষা self-defence
আত্মশক্তি spirit
আত্ম-শৃংখলা self-discipline
আত্ম সচেতন self-conscious
আত্মসন্তুষ্ট smug
আত্মসমর্পণ surrender
আত্মহত্যা suicide
আত্মা soul
আত্মীয় relative
আদর্শ ideal, model
আদর্শগতভাবে ideally
আদর্শ স্থানীয় icon
আদা ginger
আদালত court
আদিম primitive
আদেশ command, order
আদেশ দেওয়া boss around, order
আদ্যক্ষর initials
অধ-ঘন্টা half-hour
অধিসিদ্ধ rare
আধা half
আধা-আধা fifty-fifty
আধুনিক modern, trendy,
   up-to-date
আধুনিক ভাষা modern languages
আধুনিক সুবিধা mod cons
আধুনিকীকরণ modernize
আধ্যাত্মিক spiritual
আনকোরা নতুন brand-new
আনন্দ bliss, delight, joy, pleasure
আনন্দ উপভোগ করা enjoy
আনন্দজনক merry
আনন্দদায়ক sweet
আনন্দধ্বনি! hooray!
আনন্দ প্রদান করা entertain
আনন্দ প্রদানকারী entertainer
আনন্দভ্রমণ outing
আনন্দমেলা funfair
আনন্দহীন bleak
আনন্দিত delighted, glad,
   pleased
আনন্দে চিৎকার করা cheer
আনন্দের চিৎকার cheer
আনন্দের ব্যাপার happily
আনারস pineapple
আনুকূল্য favour
আনুগত্য loyalty

আনুপাতিক proportional
আনুমানিক approximate
আনুমানিকভাবে approximately, supposedly
আনুষ্ঠানিক ritual
আনুষ্ঠানিক ক্রিয়াকর্ম ritual
আন্তর্জাতিক international
আন্দাজ guess
আন্দাজ করা guess
আন্দিজ পর্বতমালা Andes
আপডেট করা update
আপৎকালীন অবতরণ emergency landing
আপৎকালীন বহিরাগমন emergency exit
আপত্তি objection
আপদ nuisance
আপনাদের নিজেদের yourselves
আপনার yours
আপনার/তোমার your
আপনি/তুমি নিজে yourself
আপাতরূপে apparently
আপেল apple
আপেলের পিঠা apple pie
আপোস-আলোচনা negotiations
আপোস-আলোচনায় অংশগ্রহণকারী ব্যক্তি negotiator
আপোস করা compromise
আপোস compromise
আফগানিস্তান-বাসী Afghan
আফগানিস্তান সম্পর্কিত Afghan
আফিম গাছ poppy
আফ্রিকান Africa, Afrikaans
আফ্রিকার অধিবাসী African
আফ্রিকার শ্বেতাঙ্গ অধিবাসী Afrikaner
আফ্রিকা সম্পর্কিত African
আব wart
আবছা faint, tinted
আবর্জনা junk, refuse, rubbish
আবর্জনা জড়ো করবার জায়গা rubbish dump
আবর্জনা ফেলার পাত্র bin, dustbin
আবশ্যক compulsory
আবহাওয়া weather
আবহাওয়ার পূর্বাভাস weather forecast
আবাসিক boarder, resident
আবিষ্কার invention
আবিষ্কারক inventor
আবিষ্কার করা explore, invent
আবিষ্কার করা discover
আবেগ emotion
আবেগবর্ণ sentimental
আবেগপ্রবণ soppy
আবেগময় emotional, moving
আবেদন application

আবেদন করা apply
আবেদনকারী applicant
আবেদনপত্র application form
আবেশ obsession
আভাস hint
আভেন-দস্তানা oven glove
আভেন-বিরোধী ovenproof
আম mango
আমদানি import
আমদানি করা import
আমন্ত্রণ invitation
আমন্ত্রণ করা invite
আমরা we
আমরা নিজেরা ourselves
আমলাতন্ত্র bureaucracy
আমাকে one
আমাদের our, ours, us
আমাদের নিজেদের ourselves
আমার mine
আমি I
আমেরিকা বাসী American
আমেরিকা মহাদেশ America
আমেরিকার ফুটবল খেলা American football
আমেরিকা সম্পর্কিত American
আমোদজনক entertaining
আয় income
আয়কর income tax
আয়তকার rectangular
আয়তক্ষেত্র rectangle
আয়তনের একক cubic
আয়তাকার oblong
আয়না mirror
আয়ার্ল্যান্ড দেশীয় Irish
আয়ার্ল্যান্ডের উত্তরপূর্ব অঞ্চল Northern Ireland
আয়ার্ল্যান্ডের ভাষা Irish
আয়োজক sponsor
আয়োজন করা arrange, organize, sponsor
আয়োজন সম্পূর্ণ করা finalize
আর কি else
আর নয় anymore
আরবদেশীয় Arabic
আরব দেশের Arab
আরবি ভাষা Arabic
আরবীয় Arab
আরশোলা cockroach
আরাধনা করা adore
আরাম কেদারা easy chair
আরামদায়ক comfortable, cosy
আরেকজন one
আরেকবার যদি বলেন pardon?
আরো কিছুটা slightly
আরো কিছু সময় longer

আরো খারাপ worse
আরো খারাপ করা worsen
আরোগ্য-নিকেতন nursing home
আরোগ্য লাভ recovery
আরোগ্যলাভ cure
আরোগ্য লাভ করা recover
আরোগ্যলাভ করানো cure
আরো দূরে further
আরো বেশি extra
আরো ভাল করে preferably
আরোহণ climb, ride, riding
আরোহণ করা ride
আরোহী climber, rider
আর্জি petition
আর্জেন্টিনা-বাসী Argentinian
আর্জেন্টিনা সম্পর্কিত Argentinian
আর্থিক financial, monetary
আর্থিক উন্নতি prosperity
আর্থিক বছর financial year
আর্থিকভাবে সাহায্য করা provide for
আর্থিক মন্দা recession
আর্থিক সহায়তা sponsorship
আর্দ্র damp
আর্দ্রতা humidity, moisture
আর্মেনিয়া ভাষা Armenian
আর্মেনিয়া মহাদেশ America
আর্মেনিয়া সম্পর্কিত Armenian
আর্মেনীয়া-বাসী Armenian
আলগা loose
আলগা করা undo
আলজেরিয়া সম্পর্কিত Algerian
আলজেরীয় Algerian
আলবেনিয়া Albania
আলবেনিয়া সম্পর্কিত Albanian
আলবেনীয় Albanian
আলবেনীয় ভাষা Albanian
আলমারি cabinet
আলস্টার Ulster
আলাদা different, distinctive
আলাদা করা separate, take apart
আলাদা কাগজ scrap paper
আলাদাভাবে separately
আলাদা হওয়া vary
আলিঙ্গন cuddle, hug
আলিঙ্গন করা hug
আলু potato
আলুবখরা plum
আলুভাজা chips
আলুভাতে mashed potatoes
আলুর খোসা ছাড়াবার যন্ত্র potato peeler
আলোকচিত্র বিদ্যা photography
আলোকরশ্মি beam
আলোক শক্তি light
আলোকসজ্জা lighting
আলোকিত light

আলোচনা discussion
আলোচনা করা discuss
আলো জ্বালানো light
আলোর বাল্ব light bulb
আল্পস পর্বতমালা Alps
আল্লা Allah
আশঙ্কাসূচক alarming
আশপাশে around
আশা hope
আশা করা hope
আশাপ্রদ hopeful, optimistic
আশাপ্রদভাবে hopefully
আশাবাদ optimism
আশাবাদী optimist, positive
আশাহীন hopeless
আশি eighty
আশীর্বাদ করা bless
আশীর্বাদের আংটি engagement ring
আশ্চর্যজনক funny, incredible
আশ্রয় refuge, shelter
আশ্রয় খোঁজে যারা asylum seeker
আশ্রয় দান asylum
আসন seat
আসন্ন coming
আসবাবপত্র furniture
আসবাবপত্র-সজ্জিত furnished
আসল pure
আসল কথা fact
আসা come
আসা যাওয়া movement
আস্ত intact
আস্তরণ lining
আস্তাকুঁড় dump
আস্তাকুঁড়ে ফেলে দেওয়া dump
আস্থাবল stable
আস্থা confidence
আস্থাপত্র credentials
আস্থাশীল trusting
আহত injured
আহার meal
আহারের প্রথম পদ starter
ইউক্রেন দেশীয় Ukrainian
ইউক্রেনের নাগরিক Ukrainian
ইউক্রেনের ভাষা Ukrainian
ইউথ হোস্টেল youth hostel
ইউনাইটেড নেশনস এর সংক্ষিপ্তকরণ UN
ইউরোপীয় European
ইংরাজী English
ইংরেজ Englishman
ইংরেজ নারী Englishwoman
ইংল্যন্ড England
ইংল্যন্ড দেশীয় English
ইঁট brick
ইঁদুর mouse

ইউরোপীয়ান ইউনিয়ন European Union
ইউরোপের জনগণ European
ইচ্ছা will
ইচ্ছা করা wish
ইচ্ছাকৃত intentional
ইচ্ছাকৃতভাবে willingly
ইচ্ছাশক্তি willpower
ইচ্ছুক willing
ইঞ্চি inch
ইটালিয়ান ভাষা Italian
ইটালী দেশীয় Italian
ইটালীর নাগরিক Italian
ইতস্ততঃ করা hesitate
ইতিহাস history
ইতিহাসকার historian
ইত্যবসরে meantime
ইত্যাদি etc
ইথিওপিয়া দেশীয় Ethiopian
ইথিওপিয়ার জনগণ Ethiopian
ইনজেকশন jab
ইনহেলার inhaler
ইন্টারনেট ব্যবহারকারী Internet user
ইন্টারনেটের চ্যাটরুম chatroom
ইন্দোনেসিয়া দেশীয় Indonesian
ইন্দোনেসিয়ার নাগরিক Indonesian
ই-মেল করা email
ই-মেল ঠিকানা email address
ইয়েলো পেজ Yellow Pages®
ইরাক দেশীয় Iraqi
ইরাকের নাগরিক Iraqi
ইরান দেশীয় Iranian
ইরানের নাগরিক Iranian
ইলেকট্রনিক-বই e-book
ইশারা ভাষা sign language
ইসলাম ধর্ম Islam
ইসলাম ধর্ম সম্পর্কিত Islamic
ইস্টার উৎসবের জন্য ডিম Easter egg
ইস্তাহার brochure
ইস্ত্রি করা iron, ironing
ইস্ত্রি করার বোর্ড ironing board
ইস্ত্রী iron
ইস্পাত steel
ইস্রায়েল দেশীয় Israeli
ইস্রায়েলের নাগরিক Israeli
ইহুদিদের ধার্মীয় খাবার kosher
ইহুদিদের বাৎসরিক অনুষ্ঠান Passover
ইহুদী Jew
ইহুদী জাতীয় Jewish
ইহুদীদের পূজাস্থল synagogue
ঈগল জাতীয় পাখি bird of prey
ঈগল পাখি eagle
ঈর্ষা envy
ঈর্ষা করা envy
ঈর্ষান্বিত envious

ঈর্ষাপরায়ণ jealous
ঈশ্বর God
ঈশ্বর-প্রদত্ত gifted
ঈষদুষ্ণ lukewarm
উইলো গাছ willow
উঁকি মারা pry
উঁচু high
উঁচু অংশ top
উঁচু ইলেকট্রিক খুঁটি pylon
উঁচু গাছবিশেষ poplar
উঁচু চেয়ার highchair
উঁচু থেকে কোন কিছু দেখা overlook
উঁচুনীচু bumpy
উঁচু স্থান থেকে লাফানো bungee jumping
উঁচু-হিল জুতো high heels
উঁচু হিলের জুতো high-heeled
উকিল lawyer, solicitor
উকুন lice
উকো file
উগান্ডা দেশীয় Ugandan
উগান্ডার নাগরিক Ugandan
উগ্র vicious
উগ্রপন্থা terrorism
উগ্রপন্থী terrorist
উগ্রপন্থী হামলা terrorist attack
উচিত ought, should
উচ্চ আওয়াজসম্পন্ন পুরুষ গায়ক tenor
উচ্চ আওয়াজে loudly
উচ্চজাতের pedigree
উচ্চতা altitude, height
উচ্চপদষ্ঠ কর্মচারী mandarin
উচ্চমার্গের classic
উচ্চ-শিক্ষা higher education
উচ্চস্বরে aloud
উচ্চভিলাষ ambition
উচ্চভিলাষী ambitious
উচ্চারণ pronunciation
উচ্চারণ করা pronounce
উচ্ছ্বসিত হয়ে কথা বলা rave
উচ্ছ্বাস ecstasy
উচ্ছ্বসময় rave
উজ্জল bright, shiny, vivid
উজ্জল নয় light
উজ্জল হওয়া shine
উট camel
উটপাখি ostrich
উঠিয়ে নেওয়া pick up
উঠে দাঁড়ান stand up
উঠে পড়া get up
উড়ে চলে যাওয়া fly away
উৎকৃষ্টতর better
উৎক্ষেপণ launch
উৎপন্ন করা produce
উৎপাদন production

উৎপাদনশীলতা productivity
উৎপাদিত দ্রব্য product
উৎফুল্ল cheerful
উৎস থেকে আসা come from
উৎসব festival
উৎসব পালন celebration
উৎসব পালন করা celebrate
উৎসর্গ dedication
উৎসর্পিত dedicated
উৎসর্গীকৃত devoted
উৎসাহ encouragement
উৎসাহজনক encouraging, interesting
উৎসাহ প্রদান করা encourage
উত্তর answer, north, reply
উত্তর আফ্রিকা দেশীয় North African
উত্তর আফ্রিকার অধিবাসী North African
উত্তর আমেরিকা দেশীয় North American
উত্তর আমেরিকার অধিবাসী North American
উত্তরদিক north
উত্তর দেওয়া account for, answer, reply
উত্তর দেওয়া যন্ত্র answering machine
উত্তর দেওয়া যন্ত্র (ফোনের সাথে সংযুক্ত) answerphone
উত্তরপশ্চিম northwest
উত্তরপূর্ব northeast
উত্তরমুখী northbound
উত্তর মেরু North Pole
উত্তর সাগর North Sea
উত্তরাঞ্চল northern
উত্তরাধিকার inheritance
উত্তরাধিকার সূত্রে প্রাপ্ত inherit
উত্তরাধিকারিণী heiress
উত্তরাধিকারী heir, successor
উত্তাল turbulence
উত্তীর্ণ pass
উত্তেজক gripping
উত্তেজনাপ্রবণ exciting
উত্তেজিত excited
উত্ত্যক্ত করা tease
উদর tummy
উদার generous, liberal
উদারতা generosity
উদাহরণ example, instance
উদ্দীপনা zest
উদ্দেশ্য cause, intention, motive, objective, purpose
উদ্দেশ্য করা point
উদ্দেশ্যহীন pointless
উদ্দেশ্যহীনভাবে কিছু করা mess about

উদ্ধত arrogant
উদ্ধার rescue
উদ্ধার করা rescue
উদ্ধৃতি quotation
উদ্ধৃতি চিহ্ন quotation marks
উদ্ধৃতি দেওয়া quote
উদ্বাস্তু refugee
উদ্বিগ্ন হওয়া fret
উদ্বেগ anxiety
উদ্বেগমুক্ত relieved
উদ্ভট absurd, awkward, clumsy
উদ্ভব origin
উদ্ভাবন innovation
উদ্ভাবন করা devise
উদ্ভাবনমূলক innovative
উদ্ভাবনশক্তিবিশিষ্ট ingenious
উদ্ভিদ plant
উদ্ভিদসমূহ vegetation
উদ্যোগ initiative, operation
উধাও হয়ে যাওয়া vanish
উনবিংশ nineteen
উনবিংশতম nineteenth
উনুনের শিক grill
উন্নত advanced
উন্নততর superior
উন্নতি development, improvement, progress
উন্নতি করা improve
উন্নয়নশীল দেশ developing country
উন্মত্ত crazy, nutter
উন্মাদ lunatic
উন্মুক্ত open
উন্মোচন করা bare
উপকথা legend
উপকরণ ingredient
উপকারী helpful
উপকূল coast
উপকূলরক্ষী coastguard
উপগ্রহ satellite
উপগ্রহ ডিশ satellite dish
উপগ্রহ ভিত্তিক পথ নির্দেশিকা sat nav
উপজাতি tribe
উপত্যকা valley
উপদেশ দেওয়া advise
উপদ্বীপ peninsula
উপন্যাস novel
উপভাষা dialect
উপভোগ্য enjoyable
উপযুক্ত decent, fit, suitable
উপযুক্ত হওয়া suit
উপরিভাগ surface
উপলব্ধি করা realize
উপসাগর bay
উপসাগরীয় রাজ্য Gulf States
উপস্থাপক presenter

উপস্থাপনা presentation
উপস্থিত present
উপস্থিত হওয়া attend, show up
উপস্থিতি attendance, presence
উপহার gift, present, treat
উপাদান component, element, material
উপায় way
উপুড় হয়ে বসা crouch down
উভগামী রাস্তা dual carriageway
উভয় both
উভয়েই নয় neither
উরুগুয়ের বসবাসকারী Uruguayan
উরুগুয়ে সম্পর্কিত Uruguayan
উর্ধ্বতন superior
উর্বর fertile
উলঙ্গ naked
উলনেট্ woollens
উল্কাপিন্ড meteorite
উল্কি tattoo
উল্টো reverse
উল্টো করা reverse
উল্টোদিকে backwards
উল্লম্ব vertical
উল্লেখ করা mention
উল্লেখযোগ্য highlight
উষ্ণ warm
উরু thigh
ঋণ debt, loan
ঋতু season
এ in
এই the, this
এইখানি this
এইলি these
এইটি this
এইমাত্র just
এই রকম such
এইরকম such
এই শর্তে provided
এক one
এক-অষ্টমাংশ eighth
একই দিনে ফেরার টিকিট day return
একই রকম stereotype
একক singular, solo
একক বাজনা concerto
একক শিল্পী soloist
একগুঁয়ে stubborn
একঘেয়েমি bored
একঘেয়েমি করে তোলা bore
একঘেয়েমি monotonous
এক-চতুর্থাংশ quarter
একচেটিয়া monopoly
এক জন করে খেলা, সিংগলস singles
একজাতীয় কুকুর poodle

একজাতীয় ক্ষুদ্র নিশাচর প্রাণী badger
একজাতীয় গাছ geranium
একজাতীয় চিরহরিৎ গুল্ম holly
একটানা constant
একটি an, single
একটি জলের ক্রীড়া windsurfing
একটি যন্ত্রবিশেষ plane
একটি সম্ভাষণ hi!
একতলা ground floor
এক তৃতীয়াংশ third
একত্রিত হওয়া get together,
   meet up
একত্রীকরণ round up
একদম ঠিক all right
এক-দশমাংশ tenth
একদিকের টিকিট single ticket
এক দৃষ্টে তাকানো stare
একদৃষ্টে তাকানো gaze
এক দেওয়ালের বাড়ি semi-detached
   house
একধরণের কমলালেবু clementine
একধরণের কাপড় felt
একধরণের কুকুর collie
এক ধরণের গাছ lilac
একধরণের গাছ beech
একধরণের চিরসবুজ গাছ yew
এক ধরণের জলের পাইপ hose
একধরণের জুয়াখেলা roulette
একধরণের জ্বর hay fever
এক ধরণের পাতা spaghetti
একধরণের পোকা ladybird
একধরণের ফাইল ring binder
এক ধরণের ফুলের গাছ lily of the
   valley
একধরণের মোটা কাপড় canvas
এক ধরনের ধাঁধা jigsaw
এক ধরনের পাথর sandstone
একধরনের বিষাক্ত সাপ rattlesnake
এক ধরনের শামুক scallop
এক ধরনের সব্জি artichoke
একজরে দেখা glance
একনায়ক dictator
একপক্ষকাল fortnight
একপশলা বৃষ্টি shower
একপায়ে লাফানো hop
একপাল litter
একপাশে aside
একপ্রকার আঁটসাঁট পোশাক tights
একপ্রকার কমলালেবু tangerine
একপ্রকার গ্যাস chlorine
একপ্রকার বাদ্যযন্ত্র banjo, French
   horn, oboe
একপ্রকার মদ্য rosé, rum
একপ্রকার যন্ত্র pliers
একপ্রকার সাইকেল tandem

একপ্রকার সামুদ্রিক মাছ cod
একপ্রকার সুগন্ধি লতা thyme
একপ্রকার স্যালাড coleslaw
একপ্রকারের গাছ carnation
এক প্রজাতির প্রাণী breed
একবার once
একবারের জন্য one-off
একমত হওয়া agree
একমাত্র only
এক রকম same
একরূপ identical
একলা unattended
একলা মা বা বাবা single parent
একশো hundred
একশো কোটি billion
এক সঙ্গে simultaneous,
   simultaneously
এক-সহস্রাংশ thousandth
একসাথে together
একা alone
একাকিত্ব loneliness
একাকী lonely
একাদশ eleventh
একান্তভাবে exclusively
এক্স-রে করা X-ray
এখন now
এখনও yet
এখনো still
এখানে here
এগারো eleven
এগিয়ে থাকা lead
এগিয়ে যাওয়া advance, go ahead
এ ছাড়া apart from
এছাড়া too
এছাড়াও also, besides
এটি it
এডস্ রোগ AIDS
এড়িয়ে যাওয়া avoid
এদিক-ওদিক বিচরণকারী ব্যক্তি
   rambler
এপ্রিল April
"এপ্রিল ফুল" দিবস April Fools' Day
এবং and
এমনকি either, even
এয়ারস্পেস airspace
এর of, to
এর মধ্যে already
এরপর next
এর মধ্যে meanwhile
এরোপ্লেন যাত্রা flight
এলোমেলো random
এলোমেলো অবস্থা muddle
এশিয়া Asia
এশিয়ার অধিবাসী Asian
এশিয়া সম্পর্কিত Asian

এস এম এস (মোবাইলে বার্তা পাঠানো)
   SMS
এস্টোনিয়া দেশীয় Estonian
এস্টোনিয়ান Estonian
এস্টোনিয়ার জনগণ Estonian
ঐকতান concert
ঐক্যবদ্ধ হওয়া unite
ঐচ্ছিক optional
ঐতিহাসিক historical
ঐতিহ্য heritage, tradition
ওই that
ওইগুলি those
ওক গাছ oak
ওকগাছের ফল acorn
ওজন weight
ওজন করা weigh
ওজর alibi
ওজোনের স্তর ozone layer
ওটাও না nor
ওঠা rise
ওঠানো raise
ওড়না veil
ওড়া float, fly
ওপর-ওপর superficial
ওপরতলা upstairs
ওপরদিকে upwards
ওপরে above, on, over, up, upon
ওপরের upper
ওপরের অংশ top
ওপরের অংশ নিচের দিকে করা upside
   down
ওপারে across
ওয়াইনের গ্লাস wineglass
ওয়াইনের তালিকা wine list
ওয়াটার-কি water-skiing
ওয়াডের প্রহরী warden
ওয়ালপেপার wallpaper
ওয়েব Web
ওয়েব ব্রাউজার web browser
ওয়েলস্ দেশীয় Welsh
ওয়েলস্ ভাষা Welsh
ওয়েস্ট ইন্ডিজ দেশীয় West Indian
ওয়েস্ট ইন্ডিজ নাগরিক West Indian
ওষুধ drug, medicine
ওষুধের দোকান chemist
ওষ্ঠ্যাগ্রন lip
ওস্তাদি রপ্ত করা master
ঔপন্যাসিক novelist
ঔষধ প্রস্তুতকারক pharmacist
ঔষধবর্জিত চিকিৎসা therapy
ঔষধ ব্যবহারের নির্দেশ দেওয়া
   prescribe
ঔষধ ব্যবহারের নির্দেশিকা prescription
ঔষধালয় pharmacy
ঔষধি herbs

কংকাল	skeleton	কবজি-বন্ধনী	bracelet	করা	commit, do
কংক্রিট	concrete	কবর	grave	করাত	saw
কংগো	Congo	কবরখানা	cemetery, graveyard	করুণ	pathetic
ককটেল/মদের সংমিশ্রণ	cocktail	কবর দেওয়া	bury	করুণা	pity
ককপিট/বিমানচালনা স্থান	cockpit	কবরের পাথর	gravestone	করুণা করা	pity
কংকেশাস পর্বতমালা	Caucasus	কবলে	clutch	কর্কগাছ	cork
কখন?	when	কবি	poet	কর্কট রাশি	Cancer
কখনও নয়	never	কবিতা	poem, poetry	কর্ডুরয়	corduroy
কখনও সখনও	occasional, rarely	কম	less, low	কর্নফ্লেক্স	cornflakes
কখেনো	sometime	কম-অ্যালকোহলযুক্ত	low-alcohol	কর্তব্যনিষ্ঠ	conscientious
কখেনো কখেনো	sometimes	কম করা	minimize	কর্তৃপক্ষ	employer, management
কচি বাছুর	veal	কমদামী	economical	কর্দমাক্ত	muddy
কচুরিপানা	hyacinth	কমপক্ষে	at least, minimum	কর্নেল	colonel
কচ্ছপ	tortoise, turtle	কম ফ্যাটযুক্ত	low-fat	কর্পদকহীন	ruin
কটূক্তি	malicious, swearword	কম মূল্য প্রাপ্তি	underpaid	কর্পোরাল	corporal
কঠিন	difficult, hard, solid, stark, tricky	কমলা খয়েরি রবিশিষ্ট	ginger	কর্ম	act
		কমলারঙ	orange	কর্ম অভিজ্ঞতা	work experience
কঠিন দীর্ঘযাত্রা	trek	কমলালেবু	orange	কর্মকর্তা	boss
কঠিন পথে চলা	trek	কমলালেবু জাতীয় ফল	mandarin	কর্মক্ষেত্র	workplace
কঠিন পরীক্ষা	ordeal	কমলালেবুর জ্যাম	marmalade	কর্মচারী	employee, staff
কঠোর	hard, strict	কমলালেবুর রস	orange juice	কর্মরত	engaged
কঠোর ভাবে	strictly	কম লীডযুক্ত	unleaded	কর্মশক্তি	energy
কড জাতীয় মাছ	haddock	কম লীডযুক্ত পেট্রল	unleaded petrol	কর্মসূচী	scheme
কড়া পাউরুটি	rusk	কম সম্ভবনাযুক্ত	unlikely	কর্মহীন	jobless
কণা	grain	কম হওয়া	shortfall	কর্মী	worker
কণ্ঠস্বর	voice	কমানো	cut down	কর্মীদের বিশ্রাম ঘর	staffroom
কণ্ডরা	tendon	কমে যাওয়া	come down, diminish, drop, go down	কর্মীবাহিনী	workforce
কত	how			কলম	fountain pen
কথা	talk	কম্পমান	unsteady	কলম্বিয়া	Colombia
কথা বলা	talk	কম্পাস	compass	কলম্বিয়া-বাসী	Colombian
কথিত	alleged	কম্পিউটার	computer	কলম্বিয়ার সাথে সম্পর্কিত	Colombian
কথোপকথন	conversation	কম্পিউটার গেম	computer game	কলা	banana
কথোপকথন করা	talk to	কম্পিউটার বিজ্ঞান	computer science	কলার	collar
কদাচিৎ	seldom	কম্পিউটার ব্যবহার	computing	কলেজ	college
কন্টাক্ট লেন্স	contact lenses	কম্পিউটার সার্ভার	server	কল্পনা	imagination
কনভয়/সাঁজোয়া গাড়ি	convoy	কম্পিউটারে ছাপা কাগজ	printout	কল্পনা করা	fancy, imagine
কনভেয়ার বেল্ট	conveyor belt	কম্পিউটারে ব্যবহৃত স্মাইলি	smiley	কল্পবিজ্ঞান	science fiction, sci-fi
কনিষ্ঠ	junior	কম্পিউটারের কারসর	cursor	কল্পিত	imaginary
কনুই	elbow	কম্পিউটারের সফটওয়্যার	software	কষ্টকর	stressful, wrench
কনে	bride	কম্পিউটারের সার্চ ইঞ্জিন	search engine	কষ্টকর দীর্ঘপথ	tramp
কনের সহচরী	bridesmaid			কষ্ট পাওয়া	suffer
কন্ডিশনার	conditioner	কম্পিউটারের স্ক্রীনসেভার	screensaver	কষ্টসহিষ্ণু	tough
কন্ডোম	condom	কম্বল	blanket	কসাই	butcher
কন্দ	bulb	কয়লা	coal	কসাইয়ের দোকান	butcher
কন্যা	daughter	কয়লাখনি	colliery	কাঁকড়া	crab
কন্যা রাশি	Virgo	কয়েকটি	few	কাঁকর	grit, stone
কপাল	forehead	কয়েদী	prisoner	কাঁচ	glass
কপিরাইট	copyright	কয়েন রাখবার কৌটো	piggybank	কাঁচঘর	conservatory
কফি	coffee	কর	tax	কাঁচা	raw
কফিন/শবাধার	coffin	করণীয় কাজ	commission	কাঁচি	scissors
কফির টেবিল	coffee table	করতে চাওয়া	mean	কাঁটা	thorn
কফির পাত্র	coffeepot	করতে পারা	can, may	কাঁটাগাছ	hawthorn
কফির বীজ	coffee bean	করদাতা	taxpayer	কাঁটাগাছবিশেষ	thistle
কব্জা	hinge	করমুক্ত	duty-free	কাঁটা-চামচ	cutlery
কবজি	wrist	করমুক্ত জিনিস	duty-free	কাঁটাচামচ	fork

কাঁটা তার barbed wire
কাঁদা cry, sob
কাঁদানে গ্যাস tear gas
কাঁধ shoulder
কাঁধের পিছন দিক shoulder blade
কাঁপা shake, tremble
কাঁসা bronze
কাউকে anyone
কাউকে বিশ্বাস করা rely on
কাউবয় cowboy
কাক crow
কাকতাড়ুয়া scarecrow
কাগজ paper
কাগজের কাটা অংশ cutting
কাছ থেকে from
কাছাকাছি close, near
কাছে near
কাছে আসা come up
কাছেই nearby
কাজ assignment, duty, job, task, work
কাজ করা act, work
কাজ করার জায়গা workspace
কাজ খোঁজার জায়গা job centre
কাজু cashew
কাজে ফাঁকি দেওয়া skive
কাজের অনুমতিপত্র work permit
কাটলেট cutlet
কাটা cut
কাটা চিহ্ন cut
কাটানো go through
কাটার যন্ত্র clippers
কাঠ timber, wood
কাঠকয়লা charcoal
কাঠনির্মিত wooden
কাঠবাদাম almond
কাঠবিড়ালী squirrel
কাঠামো frame, structure
কাঠের কাজ carpentry, woodwork
কাঠের গুঁড়ি log
কাঠের গুঁড়ো sawdust
কাঠের জুতো clog
কাণ্ডজ্ঞানহীন tactless
কাতুকুতু দেওয়া tickle
কাদা mud, slush
কাদামাখা ডোবা puddle
কান ear
কানাডা Canada
কানাডা-বাসী Canadian
কানাডার সঙ্গে সম্পর্কিত Canadian
কানে তালা লাগার মত আওয়াজ deafening
কানে ব্যথা earache
কানের গ্রাহকযন্ত্র earphones
কানের ঢল earring

কানের পর্দা eardrum
কানের প্লাগ earplugs
কানে শোনার যন্ত্র hearing aid
কাণ্ডজ্ঞানহীন senseless
কাপ cup
কাপড় cloth, fabric, material
কাপড় কাচার পাউডার detergent
কাপড় ধোওয়া washing
কাপড় ধোওয়ার পাউডার washing powder
কাপড় ধোওয়ার মেশিন washing machine
কাপড় শুকোনোর ড্রায়ার tumble dryer
কাপড় শুকোনোর যন্ত্র spin drier
কাপড় শুকোবার দড়ি washing line
কাপুরুষ coward
কাপুরুষোচিত cowardly
কাবাব kebab
কামড় bite
কামড়ানো bite
কামান mortar
কাম্বোডিয়া Cambodia
কাম্বোডিয়া-বাসী Cambodian
কাম্বোডিয়ার সাথে সম্পর্কযুক্ত Cambodian
কার whose
কারখানা factory, plant, workshop
কারণ because, reason
কারণে due to, owing to
কারাগার jail, prison
কারাগারের কর্মকর্তা prison officer
কারাবাস করা jail
কারি curry
কারি পাউডার curry powder
কাফলিঙ্ক্স হাতের বোতাম cufflinks
কারোর জন্য প্রতীক্ষা করা wait up
কারোর নিজের one's
কারোর নিজের হওয়া belong to
কারোর পক্ষে on behalf of
কারোর প্রতি বিদ্বেষ venom
কার্টুন cartoon
কার্টুন ফিল্ম cartoon
কার্ড card
কার্ড-ফোন cardphone
কার্ডবোর্ড/কাগজের বক্স carton
কার্তুজ cartridge
কার্পেট carpet
কার্ফ্যু curfew
কার্বরেটর carburettor
কার্যকরী efficient
কার্যকলাপ proceedings
কার্যক্রম programme
কার্যনির্বাহী acting
কালসিটে bruise

কালা deaf
কালি ink
কালো black
কালো কফি black coffee
কালো কিসমিস blackcurrant
কালোজাম blackberry
কাল্পনিক কাহিনী fiction
কাশি cough
কাশির ওষুধ cough mixture
কাশি হওয়া cough
কাস্টার্ড custard
কাস্তে বা মেশিন দিয়ে ঘাস কাটা mow
কাহিনী tale
কি what
কিউবা প্রজাতন্ত্র Cuba
কিউবা-বাসী Cuban
কিউবার সঙ্গে সম্পর্কিত Cuban
কিছুক্ষণ while
কিছু জিনিস something
কিছু some
কিছু নয় none
কিছু না nothing
কিছু বোনা knitting
কিছু সময় part-time
কিছুর ওপরে onto
কিছুর মধ্যে onto
কিছুর মধ্যে খোঁজা look up
কিছুর রং colouring
কিনা whether
কিন্তু but
কি বোঝাতে ব্যবহৃত হয় what
কি ভীষণ! such
কিমা mince
কিমি/ঘণ্টা km/h
কিলো kilo
কিলোমিটার kilometre
কিশমিশ sultana
কিশোর বা কিশোরী teenager
কিশমিস্ raisin
কিস্তি instalment
কুঁড়ি blossom
কুঁড়ে lazy
কুঁড়েঘর hut
কুকার cooker
কুকুর dog, sheepdog
কুকুরছানা puppy
কুকুরের ঘর kennel
কুকুরের প্রজাতি spaniel
কুচকাওয়াজ parade
কুঞ্চন curl
কুটিকুটি করে ছেঁড়া rip up
কুটোর আগুন bonfire
কুঠার axe
কুড়মুড়ে বিস্কুট cracker
কুড়ি twenty

কুৎসিত ugly
কুমড়ো pumpkin
কুমারী Miss, virgin
কুমির crocodile
কুমির প্রজাতির alligator
কুম্ভ রাশি Aquarius
কুয়াশা fog, mist
কুয়াশাছন্ন misty
কুয়াশাপূর্ণ foggy
কুয়েত দেশীয় Kuwaiti
কুয়েতের নাগরিক Kuwaiti
কুয়ো well
কুরুশে বোনা crochet
কুল আঁটি bunion
কুলি porter
কুসংস্কার superstitious
কুস্তি wrestling
কুস্তিগির wrestler
কূটনীতিক diplomat
কূটনৈতিক diplomatic
কৃত done
কৃতজ্ঞ grateful
কৃতদাস slave
কৃত্রিম artificial
কৃত্রিম দাঁত dentures
কৃপণ miser, stingy
কৃষক farmer
কৃষি agriculture
কৃষিভিত্তিক agricultural
কৃষ্ণসার হরিণ antelope
কে who
কেউ somebody
কেউই নয় neither
কেউ নয় no one
কেঁচো worm
কেক cake, pastry
কেক (মিষ্টিদ্রব্য) sponge
কেকের ওপরে মিষ্টি দেওয়া icing
কেটলী kettle
কেটে দেওয়া cross out
কেটে নেওয়া deduct
কেটে ফেলা cut
কেতা fashion
কেতাদুরস্ত fashionable
কেন why
কেনা buy
কেনাকাটা shopping
কেনাকাটার স্থান shopping centre
কেনিয়া দেশীয় Kenyan
কেনিয়ার নাগরিক Kenyan
কেন্দ্র centre
কেন্দ্রীয় central
কেন্দ্রীয় তাপ পরিবহন ব্যবহা central
  heating
কেবল mere

কেবলচালিত গাড়ী cable car
কেবল টিভি cable television
কেবল/প্লাস্টিক মোড়া ইলেকট্রিকের
  তার cable
কেবলমাত্র only
কেবলমাত্র তাদের theirs
কেবিন cabin
কেমন how
কেলেংকারী scam, scandal
কেশবিন্যাস hairdo, hairstyle
কেশবিন্যাসকারী hairdresser
কেশবিন্যাসকারীর দোকান hairdresser
কৈশোর teens
কোঁচকানো curly
কোক Coke®
কোকিল cuckoo
কোকো cocoa
কোকো বীজের তৈরী মিষ্টান্ন chocolate
কোচ couch
কোট coat
কোট ঝোলাবার হ্যাঙ্গার coathanger
কোটিপতি millionaire
কোণ angle, corner
কোথাও থাকা stay
কোথাও না nowhere
কোথা থেকে where
কোথায়? where
কোদাল spade
কোন any
কোন? which
কোন একজন someone
কোন এক স্থান someplace
কোন কিছুর অন্তর্ভুক্ত belong
কোন কিছুর ওপরে ঝোঁকা bend over
কোন কিছুর নিচে underneath
কোন কিছু শোনা listen
কোনখানে somewhere
কোন জায়গায় there
কোন জিনিস anything
কোনটা which
কোনটাই নয় neither ... nor
কোনদিনও ever
কোন বস্তুর আয়তাকার টুকরো block
কোন ব্যক্তি নয় nobody
কোন স্থানে at
কোনাকুনি diagonal
কোনামোড়া মাদুর fitted sheet
কোমর waist
কোমল soft
কোমা coma
কোম্পানী company
কোম্পানীর গাড়ি company car
কোম্পানীর সেয়ার stock
কোয়েল quail
কোরান Koran

কোরানো grate
কোরিয়া দেশীয় Korean
কোরিয়ার ভাষা Korean
কোরিয়ার মানুষ Korean
কোল lap
কোলাহল noise
কোলাহলপূর্ণ noisy
কোলাহলপূর্ণ অনুষ্ঠান bash
কোলাহলপূর্ণ আওয়াজ racket
কোলেস্টেরল cholesterol
কোষ cell
কোষাধ্যক্ষ cashier, treasurer
কোষ্ঠকাঠিন্যযুক্ত constipated
কোষ্ঠশোধক পদার্থ laxative
কোষ্ঠী horoscope
কোস্টা রিকা Costa Rica
কৌটো can
কৌটো খোলার যন্ত্র tin opener
কৌটোয় সংরক্ষিত tinned
কৌতুক joke
কৌতুক করা mock
কৌতুক বোধ sense of humour
কৌতুককুশলী comedian
কৌতুহলী curious, inquisitive, nosy
কৌশল know-how, tactics,
  technique, trick
কৌশলী tactful
কৌশলে চালনা করা manipulate
ক্যাকটাস/কাঁটাওয়ালা গাছ cactus
ক্যাটালগ/জিনিসের তালিকা catalogue
ক্যানটিন/ভোজনালয় canteen
ক্যানারি canary
ক্যানারিস দ্বীপপুঞ্জ Canaries
ক্যানেস্তারা canister
ক্যান্সার cancer
ক্যাপটেন captain
ক্যাফিন caffeine
ক্যান-কর্ডার/বহনযোগ্য ভিডিও ক্যামেরা
  camcorder
ক্যামেরা camera
ক্যামেরুন Cameroon
ক্যাম্পার camper
ক্যারাট/সোনা-হীরের ওজনের মাপ carat
ক্যারাভ্যান caravan
ক্যারামেল caramel
ক্যারিবিয়ান দ্বীপপুঞ্জের সঙ্গে সম্পর্কিত
  Caribbean
ক্যারিবিয়ান সাগর Caribbean
ক্যালসিয়াম calcium
ক্যালেন্ডার/তারিখ, দিন সম্বলিত তালিকা
  calendar
ক্যাসিনো casino
ক্যাসেট cassette
কুরিয়ার courier
ক্রম sequence

ক্রমশ অবনতি হওয়া deteriorate
ক্রমাগত steady
ক্রমিক consecutive, gradual
ক্রয় করা purchase
ক্রস-ওয়ার্ড crossword
ক্রস-কান্ট্রি ক্রীড়া cross-country
ক্রাচ crutch
ক্রিকেট খেলা cricket
ক্রিম cream
ক্রিয়া action, verb
ক্রিয়াকলাপ activity
ক্রিয়ার কাল tense
ক্রীড়া athletics, sport
ক্রীড়াবিদ athlete, sportsman
ক্রীড়াবিষয়ক athletic
ক্রীড়াহল stadium
ক্রীম-কেক gateau
ক্রু-কাট চুল crew cut
ক্রুদ্ধ resentful
ক্রুদ্ধ হওয়া resent
ক্রুশ cross
ক্রুশে ঝোলানো যীশুর মূর্তি crucifix
ক্রেডিট কার্ড credit card
ক্রেতা buyer, customer
ক্রেনবেরি cranberry
ক্রেন (যন্ত্র) crane
ক্রেশ crèche
ক্রোধ anger
ক্রোধাম্বিত glaring
ক্রোধোন্মত্ত furious
ক্রোমিয়াম chrome
ক্রোয়েশিয়ার সাথে সম্পর্কিত Croatian
ক্রোয়েশিয়া Croatia
ক্রোয়েশিয়ান Croatian
ক্রোয়েশিয়া-বাসী Croatian
ক্লান্ত exhausted, strained, tired
ক্লান্তিকর tiring
ক্লান্তিময় অবস্থা boredom
ক্লাব club
ক্লিপ clip
ক্লোকরুম cloakroom
ক্লারিওনেট বাদ্যযন্ত্র clarinet
ক্ষণভঙ্গুর fragile
ক্ষণিক momentary
ক্ষণিকের জন্য momentarily
ক্ষত চিহ্ন scar
ক্ষতি loss
ক্ষতিকর harmful, sinister
ক্ষতি করা damage, harm
ক্ষতিপূরণ compensation
ক্ষতিপূরণ দেওয়া compensate
ক্ষমতা power
ক্ষমা apology, mercy
ক্ষমা করা forgive, pardon?
ক্ষমা চাওয়া apologize

ক্ষয় decay
ক্ষয় করা ruin
ক্ষয়ক্ষতি damage
ক্ষিপ্ত mad
ক্ষীণভাবে remotely
ক্ষুদ্র minor, tiny
ক্ষুদ্র দলা pellet
ক্ষুদ্র নকল miniature
ক্ষুদ্রাতিক্ষুদ্র প্রাণী organism
ক্ষুধা hunger
ক্ষুধার ইচ্ছা appetite
ক্ষুধার্ত hungry
ক্ষেত্র case, sector
ক্ষেপণাস্ত্র missile
খচ্চর mule
খড় hay, straw
খড় ছাওয়া চাল thatched
খড়ি chalk
খড়ের গাদা haystack
খনক যন্ত্র digger
খনি mine
খনিজদ্রব্য mineral
খনিজ মেশা প্রাকৃতিক জল mineral water
খনিজীবী miner
খনি সম্বন্ধীয় mining
খণ্ড chunk
খণ্ডকাল part-time
খণ্ডিত broken
খণ্ডিত অংশ module
খবর news
খবরের কাগজ paper
খর rapids
খরগোশ hare, rabbit
খরচ expenses
খরচ করবার সামর্থ্য afford
খরচসাধ্য affordable
খরা drought
খলনায়ক villain
খসড়া draft
খাঁচা cage
খাঁটি real
খাওয়া eat
খাওয়ানো feed
খাজাঞ্চি teller
খাটসংলগ্ন টেবিল bedside table
খাটসংলগ্ন ল্যাম্প bedside lamp
খাটো shrunken
খাড়া steep
খাতাপত্র-কাগজকলম stationery
খাদ ditch
খাদান quarry
খাদ্য food
খাদ্য তালিকা menu
খাদ্য বা পানীয় রাখবার পাত্র basin

খাদ্যসংযম করা diet
খাদ্য সরবরাহের ব্যবসা catering
খাদ্যে বিষক্রিয়া food poisoning
খাবার diet
খাবার ঘর dining room
খাবার বওয়ার গাড়ী dining car
খাবার সময় mealtime
খাম envelope
খামার farm
খামার-বাড়ী farmhouse
খারাপ bad, lousy, second-rate, shabby, sloppy
খারাপ কিছু ঘটা cause
খারিজ করা dismiss, overrule
খাল canal
খালাস করা unload
খালি bare, blank, empty, vacant
খালি করা empty, evacuate, vacate
খালি-পা barefoot
খালি পায়ে barefoot
খালি সময় spare time
খিঁচুনি spasm
খিটখিটে irritable
খিলখিলিয়ে হাসা giggle
খিলান arch
খুঁজে পাওয়া spot
খুঁজে বার করা find out
খুঁটি pole, post
খুঁড়িয়ে চলা limp
খুঁত flaw
খুচরো বিক্রি retail
খুচরা বিক্রি করা retail
খুচরো বিক্রির দাম retail price
খুচরো বিক্রেতা retailer
খুন murder
খুন করা murder
খুনি thug
খুনী murderer
খুব extremely, very
খুব আঁটো, চামড়ার সাথে লেপে থাকে skin-tight
খুবই কম বা না hardly
খুব কম barely
খুব কষ্টে কাজ করা slave
খুব গুরুত্বপূর্ণ vital
খুব ছোট skimpy
খুব জোরে much
খুব বড় আকারের gigantic
খুব বেশি many, too
খুব ভাল super
খুব রোগা skinny
খুব শুকনো bone dry
খুব সুন্দর fantastic
খুরপী trowel
খুলে ফেলা apart, unroll

খুশী content
খুসকি dandruff
খেই ধরানোর ইঙ্গিত cue
খেয়াতরী ferry
খেলনা toy
খেলনা ঘোড়া rocking horse
খেলায়াড়দের ঘর pavilion
খেলা game
খেলা করা play
খেলার জন্য জায়গা pitch
খেলার জায়গা court
খেলার জুতো trainers
খেলার পোশাক sportswear
খেলার মাঠ playground, playing
    field
খেলার সময় playtime
খেলাসুলভ playful
খেলোয়াড় player
খেলোয়াড় সুলভ sporty
খেলোয়ার যে সার্ভ করে server
খোঁজ পাওয়া track down
খোঁজা find, look for
খোঁড়া dig, lame
খোদাই করা print
খোদাই করা অক্ষর inscription
খোবানি apricot
খোয়ারি hangover
খোলস shell
খোলসমইন পোকা slug
খোলা open, shell
খোলাখুলিভাবে frankly
খোলা থাকার সময় opening hours
খোলা মনের broad-minded
খোসা peel, skin
খোসা ছাড়ানো peel
খোসোসমেত স্কাকা আলু
    jacket potato
খ্যাতি fame
খ্রীষ্টধর্ম Christianity
খ্রীষ্টধর্মের গান carol
খ্রীষ্টধর্মের সাথে সম্পর্কিত Christian
খ্রীষ্টপূর্ব BC
খ্রীষ্টমাসে সাজানোর গাছ Christmas
    tree
খ্রীষ্টানদের উৎসব carnival
গঁদের আঠা resin
গগনচুম্বী ভবন skyscraper
গচ্ছিত টাকার পরিমাণের থেকে বেশি
    টাকা তোলা overdraft, overdrawn
গঠন composition
গঠন করা construct
গঠনমূলক constructive
গড় average
গড়পড়তা মান average
গড়িয়ে দেওয়া roll

গড়িয়ে পড়া slide
গণছুটি public holiday
গণতন্ত্র democracy
গণতান্ত্রিক democratic
গণনা calculation, estimate
গণনা করা calculate, estimate
গণিত maths
পণ্য করা treat
পণ্যমান্য important
গত last
গতকাল yesterday
গতি pace, rate, speed
গতি কম করা slow down
গতি পরিমাপ speedometer
গতিবর্ধক accelerator
গতি বাড়ানো accelerate, speed up
গতিবৃদ্ধি acceleration
গতিসীমা speed limit
গদা club
গদি mattress
গদিআঁটা cushion
গন্তব্যস্থান destination
গন্ধ smell
গন্ধ ছাড়া smell
গন্ধ পাওয়া smell
গবাদি পশু cattle
গবেষণা research
গভীর deep
গভীরতা depth
গভীর প্রতিক্রিয়া repercussions
গভীরভাবে deeply
গম wheat
গমনের যোগ্য accessible
গমে অ্যালার্জি wheat intolerance
গম্ভীর reserved
গম্ভীর গলার লোক bass
গয়না jewel
গরগর আওয়াজ করা purr
গরগর করা growl
গরম hot, sweltering
গরম করা heat, warm up
গরম জলের বোতল hot-water bottle
গরমের ছুটি summer holidays
গরমের দিন summertime
গরাদ bar
গরিলা gorilla
গরু cow
গরুর গাড়ি cart
গরুর মাংস beef
গর্জন করা howl, snarl
গর্ত hole, pothole
গর্ত করা drill
গর্ব pride
গর্ব করা boast
গর্বিত proud

গর্ভবতী pregnant
গর্ভবতী নারীর পরিচর্যা antenatal
গর্ভবস্থা pregnancy
গলদা চিংড়ি lobster
গলফ খেলা golf
গলফ খেলার ক্লাব golf club
গলফ শেখার ক্লাব golf club
গলফের শুরুর স্থান tee
গলা melt, neck, throat
গলা টিপে মারা strangle
গলাধঃকরণ swallow
গলানো melt
গলাবন্ধনী collar
গলার হাড় collarbone
গলি lane
গলে যায় soluble
গল্প story
গল্পের অথবা ফিল্মের চরিত্র character
গহনা jewellery
গাঁদাফুল marigold
গাছ tree
গাছের গুঁড়ি trunk
গাছের টব plant pot
গাছের দোকান garden centre
গাজর carrot
গাজর প্রজাতির সব্জি parsnip
গাড়ি saloon
গাড়ি চলাচলের ছোট রাস্তা slip road
গাড়ি চালক motorist
গাড়িচালক driver
গাড়িচালনার পাঠক্রম driving lesson
গাড়িচালনার লাইসেন্স driving licence
গাড়িচালনার শিক্ষক driving
    instructor
গাড়িতে ভ্রমণ drive
গাড়িতে লিফট lift
গাড়িতে লিফট নেওয়া hitchhike,
    hitchhiking
গাড়িতে লিফট নেওয়া ব্যক্তি hitchhiker
গাড়ি পার্ক করা park
গাড়ি বারান্দা driveway
সৎ honest
সৎ ছেলে stepson
সৎ বাবা stepfather
সৎ বোন stepsister
সৎ ভাই stepbrother
সৎভাবে honestly
সৎ মা stepmother
সৎ মেয়ে stepdaughter
গাড়ি-বারান্দা porch
গাড়ি সারাবার জায়গা garage
গাড়ির আলো sidelight
গাড়ির গিয়ার gear
গাড়ির ডানদিকে স্টিয়ারিং right-hand
    drive

গাড়ির দুধারে লাগানো আয়না **wing mirror**
গাড়ির সামনের কাচ **windscreen**
গাড়ির সামনের কাচ পরিষ্কার করবার ওয়াইপার **windscreen wiper**
গাড়ির স্টিয়ারিং **steering**
গাড়ি দুর্ঘটনা **crash**
গাড়ী ধোওয়ার জায়গা **car wash**
গাড়ী পারাপারের নৌকা **car ferry**
গাড়ি-ভাড়া **car rental**
গাড়ির চাকায় ফুটো **puncture**
গাড়ির চাকার রড **axle**
গাড়ি থেকে নির্গত দূষণ কম করবার সরঞ্জামবিশেষ **catalytic converter**
গাড়ী রাখবার জায়গা **car park**
গাড়ির চাবি **car keys**
গাড়ির বিমা **car insurance**
গাঢ় **dark**
গাঢ় নীল রং **navy**
গাদা **stack**
গাদাগাদি করে **squeeze in**
গাদাগাদি করে ভরা **jammed**
গাধা **donkey**
গান **song**
গান দেওয়া **sing**
গান গাওয়া **singing**
গানের আলবাম **album**
গানের কথা **lyrics**
গায়ক **singer**
গায়ক পক্ষী **thrush**
গায়ের রং **complexion**
গাল **cheek**
গালিগালাজের ভাষা **slang**
গালি দেওয়া **swear**
গালের হাড় **cheekbone**
গিঁট **knot**
গিঁট দেওয়া **do up**
গিনিপিগ হিসাবে ব্যবহৃত **guinea pig**
গির্জার অনুষ্ঠান **Mass**
গিলে খাওয়া **swallow**
গিলে নেওয়া **swallow**
গীর্জা **church**
গুগল করা **google**
গুচ্ছ **set**
গুজব **rumour**
গুটিয়ে ফেলা **wrap up**
গুণ **multiplication**
গুণগুণ করা **hum**
গুণমান **quality**
গুঠন **hood**
গুদান **store**
গুদামঘর **warehouse**
গুদামজাত করা **store**
গুদামে রাখা **storage**
গুনমানের মাপকাঠি **standard**

গুনে নেওয়া **count**
গুপ্তচর **spy**
গুপ্তচরের কাজ করা **spy**
গুবরেপোকা **beetle**
গুরুতর **major, serious**
গুরুতরভাবে **heavily, seriously**
গুরুত্ব **importance, significance**
গুরুত্ব আরোপ করা **underline**
গুরুত্বপূর্ণ **crucial, important, momentous, significant**
গুরুত্বপূর্ণ আবেদন **appeal**
গুরুত্বহীন **unimportant**
গুলি করা **shoot**
গুলি করার ঘটনা **shooting**
গুলি চালনা **shot**
গুলিয়ে ফেলা **confuse, mix up**
গুল্ম **bush**
গুহা **cave**
গৃহকর্তা **host**
গৃহপালিত **tame**
গৃহবধূ **housewife**
গৃহযুদ্ধ **civil war**
গৃহশিক্ষক **tutor**
গৃহশিক্ষা **tuition**
গৃহহীন **homeless**
গৃহাকুল **homesick**
গৃহাভ্যন্তর **indoors**
গেঁটেবাত **arthritis**
গোঁফ **moustache, whiskers**
গোঙানি **moan**
গোছানো করা **tidy up**
গোটা **whole**
গোড়াতে **originally**
গোড়ালি **ankle, heel**
গোপন **hidden, secret**
গোপন করা **hide**
গোপন তথ্য ফাঁস না করার বদলে **blackmail**
গোপন তথ্য ফাঁস না করার বদলে টাকা নেওয়া **blackmail**
গোপনভাবে **secretly**
গোপনীয় **confidential, secret**
গোপনীয়তা **privacy**
গোপনে **confidence**
গোপালকের জীবনকাহিনী **western**
গোবরাট **windowsill**
গোমড়ামুখো **sulky**
গোয়েন্দা **detective, scout**
গোয়েন্দাগিরি **espionage**
গোয়েন্দা বিভাগ **secret service**
গোল **round**
গোলকধাঁধা **maze**
গোলমরিচ **pepper**
গোলমরিচ পেষার যন্ত্র **peppermill**
গোলরক্ষক **goalkeeper**

গোলাপ ফুল **rose**
গোলাপী **pink**
গোলাবাড়ি **barn**
গোসাপ-জাতীয় প্রাণী **newt**
গৌরবপূর্ণ **glorious**
গ্যারান্টি দেওয়া **guarantee**
গ্যারেজ **garage**
গ্রহাগার **library**
গ্রহাগারিক **librarian**
গ্রহি **gland**
গ্রহ **planet**
গ্রহণ করা **accept**
গ্রহণযোগ্য **acceptable**
গ্রহীতা **recipient**
গ্রাফ **graph**
গ্রাম **village**
গ্রাম (ওজনের একক) **gram**
গ্রামাঞ্চল **country**
গ্রামীণ **rural**
গ্রাহক **client, consumer**
গ্রীক ভাষা **Greek**
গ্রীজযুক্ত **greasy**
গ্রীষ্মকাল **summer**
গ্রীষ্মপ্রধান স্থান **tropical**
গ্রীসদেশীয় **Greek**
গ্রীসের অধিবাসী **Greek**
গ্রেপ্তার **arrest**
গ্রেপ্তার করা **arrest**
গ্লাইডার **glider**
গ্লাইডারে ওড়া **gliding**
গ্লাস **glass**
ঘটনা **affair, event, incident, occurrence**
ঘটনা অনুযায়ী **topical**
ঘটনাকাল **occasion**
ঘটনাবহুল **eventful**
ঘটনার পরিণাম **result**
ঘটা **happen, occur**
ঘড়ি **clock**
ঘড়ির কাঁটার অভিমুখে **clockwise**
ঘড়ির কাঁটার বিপরীতমুখে **anticlockwise**
ঘন **dense, thick**
ঘনক **cube**
ঘনত্ব **density**
ঘন শ্যামল **lush**
ঘন সন্নিবদ্ধ **compact**
ঘনীভবন **condensation**
ঘণ্টা **bell, hour**
ঘণ্টীয় **hourly**
ঘর **room**
ঘরে পরিষেবা **room service**
ঘরোয়া **casual, informal**
ঘরোয়াভাবে **casually**
ঘর্মাক্ত **sweaty**

ঘষা rub
ঘসটে চলা shuffle
ঘসে ঘসে মোছা scrub
ঘা sore
ঘায়রা kilt
ঘাটতি deficit, lack, shortage
ঘাতক killer
ঘানা দেশীয় Ghanaian
ঘানার জনগণ Ghanaian
ঘাম perspiration, sweat
ঘামনাশক পদার্থ antiperspirant
ঘামা sweat
ঘাস grass
ঘাস কাটার মেশিন lawnmower
ঘাস কাটার যন্ত্র mower
ঘিরে ফেলা surround
ঘুষি punch
ঘুষি মারা punch
ঘুড়ি kite
ঘুম sleep
ঘুম ঘোর sleepy
ঘুমত্ত asleep
ঘুমপাড়ানি ওষুধ tranquillizer
ঘুমপাড়ানি গান lullaby
ঘুমানোর সময় bedtime
ঘুমিয়ে পড়া doze off
ঘুমিয়ে হাঁটা sleepwalk
ঘুমের বড়ি sleeping pill
ঘুমোনো sleep
ঘুমোনোর ব্যবস্থা সহ রেলের কামরা sleeping car
ঘুরিয়ে খোলা unscrew
ঘুরিয়ে নেওয়া swerve
ঘুরিয়ে বাঁধা wind
ঘুরে বেড়ান stroll
ঘুরে বেড়ানো wander
ঘুরে যাওয়া turn, wind
ঘুষ bribery
ঘুষ দেওয়া bribe
ঘুসি মারা thump
ঘূর্ণিঝড় tornado
ঘৃণা hatred
ঘৃণা করা hate, loathe
ঘেঁটে দেখা browse
ঘোটকী mare
ঘোড়দৌড় horse racing
ঘোড়দৌড়ের মাঠ racecourse
ঘোড়সওয়ার jockey
ঘোড়া horse
ঘোড়ায় চড়া horse riding
ঘোড়ায় জিন saddle
ঘোড়ার নাল horseshoe
ঘোড়ার পিঠে লাফিয়ে চলা gallop
ঘোড়ার স্বচ্ছন্দ দৌড় canter
ঘোষণা announcement

ঘোষণা করা announce
ঘোষণা বা প্রচার advert
ঘোষণা করা declare
ঘ্যানঘ্যান করা nag
চওড়া broad, wide
চওড়াভাবে wide
চওড়া রাস্তা avenue
চকচকে কাগজ tinsel
চকিতের দেখা glance
চক্র circle, cycle, round
চক্রাকার circular
চক্রাকারে round
চঞ্চল energetic
চটচটে আঠালো মিষ্টি পদার্থ treacle
চটজলদি তৈরি ready-cooked
চড় মারা slap, smack
চড়াই পাখি sparrow
চতুর চাহনি sly
চতুর্থ fourth
চতুর্দশ fourteen
চতুর্দশতম fourteenth
চতুর clever
চন্দ্রমল্লিকা ফুল chrysanthemum
চপ্পল sandal, slipper
চমৎকার splendid
চরবৃত্তি spying
চরম extreme
চরমপন্থা extremism
চরমপন্থী extremist
চরম মাথাব্যথা migraine
চরিত্র character
চর্মরোগ eczema
চলচ্চিত্র film, movie
চলচ্চিত্র-তারকা film star
চলতে থাকা continue
চলনশীল mobile
চলমান বাড়ি mobile home
চলাকালীন during
চলে যাওয়া away, go away, out
চল্লিশ forty
চশমা glasses, spectacles
চশমা-বিক্রেতা optician
চা tea
চাঁদ moon
চাঁদা subscription
চাওয়া ask for, long, seek, want
চাকর servant
চাকা wheel
চাকার নাভিখানের ঢাকনা hubcap
চাকার স্পোক spoke
চাকা লাগানো মোড়া চেয়ার buggy
চাকুরী employment
চা খাবার সময় teatime
চা-চামচ teaspoon
চাঞ্চল্যসৃষ্টিকারী sensational

চাটা lick
চাতাল landing
চাদর sheet
চাপ pressure, strain, stress
চাপ দেওয়া press, strain
চাপ সৃষ্টি করা pressure, stress
চাপা দেওয়া run over
চা-পান tea
চাপা রাগে চুপ থাকা sulk
চাপে পড়া stressed
চাবি key
চাবির রিং keyring
চাবুক whip
চা ব্যাগ tea bag
চামচ spoon
চামচ ভর্তি spoonful
চামড়া leather, skin, suede
চায়ের কাপ teacup
চায়ের কেটলি teapot
চায়ের প্লেট saucer
চার four
চার পায়ক quartet
চারিধারে around
চারিপাশে তাকানো look round
চারুকলা art
চারুকলা বিদ্যালয় art school
চাল rice
চালনা করা operate
চালাক clever
চালান invoice, shipment
চালান দেওয়া invoice
চালানো drive
চালিয়ে যাওয়া carry on, continue, go on, keep
চালু on
চালু করা start off, switch on, turn on
চালু খাতা current account
চাষ farming
চাহিদা need, requirement
চাহিদাপূর্ণ demanding
চাহিদামাফিক customized
চিংড়িমাছ prawn, shrimp
চিউইং গাম/চিবানোর মিষ্টি গাম chewing gum
চিকিৎসাকার্যের সহায়ক paramedic
চিকিৎসা treatment
চিকিৎসাবিদ্যা বিষয়ক medical
চিকিৎসালয় clinic, infirmary
চিঠি letter, mail
চিঠি পাঠানো mail
চিড়িয়াখানা zoo
চিৎকার shout, shriek
চিৎকার করা bark, shout, yell
চিৎকার করে ডাকা call

চিতাবাঘ leopard, panther
চিত্তবিনোদনের জায়গা amusement arcade
চিত্র drawing, painting, picture
চিত্রকর painter
চিত্রগ্রাহক photographer
চিত্রগ্রাহক/ক্যামেরা-ম্যান cameraman
চিনতে পারা recognize
চীনামাটির তৈরী ceramic
চিনি sugar
চিনি-বিহীন sugar-free
চিনির পরিবর্ত sweetener
চিনির শিরা syrup
চিন্তা concern
চিন্তা করা reckon, think, worry
চিন্তা না করা bother
চিন্তাভাবনা ভাগ করে নেওয়ার অনুভূতি communion
চিন্তার বিষয় worrying
চিন্তিত concerned, worried
চিবানো chew
চিমটি tweezers
চিমটি কাটা pinch
চিমনি chimney
চিরকূট slip
চিরদিন forever
চিরন্তন eternal
চিরাচরিত traditional
চিরুনি comb
চিলির অধিবাসী Chilean
চিলির সাথে সম্পর্কিত Chilean
চিলেকোঠার ঘর attic
চিলেকোঠা loft
চিহ্ন mark
চিহ্ন sign
চিহ্নিত করা identify, indicate, mark, tick
চীন প্রজাতন্ত্র China
চীন-বাসী Chinese
চীনা ভাষা Chinese
চীনামাটি china
চীনামাটির তৈরী দ্রব্য pottery
চীনার খাবার কাঠি chopsticks
চীনেবাদাম peanut
চীনেবাদাম মাখা peanut butter
চীনেবাদামে অ্যালার্জি peanut allergy
চীনের সাথে সম্পর্কিত Chinese
চুক্তি treaty
চুন lime
চুনকাম করা whitewash
চুনাপাথর limestone
চুপ করা shut up
চুপচাপ silence, silent
চুম্বক magnet

চুম্বকীয় magnetic
চুম্বন kiss
চুম্বন করা kiss
চুরি theft
চুরি করা steal
চুরুট cigar
চুল hair
চুল আঁচড়ানো comb
চুল আটকানোর ক্লিপ hairgrip
চুলকাটা haircut
চুল কাটেন এবং স্টাইল করেন যিনি stylist
চুলকানি itch
চুলকানিযুক্ত itchy
চুল কোঁকড়ানোর সরঞ্জাম curler
চুল ঢাকার স্কার্ফ headscarf
চুল শোকানোর পদ্ধতি blow-dry
চুলে লাগানোর জেলি hair gel
চুলে লাগানোর স্প্রে hair spray
চুলের গোছা lock
চুলের ব্রাশ hairbrush
চূড়া steeple, tower
চূড়ান্ত drastic, final, ultimate
চূড়ান্ত বিশৃঙ্খলা chaos
চূড়ান্ত বিশৃঙ্খলাযুক্ত chaotic
চূড়ান্তভাবে terminally
চূর্ণ করা crush
চেঁচানো cry
চেক-ইন/নাম-ঠিকানা নিবন্ধকরণ check in
চেক এর অধিবাসী Czech
চেক প্রজাতন্ত্র Czech Republic
চেক প্রজাতন্ত্রের সঙ্গে সম্পর্কিত Czech
চেক ভাষা Czech
চেচনিয়া Chechnya
চেতনা ফিরে পাওয়া come round
চেন zip
চেন খোলা unzip
চেন টানা zip
চেনা know
চেনার মত recognizable
চেপা squeeze
চেপে যাওয়া squash
চেয়ার chair
চেয়ার-লিফট/পাহাড়ী জায়গায় এর সাহায্যে মানুষ ওঠানামা করে chairlift
চেরীফল cherry
চেষ্টা attempt, effort, try
চেষ্টা করা attempt, try
চোখ eye
চোখ টিপে ইশারা করা wink
চোখ পিটপিট করা blink
চোখে কালো পট্টি পরানো blindfold
চোখের কালো পট্টি blindfold

চোখের ছানি cataract
চোখের ড্রপ eye drops
চোখের দৃষ্টি eyesight
চোখের পাতা eyelid
চোখের মণি iris, pupil
চোখের লোম eyelash
চোয়াল jaw
চোর thief
চোরঘণ্টি burglar alarm
চোষা suck
চৌকাঠ doorstep, skirting board
চ্যাট শো/হাল্কা কথাবার্তা বলার শো chat show
চ্যাট/হাল্কা কথাবার্তা chat
চ্যাট/হাল্কা কথাবার্তা বলা chat
চ্যাটিলো ফ্লাট flat
চ্যাড/উত্তর-মধ্য আফ্রিকার একটি প্রজাতন্ত্র Chad
চ্যাপেল/খ্রীষ্টানদের ব্যক্তিগত প্রার্থনাঘর chapel
চ্যালেঞ্জ/সাহস ও ঝুঁকি challenge
ছক্কা dice
ছড়ানো spray
ছড়িয়ে দেওয়া spray, spread, stretch
ছড়িয়ে পড়া spill
ছড়িয়ে যাওয়া spread, spread out
ছড়ি staff
ছত্রাক mushroom
ছদ্মনাম alias, pseudonym
ছদ্মবেশ ধারণ করা disguise
ছন্দ rhythm
ছবি photograph
ছবি তোলা photograph
ছবি দেখান screen
ছবির কথা অনুবাদ করে নিচে লেখা subtitled
ছবির কথা অনুবাদ করে নিচে লেখা হয় subtitles
ছবির কাঠামো picture frame
ছবির নিকটবর্তী স্থান foreground
ছবির মত সুন্দর picturesque
ছবিসম্বলিত গল্প comic strip
ছয় six
ছাঁকনি filter
ছাঁকনী sieve
ছাঁকা filter
ছাঁকা তেলে ভাজা deep-fry
ছাঁচ model, mould
ছাঁটা trim
ছাঁটাই redundancy
ছাঁটাই হওয়া redundant
ছাইদানি ashtray
ছাউনিতে থাকা camping
ছাউনি ফেলা camp

ছাউনিস্থল campsite
ছাগল goat
ছাড় concession, discount, rebate
ছাড়া besides, do without, except,
  excluding
ছাড়ানো cut off
ছাড়িয়ে beyond
ছাতা mould, umbrella
ছাতা পড়া mouldy
ছাত্র-ছাত্রী student
ছাত্রছাত্রী pupil
ছাত্রছাত্রীর জন্য ছাড় student
  discount
ছাদ ceiling, roof, terrace
ছাদের নিচে জায়গা headroom
ছাপা print
ছাপার ভুল misprint
ছায়া shadow
ছায়ার নিচে shade
ছারপোকা bug
ছিঁড়ে ফেলা tear
ছিদ্র piercing
ছিদ্রযুক্ত পাত্র colander
ছিনতাই করা mug
ছিনিয়ে নেওয়া snatch
ছিপ fishing rod
ছিপের সাহায্যে মাছ ধরা angling
ছুঁচো mole
ছুঁয়ে ফেলা catch up
ছুটি holiday, leave, time off
ছুটে যাওয়া dash
ছুতো pretext
ছুতোর carpenter, joiner
ছুরি knife
ছুরিকাঘাত stab
ছেঁড়া tear
ছেড়ে আসা leave
ছেড়ে দেওয়া give up, quit, skip,
  waive
ছেড়ে যাওয়া parting
ছেদচিহ্ন comma
ছেদবতী চিহ্ন punctuation
ছেনি chisel
ছেলে lad
ছেলে বন্ধু boyfriend
ছেলে বা মেয়েদের জাঙিয়া briefs
ছোঁড়া throw
ছোঁ মেরে নেওয়া grab
ছোঁয়াচে catching, contagious
ছোট little, short, small
ছোট গল্প short story
ছোট গোলাকৃতি কেক bun
ছোট ছেলে বা লোক chap
ছোট টুকরো chip
ছোট টুকরো করা chop

ছোট ট্যাক্সি minicab
ছোট তীক্ষ্ণদন্তী প্রাণী gerbil
ছোট দোকান kiosk
ছোট প্যাকেট pack
ছোট ফ্ল্যাটবাড়ি studio flat
ছোট বাড়ি cottage
ছোট বিক্রেতা vendor
ছোট বিজ্ঞাপন small ads
ছোট বীজ pip
ছোট মাথাওয়ালা পেরেক thumbtack
ছোট মোরগ cockerel
ছোট রাস্তা shortcut
ছোট সামুদ্রিক মাছ anchovy
ছোট হয়ে যাওয়া shrink
ছোট্ট চীনা কুকুর Pekinese
ছোট্ট ভুল slip up
ছোলার ডাল chickpea
জংলি ফুলের গাছ heather
জই oats
জপ jug
জগিং করা jogging
জঘন্য awful, disgraceful, hideous,
  nasty, obnoxious, repulsive
জঙ্গল jungle, wood
জঞ্জাল ফেলার স্থান litter bin
জটিল complex, complicated
জটিলতা complication
জড়িয়ে থাকা involve
জড়িয়ে ধরা cuddle
জড়ো হওয়া gather
জনগণ people, public
জনগণনা census
জনগণের ব্যবহৃত যানবাহন public
  transport
জনগোষ্ঠীগত ethnic
জনপ্রিয় popular
জনপ্রিয়তা popularity
জনবহুল busy, crowded
জনবাহুল congestion
জনমত public opinion
জনমানববিহীন দ্বীপ desert island
জনসংখ্যা population
জনসমীক্ষা opinion poll
জনসম্পর্ক public relations
জন্তু animal
জন্ম birth
জন্মদিন birthday
জন্মনিয়ন্ত্রক contraceptive
জন্মনিয়ন্ত্রণ contraception
জন্ম পরিচয়পত্র birth certificate
জন্মভূমি homeland, native
জন্মস্থান birthplace, place of birth
জন্য for
জবাব response

জবাব দেওয়া respond
জমকালো gorgeous
জমা deposit
জমাট-প্রতিরোধক antifreeze
জমি land, plot
জমিদার landowner
জমি বাড়ির দালাল estate agent
জমির মাপ acre
জমে যাওয়া freeze
জয়ী winning
জরাজীর্ণ worn
জরিমানা fine
জরুরী urgent
জরুরী অবস্থা emergency, urgency
জরুরী আবেদন করা appeal
জর্জরিত obsessed
জর্জিয়া দেশীয় Georgian
জর্জিয়ার জনগণ Georgian
জর্জিয়া রাষ্ট্র Georgia
জর্ডন দেশীয় Jordanian
জর্ডনের মানুষ Jordanian
জল water
জলখাবার refreshments, snack
জল ছিটান splash
জলদস্যু pirate
জল দেওয়ার পাত্র/মদ দেওয়ার পাত্র
  carafe
জল, নেলের সংযোগ করা plumbing
জলনিরোধী waterproof
জল পানের লম্বা পাত্র trough
জলপ্রপাত cataract
জলফড়িং dragonfly
জলফোস্কা blister
জলবায়ু climate
জলবায়ুর পরিবর্তন climate change
জলভরা কোষ cyst
জলময় হওয়া flood
জলযোগের দোকান snack bar
জলরং watercolour
জল শোকানোর স্থান draining board
জল স্রোত stream
জলহস্তী hippo, hippopotamus
জলাতক রোগ rabies
জলাধার reservoir
জলাভূমি marsh, swamp
জলাভূমির উত্তিজ্জ পদার্থ peat
জলে পরিপূর্ণ হওয়া flood
জলের কল tap
জলের নীচে underwater
জলের সিংক sink
জহুরী jeweller
জহুরীর দোকান jeweller
জাঁকজমকপূর্ণ elegant
জাং shin
জাইলোফোন xylophone

জাগ্রত awake
জাতি race
জাতিগত racial
জাতিবিষেধ racism
জাতিবিষেধী racist
জাতীয় national
জাতীয়করণ করা nationalize
জাতীয়তাবাদ nationalism
জাতীয়তাবাদী nationalist
জাতীয় সঙ্গীত national anthem
জাদু magic
জাদুকর conjurer, juggler, magician, sorcerer
জাদুঘর museum
জাদুগল magical
জাদুবিদ্যা magic
জাদুমন্ত্র spell
জানা know
জানানো notify
জানালা window
জানালা দরজার শাটার shutters
জানালার কাচ window pane
জানালার ধারের সীট window seat
জাপান দেশীয় Japanese
জাপানী Japanese
জাফরান saffron
জাম berry
জামা shirt
জামাইকা দেশীয় Jamaican
জামাইকার মানুষ Jamaican
জামাকাপড় clothes, clothing
জামা কাপড় খোলা strip
জামাকাপড় শুকাবার দড়ি clothes line
জামাতা son-in-law
জামিন bail
জাম্বিয়া Zambia
জাম্বিয়া দেশীয় Zambian
জাম্বিয়ার বসবাসকারী Zambian
জায়গা room, space
জায়গা দেওয়া accommodate
জায়ফল nutmeg
জার্মান ভাষা German
জার্মান মিজলস্ (হাম) German measles
জার্মানি Germany
জার্মানি দেশীয় German
জার্মানির অধিবাসী German
জাল net
জাল করা forge
জালিয়াতি forgery, fraud
জাহাজ নির্মাণ shipbuilding
জাহাজ ship
জাহাজঘাঁটি shipyard
জাহাজ দুর্ঘটনা shipwreck

জাহাজ দুর্ঘটনা থেকে বেঁচে যাওয়া shipwrecked
জাহাজ নোঙর করা moor
জাহাজযাত্রা sailing
জাহাজে প্রমোদভ্রমণ cruise
জাহাজের খোল hull
জাহাজে সাগর পার হওয়া crossing
জিজ্ঞাসা করা ask, enquire, question
জিজ্ঞাসা চিহ্ন question mark
জিজ্ঞাসাবাদ করা interrogate
জিন gene, gin
জিনগত genetic
জিনগতভাবে পরিবর্তিত genetically-modified, GM
জিনতত্ত্ব genetics
জিনিসপত্র belongings, contents
জিনিস thing
জিনিসপত্র goods
জিনিসপত্র বার করা unpack
জিনিসপত্র রাখার ট্রলি shopping trolley
জিভ tongue
জিমন্যাস্টিকে পারদর্শী gymnast
জিম্বাবোয়ে দেশীয় Zimbabwean
জিম্বাবোয়ের বসবাসকারী Zimbabwean
জিরে cumin
জীব creature
জীবন life
জীবনচরিত biography
জীবননায়ক life-saving
জীবনধারণ করা live on
জীবনধারণের মান standard of living
জীবনযাত্রার ধরণ lifestyle
জীবত্ত live
জীববিদ্যা biology
জীববিদ্যাসংক্রান্ত biological
জীবাণু bacteria, germ
জীবাণুনাশক disinfectant
জীবাণুবিয়োজ্য biodegradable
জীবাণুযুক্ত করা sterilize
জীবিকা living
জীবিত alive
জীবিত থাকা survival
জীবিত ব্যক্তি survivor
জুতো boot, shoe
জুতোর দোকান shoe shop
জুতোর পালিশ shoe polish
জুতোর ফিতে shoelace
জুন June
জুয়া gambling
জুয়াখেলা gamble
জুয়াড়ি gambler
জুলাই July
জেগে ওঠা wake up
জেগে থাকা awake

জেটি pier
জেতা win
জেদি obstinate
জেনারেল general
জেনেশুনে deliberately
জেল ক্রীম gel
জেলা district
জেলে fisherman
জেলে-নৌকা fishing boat
জেলের অধিবাসী inmate
জেহোবার সাক্ষী Jehovah's Witness
জৈব organic
জৈব রসায়ন biochemistry
জোকার clown
জোগাড় করা obtain
জোট alliance
জোড় even
জোড়া pair
জোড়াতালি দেওয়া patched
জোড়া ফিতে braces
জোড়া লাগানো fix
জোর করা force, insist, persuade
জোর করে ছেঁড়া rip
জোর দিয়ে উল্লেখ করা emphasize
জোরসহকারে roughly
জোরালো loud
জোরে ছোঁড়া pitch
জোরে জোরে পড়া read out
জোরে বলা speak up
জৌলুসময় glamorous
জ্ঞান knowledge, wisdom
জ্ঞান হারানো pass out
জ্ঞানী knowledgeable, wise
জ্বর fever
জ্বর ফোঁড়া cold sore
জ্বলে যাওয়া burn down
জ্বালা inflammation
জ্বালাতন করা pester
জ্বালানী fuel
জ্বালাযুক্ত inflamed
জ্বালিয়ে দেওয়া burn
জ্যাকেট tuxedo
জ্যামভরা কেক flan
জ্যাম রাখার জার jam jar
জ্যেষ্ঠ eldest
জ্যোতির্বিদ্যা astronomy
জ্যোতিষশাস্ত্র astrology
ঝগড়া quarrel, scrap
ঝগড়া করা quarrel, squabble
ঝটকানো flap
ঝড় storm
ঝড়বিশেষ cyclone
ঝরঝরে fluent
ঝরণা fountain, waterfall

ঝরে পড়া fall out	টাকা কেটে নেওয়া debit	টুপি cap, hat
ঝলক দেওয়া flash	টাকা দেওয়া pay	টেকনো techno
ঝলকানি flash	টাকাপয়সা money	টেকো bald
ঝলমলে bright	টাকা ফেরত দেওয়া pay back	টেডি বিয়ার teddy bear
ঝলসানো grilled, roast	টাকার পরিমাণ sum	টেনপিন বোলিং tenpin bowling
ঝলসানো চাহিত glare	টাকার ব্যাগ purse	টেনিস tennis
ঝলসে যাওয়া grill	টাকা রাখবার কাউন্টার till	টেনিস কোর্ট tennis court
ঝাঁকুনি shake	টাঙানো hang	টেনিস খেলোয়াড় tennis player
ঝাঁকুনি concussion	টাচপ্যাড touch pad	টেনিস ব্যাট tennis racket
ঝাঁপ দেওয়া dive	টাটকা fresh	টেনে আনা drag, draw, rope in
ঝাড়ু broom	টাট্টু ঘোড়া pony	টেনে ধরা pull up
ঝাড়ুদার dustman	টাট্টু ঘোড়ায় ভ্রমণ pony trekking	টেনে নিয়ে যাওয়া tow away
ঝাড়ু দেওয়া sweep	টানলে বড় হয় stretchy	টেনে বার করা pull out
ঝারি watering can	টানা pull	টেপ করা tape
ঝিঁঝিঁ পোকা cricket	টানাটানি tug-of-war	টেপ পরিমাপক tape measure
ঝিঙে courgette	টানা সেতু suspension bridge	টেপ রেকর্ডার tape recorder
ঝিনানো doze	টায়ার tyre	টেবিল table
ঝিরঝিরে হালকা বৃষ্টি drizzle	টালি tile	টেবিল ওয়াইন table wine
ঝিল lake	টালি দ্বারা বাঁধানো tiled	টেবিল ক্লথ tablecloth
ঝুঁকি risk	টি the	টেবিলচামচ tablespoon
ঝুঁকি নেওয়া risk	টিকে থাকা last	টেবিল টেনিস table tennis
ঝুঁকিপ্রবণ risky	টিউনিসিয়া Tunisia	টেরিয়ার terrier
ঝুঁকে থাকা lean	টিউনেসিয় Tunisian	টেলিফোন telephone
ঝুড়ি basket	টিউনেসিয়ার নাগরিক Tunisian	টেলিফোন করা call
ঝুমকো লতা buttercup	টিউব tube	টেলিফোনের তথ্যসংলিত তালিকা
ঝুলবারান্দা balcony	টিউমার tumour	telephone directory
ঝুলে থাকা চুলের গোছা fringe	টিউলিপ ফুল tulip	টেলিফোনের প্রত্যুত্তর call back
ঝোঁক থাকা tend	টিকটিকি lizard	টেলিফোনের মাধ্যমে বিক্রয় telesales
ঝোঁকানো bent	টিকলি tag	টেলিভিশন television, telly
ঝোড়ো stormy	টিকাদান vaccination	টেলিভিশনের ধারাবাহিক soap opera
ঝোপ shrub	টিকা দেওয়া vaccinate	টেলিস্কোপ telescope
ঝোপ-ঝাড় bush	টিকিট ticket	টোকন token
ঝোপঝাড়ের সারি hedge	টিকিট অফিস box office	টোকা মারা stroke
ঝোলানো hang	টিকিট কাটার মেশিন ticket machine	টোগো (দেশ) Togo
টক sour	টিকিট বিক্রির অফিস ticket office	টোটা রাখার খোপ magazine
টন (পরিমাপ) ton	টিক চিহ্ন tick	টোল খাওয়া dent
টনসিল tonsils	টি টাওয়েল tea towel	টোল খাওয়ানো dent
টনসিলের অসুখ tonsillitis	টিন tin	টোস্ট toast
টনিক tonic	টিন ফয়েল tinfoil	টোস্ট বানানোর যন্ত্র toaster
টফি toffee	টিনের বাক্স trunk	ট্যাক্স রিটার্ন tax return
টবের গাছ pot plant	টিপে নেবানো stub out	ট্যাক্সি cab, taxi
টমেটো tomato	টিভি TV	ট্যাক্সি চালক taxi driver
টমেটো সস tomato sauce	টিয়াপাখি parrot	ট্যাঙ্কার জাহাজ tanker
টর্চ torch	টি শার্ট T-shirt	ট্যাপ নৃত্য tap-dancing
টল টলে জল sparkling water	টি-শার্ট tee-shirt	ট্যাবলেট tablet
টলমল করা stagger	টিস্যু tissue	ট্যারা squint
টহল দল patrol	টুঁটি throat	ট্যারাগন tarragon
টাঁকশাল mint	টুকরো piece, scrap, slice	ট্যালকম পাউডার talcum powder
টাই tie	টুকরো করা chip, divide	ট্রফি trophy
টাইপ করা type	টুকরো করে কাটা cut up, slice	ট্রলি trolley
টাইপ করার যন্ত্র typewriter	টুকরো করে ছিঁড়ে ফেলা tear up	ট্রাক truck
টাইপ করে যে typist	টুকরো হয়ে যাওয়া break up	ট্রাক চালক truck driver
টাইফয়েড typhoid	টুকে রাখা note down	ট্রানজিস্টার transistor
টাইম বম্ব time bomb	টুনা মাছ tuna	ট্রাফিক লাইট traffic lights
টাউন হল town hall		ট্রাভেলার্স চেক traveller's cheque

ট্রাম গাড়ি tram
ট্রাম্পোলিন (খেলার সামগ্রী) trampoline
ট্রেইনার trailer
ট্রেন train
ট্রেনে, জাহাজে ঘুমানোর স্হান berth
ট্রেনে শোওয়ার বিছানা couchette
ট্র্যাক স্যুট tracksuit
ট্রাক্টর tractor
ঠকঠক আওয়াজ rattle
ঠকানো cheat
ঠগ cheat
ঠাকুমা grandma, grandmother, granny
ঠাকুর্দা-ঠাকুমা grandparents
ঠাকুর্দা granddad, grandfather, grandpa
ঠাণ্ডা রাখার বাক্স icebox
ঠাণ্ডা cold
ঠাণ্ডা করা chill, freeze
ঠান্ডায় কাঁপা shiver
ঠাসা crammed
ঠিক right
ঠিক আছে all right, OK!
ঠিক জায়গায় রাখা put away
ঠিকঠাক okay
ঠিকঠাক চলা work
ঠিকা contract
ঠিকাদার contractor
ঠিকানা address
ঠিকানার তালিকা mailing list
ঠিকানা লেখবার বই address book
ঠেলে দেওয়া poke
ঠেসে ভর্তি করা cram
ঠোঁট beak
ঠোঁটের মলম lip salve
ঠোকা মারা knock
ঠোকা মারার আওয়াজ knock
ডগা point
ডবল বাস double bass
ডমিনিক প্রজাতন্ত্র Dominican Republic
ডাঁশপাখি midge
ডাংরি জাতীয় পোশাক overalls
ডাইনি witch
ডাইরেক্ট ডেবিট direct debit
ডাউনলোড করা download
ডাক post
ডাকচিহ্ন postmark
ডাকটিকিট stamp
ডাকনাম nickname
ডাকবাক্স postbox
ডাকবিলি কর্মী postman
ডাকবিলি মহিলা কর্মী postwoman
ডাকমূল্য postage

ডাকা call
ডাকাত mugger, robber
ডাকাতি mugging, robbery
ডাকাতি করা rob
ডাক্তার doctor
ডাক্তারখানা surgery
ডাচ ভাষা Dutch
ডান right
ডানদিকে right-hand
ডানহাতি right-handed
ডানা wing
ডায়াবেটিস diabetes
ডায়াল করা dial
ডায়াল করার কোড dialling code
ডায়ালিং টোন dialling tone
ডায়েরী diary
ডাল pulses
ডিঙ্গিনৌকো dinghy
ডিঙি নৌকা canoe
ডিঙি নৌকার প্রতিযোগিতা canoeing
ডিজিটাল ঘড়ি digital watch
ডিনারের সময় dinner time
ডিম egg
ডিম এবং ক্রীমের তৈরী খাবার mousse
ডিম পাড়া lay
ডিম রাখার বাটি eggcup
ডিমের কুসুম egg yolk
ডিমের ঝুরি scrambled eggs
ডিমের সাদা অংশ egg white
ডিমের কুসুম yolk
ডিম্বাকৃতি oval
ডিম্বাশয় ovary
ডিশ তোয়ালে dish towel
ডিশ মোছার কাপড় dishcloth
ডুব dive, diving
ডুব সাঁতার scuba diving
ডুবসাতারের নিঃশ্বাস নেবার নল snorkel
ডুবুরি diver
ডুবে যাওয়া plunge, sink
ডুবোজাহাজ submarine
ডুমুর fig
ডেকাফিনের কফি decaffeinated coffee
ডেটা data
ডেনমার্ক-বাসী Dane
ডেনমার্ক সম্বন্ধীয় Danish
ডেবিট debit
ডেয়ারী প্রস্তুত খাদ্য dairy produce
ডেয়ারী প্রস্তুত খাদ্যদ্রব্য dairy products
ডেলা lump
ডেক্ desk
ডোবানো dip
ডোরা কাটা striped, stripy
ড্যানিশ Danish

ড্যাফোডিল ফুল/হলুদ রঙের ফুল daffodil
ড্রয়ারওয়ালা আলমারি chest of drawers
ড্রাই-ক্লিন করা dry-cleaning
ড্রাম drum
ড্রামবাদক drummer
ড্রিল drill
ড্রটস খেলা draughts
ঢলঢলে বহির্বাস apron
ঢাকনা lid
ঢাকা cover
ঢাকা দেওয়া cover
ঢাল shield
ঢালা pour
ঢালু স্হান slope
ঢিবি embankment
টিনা পোষাক pinafore
ঢিলে loose, slack
ঢিলে-ঢালা পোষাক baggy
ঢিলে ঢালা শার্ট sweatshirt
ঢিলে হাফ প্যান্ট boxer shorts
ঢেঁকি seesaw
ঢেকুর burp
ঢেকুর তোলা burp
ঢেউ tide, wave
ঢেউখেলানো wavy
ঢোকার রাস্তা way in
তকতকে spotless
তখন then
তছনছ করা vandalism
তছনছকারী ব্যক্তি vandal
তছনছ হয়ে যাওয়া vandalize
তড়িত-বিজ্ঞানবিদ electrician
তড়িৎশক্তি current
তত্ত্ব theory
তত্ত্বাবধান oversight
তথাপি however
তথা documents, information
তথা অনুসন্ধান directory enquiries
তথা কার্যালয় information office
তথ্যচিত্র documentary
তথ্যতালিকা chart
তথ্যপঞ্জিকা directory
তথ্যপ্রযুক্তি IT
তথ্য বিন্যাস করা format
তথ্যভিত্তিক informative
তথ্যাবলী documentation
তদন্ত inquest, investigation
তদারক করা supervise
তদারককারী supervisor
তন্তু fibre
তন্নতন্ন করে খোঁজা hunt
তন্বী slim
তবুও nevertheless, though

তরঙ্গদৈর্ঘ্য wavelength
তরতাজা refreshing
তরতাজা করে তোলা freshen up
তরমুজ melon, watermelon
তরল liquid
তরল করবার মেশিন liquidizer
তরল রাখবার পাত্র casserole
তরল সাবান washing-up liquid
তরুণী lass
তর্ক করা debate
তর্কবিতর্ক argument, row
তর্কবিতর্ক করা argue, row
তর্কাতীত undisputed
তর্জনী index finger
তল plane
তলদেশ bottom
তলা floor
তলায় beneath, underneath
তলার দিকে bottom
তলিয়ে যাওয়া drown
তল্পিতল্পা luggage
তল্পিতল্পা রাখবার তাক luggage rack
তল্লাসী search
তল্লাসী দল search party
তহবিল funds
তাঁবু tent
তাই so
তাইওয়ান Taiwan
তাইওয়ান দেশীয় Taiwanese
তাইওয়ানের বসবাসকারী Taiwanese
তাক rack, shelf
তাকে (নারী) her
তাকে (পুরুষ) him
তাচ্ছিল্যের হাসা snigger
তাজা fresh
তাজিকিস্তান Tajikistan
তাড়া করা go after
তাড়াতাড়ি early, hastily, promptly, quick, shortly
তাড়াতাড়ি করা hurry up
তাড়াতাড়ি করে quickly
তাড়াতাড়ি চিত্র আঁকা sketch
তাড়াহুড়ো hurry
তাড়াহুড়ো করা hurry
তাড়াহুড়োর সময় rush hour
তাদের their
তাদেরকে them
তানজানিয়া Tanzania
তানজানিয়া দেশীয় Tanzanian
তানজানিয়ার অধিবাসী Tanzanian
তাপ heat
তাপমাত্রা temperature
তামা copper
তামাক tobacco
তামাক বিক্রির দোকান tobacconist

তামাটে tan
তামাসা করা kid
তার its, string, telegram, wire
তারকা star
তারকা চিহ্ন star
তার (নারী) her, hers
তারপর then
তার (পুরুষ) his
তার(পুরুষ) his
তারবিহীন cordless
তারা নিজেরা themselves
তারিখ date
তারিখের পূর্বে ব্যবহার সর্বাধিক উত্তম best-before date
তারিখের মধ্যে বিক্রি করা sell-by date
তাল beat
তাল palm
তালগোল পাকিয়ে ফেলা mix up
তালা lock, padlock
তালাওয়ালা locksmith
তালা খোলা unlock
তালা ভেঙে ঘরে ঢুকেছে break in
তালা ভেঙে ঘরে ঢোকা break in
তালা লাগানো lock
তালিকা list
তালিকাভুক্তকরণ registration
তালিকাভুক্ত করা list
তালিকাভুক্ত নয় unlisted
তালিকাভুক্ত বিষয় item
তালু palm
তাস card, playing card
তাসখেলার টেক্কা a, ace
তাস দেওয়া deal
তাসমানিয়া Tasmania
তাসের জুয়া bingo
তায়া that
তাহারা they
তাহিতি Tahiti
তিক্ত bitter
তিতিবিরক্ত হওয়া fed up
তিতির partridge
তিন three
তিনগুণ করা treble
তিন চাকার সাইকেল tricycle
তিন অংশ triple
তিনতালে নৃত্য করা waltz
তিনতালের নৃত্য waltz
তিনি (পুরুষ) he
তিব্বত Tibet
তিব্বত দেশীয় Tibetan
তিব্বতী Tibetan
তিব্বতী ভাষা Tibetan
তিমি whale
তিরস্কার করা tell off

তির্যক চিহ্ন forward slash
তিল mole
তীক্ষ্ণ sharp
তীক্ষ্ণদন্তী প্রাণীবিশেষ rodent
তীব্র মনোবেদনা grief
তীর arrow, shore
তীরচিহ্ন arrow
তীর্থযাত্রী pilgrim
তীর্থস্থান pilgrimage
তুচ্ছ trivial
তুতে turquoise
তুমি you
তুরস্ক দেশীয় Turkish
তুরস্ক (দেশ) Turkey
তুরস্কের লোক Turk
তুর্কী ভাষা Turkish
তুলনা comparison
তুলনা করা compare
তুলনামূলকভাবে comparatively, relatively
তুলনীয় comparable
তুলসী basil
তুলা Libra
তুলে আনা fetch
তুলে ধরা boost, lift
তুলোয় জড়ানো কাঠি cotton bud
তুলোর বল cotton wool
তুষ bran
তুষার ঝড় snowstorm
তুষারঝড় blizzard
তুষারপাত frost
তৃণভূমি meadow
তৃতীয় third
তৃতীয়তঃ thirdly
তৃপ্তিকর delightful
তৃষ্ণা thirst
তৃষ্ণার্ত thirsty
তেজপাতা bay leaf
তেল oil
তৈরী dressed
তৈরী করা make, manufacture
তৈরী হয় consist of
তৈলকূপ oil well
তৈল শোধনাগার oil refinery
তেল তোলবার পাটাতন ও যন্ত্রপাতি oil rig
তেল দেওয়া oil
তোতলানো stammer, stutter
তোয়ালে towel
তোলা pick
তোমোদোদ flatter
ত্বক-পরিষ্কারক cleanser
ত্বকে দাপ zit
ত্বরিত prompt
ত্রয়ী triplets

ত্রয়োদশ thirteen
ত্রয়োদশতম thirteenth
ত্রিনিদাদ এন্ড টোবাগো, (দেশ) Trinidad and Tobago
ত্রিভুজ triangle
ত্রিমাত্রিক three-dimensional
ত্রিশ thirty
ত্রুটি defect, error, fault, shortcoming, slip
ত্রুটিযুক্ত faulty, inaccurate
ত্রুটিহীনতা perfection
থলে satchel, shopping bag
থাইল্যান্ড Thailand
থাইল্যান্ড দেশীয় Thai
থাইল্যান্ডের নাগরিক Thai
থাইল্যান্ডের ভাষা Thai
থাকা be, keep, stay
থাবা claw, paw
থামা pause, stop
থামানো stop
থার্ড পার্টি ইন্সিওরেন্স third-party insurance
থার্মোমিটার thermometer
থার্মোস Thermos®
থার্মোস্ট্যাট thermostat
থিতু হওয়া settle down
থিম পার্ক theme park
থুতনি chin
থুথু spit
থুথু ফেলা spit
থেকে from, since
থেকে যাওয়া remain
থেমে যাওয়া halt
দই yoghurt
দক্ষ expert, skilful
দক্ষতা skill
দক্ষতার সাথে effectively, efficiently
দক্ষতাসম্পন্ন skilled
দক্ষিণ আফ্রিকার নাগরিক South African
দক্ষিণ south
দক্ষিণ আফ্রিকা South Africa
দক্ষিণ আফ্রিকা দেশীয় South African
দক্ষিণ আমেরিকা South America
দক্ষিণ আমেরিকার South American
দক্ষিণ আমেরিকার মানুষ South American
দক্ষিণ কোরিয়া South Korea
দক্ষিণদিক south
দক্ষিণদিকে south
দক্ষিণ-পন্থী right-wing
দক্ষিণপশ্চিম southwest
দক্ষিণপূর্ব southeast
দক্ষিণ মুখী southbound
দক্ষিণ মেরু South Pole

দক্ষিনাঞ্চলীয় southern
দখল করা conquer
দখল নেওয়া take over
দড়ি rope
দড়িতে জামাকাপড় আটকাবার ক্লিপ clothes peg
দত্তকগ্রহণ adoption
দত্তক নেওয়া adopt
দত্তকরূপে গৃহীত adopted
দণ্ড rod
দণ্ডিত করা penalize
দন্ত-চিকিৎসক dentist
দন্ত বিষয়ক dental
দফা clause
দমকলকর্মী fireman
দমকলবাহিনী fire brigade
দমনাত্মক হওয়া crack down on
দম ফুরানো wind
দম বন্ধ হয়ে আসা suffocate
দম্পতি couple
দয়া kindness
দয়া করে kindly
দয়ালু kind
দর-কষাকষি করা haggle
দরকার হওয়া require
দরকারী useful
দরজা door, gate
দরজারক্ষী doorman
দরজার বেল doorbell
দরজার হাতল door handle
দরদী caring
দরদাম bargain
দরিদ্র poor
দর্জি tailor
দর্শক audience, onlooker, spectator, viewer
দর্শনকেন্দ্রিক visual
দর্শনবিষ্ণুঃ philosophy
দল bunch, group, party, side, team
দলিল will
দশ ten
দশক decade
দশম tenth
দশমিক decimal, metric
দশলক্ষ million
দস্তা zinc
দস্তানা glove
দস্তানা বিশেষ mitten
দাঁড়কাক raven
দাঁড় চালানো paddle
দাঁড় বওয়া row
দাঁড়ান stand
দাঁড়ি full stop
দাঁড়িপাল্লা scales
দাঁড়িয়ে যাওয়া stuck

দাঁত tooth
দাঁত কাঠি toothpick
দাঁত বার করে হাসা grin
দাঁতব্যথা toothache
দাঁত মাজার ব্রাশ toothbrush
দাঁতের মাজন toothpaste
দাঁতের সুতো dental floss
দাগ mark, smudge, spot, stain
দাগ ওঠানোর উপাদান stain remover
দাগ দিয়ে রাখা tick off
দাগ লাগা stain
দাঙ্গা riot
দাঙ্গা লাগা riot
দাড়ি beard
দাড়ি কামানো shave
দাড়ি কামানোর ক্রীম shaving cream
দাড়ি কামানোর ফোম shaving foam
দাড়ি কামানোর মেসিন shaver
দাড়ি না কামানো unshaven
দাতব্য প্রতিষ্ঠান charity
দাতা donor
দান করা donate
দানব monster
দানাশস্য grain, rye
দাবা chess
দাবি claim, demand
দাবি করা call for, claim, demand
দাবিপত্র claim form
দাম বাড়া go up
দামী expensive
দামী জিনিস valuables
দায়বদ্ধ accountable
দায়িত্ব responsibility
দায়িত্বজ্ঞানহীন irresponsible
দায়িত্বশীল responsible
দারিদ্র্য poverty
দারুচিনি cinnamon
দারুণ cool, fabulous, terrific, tremendous, wonderful
দারুণ সুন্দর lovely
দালান corridor, hallway
দালাল broker
দিক aspect, dimension, direction, side
দিকচিহ্ন landmark
দিক পরিবর্তন turn, turning
দিগন্ত horizon
দিন day
দিনের বেলা day, daytime
দিবানিদ্রা snooze
দীর্ঘ long
দীর্ঘ সময় long
দুই two
দুই ফোকাস যুক্ত চশমা bifocals
দুই বা তার আশেপাশে couple

ই রঙ এর চোকো ডিজাইন	checked	দূতাবাস	embassy	দোকানের বাইরে নিয়ে যাওয়ার খাবার	take away
ই শয্যা	twin beds	দূর	far	দোভাষী	interpreter
খ	misery	দূরত্ব	distance	দোল খাওয়া	rock, sway, swing
খিত	sorry!	দূরনিয়ন্ত্রণ	remote control	দোলনা	cradle, sling
খিত	sad	দূরবীন	binoculars	দোলনা বিছানা	hammock
খিত হয়ে	sadly	দূরে	distant	দোলা	swing
স্চিন্তামুক্তকর	reassuring	দূরে থাকা	keep out	দোষ	blame
স্চিন্তা করা	reassure	দূরের জিনিস যে দেখতে পায় না	near-sighted	দোষারোপ	allegation
সাহসপূর্ণ	adventurous	দূষণ	pollution	দোষারোপ করা	accuse, blame, condemn
স্বপ্ন	nightmare	দূষিত	polluted	দোষী	culprit, guilty
ক্রাজ্জ চিস	cheese	দূষিত করা	pollute	দৌড়	run, running
ট	double	দৃঢ়	firm	দৌড় প্রতিযোগিতা	race, sprint
টির মধ্যে একটি	either	দৃঢ়তেজ	dynamic	দৌড় প্রতিযোগিতায় অংশগ্রহণ করা	race
টির মধ্যে কোনটি নয়	neither	দৃঢ়প্রতিজ্ঞ	determined	দৌড় প্রতিযোগিতার ট্র্যাক	racetrack
ট রাস্তার সংযোগস্থল	crossroads	দৃশ্য	scene	দৌড় প্রতিযোগী	racer
তলা বিছানা	bunk beds	দৃষ্টি	sight	দৌড়বীর	runner
ধ	milk	দৃষ্টিকোণ	viewpoint	দৌড়ানো	run
ধ দেওয়া	milk	দৃষ্টিগোচর	visible	দৈনন্দিন কার্যসূচী	routine
ধের চকলেট	milk chocolate	দৃষ্টিগোচরতা	visibility	দৈনিক	daily
ধের দাঁত পড়া	teethe	দৃষ্টিপাত	look	দৈবক্রমে	accident
ধের সরবত	milkshake	দৃষ্টিভঙ্গী	outlook, standpoint	দৈর্ঘ্য	length
পায়ে লাফানো	hop	দেউলিয়া	bankrupt	দৈহিক শাস্তি	corporal punishment
-পারা কাঁচের জানালা	double glazing	দেওয়া	give, hand, provide	দ্বন্দ্ব	conflict
বার	twice	দেওয়াল	wall	দ্বন্দ্ব হওয়া	clash
রারোগ্য	chronic	দেওর	brother-in-law	দ্বাদশ	twelfth
র্গ	castle, fort	দেখতে	look	দ্বারপাল	janitor
র্গ	odour, stink	দেখতে পাওয়া	notice	দ্বারা	by
র্গ ছড়ানো	stink	দেখভাল করা	care	দ্বিখণ্ড হওয়া	split
র্গনাশক	deodorant	দেখভাল করেন যিনি	caretaker	দ্বিগুণ	double
র্গযুক্ত	foul, smelly	দেখা	look, see	দ্বিতীয়	second
র্গপরিখা	moat	দেখানো	show	দ্বিতীয়তঃ	secondly
ঘটনা	accident, mishap	দেবদূত	angel	দ্বিতীয় বিজেতা	runner-up
ঘটনাক্রমে	accidentally	দেরাজ	cupboard	দ্বিতীয় শ্রেণী	second class
ঘটনাজনিত অবস্থা	accidental	দেরি	late	দ্বিধা	suspense
ঘটনাজনিত জরুরী বিভাগ	accident and emergency	দেরি	delay	দ্বিধাগ্রস্ত	bewildered
ঘটনাজনিত বিমা	accident insurance	দেরি করা	delay, put off	দ্বিধাবিত	indecisive
ঘটনায় আহত/দুর্ঘটনায় নিহত	casualty	দেরিতে	late	দ্বিপ্রহর	noon
নীতি	corruption	দেশ	country, nation, state	দ্বীপ	island
নীতিগ্রস্ত	corrupt	দেশভক্ত	patriotic	দ্বেষ	spite
র্বল	frail, poorly, shaky, weak	দেশলাই কাঠি	match	দ্বৈভাষিক	bilingual
র্বলতা	vice, weakness	দেশান্তরে পাঠানো	deport	দ্রবীভূত হওয়া	dissolve
র্ভাগ্য	misfortune	দেশান্তরে যাওয়া	emigrate	দ্রাক্ষালতা	vine
র্ভাগ্যবশতঃ	unfortunately	দেশি মদ	house wine	দ্রাঘিমাংশ	longitude
র্ভিক্ষ	famine	দেশী	domestic	দ্রুত	fast
র্মূল্য	dear	দেহ	body	দ্রুত গতি	speeding
র্মূল্য বস্তুর দোকান	antique shop	দেহরক্ষী	bodyguard	দ্রুতগতিতে মারা	swat
র্লভ	rare	দেহের উপরিভাগের অন্তর্বাস	vest	দ্রুতগামী গাড়ির জন্য রাস্তা	motorway
ষ্ট	evil	দেহের ডাক্তারি পরীক্ষা	physical	দ্রুত দৌড়	sprint
ষ্ট	naughty	দোকান	shop, stall	দ্রুত ধাবিত হওয়া	rush
হুদিভরর্ব কৌতুক	prank	দোকান থেকে চুরি করা	shoplifting	দ্রুত বেগে চলা	trot
ত	ambassador	দোকানদার	shopkeeper	দ্রুতভাবে	fast
		দোকান সহায়ক	shop assistant	দ্রুত ধাবন	rush
		দোকানের কাউন্টার	counter	ধনসম্পত্তি	treasure
		দোকানের প্রদর্শনী	shop window		

ধনী rich
ধনুক bow
ধনুরাশি Sagittarius
ধনুষ্টংকার tetanus
ধনে coriander
ধন্যবাদ thanks!
ধন্যবাদ দেওয়া thank
ধমনী artery
ধরণ kind, pattern, sort
ধরা catch, hold
ধরে included
ধরে নেওয়া যাক supposing
ধরে রাখা hold on
ধর্ম religion
ধর্মঘট strike
ধর্মঘট পালন করা strike
ধর্মঘটী striker
ধর্মতত্ত্ব theology
ধর্ষণ rape
ধর্ষণকারী rapist
ধর্ষিত হওয়া rape
ধসে পড়া collapse
ধাঁধা puzzle
ধাক্কা bump
ধাতু metal
ধাতুর আওয়াজ click
ধাতুর কৌটো tin
ধাতুর বাদ্যযন্ত্র triangle
ধাতুরূপ conjugation
ধাত্রী midwife
ধাপ step
ধাপ কাটা terraced
ধাপ্পা bluff
ধাপ্পা দেওয়া bluff
ধাবক sprinter
ধার credit
ধার করা borrow, owe
ধারণ করে contain
ধারণ ক্ষমতা hold
ধারণা idea, impression
ধার দেওয়া lend, loan
ধারাবাহিক continuous, sequel, serial
ধারাবাহিক, পরপর successive
ধারালো দাঁত tooth
ধারালো sharp
ধারালো টুকরো splinter
ধারালো বস্তু dart
ধার্মিক religious
ধীরগতি slow
ধীরে ধীরে slowly
ধুয়ে ফেলা rinse
ধুলো dirt, dust
ধুলো ঝাড়া dust
ধুলোবালি তুষে নেবার বৈদ্যুতিক যন্ত্র
    Hoover®

ধুলোমাখা dusty
ধুমকেতু comet
ধূমপান smoking
ধূমপান-বর্জিত non-smoking
ধূমপায়ী smoker
ধূর্ত cunning
ধূলিস্মাৎ করে দেওয়া pull down
ধূসর grey
ধেড়ে ইঁদুর rat
ধেড়ে ইঁদুরের মত প্রাণী hamster
ধৈর্য patience
ধৈর্যশীল patient
ধৈর্যহীনতা impatience
ধৈর্য ধরা bear up
ধোঁয়া fumes, smoke
ধোঁয়াচ্ছন্ন smoked
ধোঁয়া বার হওয়া smoke
ধোঁয়ার কালি soot
ধোঁয়ার সতর্কতা smoke alarm
ধোয়া wash
ধৌতকরণ rinse, washing-up
ধ্বংস destruction, wreck
ধ্বংস করা wreck
ধ্বংস করে দেওয়া destroy
ধ্বংসাবশেষ wreckage
ধ্বনি note
ধ্যান meditation
নকল clone, dummy, fake,
    imitation, mock
নকল করা copy, Imitate, mimic,
    model
নকল সৃষ্টি করা clone
নক্ষত্র star
নখ nail
নখ কাটার কাঁচি nail scissors
নখের ব্রাশ nailbrush
নগণ্য trifle
নগদ cash
নগদ নিবন্ধকরণের যন্ত্র cash register
নগদ-পরিবেশক cash dispenser
নগর পরিকল্পনা town planning
নগ্ন nude
নগ্ন অবস্থা nude
নজর করা observe
নজরদার invigilator
নঞর্থক negative
নতুন new
নতুন জামা পরা dress up
নতুবা either ... or
নথিপত্র document
নদী river
নদীর পাড় bank
ননদ, শ্যালিকা, বৌদি sister-in-law
নিনি cream
নবজাত newborn

নববর্ষ New Year
নবম ninth
নবাগত newcomer
নবীকরণযোগ্য renewable
নব্বই ninety
নমনীয় flexible
নমনীয় সময় flexitime
নমুনা sample
নম্র polite
নম্রতা politeness
নম্রভাবে politely
নয় nine
নয়নাভিরাম spectacular
নয় ভাগের এক ভাগ ninth
নরওয়ে দেশীয় Norwegian
নরওয়ের অধিবাসী Norwegian
নরওয়ের ভাষা Norwegian
নরক hell
নরম soft, tender
নরম জিনিসের তৈরী টুপি beret
নরম মাটি bog
নর্তক/নর্তকী dancer
নল tube
নলখাগড়া reed
নলের মিস্ত্রি plumber
নষ্ট করা sabotage, spoil, squander
নষ্ট করে দেওয়া spoil
নষ্টামি mischief
না no, not
নাইজেরিয়া দেশীয় Nigerian
নাইজেরিয়ার অধিবাসী Nigerian
নাক nose
নাকউঁচু লোক snob
নাকচ করা turn down
নাক ডাকা snore
নাক থেকে রক্তক্ষরণ nosebleed
নাকের হাড় sinus
না খেয়ে থাকা starve
নাগরদোলা merry-go-round
নাগরিক citizen
নাগরিক অধিকার civil rights
নাগরিকত্ব citizenship, nationality
নাগাল পাওয়া reach
নাচ করা dance
নাট nut
নাটক drama, play
নাটকীয় dramatic
নাটকের চরিত্র cast
নাটককার playwright
নাড়ান stir
নাড়িভুঁড়ি gut
নাতনি granddaughter
নাতি grandson
নাতি অথবা নাতনি grandchild
না পর্যন্ত until

...পিত barber	নিচের তলার downstairs	নির্দিষ্ট স্থান slot
...বালক underage	নিছক sheer	নির্দেশ directions
...বি sailor, seaman	নিজে থেকে itself	নির্দেশক instructor
...ভি belly button, navel	নিজে (নারী) herself	নির্দেশপুস্তক manual
...ম name	নিজে (পুরুষ) himself	নির্দেশ দেওয়া direct, instruct
...মডাক reputation	নিজে oneself, own	নির্দেশত কাজ করা carry out
...মডাকা roll call	নিজের জায়গায় ম্যাচ home match	নির্দেশাবলী briefing, instructions
...মমার hardly	নিতম্ব bottom, buttocks, hip	নির্দেশিকা handbook
...ম্য land	নিতান্ত ক্ষুদ্র miniature	নির্দোষ innocent
...ম্যার দেওয়া mark	নিদ্রাচ্ছন্ন drowsy	নির্বাক নাটক pantomime
...ম্যক hero	নিদ্রাহীনতা insomnia	নির্বাচকমণ্ডলী electorate
...ম্যিকা heroine	নিবন্ধভুক্ত register	নির্বাচন election, selection, vote
...রকেল coconut	নিবন্ধিত registered	নির্বাচন করা elect, select, vote
...রী female	নিবন্ধিত করা register	নির্বাচনকেন্দ্র constituency
...রীবাদী feminist	নিবন্ধীকরণ কার্যালয় registry office	নির্বাপকযন্ত্র extinguisher
...রীর বিবাহপূর্ব নাম maiden name	নিবারক repellent	নির্বাসন exile
...রী-সংক্রান্ত feminine	নিবারণ prevention	নির্বাহক executive
...লপোষ bib	নিয়তি destiny	নির্বাহ করা cope
...লি ঘা ulcer	নিয়ন্ত্রণ check, control	নির্বোধ daft
...লিশ accusation	নিয়ন্ত্রণ করা control	নির্ভর করা depend
...লী drain	নিয়ম code, rule	নির্ভরযোগ্য authentic
...শকতা devastated, sabotage	নিয়মানুগ formal	নির্মম ruthless
...শকতামূলক devastating	নিয়মানুগতা formality	নির্মাণ construction
...সপাতি pear	নিয়মিত regular	নির্মাণ করা build, put up
...সারন্ধ্র nostril	নিয়মিতভাবে regularly	নির্মাণকর্তা builder
...স্তিক atheist	নিয়ে নেওয়া collect	নির্মাণ স্থল building site
...হলে otherwise	নিয়োগ appointment, recruitment	নির্মাতা make, maker, manufacturer
...য়শব্দে quietly	নিয়োগ করা appoint, hire	নির্যাতন torture
...য়শেষ করে ফেলা use up	নিযুক্ত করা employ	নির্যাতন করা persecute, torture
...য়শেষিত হওয়া run out	নিরক্ষবৃত্ত equator	নিলম্বন suspension
...য়শ্বাস breath	নিরক্ষীয় গিনি Equatorial Guinea	নিলম্বিত করা suspend
...য়শ্বাস গ্রহণ করা breathe in	নিরপেক্ষ impartial, neutral	নিলাম auction
...য়শ্বাস নেওয়া breathe	নিরবচ্ছিন্ন continual	নিশ্চয়তা certainty
...য়শ্বাস বার করা breathe out	নিরবচ্ছিন্নভাবে continually	নিশ্চল motionless, still
...য়সন্দেহে undoubtedly	নিরস্ত করা discourage	নিশ্চিত assure, certain
...উজিল্যান্ডের আদিবাসী সন্প্রদান Maori	নিরহংকার humble	নিশ্চিতভাবে certainly, definitely, surely
...উজিল্যান্ডের অধিবাসী New Zealander	নিরাপত্তা safety, security	নিশ্চিন্ত laid-back, relaxed
...কটতম আত্মীয় next of kin	নিরাপত্তা পেটি safety belt	নিষিদ্ধ ban, banned, forbidden, prohibited, taboo
...কটত্ব proximity	নিরাপত্তা রক্ষী security guard	নিষিদ্ধ করা ban
...কটবর্তী nearby	নিরাপদ harmless, safe, secure	নিষেধ করা forbid, restrict
...কটভাবে closely	নিরামিষাশী vegetarian	নিষেধ করে prohibit
...কটে close, close by	নিরামিষে আসক্ত ব্যক্তি vegan	নিষ্কাশন drain
...কারাগুয়া দেশীয় Nicaraguan	নিরাশ disappointed	নিষ্ঠাবান sincere
...কারাগুয়ার অধিবাসী Nicaraguan	নিরাশ করা disappoint	নিষ্ঠার সঙ্গে sincerely
...কৃষ্ট inferior, mean	নিরাশাজনক disappointing	নিষ্ঠাহীন insincere
...ক্ষেপ করা toss	নিরুদিত dehydrated	নিষ্ঠুর cruel
...খুঁত perfect	নিরুদ্বেগজনিত relaxing	নিষ্ঠুরতা cruelty
...খুঁতভাবে perfectly	নিরেট solid	নিষ্ঠুরভাবে brutal
...চু lower	নির্গত গ্যাস exhaust fumes	নিষ্পত্তি ঘটানো conclude
...চুভাবে low	নির্গমন পাইপ exhaust	নিষ্পত্তিযোগ্য disposable
...চে down, under	নির্ঘণ্ট schedule	নিষ্ফল vain
...চের lower	নির্ণয় করা pick out	নিষ্ক্রিয় passive
...চের অংশ ওপরের দিকে করা upside down	নির্ণায়ক decisive	নিস্তব্ধ silent
	নির্দিষ্ট particular	
	নির্দিষ্ট সময়সীমা deadline	

নিষ্পত্তি করা settle
নীচু low
নীচে below
নীচে ঝোঁকা bend down
নীচে পড়া fall down
নীতি morals, principle
নীতিকৌশল strategy
নীরস dull
নীল blue
নীলা sapphire
নিলাম bid
নিলাম করা bid
নুড়ি gravel, pebble
নুন salt
নুয়ে পড়া bend
নৃতত্ত্ববিদ্যা anthropology
নৃত্য dance
নৃত্যকলা dancing
নেউল ferret
নেওয়া take
নেকড়ে wolf
নেড়ামাথা skinhead
নেতা leader
নেতিবাচক negative
নেতৃত্ব দেওয়া head
নেদারল্যান্ড দেশীয় Dutch
নেদারল্যান্ডের নারী Dutchwoman
নেদারল্যান্ডের পুরুষ Dutchman
নেলপালিশ nail polish
নেশাগ্রস্ত drunk, tipsy
নেশার প্রতি আসক্ত addicted
নেশাসক্ত addict
নৈতিক ethical, moral
নৈরাশ্যবাদী pessimist
নৈর্ব্যক্তিক impersonal
নৈশ জীবন nightlife
নৈশ বিদ্যালয় night school
নৈশভোজ dinner, supper
নোংরা filthy, messy
নোংরা ফেলবার ঝুড়ি wastepaper basket
নোঙর করা ভাসমান বস্তু buoy
নোঙর anchor
নোট করা jot down
নোনতা salty
নোনতা খাবার savoury
নোনাজল saltwater
নৌকা boat
নৌকা উলটে যাওয়া capsize
নৌকা বাঁধার পাটাতন quay
নৌকা বাওয়া rowing
নৌকা করে পাড়ি দেওয়া sail
নৌ-বাহিনী navy
নৌ-বাহিনী সংক্রান্ত naval
ন্যাকড়া rag

ন্যাতা mop
ন্যাতা দেওয়া mop up
ন্যাপকিন serviette
ন্যায়পরতা fairness
ন্যায়সঙ্গত right
ন্যায্য fair
ন্যূনতম least
পকেট ছুরি penknife
পকেটমার pickpocket
পকেটে রাখবার ক্যালকুলেটর pocket calculator
পক্ষপাতদুষ্ট biased
পক্ষীবিশেষ pheasant, wren
পচা rotten
পচে যাওয়া rot
পছন্দ choice, preference
পছন্দ করা like, love, prefer
পঞ্চাশ fifty
পটি potty
পঠন reading
পড়তে অসুবিধা dyslexic
পড়া look at, read
পড়ানো teach
পড়ার অযোগ্য illegible
পতন fall
পতাকা flag
পত্রবন্ধু penfriend
পত্রলিখন correspondence
পত্রিকা magazine
পথ path
পথ কর toll
পথকর road tax
পথচারীদের যাওয়ার স্থান pedestrian crossing
পথ দেখানো কুকুর guide dog
পথ দেখিয়ে নিয়ে যাওয়া lead
পথ নির্দেশ signpost
পথনির্দেশমূলক চিহ্ন road sign
পথপ্রদর্শক guide
পথপ্রদর্শিত ভ্রমণ guided tour
পদক medal
পদক্ষেপ ফেলা step
পদচারণা footstep
পদত্যাগ করা resign
পদবী surname
পদমর্যাদা post, rank
পদযাত্রা hiking
পদযাত্রী pedestrian
পদযুগল feet
পদাতিক সৈন্য infantry
পদার্থ substance
পদার্থবিদ physicist
পদার্থবিদ্যা physics
পদ্ধতি method
পনির cottage cheese

পনের fifteen
পনের নম্বর fifteenth
পছা নেওয়া resort to
পবিত্র holy, sacred
পরিবহন transport
পয়ঃপ্রণালী sewer
পয়সা রাখার ব্যাগ wallet
পয়েন্ট point
পরচর্চা gossip
পরচর্চা করা gossip
পরচুল toupee
পরচুলা wig
পরপর গোনা count
পরবর্তী following, next
পরমাণু atom
পরমাণুসংক্রান্ত atomic
পরম্পরাগত classical
পরা wear
পরাগরেণু pollen
পরাজয় defeat
পরাজিত loser
পরাজিত করা defeat, overcome
পরামর্শ advice, consult, suggestion, tip
পরামর্শদাতা consultant
পরামর্শ দেওয়া suggest
পরিকল্পক designer
পরিকল্পনা design, layout, plan, planning
পরিকল্পনা করা design
পরিকাঠামো infrastructure
পরিচয় background, identity, introduction
পরিচয় করানো introduce
পরিচয়-পত্র ID card, identity card
পরিচারিকা maid
পরিচালক conductor, director, manager
পরিচালন অধিকর্তা managing director
পরিচালনা conduct
পরিচালনা করা handle, manage
পরিচালনীয় manageable
পরিচালিকা manageress
পরিচিত familiar, known
পরিণত grown-up, mature
পরিণত ছাত্র mature student
পরিণত হওয়া get, turn
পরিণতি result
পরিণত হওয়া consequence
পরিণামে accordingly, consequently
পরিত্যাগ abandon
পরিদর্শক inspector
পরিধানের স্যুট suit
পরিপার্শ্ব precinct

পরিপূর্ণ full
পরিপ্রেক্ষিত perspective
পরিবর্ত substitute
পরিবর্তন change, modification, replacement, shift
পরিবর্তন করা modify, switch
পরিবর্তনযোগ্য changeable, variable
পরিবর্তন গণিতপথ diversion
পরিবর্তে alternatively, instead
পরিবর্তিত হওয়া varied
পরিবর্ধন enlargement
পরিবহন করা transport
পরিবার family, household
পরিবহিত মালপত্র freight
পরিবেশ environment, surroundings
পরিবেশ অনুকূল environmentally friendly
পরিবেশক dispenser
পরিবেশ সুরক্ষা সংক্রান্ত environmental
পরিবেশে কার্বন-ডাই-অক্সাইডের পরিমাপক carbon footprint
পরিমাণ of, quantity, volume
পরিমাণ/টাকার অঙ্কের পরিমাণ amount
পরিমাণ নির্ণয় করা quantify
পরিমাপ measurements
পরিমাপ করা measure
পরিমার্জনা revision
পরিমার্জনা করা revise
পরিমিত modest
পরিমিত ব্যয় করা economize
পরিযান migration
পরিযায়ী migrant
পরিশেষে ultimately
পরিশোধ repayment
পরিশোধ করা repay
পরিশোধনীয় payable
পরিষদ council
পরিষদ-সদস্য councillor
পরিষদীয় ভবন council house
পরিষেবা service
পরিষেবা শুল্ক service charge
পরিষ্কার clean
পরিষ্কার করবার লোশন cleansing lotion
পরিষ্কার করা clean, clear up, wash up
পরিষ্কার পরিচ্ছন্ন tidy
পরিষ্কার পরিচ্ছন্ন করা tidy
পরিসংখ্যান statistics
পরিস্থান circumstances, situation
পরিহাস irony
পরী fairy
পরীক্ষক examiner
পরীক্ষা exam, examination, experiment, test

পরীক্ষা করা check, examine, inspect, test, try
পরীক্ষামূলক সময় trial period
পরীক্ষার নল test tube
পরীক্ষার পড়া swot
পরীক্ষার ফলাফল report
পরে after, afterwards, later, past
পরে নয় no
পরের পৃষ্ঠায় দেখুন PTO
পরোক্ষ indirect
পর্তুগাল দেশীয় Portuguese
পর্তুগীজ ভাষা Portuguese
পর্দা curtain, screen
পর্ব episode, period
পর্বত mountain
পর্বতময় mountainous
পর্বতমালা range
পর্বতারোহণ mountaineering
পর্বতারোহন climbing
পর্বতারোহী mountaineer
পর্যটক tourist
পর্যটন tourism
পর্যটন দপ্তর tourist office
পর্যন্ত till, until
পর্যবেক্ষক observer
পর্যবেক্ষণশীল observant
পর্যবেক্ষণাগার observatory
পর্যায় stage
পর্যায়ক্রমে gradually
পর্যালোচনা review
পলায়ন escape
পলায়ন করা escape, flee, run away
পলিথিনের ব্যাগ polythene bag
পলিনেশিয়া দেশীয় Polynesian
পলিনেশিয়া ভাষা Polynesian
পলিনেশিয়ার অধিবাসী Polynesian
পলেস্তারা plaster
পশম wool
পশমনির্মিত woollen
পশমের বস্ত্র tartan
পশু-চিকিৎসক vet
পশ্চাদ্ধাবন chase
পশ্চাদ্ধাবন করা chase
পশ্চাৎ rear
পশ্চাৎ দর্শনযোগ্য আয়না rear-view mirror
পশ্চিম west
পশ্চিম দিকে west
পশ্চিমদিকে westbound
পশ্চিমাংশ west
পশ্চিমাঞ্চল western
পা foot, leg
পাইট pint
পাঁচ five
পাঁচ নম্বর fifth

পাঁজর rib
পাই pie
পাইকারি wholesale
পাইকারি হারে ক্রয়বিক্রয় wholesale
পাই চার্ট pie chart
পাইন গাছ pine
পাইপ pipe
পাইপলাইন pipeline
পাইলট লাইট pilot light
পাউরুটি bread, loaf
পাউরুটি রাখার জায়গা bread bin
পাওয়া come in, get, receive
পাকস্থলী stomach
পাকা ripe
পাকা চুলওয়ালা লোক grey-haired
পাকানো বস্ত roll
পাকিস্তান Pakistan
পাকিস্তান দেশীয় Pakistani
পাকিস্তানী Pakistani
পাখি bird
পাগল mad, maniac
পাগল লোক madman
পাগলামি madness
পাগলের মত madly
পাঙ্ক মিউজিক্যাল punk
পাচক cook
পাচার smuggling
পাচার করা smuggle
পাচারকারী smuggler
পাছা bum
পাছায় চুটি মারা spank
পাটাতন board, platform
পাঠ lesson
পাঠক reader
পাঠক্রম curriculum
পাঠানো send
পাঠিয়ে দেওয়া forward, send off
পাঠ্যক্রম syllabus
পাঠ্যবই textbook
পাড়া neighbourhood
পাণ্ডুলিপি manuscript
পাত sheet
পাতলা dilute, thin
পাতলা আলুভাজা crisps
পাতলা করা dilute
পাতলা সুট shell suit
পাতলুন trousers
পাতা leaf
পাতাবহা গাছ elm
পাতিলেবু lime
পাতিলেবুর খোসা zest
পাতিহাঁস duck
পাত্র bowl, container, pan, pot, tray
পাথর rock, stone
পান করা drink

পানীয় drink
পানীয় জল drinking water
পাণ্ডা panda
পাফ পেস্ট্রি puff pastry
পাবলিক স্কুল public school
পাম্প করা pump
পায়জামা pyjamas
পায়রা pigeon
পায়া leg
পায়ে চলা hike
পায়ের আঙুল toe
পায়ের চিকিৎসক chiropodist
পায়ের ছাপ footprint
পায়ের ডিম calf
পায়ে হাঁটা walk
পারকসন percussion
পারদ mercury
পারদর্শী good
পারমাণবিক nuclear
পারমাণবিক চুল্লি reactor
পারমাণবিক বোমা atom bomb
পারস্যের Persian
পার হওয়া cross
পা রাখা tread
পারিশ্রমিক fee
পার্ক park
পার্কিং parking
পার্কিং টিকিট parking ticket
পার্কিং মিটার parking meter
পার্টি party
পার্টিতে মজা করা party
পার্থক্য difference, distinction
পার্থক্য নির্দেশ করা distinguish
পার্শ্ব perm
পার্শ্ব প্রতিক্রিয়া side effect
পার্শ্ব রাস্তা side street
পার্শ্ব রেখা touchline
পার্সলে parsley
পার্সোনাল অর্গানাইজার personal organizer
পাল flock, sail
পালংশাক spinach
পালক feather
পালকের তৈরী লেপ duvet
পাল তোলা নৌকা sailing boat
পালন upbringing
পালন করা foster
পালাক্রম alternate
পালাক্রমিক alternative
পালিত সন্তান foster child
পালিশ polish
পালিশ করা polish
পারা দেওয়া keep up
পাশ side
পাশ দিয়ে sideways

পাশে beside, next to
পাসওয়ার্ড password
পাসপোর্ট passport
পাস্তা pasta
পাঞ্জরীকরণ pasteurized
পাহাড় hill
পাহাড়ে চড়া rock climbing, uphill
পাহাড়ে চড়ার বাইক mountain bike
পাহাড়ের ঢাল cliff
পাহাড়ে হেঁটে বেড়ানো hill-walking
পাহারা দেওয়া guard
পিঁপড়ে ant
পিঁয়াজ onion
পি এইচ ডি PhD
পিকনিক picnic
পিক্সেল pixel
পিঙ্গল tanned
পিচ্ছিল slippery
পিছন দিকের দরজা ওপরের দিকে খোলা যায় এমন গাড়ি hatchback
পিছনে after, back, behind
পিছনে ঘোরানো rewind
পিছনে ঠেলা push
পিছনের rear
পিছনের দিকে backwards
পিছলে পড়া slip
পিছলে যাওয়া skid
পিঠ back
পিঠ নেওয়ার ব্যাগ rucksack
পিঠে ব্যথা backache
পিঠের ব্যথা/কোমরের ব্যথা back pain
পিঠের হাড় সরে যাওয়া অবস্থা slipped disc
পি ডি এফ PDF
পিতল brass
পিতলের বাদ্যযন্ত্রের বাদক সম্প্রদায় brass band
পিতা বা মাতা parent
পিতৃত্ব লাভের জন্য প্রাপ্ত ছুটি paternity leave
পিজ্জা pizza
পিতাশয় gall bladder
পিতাশয়ে পাথর gallstone
পিন pin
পিন নম্বর PIN
পিপে barrel
পিয়ানো piano
পিয়ানোবাদক pianist
পিরেনিজ পর্বতাঞ্চলের অধিবাসী Basque
পি সি PC
পিসি, মাসি, কাকিমা, জেঠিমা aunt, auntie
পিস্টন piston
পিস্তল pistol
পীচ ফল nectarine

পীচফল peach
পুঁজ pus
পুঁজভর্তি ফোড়া abscess
পুঁজিবাদ capitalism
পুঁতি bead
পুকুর pond
পুঙ্খানুপুঙ্খ thorough
পুঙ্খানুপুঙ্খরূপে thoroughly
পুড়ে যাওয়া burn
পুতুল doll
পুতুলনাচ puppet
পুত্র son
পুত্রবধূ daughter-in-law
পুদিনা mint
পুনঃপ্রদর্শন replay
পুনঃপ্রদর্শন করা replay
পুনরাক্রমণ relapse
পুনরাবৃত্তি repeat
পুনরাবৃত্তি করা repeat
পুনরাবৃত্তিমূলক repetitive
পুনরায় গরম করা heat up
পুনরায় তেল নেওয়া refuel
পুনরায় পরীক্ষা দেওয়া resit
পুনরায় প্রাণসঞ্চার করা revive
পুনরায় ভর্তি করা refill
পুনরায় লাভ করা regain
পুনরারম্ভ করা resume
পুনরুদ্ধার করা restore
পুনর্গঠন remake
পুনর্গঠন করা redo, reorganize, restructure
পুনর্নবীকরণ করা renew
পুনর্নিমাণ rebuild
পুনর্বার again
পুনর্বিবাহ remarry
পুনর্বিবেচনা reconsider
পুনর্ব্যবহার reuse
পুনর্ব্যবহারযোগ্য recycling
পুনর্ব্যবহারযোগ্য করে তোলা recycle
পুনর্মিলন উৎসব reunion
পুনঃসজ্জিত করা redecorate
পুনশ্চ NB
পুরস্কার award
পুরস্কার prize, reward
পুরস্কার দেওয়া present
পুরস্কার প্রদান prize-giving
পুরস্কার প্রাপক prizewinner
পুরাতত্ত্ব archaeology
পুরাতাত্ত্বিক archaeologist
পুরানো old, out of date
পুরানো আমলের old-fashioned
পুরানো জিনিসের বাজার flea market
পুরিয়া sachet
পুরু thick
পুরুত্ব thickness

পুরুষ bloke, male, man
পুরুষদের বৈশ ভোজ stag night
পুরুষদের শৌচালয় gents
পুরুষ-পুলিশ policeman
পুরুষ ভেড়া ram
পুরুষালী মেয়ে tomboy
পুরুষোচিত masculine
পুরোন ধাঁচের stuffy
পুরোনো বড় বাড়ি stately home
পুরোপুরি gross
পুরোপুরিভাবে absolutely
পুলিশ police
পুলিশ অফিসার police officer
পুলিশকর্মী cop
পুলিশ স্টেশন police station
পুলিশের গাড়ি patrol car
পুলিশের চর grass
পুস-আপ push-up
পুষ্টি nutrition
পুষ্টিকর nutritious
পুষ্টিদায়ক nutrient
পুস্তিকা booklet, leaflet, pamphlet
পূজা করা worship
পূরণ করা fill in
পূর্ণ করা fill up, fulfil
পূর্ণিমা full moon
পূর্ব eastern
পূর্ব এশিয়া Orient
পূর্ব এশিয়া সম্পর্কিত oriental
পূর্বকল্পিত ধারণা prejudice
পূর্বকল্পিত ধারণার বশবর্তী prejudiced
পূর্বকালে formerly
পূর্ব থেকে beforehand
পূর্ব-দিক east
পূর্ব-দিকে east, eastbound
পূর্বনির্দিষ্ট তারিখ due
পূর্বনির্দিষ্ট সাক্ষাৎ rendezvous
পূর্বপথ অনুসরণ করা retrace
পূর্বপুরুষ ancestor
পূর্বপ্রদত্ত prepaid
পূর্ববর্তী preceding
পূর্বাগ্রহ preoccupied
পূর্বসূরী predecessor
পূর্বাভাষ forecast
পূর্বাশিকা premonition
পূর্বে earlier, east, previously
পৃথক separate
পৃথিবী earth, world
পৃষ্ঠা page
পেঁচা owl
পেঁয়াজের মত গন্ধবিশিষ্ট গুল্ম spring onion
পেঁয়াজের মত গন্ধবিশিষ্ট গুল্ম chives
পেঁয়াজের মত সজি leek
পেগ peg
পেঙ্গুইন penguin

পেছন ফেরা turn back
পেছনে back, behind
পেছনে ঝোলানোর ব্যাগ backpack
পেছনে ঝোলানো ব্যগ নিয়ে যাওয়া ভ্রমণকারী backpacker
পেছনে থাকা lag behind
পেছনের দিকে back, behind
পেছনে সরা move back
পেজ page
পেট abdomen, belly
পেট খারাপ diarrhoea
পেটসংক্রান্ত coeliac
পেটের ব্যথা stomachache
পেট্রল petrol
পেট্রল ট্যাঙ্ক petrol tank
পেট্রল স্টেশন petrol station
পেট্রোল পাম্প service station
পেতলের বাদ্য trombone
পেনডেন্ট pendant
পেনশন pension
পেনশনভোগী old-age pensioner
পেনসিল pencil
পেনসিল কাটার কল pencil sharpener
পেনসিল কেস pencil case
পেনিসিলিন penicillin
পেপারওয়েট paperweight
পেপারক্লিপ paperclip
পেফোন payphone
পেমেন্ট payment
পেরিয়ে যাওয়া go by
পেরু Peru
পেরু দেশীয় Peruvian
পেরুর অধিবাসী Peruvian
পেরেক nail
পেরেকের মাথা stud
পেলিকান ক্রসিং pelican crossing
পেলিকান পাখি pelican
পেশা career, occupation, profession
পেশাগত professional
পেশাগতভাবে professionally
পেশাদার professional
পেশী muscle
পেশীবহুল muscular
পেষা grind
পেষাইকল mill
পেষ্ট্রি shortcrust pastry
পেস্ট paste
পেস্ট্রি tart
পোকা insect, pest, stick insect
পোকানাশক ওষুধ pesticide
পোকার ডিম maggot
পোড়ার ক্ষত burn
পোতাশ্রয় dock, harbour
পোলিশ ভাষা Polish

পোল্যান্ডের Polish
পোল্যান্ডের নাগরিক Pole
পোশাক costume
পোশাক পরিবর্তনের ঘর changing room
পোশাকের আলমারি wardrobe
পোষাক dress, garment, outfit
পোষাক খোলা undress
পোষাক পরিবর্তন করা change
পোষ্য pet
পৌঁছানো get, get in go round, reach
পৌঁছে যাওয়া arrive
পৌনঃপুনিক recurring
প্যাক pack
প্যাক করা খাবার packed lunch
প্যাডেল pedal
প্যাডলিং পুল paddling pool
প্যারাগুয়ে Paraguay
প্যারাগুয়ে দেশীয় Paraguayan
প্যারাগুয়ের মানুষ Paraguayan
প্যারাফিন paraffin
প্যারাসুট parachute
প্যালেস্টাইন দেশীয় Palestinian
প্যালেস্টাইনের নাগরিক Palestinian
প্যাশন ফ্রুট passion fruit
প্রকল্প project
প্রকার manner, type
প্রকাশক publisher
প্রকাশ করা disclose, express, reveal
প্রকাশনা publication
প্রকাশনা করে publish
প্রকাশ পাওয়া appear
প্রকাশিত করা develop
প্রকাশিত হওয়া come out
প্রকৃত actual, genuine, virtual
প্রকৃতঅর্থে actually
প্রকৃতপক্ষে really
প্রকৃতি nature
প্রকৃতিবিদ naturalist
প্রকৃত real
প্রকোপ outbreak
প্রকোষ্ঠ glove compartment
প্রক্রিয়া process
প্রচন্ড intense, stifling
প্রচন্ড ক্ষুধার্ত ravenous
প্রচন্ড জোরে আওয়াজ bang
প্রচন্ড জোরে ধাক্কা মারা ram
প্রচন্ড ভয় fright
প্রচন্ড ভয় পাওয়া frighten
প্রচন্ডভাবে awfully
প্রচন্ড ভীত frightened
প্রচন্ড উত্তেজনাকর frightening
প্রচন্ড রাগ rage
প্রচলিত usual

প্রচলিত ফ্যান বহির্ভূত unfashionable
প্রচার canvass, promotion, propaganda, publicity
প্রচার করা promote
প্রচারমাধ্যম media
প্রচুর lot, plenty
প্রচুর পরিমানে মজুত করা stock up
প্রচুরসংখ্যক numerous
প্রজন্ম generation
প্রজাতন্ত্র republic
প্রজাতি species
প্রজাপতি butterfly
প্রজ্বলন ignition
প্রণোদক incentive
প্রতারণা rip off
প্রতারণা করা trick
প্রতি per, to
প্রতিকূল hostile
প্রতিকৃতি portrait
প্রতিক্রিয়া feedback, reaction
প্রতিক্রিয়া জানানো react
প্রতি ঘন্টায় hourly
প্রতিজ্ঞা promise
প্রতিজ্ঞা করা promise
প্রতিটি either, every
প্রতিদ্বন্দিতা rivalry
প্রতিদ্বন্দী rival
প্রতিদ্বন্দী দল rival
প্রতিধ্বনি echo
প্রতিনিধি delegate, representative
প্রতিনিধিত্ব করা represent
প্রতিনিধি নিয়োগ করা delegate
প্রতিপক্ষ adversary
প্রতিফলন reflection
প্রতিফলিত হওয়া reflect
প্রতিবন্ধক barrier, curb
প্রতিবর্ত ক্রিয়া reflex
প্রতিবাদ protest
প্রতিবাদ করা protest
প্রতিবাদী defendant
প্রতিবিম্ব image
প্রতিবেদক reporter
প্রতিবেদন report
প্রতিবেদন করা report
প্রতিবেশী neighbour
প্রতিবেশী অঞ্চল vicinity
প্রতিভা genius, talent
প্রতিভাবান talented
প্রতিযোগিতা championship, competition, contest, tournament
প্রতিযোগিতাবিশেষ pentathlon
প্রতিযোগিতামূলক competitive
প্রতিযোগিতায় নামা compete
প্রতিযোগী competitor, contestant

প্রতিরক্ষা defence
প্রতিরূপ replica
প্রতিরোধ করা prevent
প্রতিরোধ ক্ষমতা immune system
প্রতিলিপি copy, transcript
প্রতিশোধ revenge
প্রতিষ্ঠান institute
প্রতিস্থাপন transplant
প্রতিহিংসা remedy
প্রতীক symbol
প্রতীক্ষা করা wait
প্রতীক্ষা তালিকা waiting list
প্রতীক্ষালয় waiting room
প্রত্যক্ষ হওয়া turn out
প্রত্যক্ষ apparent
প্রত্যয় confidence
প্রত্যয় জাগানো convince
প্রত্যয় জাগায় এমন convincing
প্রত্যয়ী confident
প্রত্যাখ্যান refusal
প্রত্যাখ্যান করা refuse
প্রত্যাহার withdrawal
প্রত্যাহার করা withdraw
প্রত্যেক each
প্রত্যেকটি each
প্রত্যেক স্থানে everywhere
প্রত্যেকে everyone
প্রথম first
প্রথমত firstly
প্রথম নাম first name
প্রথম শ্রেণী first-class
প্রথমে first
প্রথাবহির্ভূত unconventional
প্রথাসিদ্ধ conventional
প্রদর্শন demo, demonstration
প্রদর্শন করা demonstrate, display, show
প্রদর্শনকারী demonstrator
প্রদর্শনী display, showing
প্রদান delivery
প্রদান করা deliver
প্রধান chief, head, lead
প্রধান গায়ক lead singer
প্রধানত mainly
প্রধান পণ্য staple
প্রধান মন্ত্রী prime minister
প্রধানশিক্ষক principal
প্রধান শিক্ষক/শিক্ষিকা headteacher
প্রপিতামহ great-grandfather
প্রপিতামহী great-grandmother
প্রবঞ্চনা rip off
প্রবণতা instinct, tendency, trend
প্রবন্ধ article, essay
প্রবল অনুশোচনা remorse
প্রবল আকর্ষণ mania

প্রবল ঝড় gale
প্রবল-বর্ষণ downpour
প্রবাদ proverb
প্রবাল coral
প্রবাহ current, flow
প্রবাহিত হওয়া blow
প্রবৃত্তি দমন inhibition
প্রবেশ entry
প্রবেশ করতে দেওয়া let in
প্রবেশ করা enter, move in
প্রবেশ করানো inject
প্রবেশদ্বার entrance
প্রবেশদ্বারে ফোন entry phone
প্রবেশ-মূল্য entrance fee
প্রবেশাধিকার admittance
প্রভাত dawn
প্রভাব effect, impact, influence
প্রভাবিত কবা affect, influence
প্রভু master
প্রভুত্বপরায়ণ bossy
প্রমত্ত frantic
প্রমাণ proof
প্রমাণ করা prove
প্রমোদতরণী yacht
প্রয়োজন necessary, need
প্রয়োজনীয় essential
প্রয়োজনীয়তা necessity
প্রযুক্তি technology
প্রযুক্তিগত technological
প্রযুক্তিবিদ/ইঞ্জিনিয়ার engineer
প্রযুক্তিবিদ্যা/ইঞ্জিনিয়ারিং engineering
প্রযোজক producer
প্রলুব্ধকর tempting
প্রলুব্ধ করা tempt
প্রলোভন temptation
প্রশংসা compliment
প্রশংসা করা appreciate, compliment, praise
প্রশংসায় তুষ্ট flattered
প্রশান্ত Pacific Ocean
প্রশাসন administration
প্রশাসনিক administrative
প্রশিক্ষক coach, trainer
প্রশিক্ষণ training
প্রশিক্ষণ দেওয়া train
প্রশিক্ষণ পাঠ্যসূচী training course
প্রশিক্ষণ প্রাপ্ত trained
প্রশ্ন query, question
প্রশ্ন করা query
প্রশ্ন করা/চ্যালেঞ্জ গ্রহণ করা challenge
প্রসঙ্গ context, reference, topic
প্রসঙ্গ উল্লেখ করা refer
প্রসাধনী থলে toilet bag
প্রসাধনী সামগ্রী toiletries
প্রসার range

প্রসারিত হওয়া stretch
প্রসূতি ছুটি maternity leave
প্রসূতি হাসপাতাল maternity hospital
প্রস্তাব offer, proposal, resolution
প্রস্তাব করা propose
প্রস্তাব দেওয়া offer
প্রস্তাব রাখা approach
প্রস্তুত prepared, ready
প্রস্তুত হওয়া prepare
প্রস্তুতি preparation
প্রস্থান departure
প্রস্থান করা depart, leave
প্রস্থানের জায়গা departure lounge
প্রস্রাব urine
প্রস্রাবনালির সংক্রমণ cystitis
প্রাকৃতিক গ্যাস natural gas
প্রাকৃতিক দুর্যোগ disaster
প্রাকৃতিক দৃশ্য scenery
প্রাকৃতিক সম্পদ natural resources
প্রাক্তন former, previous
প্রাক্তন-স্ত্রী ex-wife
প্রাক্তন স্বামী ex-husband
প্রাক-বড়দিন Christmas Eve
প্রাগৈতিহাসিক prehistoric
প্রাঙ্গণ premises
প্রাচীনকালের, ancient
প্রাচীনকালের দুর্মূল্য বস্তু antique
প্রাণঘাতী malignant
প্রাণবত lively
প্রাণীকুল fauna
প্রাণীতত্ত্ব zoology
প্রাতকালীন বিবমিষা morning sickness
প্রাতরাশ breakfast
প্রাথমিক basics
প্রাথমিক চিকিৎসা first aid
প্রাথমিক চিকিৎসার বাক্স first-aid kit
প্রাথমিক চিত্রাঙ্কন sketch
প্রাথমিকভাবে primarily
প্রাথমিক স্কুল primary school
প্রাধান্য দেওয়া highlight
প্রান্ত edge, terminal, tip
প্রান্তরেখা outline
প্রাপক receiver
প্রাপ্ত বয়স্ক adult
প্রাপ্তিস্বীকার acknowledgement
প্রামাণ্য তথ্য evidence
প্রায় about, almost, around, nearly, practically
প্রায়ই often
প্রায়োগিক technical
প্রারম্ভ outset
প্রারম্ভিক early, initial
প্রার্থনা prayer
প্রার্থনা করা pray

প্রার্থনা হল shrine
প্রার্থী candidate
প্রাসঙ্গিক relevant
প্রাসাদ palace
প্রিয় dear
প্রিয়তম darling
প্রিয়পাত্র favourite
প্রুফ সংশোধন proof
প্রেম romance
প্রেমিকা girlfriend
প্রেমে পড়া fall for
প্রেমের অভিনয় করা flirt
প্রেমের অভিনয়ে দক্ষ flirt
প্রেরক sender
প্রেরণ করা issue, post
প্রেরণা motivation
প্রোগ্রাম করা program
প্লাগ খুলে ফেলা unplug
প্লাগ ঢোকানো plug in
প্লাগের গর্ত plughole
প্লাজমা টিভি plasma TV
প্লাজমা স্ক্রীন plasma screen
প্লাবন flooding
প্লাস্টার plaster
প্লেট plate
প্লে-স্টেশন PlayStation®
প্লাস্টিকের ব্যাগ carrier bag
প্ল্যাটিনাম platinum
প্লাস্টিক plastic
প্লাস্টিক ব্যাগ plastic bag
প্লাস্টিক সার্জারি plastic surgery
ফটো photo
ফটো অ্যালবাম photo album
ফটোকপি photocopy
ফটোকপি করা photocopy
ফটোকপির যন্ত্র photocopier
ফড়িং grasshopper
ফরাসী ওয়াইন champagne
ফরাসী ভদ্রমহিলা Frenchwoman
ফরাসী ভদ্রলোক Frenchman
ফরাসী ভাষা French
ফর্সা blonde
ফল fruit
ফল ও সজ্জিবিক্রেতা greengrocer
ফলত eventually
ফলাফল outcome
ফলের বাগান orchard
ফলের রস fruit juice
ফলের শাঁস core
ফলোৎপাদক effective
ফসল crop, harvest
ফসল কাটা harvest
ফাঁক crack, gap
ফাঁকা bare, clear
ফাঁকা চেক blank cheque

ফাঁদ trap
ফাঁপা hollow
ফাইল file
ফাইলবন্ধ করা file
ফাটল crack
ফাটল ধরা crack
ফাটলযুক্ত cracked
ফানেল funnel
ফায়ারপ্লেসের ওপরে অবস্থিত তাক mantelpiece
ফার fur
ফার গাছ fir tree
ফারের কোট fur coat
ফারের জ্যাকেট anorak
ফারো দ্বীপপুঞ্জ Faroe Islands
ফালা ফালা করে কাটা hack
ফিকে লাল mauve
ফিজিওথেরাপি physiotherapy
ফিজিওথেরাপিস্ট physiotherapist
ফিট হওয়া seizure
ফিতা strap, tape
ফিতে gauge, lace, ribbon
ফিতে দিয়ে মাপা gauge
ফিনফিনে see-through
ফিনল্যান্ড দেশীয় Finnish
ফিনল্যান্ডের জনগণ Finn
ফিনিশীয় ভাষা Finnish
ফিরিয়ে আনা bring back
ফিরিয়ে দেওয়া return
ফিরে আসা come back
ফিরে পাওয়া get back
ফিরে যাওয়া return
ফিলিপিন্স দেশীয় Filipino
ফিলিপিন্সের অধিবাসী Filipino
ফিলে fillet
ফিলে তৈরী করা fillet
ফিসফিস করা whisper
ফুঁ দেওয়া blow
ফুঁপিয়ে কাঁদা weep
ফুটপাথ pavement
ফুটবল football
ফুটবল খেলোয়াড় football player
ফুটবল ম্যাচ football match
ফুটে ছিটকানো boil over
ফুটো leak
ফুটো করা pierce, prick
ফুটো হয়ে যাওয়া leak
ফুল flower
ফুলকপি cauliflower
ফুলদানি vase
ফুল দেওয়া flower
ফুলবিক্রেতা florist
ফুলের তোড়া bouquet
ফুসকুড়ি rash
ফুসফুস lung

ফেটানো ক্রিম whipped cream
ফেটানো ময়দা, ডিম ইত্যাদি batter
ফেটানোর মেশিন whisk
ফেটি band
ফেনার ঢেউ surf
ফেরত return
ফেরত দেওয়া give back
ফেরত নেওয়া take back
ফেরত পাঠানো send back
ফেরত মূল্য refund
ফেরি যান shuttle
ফেলা দেওয়া throw away, throw out
ফেলে দেওয়া ditch
ফেল্ট-টিপ পেন felt-tip
ফোঁটা drip
ফোঁটা ফোঁটা করে পড়া drip
ফোটা boil
ফোটানো boil, boiling
ফোটো snapshot
ফোন phone
ফোন করা phone, ring, ring up
ফোনকল phone call
ফোনকার্ড phonecard
ফোন নম্বর phone number
ফোনবক্স phonebox
ফোন রেখে দেওয়া hang up
ফোন নাদের তালিকা phonebook
ফোনের জবাবী ফোন phone back
ফোনের জবাবে ফোন করা ring back
ফোনের বিল phone bill
ফোনের রিসিভার receiver
ফোনের শব্দ সৃষ্টি করার যন্ত্র beeper
ফোলা swollen
ফ্যাকাশে fair
ফ্যাকাসে pale
ফ্যাক্স পাঠানো fax
ফ্রান্স France
ফ্রান্সেদনীয় French
ফ্রুট স্যালাড fruit salad
ফ্লেমিংগো পাখি flamingo
বংশগত hereditary
বংশবৃদ্ধি করা breed
বই book
বইয়ের তাক bookcase
বইয়ের দোকান bookshop
বই রাখার তাক bookshelf
বকবক করা waffle
বকবকানি waffle
বকশিশ দেওয়া tip
বকশিশ tip
বকাঝকা করা scold
বকেয়া arrears
বক্তা speaker
বক্ষবন্ধনী bra
বক্ষস্থল chest

বক্সার boxer
বখাটে spoilt
বগল armpit
বজায় রাখা maintain
বজ্র thunder
বজ্রপাত lightning
বজ্রপাতযুক্ত thundery
বজ্রবিদ্যুৎসহ ঝোড়ো বৃষ্টি
    thunderstorm
বটসোয়ানা Botswana
বড় elder, large
বড় আধার tank
বড় ইঁদুরের মত ধারালো দাঁতওয়ালা প্রাণী
    beaver
বড় এরোপ্লেন jumbo jet
বড় করে তোলা bring up
বড় গির্জা cathedral
বড়জোর scarcely
বড়দিন Xmas
বড়দিন Christmas
বড়দিনের শুভেচ্ছা কার্ড Christmas
    card
বড়দোকান supermarket
বড় পাখি turkey
বড় বাড়ি villa
বড় বাস coach
বড় ব্যাগ holdall
বড় মাংসের টুকরো joint
বড় মাথাবিশিষ্ট bigheaded
বড় মাল গাড়ী HGV
বড় মোরগ cock
বড়হাতের অক্ষর capital
বড়ি pill
বড়ো বিষয় matter
বৎসর year
বদমেজাজি grumpy
বদরাগী bad-tempered
বদল করা replace
বদলানো substitute
বদলানো change
বদলে instead of
বদহজম indigestion
বদ্ধ blocked
বনাম versus
বনেট bonnet
বন্দর port
বন্দি hostage
বন্দুক gun, shotgun
বন্দোবস্ত করা mount
বন্ধক mortgage
বন্ধক দেওয়া mortgage
বন্ধ করা close, off, seal, shut,
    switch off
বন্ধ করে দেওয়া, পাট তুলে নেওয়া
    shut down

বন্ধকি মহাজন pawnbroker
বন্ধন bond
বন্ধনী brace, brackets
বন্ধ হওয়া stop
বন্ধু friend, pal
বন্ধুত্ব friendship
বন্ধুভাবাপন্ন friendly
বন্ধের অবস্থা closure
বন্ধের সময় closing time
বন্ধ্যা infertile
বন্য wild
বন্যজীবন wildlife
বন্য পাখিদের নিরীক্ষণ birdwatching
বন্যা flood
বমি করা throw up, vomit
বমিভাব nausea
বয়ঃসন্ধিকাল adolescence
বয়ঃসন্ধিতে উপনীত adolescent
বয়লার boiler
বয়স age
বয়সের সীমা age limit
বয়স্ক aged, old
বয়স্কদের হাঁটার সহায়ক Zimmer®
    frame
বয়স্ক শিক্ষা adult education
বয়োজ্যেষ্ঠ elderly
বর bridegroom
বরং rather
বরখাস্ত sack
বরখাস্ত করা lay off, sack
বরফ ice, snow
বরফজমা frozen
বরফ পড়া snow
বরফ সরানোর যন্ত্র snowplough
বরফে খেলবার উপযুক্ত হকি ice hockey
বরফে চলার গাড়ি sledge
বরফের উপর কেটিং ice-skating
বরফের ওপর খেলা tobogganing
বরফের কুঁচি snowflake
বরফের গোলা snowball
বরফের টুকরো ice cube
বরফের ধস avalanche
বরফের মনুষ্যাকৃতি snowman
বরফের লিলি ice lolly
বরবটি broad bean
বরাবর along
বরিষ্ঠ senior
বরিষ্ঠ নাগরিক senior citizen
বর্গক্ষেত্র square
বর্গাকার square
বিজ্ঞিতাংশ stub
বর্ণনা করা describe
বর্ণ বিভাজন syllable
বর্ণময় colourful
বর্ণমালা alphabet

বর্ণাস্ক colour-blind
বর্তনী circuit
বর্তমান current, present
বর্তমানে currently, presently
বর্বর achar barbaric
বর্ম armour
বর্ণময় rainy
বর্ষাকাল monsoon
বর্ষাতি mac, raincoat
বহিদেশীয় alien
বল ball
বলকান উপদ্বীপ সম্বন্ধীয় Balkan
বলতে পারা tell
বলনৃত্য ball
বলরুম নৃত্য ballroom dancing
বলা mean, say, speak, state, tell
বলিদান sacrifice
বলিভিয়া Bolivia
বলিভিয়ার বাসিন্দা Bolivian
বলিভিয়া সংক্রান্ত Bolivian
বলিরেখা wrinkle
বলিরেখাযুক্ত wrinkled
বল্গা হরিণ reindeer
বসতিহীন uninhabited
বসনিয়া এবং হার্জেগোভিনা Bosnia-
  Herzegovina
বসনিয়ার বাসিন্দা Bosnian
বসনিয়া সংক্রান্ত Bosnian
বসন্তকাল spring
বসন্তকালের ফুল crocus
বসন্ত কালের সময় springtime
বসন্ত রোগ chickenpox
বসবাসের জন্য নির্দিষ্ট residential
বসা sit
বসান set
বসার ঘর living room, sitting room
বসার টুল stool
বসার স্থান stand
বসুন sit down
বস্তা sack
বস্তি slum
বস্তু object, stuff
বস্ত্র textile
বহন করা bear, bring, carry
বহনযোগ্য portable
বহনযোগ্য খাট camp bed
বহর width
বহিস্থ exterior, outdoor
বহিরঙ্গনে outdoors
বহিরাগত external
বহির্গামী outgoing
বহিষ্কার করা relegate
বহিষ্কৃত করা exclude
বহু host

বহু গাড়ীর মধ্যে পথ দুর্ঘটনা pile-up
বহুজাতিক multinational
বহুতল ভবন high-rise
বহুদূর ব্যাপী extensively
বহুবচন plural
বহুমুখী দক্ষতার অধিকারী versatile
বহুমূত্র রোগী diabetic
বহুমূত্র সংক্রান্ত diabetic
বহুলোকের সমষ্টি pool
বাইচের নৌকা rowing boat
বাইপাস bypass
বাইবেল Bible
বাইরে out, outside
বাইরে ঝোঁকা lean out
বাইরে বেরিয়ে আসা out
বাঁক bend
বাঁকা sarcastic
বাঁচাও! help!
বাঁচানো save
বাঁচিয়ে রাখা save
বাঁদর monkey
বাঁ সিংকে left
বাঁ-দিকে left
বাঁ-দিকে গাড়ি চালানো
  left-hand drive
বাঁ দিকে হেলানো একটি চিহ্ন backslash
বাঁধ dam
বাঁধন খোলা untie
বাঁধা staple, tie, tight
বাঁধাকপি cabbage
বাঁধাকপির মত দেখতে সবজি Brussels
  sprouts
বাঁশ bamboo
বাঁশি flute, whistle
বাঁ-হাত left-hand
বাঁ-হাতি left-handed
বাইরে যাওয়া go out
বাইরে যাওয়ার রাস্তা exit
বাইরের outside
বাইরের দিক outside
বাংক bunk
বাংলাদেশ Bangladesh
বাংলাদেশি Bangladeshi
বাংলাদেশীয় Bangladeshi
বাংলো bungalow
বাক speech
বাকি left, rest
বাক্য sentence
বাক্স box, case
বাগদা চিংড়ি scampi
বাগধারা phrase
বাগান garden
বাগান করবার যন্ত্র rake
বাগান-পরিচর্যা gardening
বাগানে বসার স্থান patio

বাঘ tiger
বাচাল talkative
বাচ্চা toddler
বাচ্চা ঘোড়া foal
বাচ্চার খাট cot
বাছাই shortlist, sort out
বাছাই করা choose, pick
বাছাই করা হয়েছে chosen
বাছুর calf
বাজানো play
বাজার market, marketplace
বাজি bet
বাজি ধরা bet
বাজী budgie
বাজে ছোকরা brat
বাজে ব্যবহার করা ill-treat
বাজে ভাবে badly
বাজেয়াপ্ত করা confiscate
বাড়তি spare
বাড়তি ওজন overweight
বাড়তি থাকা spare
বাড়তি সময় overtime
বাড়া grow, mount up
বাড়ানো exaggerate, grow
বাড়ি home, house
বাড়িওয়ালা landlord
বাড়িওয়ালি landlady
বাড়িতে করা DIY
বাড়িতে তৈরী home-made
বাড়িতে থাকা stay in
বাড়িয়ে তোলা multiply
বাড়ির কাজ housework
বাড়ির ঠিকানা home address
বাড়ির মাটির তলার অংশ basement
বাড়ীর ছাদের পাইপ drainpipe
বাণী saying
বাত rheumatism
বাতাপি লেবু grapefruit
বাতাস wind
বাতাস ভরা inflatable
বাতাসযুক্ত windy
বাতি light
বাতিকগ্রস্ত neurotic
বাতিল cancellation, void
বাতিল করা call off, cancel, delete,
  reject, rule out, scrap
বাদক player
বাদ দেওয়া leave out
বাদাম chestnut
বাদামী brown
বাদামী লাল maroon
বাদামের অ্যালার্জি nut allergy
বাদুড় bat, vampire
বাদ্য যন্ত্র trumpet
বাদ্যযন্ত্র cornet, instrument

বাধা block, hurdle, interruption, obstacle, resistance, setback
বাধা দেওয়া interrupt, resist
বাধার সৃষ্টি করা obstruct
বাধ্য obedient
বাধ্য করা make
বানান spelling
বানান করা spell
বানান পরীক্ষক spellchecker
বানানো develop
বান্ডিল package
বাপি daddy
বাবা dad, father
বামন dwarf
বামপন্থী left-wing
বাম্পার bumper
বায়ু air
বায়ু-চলাচল ventilation
বায়ুচালিত বাদ্যযন্ত্র woodwind
বায়ুনিরোধী airtight
বায়ুমন্ডল atmosphere
বারংবার frequent
বারংবারতা frequency
বার করে দেওয়া lock out
বারবার repeatedly
বারান্দা passage
বারো dozen, twelve
বার্গার burger
বার্তা message, text message
বার্তা পাঠানো text
বার্তাবাহক messenger
বার্নিশ lacquer, varnish
বার্নিশ করা varnish
বার্বাডোজ দ্বীপ Barbados
বারির বাসিন্দা burgle
বাসীজ ভাষা burgle
বার্লি barley
বার্ষিক annual, yearly
বার্ষিকভাবে annually
বার্ষিক সাধারণ সভা AGM
বার্ষিকী anniversary
বালক boy
বালতি bucket
বালি ভরা গর্ত sandpit
বালির পাহাড় sand dune
বালিশ pillow
বালিশের ঢাকা pillowcase
বালু sand
বাষ্প steam
বাস bus
বাস কন্ডাক্টর bus conductor
বাস করা live, occupy
বাস টিকিট bus ticket
বাস স্টপ bus stop
বাস স্টেশন bus station

বাসস্থান accommodation
বাসা home, nest
বাসি stale
বাসিন্দা inhabitant
বাক্স ভাষা Basque
বাক্স সংশ্লীয় Basque
বাস্কেটবল basketball
বাস্তব practical
বাস্তবতা reality
বাস্তবধর্মী realistic
বাস্তব্যবিদ্যা-বিষয়ক ecological
বাস্তুতন্ত্র ecology
বাস্তুতন্ত্র যোগ্য ecofriendly
বাহন vehicle
বাহামাস দ্বীপপুঞ্জ Bahamas
বাহরিন Bahrain
বাহু arm
বাৎসরিক yearly
বিংশতি twentieth
বিকল হয়ে যাওয়া break down
বিকল্প alternative, option
বিকিনি bikini
বিকিরণ radiation
বিক্রয় মারফত টাকা পাওয়া takings
বিক্রয় মূল্য selling price
বিক্রি sale
বিক্রি করা sell
বিক্রি করে দেওয়া sell off
বিক্রিত কোম্পানী buyout
বিক্রি প্রতিনিধি sales rep
বিক্রি শেষ sold out
বিক্রি সহায়ক sales assistant
বিক্রি হয়ে যাওয়া sell out
বিক্রেতা salesperson
বিক্রেতা (পুরুষ) salesman
বিক্রেতা (মহিলা) saleswoman
বিখ্যাত famous, renowned
বিখ্যাত ব্যক্তি celebrity
বিগত gone, past
বিচক্ষণতা discretion, tact
বিচলিত nervous, upset
বিচলিত করা upset
বিচার trial
বিচারক judge, magistrate
বিচার করা judge
বিচারবুদ্ধি সম্পন্ন sensible
বিচারের মাপকাঠি criterion
বিচ্ছিন্ন isolated
বিচ্ছিন্ন করা disconnect
বিচ্ছেদ separation
বিছানা bed, bedding
বিছানার চাদর bedclothes, bedspread
বিছানার চাদর এবং বালিশ bed linen
বিছিন্ন করা off

বিছিন্ন বাড়ি detached house
বিছুটি nettle
বিছে scorpion
বিজয় triumph, victory
বিজয়প্রাপ্ত হওয়া triumph
বিজয়ী winner
বিজোড় odd
বিজ্ঞান science
বিজ্ঞানসম্মত scientific
বিজ্ঞানী scientist
বিজ্ঞাপন ad, advertisement, commercial
বিজ্ঞাপন দেওয়া advertise, advertising
বিজ্ঞাপন বিরতি commercial break
বিড়ম্বনাময় ironic
বিড়াল cat
বিতরণ করা give out, send out
বিতরণকারী distributor
বিতর্ক debate
বিতর্কমূলক controversial
বিতাড়িত করা expel
বিদায় bye!, farewell!
বিদায়ধ্বনি cheerio!
বিদায় সম্ভাষণ bye-bye!
বিদায়-সম্ভাষণ goodbye!
বিদেশ abroad, foreign, overseas
বিদেশী exotic, foreigner
বিদ্বেষ grudge
বিদ্বেষী spiteful
বিদ্যালয় school
বিদ্যুতবাহী তার flex
বিদ্যুত সরবরাহে ঘাটতি power cut
বিদ্যুতের সুইচ switch
বিদ্যুৎ শক্তি electricity
বিদ্যুৎশক্তি পরিবাহিত হওয়া charge
বিদ্যুৎশক্তির পরিমাণ বোঝাতে charge
বিধবা widow
বিধান legislation
বিধিনিয়ম regulation
বিনয়ী cheeky
বিনামূল্যে free
বিনিময় swap
বিনিময় করা exchange
বিনিময়যোগ্য convertible
বিনিময় হার exchange rate
বিনিয়োগ investment
বিনিয়োগ করা invest
বিনিয়োগকারী investor
বিনুনি plait
বিনোদন শিল্প show business
বিন্দু dot, drop
বিন্যাস format
বিপক্ষে against
বিপজ্জনক dangerous

বিপজ্জনক দৃশ্যের নেপথ্য অভিনেতা stuntman
বিপণন marketing
বিপত্নীক widower
বিপদ danger
বিপদ ডেকে আনা endanger
বিপরীত opposite
বিপরীত কথা বলা contradict
বিপরীত দিকে back
বিপরীতভাবে vice versa
বিপরীতে contrary
বিপাক metabolism
বিপুল ভোটে landslide
বিপ্লব revolution
বিবরণ account, description
বিবর্ণ হয়ে যাওয়া fade
বিবর্তন evolution
বিবাহ marriage, wedding
বিবাহ করা marry
বিবাহবার্ষিকী wedding anniversary
বিবাহ-বিচ্ছিন্ন divorced
বিবাহবিচ্ছেদ divorce
বিবাহিত married
বিবাহের আংটি wedding ring
বিবাহের পোষাক wedding dress
বিবাহের সার্টিফিকেট marriage certificate
বিবাহে শ্রেষ্ঠ ব্যক্তি best man
বিবিধ miscellaneous
বিবৃতি statement
বিবেক conscience
বিবেচক considerate
বিবেচনা consider
বিবেচনা করা regard
বিবেচনা করে considering
বিভাগ block, department, section
বিভাজিত বিপণী department store
বিভিন্ন various
বিভিন্ন দিশায় ঘোরা turn around
বিভিন্ন প্রসাধনী দ্রব্য cosmetics
বিভিন্ন শব্দের প্রথম অক্ষর সমন্বয়ে গঠিত শব্দ acronym
বিভীষিকা horror
বিভ্রান্ত baffled
বিভ্রান্তি confusion
বিভ্রান্তিকর misleading
বিমা insurance
বিমা করা insure
বিমাকৃত insured
বিমান aircraft, plane
বিমান ওড়া take off
বিমান-কর্মীবৃন্দ/জাহাজ-কর্মীবৃন্দ crew
বিমান চলাচল নিয়ন্ত্রক air traffic controller
বিমানচালক pilot

বিমান পরিষেবা airline
বিমানবন্দর airport
বিমান বাহিত মেল airmail
বিমানবাহিনী air force
বিমান-সফর জনিত অসুস্থতা airsick
বিমানসেবক cabin crew
বিমানসেবিকা air hostess
বিমানের আকাশ আরোহন take off
বিমা পলিসি insurance policy
বিমা সার্টিফিকেট insurance certificate
বিমুখ allergic
বিয়োগ minus
বিয়োগ করা subtract
বিয়োগান্তক tragedy
বিরক্ত annoy, disgusted
বিরক্ত করা disturb
বিরক্তিকর annoying, boring, disgusting, infuriating, irritating, revolting
বিরতি half-time, interval
বিরাট big, grand, mammoth
বিরাট বড় ভুল blunder
বিরামহীন non-stop
বিরোধিতা opposition
বিরোধিতা করা oppose
বিরোধিতামূলক opposing
বিরোধী opposed
বিরোধী পক্ষ opponent
বিল bill
বিলপ্রদান check out
বিলম্বিত delayed, overdue
বিলাস luxury
বিলাসবহুল luxurious
বিলি করা distribute
বিলিয়ার্ড billiards
বিলুপ্তি abolition
বিলোপ করা abolish, eliminate
বিশদ detail
বিশদীকরণ illustration
বিশাল enormous, extensive, giant, great, huge, massive
বিশালাকার giant
বিশিষ্ট হওয়া stand out
বিশুদ্ধ sterile
বিশৃংখল shambles
বিশৃঙ্খল mess
বিশৃঙ্খল করা mess up
বিশেষ special
বিশেষ আদালত tribunal
বিশেষ করে specially
বিশেষ কোন অঞ্চলের উদ্ভিদ flora
বিশেষজ্ঞ specialist
বিশেষ জ্ঞান লাভ করা specialize
বিশেষণ adjective

বিশেষণের বিশেষণ adverb
বিশেষত particularly
বিশেষ ধরণের typical
বিশেষভাবে especially
বিশেষ সুবিধা special offer
বিশেষ্য পদ noun
বিশ্ব উষ্ণায়ন global warming
বিশ্বকাপ World Cup
বিশ্বকোষ encyclopaedia
বিশ্ববিদ্যালয় uni, university
বিশ্ববিদ্যালয় বা কলেজ চত্বর campus
বিশ্বব্যাপী global
বিশ্বব্রহ্মাণ্ড universe
বিশ্বস্তভাবে faithfully
বিশ্বায়ন globalization
বিশ্বাস belief, faith, trust
বিশ্বাস-উৎপাদক persuasive
বিশ্বাস করা believe, trust
বিশ্বাসঘাতকতা করা betray, deceive
বিশ্বাসযোগ্য credible, reputable
বিশ্বাস রাখা believe
বিশ্বাসী faithful, reliable
বিশ্রাম relaxation
বিশ্রাম নেওয়া relax, rest, unwind
বিশ্রামপূর্ণ restful
বিশ্রামহীন restless
বিশ্রী vile
বিশ্লেষণ analysis
বিশ্লেষণ করা analyse
বিষ poison
বিষ দেওয়া poison
বিষনাশক পদার্থ antidote
বিষয় content, issue, subject
বিষয়বস্তু theme
বিষয়ে concerning
বিষক্ত poisonous, toxic
বিষাক্ত ছত্রাক toadstool
বিস্কুট biscuit
বিস্কুটের গুঁড়ো crumb
বিস্তারিত detailed
বিস্তীর্ণ পতিত ভূমি moor
বিস্তৃত comprehensive
বিস্ফোরক explosive
বিস্ফোরণ blast, explosion
বিস্ফোরণ করা blow up
বিস্ফোরণ ঘটা explode, go off
বিস্ফোরিত হওয়া burst
বিস্ময় amaze, astonish, surprise
বিস্ময়কর amazing, astonishing, surprising
বিস্ময়করভাবে surprisingly
বিস্ময়সূচক চিহ্ন exclamation mark
বিস্মিত amazed, astonished, stunned, surprised
বিস্মিত করা startle

বিস্মৃত forgotten
বীজ seed
বীট beetroot
বীণা harp
বীর/ঔটিযুক্ত ফলধারী লতা bean
বীয়ার beer
বুকজ্বালা করা heartburn
বুকমার্ক bookmark
বুকে হেঁটে চলা creep
বুঝতে পারা understand
বুঝদার understanding
বুড়ো আঙুল thumb
বুদবুদ bubble
বুদ্ধ Buddha
বুদ্ধিমান brainy, intelligent
বুদ্ধি সম্পর্কিত intellectual
বুদ্ধ্যাঙ্ক IQ
বুদবুদধরা পানীয় fizzy
বুধবার Wednesday
বুনো হাঁস grouse
বুফে গাড়ি buffet car
বুলগেরিয়া Bulgaria
বুলগেরিয়ার ভাষা Bulgarian
বুলগেরিয়ার বাসিন্দা Bulgarian
বুলগেরিয়া সংক্রান্ত Bulgarian
বুলিমিয়া bulimia
বুলেট bullet
বুটেনের মুদ্রা penny
বৃত্তি scholarship
বৃত্তিমূলক vocational
বৃদ্ধি growth, increase, rise
বৃদ্ধি পাওয়া increase
বৃশ্চিকরাশি Scorpio
বৃষরাশি Taurus
বৃষ্টি rain
বৃষ্টিরোধী showerproof
বৃষ্টি পড়া rain
বৃহস্পতিবার Thursday
বৃহৎ mega
বেঁচে থাকা live, survive
বেঁচে যাওয়া leftovers
বেজি weasel
বেঁধানো pierced
বেঁকানো carve
বেকার unemployed
বেকারত্ব unemployment
বেগুন aubergine
বেগুনি রঙের lilac
বেগুনী purple
বেজিং Beijing
বেঠিক incorrect
বেড় rim
বেড়া fence
বেড়ানো sightseeing
বেড়ালছানা kitten

বেড়ে ওঠা grow up
বেঢপ outsize
বেতন pay, salary
বেতনবিহীন unpaid
বেতার radio
বেদনা উপশমকারী painkiller
বেদনাদায়ক painful
বেদনাবহ traumatic
বেদানা pomegranate
বেদি altar
বেপরোয়া হত্যাকাণ্ড massacre
বেরসিক spoilsport
বেরিয়ে থাকা stick out
বেরিয়ে যাওয়া get out
বেরিয়ে যেতে বলা clear off
বেরোবার রাস্তা way out
বেলচা shovel
বেলজিয়াম Belgium
বেলজিয়ামবাসী Belgian
বেলজিয়াম সম্বন্ধীয় Belgian
বেলারুস Belarus
বেলারুসবাসী Belarussian
বেলারুস সম্বন্ধীয় Belarussian
বেলারুসীয় Belarussian
বেলুন balloon
বেল্ট belt
বেল্টে লাগানো ছোট ব্যাগ bum bag
বেশ quite
বেশ কিছু several
বেশ ভাল pretty
বেশ ভালভাবে prettily
বেশি more, surplus
বেশি করে ফেলা overdone
বেশিক্ষণ জেগে থাকা stay up
বেশি পয়সা নেওয়া overcharge
বেশিরভাগ most
বেশি সময় ধরে ঘুমানো oversleep
বেসবল টুপি baseball cap
বেসরকারি private
বেসরকারিকরণ privatize
বেসরকারী unofficial
বেহালা violin
বেহালাবাদক violinist
বোকা blunt, fool, silly, stupid
বোকা বানানো fool
বোকাবোকা nonsense
বোঝা burden
বোঝাই করা load
বো-টাই bow tie
বোতল bottle
বোতল খোলার জিনিষ bottle-opener
বোতল খোলার যন্ত্র can opener
বোতল রাখার স্থান bottle bank
বোতলের ছিপি খোলার সরঞ্জাম corkscrew

বোতাম button, key
বোতামওয়ালা উলের পোশাক cardigan
বোধ sense
বোধ করা feel
বোধগম্য understandable
বোধশক্তি comprehension
বোন sister
বোনা knit
বোনার কাঁটা knitting needle
বোনাস bonus
বোবা dumb
বোমা bomb
বোমাবর্ষণ bombing
বোমাবাজি করা bomb
বোর্ড-গেম board game
বোর্ড/পর্ষদ board
বোর্ডিং স্কুল boarding school
বোলতা wasp
বোল্ট bolt
বৌদ্ধ Buddhist
বৌদ্ধ ধর্ম Buddhism
বৌদ্ধ ধর্ম সংক্রান্ত Buddhist
বৈঁচিজাতীয় ছোট ফল gooseberry
বৈচিত্র্য variety
বৈঠক meeting
বৈঠা oar
বৈদ্যুতিক electric, electrical
বৈদ্যুতিক কম্বল electric blanket
বৈদ্যুতিক ঝটকা electric shock
বৈদ্যুতিক সিঁড়ি escalator
বৈদ্যুতিন electronic
বৈদ্যুতিন যোগাযোগব্যবস্থা telecommunications
বৈধ valid
বৈপরীত্য contradiction
বৈপ্লবিক revolutionary
বৈবাহিক অবস্থা marital status
বৈশিষ্ট্য characteristic, feature, speciality
বৈশিষ্ট্যসূচক peculiar
বৈষম্য discrimination
বৈসাদৃশ্য contrast
ব্যক্তি personal
ব্যক্তিগত personal
ব্যক্তিগত ড্রাইভার chauffeur
ব্যক্তিগতভাবে personally
ব্যক্তিগত সম্পত্তি private property
ব্যক্তিগত সহায়ক personal assistant
ব্যক্তিগত স্টিরিও personal stereo
ব্যক্তিত্ব personality
ব্যক্তিবিশেষ individual
ব্যঙ্গ humour
ব্যঙ্গ করা scoff
ব্যঞ্জনবর্ণ consonant
ব্যতিক্রম exception

ব্যথা ache, pain, sore
ব্যথা করা ache
বথানাশক ওষুধ aspirin
ব্যথায় ককিয়ে ওঠা groan
ব্যবধান margin
ব্যবধানে apart
ব্যবসা trade
ব্যবসা-প্রতিষ্ঠান firm
ব্যবসায় business
ব্যবসায়িক প্রতিষ্ঠান একত্রিত হওয়া merger
ব্যবসায়িক ব্যাংক merchant bank
ব্যবসায়ী businessman
ব্যবস্থা system
ব্যবস্থাপনা arrangement
ব্যবহার use
ব্যবহার করতে পারা access
ব্যবহার করা exploit, secondhand, use
ব্যবহারকারী user
ব্যবহারকারী-সহায়ক user-friendly
ব্যবহারিক প্রমাণের পরিক্ষা try out
ব্যবহৃত used
ব্যয় expenditure
ব্যয় করা spend
ব্যর্থ হওয়া miss
ব্যস্ত busy
ব্যস্ত থাকার টোন engaged tone
ব্যস্ত সিগনাল busy signal
ব্যাকরণ grammar
ব্যাকরণগত grammatical
ব্যাখ্যা explanation
ব্যাখ্যা করা explain, interpret
ব্যাগ/থলে bag
ব্যাঙ frog, toad
ব্যাঙ্ক bank
ব্যাঙ্ক অ্যাকাউন্ট bank account
ব্যাঙ্ক ব্যালেন্স bank balance
ব্যাঙ্কের অ্যাকাউন্ট account
ব্যাঙ্কের উচ্চপদস্থ কর্মচারী banker
ব্যাঙ্কের চেক cheque
ব্যাঙ্কের চেকবই chequebook
ব্যাঙ্কের ছুটির দিন bank holiday
ব্যাঙ্কের টাকা note
ব্যাঙ্কের নোট বা মুদ্রা banknote
ব্যাঙাচি tadpole
ব্যাজ badge
ব্যাডমিন্টন badminton
ব্যান্ড band
ব্যান্ডেজ bandage
ব্যান্ডেজ করা bandage
ব্যাপক intensive, widespread
ব্যাপক পরিষ্কার করা spring-cleaning
ব্যাপার matter
ব্যাপারী dealer

ব্যায়াম exercise
ব্যালে নর্তক/নর্তকী ballet dancer
ব্যালে নর্তকী ballerina
ব্যালে নৃত্য ballet
ব্যালে নৃত্যের জুতো ballet shoes
ব্যাস diameter
ব্যাস ড্রাম বাদ্যযন্ত্র bass drum
ব্যাসুন bassoon
ব্যাহত করা disrupt
ব্রণ acne, pimple
ব্রাউজার browser
ব্রাজিল Brazil
ব্রাজিল সংক্রান্ত Brazilian
ব্রাজিলের বাসিন্দা Brazilian
ব্রাশ করা brush
ব্রিটেন Britain
ব্রিটেন সংক্রান্ত British
ব্রিটেনের বাসিন্দা British
ব্রিটেনের মুদ্রা sterling
ব্রেক brake
ব্রেক কষা brake
ব্র্যান্ড brand
ব্র্যান্ডি brandy
ব্র্যান্ডের নাম brand name
ব্লগ লেখা blog
ব্লাউজ blouse
ব্লাশার blusher
ব্লেজার blazer
ব্লেড blade
ভদ্র gentle, sober
ভদ্রভাবে gently
ভদ্রমহিলা lady
ভদ্রলোক gentleman
ভবঘুরে tramp
ভবন building
ভবিষ্যত future
ভবিষ্যতে করা হবে shall
ভবিষ্যদ্বাণী করা foresee, predict
ভয় fear, scare
ভয়ঙ্কর dreadful, horrendous, horrifying
ভয় দেখানো intimidate, scare
ভয় দেখিয়ে টাকা আদায় hold up
ভয় পাওয়া fear, shudder
ভয় পাওয়ার মত scary
ভয়ার্ত edgy
ভয়ানক gruesome, horrible, shocking
ভয়াবহ সিনেমা horror film
ভয়ার্ত চিৎকার scream
ভয়ে চিৎকার করা scream
ভয়ে বা শীতে গায়ে কাঁটা দেওয়া goose pimples
ভর্তুকি subsidy

ভর্তুকি দেওয়া subsidize
ভরসা করা count on
ভরসায় থাকা lean on
ভর্তি admission
ভর্তি করা fill
ভর্তি হওয়া admit
ভাঁজ crease, fold
ভাঁজ করা fold
ভাঁজ করে বসা kneel down
ভাঁজযুক্ত creased
ভাই brother
ভাইঝি/ভাগ্নী niece
ভাইবোন siblings
ভাইরাসবাহিত রোগ flu
ভাগ division, make up
ভাগ করা divide
ভাগ করে নেওয়া share
ভাগ্নে/ভাইপো nephew
ভাগ্য fate, luck
ভাগ্যবশতঃ luckily
ভাগ্যবান lucky
ভাগ্যহীন unlucky
ভাঙা break, broken down
ভাজা fried, fry
ভাজার পাত্র frying pan
ভাটিখানা brewery, distillery
ভাড়া fare, hire, rent
ভাড়া গাড়ী car hire
ভাড়াটে tenant
ভাড়া দেওয়া rent
ভাড়ার অর্থ rental
ভাতা dole
ভাতার জন্য আবেদন sign on
ভান করা pretend
ভাবময় sensuous
ভায়োলা viola
ভার load
ভারত India
ভারত মহাসাগর Indian Ocean
ভারতীয় Indian
ভারতীয় নাগরিক Indian
ভারসাম্য balance
ভারা scaffolding
ভারি heavy
ভারোত্তোলক weightlifter
ভারোত্তোলন weightlifting
ভাল good, well
ভালোবাসা love
ভালসমত fairly
ভালো fine
ভালো আচরণ করা behave
ভালোবাসা love
ভাল্লুক bear
ভাষণ address, lecture
ভাষণ দেওয়া lecture

ভাষা language	ভূমধ্যসাগর সম্বন্ধীয় Mediterranean	মজার fun, funny
ভাষাতত্ত্ববিদ linguist	ভূমণ্ডল globe	মজুত reserve
ভাষা শেখার স্কুল language school	ভূমিকম্প earthquake	মজুত রাখা stock
ভাষা সংক্রান্ত linguistic	ভূমিকা role	মজুর workman
ভাষ্যকার commentator	ভূমিসাৎ করা demolish	মজুরী wage
ভাষ্যপাঠ commentary	ভেঙে টুকরো টুকরো হওয়া smash	মজ্জা marrow
ভাসমান তেলের আবরণ oil slick	ভেঙে ফেলা knock down	মট MOT
ভাসা float	ভেঙে যাওয়া break, snap	মটর peas
ভাস্কর sculptor	ভেজা soaked	মটরশুটি mangetout
ভাস্কর্য sculpture	ভেড়া lamb	মঠ monastery
ভিক্ষা করা beg	ভেড়া-ছাগলের মাংস red meat	মডেল model
ভিক্ষুক beggar	ভেড়ার পাল fleet	মণি jewel
ভিজা moist	ভেড়ি ewe	মত as ... as
ভিজিটর কেন্দ্র visitor centre	ভেতরে inside, into	মতাদর্শ ideology
ভিজিয়ে রাখা soak	ভেতরে ঢুকে যাওয়া go in	মতামত opinion, point, view
ভিজে wet	ভেতরের অংশ interior	মথ moth
ভিজে জবজবে হওয়া drench	ভেতরের শক্তি spirits	মদ booze, liqueur
ভিজে ন্যাতানো soggy	ভেনিজুয়েলা দেশীয় Venezuelan	মদ দিয়ে বানানো পানীয় punch
ভিড়ে ঠাসা packed	ভেনিজুয়েলার বসবাসকারী Venezuelan	মদ্যপান করে গাড়ী চালানো drink-driving
ভিত base, foundations	ভেন্ডিং মেশিন vending machine	
ভিতর inside	ভেড়ার ছাল sheepskin	মদ্যপানে অনিচ্ছুক teetotal
ভিত্তি basis, ground	ভেলা raft	মদ্যবিশেষ aperitif, port, whisky, wine
ভিত্তি করে based	ভেষজ চা herbal tea	
ভিনিগার মাখানো খাবার vinaigrette	ভোঁদড় otter	মধু honey
ভিয়েতনাম দেশীয় Vietnamese	ভোগদখল possession	মধুচন্দ্রিমা honeymoon
ভিয়েতনামের নাগরিক Vietnamese	ভোগদখল করা possess	মধুর charming
ভিয়েতনামের ভাষা Vietnamese	ভোজ্য edible	মধুর সুর melody
ভীত afraid, scared	ভ্যাকুয়াম ক্লিনার দিয়ে পরিষ্কার করা hoover, vacuum	মধ্য mid
ভীতি phobia		মধ্য-আফ্রিকান প্রজাতন্ত্র Central African Republic
ভীতিজনক threatening	ভ্যান পাড়ি van	
ভীষণ so, such	ভ্যালেন্টাইনস দিবস Valentine's Day	মধ্য-আমেরিকা Central America
ভূজাগাছ birch	ভ্রমণ backpacking, tour, travel, travelling, trip	মধ্যপন্থী moderate
ভুট্টা corn, maize, sweetcorn		মধ্যপ্রাচ্য Middle East
ভুট্টার গুঁড়ো cornflour	ভ্রমণ করা tour, travel	মধ্যবয়স্ক middle-aged
ভুতুড়ে haunted	ভ্রমণকারী traveller	মধ্যবর্তী intermediate
ভুরু eyebrow	ভ্রমণ নির্দেশক tour guide	মধ্যবিত্ত middle-class
ভুরু কোঁচকানো frown	ভ্রমণবীমা travel insurance	মধ্যযুগ mediaeval, Middle Ages
ভুল mistake, mistaken, wrong	ভ্রমণ ব্যবহার দোকান travel agent	মধ্যরাত্রি midnight
ভুল করা mistake, slip up	ভ্রমণ সংস্থা travel agency	মধ্যাহ্ন midday
ভুল বোঝা misunderstand	ভ্রান্তি illusion	মধ্যাহ্নভোজ lunch
ভুল বোঝাবুঝি misunderstanding	ভ্রাম্যমাণ বিক্রেতা rep	মধ্যাহ্নভোজ-বিরতি lunch break
ভুলভাবে mistakenly	ভ্রূণ foetus	মধ্যাহ্নভোজের নির্ধারিত সময় lunchtime
ভুল শুধরানো correct	মই ladder	
ভুল জায়গায় রাখা mislay	মই বা সিঁড়ি stepladder	মধিখানে halfway
ভুলে যাওয়া forget	মকর রাশি Capricorn	মধ্যে among, between, in, into, middle, through, within
ভূগর্ভ underground	মক্কা Mecca	
ভূগর্ভস্থ underground	মগ mug	মন mind
ভূগর্ভস্থ পথ underpass	মঙ্গলবার Tuesday	মনঃসংযোগ concentration
ভূগর্ভস্থ পায়ে হাঁটার পথ subway	মচকানো sprain	মনঃসংযোগ করা concentrate
ভূগর্ভস্থ স্টেশন underground station	মচকে যাওয়া sprain	মনখারাপ depressed
ভূগোল geography	মজবুত sound	মনন thought
ভূত ghost	মজবুত করা strengthen	মননশীল thoughtful
ভূ-তত্ত্ব geology	মজবুতভাবে strongly	মননহীন thoughtless
ভূদৃশ্য landscape	মজা fun	মনভরানো impressive
ভূমধ্যসাগর Mediterranean	মজা করা joke	মন ভরিয়ে দেওয়া impress

মনশ্চক্ষুতে দেখা visualize
মনছ করা intend
মনুষ্যজাতি mankind
মনুষ্যনির্মিত man-made
মনে করা mind, suppose, think
মনে করানো remind
মনে রাখা memorize
মনে হওয়া seem
মনোচিকিৎসক psychiatrist
মনোনয়ন nomination
মনোনীত nominate
মনোবল morale
মনোবাসনা wish
মনোবিজ্ঞান psychology
মনোবিদ psychologist
মনোবৃত্তি mentality
মনোমুগ্ধকর fascinating
মনোযোগ attention
মনোরম fine, pleasant, quaint
মনোরোগ সংক্রোত psychiatric
মন্তব্য comment, remark
মন্তব্য করা comment
মন্ত্রক ministry
মন্ত্রী minister
মন্দ bad, wicked
মন্দা সময় off-peak, off-season
মন্দির temple
মন্দিরা cymbals
ময়দা flour
ময়দার তাল dough
ময়দার মিষ্টি doughnut
ময়লা dirty
ময়লা তোলার পাত্র dustpan
ময়শ্চারাইজার moisturizer
ময়ূর peacock
মরক্কো দেশীয় Moroccan
মরক্কোবাসী Moroccan
মরচে rust
মরচে ধরা rusty
মরচে পরে না এমন ধাতু stainless steel
মরিটানিয়া Mauritania
মরিয়া desperate
মরিয়া ভাবে desperately
মরুদ্যান oasis
মরুভূমি desert
মর্মঘাতী appalling
মর্মস্পর্শী tragic
মর্যাদা dignity, prestige
মর্যাদাপূর্ণ prestigious
মলদোভার মানুষ Moldovan
মলম ointment
মলাট দেওয়া বই paperback
মল্ট হুইস্কি malt whisky
মশলা spice

মশলাযুক্ত spicy
মশা mosquito
মসজিদ mosque
মসৃণ even, smooth
মসৃণ করা file
মস্তান bully
মস্তানি করা bully
মস্তিষ্ক brain
মহাকাশ space
মহাকাশচারী astronaut
মহাকাশযান spacecraft
মহাদেশ continent
মহামান্য majesty
মহামারী epidemic
মহাশয় sir
মহাসমুদ্র ocean
মহিমা glory
মহিলা female, woman
মহিলা খেলোয়াড় sportswoman
মহিলাদের ladies
মহিলা পুলিশ policewoman
মহিলা ব্যবসায়ী businesswoman
মহিলা সাফাইকর্মী cleaning lady
মহিলা সৈনিক servicewoman
মহোদয়া madam
মহৎ great
মা mother, mum, mummy
মাংস meat
মাংস ঝলসানোর উনুন barbecue
মাংস বা সব্জির পুরভরি dumpling
মাংসের ছোট ছোট বল meatball
মাংসের ছোট টুকরো chop
মাংসের ঝোল broth
মাংসের ফালি steak
মাংসের রসা gravy
মাউস mouse
মাকড়সা spider
মাকড়সার জাল cobweb
মাখন butter
মাখন জাতীয় খাবার spread
মাখন তোলা দুধ skimmed milk
মাছ fish, trout
মাছধরা fish, fishing
মাছ ধরার দড়ি fishing tackle
মাছবিক্রেতা fishmonger
মাছরাঙা kingfisher
মাছি fly
মাঝারি medium
মাঝারি-মাপের medium-sized
মাঝে মধ্যে occasionally
মাটি clay, soil
মাটিতে পড়ে যাওয়া fall
মাঠ field
মাঠা তোলা দুধ semi-skimmed milk
মাড় gluten

মাতাল drunk
মাতৃভাষা mother tongue
মাতৃভাষা বক্তা native speaker
মাতৃ সম্পর্কীয় maternal
মাত্রা degree, dose, extent, level
মাথা head
মাথা এবং বুকের মূর্তি bust
মাথা ঘোরা dizzy
মাথা ঝোঁকানো bow
মাথাব্যথা headache
মাথা নেড়ে সম্মতি জানানো nod
মাথার খুলি skull
মাথা হেলানো tip
মাদি কুকুর bitch
মাদুর mat
মাধুর্যমিষ্ট graceful
মাধুর্যময় cute
মাধুর্য charm
মাধ্যমিক বিদ্যালয় secondary school
মান grade
মানচিত্র map
মানচিত্রের বই atlas
মানদণ্ড scale
মানব human
মানবতাবাদী humanitarian
মানবাধিকার human rights
মানসিক mental, psychological
মানসিক চিকিৎসালয় mental hospital
মানসিক বিষাদ depression
মানসিক বিষাদগ্রস্ত depressing
মানসিকভাবে ভেঙে পড়া heartbroken
মানানসই fit
মানিয়ে নেওয়া adapt
মানুষ human being
মান্য করা obey
মাপে হওয়া fit
মাফলার scarf
মামলা করা sue
মাম্পস্ mumps
মারা beat
মারাত্মক fatal
মারা যাওয়া die
মার্কসবাদ Marxism
মার্কা trademark
মার্কিন যুক্তরাষ্ট্র United States, US, USA
মার্চ March
মার্চ করা march
মার্জনা excuse
মার্জনা করা excuse
মার্জিত tasteful
মাল্টা Malta
মাল্টা দেশীয় Maltese
মাল্টার মানুষ Maltese
মালদোভিয় Moldovan

মালপত্র baggage, cargo
মালপত্র বহনের ভ্যান removal van
মালপত্রের তালিকা inventory
মালবাহী নৌকা barge
মালয়েশিয়া দেশীয় Malaysian
মালয়েশিয়ার অধিবাসী Malaysian
মালিক owner
মালিকানা লাভ করা own
মালী gardener
মাস month
মাসিক menstruation, monthly
মাস্তুল mast
মিছিল procession
মিটার metre
মিতব্যয়িতা austerity
মিথুন রাশি Gemini
মিথ্যাকথা lie
মিথ্যাবাদী liar
মিথ্যা সাক্ষী perjury
মিনা করা engrave
মিনিট minute
মিনিবাস minibus
মিলনস্থল joint
মিলিত চুক্তি agreement
মিলিত হওয়া merge
মিলিমিটার millimetre
মিশর Egypt
মিশর দেশীয় Egyptian
মিশরবাসী Egyptian
মিশ্র mixed
মিশ্রক blender
মিশ্রণ mix, mixture
মিশ্র স্যালাড mixed salad
মিশ্রিত mix
মিশ্রিত দস্তা pewter
মিষ্টদ্রব্য sweet
মিষ্টি afters, pretty, sweet
মিষ্টজলের মাছ freshwater fish
মিষ্টিদ্রব্য sweets
মিস্ত্রি mechanic
মিহি fine
মীনরাশি Pisces
মুকুট crown
মুক্তা pearl
মুক্ত হওয়া release
মুক্তি release
মুক্তি দেওয়া free
মুক্তিপণ ransom
মুক্তি পাওয়া get off
মুখ face, mouth
মুখ ধোয়ার বেসিন washbasin
মুখ ধোয়ার তরল প্রতিষেধক
   mouthwash
মুখপাত্র spokesperson
মুখপাত্র (পুরুষ) spokesman

মুখপাত্র (মহিলা) spokeswoman
মুখমণ্ডল-সম্পর্কিত facial
মুখরোচক খাবারের দোকান
   delicatessen
মুখী face
মুখে দাগ আছে যার spotty
মুখের তোয়ালে face cloth
মুখের ভাব expression
মুখোমুখি level, opposite
মুখোমুখি ধাক্কা লাগা crash
মুখোমুখি ধাক্কা লাগানো crash
মুখোমুখি সংঘর্ষ collision
মুখোমুখি সংঘর্ষ হওয়া collide
মুখোশ mask
মুখোশধারী masked
মুখ্য chief, main, primary,
   principal
মুখ্য কার্যালয় head office,
   headquarters
মুখ্যগায়ক/গায়িকা soprano
মুগ্ধ impressed
মুচমুচে crispy
মুচমুচে ভাবযুক্ত crisp
মুছে ফেলা erase, wipe up
মুদি grocer
মুদিখানার grocer
মুদিখানায় লভ্য সামগ্রী groceries
মুদ্রণ print
মুদ্রণযন্ত্র printer
মুদ্রা coin, currency
মুদ্রাকর a printer
মুদ্রার বিনিময় হার rate of exchange
মুনাফা return
মুরগী chicken, hen
মুরগীর বাচ্ছা chick
মুরগীর মাংস chicken
মুলো horseradish
মুষ্টিযুদ্ধ boxing
মুসলমান Moslem
মুসলিম Moslem
মুহূর্ত moment
মূত্রাশয় bladder
মূদ্রাহ্রাস devaluation
মূর্খ idiot
মূর্খামি idiotic
মূর্ত abstract
মূর্তি statue
মূল root
মূল খাবার main course
মূলতঃ basically
মূলধন capital
মূল ভূখণ্ড mainland
মূল রাস্তা main road
মূল সঙ্গীতে শব্দযোগ dubbed
মূলো radish

মূল্য charge, cost, price, value,
   worth
মূল্য ধার্য করা charge
মূল্যফেরত change
মূল্য ফেরত দেওয়া refund
মূল্যবান precious, valuable
মূল্যবৃদ্ধি inflation
মূল্যহীন worthless
মূল্যায়ন করা rate
মূল্যে cost
মূল্যের তালিকা price list
মৃত dead
মৃত্তিকা earth
মৃত্যু death
মৃত্যুদণ্ড capital punishment,
   execution
মৃত্যুদণ্ড দেওয়া execute
মৃদু mild
মৃদু বাতাস breeze
মে May
মেক্সিকান Mexican
মেক্সিকো সম্বন্ধীয় Mexican
মেঘ cloud
মেঘাচ্ছন্ন cloudy, overcast
মেচেতা freckles
মেজাজ mood, temper
মেজাজী moody
মেঝে floor
মেঝে/ভূতল ground
মেদবহুল flabby
মেধা intelligence
মেধাবী brilliant, intellectual
মেনথল peppermint
মেনিনজাইটিস meningitis
মেনে নেওয়া yield
মেমরী কার্ড memory card
মেয়র mayor
মেয়ে girl
মেয়েদের অন্তর্বাস knickers
মেয়েদের সাঁতারের পোশাক swimsuit
মেরামত repair
মেরামত করা fix, mend, renovate,
   repair
মেরামত করান service
মেরামতির কিট repair kit
মেরুদণ্ড backbone, spinal cord
মেরুদেশীয় polar
মেরে ফেলা kill
মেলা fair, match
মেলাপ্রাঙ্গন fairground
মেশানো add
মেশিন machine
মেশিন-গান machine gun
মেশিনে ধোয়া যায় এমন machine
   washable

মেষ sheep
মেষ পালক shepherd
মেষ রাশি Aries
মেহপনি mahogany
মোঙ্গোলিয়ান ভাষা Mongolian
মোঙ্গোলীনিবাসী Mongolian
মোঙ্গোলীয় Mongolian
মোড়ান twist
মোচাকৃতি conifer
মোছা wipe
মোছার কাপড় cloth
মোজা sock
মোজাইক mosaic
মোট total
মোটর motor
মোটরগাড়ী car
মোটরগাড়ী রেসের চালক racing driver
মোটর দৌড় প্রতিযোগিতা motor racing
মোটরবাইক motorbike
মোটরবোট motorboat
মোটর মিস্ত্রি motor mechanic
মোটরসাইকেল motorcycle
মোটরসাইকেল চালক motorcyclist
মোট লেনদেন turnover
মোটা coarse, fat
মোটা বেতন প্রাপ্ত well-paid
মোটামুটি so-so
মোটাসোটা chubby, plump
মোটেল motel
মোড়ক foil, packaging, packet, parcel
মোড়ক খোলা unwrap
মোড়া wrap
মোড়ার কাগজ wrapping paper
মোবাইল ক্যামেরা-ফোন camera phone
মোবাইল নাম্বার mobile number
মোবাইল ফোন mobile phone
মোবাইলে ব্যবহৃত কার্ড top-up card
মোম wax
মোমবাতি candle
মোমবাতিদানি candlestick
মোম-রং crayon
মোষ buffalo
মৌখিক oral
মৌমাছি bee
মৌরী aniseed
মৌরীজাতীয় শাক fennel
মৌলিক basic, original
মৌসুমী seasonal
ম্যাচ match
ম্যাটমেটে marinade
ম্যারিনেড করা marinade
মৎসকন্যা mermaid
মৎসশিকারি angler

যক্ষ্মা TB, tuberculosis
যখন when, while
যখনই as, whenever
যখন থেকে since
যতক্ষণ পর্যন্ত till
যত তাড়াতাড়ি সম্ভব asap
যতিচিহ্ন colon
যত্ন care
যত্ন নেওয়া care
যথাক্রমে respectively
যথাযথভাবে exactly
যথাযথ appropriate, truly
যথার্থ accurate, definite, right
যথার্থতা accuracy
যথার্থভাবে accurately
যথাস্থানে থাকা belong
যথেষ্ট enough
যদি if
যদিও although
যদি না unless
যন্ত্র device, instrument
যন্ত্রকুশলী technician
যন্ত্র কৌশল mechanism
যন্ত্রগণক calculator
যন্ত্রপাতি apparatus, machinery
যন্ত্রাংশ spare part
যবের পায়েস porridge
যমজ twin
যা অন্য উপাদানকে গলায় solvent
যাইহোক anyhow, anyway
যাওয়া go
যা কিছু whatever, whichever
যাকে whom
যাচাই করা try on
যাতায়াত round trip
যাতায়াত করা commute
যাতায়াতকারী commuter
যাতে so
যাতে শব্দ হয় না silencer
যাত্রা journey
যাত্রাপথ course
যাত্রার সহযোগিনী flight attendant
যাত্রা শুরু করা set out
যাত্রী passenger
যাত্রীদের পরিচারক steward
যাত্রীবাহী জাহাজ liner
যা দিয়ে চার্জ করা হয় charger
যান craft
যানজট traffic jam
যান নিয়ন্ত্রক traffic warden
যানবাহন traffic
যানবাহনে চড়া take
যান্ত্রিক mechanical
যাযাবর সম্প্রদায় gypsy
যা যোগ করা হয় additive

যার whose
যীশু Jesus
যীশু খ্রীষ্ট Christ
যীশুর অনুগামী Christian
যুক্ত attached
যুক্ত করা attach, join
যুক্তরাজ্য United Kingdom
যুক্ত হওয়া plus
যুক্তি দিয়ে বোঝানো justify
যুক্তিবুদ্ধিসম্পর্ন rational
যুক্তিসংগত logical
যুক্তিসম্পর্ন reasonable
যুক্তিসম্পর্নভাবে reasonably
যুদ্ধ battle, war
যুদ্ধকালীন নিষ্প্রদীপ অবস্থা blackout
যুদ্ধজাহাজ battleship
যুদ্ধের ট্যাংক tank
যুব সঙ্ঘ youth club
যে অন্য লিঙ্গের পোশাক পড়ে transvestite
যে কেউ any, anybody, whoever
যে কোন any
যে কোন জায়গায় anywhere
যে কোন রকমে somehow
যে কোন সময় anytime
যে গাড়ির চার চাকায় শক্তি আসে four-wheel drive
যে ঘরবাড়ি সাজায় decorator
যেটা that
যেটা হল i.e.
যে সার্ফিং করে surfer
যোগ করা add, add up, sum up
যোগদান করা get into
যোগদান দেওয়া join
যোগফল total
যোগব্যায়াম yoga
যোগান supplies
যোগাযোগ contact
যোগাযোগ করা contact
যোগাযোগ স্থাপন communication
যোগাযোগ স্থাপন করা communicate
যোগ্যতা qualification
যোগ্যতা অর্জন করা qualify
যোগ্যতাসম্পর্ন competent
যোগ্য হওয়া deserve
যোজনা conjunction
যৌথ joint
যৌথ খাতা joint account
যৌথ শয়নাগার dormitory
যৌবনে youth
যৎসামান্য minimal
রং colour, dye
রং করা dye
রং ফিকে হওয়া bleached
রওনা দেওয়া set off

রক্ত blood
রক্তচাপ blood pressure
রক্তচোষা পতঙ্গ flea
রক্ত দূষণ blood poisoning
রক্ত পরীক্ষা blood test
রক্তপাত bleed
রক্তাল্পতার রোগী anaemic
রক্তিম scarlet
রক্তিম আভা flush
রক্তের গ্রুপ blood group
রক্ষক defender
রক্ষণশীল conservative
রক্ষণাবেক্ষণ maintenance
রক্ষা করা defend, protect
রক্ষী guard
রঙ paint
রঙ paint
রঙ করার তুলি paintbrush
রঙিন কাঁচ stained glass
রঙ্গমঞ্চ theatre
রচনাংশ passage
রজঃস্রাবে ব্যবহৃত ন্যাকড়া tampon
রজোনিবৃত্তি menopause
রণনীতি বিষয়ক strategic
রত্ন gem
রন্ধনকার্য cooking
রন্ধনপ্রণালী recipe
রন্ধনপ্রণালীর বই cookery book
রপ্তানি export
রপ্তানি করা export
রফা deal
রফা করা negotiate
রবার rubber
রবার দস্তানা rubber gloves
রবিন পাখি robin
রবিবার Sunday
রমজান Ramadan
রয়েছে have
রস juice
রসময় witty
রসায়ন chemistry
রসায়নবিদ chemist
রসিক humorous
রসিকতা wit
রসিদ receipt, voucher
রসুন garlic
রাখা keep, put
রাগারাগি tantrum
রাগী angry
রাজকীয় royal
রাজকুমার prince
রাজকুমার পরিচালিত রাজ্য Wales
রাজকুমারী princess
রাজতন্ত্র monarchy
রাজত্ব করা rule

রাজধানী capital
রাজনীতি politics
রাজনীতিক politician
রাজনৈতিক political
রাজসিক magnificent
রাজস্ব revenue
রাজহংস swan
রাজা king, monarch
রাজ্য kingdom
রাণী queen
রাত night
রাতপোষাক nightdress
রাতের শিফট night shift
রানওয়ে runway
রান্না করবার পদ্ধতি cookery
রান্না করা cook
রান্না করা গরুর মাংস beefburger
রান্নাঘর kitchen
রান্নার খুন্তি spatula
রান্নার বই cookbook
রামধনু rainbow
রায় sentence, verdict
রাশিচক্র zodiac
রাশিয়া দেশীয় Russian
রাশিয়ার অধিবাসী Russian
রাষ্ট্রদূত consul
রাষ্ট্রদূতের অফিস consulate
রাষ্ট্রপতি president
রাষ্ট্রসংঘ United Nations
রাষ্ট্রীয় পার্ক national park
রাসায়নিক উপাদান steroid
রাসায়নিক বস্তু chemical
রাস্তা road, street, way
রাস্তা অবরোধ করা block
রাস্তাবদল করা turn off
রাস্তা বন্ধ roadblock
রাস্তা সারাই roadworks
রাস্তায় out-of-doors
রাস্তায় গাড়ি খারাপ হলে থামানোর জায়গা
    hard shoulder
রাস্তায় চালকের ক্রোধ road rage
রাস্তায় পড়ে থাকে বরফের টুকরো black
    ice
রাস্তার আলো streetlamp
রাস্তার গায়ক busker
রাস্তার ধার kerb
রাস্তার ধারে গলি layby
রাস্তার পিচ tarmac
রাস্তার মানচিত্র street map
রাস্তার মোড় roundabout
রাস্তার ম্যাপ road map
রাস্পবেরির ফল raspberry
রিং রোড ring road
রিচার্জ করা recharge

রিটার্ন টিকিট return
রীতিনীতি custom
রুক্ষ rough
রুটিওয়ালা baker
রুটি তৈরী করার পদ্ধতি baking
রূপচর্চার স্হান beauty salon
রূপান্তরিত হওয়া become
রূপো silver
রুমাল handkerchief, hankie, napkin
রুলার ruler
রুশ ভাষা Russian
রূঢ় harsh, rude
রূপ form
রূপকথা fairytale
রূপান্তর makeover
রূপান্তর convert, transition
রূপান্তর করা transform
রেকর্ড record
রেকর্ড করা record
রেকর্ডভুক্ত ডেলিভারি recorded
    delivery
রেকর্ডার recorder
রেকর্ডিং recording
রেখাচিত্র diagram
রেগে যাওয়া cross
রেড ওয়াইন red wine
রেড ক্রস Red Cross
রেড সী Red Sea
রেডিয়ো নিয়ন্ত্রিত radio-controlled
রেলগাড়ির ইঞ্জিন engine
রেলগাড়ী carriage
রেল স্টেশন station
রেলের কামরা compartment
রেশম silk
রেসের ঘোড়া racehorse
রেস্তোরা café, restaurant
রোগ disease
রোগ নির্ণয় diagnosis
রোগা thin
রোগী patient
রোজ daily
রোজগার earnings
রোজগার করা earn
রোদ চশমা sunglasses
রোদশমা goggles
রোদ থেকে সুরক্ষার তেল suntan oil
রোদ থেকে সুরক্ষার লোশন suntan
    lotion
রোদে পুড়ে যাওয়া sunburnt
রোদে পোড়া sunburn
রোদে বিবর্ণ suntan
রোধনিরোধী ক্রিম sunscreen
রোপণ করা plant
রোম দেশীয় Roman
রোমাঞ্চ thrill

রোমাঞ্চকর thrilling
রোমাঞ্চকর কাহিনী thriller
রোমাঞ্চিত thrilled
রোমানিয়া দেশীয় Romanian
রোমানিয়া ভাষা Romanian
রোমানিয়ার অধিবাসী Romanian
রৌদ্রস্নান sunbathe
রৌদ্রোজ্জ্বল sunny
র্যাকেট (টেনিসের ব্যাট) racquet
র্যাডার radar
লক্ষণ symptom
লক্ষ্য aim, focus, goal, target
লক্ষ্য করা watch
লক্ষণীয় noticeable, striking
লক্ষ্য না করা miss
লক্ষ্য নিবদ্ধ করা focus
লক্ষ্য রাখা look after
লক্ষ্য স্থির করা aim
লগ-আউট করা log out
লগ-ইন করা log in
লকা chilli, pepper
লঙ্কাগুঁড়ো paprika
লজ্জা shame
লজ্জা পাওয়া blush
লজ্জিত ashamed
লজ্জিত হওয়া embarrassed
লড়াই fight
লড়াই করা fight
লন lawn
লবঙ্গ clove
লবণে জারিত শুয়োরের মাংস bacon
লভ্য available
লভ্যতা availability
লম্বা long, tall
লম্বা গলাওয়ালা হাঁস goose
লম্বাগোছের বীন runner bean
লম্বা বৃন্তওয়ালা গাছ rhubarb
লম্বা রাবারের জুতো wellingtons
লম্বা লম্বা ফালি strip
লরি lorry
লরিচালক lorry driver
লাইন line, queue
লাইনে দাঁড়ানো queue
লাইবেরিয়া দেশীয় Liberian
লাইবেরিয়ার মানুষ Liberian
লাগাম reins
লাঙল plough
লাজুক shy
লাঠি stick
লাথি kick
লাথি মারা kick
লাফানো bounce, gallop, jump, leap
লাফিয়ে চলা skip
লাভ gain, profit
লাভ করা gain

লাভজনক profitable
লাল red
লাল চাল brown rice
লাল চুলওয়ালা মহিলা redhead
লাল চুলওয়ালা লোক red-haired
লালচে বাদামী auburn
লাল পাউরুটি brown bread
লাল বেরী জাতীয় ফল redcurrant
লাল হয়ে যাওয়া flush
লালা saliva
লাশ corpse
লিঙ্গ sex
লিখিত বস্তু text
লিখিত বিবরণ record
লিখিত বিবরণ রাখা record
লিখে রাখা write down
লিঙ্গ gender
লিজ দেওয়া lease
লিথুয়ানিয়া দেশীয় Lithuanian
লিথুয়ানিয়া ভাষা Lithuanian
লিথুয়ানিয়ার মানুষ Lithuanian
লিবিয়া দেশীয় Libyan
লিবিয়াবাসী Libyan
লিলিফুল lily
লুকিয়ে থাকা hide
লুকিয়ে চলা dodge
লুকিয়ে রাখা hide
লুকোচুরি খেলা hide-and-seek
লুপ্ত extinct
লুফে নেওয়া catch
লেই paste
লেখক author, writer
লেখা write, writing
লেখা পড়া করা study
লেখার কাগজ writing paper
লেখার কাজ paperwork
লেজ tail
লেনদেন transaction
লেন্ট পর্ব Lent
লেন্স lens
লেপ quilt
লেবানন দেশীয় Lebanese
লেবাননের মানুষ Lebanese
লেবু lemon
লেবুর সরবত lemonade
লেস lace
লোক guy
লোককথা folklore
লোককে দেখানো show
লোকঠকানো fake
লোক দেখানো show off, stunt
লোকবল manpower
লোকসঙ্গীত folk music
লোকের ভিড় crowd
লোভনীয় lucrative

লোভী greedy
লোমওয়ালা hairy
লোমশ চামড়া fleece
লোহা iron
লোহার জিনিসের ব্যবসায়ী ironmonger
ল্যাংপেকে lanky
ল্যাঞ্জেঝোলা পাখি magpie
ল্যাটভিয়ান Latvian
ল্যাটভিয়া সংক্রান্ত Latvian
ল্যাটিন আমেরিকীয় Latin American
শংসাপত্র certificate
শক্ত hard, stiff, strong
শক্ত করে বাঁধা tie up
শক্ত কাগজের বোর্ড cardboard
শক্তি energy, force, power, strength
শক্তিবলে এলাকা দখল occupation
শক্তিশালী powerful
শখ hobby
শঙ্কিত apprehensive
শঙ্কু cone
শণের কাপড় linen
শতকরা per cent
শতবর্ষ century
শতবার্ষিকী centenary
শতরঞ্জি rug
শতাংশ percentage
শত্রু enemy
শত্রুতা করা spite
শত্রুভাবাপন্ন করে তোলা antagonize
শনিবার Saturday
শপথ oath
শবদেহ সংস্কারকারী undertaker
শবাগার morgue
শব্দ sound, term, word
শব্দ করে নাক টানা sniff
শব্দভাণ্ডার vocabulary
শব্দানুবাদ সম্বলিত বই phrasebook
শয়তান Devil
শরৎকাল autumn
শরীরচর্চা bodybuilding
শরীরে রক্তদান transfusion
শরীরের পেছনের অংশ backside
শর্করা carbohydrate
শর্টহ্যান্ড লেখা shorthand
শর্তহীন unconditional
শর্তাধীন conditional, provisional
শর্তাধীনে ছাড়া পাওয়া parole
শল্যচিকিৎসক surgeon
শসা cucumber
শস্যদানা cereal
শস্যদানা থেকে তৈরি খাবার cereal
শহর city, town
শহরতলি outskirts
শহরতলি suburb
শহরতলি সংক্রান্ত suburban

শহর থেকে দূরে countryside
শহরের কেন্দ্রস্থল town centre
শহরের ব্যস্ততম স্থান city centre
শহীদ martyr
শাওয়ার shower
শাখা branch
শাগরেদ accomplice
শাটলকক shuttlecock
শান্ত calm, quiet
শান্ত করা/শান্ত হওয়া calm down
শান্তকারী sedative
শান্তি peace
শান্তিপূর্ণ peaceful
শামুক snail
শারীরিক physical
শারীরিক কসরতে দক্ষ acrobat
শারীরিক পরীক্ষা check-up, medical
শারীরিক শক্তি stamina
শাল shawl
শালগম swede, turnip
শাশুড়ি mother-in-law
শাসক ruler
শাসিত অঞ্চল territory
শাস্তি punishment
শাস্তি দেওয়া punish
শাস্তি প্রদান sentence
শিক skewer
শিকার prey, victim
শিকার করা hunt, hunting
শিকার যাত্রা safari
শিকারি hunter
শিক্ষক teacher
শিক্ষকতা teaching
শিক্ষা education
শিক্ষাগত academic, educational
শিক্ষানবিশ beginner, trainee
শিক্ষাপ্রতিষ্ঠান academy
শিক্ষাবর্ষ academic year
শিক্ষাবর্ষের ভাগ term
শিক্ষার বেতন tuition fees
শিক্ষানী/ছাত্রানী apprentice, learner
শিক্ষার্থী ড্রাইভার learner driver
শিক্ষাছল tutorial
শিক্ষিত educated
শিখ Sikh
শিখর spire
শিখর সম্মেলন summit
শিখ সম্প্রদায়ের Sikh
শিঙ horn
শিবির/ছাউনি camp
শিম্পাঞ্জি chimpanzee
শিয়াল fox
শিরদাঁড়া spine
শিরস্ত্রাণ helmet
শিরা vein

শিরিশ কাগজ sandpaper
শিরোনাম caption, headline, title
শিলা hail
শিলার টুকরো rock
শিল্প industry
শিল্প এলাকা industrial estate
শিল্পকর্ম work of art
শিল্পঘন/সপন্ন artistic
শিল্প গ্যালারি art gallery
শিল্প-প্রদর্শনী exhibition
শিল্প-সংক্রান্ত industrial
শিল্পী artist
শিশু child, kid
শিশু-আলয় nursery
শিশু পরিচর্যা babysitting
শিশু পরিচর্যা করা babysit
শিশু-পরিচর্যাকারী babysitter
শিশু-পরিচর্যাকারী nanny
শিশু ছড়া nursery rhyme
শিশুদের দুধ baby milk
শিশুদের দুধ খাওয়ার বোতল baby's
  bottle
শিশুদের পরিষ্কার করার তোয়ালে baby
  wipe
শিশুদের লেংটি nappy
শিশু-পালক/শিশু-পালয়িত্রী
  childminder
শিশু বিদ্যালয় nursery school,
  playgroup
শিশু-বিদ্যালয় infant school
শিশুর যত্ন childcare
শিশুসুলভ childish
শিশু baby
শিস দেওয়া whistle
শীঘ্র soon
শীতকাল winter
শীতকালের খেলা winter sports
শীততাপ নিয়ন্ত্রণ air conditioning
শীততাপ নিয়ন্ত্রিত air-conditioned
শীত বস্ত্র sweater
শীতল cool
শীত লাগা cold
শীর্ষ peak
শীর্ষস্থান top
ষটকি মাছ kipper
ষটজাতীয় গাছের বীজ lentils
ষঁড় trunk
ষঁড়যুক্ত বড় মৌমাছি bumblebee
ষঁড়খানা bar
ষ্রোপোকার caterpillar, grub
শুকনো dried, dry
শুকনো কালো আঙুর currant
শুকনো খাবার stock cube
শুকনো খেঁজুর prune
শুকনো পাউরুটি breadcrumbs

শুকানো dry
শুকিয়ে যাওয়া wilt
শুক্রাণু sperm
শুধরানো rectify
শুধু পথচারীদের জন্য করা স্থান
  pedestrianized
শুধু পথচারীদের জন্য স্থান pedestrian
  precinct
শুধুমাত্র সাইকেলের জন্য রাস্তা cycle
  path
শুনছেন! hello!
শুভেচ্ছা toast
শুয়ে থাকা lie
শুরু beginning
শুরু করা begin, kick off, start
শুরু করার সময় kick off
শুরুতে initially
শুরুর first
শুরু হওয়া start
শুল্ক surcharge, tariff
শুল্ক অধিকারিক customs officer
শুল্ক বিভাগ customs
শূন্য nil, zero
শূন্য void
শূন্যপদ vacancy
শূন্য সংখ্যা nought
শূন্যস্থান blank
শূয়োর pig
শূয়োরের লেজ pigtail
শৃঙ্খল chain
শেখা learn
শেড shed
শেয়ার দালাল stockbroker
শেয়ার ধারক shareholder
শেয়ার বাজার stock market
শেয়ার বিনিময় কেন্দ্র
  stock exchange
শেরী মদ sherry
শেষ last, over
শেষ করা finish
শেষ প্রান্ত ultimatum
শেষ প্রান্ত dead end
শেষবেলা late
শেষ হওয়া end
শেষ হয়ে যাওয়া expire
শেষের আগেরটা penultimate
শৈলী style
শৈশব childhood
শোক mourning
শোকসংবাদ obituary
শোচনীয় miserable
শো জাম্পিং show jumping
শোধ করে দেওয়া reimburse
শোধনাগার refinery
শোনা hear, listen

শোয়া এবং জলখাবার bed and breakfast
শোয়ানো lay
শোয়ার ঘর bedroom
শোষণ exploitation
শৌখিন fancy
শৌচাগার lavatory, toilet
শৌচাগারে ব্যবহৃত কাগজ toilet paper
শৌচাগারে ব্যবহৃত কাগজের রোল toilet roll
শৌচালয় loo
শ্বশুর father-in-law
শ্বশুরবাড়ি in-laws
শ্বাস-প্রশ্বাস breathing
শ্বাসরোধ হওয়া choke
শ্বেতভালুক polar bear
শ্বেতসার starch
শ্মশান crematorium
শ্মশ্রুময় bearded
শ্যাওলা moss
শ্যাম্পু shampoo
শ্রদ্ধা admiration, regard, respect
শ্রদ্ধা করা admire, respect
শ্রদ্ধেয় respectable
শ্রবণশক্তি hearing
শ্রম labour
শ্রমিক labourer
শ্রমিক নেতা trade unionist
শ্রমিকশ্রেণী working-class
শ্রমিক সংঘ trade union
শ্রী Mr
শ্রীমতী Mrs
শ্রীযুক্তা Ms
শ্রীলংকা (দেশ) Sri Lanka
শ্রুতিলিপি dictation
শ্রেণি class
শ্রেণিকক্ষ classroom
শ্রেণিকক্ষ-সহায়ক classroom assistant
শ্রেণিবিভাগ category
শ্রেষ্ঠ best
শ্রেষ্ঠ কৃতি masterpiece
শ্রেষ্ঠ প্রতিযোগি/প্রথমশ্রেণীর বিজয়ী champion
শ্রেষ্ঠ ব্যক্তি বা বস্তু pick
শ্রোণী pelvis
শ্রোতা listener
ষড়যন্ত্র conspiracy
ষড়যন্ত্র করা plot
ষষ্ঠ sixth
ষাঁড় bull
ষাট sixty
ষান্মাসিক half-term
ষোড়শ sixteenth
ষোল sixteen
সংকট dilemma

সংকটজনক critical
সংকটমুহূর্ত crisis
সংকীর্ণ narrow
সংকীর্ণ পরিখা ravine
সংকীর্ণমনা narrow-minded
সংকীর্ণ রাস্তা alley
সংকেত sign, signal
সংকেত দেওয়া hint, signal
সংক্রমণ infection
সংক্রমণরোধী ওষুধ antibiotic
সংক্রামক infectious
সংক্ষিপ্ত concise
সংক্ষিপ্তকরণ, abbreviation
সংক্ষিপ্তাকারে briefly
সংখ্যা number
সংখ্যালঘু minority
সংগত advisable
সংগতি means
সংগম junction
সংগীত music, musical
সংগীত-বিষয়ক musical
সংগ্রহ assortment, collection
সংগ্রহ করা collect
সংগ্রাম fighting, struggle
সংগ্রাম করা struggle
সংগ্রাহক collector
সংঘবদ্ধ হওয়া club together
সংঘর্ষ বিরতি truce
সংজ্ঞা definition
সংবাদকর্মী newsagent
সংবাদপত্র newspaper, press
সংবাদপত্র বিলি paper round
সংবাদপাঠক newsreader
সংবাদ বিবৃতি বোর্ড bulletin board
সংবাদ-সম্মেলন press conference
সংবিধান constitution
সংবেদনশীল sensitive
সংমিশ্রণ combination
সংমিশ্রিত করা combine
সংযম moderation
সংযুক্ত আরব আমিরশাহী United Arab Emirates
সংযুক্তি attachment
সংযোগ connection
সংযোগ করা link
সংরক্ষক preservative
সংরক্ষণ booking, conservation, reservation
সংরক্ষণ করা book
সংরক্ষণাগার archive
সংরক্ষিত canned
সংরক্ষিত রাখা reserve
সংলগ্ন adjacent, twinned
সংলাপ dialogue
সংশোধন correction

সংসদ parliament
সংসার-খরচ cost of living
সংস্করণ edition, version
সংস্কৃতি culture
সংস্থা institution, organization
সংস্থা-গাড়ী estate car
সংস্থার কর্মীবৃন্দ personnel
সই initial
সওনা এক ধরনের বাষ্পস্নান sauna
সকল all
সকলেই everybody
সকাল morning
সকেট (সরঞ্জাম) socket
সক্রিয় active
সক্ষম able
সঙ্গ দেওয়া accompany
সঙ্গরোধ quarantine
সঙ্গী associate, companion, mate
সঙ্গীত symphony
সঙ্গে along, with
সঙ্গে নিয়ে যাওয়া escort
সচিব secretary
সচেতন aware, conscious
সচেতনতা consciousness
সজারুজাতীয় ছোট প্রাণী hedgehog
সজোরে ছুঁড়ে দেওয়া fling
সজোরে ধাক্কা মারা bang, bash
সজোরে বন্ধ করা slam
সঞ্চয় savings
সঞ্চারণ drift
সঞ্চালন circulation
সঠিক correct, exact, precise, proper, true
সঠিকভাবে correctly, precisely, properly, rightly
সততা honesty
সতর্ক alert, careful
সতর্ক করা alert, warn
সতর্কতা precaution, warning
সতর্ক বার্তা SOS
সতর্কবার্তা alarm
সতর্কভাবে carefully
সতর্ক হওয়া watch out
সতেরো seventeen
সত্তর seventy
সত্ত্বেও despite
সত্য true, truth
সত্যবাদী truthful
সত্যসত্যই really
সত্যি indeed
সদন্ত-হাসি grin
সদর দপ্তর HQ
সদস্য member
সদস্যতা membership
সদস্যতা পত্র membership card

সদৃশ symmetrical
সদৃশ হওয়া resemble, take after
সনাক্তকরণ identification
সন্ত saint
সন্তান প্রসবে ব্যর্থতা miscarriage
সন্তুষ্ট satisfied
সন্তুষ্টি satisfaction
সন্তোষজনক satisfactory
সন্ত্রস্ত terrified
সন্ত্রস্ত হওয়া terrify
সন্দেহ doubt
সন্দেহ করা doubt, suspect
সন্দেহজনক doubtful, dubious
সন্দেহ বাতিক sceptical
সন্দেহবাতিক suspicious
সন্দেহভাজন suspect
সন্ধান করা search
সন্ধিস্থাপন ally
সন্ধ্যা dusk
সন্ধ্যাবেলা evening
সন্ন্যাসী monk
সন্ন্যাসিনী nun
সপ্তদশ seventeenth
সপ্তম seventh
সপ্তাহ week
সপ্তাহান্ত weekend
সপ্তাহের কাজের দিন weekday
সফরসূচি itinerary
সফল হওয়া successful
সফল successful
সফলভাবে successfully
সফল হওয়া blossom, succeed
সবকিছু everything
সবজান্তা know-all
সবজি vegetable
সবথেকে খারাপ worst
সবথেকে ছোট youngest
সবল strong
সবশুদ্ধ altogether
সবুজ green
সবেতন paid
সজি sprouts
সভাপতি chairman
সভার বিষয়তালিকা agenda
সভ্যতা civilization
সমকক্ষ match
সমকোণ right angle
সমগ্র entire
সমচতুর্ভুজ diamond
সমতলভূমি plain
সমবেত গায়কবৃন্দ choir
সমমূল্য equivalent
সময় spell, time
সময় দেওয়া put in
সময়-পরিমাপক যন্ত্র timer
সময় বের করা fit in

সময়-মান মণ্ডল time zone
সময় সারণী timetable
সময়সীমা duration
সময়ানুবর্তী punctual
সময়ে on time
সমর্থ capable
সমর্থক supporter
সমর্থন support
সমর্থন করা back up, support
সমষ্টিগত collective
সমসাময়িক contemporary
সমস্ত all
সমস্যা problem, trouble
সমস্যা সৃষ্টিকারী troublemaker
সমাগম advent
সমাজ society
সমাজতন্ত্র socialism
সমাজবাদী socialist
সমাজ বিজ্ঞান sociology
সমাজ সেবা social services
সমাজসেবী social worker
সমাধান solution
সমাধান করা solve
সমাধান খোঁজা figure out, work out
সমাধি সৌধ tomb
সমান equal
সমান করা equal, equalize
সমানভাবে ভাগ করে দেওয়া share out
সমান্তরাল parallel
সমাপ্ত finished
সমাপ্তি end, ending, finish
সমাবেশ assembly, rally
সমালোচক critic
সমালোচনা criticism
সমালোচনা করা criticize, slag off
সমিতি association, collective
সমীকরণ equation
সমীক্ষক surveyor
সমীক্ষা poll, survey
সমীক্ষার প্রশ্নাবলী questionnaire
সমুদ্র sea
সমুদ্রতট beach
সমুদ্র তীর seashore
সমুদ্রতীরে seaside
সমুদ্রপৃষ্ঠ sea level
সমুদ্র সম্বন্ধীয় maritime
সমুদ্র ভ্রমণের ফলে অসুস্থ seasick
সমুদ্রের জল sea water
সমুদ্রের ঢেউয়ে খেলা surfing
সমেত inclusive
সম্পত্তি estate
সম্পদ asset, property, resource, wealth
সম্পদশালী wealthy
সম্পর্ক link, relation, relationship

সম্পর্ক ছিন্ন করা split up
সম্পর্কিত related
সম্পর্কিত ভাই-বোন cousin
সম্পর্কে regarding
সম্পাদক editor
সম্পাদন করা perform
সম্পাদিত কার্য performance
সম্পূরক complementary
সম্পূর্ণ complete, whole
সম্পূর্ণভাবে completely, dead, entirely, fully
সম্পূর্ণরূপে throughout, totally
সম্পূর্ণ সময় full-time
সম্পূর্ণ সময়ের full-time
সম্প্রচার broadcast
সম্প্রচার করা broadcast
সম্প্রদায় community, sect
সম্প্রসারণ extension
সম্বদ্ধে about, of
সম্ভব possible, probable
সম্ভবত likely
সম্ভবতঃ maybe, possibly, presumably, probably
সম্ভবপর feasible
সম্ভাবনা possibility, potential, probability, prospect
সম্ভাবনাময় promising
সম্ভাব্য might, potential
সম্ভাষণ greeting
সম্ভাষণ করা greet
সম্ভাষণ জানানো hail
সম্মতিসূচক okay
সম্মান honour
সম্মানসূচক complimentary
সম্মুখ front
সম্মেলন conference
সম্রাট emperor
সযত্নে পরীক্ষা করা scan
সয়া soya
সয়া সস soy sauce
সরকার government
সরকারি পথ right of way
সরকারি রাজম্ববর্ষ fiscal year
সরকারী রাজম্বসংক্রান্ত fiscal
সরঞ্জাম appliance, equipment, gear
সরবত sorbet
সরবরাহ supply
সরবরাহ করা supply
সরবরাহকারী supplier
সরল simple
সরলভাবে simply
সরলীকরণ simplify
সরাইখানা inn
সরানো move, shift
সরাসরি direct

সরাসরিভাবে directly
সরিয়ে নেওয়া take away
সরিয়ে রাখা away, put aside
সরীসৃপ reptile
সরু পর্ত aperture
সরু পিরিপথ pass
সরু দড়ি string
সরু নল straw
সরু পথ track
সরু সরু রেখা stripe
সরে আসা back out
সর্দি cold
সর্দিগর্মি sunstroke
সর্দি, নাসিকা ও গলার প্রদাহ catarrh
সর্বদা always
সর্বনাম pronoun
সর্বনাশা disastrous
সর্বশেষে lastly
সর্বশ্রেষ্ঠ best
সর্বসম্মত unanimous
সর্বসম্মতি consensus
সর্বস্ব broke
সর্বাধিক maximum, most
সর্বাধিক বিক্রয় bestseller
সর্বোচ্চ maximum
সর্বোত্তম classic
সর্ষেজাতীয় গাছ rape
সশস্ত্র armed, equipped
সশস্ত্রবাহিনী/পুলিস-প্রশিক্ষণপ্রাপ্ত ছেলে/
পুলিস-প্রশিক্ষণপ্রাপ্ত মেয়ে cadet
সশস্ত্র সেনাবাহিনীর প্রাক্তন কর্মী veteran
সস dip
সস (খাদ্য দ্রব্য) sauce
সসপ্যান (পাত্র) saucepan
সসেজ (মাংস জাতীয় খাবার)
    sausage
সস্তা cheap, inexpensive
সস্তার বিপণি charity shop
সস্নেহ affectionate
সহ including, with
সহকর্মী colleague
সহকারী প্রধান deputy head
সহঘটন coincidence
সহঘটিত coincide
সহজ easy
সহজদাহ্য flammable
সহজেই easily
কাঁতুকুতু লাগে এমন
    ticklish
সহপাঠী classmate
সহমত পোষণ করা agreed
সহযোগিতা cooperation
সহযোগিতা করা collaborate
সহযোগী associate
সহস্র thousand

সহস্রতম thousandth
সহস্র বছর millennium
সহানুভূতি sympathy
সহানুভূতি প্রদর্শন sympathize
সহানুভূতিশীল sympathetic
সহায়ক assistant, back up
সহায়ক দণ্ড splint
সহায়ক বস্তু accessory
সহায়তা assistance
সহিষ্ণু tolerant
সাঁতার swimming
সাঁতার কাটা swim
সাঁতার কাটার জলাশয় swimming pool
সাঁতার কাটার পরিধান bathing suit
সাঁতারু swimmer
সাঁতারের পোশাক wetsuit
সাঁতারের পোশাক swimming
    costume
সাঁতারের প্যান্ট swimming trunks
সাংকেতিক লিখন পদ্ধতি morse code
সাংঘাতিক grim, outrageous,
    terrible
সাংঘাতিকভাবে terribly
সাংবাদিক correspondent, journalist
সাংবাদিকতা journalism
সাংস্কৃতিক cultural
সাইকেল cycle
সাইকেল গলি cycle lane
সাইকেল চড়া cycle
সাইকেল-চালক cyclist
সাইকেল চালানো cycling
সাইকোথেরাপি psychotherapy
সাইড বোর্ড, আলমারী sideboard
সাইপ্রাস একটি দ্বীপ Cyprus
সাইপ্রাসের নাগরিক Cypriot
সাইপ্রাসের সঙ্গে সম্পর্কযুক্ত Cypriot
সাইবার কাফে cybercafé
সাইবার ক্রাইম cybercrime
সাইবেরিয়া Siberia
সাইরেন siren
সাক্ষাতের সময় visiting hours
সাক্ষাৎ visit
সাক্ষাৎ করা meet, see, visit
সাক্ষাৎকার interview
সাক্ষাৎকার গ্রহণকারী interviewer
সাক্ষাৎকার নেওয়া interview
সাক্ষাৎকারী visitor
সাক্ষী witness
সাপ্রতীরের রাস্তা promenade
সাগ্রহে readily
সাজগোজ করা dress
সাজসরঞ্জাম kit
সাজা penalty
সাজানো decorate
সাজার জায়গা dresser

সাজিয়ে রাখা arrange
সাত seven
সাত ভাগের এক ভাগ seventh
সাদা white
সাদা এবং পরিষ্কার করার রাসায়নিক
    bleach
সাদা ঘুঘু dove
সাদা পাপড়িযুক্ত বুনো ফুল daisy
সাদামাটি plain
সাদৃশ্য resemblance, similarity
সাধারণ common, general, ordinary,
    standard
সাধারণ অ্যানেস্থেসিয়া general
    anaesthetic
সাধারণ চকোলেট plain chocolate
সাধারণ চিকিৎসক GP
সাধারণ জ্ঞান general knowledge
সাধারণতঃ generally, normally,
    usually
সাধারণ নাগরিক যে সশস্ত্র বাহিনীর সদস্য
    নয় civilian
সাধারণ নির্বাচন general election
সাধারণ বুদ্ধি common sense
সাধারণ রূপ দেওয়া generalize
সাধারণ শ্রেণী economy class
সাধাসিধে naive
সান ক্রীম suncream
সানবেড sunbed
সানব্লক ক্রীম sunblock
সান রুফ,গাড়িতে আলো বাতাস আসার
    ছান sunroof
সান্ধ্য ক্লাস evening class
সান্ধ্য পোষাক evening dress
সাপ snake
সাফ করা clear
সাফল্য achievement, success
সাফল্যলাভ করা pass
সাফাই cleaning
সাফাই কর্মী cleaner
সাবধান cautious
সাবধানতা caution
সাবধানভাবে cautiously
সাবান soap
সাবান জলে স্নান bubble bath
সাবানদানি soap dish
সাবানের গুঁড়ো soap powder
সাবাস well done!
সামগ্রিক overall
সামঞ্জস্যপূর্ণ compatible
সামঞ্জস্যপূর্ণ balanced, matching
সামনাসামনি opposite
সামনে ahead, before, front
সামনে ঝোঁকা lean forward
সামনে বাওয়া move forward
সামনের দিকে forward

সামনে রাখা put forward
সাময়িকভাবে ধরে নেওয়া presume
সামরিক যুদ্ধবিরতির ব্যবহ ceasefire
সামরিক military
সামর্থ্য ability, capacity
সামলানো deal with, tackle
সামনে রাখা tackle
সামাজিক sociable, social
সামাজিক অনুষ্ঠান ceremony
সামাজিক নিরাপত্তা social security
সামান্য slight
সামুদ্রিক উদ্ভিদ seaweed
সামুদ্রিক ক্রীড়া surf
সামুদ্রিক খাবার seafood
সামুদ্রিক পলদচিংড়ি crayfish
সামুদ্রিক মাছ swordfish
সামুদ্রিক মৎসবিশেষ mackerel,
    whiting
সাম্প্রতিক recent
সাম্প্রতিককালে lately, recently
সাম্প্রতিক বিষয়াবলী current affairs
সাম্য equality
সাম্যবাদ communism
সাম্যবাদ-সম্পর্কিত communist
সাম্যবাদী communist
সাম্রাজ্য empire
সার fertilizer, manure
সার্ডিন মাছ sardine
সারণী table
সারস crane, heron
সারসংক্ষেপ করা summarize
সারাংশ summary
সারি rank, row
সার্কাস circus
সার্জেন্ট sergeant
সার্ফবোর্ড surfboard
সার্বীয় Serbian
সার্বিয়া Serbia
সার্বিয়ার নাগরিক Serbian
সার্বিয়ার ভাষা Serbian
সার্ভ (খেলার ক্ষেত্রে) serve
সার্ভিস এলাকা service area
সালিসি arbitration
সাশ্রয় save up
সাহস courage, nerve
সাহস করা dare
সাহসিকতা bravery
সাহসিকতাপূর্ণ/ঝুঁকিপূর্ণ challenging
সাহসী brave, courageous, daring
সাহায্য করা help!
সাহায্য backing, help!
সাহারা মরুভূমি Sahara
সাহিত্য literature
সাহিত্যে স্নাতক BA
সিঁড়ি staircase, stairs

সিঁড়ি বেয়ে নিচে downstairs
সিঁড়ির রেলিং banister
সিঁধকাটা চোর burglar
সিঁধকেটে চুরি burglary
সিঁধকেটে ঢোকা burgle
সিংহ lion
সিংহরাশি Leo
সিংহশাবক cub
সিংহাসন throne
সিংহী lioness
সি.ই.ও./"চিফ এক্সিকিউটিভ অফিসার"
    CEO
সিগারেট cigarette
সিগারেট ধরাবার সরঞ্জাম cigarette
    lighter
সিগাল seagull
সিজন টিকিট season ticket
সিডার/আপেল থেকে প্রস্তুত সুরা
    cider
সিডি CD
সিডি-কপি করার যন্ত্র CD burner
সিডি বাজানোর যন্ত্র CD player
সিদ্ধ boiled
সিদ্ধ ডিম boiled egg
সিদ্ধান্ত conclusion, decision
সিনেমা cinema
সিন্দুক chest, safe
সিন্ধুঘোটক walrus
সি.ভি./ব্যক্তিগত বিবরণ curriculum
    vitae, CV
সিমেন্ট cement
সিরিজ series
সিরিঞ্জ syringe
সিরিয়া (দেশ) Syria
সিরিয়া দেশীয় Syrian
সিরিয়ার নাগরিক Syrian
সিলিকন চিপ silicon chip
সিলিকনের ছোট টুকরো chip
সিলিন্ডার/চোঙ cylinder
সিস্টেম অ্যানালিস্ট systems analyst
সীমা limit, range
সীমানা border
সীমান্ত অঞ্চল frontier
সীমারেখা boundary
সীমিত সমর্থন qualified
সীল (জলচর প্রাণী) seal
সীলমোহর seal
সীলমোহর লাগান stamp
সীসা lead
সীসা ছাড়া lead-free
সুইচ বোর্ড switchboard
সুইডেন Sweden
সুইডেন দেশীয় Swedish
সুইডেনের ভাষা Swedish
সুইডেনের লোক Swede

সুইজারল্যান্ড, (দেশ) Switzerland
সুইজারল্যান্ডের Swiss
সুইজারল্যান্ডের নাগরিক Swiss
সুখ happiness
সুখী happy
সুগন্ধ aroma, flavour
সুগন্ধকারী বস্ত flavouring
সুগন্ধ-চিকিৎসা aromatherapy
সুগন্ধি পুষ্পলতা honeysuckle
সুগন্ধী perfume, scent
সুটকেস suitcase
সুড়ঙ্গ trench, tunnel
সুতরাং therefore
সুতির কাপড় cotton, denim,
    dungarees
সুতির কাপড়ের প্যান্ট denims
সুতো cotton, thread
সুদ interest
সুদর্শন handsome
সুদান Sudan
সুদান দেশীয় Sudanese
সুদানের নাগরিক Sudanese
সুদূর remote
সুদূর প্রাচ্য Far East
সুদের হার interest rate
সুনিশ্চিত করা ensure
সুনামি tsunami
সুনির্দিষ্ট specific
সুনির্দিষ্ট করা specify
সুনির্দিষ্টভাবে specifically
সুনিশ্চিতকরণ confirmation
সুনিশ্চিত করা confirm
সুন্দর beautiful, great, nice
সুন্দর আচরণবিশিষ্ট well-behaved
সুন্দরভাবে beautifully
সুন্দরস্থান beauty spot
সুন্দর স্বভাব-বিশিষ্ট good-natured
সুপ, ঝোল soup
সুপরিকল্পিত systematic
সুপরিচিত well-known
সুপারিশ recommendation
সুপারিশ করা recommend
সুফলদায়ক rewarding
সুবিচার justice
সুবিধা benefit
সুবিধাজনক convenient, handy
সুবিধা ভোগ করা benefit
সুবিন্যস্ত neat
সুবিন্যস্তভাবে neatly
সুমেরু অঞ্চল Arctic
সুমেরু বলয় Arctic Circle
সুমেরু মহাসাগর Arctic Ocean
সুযোগ advantage, chance,
    opportunity, privilege
সুযোগ-সুবিধা facilities

সুযোগসুবিধা amenities
সুর tune
সুরক্ষা protection
সুরক্ষা-বন্ধনী seatbelt
সুরস্রষ্টা composer
সুরা alcohol
সুরাপানে আসক্ত alcoholic
সুরা-বর্জিত alcohol-free
সুরাসক্ত alcoholic
সুন্দী good-looking
সুসম্পর্ক বজায় রাখা get on
সুহ well
সুহ বোধ করা better
সুহ রাখা keep-fit
সুহসবল healthy
সুস্পষ্ট obvious
সুস্পষ্টই obviously
সুস্বাদু delicious, tasty
সুস্বাদু করে তোলা seasoning
সূক্ষ delicate
সূক্ষ subtle
সূক্ষ নরম উল cashmere
সূচ needle
সূচক indicator
সূচক সংখ্যা index
সূচনা notice, start
সূচ ফুটিয়ে চিকিৎসা acupuncture
সূচিত করা point out
সূচীপত্র index
সূচীশিল্প embroidery
সূচীশিল্পের দ্বারা সাজানো embroider
সূত্র clue, formula
সূর্য ওঠা sunrise
সূর্যকিরণ sunshine
সূর্যমুখী sunflower
সূর্যরশ্মি sunlight
সূর্যাস্ত sunset
সূর্যের দিকে মুখ করে তাকালে বাঁদিক
  north
সূর্য sun
সৃষ্টি creation
সৃষ্টি করা create
সৃষ্টিশীল creative
সেঁকা bake
সেঁকা আলু baked potato
সেঁকা খাবার baked
সেঁটে দেওয়া paste
সেকেন্ড second
সেখানে there
সে গুলির কিছু some
সেটি, বসার আসন settee
সেতু bridge
সেনাবাহিনী army
সেনেগাল দেশ Senegal
সেনেগালীয় Senegalese

সেনেগালের নাগরিক Senegalese
সেন্ট cent
সেপ্টিক ট্যাংক septic tank
সেপ্টেম্বর মাস September
সেফটি পিন safety pin
সেবা serve
সেবিকা nurse
সেভিং ব্যাগ sponge bag
সেমি কোলন/অর্ধ বিরাম semi-colon
সেমিফাইনাল semifinal
সেমিস্টার semester
সে (মেয়ে) she
সেরা মরশুম high season
সেরে যাওয়া heal
সেলাই stitch
সেলাই এর কাজ sewing
সেলাই করা seam, sew, sew up,
  stitch
সেলাই মেসিন sewing machine
সেলার/মাটির নিচে ঘর cellar
সেলুন গাড়ি saloon car
সেলো/একতারার বাদ্যবিশেষ cello
সেলোটেপ® Sellotape®
সৈকতে শিশুদের বানানো বালির ঘর
  sandcastle
সৈনিক serviceman, soldier
সৈন্য troops
সৈন্যদলের চলন straight, upright
সোজাভাবে straight on
সোনা gold
সোনালী golden
সোফা (আসবাব পত্র) sofa
সোফা তথা বিছানা sofa bed
সোমবার Monday
সোমালিয়া (দেশ) Somalia
সোমালিয়ার নাগরিক Somali
সোমালী ভাষা Somali
সোমালীয় Somali
সোয়াজিল্যান্ড Swaziland
সৌদি আরব Saudi Arabia
সৌদি আরবীয় Saudi, Saudi Arabian
সৌদি আরবের মানুষ Saudi, Saudi
  Arabian
সৌন্দর্য beauty
সৌন্দর্যবর্ধক-শল্যচিকিৎসা cosmetic
  surgery
সৌভাগ্য fortune
সৌভাগ্যবশতঃ fortunately
সৌভাগ্যবান fortunate
সৌম্য দর্শন smart
সৌর solar
সৌর জগৎ solar system
সৌর শক্তি solar power
স্কটল্যান্ড (দেশ) Scotland

স্কটল্যান্ড দেশীয় Scots, Scottish
স্কটল্যান্ডের পুরুষ Scotsman
স্কটল্যান্ডের মহিলা Scotswoman
স্কটিশ বংশোদ্ভূত Scot
স্কার্ট skirt
স্কার্টের নিচে পরবার পোষাক underskirt
স্কি খেলতে উঁচু স্থানে নিয়ে যাবার লিফট
  ski lift
স্কি খেলা ski, skiing
স্কি খেলে যে ব্যক্তি skier
স্কিজোফ্রেনিয়ার রোগী schizophrenic
স্কি, (বরফের খেলার উপকরণ) ski
স্কুইড squid
স্কুটার scooter
স্কুল-পরবর্তী শিক্ষা further education
স্কুল পালানো play truant
স্কুল শিক্ষক schoolteacher
স্কুলের কাজ homework
স্কুলের ছাত্র schoolboy
স্কুলের পোশাক school uniform
স্কুলের বই schoolbook
স্কুলের ছাত্রছাত্রী schoolchildren
স্কুলের ব্যাগ schoolbag
স্কুলের মেয়ে schoolgirl
স্কেট করা skate
স্কেট বোর্ড skateboard
স্কেট বোর্ডে চড়া skateboarding
স্কেটিং এর জুতো rollerskates
স্কেটিং এর জুতো পরে স্কেটিং করা
  rollerskating
স্কেটিং এর স্থান rink
স্কেটিং করবার জন্য তৈরি করা ice rink
স্কেটিং করা skating
স্কেটিং করার স্থান skating rink
স্কোয়াশ খেলা squash
স্কোর করা score
স্কোর (খেলার ফলাফল) score
স্ক্যান (ডাক্তারী পরীক্ষা) scan
ক্যান্ডিনেভিয়া (স্থানের নাম)
  Scandinavia
স্ক্যানার যন্ত্র scanner
স্ক্যান্ডেনেভিয় Scandinavian
স্ত্রী-পুরুষবাদী sexist
স্ক্রু screw
স্ক্রুড্রাইভার screwdriver
স্ক্র্যাপ বই scrapbook
স্টপ ওয়াচ stopwatch
স্টিউ stew
স্টিকার sticker
স্টিয়ারিং চাকা steering wheel
স্টিরিও stereo
স্টুডিও studio
স্টেপল staple
স্টেপলার stapler

স্টেশনারি দোকান stationer
স্টোভ stove
স্ট্রবেরি ফল strawberry
স্ট্রেচার stretcher
স্ট্রোক (অসুখ) stroke
স্তন breast
স্তন্য পান করানো breast-feed
স্তন্যপায়ী mammal
স্তম্ভ column, pillar
স্তর layer
স্তুতিমূলক গান anthem
স্তূপ heap
স্তূপ pile
স্ত্রী wife
স্ত্রী-পুরুষবাদ sexism
স্ত্রীলোক-বিশেষজ্ঞ gynaecologist
স্থগিত রাখা postpone, put back
স্থপতি architect
স্থল site
স্থান place, rank, spot, venue
স্থানান্তর move
স্থানান্তরণ transit
স্থানান্তরে যাওয়া move
স্থানীয় local
স্থাপত্যবিদ্যা architecture
স্থাপন placement
স্থাপন করা place
স্থায়ী fixed, permanent
স্থায়ী আদেশ standing order
স্থায়ীভাবে permanently
স্থিতাবস্থা status quo
স্থিতিশীল stable
স্থিতিশীলতা stability
স্থিতিস্থাপক elastic, elastic band
স্থির করা decide
স্থির জলের পুকুর pool
স্থির ব্যয় overheads
স্থূল obese
স্থূল কারুকার্যময় vulgar
স্থূলভাবে grossly
স্নাতক graduate
স্নাতকত্ব লাভ graduation
স্নাতক পাঠরত undergraduate
স্নাতকোত্তর ছাত্র postgraduate
স্নান করা bathe
স্নান করার তোয়ালে bath towel
স্নানঘর bathroom
স্নানাগার baths
স্নানের তরল সাবান shower gel
স্নানের পরে পরার জন্য পরিধান bathrobe
স্নানের পাত্র bath
স্নানের বড় গামলা bathtub
স্নানের সময় পরবার টুপি shower cap
স্নায়ু nerve

স্নায়ুচাপপ্রণত uptight
স্নায়ুচাপ পীড়ন tension
স্নায়ুচাপে পীড়িত tense
স্নায়ুর ওপর চাপসূচিকারী nerve-racking
স্নুকার খেলা snooker
স্নেহপদার্থ fat
স্পঞ্জ sponge
স্পটলাইট spotlight
স্পন্দিত হওয়া throb
স্পর্শ করা touch
স্পর্শ কাতর touchy
স্পষ্ট clear, legible
স্পষ্ট করা clarify
স্পষ্টভাষী outspoken, straightforward
স্পষ্টরূপে clearly
স্পা spa
স্পার্ক প্লাগ, গাড়ির যন্ত্রাংশ spark plug
স্পীডবোট speedboat
স্পেন Spain
স্পেনীয় বা স্পেনের Spanish
স্পেনের বংশোদ্ভুত Spaniard
স্পেনের ভাষা Spanish
স্প্যানার spanner
স্প্রিং spring
স্প্রিংকলার sprinkler
স্প্রেডশীট কম্পিউটার প্রোগ্রাম spreadsheet
স্ফটিক crystal
স্ফুলিঙ্গ spark
স্ব-আশ্বাসযুক্ত self-assured
স্বচ্ছ clear, transparent
স্বচ্ছ কাগজ tracing paper
স্বচ্ছল well-off
স্বজনহীন lonesome
স্বতঃস্ফূর্ত spontaneous
স্ব-নিযুক্ত self-employed
স্বনির্ভর freelance
স্বনির্ভরভাবে freelance
স্বপরিবেশন self-service
স্বপ্ন dream
স্বপ্ন দেখা dream
স্ব-ব্যবস্থাপনা self-catering
স্বয়ংক্রিয় automatic
স্বয়ংক্রিয়ভাবে automatically
স্বয়ং পরিবেশন ভোজ buffet
স্বয়ংপরিবেশন রেস্তোরাঁ cafeteria
স্বরনালির প্রদাহ laryngitis
স্বরবর্ণ vowel
স্বরলিপি score
স্বর-পরীক্ষা পরীক্ষা audition
স্বর্গ heaven, paradise
স্বর্গীয় late
স্বল্প scarce

স্বল্প কালের জন্য থামা stopover
স্বল্পমেয়াদী short
স্বল্পসময়ের ঘুম nap
স্বল্পস্থায়ী brief
স্বশাসিত autonomous
স্বস্তি relief
স্বস্তি পাওয়া relieve
স্বাক্ষর signature
স্বাক্ষর করা sign
স্বাগত welcome!
স্বাগত জানানো welcome!
স্বাগত-সম্ভাষণ welcome!
স্বাদ taste
স্বাদ নেওয়া taste
স্বাদহীন tasteless
স্বাধীন free
স্বাধীনতা freedom, independence, liberation
স্বাধীন independent
স্বাভাবিক natural, normal
স্বাভাবিকভাবে naturally
স্বামী husband
স্বামী বা স্ত্রী spouse
স্বায়ত্তশাসন autonomy
স্বার্থ interest
স্বার্থপর selfish, shellfish
স্বাস্থ্য health
স্বাস্থ্যকর healthy
স্বাস্থ্যবিধি hygiene
স্বীকার করা admit, confess, own up
স্বীকারোক্তি confession
স্বেচ্ছাপ্রণোদিত voluntary
স্বেচ্ছায় deliberate, voluntarily
স্বেচ্ছায় সরে আসা opt out
স্বেচ্ছাপ্রেম volunteer
স্বেচ্ছাসেবী volunteer
স্মরণ করা remember
স্মরণচিহ্ন reminder
স্মরণার্থ চিহ্ন memento
স্মরণীয় souvenir
স্মরণীয় remarkable
স্মরণীয়ভাবে remarkably
স্মারকলিপি note
স্মারকলিপি memo
স্মারণিক memorial
স্মার্ট ফোন smart phone
স্মিয়ার পরীক্ষা smear
স্মৃতি memory
স্মৃতিফলক plaque
স্মৃতিশক্তি memory
স্মৃতিস্তম্ভ monument
সাঁতস্যাঁতে humid
স্যাক্সোফোন (বাদ্য যন্ত্র) saxophone
স্যাডল থলে saddlebag
স্যান ম্যারিনো দেশ San Marino

হিমেল বৃষ্টি হওয়া sleet
হিরে diamond
হিসাব নিরীক্ষক auditor
হিসাব নিরীক্ষণ audit
হিসাব নিরীক্ষণ করা audit
হিসাবরক্ষক accountant
হিসাবশাস্ত্র accountancy
হিসাবী thrifty
হিসাবে as
হুডখোলা গাড়ী convertible
হুমকি threat
হুমকি দেওয়া threaten
হুল sting
হুল ফোটান sting
হৃদয়স্পর্শী touching
হৃদরোগে আক্রান্ত হওয়া heart attack
হৃৎস্পন্দন pulse
হৃৎপিণ্ড heart
হেঁচকি hiccups
হেঁটে বেড়াবার স্থান walkway
হেজল গাছের বাদাম hazelnut
হেমারয়েড haemorrhoids
হেরিংমাছ herring
হেলান দেওয়া against
হেলানো reclining
হেলাফেলা করা despise
হেল্পলাইন helpline
হোঁচট খাওয়া stumble, trip
হোটেল hotel
হোটেল ভাড়া রাতের খাওয়া ছাড়া half
    board
হোটেলের পরিচারক waiter
হোটেলের পরিচারিকা chambermaid
হোটেলের পাচক chef
হোটেলের বিল মেটানো check out
হোটেলের মহিলা পরিচারক waitress
হোটেলের সুইট suite
হোমিওপ্যাথি সংক্রান্ত homeopathic
হোসপাইপ hosepipe
হ্যাঁ! yes!
হ্যাঁচকা মারা wrench
হ্যাং-গ্লাইডারে ওড়া hang-gliding
হ্যান্ডবল handball
হ্যান্ডস্-ফ্রী কিট hands-free kit
হ্রাস decrease, reduction
হ্রাসকরণ cutback
হ্রাস করা reduce
হ্রাস পাওয়া decrease

স্যানিটারি টাওয়েল **sanitary towel**
স্যাণ্ডউইচ **sandwich**
স্যামন মাছ **salmon**
স্যালাড **salad**
স্যালাডের মশলা **salad dressing**
স্যালাডের সেলেরি **celery**
স্যালামী **salami**
স্রোতের টান **drift**
স্লট মেসিন **slot machine**
স্লাইড (বাচ্চাদের খেলার উপকরণ) **slide**
স্লিপিং ব্যাগ **sleeping bag**
স্লেজ গাড়িতে চড়া **sledging**
স্লেট পাথর **slate**
স্লোভাক ভাষা **Slovak**
স্লোভাকিয় **Slovak**
স্লোভাকিয়া (দেশ) **Slovakia**
স্লোভাকিয়ার নাগরিক **Slovak**
স্লোভেনিয় ভাষা **Slovenian**
স্লোভেনিয়া (দেশ) **Slovenia**
স্লোভেনিয়া দেশীয় **Slovenian**
স্লোভেনিয়ার মানুষ **Slovenian**
হওয়া **be**
হজম **digestion**
হজম করা **digest**
হট্টগোল **din**
হঠাৎ **sudden**
হঠাৎকরে **suddenly**
হঠাৎ দেখা হওয়া **bump into**
হঠাৎ বৃদ্ধি পাওয়া **surge**
হতবাক **shock, speechless**
হতবাক হওয়া **shock**
হতবুদ্ধিকর **confusing, puzzling**
হতবুদ্ধি হওয়া **puzzled**
হতভম্ব **confused**
হতাশ করা **let down**
হতাশা **despair**
হতাশাগ্রস্ত **frustrated**
হতাশাজনক **dismal**
হতাশাবাদ সংক্রান্ত **pessimistic**
হেতে চলেছে **go**
হেতে দেওয়া **let**
হেতে পারা **may**
হবু-বউ **fiancée**
হবু-বর **fiancé**
হবে **will**
হবেই **have to**
হয়ত **perhaps**
হয়রান করা **pick on**
হয়রানি **harassment**
হয়ে **via**
হরমোন **hormone**
হরিণ **deer**
হরিণের মাংস **venison**
হর্ণ **horn**
হলকর্ষণ করা **plough**

হলঘর **hall**
হলদে ফুলবিশেষ **primrose**
হলুদ **yellow**
হলুদ ফুলযুক্ত গাছ **dandelion**
হলুদ রং এর মণি **amber**
হস্তগত করা **take**
হস্তশিল্পী **craftsman**
হস্তান্তর, বদলী **transfer**
হস্তান্তরিত করা **pass**
হাঁচি **sneeze**
হাঁটা **walk, walking**
হাঁটার লাঠি **walking stick**
হাঁটু **knee**
হাঁটু-পাড়া **kneel**
হাঁপানি **asthma**
হাঁফ ছাড়া **sigh**
হাঁফ ছেড়ে বাঁচা **sigh**
হাঙর মাছ **shark**
হাই তোলা **yawn**
হাইলাইটার কলম **highlighter**
হাওয়া কল **windmill**
হাওয়াবাদিত বাদ্যযন্ত্র **bagpipes**
হাওয়াভরা ড্রিল **pneumatic drill**
হাওয়া ভর্তি করা **pump up**
হাওয়াভর্তি ব্যাগ **airbag**
হাওয়া-মিঠাই **candyfloss**
হাওয়ার দমক **draught**
হাঙ্গেরী দেশীয় **Hungarian**
হাঙ্গেরীর মানুষ **Hungarian**
হাজির হওয়া **turn up**
হাড় **bone**
হাত **hand**
হাত ও নখের যত্ন **manicure**
হাত ও নখের যত্ন নেওয়া **manicure**
হাতওয়ালা বালতি **pail**
হাতকড়া **handcuffs**
হাতখরচ **pocket money**
হাতঘড়ি **watch**
হাতঘড়ির ব্যাণ্ড **watch strap**
হাত-ছাড়া করা **part with**
হাতড়ানো **grope**
হাততালি দিয়ে প্রশংসা **applause**
হাততালি দেওয়া **clap**
হা৩৩তালির মাধ্যমে প্রশংসা করা **applaud**
হাত নাড়া **wave**
হাত নাড়ানো **wave**
হাতব্যাগ **handbag**
হাতল **handle, handlebars, knob, rail**
হাতলওয়ালা শিশুদের খাট **carrycot**
হাতা **ladle, sleeve**
হাতা কাটা **sleeveless**
হাতি **elephant**
হাতিয়ার **tool**

হাতির দাঁত **ivory**
হাতুড়ি **hammer**
হাতে বওয়ার তল্লিতল্পা **hand luggage**
হাতে বানানো **handmade**
হাতের মুঠির মধ্যে আসা **grip**
হাতের মুঠো **fist**
হাতের লেখা **handwriting**
হাতে লেখা **scribble**
হাফ প্যান্ট **shorts, trunks**
হাফ হাতা জামা **short-sleeved**
হাবভাব **attitude**
হাম **measles**
হামাগুড়ি দেওয়া **crawl, creep**
হার মানা **give in**
হারিয়ে দেওয়া **beat**
হারিয়ে যাওয়া **lose, lost**
হারিয়ে যাওয়া গৃহপালিত জন্তু **stray**
হার্ডবোর্ড **hardboard**
হালকা আঁচে রান্না করা **simmer**
হালকা ওজনের হাঁটু পর্যন্ত ঢাকা বর্ষাতি **cagoule**
হালকা বিয়ার **lager**
হালকা ভাসমান বস্তু **float**
হালকা হলদে-বাদামী রঙ **beige**
হালিম শাক **watercress**
হাল্কা **light**
হাল্কা কাঠের বোর্ড **toboggan**
হাল্কা ঘুমোনো **snooze**
হাল্কা পানীয় **soft drink**
হাসপাতাল **hospital**
হাসপাতালের ঘর **ward**
হাসা **laugh, smile**
হাসানো **amuse**
হাসি **laugh, smile**
হাসিখুশি **jolly**
হাসির শব্দ **laughter**
হাস্যকর **ridiculous**
হাস্যরস **comedy**
হাস্যরসসমৃদ্ধ **comic**
হাস্যরসাত্মক নাটক **sitcom**
হাস্যরসাত্মক বই **comic book**
হিঁচে শাক **cress**
হিংসা **violence**
হিংস্র **violent**
হিংস্র **fierce**
হিটিং **heating**
হিন্দু **Hindu**
হিন্দুধর্ম **Hinduism**
হিন্দুধর্ম সংক্রান্ত **Hindu**
হিপ্পি **hippie**
হিমবাহ **glacier**
হিমশীতল **freezing, icy**
হিমশৈল **iceberg**
হিমেল **frosty**
হিমেল বৃষ্টি **sleet**